EMF

eclipse

the eclipse series

SERIES EDITORS Erich Gamma ▪ Lee Nackman ▪ John Wiegand

Eclipse is a universal tool platform, an open extensible integrated development environment (IDE) for anything and nothing in particular. Eclipse represents one of the most exciting initiatives hatched from the world of application development in a long time, and it has the considerable support of the leading companies and organizations in the technology sector. Eclipse is gaining widespread acceptance in both the commercial and academic arenas.

The Eclipse Series from Addison-Wesley is the definitive series of books dedicated to the Eclipse platform. Books in the series promise to bring you the key technical information you need to analyze Eclipse, high-quality insight into this powerful technology, and the practical advice you need to build tools to support this evolutionary Open Source platform. Leading experts Erich Gamma, Lee Nackman, and John Wiegand are the series editors.

Titles in the Eclipse Series

For more information on books in this series visit www.awprofessional.com/series/eclipse

EMF

Eclipse Modeling Framework
Second Edition

Dave Steinberg
Frank Budinsky
Marcelo Paternostro
Ed Merks

✦Addison-Wesley

Upper Saddle River, NJ • Boston • Indianapolis • San Francisco •
New York • Toronto • Montreal • London • Munich • Paris • Madrid •
Cape Town • Sydney • Tokyo • Singapore • Mexico City

Many of the designations used by manufacturers and sellers to distinguish their products are claimed as trademarks. Where those designations appear in this book, and the publisher was aware of a trademark claim, the designations have been printed with initial capital letters or in all capitals.

The authors and publisher have taken care in the preparation of this book, but make no expressed or implied warranty of any kind and assume no responsibility for errors or omissions. No liability is assumed for incidental or consequential damages in connection with or arising out of the use of the information or programs contained herein.

The publisher offers excellent discounts on this book when ordered in quantity for bulk purchases or special sales, which may include electronic versions and/or custom covers and content particular to your business, training goals, marketing focus, and branding interests. For more information, please contact:

U.S. Corporate and Government Sales
(800) 382-3419
corpsales@pearsontechgroup.com

For sales outside the United States please contact:

International Sales
international@pearson.com

Visit us on the Web: informit.com/aw

Library of Congress Cataloging-in-Publication Data:

EMF : Eclipse Modeling Framework / Dave Steinberg ... [et al.].
   p. cm.
   ISBN 0-321-33188-5 (pbk. : alk. paper) 1. Computer software--Development. 2. Java (Computer program language) I. Steinberg, Dave.

   QA76.76.D47E55 2008
   005.13'3--dc22

                                    2007049160

ISBN-13: 978-0-321-33188-5
ISBN-10: 0-321-33188-5
Text printed in the United States on recycled paper at Edwards Brothers in Ann Arbor, Michigan
First printing December 2008

Contents

v

Foreword

by Richard C. Gronback

Modeling can mean very different things to different people, even within the discipline of software engineering. Some will immediately think of the Unified Modeling Language (UML), others will think of Model-Driven Architecture (MDA), while others may remember the days of CASE tools. With increasing frequency, those familiar with the Eclipse community think of the Eclipse Modeling Framework (EMF), which provides a solid basis for application development through the use of pragmatic modeling and code generation facilities.

From its beginnings within the Tools Project at Eclipse, EMF's reputation for high quality and unparalleled community support quickly led to several complementary modeling projects forming at Eclipse. Code generators, graphical diagramming frameworks, model transformation, validation, and search are just a few that have built upon EMF and now are contained within the Eclipse Modeling Project. The growth and success of this top-level project is due in large part to the strength of its core component, EMF.

In many ways, the EMF project is a model for other Eclipse projects (pun intended). From the tireless efforts of its committers in answering questions on the project's newsgroup, to the professionalism and openness of its development in terms of API, features, performance, and documentation, EMF is a tough act to follow. The diversity of the Modeling community that has grown up around EMF makes it a poster child for collaboration, including individual contributors, commercial vendors, and academic institutions. Further evidence of EMF's value to Eclipse is its anticipated use in e4, the next Eclipse platform. At present, e4 developers have plans to leverage the capabilities of EMF to provide a consistent model-based foundation and runtime; clearly, a step forward for model-driven software development.

With so much technology built upon EMF, understanding its architecture and capabilities are essential to using it successfully. For years, the first edition of this book has been an important resource for many developers building their applications with EMF and extending EMF's own capabilities. With the introduction of this second edition, the many enhancements made to EMF in the interim are now documented and able to be leveraged effectively. The API section has been replaced by new chapters covering EMF persistence, client programming, change recording, validation, and Rich Client Platform (RCP) development. In addition to updating the original material, this new edition covers the latest features of EMF versions 2.3 and 2.4, including generics, content types, and REST APIs. It is a most welcome second edition.

I hope you find this second edition as valuable as I do.

Richard C. Gronback
Chief Scientist, Borland Software Corporation
November 2008

Foreword

by Mike Milinkovich

The Eclipse Modeling Framework is an exemplary open source project in many respects. We at the Eclipse Foundation have a number of ways to value the contributions of any one project to our community. Our criteria include industry adoption, robust technology, stability as an extensible platform, and open and transparent project leadership. In all of these ways and more, EMF has for many years been one of the very best of Eclipse.

With respect to industry adoption, I have often marveled at the amazing success of EMF. A large part of my role at the Eclipse Foundation is to travel and speak with adopters of Eclipse technology. Whether I am speaking to startups, enterprises or established software vendors, everywhere I go EMF is on the list of key Eclipse technologies being used. Its ability to simplify the development of complex software applications and products has been widely recognized. Rarely has a single framework driven so much developer productivity in so many domains.

This adoption has largely been driven by a very simple value proposition: EMF is great technology. Careful attention has been paid to EMF's architecture, the completeness of its APIs, its flexibility, and its performance. And performance is key for any technology that is going to be used in real world applications.

As a platform, EMF has transformed the modeling tools industry. Leading model tools vendors such as Borland and IBM have based their products on EMF, making a strategic decision that EMF is their core modeling framework of the future. Almost every new modeling product that I have seen over the past four years has been based on EMF.

So, EMF has clearly seen enormous adoption in the industry, but that is only half the story. We look at EMF as a community success story as well. The EMF team has always done an excellent job of interacting with community. Ed Merks, the leader of the project and one of the authors of this book, is famous throughout the Eclipse community for his prompt responses to any adopter's inquiry about EMF. That leadership-by-example has resulted in the entire EMF team being one of the most community-focused at Eclipse.

EMF is an enormous Eclipse community success story and I am certain that this book will help further that success.

Mike Milinkovich
Executive Director, Eclipse Foundation
November 2008

Preface

This book is a comprehensive introduction and developer's guide to the Eclipse Modeling Framework (EMF). EMF is a powerful framework and code generation facility for building Java applications based on simple model definitions. Designed to make modeling practical and useful to the mainstream Java programmer, EMF unifies three important technologies: Java, XML, and UML. Models can be defined using a UML modeling tool or an XML Schema, or even by specifying simple annotations on Java interfaces. In this last case, the developer writes just a subset of abstract interfaces that describe the model, and the rest of the code is generated automatically and merged back in.

By relating modeling concepts to the simple Java representations of those concepts, EMF has successfully bridged the gap between modelers and Java programmers. It serves as a gentle introduction to modeling for Java programmers and at the same time as a reinforcement of the modeler's theory that a great deal of coding can be automated, given an appropriate tool. This book shows how EMF is such a tool. It also shows how using EMF lets you do more with your models that you might have thought possible.

EMF provides a runtime framework that allows any modeled data to be easily validated, persisted, and edited in a UI. Change notification and recording are supported automatically. Metadata is available to enable generic processing of any data using a uniform, reflective API. With all of these features and more, EMF is the foundation for data sharing and fine-grained interoperability among tools and applications in Eclipse, in much the same way that Eclipse is itself a platform for integration at the component and UI level. Numerous organizations are currently using Eclipse, EMF, and the growing number of EMF-based technologies in the Eclipse Modeling Project as the foundation for their own commercial and open source offerings.

This book assumes the reader is familiar with object-oriented programming concepts and specifically with the Java programming language. Previous exposure to modeling technologies such as UML, although helpful, is not required. Part I (Chapters 1 to 4) provides a basic overview of the most important concepts in EMF and modeling. This part teaches someone with basic Java programming skills everything needed to start using EMF to model and build an application. Part II (Chapters 5 to 9) presents a thorough overview of EMF's metamodel, Ecore, followed by details of the mappings between Ecore and the other supported model-definition forms: UML, annotated Java, and XML Schema. Part III (Chapters 10 to 13) includes detailed analyses of EMF's code generator patterns and tools, followed by an end-to-end example of a non-trivial EMF application. Finally, Part IV (Chapters 14 to 21) takes a close look at EMF's runtime framework and discusses important EMF programming techniques.

The bulk of this book is based on EMF 2.2, the last version to support the venerable Java 1.4 language. In version 2.3, EMF adopted key language features of Java 5.0, making it incompatible with previous Java runtimes. EMF 2.2, which was current while much of this book was written, is therefore still popular and an excellent base for learning about the framework. The code in Chapters 1 to 20 is based on that version, but due to EMF's backward compatibility, all examples run without change on version 2.4, the latest at the time of this book's release. Chapter 21 focuses specifically on changes in EMF 2.3 and 2.4 and, as such, uses 2.4 as the basis for its examples.

Conventions Used in This Book

The following formatting conventions are used throughout this book:

Bold—Used for the names of model elements, such as packages, classes, attributes, and references; and of user-interface elements, including menus, buttons, tabs, and text boxes.

Italic—Used for filenames and URIs, as well as for placeholder text that is meant to be replaced by a particular name. New terms are often italicized for emphasis. Also, in Chapter 9's example mappings, items shown purely to provide context appear in italics.

`Courier`—Used for all code samples and for in-text references to code elements, including the names of Java packages, classes, interfaces, methods, fields, variables, and keywords. Plug-in names, command lines, and elements of non-Java files, including XML, also appear in this font.

`Courier Bold`—Used to emphasize portions of code samples, usually new insertions or changes.

~~`Courier Strikethrough`~~—Used in code samples to indicate that text should be deleted.

Online Examples

The Web site for this book is located at *http://www.informit.com/ title/9780321331885*. All of the example models and code used throughout this book can be downloaded from there. The site will also provide an errata list, and other news related to the book.

Eclipse and EMF are required to use the examples. You can download one of several Eclipse packages (we recommend Eclipse Classic) at *http://www.eclipse.org/downloads/* and the all-in-one EMF SDK at *http://www.eclipse.org/modeling/emf/downloads/*.

Acknowledgments

This book would not have been possible without the contributions of many people. First and foremost, we must thank those who reviewed our early drafts, pointed out our errors, and helped us improve our writing with their thoughtful feedback: Chris Aniszczyk, Chris Daly, Kenn Hussey, Elena Litani, and Kevin Williams. Kenn and Elena, in particular, also deserve acknowledgement for their major contributions to EMF as committers on the project. We also thank Stefan Baramov and Reinhold Bihler for their feedback on the Rough Cuts version of the book. We are grateful to Richard Gronback and Mike Milinkovich for their kind and insightful Forewords. A big thanks also goes to Greg Doench and Michelle Housley at Pearson, and to our production manager Mary Sudul, for their skill and patience in steering us through this process.

Of course, there are many more people who have contributed to EMF, and without them, this book would have been much shorter and not nearly as interesting. Thanks to Lucas Bigeardel, Boris Bokowski, Nick Boldt, Steve Brodsky, Cedric Brun, Ian Bull, Christian Damus, Dmitry Denisov, Raymond Ellersick, Tim Grose, Michael Hanner, Anthony Hunter, Sridhar Iyengar, Bernd Kolb, Daniel Leroux, Kim Letkeman, Martin Nally, Frederic Plante, Bertrand Portier, Barbara Price, Tom Schindl, David Sciamma, Neil Skrypuch, Eike Stepper, and Martin Taal. EMF truly is a community effort, and there are countless members of the community who have contributed in various ways. It would be impossible to name them all, but we are deeply appreciative of everyone who has reported bugs, offered patches, provided feedback, written articles, answered other users' questions, promoted EMF, and created or contributed to related components in the Eclipse Modeling Project. Thanks also to the wider Eclipse community, and to all the talented people at the Eclipse Foundation who have nurtured and supported it.

Finally, we wish to express our love and appreciation to our partners, spouses, and families. Writing this book was no small task, and we couldn't have done it without their support.

References

[1] "Eclipse Platform Technical Overview." Object Technology International, Inc., February 2003, *http://www.eclipse.org/whitepapers/eclipse-overview.pdf*.

[2] "XML Schema Part 0: Primer," Second Edition. W3C, October 2004, *http://www.w3.org/TR/xmlschema-0/*.

[3] E. Gamma, R. Helm, R. Johnson, and J. Vlissides. *Design Patterns: Elements of Reusable Object-Oriented Software*. Addison-Wesley, Reading, MA, 1995.

[4] J. Bloch. *Effective Java Programming Language Guide*. Addison-Wesley, Reading, MA, 2001.

[5] "Namespaces in XML 1.0," Second Edition. W3C, August 2006, *http://www.w3.org/TR/2006/REC-xml-names-20060816/*.

[6] J. Gosling, B. Joy, G. Steele, and G. Bracha. *The Java Language Specification, Third Edition*. Addison-Wesley, 2005.

[7] "XML Schema Part 2: Datatypes," Second Edition. W3C, October 2004, *http://www.w3.org/TR/xmlschema-2/*.

[8] "XML Schema Part 1: Structures," Second Edition. W3C, October 2004, *http://www.w3.org/TR/xmlschema-1/*.

PART I

EMF Overview

CHAPTER 1

Eclipse

Before we can begin to describe the Eclipse Modeling Framework (EMF), a basic introduction to Eclipse would seem in order. If you're already familiar with Eclipse, you can skip this chapter and go straight to Chapter 2, which is the "real" Chapter 1 from the EMF perspective.

Eclipse is an open source software project, the purpose of which is to provide a highly integrated tool platform. The work in Eclipse includes a core project, which includes a generic framework for tool integration, and a Java development environment built using it. Other projects extend the core framework to support specific kinds of tools and development environments. The projects in Eclipse are implemented in Java and run on many operating systems including Windows, Mac OSX, and Linux.

By involving committed and enthusiastic developers in an environment organized to facilitate the free exchange of technology and ideas, Eclipse is hoping to create the best possible integration platform. The software produced by Eclipse is made available under the Eclipse Public License (EPL), which contains a good deal of legalese, but in loose terms permits you to use, modify, and redistribute the software for free, and also to distribute it alongside proprietary components as part of a commercial product. The EPL is Open Source Initiative (OSI)-approved and recognized by the Free Software Foundation as a free software license. Any software contributed to Eclipse must also be licensed under the EPL.

The development of Eclipse is overseen by the Eclipse Foundation, an independent, non-profit organization. The foundation's membership includes more than 100 companies that support Eclipse and provide commercial Eclipse-based offerings, as well as individual code committers without corporate representation. The Eclipse Foundation operates in accordance with a series of bylaws and a development process that define the roles and responsibilities of the various participants including the Board of Directors, the Eclipse Management

Organization, the Project Management Committees, the membership, and users and developers of Eclipse.

1.1   The Projects

The development work in Eclipse is divided into numerous top-level projects, including the Eclipse Project, the Modeling Project, the Tools Project, and the Technology Project. The Eclipse Project contains the core components needed to develop using Eclipse. Its components are essentially fixed and downloadable as a single unit referred to as the Eclipse Software Development Kit (SDK). The components of the other projects are used for specific purposes and are generally independent and downloaded individually. New projects are created and new components are added to existing projects on an ongoing basis.

1.1.1   The Eclipse Project

The Eclipse Project supports the development of a platform, or framework, for the implementation of integrated development environments (IDEs) and other applications. The Eclipse framework is implemented using Java but is used to implement development tools for other languages as well (e.g., C++, XML, etc.).

The Eclipse Project itself is divided into four main subprojects: Equinox, the Platform, the Java Development Tools (JDT), and the Plug-in Development Environment (PDE). Collectively, the four subprojects provide everything needed to extend the framework and develop tools based on Eclipse.

Equinox and the Platform are the core components of Eclipse and, together, are considered by many to *be* Eclipse. Equinox is an implementation of the OSGi R4 core framework specification,[1] which provides the component model on which all of Eclipse is based. The Platform defines additional core frameworks and services required to support the integration of tools. These services include, among others, a standard workbench user interface and mechanisms for managing projects, files, and folders. We describe the platform in more detail in Section 1.2.

The JDT is a full-function Java development environment built using Eclipse. Its tools are highly integrated and representative of the power of the Eclipse Platform. It can be used to develop Java programs for Eclipse or other target platforms. The JDT is even used to develop the Eclipse Project itself.

The PDE provides views and editors to facilitate the creation of plug-ins for Eclipse. The PDE builds on and extends the JDT by providing support for the

---

[1] The OSGi specifications are available at *http://www2.osgi.org/Specifications/HomePage.*

non-Java parts of the plug-in development activity, such as registering plug-in extensions, and so on.

1.1.2   The Modeling Project

The Eclipse Modeling Project is the focal point for the evolution and promotion of model-based development technologies at Eclipse. At its core is EMF, the subject of this book, which provides the basic framework for modeling. Other modeling sub-projects build on top of the EMF core, providing such capabilities as model tranformation, database integration, and graphical editor generation. Also included are a number of implementations of important modeling standards. For example, the UML2 project provides an EMF-based implementation of the UML 2.x metamodel.

1.1.3   The Tools Project

The Eclipse Tools Project develops a wide range of exemplary, extensible development tools based on the Eclipse Platform. It includes a rather broad range of sub-projects. Some provide tools for working with other languages, including C/C++, COBOL, and PHP. Others, like the Graphical Editing Framework (GEF), provide common support for larger categories of Eclipse tools. EMF also began its life as a part of the Tools Project, before the Modeling Project was formed.

1.1.4   The Technology Project

The Eclipse Technology Project provides an opportunity for researchers, academics, and educators to become involved in the ongoing evolution of Eclipse. This project serves as a temporary home for new or experimental work, which may reach its natural conclusion or move into another project on reaching maturity. The other top-level projects may also contain so-called incubator projects for this purpose.

1.1.5   Other Projects

A growing number of other projects support and provide more specialized types of tools. These include the Data Tools Platform Project, the Device Software Development Platform Project, and the Eclipse Web Tools Platform Project, to name just a few.

1.2   The Eclipse Platform

The Eclipse Platform is a framework for building IDEs. It's been described as "an IDE for anything, and nothing in particular,"[1] which is pretty much the way you could think of any framework. It simply defines the basic structure of an IDE. Specific tools extend the framework and are plugged into it to define a particular IDE collectively.

In fact, the architecture of the platform allows for a subset of its components to be used to help build just about any application at all.

1.2.1   Plug-In Architecture

In Eclipse, the basic unit of function, or a component, is called a *plug-in*. The Eclipse Platform itself and the tools that extend it are both composed of plug-ins. A simple tool might consist of a single plug-in, but more complex tools are typically divided into several. Each plug-in contributes functionality that can be invoked by the user or reused and extended by other plug-ins.

The platform runtime engine is responsible for discovering and running plug-ins. It is implemented atop the OSGi Service Platform, which provides a flexible, standard component framework allowing plug-ins to be installed and removed without restarting the platform. The OSGi term for a component is *bundle*, so you will often see this term used interchangeably with plug-in.

From a packaging perspective, a plug-in includes everything needed to run the component, such as Java code, images, translated text, and the like. It also includes two manifest files.[2] The OSGi bundle manifest file, named *META-INF/MANIFEST.MF*, identifies the plug-in and provides, among other things, dependency information. It includes the following:

○ **Required bundles.** Its dependencies on other plug-ins.

○ **Exported packages.** The packages that it makes visible to other plug-ins.

The plug-in manifest file, named *plugin.xml*, declares the interconnections to other plug-ins. It can define the following:

○ **Extension points.** Declarations of functionality that it makes available to other plug-ins.

○ **Extensions.** Use (implementation) of other plug-ins' extension points.

---

[2] The OSGi-based runtime was introduced in Eclipse 3.0. Prior to this, a single plug-in manifest file was used. For backward compatibility, the Eclipse Platform and EMF still support this simpler, but less flexible, approach.

The platform runtime manages the life cycle of the plug-ins and matches extensions with their corresponding extension points. It uses class loaders to enforce the visibility declared in the manifest files and provides a registry that plug-ins can consult to discover the extensions to their extension points.

1.2.2   Workspace Resources

Integrated Eclipse tools work with ordinary files and folders, but they use a higher level application programming interface (API) based on resources, projects, and a workspace. A *resource* is the Eclipse representation of a file or folder that provides the following additional capabilities:

1. Change listeners can be registered to receive resource change notifications (called resource deltas).

2. *Markers,* such as error messages or to-do lists, can be added to a resource.

3. The previous content, or history, of a resource can be tracked.

A *project* is a special folder-type resource that maps to a user-specified folder in the underlying file system. The subfolders of the project are the same as in the physical file system, but projects are top-level folders in the user's virtual project container, called the *workspace*. Projects can also be tagged with a particular personality, called a *nature*. For example, the Java nature is used to indicate that a project contains the source code for a Java program.

1.2.3   Platform UI

The Eclipse user interface (UI) framework, known as Platform UI, consists of two general-purpose toolkits, SWT and JFace; and a customizable workbench UI structure. Platform UI also provides a workbench instantiation configured for use as an IDE.

SWT

Standard Widget Toolkit (SWT) is an operating system (OS)-independent widget set and graphics library, implemented using native widgets wherever possible. This is unlike Java's Abstract Window Toolkit (AWT), which provides a native implementation only for low-level widgets like lists, text fields, and buttons (i.e., the lowest common denominator of all the OSs), and defers to Swing's emulated widgets for the rest. In SWT, emulated widgets are only used where no native implementation is possible, resulting in a portable API with as much native look and feel as possible.

JFace

JFace is a higher level toolkit, implemented using SWT. It provides classes to support common UI programming tasks such as managing image and font registries, dialog boxes, wizards, progress monitors, and so on. The JFace API does not hide SWT, but rather works with and expands on it.

A particularly valuable part of JFace is its set of standard viewer classes. Viewer classes for lists, trees, and tables work with corresponding SWT widgets, but provide a higher level connection to the data they're displaying. For example, they include convenient mechanisms for populating themselves from a data model and for keeping themselves in sync with changes to the model.

Another widely used part of JFace is its action framework, which is used to add commands to menus and toolbars. The framework allows you to create an action (to implement a user command), and then contribute the action to a toolbar, menu bar, or context menu. You can even reuse the same action in all three places.

Workbench

The workbench is the main window that the user sees when running the Eclipse IDE, or any other Eclipse-based application; it's sometimes referred to as the Eclipse desktop.[3] It is itself implemented using SWT and JFace.

A workbench window is composed primarily of *editors* and *views*. Eclipse editors work in the usual way, but they are integrated into the workbench window instead of launched externally in their own window. Views are used to present more, or different, information about the contents of the active editor or about the object selected in an editor or another view. Typically, only one instance of a view can exist at a time, and it is immediately updated based on the state of the workbench. Likewise, any changes made in a view typically take effect immediately, without requiring a save action. When activated, editors and views can contribute actions to the workbench's menus and toolbar.

The arrangement of views and editors in the workbench window can be customized to suit a role or task. A particular default arrangement is called a *perspective* in Eclipse. The user can change the arrangement of a perspective and save the result for future use.

The primary way to extend the Eclipse Platform is using extension points provided by the workbench. These extension points allow tools to add new editors, views, or perspectives to the workbench. Tools can also customize existing editors, views, or perspectives for their own purposes.

---

[3] Although primarily intended for graphical user interface (GUI)-based development, the Eclipse Platform can also be used to implement non-GUI applications by running a "headless" workbench.

IDE

The IDE is an instantiation of the generic workbench described earlier. It configures the workbench with appropriate views, editors, and perspectives for an IDE.

For example, the IDE provides a Navigator view, based on the workspace model, for navigating the tree of resources in the workspace and for performing common actions on those resources, like deletion, copying, and renaming.

The IDE also provides IDE-specific menu and toolbar items, preference pages, and other extensions.

1.2.4 Rich Client Platform

The Eclipse Platform provides so much useful functionality that it would be a shame if much of it couldn't be reused outside of the context of an IDE. Fortunately, the Eclipse Rich Client Platform (RCP) allows exactly this kind of reuse.

RCP refers to the minimal set of plug-ins needed to build a rich client application. Such applications are still based on a dynamic plug-in model, and have workbench-based UIs built on SWT and JFace. However, they specify their own workbench configuration and typically do not require the workspace resource model.

There are a number of other components provided by the Eclipse Platform that can be used by RCP applications, including the standard Outline and Property views, the help system, the update manager, text editors, and the welcome page. EMF is also well suited for use in RCP applications, as Chapter 20 details.

1.3 More Information

If you want to learn more about Eclipse, you can visit the Eclipse Web site at *http://www.eclipse.org/*. There you will find plenty of detailed information—technical, organizational, and legal. You can download the software, sign up to join user newsgroups, or even find out how to participate in the projects. Eclipse is an open source project, the very success of which depends on the active participation of a vibrant user community.

CHAPTER 2

Introducing EMF

Simply put, the Eclipse Modeling Framework (EMF) is a modeling framework that exploits the facilities provided by Eclipse. By now, you probably know what Eclipse is, given that you either just read Chapter 1, or you skipped it, presumably because you already knew what it was. You also probably know what a framework is, because you know what Eclipse is, and Eclipse is itself a framework. So, to understand what EMF really is, all you need to know is one more thing: What is a model? Or better yet, what do we mean by a model?

If you're familiar with things like class diagrams, collaboration diagrams, state diagrams, and so on, you're probably thinking that a model is a set of those things, probably defined using Unified Modeling Language (UML), the standard notation for them. You might be imagining a higher level description of an application from which some, or all, of the implementation can be generated. Well, you're right about what a model is, but not exactly about EMF's spin on it.

Although the idea is the same, a model in EMF is less general and not quite as high level as the commonly accepted interpretation. EMF doesn't require a completely different methodology or any sophisticated modeling tools. All you need to get started with EMF are the Eclipse Java Development Tools. As you'll see in the following sections, EMF relates modeling concepts directly to their implementations, thereby bringing to Eclipse—and Java developers in general— the benefits of modeling with a low cost of entry.

2.1   Unifying Java, XML, and UML

To help understand what EMF is about, let's start with a simple Java programming example. Say that you've been given the job of writing a program to manage purchase orders for some store or supplier.[1] You've been told that a purchase order includes a "bill to" and "ship to" address, and a collection of (purchase) items. An item includes a product name, a quantity, and a price. "No problem," you say, and you proceed to create the following Java interfaces:

```java
public interface PurchaseOrder
{
  String getShipTo();
  void setShipTo(String value);

  String getBillTo();
  void setBillTo(String value);

  List getItems(); // List of Item
}

public interface Item
{
  String getProductName();
  void setProductName(String value);

  int getQuantity();
  void setQuantity(int value);

  float getPrice();
  void setPrice(float value);
}
```

Starting with these interfaces, you've got what you need to begin writing the application UI, persistence, and so on.

Before you start to write the implementation code, your boss asks you, "Shouldn't you create a 'model' first?" If you're like other Java programmers we've talked to, who didn't think that modeling was relevant to them, then you'd probably claim that the Java code is the model. "Describing the model using some formal notation would have no added value," you say. Maybe a class diagram or two would fill out the documentation a bit, but other than that it

---

1. If you've read much about XML Schema, you'll probably find this example quite familiar, as it's based on the well-known example from the World Wide Web Consortium's XML Schema primer [2]. We've simplified it here, but in Chapter 4 we'll step up to the real thing.

simply doesn't help. So, to appease the boss, you produce the UML diagram shown in Figure 2.1.[2]

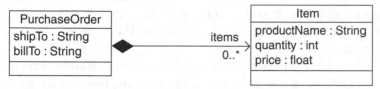

Figure 2.1   UML diagram of interfaces.

Then you tell the boss to go away so you can get down to business. (As you'll see later, if you had been using EMF, you would already have avoided this unpleasant little incident with the boss.)

Next, you start to think about how to persist this "model." You decide that storing the model in an XML file would be a good solution. Priding yourself on being a bit of an XML expert, you decide to write an XML Schema to define the structure of your XML document:

```
<?xml version="1.0" encoding="UTF-8"?>
<xsd:schema xmlns:xsd="http://www.w3.org/2001/XMLSchema"
            xmlns:po="http://www.example.com/SimplePO"
            targetNamespace="http://www.example.com/SimplePO">
  <xsd:complexType name="PurchaseOrder">
    <xsd:sequence>
      <xsd:element name="shipTo" type="xsd:string"/>
      <xsd:element name="billTo" type="xsd:string"/>
      <xsd:element name="items"  type="po:Item"
                   minOccurs="0" maxOccurs="unbounded"/>
    </xsd:sequence>
  </xsd:complexType>

  <xsd:complexType name="Item">
    <xsd:sequence>
      <xsd:element name="productName" type="xsd:string"/>
      <xsd:element name="quantity" type="xsd:int"/>
      <xsd:element name="price" type="xsd:float"/>
    </xsd:sequence>
  </xsd:complexType>
</xsd:schema>
```

---

2. If you're unfamiliar with UML and are wondering what things like the little black diamond mean, Appendix A provides a brief overview of the notation.

Before going any further, you notice that you now have three different representations of what appears to be pretty much (actually, exactly) the same thing: the "data model" of your application. Looking at it, you start to wonder if you could have written only one of the three (i.e., Java interfaces, UML diagram, or XML Schema), and generated the others from it. Even better, you start to wonder if maybe there's even enough information in this "model" to generate the Java implementation of the interfaces.

This is where EMF comes in. EMF is a framework and code generation facility that lets you define a model in any of these forms, from which you can then generate the others and also the corresponding implementation classes. Figure 2.2 shows how EMF unifies the three important technologies: Java, XML, and UML. Regardless of which one is used to define it, an EMF model is the common high-level representation that "glues" them all together.

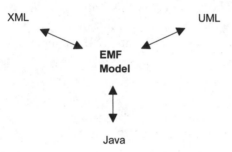

Figure 2.2   EMF unifies Java, XML, and UML.

Imagine that you want to build an application to manipulate some specific XML message structure. You would probably be starting with a message schema, wouldn't you? Wouldn't it be nice to be able to take the schema, press a button or two, and get a UML class diagram for it? Press another button, and you have a set of Java implementation classes for manipulating the XML. Finally, press one more button, and you can even generate a working editor for your messages. All this is possible with EMF, as you'll see when we walk through an example similar to this in Chapter 4.

If, on the other hand, you're not an XML Schema expert, you might choose to start with a UML diagram, or simply a set of Java interfaces representing the message structure. The EMF model can just as easily be defined using either of them. If you want, you can then have an XML Schema generated for you, in addition to the implementation code. Regardless of how the EMF model is provided, the power of the framework and generator will be the same.

2.2 Modeling vs. Programming

So is EMF simply a framework for describing a model and then generating other things from it? Well, basically yes, but there's an important difference. Unlike most tools of this type, EMF is truly integrated with and tuned for efficient programming. It answers the often-asked question, "Should I model or should I program?" with a resounding, "Both."

"To model or to program, that is not the question."

How's that for a quote? With EMF, modeling and programming can be considered the same thing. Instead of forcing a separation of the high-level engineering and modeling work from the low-level implementation programming, it brings them together as two well-integrated parts of the same job. Often, especially with large applications, this kind of separation is still desirable, but with EMF the degree to which it is done is entirely up to you.

Why is modeling interesting in the first place? Well, for starters it gives you the ability to describe what your application is supposed to do (presumably) more easily than with code. This in turn can give you a solid, high-level way both to communicate the design and to generate part, if not all, of the implementation code. If you're a hard-core programmer without a lot of faith in the idea of high-level modeling, you should think of EMF as a gentle introduction to modeling, and the benefits it implies. You don't need to step up to a whole new methodology, but you can enjoy some of the benefits of modeling. Once you see the power of EMF and its generator, who knows, we might even make a modeler out of you yet!

If, on the other hand, you have already bought into the idea of modeling, and even the Model Driven Architecture (MDA) big picture,[3] you should think of EMF as a technology that is moving in that direction, but more slowly than immediate widespread adoption. You can think of EMF as MDA on training wheels. We're definitely riding the bike, but we don't want to fall down and hurt ourselves by moving too fast. The problem is that high-level modeling languages need to be learned, and because we're going to need to work with (e.g., debug) generated Java code anyway, we now need to understand the mapping between them. Except for specific applications where things like state diagrams, for example, can be the most effective way to convey the behavior, in the general case, good old-fashioned Java programming is the simplest and most direct way to do the job.

---

3. MDA is described in Section 2.6.4.

From the last two paragraphs, you've probably surmised that EMF stands in the middle between two extreme views of modeling: the "I don't need modeling" crowd, and the "Modeling rules!" crowd. You might be thinking that being in the middle implies that EMF is a compromise and is reduced to the lowest common denominator. You're right about EMF being in the middle and requiring a bit of compromise from those with extreme views. However, as the designers of EMF, we truly feel that its exact position in the middle represents the right level of modeling at this point in the evolution of software development technology. We believe that EMF mixes just the right amount of modeling with programming to maximize the effectiveness of both. We must admit, though, that standing in the middle and arguing out of both sides of our mouths can get tiring!

What is this right balance between modeling and programming? An EMF model is essentially the Class Diagram subset of UML; that is, a simple model of the classes, or data, of the application. From that, a surprisingly large portion of the benefits of modeling can be had within a standard Java development environment. With EMF, there's no need for the user, or other development tools (e.g., a debugger), to understand the mapping between a high-level modeling language and the generated Java code. The mapping between an EMF model and Java is natural and simple for Java programmers to understand. At the same time, it's enough to support fine-grained data integration between applications; next to the productivity gain resulting from code generation, this is one of the most important benefits of modeling.

2.3 Defining the Model

Let's put aside the philosophy for now and take a closer look at what we're really describing with an EMF model. We saw in Section 2.1 that our conceptual model could be defined in several different ways; that is, in Java, UML, or XML Schema. But, what exactly are the common concepts we're talking about when describing a model? Let's look at our purchase order example again. Recall that our simple model included the following:

1. **PurchaseOrder** and **Item**, which in UML and Java map to class definitions, but in XML Schema map to complex type definitions.

2. **shipTo**, **billTo**, **productName**, **quantity**, and **price**, which map to attributes in UML, `get()`/`set()` method pairs (or bean properties, if you want to look at it that way) in Java, and in the XML Schema are nested element declarations.

3. **items**, which is a UML association end or reference, a `get()` method in Java, and in XML Schema, a nested element declaration of another complex type.

As you can see, a model is described using concepts that are at a higher level than simple classes and methods. Attributes, for example, represent pairs of methods, and as you'll see when we look deeper into the EMF implementation, they also have the ability to notify observers (e.g., UI views) and be saved to, and loaded from, persistent storage. References are more powerful yet, because they can be bidirectional, in which case referential integrity is maintained. References can also be persisted across multiple resources (documents), where demand load and proxy resolution come into play.

To define a model using these kinds of "model parts" we need a common terminology to describe them. More important, to implement the EMF tools and generator, we also need a model for the information. We need a model for describing EMF models; that is, a metamodel.

2.3.1 *The Ecore (Meta) Model*

The model used to represent models in EMF is called Ecore. Ecore is itself an EMF model, and thus is its own metamodel. You could say that makes it a meta-metamodel. People often get confused when talking about meta-metamodels (metamodels in general, for that matter), but the concept is actually quite simple. A metamodel is simply the model of a model, and if that model is itself a metamodel, then the metamodel is in fact a meta-metamodel.[4] Got it? If not, don't worry about it, as it's really just an academic issue anyway.

A simplified subset of the Ecore metamodel is shown in Figure 2.3. This diagram only shows the parts of Ecore needed to describe our purchase order example, and we've taken the liberty of simplifying it a bit to avoid showing base classes. For example, in the real Ecore metamodel the classes **EClass**, **EAttribute**, and **EReference** share a common base class, **ENamedElement**, which defines the **name** attribute that here we've shown explicitly in the classes themselves.

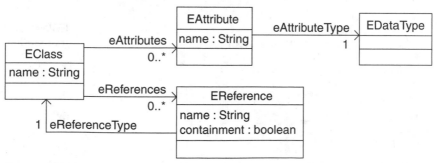

Figure 2.3 A simplified subset of the Ecore metamodel.

---

4. This concept can recurse into meta-meta-metamodels, and so on, but we won't go there.

As you can see, there are four Ecore classes needed to represent our model:

1. **EClass** is used to represent a modeled class. It has a name, zero or more attributes, and zero or more references.

2. **EAttribute** is used to represent a modeled attribute. Attributes have a name and a type.

3. **EReference** is used to represent one end of an association between classes. It has a name, a boolean flag to indicate if it represents containment, and a reference (target) type, which is another class.

4. **EDataType** is used to represent the type of an attribute. A data type can be a primitive type like `int` or `float` or an object type like `java.util.Date`.

Notice that the names of the classes correspond most closely to the UML terms. This is not surprising because UML stands for Unified Modeling Language. In fact, you might be wondering why UML isn't "the" EMF model. Why does EMF need its own model? Well, the answer is quite simply that Ecore is a small and simplified subset of full UML. Full UML supports much more ambitious modeling than the core support in EMF. UML, for example, allows you to model the behavior of an application, as well as its class structure. We'll talk more about the relationship of EMF to UML and other standards in Section 2.6.

We can now use instances of the classes defined in Ecore to describe the class structure of our application models. For example, we describe the purchase order class as an instance of **EClass** named "PurchaseOrder". It contains two attributes (instances of **EAttribute** that are accessed via **eAttributes**) named "shipTo" and "billTo", and one reference (an instance of **EReference** that is accessed via **eReferences**) named "items", for which **eReferenceType** (its target type) is equal to another **EClass** instance named "Item". These instances are shown in Figure 2.4.

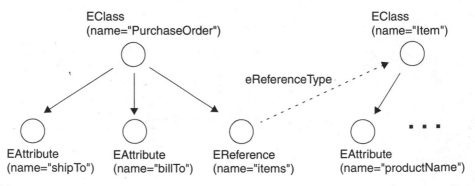

Figure 2.4 The purchase order Ecore instances.

When we instantiate the classes defined in the Ecore metamodel to define the model for our own application, we are creating what we call an *Ecore model*.

2.3.2 Creating and Editing the Model

Now that we have these Ecore objects to represent a model in memory, EMF can read from them to, among other things, generate implementation code. You might be wondering, though, how do you create the model in the first place? The answer is that you need to build it from whatever input form you start with. If you start with Java interfaces, EMF will introspect them and build the Ecore model. If, instead, you start with an XML Schema, then the model will be built from that. If you start with UML, there are three possibilities:

1. **Direct Ecore editing.** EMF includes a simple tree-based sample editor for Ecore. If you'd rather use a graphical tool, the Ecore Tools project[5] provides a graphical Ecore editor based on UML notation. Third-party options are also available, including Topcased's Ecore Editor (*http://www.topcased.org/*), Omondo's EclipseUML (*http://www.omondo.com/*) and Soyatec's eUML (*http://www.soyatec.com/*).

2. **Import from UML.** The EMF Project and EMF Model wizards provide an extensible framework, into which model importers can be plugged, supporting different model formats. EMF provides support for Rational Rose (*.mdl* files) only. The reason Rose has this special status is because it's the tool that was used to "bootstrap" the implementation of EMF itself. The UML2 project[6] also provides a model importer for standard UML 2.x models.

3. **Export from UML.** This is similar to the second option, but the conversion support is provided exclusively by the UML tool. It is invoked from within the UML tool, instead of from an EMF wizard.

As you might imagine, the first option is the most desirable. With it, there is no import or export step in the development process. You simply edit the model and then generate. Also, unlike the other options, you don't need to worry about the Ecore model being out of sync with the tool's own native model. The other

---

5. Ecore Tools is a component of the EMF Technology (EMFT) project, which is itself a subproject of the Eclipse Modeling Project. EMFT is an incubator project for new technologies that extend or complement EMF. The Web site for Ecore Tools is *http://www.eclipse.org/modeling/emft/?project=ecoretools*.

6. UML2 is another component in the Eclipse Modeling Project. It provides an EMF-based implementation of the UML 2.x metamodel and can be found at *http://www.eclipse.org/modeling/mdt/?project=uml2*.

two approaches require an explicit reimport or reexport step whenever the UML model changes.

The advantage of the second and third options is that you can use the UML tool to do more than just your EMF modeling. You can use the full power of UML and whatever fancy features the particular tool has to offer. If it supports its own code generation, for example, you can use the tool to define your Ecore model, and also to both define and generate other parts of your application. As long as a mechanism for conversion to Ecore is provided, that tool will also be usable as an input source for EMF and its generator.

2.3.3 XMI Serialization

By now you might be wondering what the serialized form of an Ecore model is. Previously, we've observed that the "conceptual" model is represented in at least three physical places: Java code, XML Schema, or a UML diagram. Should there be just one form that we use as the primary, or standard, representation? If so, which one should it be?

Believe it or not, we actually have yet another (i.e., a fourth) persistent form that we use as the canonical representation: XML Metadata Interchange (XMI). Why did we need another one? We weren't exactly short of ways to represent the model persistently.

For starters, Java code, XML Schema, and UML all carry additional information beyond what is captured in an Ecore model. Moreover, none of these forms is required in every scenario in which EMF can be used. Java code was the only one required in our running example, but as we will soon see, even it is optional in some cases. So, what we need is a direct serialization of Ecore, which doesn't add any extra information. XMI fits the bill here, as it is a standard for serializing metadata concisely using XML.

Serialized as an Ecore XMI file, our purchase order model looks something like this:

```
<?xml version="1.0" encoding="UTF-8"?>
<ecore:EPackage xmi:version="2.0" xmlns:xmi="http://www.omg.org/XMI"
    xmlns:xsi="http://www.w3.org/2001/XMLSchema-instance"
    xmlns:ecore="http://www.eclipse.org/emf/2002/Ecore" name="po"
    nsURI="http://www.example.com/SimplePO" nsPrefix="po">
  <eClassifiers xsi:type="ecore:EClass" name="PurchaseOrder">
    <eStructuralFeatures xsi:type="ecore:EAttribute" name="shipTo"
        eType="ecore:EDataType
            http://www.eclipse.org/emf/2002/Ecore#//EString"/>
    <eStructuralFeatures xsi:type="ecore:EAttribute" name="billTo"
        eType="ecore:EDataType
```

```
                    http://www.eclipse.org/emf/2002/Ecore#//EString"/>
      <eStructuralFeatures xsi:type="ecore:EReference" name="items"
         upperBound="-1" eType="#//Item" containment="true"/>
    </eClassifiers>
    <eClassifiers xsi:type="ecore:EClass" name="Item">
      <eStructuralFeatures xsi:type="ecore:EAttribute"
         name="productName"
         eType="ecore:EDataType
                    http://www.eclipse.org/emf/2002/Ecore#//EString"/>
      <eStructuralFeatures xsi:type="ecore:EAttribute" name="quantity"
         eType="ecore:EDataType
                    http://www.eclipse.org/emf/2002/Ecore#//EInt"/>
      <eStructuralFeatures xsi:type="ecore:EAttribute" name="price"
         eType="ecore:EDataType
                    http://www.eclipse.org/emf/2002/Ecore#//EFloat"/>
    </eClassifiers>
  </ecore:EPackage>
```

Notice that the XML elements correspond directly to the Ecore instances back in Figure 2.4, which makes perfect sense because this is a serialization of exactly those objects. Here we've hit an important point: because Ecore metadata is not the same as, for example, UML metadata, XMI serializations of the two are not the same either.[7]

2.3.4 Java Annotations

Let's revisit the issue of defining an Ecore model using Java interfaces. Previously we implied that when provided with ordinary Java interfaces, EMF "would" introspect them and deduce the model properties. That's not exactly the case. The truth is that given interfaces containing standard get() methods,[8] EMF *could* deduce the model attributes and references. EMF does not, however, blindly assume that every interface and method in it is part of the model. The reason for this is that the EMF generator is a code-merging generator. It generates code that not only is capable of being merged with user-written code, it's *expected* to be.

Because of this, our PurchaseOrder interface isn't quite right for use as a model definition. First of all, the parts of the interface that correspond to model elements whose implementation should be generated need to be indicated. Unless explicitly marked with an @model annotation in the Javadoc comment, a method

---

7. When we spoke of exporting a model for use with EMF in the previous section, we were really talking about exporting to Ecore XMI, specifically.

8. EMF uses a subset of the JavaBeans simple property accessor naming patterns. For more information, see Section 7.1 of the specification at *http://java.sun.com/products/javabeans/docs/spec.html*.

is not considered to be part of the model definition. For example, interface `PurchaseOrder` needs the following annotations:

```
/**
 * @model
 */
public interface PurchaseOrder
{
  /**
   * @model
   */
  String getShipTo();

  /**
   * @model
   */
  String getBillTo();

  /**
   * @model type="Item" containment="true"
   */
  List getItems();
}
```

Here, the `@model` tags identify **PurhaseOrder** as a modeled class, with two attributes, **shipTo** and **billTo,** and a single reference, **items.** Notice that both attributes, **shipTo** and **billTo,** have all their model information available through Java introspection; that is, they are simple attributes of type `String`. No additional model information appears after their `@model` tags, because only information that is different from the default needs to be specified.

There is some non-default model information needed for the **items** reference. Because the reference is multiplicity-many, indicated by the fact that `getItems()` returns a `List`, we need to specify the target type of the reference as `type="Item"`.[9] We also need to specify `containment="true"` to indicate that we want purchase orders to be a container for their items and serialize them as children.

Notice that the `setShipTo()` and `setBillTo()` methods are not required in the annotated interface. With the annotations present on the `get()` method, we don't need to include them; once we've identified the attributes (which are settable by default), the `set()` methods will be generated and merged into the interface if they're not already there.

---

9. Note that beginning with Java 5.0, generics can be used to specify a list's item type. Generics have only been supported in EMF since version 2.3. You'll see the older form, with a raw list type, throughout most of this book, both as the Java specification for a multiplicity-many reference and in the code generated from it. Chapter 21, which focuses specifically on EMF 2.3 and 2.4, details the new generics-based form.

2.3.5   *The Ecore "Big Picture"*

Let's recap what we've covered so far.

1. Ecore, and its XMI serialization, is the center of the EMF world.

2. An Ecore model can be created from any of at least three sources: a UML model, an XML Schema, or annotated Java interfaces.

3. Java implementation code and, optionally, other forms of the model can be generated from an Ecore model.

We haven't talked about it yet, but there is one important advantage to using XML Schema to define a model: given the schema, instances of the model can be serialized to conform to it. Not surprisingly, in addition to simply defining the model, the XML Schema approach is also specifying something about the persistent form of the instances.

One question that comes to mind is whether there are other persistent model forms possible. Couldn't we, for example, provide a relational database (RDB) Schema and produce an Ecore model from it? Couldn't this RDB Schema also be used to specify the persistent format, similar to the way XML Schema does? The answer is, quite simply, yes. This is one type of function that EMF is intended to support, and certainly not the only kind. The "big picture" is shown in Figure 2.5.

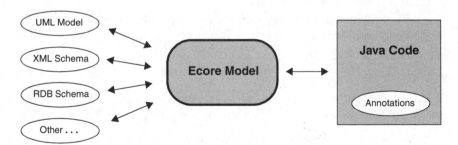

Figure 2.5   An Ecore model and its sources.

2.4   Generating Code

The most important benefit of EMF, as with modeling in general, is the boost in productivity that results from automatic code generation. Let's say that you've defined a model, for example the purchase order Ecore model shown in Section 2.3.3, and are ready to turn it into Java code. What do you do now? In Chapter 4, we'll walk through this scenario and others where you start with other forms of the model (e.g., Java interfaces). For now, suffice to say that it only involves a few mouse clicks. All you need to do is create a project using the EMF Project wizard, which automatically launches the generator, and select **Generate Model Code** from a menu.

2.4.1 Generated Model Classes

So what kind of code does EMF generate? The first thing to notice is that an Ecore class (i.e., an **EClass**) actually corresponds to two things in Java: an interface and a corresponding implementation class. For example, the **EClass** for **PurchaseOrder** maps to a Java interface:

```
public interface PurchaseOrder ...
```

and a corresponding implementation class:

```
public class PurchaseOrderImpl extends ... implements PurchaseOrder {
```

This interface–implementation separation is a design choice favored by EMF. Why do we advocate this approach? The reason is simply that we believe it's the best pattern for any model-like API. For example, the Document Object Model (DOM) is like this and so is much of Eclipse. It's also a necessary pattern to support multiple inheritance in Java.

The next thing to notice about each generated interface is that it extends directly or indirectly from the base interface `EObject` like this:

```
public interface PurchaseOrder extends EObject {
```

`EObject` is the EMF equivalent of `java.lang.Object`; that is, it's the base of all modeled objects. Extending `EObject` introduces three main behaviors:

1. **eClass()** returns the object's metaobject (an `EClass`).
2. **eContainer()** and **eResource()** return the object's containing object and resource.
3. **eGet()**, **eSet()**, **eIsSet()**, and **eUnset()** provide an API for accessing the objects reflectively.

The first and third items are interesting only if you want to generically access the objects instead of, or in addition to, using the type-safe generated accessors. We'll look at how this works in Sections 2.5.3 and 2.5.4. The second item is an integral part of the persistence API that we will describe in Section 2.5.2.

Other than that, EObject has only a few convenience methods. However, there is one more important thing to notice; EObject extends yet another interface:

```
public interface EObject extends Notifier {
```

The Notifier interface is also quite small, but it introduces an important characteristic to every modeled object; model change notification as in the Observer design pattern [3]. Like object persistence, notification is an important feature of an EMF object. We'll look at EMF notification in more detail in Section 2.5.1.

Let's move on to the generated methods. The exact pattern that is used for any given feature (i.e., attribute or reference) implementation depends on the type and other user-settable properties. In general, the features are implemented as you'd expect. For example, the get() method for the **shipTo** attribute simply returns an instance variable like this:

```
public String getShipTo()
{
  return shipTo;
}
```

The corresponding set() method sets the same variable, but it also sends a notification to any observers that might be interested in the state change:

```
public void setShipTo(String newShipTo)
{
  String oldShipTo = shipTo;
  shipTo = newShipTo;
  if (eNotificationRequired())
    eNotify(new ENotificationImpl(this,
                          Notification.SET,
                          POPackage.PURCHASE_ORDER__SHIP_TO,
                          oldShipTo, shipTo));
}
```

Notice that, to make this method more efficient when the object has no observers, the relatively expensive call to eNotify() is avoided by the eNotificationRequired() guard.

More complicated patterns are generated for other types of features, especially bidirectional references where referential integrity is maintained. In all cases, however, the code is generally as efficient as possible, given the intended semantic. We'll cover the complete set of generator patterns in Chapter 10.

The main message you should go away with is that the generated code is clean, simple, and efficient. EMF does not pull in large base classes, or generate inefficient code. EMF's runtime framework is lightweight, as are the objects generated for your model. The idea is that the code that's generated should look pretty much like what you would have written, had you done it by hand. However, because it's generated, you know it's correct. It's a big time saver, especially for some of the more complicated bidirectional reference handshaking code, which might otherwise be fairly difficult to get right.

Before moving on, we should mention two other important classes that are generated for a model: a factory and a package. The generated factory (e.g., POFactory) includes a create method for each class in the model. The EMF programming model strongly encourages, but doesn't require, the use of factories for creating objects. Instead of simply using the new operator to create a purchase order, you should do this:

```
PurchaseOrder aPurchaseOrder =
  POFactory.eINSTANCE.createPurchaseOrder();
```

The generated package (e.g., POPackage) provides convenient accessors for all the Ecore metadata for the model. You might already have noticed, in the implementation of setShipTo() shown earlier, the use of POPackage. PURCHASE_ORDER__SHIP_TO, a static int constant representing the **shipTo** attribute. The generated package also includes convenient accessors for the **EClass**es, **EAttribute**s, and **EReference**s. We'll look at the use of these accessors in Section 2.5.3.

2.4.2   Other Generated "Stuff"

In addition to the interfaces and classes described in the previous section, the EMF generator can optionally generate the following:

1. A skeleton adapter factory[10] class (e.g., POAdapterFactory) for the model. This convenient base class can be used to implement adapter factories that need to create type-specific adapters; for example, a PurchaseOrderAdapter for **PurchaseOrders**, an ItemAdapter for **Items**, and so on.

2. A convenience switch class (e.g., POSwitch) that implements a "switch statement"-like callback mechanism for dispatching based on an object's

---

10. Adapters and adapter factories are described in Section 2.5.1.

type (i.e., its **EClass**). The adapter factory class, as just described, uses this switch class in its implementation.

3. Plug-in manifest files and property files, so that the model can be used as an Eclipse plug-in.

If all you're interested in is generating a model, this is the end of the story. However, as we'll see in Chapters 3 and 4, the EMF generator can, using the EMF.Edit extensions to the EMF core, generate adapter classes that enable viewing and command-based, undoable editing of a model. It can even generate a complete working editor for your model. We will talk more about EMF.Edit and its capabilities in the following chapter. For now, we just stick to the basic modeling framework itself.

2.4.3 Regeneration and Merge

The EMF generator produces files that are intended to be a combination of generated pieces and handwritten pieces. You are expected to edit the generated classes to add methods and instance variables. You can always regenerate from the model as needed and your additions will be preserved during the regeneration.

EMF uses @generated markers in the Javadoc comments of generated interfaces, classes, methods, and fields to identify the generated parts. For example, getShipTo() actually looks like this:

```
/**
 * @generated
 */
public String getShipTo() { ...
```

Any method that doesn't have this @generated tag (i.e., anything you add by hand) will be left alone during regeneration. If you already have a method in a class that conflicts with a generated method, your version will take precedence and the generated one will be discarded. You can, however, redirect a generated method if you want to override it but still call the generated version. If, for example, you rename the getShipTo() method with a Gen suffix:

```
/**
 * @generated
 */
public String getShipToGen() { ...
```

Then if you add your own `getShipTo()` method without an `@generated` tag, the generator will, on detecting the conflict, check for the corresponding `Gen` version and, if it finds one, redirect the generated method body there.

The merge behavior for other things is generally reasonable. For example, you can add extra interfaces to the `extends` clause of a generated interface (or the `implements` clause of a generated class) and specify that they should be retained during regeneration. The single extends class of a generated class, however, will always be overwritten by the model's choice. We'll look at code merging in more detail in Chapter 10.

2.4.4   The Generator Model

Most of the data needed by the EMF generator is stored in the Ecore model. As we saw in Section 2.3.1, the classes to be generated and their names, attributes, and references are all there. There is, however, more information that needs to be provided to the generator, such as where to put the generated code and what prefix to use for the generated factory and package class names, that isn't stored in the Ecore model. All this user-settable data also needs to be saved somewhere so that it will be available if we regenerate the model in the future.

The EMF code generator uses a generator model to store this information. Like Ecore, the generator model is itself an EMF model. Actually, a generator model provides access to all of the data needed for generation, including the Ecore part, by wrapping the corresponding Ecore model. That is, generator model classes are decorators [3] of Ecore classes. For example, `GenClass` decorates `EClass`, `GenFeature` decorates `EAttribute` and `EReference`, and so on.

The significance of all this is that the EMF generator runs off of a generator model instead of an Ecore model; it's actually a generator model editor.[11] When you use the generator, you'll be editing a generator model, which in turn indirectly accesses the Ecore model from which you're generating. As you'll see in Chapter 4 when we walk through an example of using the generator, there are two model resources (files) in the project: an *.ecore* file and a *.genmodel* file. The *.ecore* file is an XMI serialization of the Ecore model, as we saw in Section 2.3.3. The *.genmodel* file is a serialized generator model with cross-document references to the *.ecore* file. Figure 2.6 shows the conceptual picture.

---

11. It is, in fact, an editor generated by EMF, like the ones we'll be looking at in Chapter 4 and later in the book.

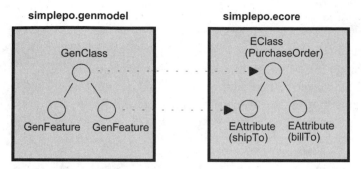

Figure 2.6 The .genmodel and .ecore files.

Separating the generator model from the Ecore model like this has the advantage that the actual Ecore metamodel can remain pure and independent of any information that is only relevant for code generation. The disadvantage of not storing all the information right in the Ecore model is that a generator model might get out of sync if the referenced Ecore model changes. To handle this, the generator model elements are able to automatically reconcile themselves with changes to their corresponding Ecore elements. Users don't need to worry about it.

2.5 The Runtime Framework

In addition to simply increasing your productivity, building your application using EMF provides several other benefits, such as model change notification, persistence support including default XMI serialization, and an efficient reflective API for manipulating EMF objects generically. Most importantly, EMF provides the foundation for interoperability with other EMF-based tools and applications.

2.5.1 *Notification and Adapters*

In Section 2.4.1, we saw that every generated EMF class is also a `Notifier`; that is, it can send notification whenever an attribute or reference is changed. This is an important property, allowing EMF objects to be observed, for example, to update views or other dependent objects.

Notification observers (or listeners) in EMF are called adapters because in addition to their observer status, they are often used to extend the behavior (i.e., support additional interfaces without subclassing) of the object they're attached to. An adapter, as a simple observer, can be attached to any `EObject` (e.g., a `PurchaseOrder`) by adding to its adapter list like this:

```
Adapter poObserver = ...
aPurchaseOrder.eAdapters().add(poObserver);
```

After doing this, the `notifyChanged()` method will be called, on poObserver, whenever a state change occurs in the purchase order (e.g., if the `setBillTo()` method is called), as shown in Figure 2.7.

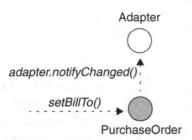

Figure 2.7 Calling the notifyChanged() method.

Unlike simple observers, attaching an adapter as a behavior extension is normally done using an adapter factory. An adapter factory is asked to adapt an object with an extension of the required type, something like this:

```
PurchaseOrder aPurchaseOrder = ...
AdapterFactory somePOAdapterFactory = ...
Object poExtensionType = ...
if (somePOAdapterFactory.isFactoryForType(poExtensionType))
{
  Adapter poAdapter =
    somePOAdapterFactory.adapt(aPurchaseOrder, poExtensionType);
  ...
}
```

Often, the `poExtensionType` represents some interface supported by the adapter. For example, the argument could be the actual `java.lang.Class` for an interface of the chosen adapter. The returned adapter can then be downcast to the requested interface, like this:

```
POAdapter poAdapter =
  (POAdapter)somePOAdapterFactory.adapt(someObject,
                                  POAdapter.class);
```

If the adapter of the requested type is already attached to the object, then `adapt()` will return the existing adapter; otherwise it will create a new one.

In EMF, the adapter factory is the one responsible for creating the adapter; the EMF object itself has no notion of being able to adapt itself. This approach allows greater flexibility to implement the same behavioral extension in more than one way, as different factories can return different implementation for a given extension type.

As you can see, an adapter must be attached to each individual `EObject` that it wants to observe. Sometimes, you might want to be informed of state changes to any object in a containment hierarchy, a resource, or even any of a set of related resources. Rather than requiring you to walk through the hierarchy and attach your observer to each object, EMF provides a very convenient adapter class, `EContentAdapter`, that can be used for this purpose. It can be attached to a root object, a resource, or even a resource set, and it will automatically attach itself to all the contents. It will then receive notification of state changes to any of the objects and will even respond to content change notifications itself, by attaching or detaching itself as appropriate.

Adapters are used extensively in EMF as observers and to extend behavior. They are the foundation for the UI and command support provided by EMF.Edit, as we will see in Chapter 3. We'll also look at how they work in much more detail in Chapter 16.

2.5.2 Object Persistence

The ability to persist and reference other persisted objects, is one of the most important benefits of EMF modeling; it's the foundation for fine-grained data integration between applications. EMF provides simple, yet powerful, mechanisms for managing object persistence.

As we've seen earlier, Ecore models are serialized using XMI. Actually, EMF includes a default XMI serializer that can be used to persist objects generically from any model, not just Ecore. Even better, if your model is defined using an XML Schema, EMF allows you to persist your objects as an XML instance document conforming to that schema. The persistence framework, combined with the code generated for your model, handles all this for you.

Above and beyond the default serialization support, EMF allows you to save your objects in any persistent form you like. In this case you'll also need to write the actual serialization code yourself, but once you do that the model will transparently be able to reference (and be referenced by) objects in other models and documents, regardless of how they're persisted.

When we looked at the properties of a generated model class in Section 2.4.1, we pointed out that there are two methods related to persistence: `eContainer()` and `eResource()`. To understand how they work, let's start with the following example:

```
PurchaseOrder aPurchaseOrder =
  POFactory.eINSTANCE.createPurchaseOrder();
aPurchaseOrder.setBillTo("123 Maple Street");

Item aItem = POFactory.eINSTANCE.createItem();
aItem.setProductName("Apples");
aItem.setQuantity(12);
aItem.setPrice(0.50);

aPurchaseOrder.getItems().add(aItem);
```

Here we've created a **PurchaseOrder** and an **Item** using the generated classes from our purchase order model. We then added the **Item** to the **items** reference by calling `getItems().add()`.

Whenever an object is added to a containment reference, which **items** is, it also sets the container of the added object. So, in our example, if we were to call `aItem.eContainer()` now, it would return the purchase order, `aPurchaseOrder`.[12] The purchase order itself is not in any container, so calling `eContainer()` on it would return `null`. Note also that calling the `eResource()` method on either object would also return `null` at this point.

Now, to persist this pair of objects, we need to put them into a resource. Interface `Resource` is used to represent a physical storage location (e.g., a file). To persist our objects, all we need to do is add the root object (i.e., the purchase order) to a resource like this:

```
Resource poResource = ...
poResource.getContents().add(aPurchaseOrder);
```

After adding the purchase order to the resource, calling `eResource()` on either object will return `poResource`. The item (`aItem`) is in the resource via its container (`aPurchaseOrder`).

Now that we've put the two objects into the resource, we can save them by simply calling `save()` on the resource. That seems simple enough, but where did we get the resource from in the first place? To understand how it all fits together we need to look at another important interface in the persistence framework: `ResourceSet`.

A `ResourceSet`, as its name implies, is a set of resources that are accessed together to allow for potential cross-document references among them. It's also

---

12. Notice how this implies that a containment association is implicitly bidirectional, even if, like the **items** reference, it is declared to be one-way. We discuss this issue in more detail in Chapter 10.

the factory for its resources. So, to complete our example, we would create the resource, add the purchase order to it, and then save it like this:[13]

```
ResourceSet resourceSet = new ResourceSetImpl();
URI fileURI =
  URI.createFileURI(new File("mypo.xml").getAbsolutePath());
Resource poResource = resourceSet.createResource(fileURI);
poResource.getContents().add(aPurchaseOrder);
poResource.save(null);
```

Class `ResourceSetImpl` chooses the resource implementation class using an implementation registry. Resource implementations are registered, globally or local to the resource set, based on a URI scheme, file extension, or other possible criteria. If no specific resource implementation applies for the specified URI, then EMF's default XMI resource implementation will be used.

Assuming that we haven't registered a different resource implementation, after saving our simple resource, we'd get an XMI file, *mypo.xml*, that looks something like this:

```
<?xml version="1.0" encoding="UTF-8"?>
<po:PurchaseOrder xmi:version="2.0"
    xmlns:xmi="http://www.omg.org/XMI"
    xmlns:po="http://www.example.com/SimplePO"
    billTo="123 Maple Street">
  <items productName="Apples" quantity="12" price="0.5"/>
</po:PurchaseOrder>
```

Now that we've been able to save our model instance, let's look at how we would load it again. Loading is also done using a resource set like this:

```
ResourceSet resourceSet = new ResourceSetImpl();
URI fileURI =
  URI.createFileURI(new File("mypo.xml").getAbsolutePath());
Resource poResource = resourceSet.getResource(fileURI, true);
PurchaseOrder aPurchaseOrder =
  (PurchaseOrder)poResource.getContents().get(0);
```

Notice that because we know that the resource has our single purchase order at its root, we simply get the first element and downcast.

---

13. If you're wondering about the call to `File.getAbsolutePath()`, it's used to ensure that we start with an absolute URI that will allow any cross-document references that we might serialize to use relative URIs, guaranteeing that our serialized document(s) will be location independent. URIs and cross-document referencing are described in detail in Chapter 14.

The resource set also manages demand load for cross-document references, if there are any. When loading a resource, any cross-document references that are encountered will use a proxy object instead of the actual target. These proxies will then be resolved lazily when they are first used.

In our simple example, we actually have no cross-document references; the purchase order contains the item, and they are both in the same resource. Imagine, however, that we had modeled **items** as a non-containment reference as shown in Figure 2.8.

Figure 2.8 **items** as a simple reference.

Notice the missing black diamond on the **PurchaseOrder** end of the association, indicating a simple reference as opposed to a by-value aggregation (containment reference). If we make this change using Java annotations instead of UML, the `getItems()` method would need to change to this:

```
/**
 * @model type="Item"
 */
List getItems();
```

Now that **items** is not a containment reference, we'll need to explicitly call `getContents().add()` on a resource for the item, just like we previously did for the purchase order. We also have the option of adding it to the same resource as the purchase order, or to a different one. If we choose to put the items into separate resources, then demand loading would come into play, as shown in Figure 2.9. In Figure 2.9, Resource 1 (which could contain our purchase order, for example) contains cross-document references to Resource 2 (e.g., containing our item). When we load Resource 1 by calling `getResource()` for "uri 1", any references to objects in Resource 2 (i.e., "uri 2") will simply be set to proxies. A proxy is an uninitialized instance of the target class, but with the actual object's URI stored in it. Later, when we access the object—for example, by calling `aPurchaseOrder.getItems().get(0)`—Resource 2 will be demand loaded and the proxy will be resolved (i.e., replaced with the target object).

Although, as we saw earlier, objects in containment references are implicitly included in their container's resource by default, it is also possible to enable cross-resource containment. In Chapters 10 and 15, we'll explore this topic, and look at demand loading, proxies, and proxy resolution in greater detail.

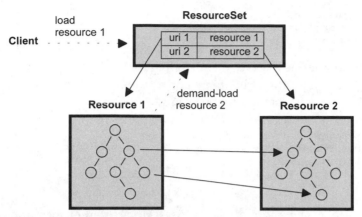

Figure 2.9   Resource set demand loading of resources.

2.5.3   The Reflective EObject API

As we observed in Section 2.4.1, every generated model class implements the EMF base interface, EObject. Among other things, EObject defines a generic, reflective API for manipulating instances:

```
public interface EObject
{
  Object eGet(EStructuralFeature feature);
  void eSet(EStructuralFeature feature, Object newValue);

  boolean eIsSet(EStructuralFeature feature);
  void eUnset(EStructuralFeature feature);

  ...
}
```

We can use this reflective API, instead of the generated methods, to read and write the model. For example, we can set the **shipTo** attribute of the purchase order like this:

```
aPurchaseOrder.eSet(shipToAttribute, "123 Maple Street");
```

We can read it back like this:

```
String shipTo = (String)aPurchaseOrder.eGet(shipToAttribute);
```

We can also create a purchase order reflectively by calling a generic create method on the factory like this:

```
EObject aPurchaseOrder =
  poFactory.create(purchaseOrderClass);
```

If you're wondering where the metaobjects, `purchaseOrderClass` and `shipToAttribute`, and the `poFactory` come from, the answer is that you can get them using generated static fields like this:

```
POFactory poFactory = POFactory.eINSTANCE;
EClass purchaseOrderClass = POPackage.Literals.PURCHASE_ORDER;
EAttribute shipToAttribute =
  POPackage.Literals.PURCHASE_ORDER__SHIP_TO;
```

The EMF code generator also generates efficient implementations of the reflective methods. They are slightly less efficient than the generated `getShipTo()` and `setShipTo()` methods (the reflective methods dispatch to the generated ones through a generated switch statement), but they open up the model for completely generic access. For example, the reflective methods are used by EMF.Edit to implement a full set of generic commands (e.g., `AddCommand`, `RemoveCommand`, `SetCommand`) that can be used on any model. We'll talk more about this in Chapter 3.

Notice that in addition to the `eGet()` and `eSet()` methods, the reflective `EObject` API includes two more methods: `eIsSet()` and `eUnset()`. The `eIsSet()` method can be used to find out if an attribute is set or not, whereas `eUnset()` can be used to unset or reset it. The generic XMI serializer, for example, uses `eIsSet()` to determine which attributes need to be serialized during a resource save operation. We'll talk more about the "unset" state, and its significance on certain models, in Chapters 5 and 10.

2.5.4   Dynamic EMF

Until now, we've only ever considered the value of EMF in generating implementations of models. Sometimes, we would like to simply share objects without requiring generated implementation classes to be available. A simple interpretive implementation would be good enough.

A particularly interesting characteristic of the reflective API is that it can also be used to manipulate instances of dynamic, non-generated, classes. Imagine if we hadn't created the purchase order model or run the EMF generator to produce the Java implementation classes in the usual way. Instead, we could simply create the Ecore model at runtime, something like this:

```
EPackage poPackage = EcoreFactory.eINSTANCE.createEPackage();

EClass purchaseOrderClass = EcoreFactory.eINSTANCE.createEClass();
purchaseOrderClass.setName("PurchaseOrder");
poPackage.getEClassifiers().add(purchaseOrderClass);

EClass itemClass = EcoreFactory.eINSTANCE.createEClass();
itemClass.setName("Item");
poPackage.getEClassifiers().add(itemClass);

EAttribute shipToAttribute =
  EcoreFactory.eINSTANCE.createEAttribute();
shipToAttribute.setName("shipTo");
shipToAttribute.setEType(EcorePackage.eINSTANCE.getEString());
purchaseOrderClass.getEStructuralFeatures().add(shipToAttribute);

// and so on ...
```

Here we have an in-memory Ecore model, for which we haven't generated any Java classes. We can now create a purchase order instance and initialize it using the same reflective calls as we used in the previous section:

```
EFactory poFactory = poPackage.getEFactoryInstance();
EObject aPurchaseOrder = poFactory.create(purchaseOrderClass);
aPurchaseOrder.eSet(shipToAttribute, "123 Maple Street");
```

Because there is no generated `PurchaseOrderImpl` class, the factory will create an instance of `EObjectImpl` instead.[14] `EObjectImpl` provides a default dynamic implementation of the reflective API. As you'd expect, this implementation is slower than the generated one, but the behavior is exactly the same.

An even more interesting scenario involves a mixture of generated and dynamic classes. For example, assume that we had generated class **PurchaseOrder** in the usual way and now we'd like to create a dynamic subclass of it.

```
EClass subPOClass = EcoreFactory.eINSTANCE.createEClass();
subPOClass.setName("SubPO");
subPOClass.getESuperTypes().add(poPackage.getPurchaseOrder());
poPackage.getEClassifiers().add(subPOClass);
```

If we now instantiate an instance of our dynamic class **SubPO**, then the factory will detect the generated base class and will instantiate it instead of

---

14. This is not entirely true. It could instantiate `EObjectImpl` directly, but instead it actually uses an instance of a simple subclass of `EObjectImpl`, `DynamicEObjectImpl`, which is tuned to provide better performance in the pure dynamic case.

`EObjectImpl`. The significance of this is that any accesses we make to attributes or references that come from the base class will call the efficient generated implementations in class `PurchaseOrderImpl`:

```
String shipTo = aSubPO.eGet(shipToAttribute);
```

Only features that come from the derived (dynamic) class will use the slower dynamic implementation. Another direct benefit of this approach is that any **SubPO** object is actually an instance of the Java interface `PurchaseOrder`, as reported by the `instanceof` operator.

The most important point of all of this is that, when using the reflective API, the presence (or lack thereof) of generated implementation classes is completely transparent. All you need is the Ecore model in memory. If generated implementation classes are (later) added to the class path, they will then be used. From the client's perspective, the only thing that will change is the speed of the code.

2.5.5   *Foundation for Data Integration*

The last few sections have shown various features of the runtime framework that support sharing of data. Section 2.5.1 described how change notification is an intrinsic property of every EMF object, and how adapters can be used to support open-ended extension. In Section 2.5.2, we showed how the EMF persistence framework uses `Resources` and `ResourceSets` to support cross-document referencing, demand loading of documents, and arbitrary persistent forms. Finally, in Sections 2.5.3 and 2.5.4 we saw how EMF supports generic access to EMF models, including ones that might be partially or completely dynamic (i.e., without generated implementation classes).

In addition to these features, the runtime framework provides a number of convenience classes and utility functions to help manage the sharing of objects. For example, a utility class for finding object cross-references (`EcoreUtil. CrossReferencer` and its subclasses) can be used to find any uses of an object (e.g., to clean up references when deleting the object) and any unresolved proxies in a resource, among other things.

All these features, combined with an intrinsic property of models—that they are higher level descriptions that can more easily be shared—provide all the needed ingredients to foster fine-grained data integration. While Eclipse itself provides a wonderful platform for integration at the UI and file level, EMF builds on this capability to enable applications to integrate at a much finer granularity than would otherwise be possible. We've seen how EMF can be used to share data reflectively, even without using the EMF code generation support. Whether dynamic or generated, EMF models are the foundation for fine-grained data integration in Eclipse.

2.6 EMF and Modeling Standards

EMF is often discussed together with several important modeling standards of the Object Management Group (OMG), including UML, MOF, XMI, and MDA. This section introduces these standards and describes EMF's relationships with them.

2.6.1 Unified Modeling Language

UML is the most widely used standard for describing systems in terms of object concepts. UML is very popular in the specification and design of software, most often software to be written using an object-oriented language. UML emphasizes the idea that complex systems are best described through a number of different views, as no single view can capture all aspects of such a system completely. As such, it includes several different types of model diagrams to capture usage scenarios, class structures, behaviors, and implementations.

EMF is concerned with only one aspect of UML, class modeling. This focus is in no way a rejection of UML's holistic approach. Rather, it is a starting point, based on the pragmatic realization that the task of translating the ideas that can be expressed in various UML diagrams into concrete implementations is very large and very complex.

UML was first standardized by the OMG in 1997. The standard's latest version is 2.1.2; it is available at *http://www.omg.org/spec/UML/2.1.2/*. The UML2 project, which like EMF belongs to the Eclipse Modeling Project, provides an EMF-based implementation of the UML metamodel.

2.6.2 Meta-Object Facility

Meta-Object Facility (MOF) concretely defines a subset of UML for describing class modeling concepts within an object repository. As such, MOF is comparable to Ecore. However, with a focus on tool integration, rather than metadata repository management, Ecore avoids some of MOF's complexities, resulting in a widely applicable, optimized implementation.

MOF and Ecore have many similarities in their ability to specify classes and their structural and behavioral features, inheritance, packages, and reflection. They differ in the area of life cycle, data type structures, package relationships, and complex aspects of associations.

MOF was first standardized in 1997, at the same time as UML. The standard, which is now at version 2.0, is available at *http://www.omg.org/spec/MOF/2.0/*.

Development experience from EMF has substantially influenced this latest version of the specification, in terms of the layering of the architecture and the structure of the semantic core. Essential Meta-Object Facility (EMOF) is the new, lightweight core of the metamodel that quite closely resembles Ecore. Because the two models are so similar, EMF is able to support EMOF directly as an alternate XMI serialization of Ecore.

2.6.3 XML Metadata Interchange

XMI is the standard that connects modeling with XML, defining a simple way to serialize models in XML documents. An XMI document's structure closely matches that of the corresponding model, with the same names and an element hierarchy that follows the model's containment hierarchy. As a result, the relationship between a model and its XMI serialization is easy to understand.

Although XMI can be, and is by default, used as the serialization format for instances of any EMF model, it is most appropriate for use with models representing metadata; that is, metamodels, like Ecore itself. We refer to·an Ecore model, serialized in XMI 2.0, as *Ecore XMI* and consider an Ecore XMI (*.ecore*) file as the canonical form of such a model.

XMI was standardized in 1998, shortly after XML 1.0 was finalized. The latest XMI specification, version 2.1.1, is available at *http://www.omg.org/spec/XMI/2.1.1/*.

2.6.4 Model Driven Architecture

MDA is an industry architecture proposed by the OMG that addresses full lifecycle application development, data, and application integration standards that work with multiple middleware languages and interchange formats. MDA unifies some of the industry best practices in software architecture, modeling, metadata management, and software transformation technologies that allow a user to develop a modeling specification once and target multiple technology implementations by using precise transformations and mappings.

EMF supports the key MDA concept of using models as input to development and integration tools: in EMF, a model is used to drive code generation and serialization for data interchange.

MDA information and key specifications are available at *http://www.omg.org/mda/*.

CHAPTER 3

Model Editing with EMF.Edit

In the previous chapter we saw how EMF can take a model definition and produce a good, easily customizable Java implementation for it. Well, that's just the beginning. Once you decide to use EMF to model your application, you can then use EMF.Edit to build very functional viewers and editors for the model. You can generate an editor that will display and edit (i.e., copy, paste, drag-and-drop, etc.) instances of your model using standard JFace viewers and a property sheet, all with unlimited undo and redo. Alternatively, you can use the reflective support in EMF.Edit to do the same kinds of editing reflectively, even with a dynamic EMF model for which you didn't generate code.

You might be thinking that this is beginning to sound like one of those infomercials: if you buy EMF in the next 24 hours, we'll throw in the free viewers, drag-and-drop, and a bonus icon directory. Well, maybe it does sound that way, but the bottom line is that EMF.Edit is simply exploiting the information that is available in the model, along with the mechanisms supplied by the EMF core, to provide greater and higher level functionality. The free functionality being offered comes naturally from the fact that we have a model, so you can rest assured that there is no "free juicer" about to be offered.

3.1   Displaying and Editing EMF Models

Let's return to the simple purchase order model we looked at in Chapter 2. Recall that it consisted of two simple classes with a containment association between them, as illustrated in Figure 3.1.

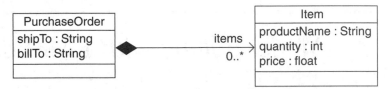

Figure 3.1   Purchase order model with containment association.

In the previous chapter we saw how EMF gives you the ability to generate Java implementations for the model classes **PurchaseOrder** and **Item**, as well as other supporting classes. We also saw how using the generated classes along with the framework classes Resource and ResourceSet, you could persist a purchase order instance and its items. For example, assuming you used the framework default (XMI) serializer, a purchase order with two items could be serialized something like this:

```
<po:PurchaseOrder xmi:version="2.0"
    xmlns:xmi="http://www.omg.org/XMI"
    xmlns:po="http://www.example.com./SimplePO"
    billTo="123 Maple Street">
  <items productName="Apples" quantity="12" price="0.5"/>
  <items productName="Oranges" quantity="24" price="0.3"/>
</po:PurchaseOrder>
```

Let's assume you save this into a file, *My.po*, somewhere in your Eclipse workspace. The next thing you might like to do is display and edit it using a purchase order editor launched in the Eclipse workbench. You could then, for example, display the containment structure in a tree view and edit the attributes in a property sheet as shown in Figure 3.2. To really leverage the power of Eclipse, you would want to "integrate" the purchase order implementation with the Eclipse desktop this way.

So what would it take to display a model in a UI like this? To understand that, we first need to understand how Eclipse viewers work in general. The following section gives a brief overview of the Eclipse UI framework's viewer classes, property sheet, and action mechanism. If you already know how they work, you might want to skip it and go straight to Section 3.1.2, where we start to look at what EMF.Edit provides to help you use the Eclipse framework to display and edit EMF models.

TreeViewer

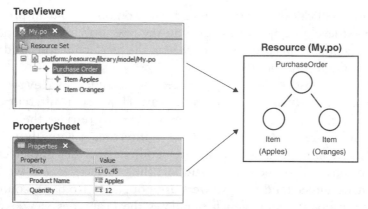

Figure 3.2   Outline and Properties views of a purchase order.

3.1.1   Eclipse UI Basics

Included in JFace, a part of the Eclipse UI framework, is a set of reusable viewer classes (e.g., `TreeViewer`) for displaying data based on structured models. Instead of querying objects directly, the JFace viewers use a content provider to navigate the content and a label provider to retrieve the label text and icons for the objects being displayed. Each viewer class uses a content provider that implements a specific provider interface. For example, a `TreeViewer` uses a content provider that implements the interface `ITreeContentProvider`, as shown in Figure 3.3.

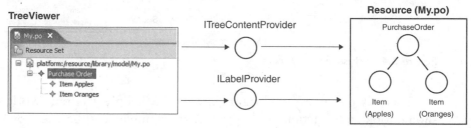

Figure 3.3   JFace viewer access to a model instance.

To display our purchase order resource in a `TreeViewer`, we start by providing the root object (the Resource object, "My.po", in this example) to the viewer. The viewer will respond by calling the `getText()` and `getImage()` methods on its label provider to retrieve the image and text, respectively. Next, the `TreeViewer` will call the `getChildren()` method on its content provider to retrieve the next level of objects to display in the tree (only the single purchase order in our example). This process of retrieving the text, icon, and children will then repeat for the rest of the tree.

In addition to class `TreeViewer`, JFace also includes `TableViewer` and `ListViewer` classes, which work the same way. They use a different content provider interface, `IStructuredContentProvider`, to retrieve their content. However, the `ITreeContentProvider` interface actually extends `IStructuredContentProvider`, so any tree content provider implementation class can also conveniently be used to support the other viewers as well.

Now that we understand how viewers are populated from a resource, let's look at how a property sheet, which populates the Properties view, works. A property sheet gets the properties of an object by first calling the `getPropertySource()` method on its associated `IPropertySourceProvider`. Figure 3.4 shows how the property source provider produces an `IPropertySource` corresponding to a specific object, for example, the "Apples" item. Next, the property sheet calls the `getPropertyDescriptors()` method on the property source to get a list of `IPropertyDescriptors` for the object's properties ("Price", "Product Name", and "Quantity"). The `IPropertyDescriptor` interface is then used by the property sheet to display and edit the properties.

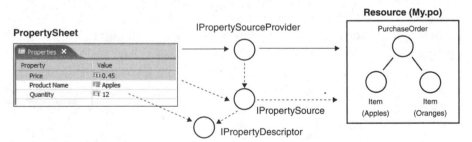

Figure 3.4 Eclipse property sheet.

There is one more important part of the Eclipse UI framework that we should look at: the action mechanism. Actions implement the `IAction` interface and represent the commands that can be run from menu items or toolbar buttons. When a menu item or toolbar button is selected, the framework invokes the associated action by calling its `run()` method. Actions also include methods to retrieve, among other things, the label and icon. For example, the `getText()` method is called by the framework to get the text for a menu item, when it is showing. The `getImageDescriptor()` method is used to get the icon to display both on menu items and toolbar buttons.

An action bar contributor is used to create and manage the actions for an editor. A subclass of `EditorActionBarContributor` is used to contribute the actions on behalf of its associated `EditorPart`. For example, to add a **New Purchase Order** item to the menu bar for a purchase order editor, `POEditor`, we would create an action bar contributor subclass, `POActionBarContributor`, and override the `contributeToMenu()` method to add (contribute) the new action. `POActionBarContributor` would be associated with `POEditor` in the workbench "registered editor" extension in the editor plug-in's manifest file.

3.1.2   EMF.Edit Support

Now that we know how views and actions work in Eclipse, we can look at how EMF.Edit helps you implement a UI for a model based on EMF.

To implement a tree viewer, like the one shown in the previous section, we need an implementation of the `ITreeContentProvider` interface that is capable of returning the children of EMF objects. We also need an implementation of `ILabelProvider` to return a suitable text string for the label, usually based on one of the Ecore attributes. For a property sheet, we need a way of producing a set of `IPropertyDescriptors` for the subset of Ecore attributes and references that should be exposed as properties. EMF.Edit supports two ways of implementing these things, one using the reflective `EObject` API, and the other using generated classes.

The reflective approach consults the Ecore model at runtime to provide a "best guess" implementation. For example, it implements the `getChildren()` method by calling `eContents()` on an `EObject` to return its contained objects. For a label, it first tries to find a "name" attribute (case insensitive) in the class, or failing that, one that includes the string "name" (e.g., "productName"). For our simple purchase order example, the reflective implementation will do pretty much what we want.

The second approach is to use the EMF generator to generate an implementation. The generated approach will, by default, produce the same behavior as the reflective implementation. This is not surprising, because the code is generated from the same Ecore model that the reflective implementation uses at runtime. With the generated approach, however, you have an opportunity to influence some of the choices before the code is generated. For example, you could pick the **quantity** attribute for the label feature instead of the default **productName**.

Generating the implementation classes also results in a much more easily customizable solution. Just like the EMF model classes described in Chapter 2, you can modify and regenerate the EMF.Edit classes any way you like. The generated classes provide convenient override points for the most common types of customizations, unlike the reflective implementation, which would require a monolithic override with lots of `instanceof` checks.

EMF.Edit also includes support for Eclipse actions, and object modification in general, based on the Command design pattern [3]. Changing the state of a modeled EMF object, by running an action or using a property descriptor, is implemented in EMF.Edit by delegating to a command. EMF.Edit includes generic implementations of a number of common commands, as well as framework support for customizing their behavior or for implementing your own specialized commands.

As shown in Figure 3.5, EMF.Edit is the bridge between the Eclipse UI framework and the EMF core.

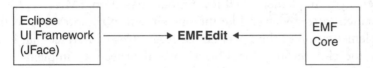

Figure 3.5   EMF.Edit connects the Eclipse UI and EMF core frameworks.

A large amount of EMF.Edit function is actually independent of the UI. To support reuse of the UI-independent parts, EMF.Edit is divided into two separate plug-ins:

1. **org.eclipse.emf.edit** is the low-level UI-independent portion.

2. **org.eclipse.emf.edit.ui** contains the Eclipse UI-dependent implementation classes.

As we'll see in the following two sections, most of the editing work is actually delegated to two very important mechanisms in the UI-independent plug-in: item providers and commands. The UI plug-in connects these mechanisms to the display, tying the implementation to the Eclipse UI framework.

3.2   Item Providers

Item providers constitute the single most important piece of EMF.Edit. They are used to adapt EMF objects, providing all of the interfaces that they need to be viewed or edited. If you think back to Chapter 2, where we saw how EMF adapters can be used as both behavioral extensions and as change observers, you can see how adapters would be just right for implementing item providers. As behavioral extensions, they can adapt the objects to implement whatever interfaces the editors and views need, and at the same time, as observers, they will be notified of state changes that they can then pass on to listening views.

Although item providers are usually EMF adapters, this is not always the case. An item provider that is "providing" for an EMF object will be an adapter, but other item providers may represent non-modeled objects, mixed into a view with modeled items. This is an important feature of EMF.Edit. It has been carefully designed to allow you to create views on EMF objects that might be structurally different from the underlying objects themselves (i.e., views that suppress objects or include additional, non-modeled objects). We'll look at this issue in Chapter 19. For now you should simply think of item providers as adapters on EMF objects, but keep in mind that the framework is actually more flexible.

Their name, "item provider", stems from the fact that they "provide" functions on behalf of individual editable "items" (objects). As you'll see in the following sections, EMF.Edit implements a delegation scheme whereby most functions involving objects are ultimately implemented in their associated item providers. Consequently, item providers need to perform four major roles:

1. Implement content and label provider functions.

2. Provide a property source (property descriptors) for EMF objects.

3. Act as a command factory for commands on their associated objects.

4. Forward EMF change notifications on to viewers.

A given item provider can implement all of these functions or just a subset, depending on what editing functions are actually required. Most commonly, however, item providers simply implement them all by subclassing the very functional EMF.Edit base class, `ItemProviderAdapter`. It implements most of the function generically, so a subclass (which can be generated, as we'll see in Section 3.4.1) only needs to implement a few methods to complete the job. EMF.Edit also provides a full function subclass, `ReflectiveItemProvider`, that implements all of the roles using the reflective `EObject` API. We'll talk about these and other implementation issues in Section 3.2.5, but first, the next four sections will describe each of the roles of an item provider.

3.2.1 Content and Label Item Providers

The first role of an item provider is to support the implementation of content and label providers for the viewers. In Section 3.1.1, we saw how Eclipse viewers use a content provider (e.g., `ITreeContentProvider`) and a label provider (e.g., `ILabelProvider`) to get the information they need from the model. EMF.Edit provides generic content and label provider implementation classes, `AdapterFactoryContentProvider` and `AdapterFactoryLabelProvider`, that delegate their implementation to item providers as shown in Figure 3.6.

Both of these classes are constructed with an adapter factory (`POItemProviderAdapterFactory` in this example), which, like any other EMF adapter factory, serves to create and locate EMF adapters of a specific type (item providers for the purchase order model, in this case).

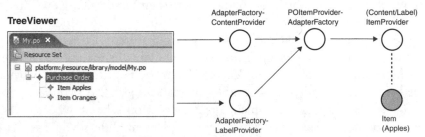

Figure 3.6 Content and label provider role of an item provider.

To service a request like `ITreeContentProvider.getChildren()`, for example, the `AdapterFactoryContentProvider` first calls `adapt()` on the `ItemProviderAdapterFactory`, which will create or return the `ItemProvider` (adapter) for the specified object. It then simply delegates to the `getChildren()` method of a corresponding item provider interface, `ITreeItemContent-Provider`. The `getChildren()` method in `AdapterFactoryContentProvider` looks something like this:

```
public Object[] getChildren(Object object)
{
  ITreeItemContentProvider adapter = (ITreeItemContentProvider)
    adapterFactory.adapt(object, ITreeItemContentProvider.class);
  return adapter.getChildren(object).toArray();
}
```

This same pattern is used for all of the content provider methods, and also by the `AdapterFactoryLabelProvider` to implement `ILabelProvider` methods (e.g., `getText()`). The adapter factory content and label providers do nothing more than simply delegate JFace provider methods to corresponding EMF content and label item provider mixin interfaces:

1. `ITreeItemContentProvider` is used to support content providers for `TreeViewers`.

2. `IStructuredItemContentProvider` is used to support content providers for other structured viewers, such as `ListViewers` and `TableViewers`.

3. `ITableItemLabelProvider` is used to support label providers for `TableViewers`.

4. `IItemLabelProvider` is used to support label providers for other structured viewers.

Notice the similarity of these interface names to those in JFace, with the word "Item" added. The EMF.Edit interfaces are in fact very similar to the corresponding JFace ones. The main reason for having the parallel set of interfaces is to avoid any dependencies on JFace. Although item providers are primarily used to implement Eclipse (JFace-based) UIs, they are completely UI independent. So, in addition to their use in support of the JFace implementation classes, `AdapterFactoryContentProvider` and `AdapterFactoryLabelProvider`, they can also be used to implement views for other UI libraries (e.g., Swing), or to implement non-UI, command-based utilities for EMF models.

3.2.2   Item Property Source

The second major role of an item provider is to act as a property source for the property sheet. Recall that the Eclipse `PropertySheet` uses an `IPropertySourceProvider` to request an `IPropertySource` for the object whose properties it wants to display and edit. In EMF.Edit, the `AdapterFactoryContentProvider` also implements the `IPropertySourceProvider` interface and is used to provide a property source to the property sheet, as shown in Figure 3.7.

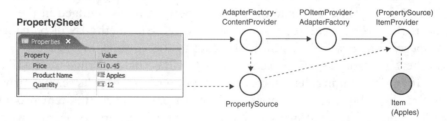

Figure 3.7   Property source role of an item provider.

Following the same pattern that we saw for `ITreeContentProvider` in the previous section, the `AdapterFactoryContentProvider` uses the adapter factory to locate an item provider, only this time one that implements the EMF.Edit item provider mixin interface `IItemPropertySource`. Again, just like the content and label provider interface, this EMF.Edit interface, `IItemPropertySource`, is very similar to its corresponding Eclipse interface, `IPropertySource`, only UI independent. Another EMF.Edit helper class, `PropertySource`, implements the actual `IPropertySource` interface needed by the property sheet. The `AdapterFactoryContentProvider` creates an instance of this class as a wrapper for the selected item provider (i.e., the `IItemPropertySource`) and then returns it to the `PropertySheet`.

This same wrapping pattern is used again when the property sheet calls the `IPropertySource.getPropertyDescriptors()` method. The `PropertySource` services the request by delegating to the `getPropertyDescriptors()` method on the item provider, which returns a set of `IItemPropertyDescriptors`. The `PropertySource` then instantiates an `IPropertyDescriptor` wrapper class, `PropertyDescriptor`, for each item property descriptor, returning these wrappers to the property sheet. The complete picture is shown in Figure 3.8.

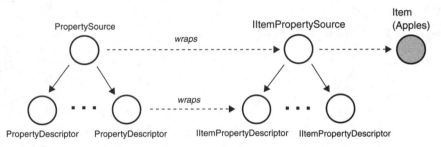

Figure 3.8   `PropertySource` and `PropertyDescriptor` **delegation.**

With this arrangement, property descriptor calls are now delegated to their "Item" equivalents. For example, if a property value is changed in the property sheet, the `PropertySource.setPropertyValue()` method will be called. The property source will then simply delegate to the `setPropertyValue()` method on the `ItemPropertyDescriptor`, which will actually change the EMF object.

If you're thinking that all this creating of wrapper objects seems fairly messy, you're right, but that's the price we have to pay to keep the item providers UI independent. The good news is that the property descriptors are the worst, and the last, of this double-object pattern.

3.2.3   Command Factory

Item providers act as the factory for commands involving their adapted objects. In this role, item providers play a critical part in the EMF.Edit command framework, which we'll look at in Section 3.3. For now, let's just say that EMF.Edit provides all the mechanisms for modifying EMF objects in an undoable way, including a full set of generic commands. The framework makes it easy to tune the command behavior for specific models by delegating their creation to item providers.

Similar to the way the Eclipse UI framework uses "provider" interfaces (e.g., `ITreeContentProvider`) to access the model, the EMF.Edit command framework also has an interface, `EditingDomain`, which it uses for the same purpose. Also, just like the content and label providers, a delegating implementation class, `AdapterFactoryEditingDomain`, is used to implement it. As shown in Figure 3.9, `AdapterFactoryEditingDomain` works the same as the other `AdapterFactory` implementation classes, only it delegates its methods to an item provider supporting the editing domain item provider mixin interface `IEditingDomainItemProvider`. We'll look at editing domains and the role of item providers in their implementation in Section 3.3.3.

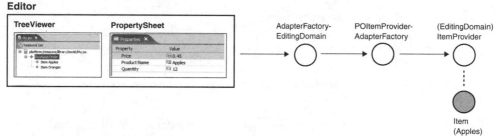

Figure 3.9   Command creation role of an item provider.

3.2.4   Change Notification

Being a standard EMF adapter, an `ItemProvider` will be notified, with a call to its `notifyChanged()` method, whenever an object that it is adapting changes state. The `ItemProvider`'s responsibility as an observer is to optionally filter uninteresting events and then to pass the remaining ones on to a central change notifier for the model, usually the `ItemProviderAdapterFactory`. The `ItemProviderAdapterFactory` implements the EMF.Edit interface `IChangeNotifier`, which allows views and other interested parties to register as listeners of the model as a whole. The design is illustrated in Figure 3.10.

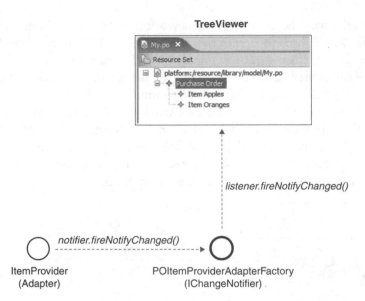

Figure 3.10   Notification flow from an `ItemProvider` to the views.

Figure 3.10 shows the flow of notification after a purchase order **Item** changes state in some way (e.g., the **productName** attribute was just set to "Apples"). In its `notifyChanged()` method, the `ItemItemProvider` (that is the `ItemProvider` for the class **Item**) passes on the change notification by calling the `fireNotifyChanged()` method on the `IChangeNotifier` (the `POItemProviderAdapterFactory` in our example), which in turn calls `fireNotifyChanged()` on all its registered listeners. In our example, the listener is a `TreeViewer`, which would now be updated to reflect the change.

That's basically all there is to it, but there are two more details worth mentioning. First, rather than simply passing along basic EMF change notifications, an `ItemProvider` can actually decorate them with information describing the extent to which viewers will need to be updated. Second, it is not the JFace viewer that actually listens for notifications from the adapter factory. Instead, the content provider associated with that viewer registers as a listener on its behalf.

As shown in Figure 3.11, the content provider responds to the `fireNotifyChanged()` call by updating the viewer according to the information provided by the `ItemProvider`. This is another function that is handled automatically for you by the EMF.Edit class `AdapterFactoryContentProvider`. It merges and queues notifications to minimize the number of viewer updates required, and translates these notifications into the appropriate calls to the standard JFace viewer APIs. All updates to viewers are performed asynchronously, allowing for the possibility that an update may cause additional resources to be loaded, resulting in another notification and update.

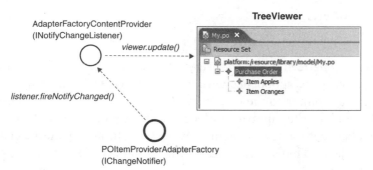

Figure 3.11   `AdapterFactoryContentProvider` updating its associated viewer.

3.2.5   Item Provider Implementation Classes

Now that we understand the various roles that item providers play, the question of how to implement them comes up. EMF.Edit provides lots of flexibility as far as this is concerned, ranging from using a single generic (reflective) item provider to having generated type-specific item providers for every class in the model.

Reflective Item Provider

In Chapter 2, we showed how Java code does not necessarily need to be generated for an EMF model. If you choose not to generate implementation classes for your model, you can still create and manipulate instances of your classes using dynamic EMF and the reflective `EObject` API. The same is true for the editing support in EMF.Edit.

You can decide to generate or to use a reflective implementation for your item providers. In fact, you can choose to use reflective item providers for some of your classes and generated ones for others. The important thing to consider is how much customization you plan to do.

Class `ReflectiveItemProvider` is the EMF.Edit generic item provider implementation, which implements essentially the same behavior as generated item providers with default generator settings. Using it is simple, but its behavior is not easily customizable. Any customization you might want to do will involve identifying the type of each object, probably via `instanceof` checks. If you use typed item provider classes whose inheritance hierarchy mirrors the model's instead, you will be able to specialize the implementation in a clean, object-oriented way.

Typed Item Providers

When using the typed item providers, there are two possible patterns:

1. The Stateful pattern, in which every object in an instance of the model has a one-to-one correspondence with its item provider. Each item provider has a target pointer to the one and only object that it is adapting. This pattern doubles the number of objects in the application, and therefore only makes sense when the item providers need to carry additional state for the objects. That's why we call it the Stateful pattern.

2. The Singleton pattern avoids most of the extra objects. With this pattern, we share a single item provider adapter for all objects of the same type. In this case, like the reflective case, each item provider has many targets.

To allow more than one object to share an item provider (i.e., for the Singleton or reflective cases), an extra argument (the object) is passed to every item provider interface method. For example, the `getChildren()` method in the `ITreeItemProvider` interface looks like this:

```
public Collection getChildren(Object object);
```

In the Stateful case, this object will always be the same as the adapter's target, so a Stateful item provider implementation could choose to ignore this argument and use the adapter target to access the object instead. However, doing the opposite (using the argument instead of the target) is a better approach because it leaves you the option of switching to the Singleton pattern in the future, without having to change the item provider itself.

3.3 Command Framework

In the previous sections, we've seen how instances of EMF models can be viewed using content and label providers, but we haven't talked much about how to change, or edit, them. Another very important feature of EMF.Edit is its support for command-based editing of EMF objects, including fully automatic undo and redo.

Note that we are not referring to Eclipse workbench commands here. Those commands are used to associate key bindings with actions, whereas EMF commands provide model-based implementations for actions. EMF commands have been around since the first release of the framework, while workbench commands were introduced only in Eclipse 3.1. EMF currently does not make use of workbench commands, so any mention of commands in this book refers to EMF commands.

The command framework in EMF is divided into two parts, the common command framework and the EMF.Edit commands. The common framework defines basic command interfaces and provides some implementation classes like a basic command stack, a compound command for composing commands from other commands, and other convenient command implementations. The commands in the common framework are very general and can be used independently of EMF.Edit. In fact, they don't even depend on EMF objects (i.e., EObjects).

The EMF.Edit commands, on the other hand, are specifically for editing EObjects. EMF.Edit includes a full set of generic command implementation classes that, using the reflective EObject API, provide support for setting attributes, adding and removing references, copying objects, and other kinds of EMF object modifications. In the next two sections we'll look at some of the most interesting commands provided by the framework. Then, in Section 3.3.3, we'll look at the rest of the infrastructure in the command framework, and how it allows you to easily customize a command's behavior for your specific model.

3.3.1 Common Command Framework

The common command framework includes the basic interfaces and implementation classes with which model-based change commands can be built and executed. Although the main use of them is in EMF.Edit, they are completely general purpose (i.e., they work with java.lang.Objects as opposed to EObjects) and therefore can be used with any model, EMF or not. The framework consists of the following classes and interfaces.

Command

Command is the base interface that all commands must implement. Most important, it includes execute(), undo(), and redo() methods that behave as one would expect. A command is tested for executability by calling the canExecute() method, which is often used to control the enablement of actions bound to the command. Not all commands can be undone; sometimes it is just too hard to maintain all the information needed to reverse the state changes caused by a command. The method canUndo() is used to check for undoability of a command. Returning false from canUndo() indicates that the undo() and redo() methods are unimplemented.

The command interface includes a few more methods, two of which are particularly interesting: getResult() and getAffectedObjects(). Implementing these two methods is optional, but they can be quite useful. The getResult() method is used by a command implementation to return what should be considered the result of its execution. This allows one to implement compound commands where the result of one command can be the input of another. For example, if a generic object copy command returns the copy as its result, then a copy-and-paste command could simply be composed from the copy command and a generic add command; the add command's input would be the copy command's result.

The second method, `getAffectedObjects()`, is used to return the objects that have been changed during the last `execute()`, `undo()`, or `redo()` call. The EMF.Edit UI framework uses the affected objects to control the UI selection to highlight the effect of the command. The `getAffectedObjects()` method often returns the same thing as `getResult()`, but not always.

Finally, it is worth mentioning that a command can supply a label and a description, which are often passed along to the action implemented by the command.

AbstractCommand

Class `AbstractCommand` is a convenient partial implementation of the `Command` interface that most commands extend. It's a small class that doesn't really do a lot; non-trivial commands need to override most of the methods anyway. However, it does provide an important implementation of the `canExecute()` method, which calls out to another protected method, `prepare()`, like this:

```
public boolean canExecute()
{
  if (!isPrepared)
  {
    isExecutable = prepare();
    isPrepared = true;
  }
  return isExecutable;
}
```

Notice that the `prepare()` method will be called only once, regardless of how often `canExecute()` is called. This is particularly significant if the enablement checking of the actual command subclass involves a lot of computation. With this design, all a subclass needs to do differently is override and put the enablement checking code in the `prepare()` method, instead of `canExecute()`.

CommandStack

`CommandStack` defines the interface for executing and maintaining commands in an undoable stack. Like `Command` itself, it includes methods to `execute()`, undo(), and redo() a command, only here it also maintains the command on the stack. The canUndo() and canRedo() methods can be used to determine if there are any commands on the stack to undo or redo, respectively. Other methods are provided to access the command at the top of the stack or the next command to undo or redo, to flush the stack, and to add change listeners to the stack.

CommandStackListener

CommandStackListener defines the interface for listening to a command stack. It includes a single method, commandStackChanged(), which a command stack invokes on any registered listeners following an execute(), undo(), redo(), or flush().

BasicCommandStack

Class BasicCommandStack is a basic implementation of the CommandStack interface. It is fully functional and can be used, as is, as the command stack for an EMF.Edit-based editor. One interesting observation relates to non-undoable commands. It can be seen when looking at the implementation of the canUndo() method in BasicCommandStack:

```
public boolean canUndo()
{
  return top != -1 && ((Command)commandList.get(top)).canUndo();
}
```

Notice that the command stack will not only return false from the canUndo() method when there are no commands to undo (i.e., top == -1), but also if the last executed command cannot be undone (i.e., (...command-List.get(top)).canUndo() returns false). This is a very important observation in that it implies that if a non-undoable command is executed, the entire stack of commands before it will no longer be undoable either. The undo list is effectively wiped out at this point, so it's important to consider this before executing a non-undoable command on the command stack.

CompoundCommand

Class CompoundCommand is probably the single most commonly used command in the framework. It's a very useful class that allows you to build higher level commands by composing them from other more basic commands. The execute() method simply calls execute(), in order, on each of the commands from which it is composed; canExecute() returns true if all the commands can execute; and so on.

In addition to delegating its implementation to the composed commands, `CompoundCommand` provides a few useful convenience methods. For example, the `appendAndExecute()` method can be used to append a command and immediately execute it. This is a particularly good way of recording a set of executed commands, which can later be reversed by simply calling `undo()` on the compound command. This technique is often used to conditionally execute commands in the `execute()` method of another command. Chapter 19 includes an example of this.

Another useful convenience method is `unwrap()`, which returns the underlying (composed) command if there is only one, or the compound command itself (i.e., `this`) otherwise. It allows you to optimize away compound commands that only have one command under them.

CommandWrapper

Class `CommandWrapper` is another useful base for creating new commands from existing ones. It simply wraps an existing command and delegates all method implementations to that command.

`CommandWrapper` is typically used to create decorators and proxies for existing commands. A decorator can override any delegating methods to alter the command's behavior or to provide a different label, description, result, or set of affected objects for the new command. A proxy delays the creation of the delegate command until `canExecute()` is called.

Other Common Commands

In addition to the classes we've just described, there are three more common command implementation classes that are less frequently used but nevertheless quite handy: `IdentityCommand`, `UnexecutableCommand`, and `StrictCompoundCommand`.

Consider the scenario in which a larger operation has been broken down into several steps, each implemented by some command, and you are writing a method that returns one of these commands. If, in a particular circumstance, your step should do nothing, you can return an `IdentityCommand`. Along the same lines, the `UnexecutableCommand` can be used to signal that your step cannot be completed, which often would result in the entire operation being cancelled.

`StrictCompoundCommand` is a subclass of `CompoundCommand` that is applicable when testing the executability of one underlying command depends on previous commands having already been executed. As a result, its implementation of `canExecute()` actually calls `execute()` on each command before testing the executability of the next.

3.3.2   EMF.Edit Commands

EMF.Edit includes a set of generic commands for modifying EMF objects. Its commands extend and build on the interfaces defined in the common command component. They use the reflective `EObject` API to operate on objects, imposing a dependency on Ecore. The following basic commands are provided:

1. `SetCommand` sets the value of an attribute or reference on an `EObject`.

2. `AddCommand` adds one or more objects to a multiplicity-many feature of an `EObject`.

3. `RemoveCommand` removes one or more objects from a multiplicity-many feature of an `EObject`.

4. `MoveCommand` moves an object within a multiplicity-many feature of an `EObject`.

5. `ReplaceCommand` replaces an object in a multiplicity-many feature of an `EObject`.

6. `CopyCommand` performs a deep copy of one or more `EObjects`.

These commands work on instances of any EMF model, and their implementations fully support undo and redo. All of these commands, except `CopyCommand`, are primitive commands that simply perform their function when called. A `CopyCommand` is composed from instances of two other special-purpose primitive commands, `CreateCopyCommand` and `InitializeCopyCommand`, which create and initialize a shallow copy object, respectively. The `CopyCommand` works by building up `CompoundCommands` composed of `CreateCopyCommands` and `InitializeCopyCommands` for the individual objects that need to be copied. It then invokes the compound commands to perform the deep copy. This approach allows easy customization of any part of the copy operation.

EMF.Edit also includes some higher level commands that are built using the basic commands we have just seen, along with some of the classes from the common command component:

1. `CreateChildCommand` allows you to create a new object and add it to a feature of an `EObject`. It uses an `AddCommand` or `SetCommand` to add the child, depending on whether the feature is multiplicity-many or not.

2. `DeleteCommand` uses one or more `RemoveCommands` to remove an `EObject` from its parent container and delete all other references to it.

3. `CutToClipboardCommand` invokes a `RemoveCommand`, and then saves the removed object on the clipboard.

4. `CopyToClipboardCommand` simply saves a pointer on the clipboard; it doesn't actually change any objects.

5. `PasteFromClipboardCommand` uses a `CopyCommand` to copy the object on the clipboard and then an `AddCommand` to add the copy to the target location.

6. `DragAndDropCommand` uses `CopyCommand`, `RemoveCommand`, and `AddCommand` to implement standard drag-and-drop operations.

There is one more command, called `ChangeCommand`, that provides a different approach to complex editing. Instead of combining basic commands to form more complicated compound commands, you can use a `ChangeCommand` to record arbitrary modifications to any number of `EObjects` in `execute()` and revert those changes in `undo()`. Under the covers, an EMF change recorder is used to produce a description of the change. We will discuss change recording in Chapter 17.

That's it for the predefined commands, but there are a couple of other interesting features of the EMF.Edit command package that we should point out. The first has to do with overrideability of the commands.

AbstractOverrideableCommand

Most of the generic EMF.Edit commands are derived from an abstract base class, `AbstractOverrideableCommand`, which is, itself, a subclass of the common `AbstractCommand`. The EMF.Edit base class adds the ability to attach another command to override it, via delegation. For example, the `execute()` method looks like this:

```
public final void execute()
{
  if (overrideCommand != null)
    overrideCommand.execute();
  else
    doExecute();
}
```

If an `overrideCommand` is attached, the `execute()` method is delegated to it, otherwise the `doExecute()` method is called. This pattern is used for all of the `Command` methods.

You might be wondering why this is needed, given that you can always override a command simply by subclassing it. The key word is "you." EMF.Edit expects you to use ordinary subclassing to customize the generic commands with any model-specific specializations you might need. At the same time, the framework reserves the ability to attach an `overrideCommand` as an orthogonal dimension of overrideability for itself.

The implication of this is that if you want to subclass an EMF.Edit override-able command, you need to override the doExecute() method instead of execute(), doUndo() instead of undo(), and so on. Other than that, you typically shouldn't need to concern yourself with the OverrideableCommand mechanism.

CommandParameter and Static Create Methods

Another special feature of the EMF.Edit command package has to do with the creation of commands. We already mentioned in Section 3.2.3 that EMF.Edit commands are created using an EditingDomain, which, in turn, delegates to item providers. The EditingDomain interface contains (among other things) a command factory method, createCommand(), that looks like this:

```
Command createCommand(Class commandClass,
                  CommandParameter commandParameter);
```

Notice that class CommandParameter is used to pass the command arguments in a generic way. To use this method to create a command you would first need to create a CommandParameter object, set the command's parameters into it, and then call the create method, passing to it the command class (e.g., SetCommand.class) and the parameters.

Rather then making clients go through all that, the EMF.Edit command framework uses a convention of providing static convenience create() methods in every command class. Using the static method, you can create a SetCommand like this:

```
Command cmd = SetCommand.create(ed, object, feature, value);
```

The static create() method will, in turn, create the CommandParameter object and call the createCommand() method on the specified EditingDomain, in this case ed, for you.

3.3.3   EditingDomain

Similar to the way that content and label providers are used to manage viewer access to objects, EMF.Edit uses an editing domain to manage an editor's command-based modification of objects. It does this by providing three main functions:

1. Creating commands, optionally deducing some of their arguments.
2. Managing the command undo stack.

3. Providing convenient access to the set of EMF resources being edited.

In Section 3.2.3 we saw that EMF.Edit's editing domain implementation class, `AdapterFactoryEditingDomain`, implements the first function, command creation, by delegating to an item provider. The second and third functions are handled by maintaining the editor's `CommandStack` and `ResourceSet`, respectively. The three roles are illustrated in Figure 3.12.

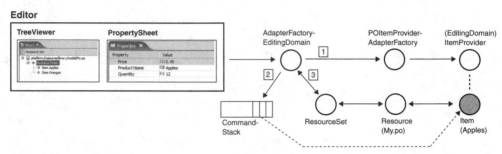

Figure 3.12   The roles of an `EditingDomain`.

Creating Commands

To understand how an editing domain handles its command creation role, let's walk through a simple example. Assume we want to remove one of the items from our purchase order, *My.po*. The `RemoveCommand`, like most EMF.Edit commands, includes several static `create()` methods. Two of them look like this:

```
public static Command create(EditingDomain domain,
                             Object owner,
                             Object feature,
                             Object value) { ...
```

```
public static Command create(EditingDomain domain,
                             Object value) { ...
```

Notice that the first one takes three arguments in addition to the `EditingDomain`: the `owner` and `feature` being removed from, and the `value` being removed. For our example we would call it like this:

```
Command cmd = RemoveCommand.create(editingDomain
                             aPurchaseOrder,
                             poPackage.getPurchaseOrder_Items(),
                             aItem);
```

In this example, we provided all the information needed to create the `RemoveCommand`. This would not be the case if we used the second `create()` method instead:

```
Command cmd = RemoveCommand.create(editingDomain, aItem);
```

Notice that here we simply pass the item to be removed, `aItem`, without specifying where to remove it from. In fact, this approach is used to create a `RemoveCommand` as part of the EMF.Edit implemention of a **Delete** action. The editing domain is then given the added responsibility of filling in the missing arguments. Let's follow through with our example to see how it does that.

As we described in the previous section, the static `create()` methods simply package up their arguments in a `CommandParameter` and then call `createCommand()` on an editing domain. The `AdapterFactoryEditingDomain` simply delegates `createCommand()` to an item provider using the familiar adapter factory delegation pattern:

```
public Command createCommand(Class commandClass,
                             CommandParameter commandParameter)
{
  Object owner = ... // get the owner object for the command
  IEditingDomainItemProvider adapter =
   (IEditingDomainItemProvider)
     adapterFactory.adapt(owner, IEditingDomainItemProvider.class);
  return adapter.createCommand(owner, this, commandClass,
                              commandParameter);
}
```

Notice that the `createCommand()` method uses the `owner` object to access the item provider to delegate to (i.e., for the object used in the `adapterFactory.adapt()` call). If we used the four-argument `create()` method, then the `owner` is known (`aPurchaseOrder`). However, if we used the two-argument method, then the editing domain will need to compute it.

If you look at the actual implementation, the way `AdapterFactory-EditingDomain` finds the `owner` looks more complicated than it is. This is because it's designed to handle, among other things, removing collections of objects at once. For example, a user might select multiple items from more than one purchase order, and then invoke a **Delete** action. The editing domain handles this case by computing all the owners involved, and then creating a `CompoundCommand` containing a `RemoveCommand` for each owner.

For any given object (to be removed), the owner is computed by calling the `getParent()` method on its item provider, another method in the

IEditingDomainItemProvider interface.[1] The effect of this is that the method createCommand() is finally called on the item provider of the purchase order (aPurchaseOrder).

In Section 3.2, we mentioned that most item providers that are also EMF adapters extend the EMF.Edit convenience base class, Item-ProviderAdapter, which provides a default implementation of many methods. Included among these is an implementation of createCommand() that handles all the standard commands provided by EMF.Edit. For our example, the item provider will first deduce the final argument, the feature (**items**), and then simply return a new RemoveCommand constructed with all four arguments. In Chapter 19, we'll look in detail at how this works and how you can easily override the generic commands with your own model-specific customizations.

Maintaining the Command Stack

The command stack plays a key role in an EMF.Edit-based editor. If a single command stack is used pervasively for all changes to the all the objects being edited, editors can also use it to enable the **Save** action (i.e., only enable it when the stack is not empty), and to both enable and execute the **Undo** and **Redo** actions.

In general, commands are created and executed in the same place. Because the editing domain serves as the command factory, it would also be an excellent holder for the command stack. Having created the command, the editing domain can then be used to access the command stack to execute it.

The only thing that we need to ensure is that the editing domain is available everywhere in the code that needs to change the objects (i.e., execute commands). For editor actions, the editing domain is readily available from the editor. For property descriptors, the editing domain needs to be located using the resource set, which brings us to the third role of the editing domain.

Accessing the ResourceSet

In its third role, the adapter factory provides convenience methods to load and save resources, as well as convenient access to the resource set. However, the real reason it provides these friendly services is so it can create a special ResourceSet that knows about it—one that implements the interface IEditingDomainProvider. This is indicated in Figure 3.12 by the arrow on both ends of the line between the editing domain and resource set.

---

1. Actually, there is also a getParent() method with the same signature in the ITreeItemContentProvider interface, which works out fine because we usually have the same item provider implementing both interfaces.

Because a resource is aware of its resource set, and an object is aware of its resource, with this arrangement we can now find the editing domain for any EMF object. This is important, in that it allows commands to be executed on objects from anywhere in the code. For example, when a property sheet change is made, the `ItemPropertyDescriptor setPropertyValue()` method will locate the editing domain from the object being changed, like this:

```
EditingDomain editingDomain = getEditingDomain(object);
```

Once it has access to the editing domain, it can then create the command and, as it also now has access to the command stack, execute it:

```
editingDomain.getCommandStack().execute(
  SetCommand.create(editingDomain, object, feature, value));
```

3.4 Generating EMF.Edit Code

In Chapter 2, we saw how EMF lets you take a model definition in any of several forms and generate Java implementation code for it. Given the same model definition, we can also use the EMF.Edit code generation support to generate item providers and other classes needed to edit instances of the model. The EMF.Edit code generator is not a separate tool; it's just another feature of the model generator. As you'll see in Chapter 4, after generating your model, you can generate the EMF.Edit parts via the **Generate Edit Code** and **Generate Editor Code** menu items.

The EMF generator will create new projects when they are needed to hold generated code. We have seen that, by default, model code is generated into the existing project that contains the Ecore and generator models. However, this is not the case for generated EMF.Edit code. As described in Section 3.1.2, EMF.Edit is divided into two separate plug-ins: the UI-independent part and the Eclipse UI-dependent part. By default, the code generated by EMF.Edit follows this same pattern. **Generate Edit Code** will generate a plug-in containing the UI-independent editing support classes, whereas **Generate Editor Code** will generate the rest into a separate plug-in that also depends on the Eclipse UI. You can, however, override this and force the generator to put everything into a single plug-in, if that's what you want.

3.4.1   Edit Generation

Invoking **Generate Edit Code** in the EMF generator will generate a complete plug-in containing the UI-independent portion of a model editor. It produces the following:

1. A set of typed item provider classes, one for each class in the model.
2. An item provider adapter factory class that creates the generated item providers. It extends the model-generated adapter factory base class described in Chapter 2.
3. A plug-in class that includes methods for locating the plug-in's resource strings and icons.
4. Two manifest files, *META-INF/MANIFEST.MF* and *plugin.xml*, declaring the plug-in's dependencies.
5. A *build.properties* file, containing information to guide the building and packaging of the plug-in.
6. A *plugin.properties* file, containing the externalized strings needed by the generated classes and the framework.
7. A directory of icons, one for each model class.

The most important of these is the set of item provider implementation classes. As described in Section 3.2.5, there are two possible item provider patterns: Stateful or Singleton. The generator gives you the option on a class-by-class basis to generate a Stateful, a Singleton, or no item provider. The chosen pattern only affects the generated `create()` method in the adapter factory and not the generated item provider itself. The generated item providers are implemented using the pattern-neutral approach described in Section 3.2.5.

Choosing not to generate an item provider for a class would be appropriate if you plan to never display instances of it or if you don't need to customize it and can therefore use EMF.Edit's reflective item provider, class `ReflectiveItemProvider`, for it.

The generated item providers mix in all the interfaces needed for basic support of the standard viewers, commands, and the property sheet. For example:

```
public class PurchaseOrderItemProvider extends ItemProviderAdapter
  implements
    IEditingDomainItemProvider,
    IStructuredItemContentProvider,
    ITreeItemContentProvider,
    IItemLabelProvider,
    IItemPropertySource
{ ...
```

It extends, either directly or indirectly, the EMF.Edit item provider base class, `ItemProviderAdapter`.

If you look at a generated item provider class, you'll notice that most of the methods from the item provider interfaces are actually implemented in the base class, either generically or by calling out to a few simple methods that are implemented in the generated subclasses. We'll cover these methods, along with all the EMF.Edit generator patterns, in detail in Chapter 11.

3.4.2   Editor Generation

Generate Editor Code is used to generate a fully functional editor plug-in that will allow you to view instances of the model using several common viewers and to add, remove, cut, copy, and paste objects, or to modify the objects in a standard property sheet, all with full undo and redo support. By default, the editor integrates into the Eclipse IDE; however, an RCP-based editor application can be generated instead.

The following artifacts are generated in the editor plug-in:

- The editor class.
- A wizard for creating new model instance documents.
- An action bar contributor that manages the popup menus, and toolbar and menu bar items.
- Optionally, an advisor class that lays out the editor UI as an RCP application.
- A plug-in class that includes methods for locating the plug-in's resource strings and icons.
- Two manifest files, *META-INF/MANIFEST.MF* and *plugin.xml*, that specify the required dependencies and extensions of various workbench extension points.
- A *build.properties* file, containing information to guide the building and packaging of the plug-in.
- A *plugin.properties* file, containing the externalized strings needed by the generated classes and the framework.
- A directory containing icons for the editor and model wizard.

The generated editor is a very functional multipage editor by default. The Outline view displays the contents of an EMF resource in a tree viewer. Each page of the editor is synchronized with it and demonstrates a different way of displaying the objects. The following pages are created:

- ○ **Selection** shows a tree viewer similar to the one in the Outline view.
- ○ **Parent** is an inverted tree showing the container path from the element selected in the Outline view back to the root.
- ○ **List** shows a list viewer containing the children of the selection in the Outline view.
- ○ **Tree** shows another tree viewer, only rooted at the current selection.
- ○ **Table** shows a table viewer containing the children of the current selection.
- ○ **TableTree** is the same, only using a table tree viewer.

The generated wizard allows you to create a new model instance document containing a single root object of one of the model's types. The generated default implementation provides a drop-down list of concrete classes in the model, from which the user selects an appropriate root.

3.4.3 Regenerating EMF.Edit Plug-Ins

When regenerating into existing projects, the EMF generator supports the same kind of merging for EMF.Edit code as it does for model code, which we described in Chapter 2. You can edit the generated classes to add methods and instance variables or to modify the generated ones. As long as you remove the `@generated` tags from any generated methods that you change, your modifications will be preserved during the regeneration.

As shown in the last two sections, EMF.Edit also generates other types of non-Java content, including property files, icons, and manifest files. Generated *plugin.properties* files contain the translated text strings (resources) referenced by the generated code. You can manually add new resource strings or edit the generated ones and then later regenerate without losing your changes. Any newly generated strings will be added, but unused ones, whether initially generated or not, will never be removed. You will need to manually remove them.

Every icon generated by EMF.Edit is a uniquely colored version of a generic icon. The generated icons are expected to be replaced by properly designed model-specific ones, and therefore, the generator will never overwrite an existing icon.

The generator also never overwrites manifest files. There is no automatic merge support either, because it's rarely needed. If you've changed a generated manifest file by hand (e.g., to add a new extension point), and then later change the model in a way that affects the file, you should rename it, run the generator to produce the new version, and then manually merge your changes into that newly generated version.

CHAPTER 4

Using EMF—A Simple Overview

Now that you have been introduced to EMF, it's time to get personally acquainted.

In Chapter 2, we explained EMF's notion of a model, examining its conceptual and concrete, serialized forms, and discussing the framework and generated Java code that realize it. In Chapter 3, we looked at EMF.Edit's contributions, primarily item providers for model objects and a command framework, and how these can form the basis for a structured editor for any EMF model. Now, let's put all of this into action.

In this chapter, we walk through the process of creating an EMF application from a data model in each of the four forms—annotated Java, UML, XML Schema, and Ecore itself—discussed in Chapter 2. Each step in the process is explained, but there is an expectation that you are already fairly familiar with the interface of the Eclipse IDE and the Java Development Tools (JDT). If this is not the case, you may wish to consult the *Workbench User Guide* and the *Java Development User Guide*, which are both available through Eclipse's help system.

We hope to show how easy it can be to go from a high-level model description, to a working implementation of that model, to a capable and feature-rich editor for it. You are encouraged to roll up your sleeves, fire up your copy of Eclipse, follow along, and see for yourself just how painless this task can be with EMF.

4.1   Example Model: The Primer Purchase Order

In Chapter 2, we saw a simple model of a purchase order that we mentioned was based on the central example from the XML Schema primer [2]. Let's expand our model, so that it includes a few more different elements of Ecore and more closely resembles the example from the primer.

Figure 4.1 shows the UML class diagram for our expanded primer purchase order model.

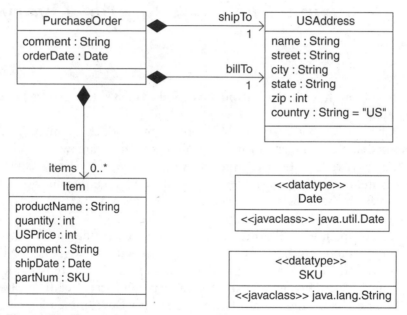

Figure 4.1   Primer purchase model in UML.

Instead of simply representing addresses with a string, we have added a class called **USAddress**, whose attributes are the components of an address in the United States. Now that addresses are represented by a class, **shipTo** and **billTo** can no longer be simple attributes of a **PurchaseOrder**. In UML, we show composition associations (also called by-value aggregations) between **PurchaseOrder** and **USAddress**; they correspond to containment references in Ecore. We have also added a number of attributes to the **PurchaseOrder** and **Item** classes. In particular, notice the **orderDate** attribute of **PurchaseOrder** and the **shipDate** and **partNum** attributes of **Item**, for which we have defined new data types. **Dates** will be represented in Java by the `java.util.Date` class and **SKUs** (stock keeping units) by `java.lang.String`. Why, you might ask, are we defining this second type, instead of simply using the built-in type for strings?

The purchase order in the XML Schema primer defines a **SKU** simple type as a restriction on string so that only values matching a certain pattern are accepted. We might wish to implement a similar restriction. As we will discuss in Chapter 18, the way to model this in EMF is as a data type with a constraint.

The last thing to mention about this purchase order model is that its constituent classes and data types all reside in a package, which we have called **ppo**. EMF requires that all classes and data types belong to a package; Java's default, nameless package is not supported. When a UML class model is converted to Ecore and there are objects that are not contained in a package, a package will be created for them.

4.2 Creating EMF Models and Projects

As we discussed in Section 1.2.2, the work that we do in Eclipse lives in the workspace, in a number of projects, or groups of related folders and files. In the context of creating Eclipse plug-ins with the Plug-in Development Environment (PDE), a project corresponds to a single plug-in.

Typically, an EMF model, which can include one or more packages, will live in one plug-in, and hence will be developed in one project, while the UI-independent and UI-dependent portions of the editor will reside in two others. We refer to these as the *model*, *edit*, and *editor* plug-ins.[1]

In keeping with the Eclipse philosophy of tool interoperability, the EMF development tools are meant to build on and be used with the JDT and PDE. As a result, an EMF project has Java and PDE natures and includes manifest files. An EMF project is distinguished from other JDT and PDE projects by the presence of a generator model file, with an extension of *.genmodel*, and one or more Ecore model files, with extensions of *.ecore*.[2]

EMF provides two wizards to help you create these model files. The EMF Model wizard creates Ecore model files based on the annotated Java files in a project, an XML Schema or a Rational Rose class model, or copied directly from existing Ecore models. A generator model file is also created to decorate the Ecore models with default code generation settings. The EMF Project wizard is similar, but it also creates a new project in the workspace as a home for the models it creates. It does not, however, support annotated Java as a model source, because that approach requires an existing project containing the source files. A third wizard, the Empty EMF Project wizard, is usually used as the starting point when specifying a model via annotated Java.

---

1. It is also possible to combine the two editor-related plug-ins, or indeed all three plug-ins, into one. In Chapter 11, we describe how.

2. Generally, these model files live in the same project as the model source, but there is no reason why they could not form their own project instead.

In the following subsections, we demonstrate the use of these wizards to create EMF models and projects from the four supported data model sources.

4.2.1 Creating an EMF Model from Annotated Java

Of the different sources from which we can create EMF models, annotated Java code certainly offers the lowest cost of entry for a couple of reasons. First, as Java programmers, we already understand the syntax. Second, the only tool that this approach requires is a familiar text editor, which can be the editor provided by the JDT, a third-party Eclipse plug-in, or the "one true editor" that you have been using since the beginning of time. This makes annotated Java a good place to start this discussion.

Figure 4.2 shows the Eclipse IDE in the Java perspective, with a single, very simple Java project in the workspace. This project, named *com.example.ppo*, was created with the Empty EMF Project wizard, and it will soon become our model plug-in.

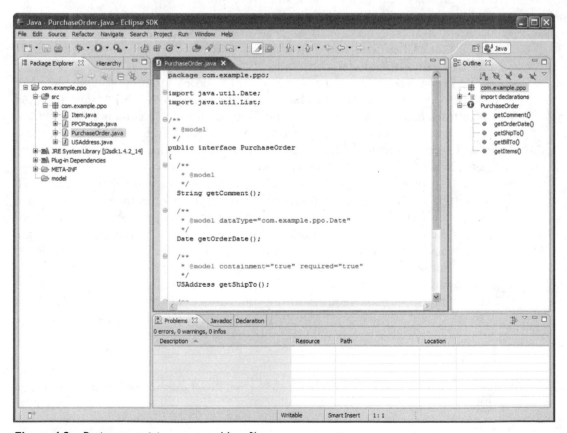

Figure 4.2 Project containing annotated Java files.

Like any other project, an EMF project is created using the **New > Project...** wizard, which can be accessed from the **File** pull-down menu, the **New Wizard** toolbar button, or the context-sensitive menu in the Navigator and Package Explorer views. The wizard's first page is shown in Figure 4.3. In the tree, expand "Eclipse Modeling Framework" and select "Empty EMF Project". Click the **Next** button to advance.

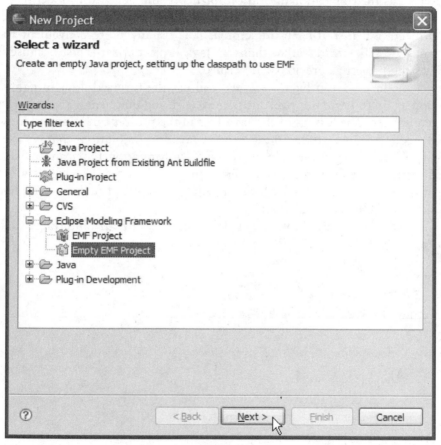

Figure 4.3   The New Project wizard.

On the single page that follows, name the project "com.example.ppo", leave the default project directory unchanged, and click **Finish**. To ensure uniqueness, we are following the recommended convention of beginning plug-in IDs with a reversed domain name—assuming, of course, that we own the *example.com* domain.

The wizard creates the project and configures it for use with EMF. In particular, a *META-INF/MANIFEST.MF* file is generated, identifying the project as a plug-in and declaring a dependency on `org.eclipse.emf.ecore`. This ensures that the class path contains any Ecore types that we might need to reference while writing Java code to describe our model.[3] When we eventually generate code, the minimal manifest file will be replaced by a more elaborate version, and a *plugin.xml* will be added. The wizard also creates a *model* directory, which serves as the conventional location for Ecore and generator model files.

Note that we can actually create a model from the interfaces in any Java project. When starting from scratch, it is usually more convenient to use the Empty EMF wizard, rather than the Java Project wizard, just because it initializes the project as previously described.

As illustrated in Figure 4.2, we will use the reversed domain name convention again to begin our package names, ensuring uniqueness in the Java package namespace. The listings of the Java files in the project can be found in Appendix B. Section 2.3.4 introduced the `@model` Javadoc annotations that we use to identify EMF model elements and to specify information that cannot be captured directly in the Java interface declarations. This code demonstrates a little more of the `@model` tag syntax, which we will now explain briefly. A complete discussion can be found in Chapter 7.

Let's begin by looking at the `PurchaseOrder` interface, defined in *PurchaseOrder.java*:

```
/**
 * @model
 */
public interface PurchaseOrder
{
  /**
   * @model
   */
  String getComment();

  /**
   * @model dataType="com.example.ppo.Date"
   */
  Date getOrderDate();

  ...
}
```

---

3. Actually, this model is simple enough that we don't actually need to reference any Ecore types to define it. In Chapter 7, we will see the more complicated model constructs that can only be defined in Java using Ecore types.

This interface is identified as representing a modeled class by the simple `@model` annotation. Its first two accessors represent attributes in the model. The `@model` tag on `getOrderDate()` carries an additional piece of information: it specifies that the type of the **orderDate** attribute should be a new data type called **Date**. Note that the Ecore data type name is qualified with the corresponding Java package. We are defining a new data type so that we can supply our own serialization and deserialization methods. Because no `dataType` property is specified in the tag on `getComment()`, the built-in Ecore data type **EString**[4] will be used as **comment**'s type.

Carrying on in the interface, we next find the accessors that define **PurchaseOrder**'s references to class **USAddress**:

```
/**
 * @model containment="true" required="true"
 */
USAddress getBillTo();

/**
 * @model containment="true" required="true"
 */
USAddress getShipTo();
```

The `containment` property, which we already saw in Chapter 2, indicates that **PurchaseOrder** will be a container for its **billTo** and **shipTo** addresses. The `required` property specifies that a valid instance of **PurchaseOrder** must define values for these two features. In Chapter 18, we'll discuss how constraints such as this can be validated.

Finally, the **items** reference is defined:

```
/**
 * @model type="Item" containment="true"
 */
List getItems();
```

Again, we see this is a containment reference. Because the return type of the method has been used to indicate that the reference is multiplicity-many, we also need the `type` property to specify its actual type.

---

4. Ecore defines data types, including **EString**, corresponding to simple Java types. These built-in Ecore types are discussed in Section 5.8.

If we looked at the Item and USAddress interfaces, we would see that they use the same kind of @model annotations to define the **Item** and **USAddress** classes and their attributes and references.

The other interface, PPOPackage, is a little different:

```
/**
 * @model kind="package"
 */
public interface PPOPackage
{
  String eNS_URI = "http://www.example.com/PrimerPO";
  String eNS_PREFIX = "ppo";
}
```

The kind property on the @model tag indicates that this interface does not represent a modeled class, but instead carries model information about the package. In particular, two special fields, eNS_URI and eNS_PREFIX, are declared to specify the namespace URI and prefix for the package. In particular, as we will see in Chapter 5, the namespace URI is used to uniquely identify the package. Package interfaces like PPOPackage are most often included in a Java model specification to specify this namespace information.

Now, let's see how all of these annotated Java files are introspected and turned into EMF models.

EMF models, like many other resources in Eclipse, are created using the New wizard, which can be accessed from the **File** pull-down menu, the **New** toolbar button, or the context-sensitive menu in the Package Explorer and Navigator views. We'll access it by right-clicking the *model* folder, and selecting **New**, then **Other...** from the pop-up menu. The wizard's first page is shown in Figure 4.4.

In the tree, expand "Eclipse Modeling Framework" and select "EMF Model". Click the **Next** button to advance to the next page.

Figure 4.4   The New wizard's opening page.

This page is illustrated in Figure 4.5. Here, we choose where to create the models and what file name to give the generator model. We will select the *model* folder, name the model "PrimerPO.genmodel", and then advance to the next page.

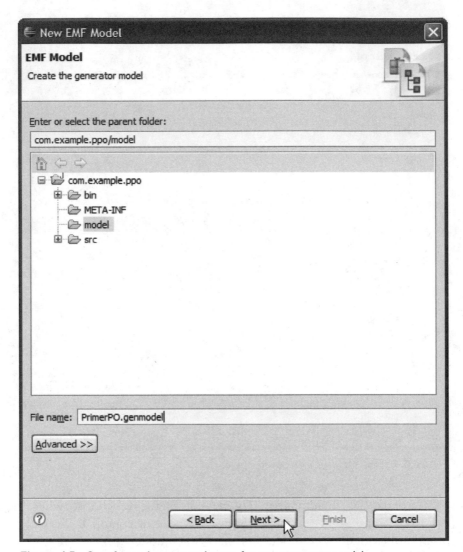

Figure 4.5 Specifying a location and name for new generator model.

On the next page, shown in Figure 4.6, we select the appropriate model importer for our model source. In this case, we want "Annotated Java".

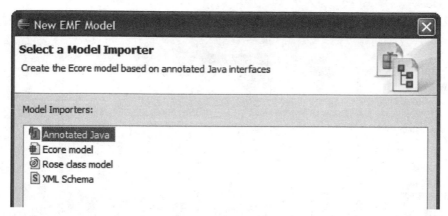

Figure 4.6 Selecting the Annotated Java model importer.

When we advance to the last page of the wizard, the source contained in the project is examined, and we are presented with the list of packages that were discovered, as illustrated in Figure 4.7. We can select which packages to model and change the file names of the Ecore models that we are creating. Because we only have one package, and the default Ecore model name looks fine, we'll just leave that package selected and click **Finish**.

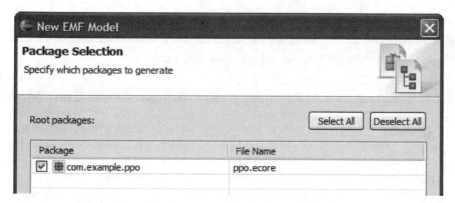

Figure 4.7 Selecting packages discovered in the annotated Java.

The wizard creates the Ecore and generator models for our package; the latter is opened in the EMF generator, as illustrated in Figure 4.8. Before we proceed to generate code from the models, let's consider how we would create these models from the other sources. Because we are going to re-create the same project in each of the following three sections, you might want to rename them in between, so that you can compare the results.

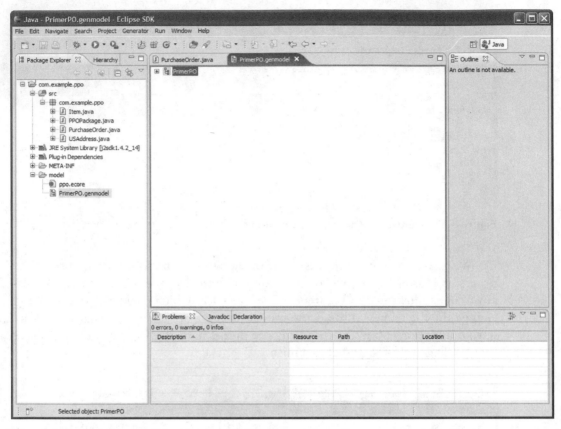

Figure 4.8   Model imported from Java and EMF generator opened.

4.2.2   Creating an EMF Project from a Rational Rose Class Model

According to the oft-quoted Chinese proverb, "a picture's worth a thousand words." Even in this chapter's simple example, the UML class model of Figure 4.1 would seem to be worth 111 lines of annotated Java code. It's a notion well understood by those who have bought into modeling. If you fall into this group and already have a visual modeling tool like Rational Rose at your disposal, you should expect to be able to use your class diagrams as input to EMF.

Before we describe how, it is worth briefly mentioning the concept of extensible model properties that is supported by Rose. For the sake of flexibility, Rose provides a mechanism for defining non-UML properties of model elements. EMF uses this mechanism—a property file—to add support for several features of the Ecore and generator models. It is highly recommended that you add the properties from the *ecore.pty* file to Rose models on which you plan to base EMF projects. This file is located in the *rose/* subdirectory of the `org.eclipse.emf.importer.rose` plug-in, in the EMF Runtime package.

Chapter 6 briefly describes how to do this. For more details on property files, see your Rational Rose documentation. Once added, these properties will be accessible via the **Ecore** tab of the specification dialog box for any class model element.

While these model properties will be discussed thoroughly in Chapter 6, let's briefly look at some of the model properties for our **ppo** package, illustrated in Figure 4.9.

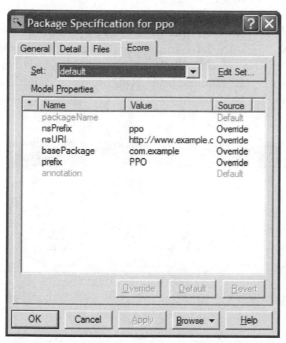

Figure 4.9   Ecore package properties in Rose.

The **nsPrefix** and and **nsURI** properties correspond directly to the Ecore package's attributes of the same name. These are exactly the same attributes that, as we saw in the previous section, could be specified via a package interface when using annotated Java to define the model. We have specified the same values here.

The **basePackage** and **prefix** are properties of the generator model; **basePackage** specifies the Java package of which the generated package will be a subpackage. In other words, it allows us to easily generate code with globally unique package names, without modeling empty, nested packages. For our purchase order package, we set its value to "com.example". Because our package is named "ppo", our generated code will go into `com.example.ppo`, the same package we used in our annotated Java example. The other property, **prefix**, is used in forming the names of the generated supporting classes for the package, which include the interface and class representing the package itself, a factory, a switch, and an adapter factory. If we did not set a value here, a default would be generated by capitalizing the first letter of the package name. Because our package name is an abbreviation, we prefer to capitalize it in its entirety and enter the value "PPO".

With that detail out of the way, let's now see exactly how we go about creating an EMF project based on this Rose model.

We will use the EMF Project wizard. Again, this is done by launching Eclipse's **New > Project** wizard, for example, from the **File** pull-down menu. The wizard's first page is shown in Figure 4.10. In the tree, expand "Eclipse Modeling Framework" and select "EMF Project". Click the **Next** button to advance. On the next page, name the project "com.example.ppo", leave the default project directory unchanged, and click **Next** again.

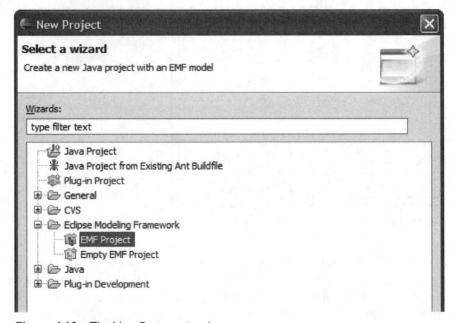

Figure 4.10   The New Project wizard.

As shown in Figure 4.11, we next select the desired model importer: "Rose class model".

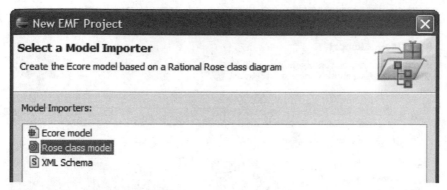

Figure 4.11   Selecting the Rose class model importer.

Figure 4.12 shows the next page, where we specify the location of the Rose model file, *PrimerPO.mdl*. The location is expressed as a Uniform Resource Identifier (URI), which can be typed in the text box. Alternatively you can select a file by clicking either the **Browse File System...** or the **Browse Workspace...** button.

URIs are strings used to locate and identify content, including on the World Wide Web. We discuss them, and EMF's extensive use of them, in Chapter 15. The URI syntax is generic, but we can limit ourselves to a small subset of it for now. A URI's form is specified by its *scheme* (the name given to its first word), which is followed by a colon. At this point, we are only interested in two schemes:

○ A *file* scheme URI includes a slash-delimited path to locate a file on a local or networked file system (e.g., on Windows, *file:/C:/eclipse/eclipse.exe*).

○ A *platform* scheme URI also includes a slash-delimited path. When its first segment is "resource," the remainder of the path identifies a resource relative to the workspace (e.g., *platform:/resource/com.example.ppo/model/*). This scheme is internal to Eclipse.

It is generally easier and less error prone to use the buttons. Given that we don't have the Rose model in the workspace, we should click the **Browse File System...** button to locate the Rose model file.

If the Rose model had included packages from separate *.cat* files and used path map symbols to locate them, we could define values for those symbols in the **Path Map** table. Because our model is contained in a single file, we need not fill in anything here. We can also accept the suggested **Generator model file name**, "PrimerPO.genmodel", and then advance to the last page of the wizard.

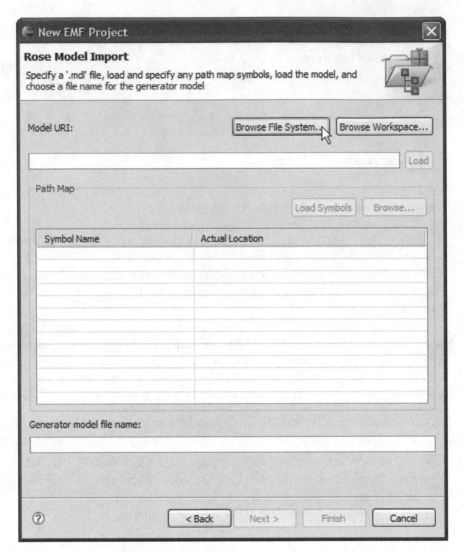

Figure 4.12   Locating the Rose model.

As when we were creating a model from annotated Java, this final page allows us to select those packages for which we wish to create Ecore models and to specify their file names. This is illustrated in Figure 4.13. We are not shown any nested packages, only those appearing as immediate children of "Logical View" in Rose. If there were more than one of these root packages, we could choose to generate a subset of them and reference dependent packages in existing projects in the workspace.[5] Note that we did not have this control when introspecting annotated Java because the references would be made explicitly via `import` statements and fully qualified class names. In any case, we still have only one package, so we will again just leave it selected and click **Finish**.

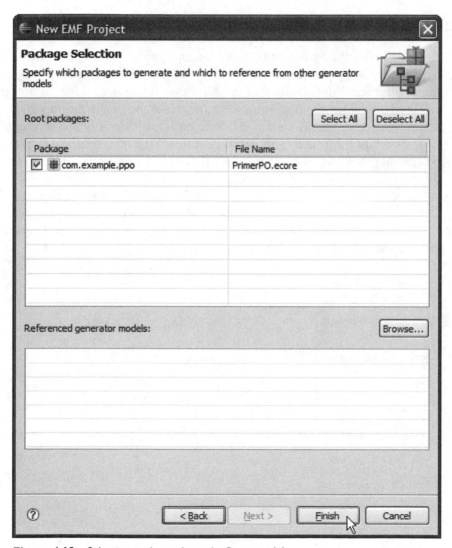

Figure 4.13   Selecting packages from the Rose model.

---

5. We will show exactly how to do this in Chapter 13.

The wizard creates our project, converts our Rose model into an Ecore model, and creates a generator model for it; once again, this model is opened in the EMF generator. If you compare the Ecore model with the one created in Section 4.2.1, you will find that they model the same package, classes, features, and data types.[6] The two generator models are also very similar.

4.2.3   Creating an EMF Project from an XML Schema

As described in Chapter 2, the design of an application may be centered on the particular XML message structure that it handles. If so, it would make sense to start with the XML Schema that specifies that structure, and from that generate an EMF model for manipulating the data contained in the messages.

Ecore's relationship with XML Schema is considerably less straightforward than its relationship with annotated Java or UML. As a result, trying to apply a simple mapping from an arbitrary XML Schema will often result in more complicated Ecore models, sometimes unnecessarily so.

In fact, the purchase order schema from the XML Schema primer illustrates this well. It defines items, an element of a PurchaseOrderType, with a type called Items. Items is a complex type consisting of a sequence of item elements. Here is the relevant portion of the schema:

```
<xsd:complexType name="PurchaseOrderType">
  <xsd:sequence>
    ...
    <xsd:element name="items" type="Items"/>
  </xsd:sequence>
  ...
</xsd:complexType>

...

<xsd:complexType name="Items">
  <xsd:sequence>
    <xsd:element name="item" minOccurs="0" maxOccurs="unbounded">
      ...
    </xsd:element>
  </xsd:sequence>
</xsd:complexType>
```

---

6. There is one small, but notable exception: the **USPrice** attribute of **Item** was named **uSPrice** in the Ecore model created from annotated Java, following the usual convention of beginning feature names with a lowercase character. In the Rose model, we were able to specify the unconventional name used in the XML Schema primer.

This structure makes perfect sense in a schema: the whole list is delimited by the `items` element, and each member of the list corresponds to a single `item` element. However, when we map complex types in XML Schema to classes in Ecore, the result is unnatural and suboptimal, as illustrated in Figure 4.14.

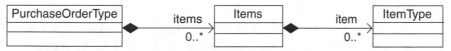

Figure 4.14   Mapping complex XML Schema types to classes in Ecore.

An extra class, **Items,** has been introduced, but all it does is hold the multiplicity-many reference to the **ItemType** class. It is unnecessary because lists are built into Ecore and implied by multiplicity-many references. Thus, we can make our schema more Ecore-friendly by leaving out the `Items` type and changing the multiplicity of `items` itself:

```
<xsd:element name="items" type="Item" minOccurs="0"
  maxOccurs="unbounded">
```

Another problem we will face is that of reversing the mapping, re-creating the XML Schema from the Ecore form. To enable this, we retain additional information about the structure of the schema in the Ecore model using annotations.[7] We will address all of these issues more completely in Chapter 9, but for now, the point is simply that an Ecore model created from an arbitrary XML Schema is going to be more complicated than an equivalent one that came from annotated Java or UML.

For the purposes of this example, we use a slightly modified, although functionally equivalent, version of the primer's purchase order schema; however, the EMF model that we create will still differ slightly from those we create from the other sources. A listing for our schema, *PrimerPO.xsd*, can be found in Appendix B.

Again, we will use the EMF Project wizard. We begin by launching the **New > Project...** wizard, expanding "Eclipse Modeling Framework", selecting "EMF Project", and then clicking **Next**. We name the project "com.example.ppo" and advance to the next page, accepting the default directory.

Here, we specify that we want to use the "XML Schema" model importer, as shown in Figure 4.15.

---

7. Ecore annotations are discussed in Chapter 5.

On the following page, shown in Figure 4.16, we specify the location of the XML Schema using a URI.

Again, we don't have the purchase order schema in the workspace, so we should click the **Browse File System...** button and locate the file in the **Open** dialog box. The file scheme URI is filled in, and we accept the default **Generator model file name**, "PrimerPO.genmodel", advancing to the last page of the wizard, shown in Figure 4.17.

Again, we simply leave the single package selected and click **Finish**. The wizard creates the new project and places in it the new Ecore model and the new generator model.

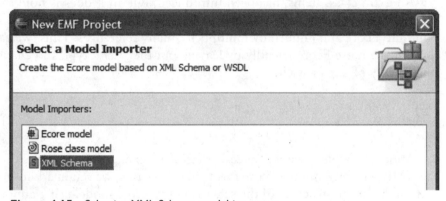

Figure 4.15   Selecting XML Schema model importer.

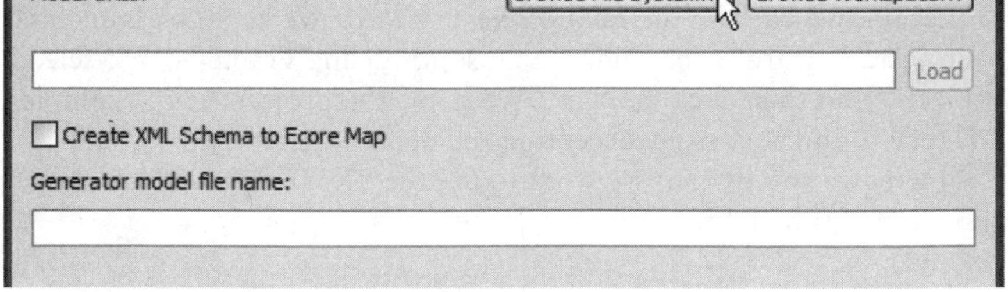

Figure 4.16   Locating the XML Schema.

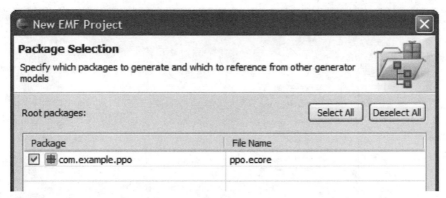

Figure 4.17 Selecting packages from the XML Schema.

4.2.4 *Creating a Generator Model for an Ecore Model*

The final scenario we will describe is the simplest. In this case, we already have an Ecore model, and we only need to create a generator model that will drive code generation for it. It will seem particularly simple because, by now, we have already seen all the relevant pages in the wizard.

As mentioned in Section 2.3.2, direct Ecore modeling is currently possible in Eclipse using EMF's tree-based sample editor, the Ecore Tools graphical editor, and various third-party offerings. Other UML tool vendors are also starting to add support for exporting an Ecore XMI model, as we described in Chapter 2. Regardless of the tool used to create it, once you have an Ecore model, you can always use the following approach to import it into EMF.[8]

Figure 4.18 shows the Eclipse IDE, again with a single *com.example.ppo* project. As in Section 4.2.1, this project was created using the Empty EMF Project wizard. This time, the Ecore model, *PrimerPO.ecore*, has already been created in the project's *model* folder. A listing of the file can be found in Appendix B.

To create a generator model, we right-click the *model* folder and select **New > Other...** from the pop-up menu. Once again, we expand "Eclipse Modeling Framework", select "EMF Model", and then advance to the next page. Again, we name the generator model "PrimerPO.genmodel", leave "model" as its folder, and click **Next**. Then, we specify that the model importer we want is "Ecore model", as illustrated in Figure 4.19.

---

8. Some tools, like EclipseUML, allow you to invoke the EMF wizard and generator directly from within them. If this is the case, you might not need to perform this step at all. You should follow the directions provided with the tool instead.

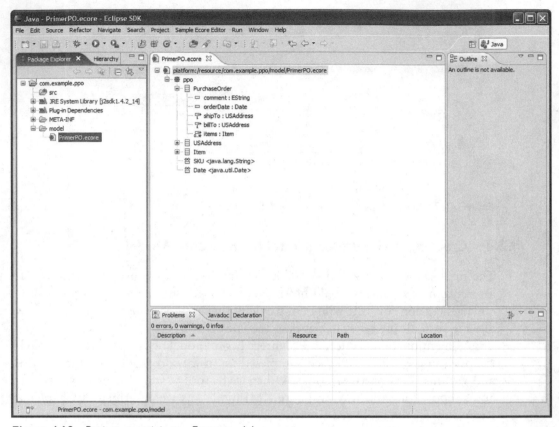

Figure 4.18   Project containing an Ecore model.

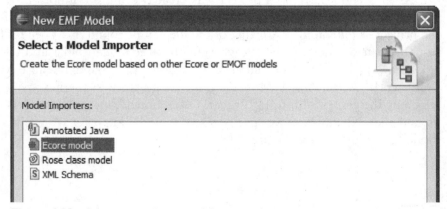

Figure 4.19   Selecting the Ecore model importer.

On the next page of the wizard, we must specify the URI for our Ecore model. Because it is located in the workspace, we click the **Browse Workspace...** button. Figure 4.20 shows the dialog box that appears, which we use to select a file. In the tree, we expand the *model* folder under *com.example.ppo* and select *PrimerPO.ecore*. When we click **OK**, a platform scheme URI will be filled in, and we can advance to the last page of the wizard.

Figure 4.20   Browsing for the Ecore model.

By now, this package selection page should seem very familiar. Once again, our single package is selected. Notice that the default name for the Ecore model file, "PrimerPO.ecore", is the same as that of the existing file we chose, so we won't really be importing it. Had we specified a different name from the original, the file would be copied. However, we only want to create the generator model, and not make a copy of the Ecore model. We click **Finish** to continue.

4.2.5 Other Formats

In the previous sections, we created Ecore representations from a number of different types of models. In each case, we had to select the appropriate model importer for the given model source. Perhaps you found yourself wondering, "Just what are these 'model importers'?"

Basically, they are registered components, each responsible for converting models described in a given format into Ecore. The EMF wizards that we have seen use an Eclipse extension point to generically provide support for any number of types of model input.

EMF provides importers for the four model formats mentioned up to this point: annotated Java, Rational Rose, XML Schema, and Ecore. You can think of these as the formats supported by EMF out of the box.

Anyone interested in providing a mechanism for converting from a specific model format to Ecore should also extend the model importer extension point, `org.eclipse.emf.importer.modelImporterDescriptors`, to contribute support for that format. For example, the UML2 project provides an additional model importer that converts standard UML models into Ecore. By installing the project into your Eclipse workbench, you will add this model importer to those already listed in the wizard, as illustrated in Figure 4.21.

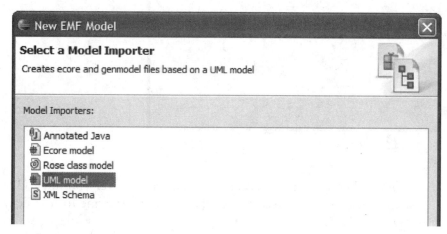

Figure 4.21   The contributed UML model importer.

Thus, although EMF doesn't provide direct support for other model formats, the doors are wide open, allowing the community to easily bring the power of EMF to users of all sorts of different tools and standards.

4.3 Generating Code

At this point, we have taken four different forms of what is essentially the same data model, and from each created an Ecore model and a generator model. These two artifacts will now drive the generation of a complete application for handling our data, purchase order records. Regardless of where our data model came from, once we've converted it into its EMF form, we proceed with code generation in the same way.

We could continue with any of the models obtained in the previous four subsections. However, we did note that there are some minor differences among them, so for the sake of clarity, we will proceed with the ones that we created from the Rose class model.

Figure 4.22 shows the Eclipse platform in the Java perspective with that familiar *com.example.ppo* project expanded to show the two model files. We have launched the EMF generator by double-clicking the generator model file, *PrimerPO.genmodel*.

The EMF generator provides a main editor view that contains a single tree of the artifacts to be generated. At the root level, there is an element labeled "PrimerPO" that represents the whole model. On expanding it, we see that it has a single child, a package called "PPO". Beneath that, we find our classes, "PurchaseOrder", "USAddress", and "Item", and our data types, "SKU" and "Date". The children of each class include its attributes, references, and operations.

The generator makes another contribution to the workbench: as you select different objects in the tree, their properties are shown in the Properties view. These properties correspond to the attributes of the generator model objects, and they affect the way code is generated. If the Properties view is not visible, you can show it by right-clicking any object in the tree and selecting **Show Properties View** from the pop-up menu.

There are a significant number of properties, offering a great deal of control over code generation. For example, we can suppress the generation of the switch and adapter factory classes (see Section 2.4.2) for a package, select between the Singleton and Stateful patterns (see Section 3.2.5) for an item provider, and specify for which features change notifications should be passed to the model's central change notifier (see Section 3.2.4). We will discuss all of the available properties in Chapter 12. For now, the defaults will do just fine.

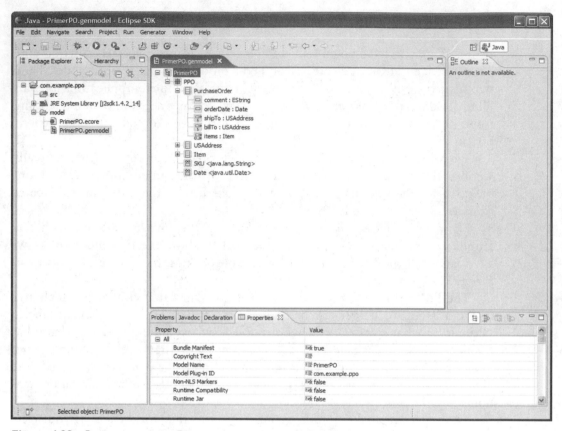

Figure 4.22 Project containing Ecore and generator models with the generator running.

To generate code, we can right-click any object in the generator tree. As illustrated in Figure 4.23, the pop-up menu contains five code generation actions: **Generate Model Code, Generate Edit Code, Generate Editor Code, Generate Test Code,** and **Generate All**. For any object in the tree, selecting one of the first four of these actions will generate all of the code associated with that object and belonging to the model, edit, editor, or test plug-in, respectively. As you might expect, selecting the last of these actions generates all of the code associated with the selected object across all four plug-ins. As an alternative to using the pop-up menu, we can select an object in the tree and then choose one of the five code generation actions from the **Generator** pull-down menu.

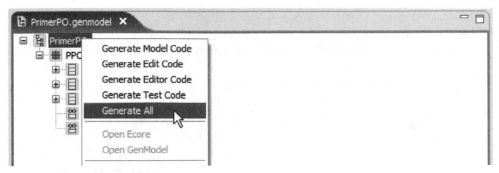

Figure 4.23   Code generation actions.

If any of the code generation actions are grayed out, it simply means that there are no artifacts to be generated for the selected object in those plug-ins, or that the current state of the properties dictate that it should not be generated.

Continuing on with our example, we would like to generate all of the code for the four plug-ins, so we simply right-click the "PrimerPO" model object and select **Generate All**.

In a few moments, after code generation is complete, we notice in the Package Explorer view that numerous artifacts have been added to our existing project, including *META-INF/MANIFEST.MF* and *plugin.xml* manifest files and three packages of generated source. Three new projects have also been created: *com.example.ppo.edit*, *com.example.ppo.editor*, and *com.example.ppo.test*. If **Build Automatically** is enabled in the **Project** menu, the application will be compiled as it is generated. Any compilation errors or warnings will be marked in the **Problems** view. There should be no errors, but you will see three warnings in the test plug-in. Don't worry: they are just indicating that the generated test scaffolding is not being used, as the actual tests have yet to be written.

If automatic building is disabled, we can compile our projects by selecting them in the Package Explorer and choosing **Build Project** from the **Project** pull-down menu.

4.4   Running the Application

To test our application, we need to launch a second instance of Eclipse, called a *runtime workbench*, in which our new plug-ins will be accessible. To do so, select one of the generated projects and, from the **Run** pull-down menu, select **Run As**, then **Eclipse Application**. The second instance of Eclipse should come up in a few moments.

In the runtime workbench, we need to create a project to hold an instance of our purchase order model. Once again, launch the New Project wizard. On the first page, expand "General" and select "Project". Click **Next**. Give the project a name, say "PPOProject", and then click **Finish**.

We can now create our purchase order using the generated PPO Model wizard. In the Navigator view, right-click the new "PPOProject", and select **New**, then **Other...** from the pop-up menu. The generated wizard was placed under "Example EMF Model Creation Wizards", along with the samples that are included with EMF. Select "PPO Model", as shown in Figure 4.24, and advance to the next page of the wizard. We can accept the suggested file name, "My.ppo".

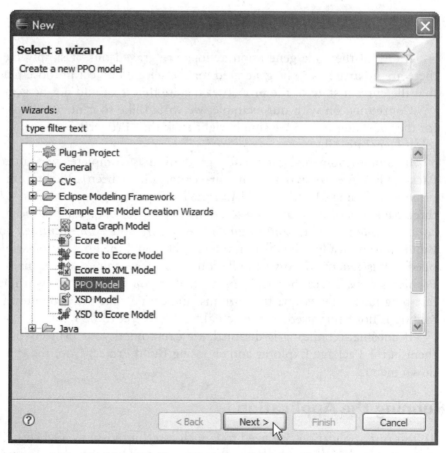

Figure 4.24   The New Wizard.

On the wizard's last page, shown in Figure 4.25, we must select one of the classes defined in the model to use as the type of the root object. This will correspond to the document element when we serialize the instance. The logical choice is "PurchaseOrder". So, select it.

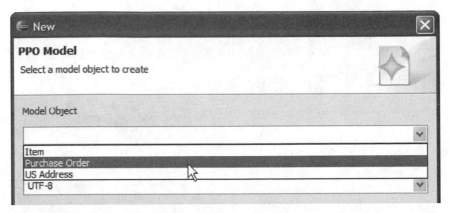

Figure 4.25   Selecting the model object.

This page also allows us to specify the encoding to use when persisting the instance as XMI. The default, "UTF-8", is appropriate for most cases, so we simply click **Finish**.

The model is created and opened in the PPO editor. Like the EMF generator, the editor presents us with a tree view of the model.[9] The root-level element corresponds to the resource. If we expand it, we see its single child, the **PurchaseOrder**-typed model object. We can add children and siblings to objects using the pop-up menu, shown in Figure 4.26, or the **PPO Editor** pull-down menu. Notice that only valid options, as determined by the class's containment references, are presented. The objects can also be cut, copied, and pasted, as well as dragged and dropped. Also, their attributes can be edited in the Properties view. Finally, notice the editor's different pages and the content that it provides to the Outline view, all of which was described in Section 3.4.2. Feel free to experiment with the editor to get a feel for all of the functionality it provides.

When you are finished, save the instance from the **File** menu or the toolbar. Close the editor. If you right-click the new file, *My.ppo*, in the Navigator view, you can select **Open With** and then **Text Editor** from the pop-up menu. This allows you to see the format of the XMI serialization.

Close the text editor and the runtime workbench.

---

9. As we mentioned in Chapter 2, the generator is actually a generated editor that has been customized.

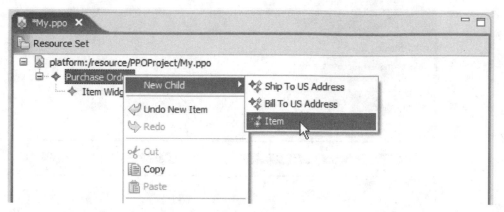

Figure 4.26   Adding objects in the generated editor.

4.5   Continuing Development

We have now seen exactly how EMF lets us take a data model, convert it to Ecore, generate code for model and editor plug-ins, and use those plug-ins to create and edit instances of the model. However, for a real application, that's just the starting point.

From here, we would want to continue to develop our model and editor in two different ways:

1. By writing new Java code and modifying the generated code.

2. By updating the original model, regenerating code based on those changes, and merging the new code into the existing code base.

EMF-generated code is meant to be modified. As explained in Section 2.4.3, code merging is done according to @generated Javadoc tags; it is the presence or absence of such tags that determines whether the associated code elements should be updated or left alone during regeneration.

However, we still need to know how to update the model from which we are generating. In general, we edit the data model in whatever form we started with, and then update the Ecore form with those changes. If the changes to the Ecore model are structural, the corresponding changes will be made to the generator model at the same time, while maintaining its existing attribute values.[10]

To perform this update of the model, we right-click the generator model in the Package Explorer and select **Reload...** from the pop-up menu, as shown in Figure 4.27.

---

10. Note that the generator model automatically adapts to changes in its associated Ecore model when it is opened in the generator. Thus, if we change the Ecore model directly, we do not need to reimport it just to update the generator model.

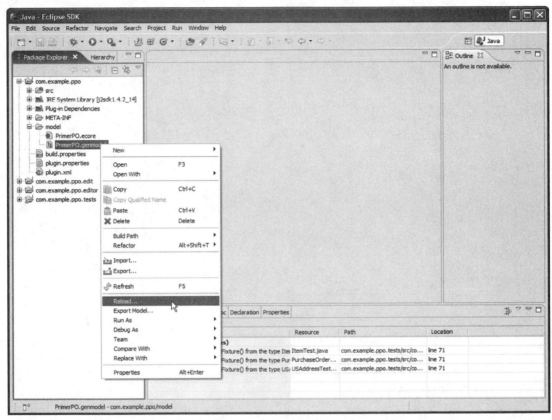

Figure 4.27   Reloading the EMF model.

We then step through the wizard, as we did when we created the model originally, reviewing the selections made at that time.

In this chapter, we have discussed how to use the EMF tools to create Ecore and generator models, to generate model and editor implementations from those models, and to continue the development of an application through model and code modifications. Together with the overview of modeling and EMF concepts and the introduction to EMF.Edit presented in the previous two chapters, this equips you well to begin working with these frameworks.

That said, there are still many details that we have yet to discuss. In the next part of the book, we will closely examine the Ecore model at the heart of EMF and its relationships with the other EMF-related technologies: Java, XML, and UML.

PART II

Defining EMF Models

CHAPTER 5

Ecore Modeling Concepts

When we create an Ecore model—whether directly or from annotated Java, UML, XML Schema, or some other source—we are defining the structure of a series of instances of that model. That is, we are specifying the types of objects that make up instances of that model, the data they contain, and the relationships between them. For example, the PrimerPO model of the previous chapter defined the structure for objects that represent purchase orders.

As we first discussed in Chapter 2, the Ecore metamodel defines the structure of the objects in an Ecore model. Modelers use the term "metamodel" for this kind of model, which, in a sense, defines a language that its instances use to describe other things.

Most of the modeling concepts that the Ecore metamodel defines should be quite familiar to avid modelers and object-oriented programmers alike. As we discussed in Chapter 2, Ecore has its roots in MOF and UML, and was designed to map cleanly to Java implementations. Essentially, if you're comfortable thinking about classes and the relationships between them, you shouldn't have too much trouble using Ecore to define your models.

Ecore supports a number of higher level concepts that are not directly included in Java. For example, Ecore models can include containment and bidirectional relationships. You are likely familiar with these concepts and have probably implemented them yourself more than once. Part of EMF's value is its ability to generate correct and efficient Java implementations for these and other constructs, saving the programmer time and effort.

The Ecore metamodel is, itself, an Ecore model. That is, Ecore acts as its own metamodel, so it is defined in terms of itself. This presents a few conceptual and implementation-related challenges, but it's generally considered a good thing. The other alternatives—defining yet another model to acts as its metamodel or "handwaving" through an informal definition—are significantly less attractive.

Moreover, we are able to treat Ecore much like any other EMF model and to reap the benefits of the EMF generator in creating and maintaining its implementation.

In this chapter, we examine Ecore in detail, with the aim of enabling you to use it effectively in defining your own Ecore models. The use of Ecore as its own metamodel inevitably influences such a discussion, as aspects of certain model elements will be described in terms of other model elements. Thus, we begin the discussion with a simplified subset of the model that you might recognize from Chapter 2. Once we understand that subset in its entirety, we can build on that understanding a complete description of the details of Ecore.

5.1   Ecore Model Uses

Before delving into the discussion of the Ecore metamodel, a word about how EMF uses Ecore models would be appropriate. Like an instance of any other model in EMF, an Ecore model can be built programmatically or loaded from a serialized form. It is generally used in two different contexts: during application development and when the application is running.

During development, the Ecore model is the primary source of information for the EMF generator, when it produces code to be used in the application. As we discussed in Chapter 2, this code includes the interfaces and classes that realize the modeled types, a factory for instantiating them, and a package that efficiently builds the Ecore model at runtime and provides convenient access to its members. The EMF generator reads Ecore models from their XMI serializations.

At runtime, the Ecore model is used by generic framework code to determine correct behavior for that particular model, and is likewise available to user-written code that needs to dynamically discover particulars of the model. The framework code that depends on the Ecore model handles not only peripheral functionalities, such as serialization, but also includes some of the basic Ecore functionality expressed in the `EObject` API. In fact, in the absence of generated code, the behavior of all dynamic model objects is completely dependent on an Ecore model. At runtime, the Ecore model can either be built programmatically or loaded from a serialization; however, the former, more efficient approach is usually taken for generated models.

In discussing the details of Ecore, we will see that most of the concepts that it defines are equally applicable in both the code generation and runtime contexts. Some concepts, however, have special significance in only one context, which we will point out as appropriate.

5.2   The Ecore Kernel

In Section 2.3.1, we presented an illustration of a simplified subset of the Ecore metamodel. We describe this, with minor additions, as the Ecore kernel, and we will use it to "bootstrap"[1] the discussion of the full model. This model is illustrated in Figure 5.1.

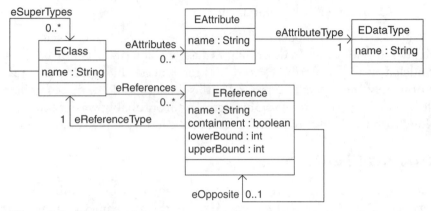

Figure 5.1   The Ecore kernel.

Note that we have created this notion of a kernel only for the purposes of this discussion. There is nothing particularly special about how these elements are defined or created in the implementation of Ecore.

Essentially, reviewing from Chapter 2, this simplified model defines four types of objects—that is, four classes:

1. **EClass** models classes themselves. Classes are identified by name and can have a number of attributes and references. To support inheritance, a class can refer to a number of other classes as its supertypes.

2. **EAttribute** models attributes, the components of an object's data. They are identified by name, and they have a type.

3. **EDataType** is used to represent simple types whose details are not modeled as classes. Instead, they are associated with a primitive or object type fully defined in Java. Data types are also identified by name, and they are used as the types of attributes.

---

1. The term *bootstrap* is commonly used to describe the process by which a system starts up, which generally involves loading a small portion of the system to support the loading and initialization of its remainder. It should bring to mind the awkward image of a person attempting to stand by pulling up on his or her own boots.

4. **EReference** is used in modeling associations between classes; it models one end of such an association. Like attributes, references are identified by name and have a type. However, this type must be the **EClass** at the other end of the association. If the association is navigable in the opposite direction, there will be another reference to represent this bidirectionality. A reference specifies lower and upper bounds on its multiplicity. Finally, a reference specifies whether it is being used to represent a stronger type of association, called containment.[2]

Notice that this model really needs to be understood as a single unit, as it is highly self-referential. In describing **EClass**, we described its attributes, which are modeled using **EAttribute**, and its references, modeled with **EReference**. Fortunately, the concepts expressed in this model should be quite familiar to modelers and object-oriented programmers, so this probably wasn't too troublesome. Now, with this subset of Ecore in hand, we can tackle the rest of the model.

5.3 Structural Features

Looking back at the Ecore kernel, you might notice a number of similarities between **EAttribute** and **EReference**: they both have names and types, and taken together, they define the state of an instance of the **EClass** that contains them. There are many more common aspects of these two classes, including, in fact, the **lowerBound** and **upperBound** attributes, which we previously showed only for **EReference**. To capture these kinds of similarities, Ecore includes a common base for the two classes, called **EStructuralFeature**. The situation is illustrated in Figure 5.2.

As Figure 5.2 shows, **EStructuralFeature** is, itself, derived from other supertypes. **ENamedElement** defines just one attribute, the **name** that we have seen in every class discussed so far. Most classes in Ecore extend this class to inherit this attribute.

Another common aspect of **EAttribute** and **EReference** that we observed is the notion of a type. Because this is also shared with other classes in Ecore, as we will soon see, the **eType** attribute is factored out into **ETypedElement**, the immediate supertype of **EStructuralFeature**. Notice that the type of **eType** is **EClassifier**, a common base class of **EDataType** and **EClass**, which were the required types for **eAttributeType** and **eReferenceType**, respectively.

---

2. Longtime users of EMF might notice a subtle change in this figure compared to, for example, the version in the first edition of this book: before EMF 2.0, **eAttributes** and **eReferences** were containment references. As we will see in Section 5.3, **EClass** now defines a single containment reference for all of the attributes and references in a class. The **eAttributes** and **eReferences** references are non-containment and provide a filtered view for backward compatibility.

ETypedElement also defines attributes related to multiplicity. That is, a typed element specifies not only what type of values it is associated with, but how many of those values it allows. The minimum and maximum number are specified by **lowerBound** and **upperBound**, respectively. Although these are defined in the model as integers, only 0 and the positive integers are legal values. In addition, **upperBound** should be greater than or equal to **lowerBound**, or it can be *unbounded*. This latter condition is indicated in the model by * and corresponds to the value -1, which is represented in the Java implementation of Ecore by the constant `ETypedElement.UNBOUNDED_MULTIPLICITY`.

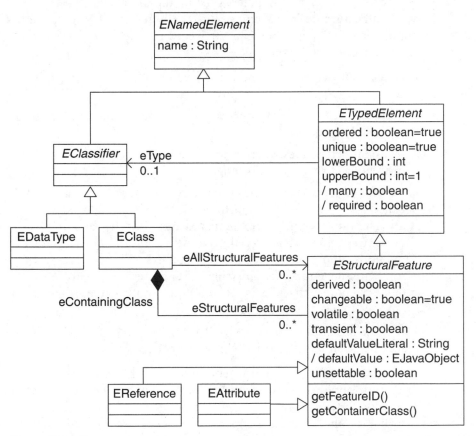

Figure 5.2 Ecore structural features.

Two other attributes of **ETypedElement** are meaningful only in the multiplicity-many case: **unique** specifies whether a single value is prevented from occuring more than once, and **ordered** specifies whether the order of values is significant. Currently, their use is limited. The behavior of a multi-valued attribute depends on its uniqueness, but references always behave as if **unique** is true. Moreover, **ordered** is ignored by all features, as a List-based implementation is always used. In the future, this attribute might be used to substitute an orderless, Collection-based implementation, instead.

EStructuralFeatures are contained by an **EClass** via its **eStructuralFeatures** reference. Notice that this reference constitutes part of a bidirectional association, the first we have seen so far. Thus, the **EClass** that contains an **EStructuralFeature** is available via its **eContainingClass** reference. In Section 5.3.2, we will see how this is actually modeled in Ecore.

In addition to what it inherits from the base classes already described, **EStructuralFeature** defines a number of attributes that characterize both attributes and references. Five boolean attributes specify how the structural feature stores and accesses values:

- **changeable** determines whether the value of the feature can be externally set.

- **derived** specifies whether the value of the feature is to be computed from other, related data.

- **transient** determines whether the feature is omitted from the serialization of the object to which it belongs.

- **unsettable** specifies whether the feature has an additional possible state, called *unset*, that is distinguishable from that of being set to any value at all. The value of this attribute also determines the semantics of EObject's eUnset() and eIsSet() reflective APIs. For an unsettable feature, these methods simply unset the feature and check if it is set, respectively. But, for a non-unsettable feature, they actually reset the feature's value to its default and test that if it is set to a non-default value, respectively.

- **volatile** specifies whether the feature has no storage directly associated with it; this is often the case for derived features. The bodies of the accessors for such features usually must be coded by hand.

Before continuing, it is worth enlarging slightly on the notion of structural features with values that are derived from those of other features. It is important to identify such features so that they can be ignored by generic framework code responsible for operations like copying and persistence. Because derived features contribute nothing new to the state of an object, it is common to make them volatile and transient as well. Moreover, to keep things simple, we often declare them to be non-changeable, only letting them be affected indirectly by changing the features from which they are derived. In fact, this is done consistently throughout Ecore itself. Thus, for the remainder of this chapter, whenever a feature is described as derived, you can assume it is also volatile, transient, and non-changeable. You can easily identify a derived attribute in a class diagram by the "/" preceding its name. Keep in mind that the derived features in the Ecore metamodel are already implemented, so you are never responsible for determining appropriate values for such features when defining a model. Similarly you will have to implement the derived features of your model manually.

For example, there are two derived attributes provided on **ETypedElement** as a convenience: **required** and **many**, which reflect whether the lower and upper bounds are non-zero and greater than one, respectively.

The last two attributes of **EStructuralFeature** have to do with the default value, the value of the feature before it is explicitly set to something else. Regardless of the type of the feature, its default value is always modeled by **defaultValueLiteral** as a string. Another attribute, **defaultValue**, can be used to access the equivalent value as a Java object of the appropriate type for the feature. This attribute is derived from **defaultValueLiteral** using the standard Ecore data type conversion mechanism, which we will discuss in Section 5.6. For a reference, **defaultValue** will always be null. Although **defaultValue** is modeled as non-changeable, there is a hand-coded convenience method in the Java implementation, `EStructuralFeature.setDefaultValue()`, which takes an object and uses the inverse of the data type conversion mechanism to set **defaultValueLiteral** to the equivalent string.

If a structural feature does not specify a non-null **defaultValueLiteral**, then the intrinsic default value of its type is used instead. As we will see in Section 5.5, **EClassifier** includes a non-changeable **defaultValue** attribute that corresponds directly to the default value of its underlying Java type. Thus, boolean-typed attributes with no default specified, such as **transient, unsettable**, and **volatile**, have a default value of false. Likewise, as an integer-typed attribute with no explicit default, **lowerBound** has a default value of 0.

Finally, we should mention the operations defined on **EStructuralFeature**: **getFeatureID** and **getContainerClass**. We will not worry about how operations are represented in Ecore until Section 5.4, so for now, we'll just say what these two operations do.

Each structural feature is identified within a class by a unique integer, called the feature ID, which is used in implementing the reflective `EObject` API. This value is set during the initialization of a static model and during a call to `getEAllStructuralFeatures()` on a dynamically defined class. Before this point, it will just be -1.

In generated models, the Java class that realizes the containing class is also significant. Where there is multiple inheritance, the feature ID should be considered relative to a particular class that defines or inherits it, and the Java class is used as a key in converting among these values. The class of the structural feature's container identifies the generated, static base value, from which we can efficiently convert to a value relative to any given subtype. This is used in the fast, switch-based, generated implementations that we discuss in Section 10.7. The feature ID and container class are made available by the **getFeatureID** and **getContainerClass** operations, respectively.

5.3.1 Attributes

Having looked at what attributes have in common with references, we will now examine what sets them apart. Figure 5.3 illustrates the unique aspects of **EAttribute**.

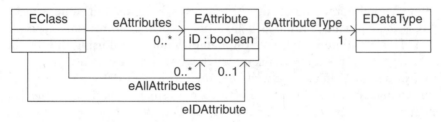

Figure 5.3   Ecore attributes.

In addition to all of the attributes it inherits from **EStructuralFeature**, **EAttribute** defines one more, **iD**,[3] which determines whether the value of the attribute can be used to uniquely identify the instance of its containing class in a given context, such as a resource.

EAttribute also defines one derived reference: **eAttributeType**, which actually refers to the same **EClassifier** as **eType**, which we described in the previous subsection. However, the type of an attribute must be a data type and not a class, so this reference casts that object to an **EDataType**.

As we saw in Figure 5.2, **EAttribute**s, along with **EReference**s, are contained by an **EClass** via its **eStructuralFeatures** reference. **EClass** defines three additional related references, **eAttributes**, **eAllAttributes**, and **eIDAttribute**. We already saw **eAttributes** in Figure 5.1; it provides a filtered view of the **eStructuralFeatures** reference, including only the **EAttribute**s from that list. For an instance of **EClass**, **eAllAttributes** includes not only its own **eAttributes**, but also those collected from the **eAttributes** references of all of its supertypes; that is, the **EClasses** accessible recursively through the **eSuperTypes** reference. As a convenience, **eIDAttribute** refers to the first **EAttribute** in **eAllAttributes** for

---

3. The unfortunate capitalization comes from the convention that structural feature names should begin with a lowercase letter. Fortunately, when code is generated for the model, this letter is capitalized in forming the accessor names isID() and setID().

which **iD** is true. All three of **eAttributes**, **eAllAttributes**, and **eIDAttribute** are derived references.

5.3.2 References

The unique aspects of **EReference** are illustrated in Figure 5.4.

EReference adds two references and three attributes to those defined by **EStructuralFeature** and its base classes. The first reference, **eReferenceType**, is analogous to **EAttribute**'s **eAttributeType**: it refers to the same **EClassifier** as **ETypedElement**'s **eType**, but cast to an **EClass**. Like its attribute analog, it is a derived reference. The other, **eOpposite**, refers to the reference representing the opposite direction of a bidirectional association. Thus, such an association is represented by the two **EReference**s, each defining the other as its **eOpposite**.

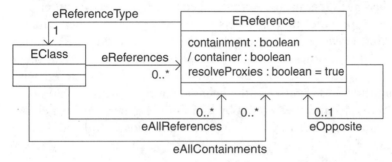

Figure 5.4 Ecore references.

We mentioned the notion of containment in Section 5.2. Known as "by-value aggregation" in UML, containment is a stronger type of association that implies a whole–part relationship: an object cannot, directly or indirectly, contain its own container; it can have no more than one container; and its life span ends with that of its container. The **containment** attribute indicates whether an **EReference** is being used in modeling such a relationship. If so, it is set on the reference from the whole to the part, that is, from the container to the contained object. If the containment relationship is explicitly bidirectional, then for the opposite reference, the derived **container** attribute is also true.

The last attribute defined by **EReference**, **resolveProxies**, relates to EMF's resource model for persistence. We described in Section 2.5.2 how, when a resource is loaded, any referenced objects that are persisted in other resources are represented by proxies. We also said that, when such an object is accessed for the first time, its resource is loaded and the real object is returned. In fact, the automatic resolution of proxies is only performed for references that define

resolveProxies to be true. This is the default and should normally be the case; however, sometimes it makes sense to dictate that a particular reference can never be cross-document. In these cases, **resolveProxies** can be set to false, permitting the use of a more efficient implementation.

EReference is also analogous to **EAttribute** in its containment relationship with **EClass**: **EClass** uses **eReferences** to provide a filtered view of the **eStructurealFeatures** containment reference, and defines **eAllReferences** to also include the references of its supertypes. Finally, **eAllContainments** refers to all of those **EReferences** accessible via **eAllReferences** for which **containment** is true. All three of these references are derived.

5.4   Behavioral Features

In addition to their structural features, Ecore can model the behavioral features of an **EClass** as **EOperation**s. Actually, Ecore only models the interfaces to those operations; it provides no constructs to express the actual behavior that operations exhibit. However, it is possible to annotate the model with an implementation specified in another language. We will look at Ecore annotations in Section 5.7 and see, specifically, how an **EOperation** can be annotated with its Java implementation.[4] Alternatively, the behavior of the operation can be left unspecified in the model and then coded by hand in the generated Java class.

EOperation is illustrated, along with the closely related **EParameter**, in Figure 5.5.

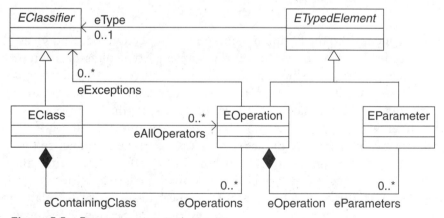

Figure 5.5   Ecore operations and parameters.

---

4. It would also be possible to annotate an operation to specify its behavior in another language. Because EMF's code generator is extensible, it could be made to convert another language into Java or to generate code that invokes an interpreter.

Like **EStructuralFeatures**, **EOperation**s are contained by an **EClass**. They are accessed via the **eOperations** containment reference. Its opposite, **eContainingClass**, provides the other half of the bidirectional association between the two classes. **EClass** also defines a derived **eAllOperations** reference to include the operations of a class and its supertypes.

An **EOperation** contains zero or more **EParameters**, accessible via **eParameters**, which model the operation's input parameters. Again, this reference constitutes half of a bidirectional association; the **EParameters** can access the **EOperation** to which they belong via the opposite reference, **eOperation**.

Both **EOperation** and **EParameter** inherit the **name** attribute and type and multiplicty data from **ETypedElement**. Recall from Section 5.3 that this includes the **eType** reference, which can refer to any **EClassifier**, whether **EClass** or **EDataType**. Here, it models the return type of an operation and the type of an input parameter. Also inherited from **ETypedElement** are the multiplicity-related attributes, including **lowerBound**, **upperBound**, **many**, **required**, **ordered**, and **unique**.

Finally, **EOperation** defines an additional reference, **eExceptions**, to zero or more **EClassifiers**, to model the types of objects that an operation can throw as exceptions.

5.5 Classifiers

Having discussed Ecore's representations of structural and behavioral features, let's now back up and take a detailed look at the classes that, taken together, they define. As we have already seen, **EClass** shares a base class with **EDataType**, so we will have to discuss the two together. That base class, **EClassifier**, acts as a common target for **ETypedElement**'s **eType** reference, allowing structural features, operations, and parameters to specify as their types either classes or data types. As illustrated in Figure 5.6, **EClassifier** also contributes a number of attributes and operations to its subtypes, which we discuss next.

First, we observe that, like everything else we have seen so far, **EClassifier** inherits a **name** attribute from **ENamedElement**.

Two of the attributes defined by **EClassifier** specify a correspondence to an ordinary, non-EMF Java class or interface; we will expand on the particular character of this correspondence for **EClasses** and for **EDataTypes** in the following subsections. Such a class or interface is specified, by name, by the **instanceClassName** attribute. A derived attribute, **instanceClass** can be used to access the Java class with that name. The relationship between these two attributes is similar to the one between **EStructuralFeature**'s **defaultValueLiteral** and **defaultValue** attributes, described in Section 5.3, in that the Java implementation also provides a hand-coded `setInstanceClass()` method that takes a Java class, but actually sets the value of **instanceClassName**.

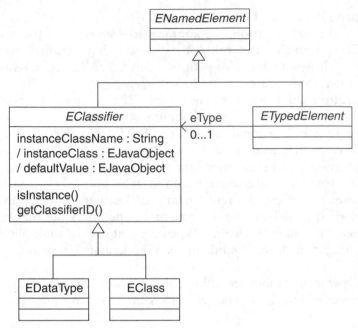

Figure 5.6   Ecore classifiers.

The last of **EClassifier**'s attributes, **defaultValue**, represents the intrinsic default value of a class or data type; that is, the default value of the Java primitive or class that realizes it. This attribute is derived from the value of **instanceClass**.

EClassifier provides an **isInstance** operation, which tests whether an arbitrary Java object, specified as a parameter, is non-null and an instance of the class or data type represented by the **EClassifier**, or of one of its subtypes. For an **EClass**, this is determined by consulting the **eAllSuperTypes** reference, which we will see in the following subsection. For an **EDataType**, it means a reflective Java `Class.isInstance()` test on the value of **instanceClass**. Finally, the **getClassifierID** operation returns an integer that is used to uniquely identify a classifier within its package. This value is set during the initialization of a static model; it will always be -1 for dynamically defined classifiers.

5.5.1   Classes

The unique aspects of **EClass** are illustrated in Figure 5.7.

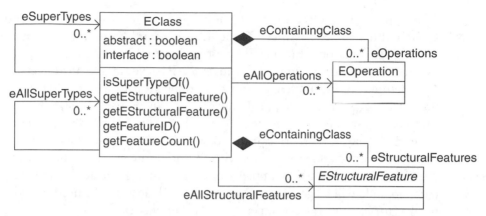

Figure 5.7 Ecore classes.

We have already discussed at some length the relationships between **EClass** and the classes that represent structural and behavioral features; let's complete that discussion now. We have seen the **eOperations** and **eStructuralFeatures** containment references, which connect an **EClass** with its **EOperation**s and **EStructuralFeature**s, as well as their opposite references, both called **eContainingClass**. We have also seen the derived **eReferences** and **eAttributes** references, each of which includes only one of the structural feature types, and **eAllReferences** and **eAllAttributes**, which also include inherited references and attributes, respectively. All that's missing is one more derived reference, **eAllStructuralFeatures**, that similarly aggregates all of the structural features defined and inherited by a class.

We saw in Section 5.2 that **EClass** provides support for multiple inheritance via its **eSuperTypes** reference. A class inherits structural and behavioral features from all of its supertypes, all of its supertypes' supertypes, and so on. This complete set of classes from which features are inherited is provided by the derived **eAllSuperTypes** reference. Because **eSuperTypes** is a proxy-resolving reference, a class can inherit from base classes defined in other Ecore documents.

The two attributes defined by **EClass** itself can be used to specify the particular type of class being modeled. If **interface** is true, the **EClass** represents an interface that declares its operations and the accessors for its attributes and references, but can provide no implementation for them. An interface cannot be instantiated. Implementation of an interface is modeled by including the interface in the **eSuperTypes** reference of a non-interface **EClass**; that class will implement the operations and the accessors for the structural features declared by the interface. If **abstract** is true, the **EClass** represents an abstract class, from which other classes can inherit features, but that cannot itself be instantiated. Ecore includes a number of abstract classes, most of which we have already seen: **ENamedElement**, **EClassifier**, **ETypedElement**, and **EStructuralFeature**. We look at the only other one, **EModelElement**, in Section 5.6.

As mentioned previously, the **instanceClassName** and **instanceClass** attributes defined by **EClassifier** establish a connection to a non-EMF Java class or interface. In particular, for an **EClass**, they can be used to specify an interface that corresponds to the class it defines. This is only applicable in the context of generated models, as there can be no such interface for classes defined dynamically. Generating code for a class with this attribute set will generally result in an implementation class that implements the named interface. If **interface** is also true, no code will be generated, but the defined class can be used elsewhere in the model, for example as the supertype of other classes.

Finally, **EClass** defines five operations that provide simple conveniences. As a shortcut for consulting the **eAllSuperTypes** reference, **isSuperTypeOf** tests whether one class extends another. The two forms of **getEStructuralFeature** return the **EStructuralFeature** from **eAllStructuralFeatures** with either a specified name or feature ID. The ID for a given **EStructuralFeature** can be looked up using **getFeatureID**, and **getFeatureCount** simply returns the total number of structural features defined and inherited by a class.

5.5.2 *Data Types*

Whereas classes define multiple structural and behavioral features, data types represent a single piece of "simple" data. This distinction is somewhat similar to that between classes and primitive types in Java. In fact, an **EDataType** models a single Java type, whether a primitive type, a Java class or interface, or even an array. This allows conceptually simple classes, like `String`, to be represented as a single unit.

In general, however, it is considered a bad idea to represent a highly complicated Java class as a data type. Instead, it is preferable to directly model the class in EMF with an **EClass** and, thus, to benefit from the framework's assistance in matters of serialization, notification, and reflection. As a general rule, if its values cannot be simply represented as a string without the use of some notation to impose structure, it probably shouldn't be modeled as a data type.[5]

It is the **instanceClassName** and **instanceClass** attributes inherited from **EClassifier** that are used to specify the Java type that is modeled by a data type.

---

5. In fact, this is more than just a rule of thumb: serialization of data type values is implemented at the level of the Ecore model, not of the resource. Thus, to be compatible with different resource types that perform different serializations, it should never impose structure.

EDataType does not add much to the attributes and operations that it inherits. In fact, it defines just one attribute, **serializable**, that indicates whether values of the type can be serialized. In other words, the value of any attribute whose **eType** is a non-serializable data type will not be persisted. Indeed, you could obtain this same result by making all such attributes transient. The difference between these two approaches is seen at development time: if a data type is serializable, a generated factory will include methods to convert values of that type to and from strings.

Enumerated Types

An enumerated type is a special data type that defines an explicit list of values, called literals, that elements of that type are allowed to assume. Figure 5.8 illustrates **EDataType**, **EEnum**, and **EEnumLiteral**, which model data types, enumerated types, and enumeration literals, respectively.

An **EEnum** specifies its valid **EEnumLiterals** via the **eLiterals** containment reference, which is bidirectional, with an opposite named **eEnum**. **EEnumLiteral** inherits a **name** attribute from **ENamedElement** and defines two more: an integer-typed **value**, and an arbitrary **literal** string that's used to represent the literal during serialization, for example. If the **literal** string is left null, then the **name** will be used to represent it, instead. In generated models, enumerated types are realized using the Type-safe Enum pattern, described by Joshua Bloch in *Effective Java Programming Language Guide* [4]. In this pattern, a Java class with no public constructor is defined for the enumerated type. The literal values are made available as static instances of this class. Also, these instances are accessible from the corresponding **EEnumLiteral**, via its **instance** attribute.

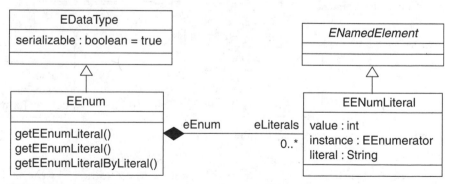

Figure 5.8   Ecore data types, enumerated types, and literals.

For convenience, **EEnum** defines three operations that return an **EEnumLiteral** from eLiterals: two forms of **getEEnumLiteral** look up the **EEnumLiteral** by name or value, and **getEEnumLiteralByLiteral** looks it up by literal string.

5.6 Packages and Factories

In Ecore, related classes and data types are grouped into packages, and a factory is used to create instances of the classes and values of the data types that belong to the package. When an Ecore model is serialized, the root element represents a package. **EPackage** and **EFactory**, which model packages and factories, are illustrated in Figure 5.9.

EPackage inherits a **name** attribute from **ENamedElement**. A package's name need not be universally unique. Instead, a URI is used to uniquely identify the package. Reflecting EMF's close relationship with XML, this URI is also used in the serialization of instance documents to identify an XML namespace [5] for the root element. This URI is specified as the value of the **EPackage**'s **nsURI** attribute; the **nsPrefix** attribute is used to define the corresponding namespace prefix.

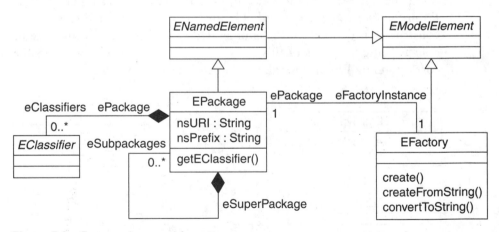

Figure 5.9 Ecore packages and factories.

The **EClassifiers** grouped by an **EPackage** are contained via the **eClassifiers** reference, which has an opposite reference called **ePackage**. A **getEClassifier** operation is also defined, to conveniently obtain one of these **EClassifiers** by name. **EPackages** support nesting, via the **eSubpackages** containment reference. An **EPackage**'s associated **EFactory** is accessed via the **eFactoryInstance** reference.

Ecore packages are closely related to Java packages. Conceptually, they serve the same purpose, and when code is generated from an Ecore model, the Java classes and interfaces that realize its classifiers are placed in packages that correspond to their Ecore counterparts. When Ecore packages are nested, the package names used in generated code are automatically formed, in the usual Java manner, by prepending their dot-separated superpackage names. Note, however, that it is not necessary to model empty, nested packages just to ensure that generated code uses universally unique package names. **GenPackage**, the generator model class that decorates **EPackage** with code generation data, provides an attribute called **basePackage** for this purpose, as we've seen in Chapter 4.

While all of the classes in Ecore that we have seen so far are subtypes of **ENamedElement**, **EFactory** directly extends **EModelElement**, the single base type for everything in Ecore. As a result, **EFactory** does not have a **name** attribute. In fact, **EFactory** does not inherit or declare any structural features except for **ePackage**, the reverse of the reference from the associated **EPackage**. Because factories do not have any further instance data, they need not be explicitly modeled or serialized; a factory can simply be demand created by its package. As a result, both of the references that model the association between **EPackage** and **EFactory** are transient.

The factory's role is purely behavioral: it defines **create**, **createFromString**, and **convertToString** operations, which instantiate classes and convert data type values to and from strings. For generated models, each of these operations is implemented using call-out methods, one for each class or data type. The mappings between data type values and their serialized forms are thus specified by changing the implementations of these `createFromString()` and `convertToString()` methods.

5.7 Annotations

Annotations constitute a mechanism by which additional information can be attached to any object in an Ecore model. **EAnnotation**, illustrated in Figure 5.10, is used to model annotations.

By subclassing **EModelElement**, all classes defined in Ecore include an **eAnnotations** reference, which can contain zero or more **EAnnotation**s. As this association is bidirectional, an **EAnnotation** can access its **EModelElement** via the opposite reference, **eModelElement**.

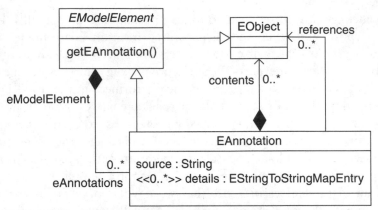

Figure 5.10   Ecore annotations.

EAnnotation defines a **source** attribute, which is typically used to store a URI representing the type of the annotation. **EModelElement** also defines a **getEAnnotation** operation, to conveniently obtain one of its **EAnnotation**s by its source. Two references, **contents** and **references**, allow an **EAnnotation** to contain or refer to any number of arbitrary EMF objects, which we model using **EObject**.[6]

The last structural feature defined by **EAnnotation** is worth describing in some detail, as it demonstrates an Ecore modeling technique that we have not yet seen: the use of map-typed features. Although there is no map type explicitly modeled in Ecore, support for such features is enabled through a special behavior of the code generator.

Figure 5.11 illustrates **EStringToStringMapEntry**, the type of the **details** feature.

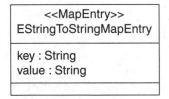

Figure 5.11   Example of a map entry class.

---

6. Notice from Figure 5.10 that **EModelElement**, the base type for Ecore, is derived from **EObject**. Because the metaobject for an **EObject** is itself an **EClass**, this is consistent with our earlier statement that Ecore is its own metamodel.

Like any other class, **EStringToStringMapEntry** is modeled using **EClass**. However, because of its <<MapEntry>> stereotype, the **EClass's instanceClassName** attribute will be set to "java.util.Map$Entry", to indicate that the class will implement a `Map.Entry`-based interface. The class also contains two particular structural features, **key** and **value**, whose types will constrain the map accordingly.

So, in general, a multi-valued containment reference[7] to a class that both implements `Map.Entry` and contains structural features named **key** and **value** tips off the generator that the pattern for a map-typed feature should be used. We will discuss this pattern in Chapter 10.

In this case, the end result is a feature called **details** that stores mappings from one string value to another. Thus, not only can an **EAnnotation** contain and reference arbitrary EMF objects, it can also store and efficiently retrieve arbitrary textual data.

EMF uses annotations to attach several different types of information to Ecore models in ways that weren't envisioned when the metamodel was first designed. Section 5.7.1 identifies these annotations. Moreover, annotations provide other applications with a great deal of flexibility to extend Ecore models for their own specific purposes.

5.7.1 Annotations in EMF

EMF annotates Ecore models for a number of different purposes. In general, annotations are used to store kinds of information that were not considered fundamental enough to be explicitly supported in the Ecore metamodel. This section summarizes all of EMF's own uses of **EAnnotations**, categorized by the source it uses for each kind.

Ecore

An Ecore-sourced **EAnnotation** is attached to an **EModelElement** to specify general-purpose model information that is relevant at both runtime and code generation time. Such an annotation is identified by a **source** of "http://www.eclipse.org/emf/2002/Ecore". This is the namespace URI for Ecore, which is available programatically as `EcorePackage.eNS_URI`.

Ecore-sourced annotations are currently only used to specify named constraints on classifiers. One such **EAnnotation** may be included on an **EClassifier**, with only one entry in its **details** map. The list of space-separated constraint

---

7. Although **details** looks like an attribute in UML, because its type is a class and not a data type, it is actually represented as a reference in Ecore. Refer to Chapter 8 for a more detailed explanation.

names appears as a single value, keyed by "constraints". Constraints are discussed in detail in Chapter 18.

GenModel

A GenModel-sourced **EAnnotation** is attached to an **EModelElement** to specify information that is only relevant when generating code, not at runtime. Such an annotation is identified by a **source** of "http://www.eclipse.org/emf/2002/GenModel". This is the namespace URI for the EMF generator model, which is available programatically as `GenModelPackage.eNS_URI`.

GenModel-sourced annotations are used for several different purposes. One such **EAnnotation** may be included on any **EModelElement**, and currently, only its **details** feature is used. Table 5.1 summarizes the recognized key–value pairs for annotations on each type of model element.

Table 5.1   GenModel-Sourced Annotation Details

Type	Key	Value
EOperation	body	The Java code that implements the operation. Fully qualified type names enclosed between <% and %> will be imported during code generation.
EModelElement	documentation	Documentation for the model element, which will be generated into a delimited section of its Javadoc.
EStructuralFeature	suppressedGetVisibility	If "true", the `get()` accessor for the feature will be suppressed from the generated interface for its containing class.
EStructuralFeature	suppressedSetVisibility	If "true", the `set()` accessor for the feature will be suppressed from the generated interface for its containing class.
EStructuralFeature	suppressedIsSetVisibility	If "true", the `isSet()` accessor for the feature will be suppressed from the generated interface for its containing class.
EStructuralFeature	suppressedUnsetVisibility	If "true", the `unset()` accessor for the feature will be suppressed from the generated interface for its containing class.

Extended Metadata

Extended metadata **EAnnotation**s are used in models that were created from XML Schema to capture details about the schema that have no other direct representation in Ecore. Such annotations are identified by a **source** of "http:///org/eclipse/emf/ecore/util/ExtendedMetaData".

Extended metadata annotations are discussed at length in Chapters 8 and 9.

XSD2Ecore

XSD2Ecore **EAnnotation**s were used before extended metadata was introduced in EMF 2.0, for much the same purpose: they were added to models created from XML Schema to capture details without a direct Ecore representation. Such annotations are identified by a **source** of "http:///org/eclipse/emf/mapping/xsd2ecore/XSD2Ecore".

Compared to extended metadata, XSD2Ecore annotations are quite basic. Extended metadata does a much better job of preserving the details of a schema, so EMF no longer produces XSD2Ecore annotations. However, they can still be found on old models. For the sake of backward compatibility, EMF's XML resource implementation still uses them, when present, to drive schema-conformant serialization.

EMOF Tags

As we first mentioned in Section 2.6.2, EMF provides for interchange between Ecore and EMOF by allowing Ecore models to be serialized as EMOF. Tags serve essentially the same purpose in EMOF as annotations do in Ecore. So, when constructing an Ecore model from an EMOF serialization, an **EAnnotation** is used in place of each tag.

EMOF tags are not tied directly to a single model element, but can refer to any number of them. So, rather than being attached directly to any model element, **EAnnotation**s representing tags are stored alongside an **EPackage**, directly in its containing resource. Such an annotation is identified by a **source** of "http://schema.omg.org/spec/mof/2.0/emof.xmi". The value of its **references** feature is the set of **EModelElement**s to which the tag refers, and its **details** map is used to record the tag's name and value, keyed by "name" and "value", respectively.

5.8 Modeled Data Types

The Ecore metamodel itself includes a number of **EDataType** instances representing all of the most common Java types, as specified in Table 5.2. Any Ecore models can refer to any of these data types and take advantage of the conversions to and from strings that are provided by Ecore's factory implementation.

Table 5.2 Java Language Types in Ecore

Ecore Data Type	Java Primitive Type or Class	Serializable
EBoolean	boolean	true
EByte	byte	true
EChar	char	true
EDouble	double	true
EFloat	float	true
EInt	int	true
ELong	long	true
EShort	short	true
EByteArray	byte[]	true
EBooleanObject	java.lang.Boolean	true
EByteObject	java.lang.Byte	true
ECharacterObject	java.lang.Character	true
EDoubleObject	java.lang.Double	true
EFloatObject	java.lang.Float	true
EIntegerObject	java.lang.Integer	true
ELongObject	java.lang.Long	true
EShortObject	java.lang.Short	true
EBigDecimal	java.math.BigDecimal	true
EBigInteger	java.math.BigInteger	true
EDate	java.util.Date	true
EJavaObject	java.lang.Object	false
EJavaClass	java.lang.Class	true
EString	java.lang.String	true

Ecore also includes a few more **EDataTypes** that allow it to completely model its own API, such as **EEList**, **EEnumerator**, **EMap**, **EResource**, and **ETreeIterator**. These are not typically used in other models. One exception, however, is **EDiagnosticChain**, which you will need to use in the signature of an **EOperation** that defines an invariant, as we will see later, in Chapter 18.

5.9   Ecore and User Models

As we looked through the classes that make up Ecore, you might have thought to yourself, "Hey, that's just like what I want to model!" This is especially likely to be the case if your aim is to represent another metamodel, as metamodels tend to share quite similar concepts of classes with data and relationships between them. You might be wondering if you can simply extend the model elements defined by Ecore, and tweak your derived classes to suit your own needs.

The answer is that this use of Ecore is strongly discouraged. Ecore was not designed to be extended in this way, and there is no guarantee that future changes to EMF will not break any classes that extend **EModelElement** or any of its subclasses. Instead, you should model something equivalent yourself.

However, you are certainly free to *use* the classifiers defined by Ecore in your models. In fact, you are strongly encouraged to use the data types listed in Table 5.2 to represent basic Java types. If your model logically references or operates on classes from Ecore, you can use those classes as the types of your own model's references, operations, and parameters.

CHAPTER 6

UML

In becoming the standard language for modeling software systems, UML has garnered wide acceptance among modeling enthusiasts and extensive support from modeling tools. If you're already comfortable with UML, this will be a convenient representation for specifying your models. However, because EMF only concerns itself with a small subset of UML, you really don't need to be a UML expert to use it to represent Ecore. The relevant UML constructs are essentially the ones that are used in a class diagram: packages, classes, attributes, associations, and operations.

EMF defines a mapping from UML version 1.4 to Ecore, which is described here. This mapping is really quite straightforward, with just a few special conventions for some properties of a few UML constructs. The UML2 project at Eclipse.org defines a similar mapping for UML 2.0, differing only in some subtle details.

Some of the features of certain Ecore model elements cannot be expressed directly in UML. For example, there is no UML equivalent for the **resolveProxies** attribute of an **EReference**. So, we must rely on extension mechanisms provided by UML itself, or by particular UML tools, to fully specify an Ecore model.

As described in Chapter 2, EMF provides out-of-box support for importing UML models created in Rational Rose. A number of other popular UML tools provide their own specialized model converters, and the UML2 project mentioned earlier includes an EMF model importer for standard UML2 models. As we explore how UML constructs map to Ecore elements in this chapter, we will come across some of the Ecore properties that have no equivalent in UML. Then, in Section 6.7, we will see how they can be expressed in Rose models. Users of other tools should refer to their documentation for details of their mapping to Ecore.

6.1   UML Packages

As you might recall from Chapter 5, the top-level element of an Ecore model is an **EPackage**. Each UML package in a model is mapped to an **EPackage**.

- ❍ By default, the name of the **EPackage** is the same as the name of the corresponding UML package.

- ❍ The **eClassifiers** reference is populated based on the UML classes contained in the UML package. The type of each **EClassifier** created depends on the corresponding UML class's stereotype. This is discussed in the following section.

- ❍ The **eSubpackages** and **eSuperPackage** references are set according to the analogous UML package relationships.

- ❍ The **nsURI** and **nsPrefix** attributes cannot be expressed directly in UML. Default values are chosen automatically based on the name of the package.

For example, the ExtendedPO3 model contains the packages illustrated in Figure 6.1.

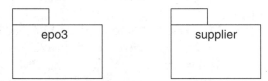

Figure 6.1   UML packages.

This maps to two **EPackages** whose name attributes are "epo3" and "supplier". Without using any tool-specific technique to specify them, the **nsURI** and **nsPrefix** for **epo3** will be "epo3" and "http:///epo3.ecore", respectively. Similarly, for **supplier,** the two attributes will be "supplier" and "http:///supplier.ecore" by default. Both packages will have empty **eSubpackages** references.

6.2   UML Specification for Classifiers

A UML class is mapped to an **EClass, EEnum,** or an **EDataType,** depending on the class's stereotype. We'll look at each of these three cases in the following sections.

6.2.1 Classes

Every UML class that has either an <<interface>> stereotype or no stereotype at all maps to an **EClass** in the **EPackage** corresponding to the UML package of the class.

- ❍ By default, the name of the **EClass** is the same as the name of the corresponding UML class.

- ❍ The **eSuperTypes** list references the **EClass**es corresponding to the UML classes that are the targets of generalization relationships. If you specify multiple generalizations for the UML class, you can attach an <<extend>> stereotype to one of them, to make it first in the **eSuperTypes** list. This is an important distinction because the EMF code generator uses the first of the **eSuperTypes** for the implementation base class of the generated Java class.

- ❍ The **eStructuralFeatures** reference is populated with the **EAttribute**s and **EReference**s derived from the UML attributes and associations for the class. These are discussed in Sections 6.3 and 6.4.

- ❍ The **eOperations** reference is populated with the **EOperation**s derived from the UML operations for the class. These are discussed in Section 6.5.

- ❍ The **instanceClassName** is set to the name of the UML attribute that has a <<javaclass>> stereotype, if such an attribute is present in the class.

- ❍ The **abstract** attribute is set to true if the UML class is abstract, as indicated in a class diagram by the italicization of its name.[1]

- ❍ The **interface** attribute of the **EClass** is set to true if the UML class has an <<interface>> stereotype.

Figure 6.2 illustrates the UML representation of **Address** and its subclasses, from the ExtendedPO2 model.

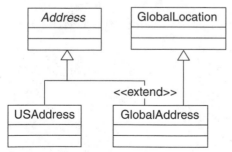

Figure 6.2 UML classes with generalization relationships.

---

1. In Rose, you can control whether a class is abstract via a check box on the **Detail** page of its **Class Specification** dialog box.

These four UML classes map to the following **EClasses**:

○ The **EClass** named "Address" has no **eSuperTypes**. Its **abstract** attribute is true and its **interface** attribute is false.

○ The **EClass** named "USAddress" has class **Address** in its **eSuperTypes** reference. Its **abstract** and **interface** attributes are false.

○ The **EClass** named "GlobalLocation" has no **eSuperTypes**, and both its **abstract** and **interface** attributes are false.

○ The **EClass** named "GlobalAddress" has **Address** and **GlobalLocation**, in that order, as its **eSuperTypes**. The <<extend>> stereotype determines this order, ensuring that the generated implementation class for **GlobalAddress** will extend the implementation class for **Address**. The **abstract** and **interface** attributes are both false for this class.

The various attributes, references, and operations for these classes are not shown in Figure 6.2. These elements will be discussed in later sections.

6.2.2 Enumerated Types

A UML class with an <<enumeration>> stereotype is mapped to an **EEnum**.

○ By default, the name of each **EEnum** is the same as the name of the corresponding UML class.

○ The **eLiterals** reference is populated with **EEnumLiterals** derived from the attributes that belong to the UML class. The name of each **EEnumLiteral** is set to the name of the UML attribute. The value of a literal, an integer, can be specified as the attribute's initial value. Otherwise, it will be assigned a sequential value by default. No type should be specified for these attributes.

For example, the ExtenedPO3 model includes the UML class shown in Figure 6.3.

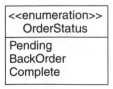

Figure 6.3 A UML class representing an enumerated type.

This maps to an **EEnum** named "OrderStatus" that contains three **EEnumLiterals**. The literals are automatically assigned sequential integer values, starting with 0. Thus, **Pending** is assigned the value 0, **BackOrder** is assigned 1, and **Complete** is assigned 2.

If you want to specify any literal values yourself, you can do so by including initial values for the UML attributes that represent those literals, as illustrated in Figure 6.4.

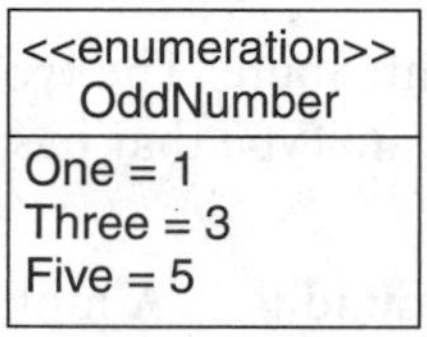

<<enumeration>> OddNumber
One = 1 Three = 3 Five = 5

Figure 6.4   Specifying values for literals.

6.2.3   *Data Types*

A UML class with a <<datatype>> stereotype is mapped to an **EDataType**. Such a class must have exactly one attribute.

○ By default, the name of the **EDataType** is the same as the name of the corresponding UML class.

○ The **instanceClassName** is set to the name of the UML class's single attribute, which must have a stereotype of <<javaclass>> and not specify a type. This value is the fully qualified name of the Java class or interface that the **EDataType** will be used to model.

○ The **serializable** attribute is set to false if the UML class is abstract, as indicated in a class diagram by the italicization of its name.

There are two data types defined in the ExtendedPO3 model. They are illustrated in Figure 6.5.

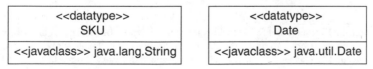

Figure 6.5   UML classes representing data types.

The **EDataType** named "SKU" is implemented by `java.lang.String`. The **EDataType** named "Date" is implemented by `java.util.Date`.

6.3   UML Specification for Attributes

Each attribute of a UML class is mapped to an **EAttribute** of the corresponding **EClass**.

- ❍ By default, the name of the **EAttribute** is the same as the name of the corresponding UML attribute.

- ❍ The **eType** corresponds to the type of the UML attribute. The type must be either a basic Java type,[2] or an **EEnum** or **EDataType** that has been defined in the model.

- ❍ By default, the **lowerBound** is 0 and the **upperBound** is 1. A multiplicity expression can also be specified explicitly, as a stereotype on the UML attribute. This is discussed further in Section 6.3.2.

- ❍ The **defaultValueLiteral** is set according to the initial value of the UML attribute, if specified. This is discussed further in Section 6.3.3.

- ❍ The **derived** attribute is set to true if the UML attribute has been tagged as derived.[3]

- ❍ By default, the **transient, volatile, unsettable,** and **iD** attributes are all false, and the **unique** and **changeable** attributes are true. There is no way to specify these attributes in standard UML.

6.3.1   Single-Valued Attributes

By default, attributes are single-valued. For example, consider the attribute of class **Supplier** that is illustrated in Figure 6.6.

---

2. Ecore has built-in **EDataTypes** for all the Java primitive types (`boolean`, `byte`, `char`, `double`, `float`, `int`, `long`, `short`) and their corresponding java.lang wrapper classes (e.g., `java.lang.Character`), as well as the `byte[]` array type and `java.lang.String` class.

3. UML supports an extension mechanism for model elements known as tagged values. UML 1.4, in particular, defines a number of built-in tagged values, one of which allows any model element to be tagged as derived. In Rose, you can control whether an attribute is derived using a check box on the **Detail** page of its **Attribute Specification** dialog box.

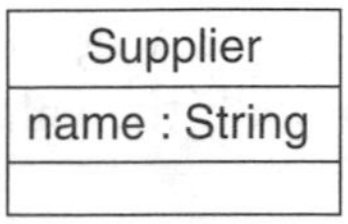

```
+---------------------+
|      Supplier       |
+---------------------+
| name : String       |
+---------------------+
|                     |
+---------------------+
```

Figure 6.6 A single-valued attribute.

The corresponding **EAttribute** has its **name** set to "name". Its **eType** is the built-in Ecore data type **EString**, which represents `java.lang.String`. The **lowerBound** and **upperBound** are 0 and 1 respectively, and **defaultValueLiteral** is null.

6.3.2 Multi-valued Attributes

To indicate that an attribute is multi-valued, we can specify a multiplicity expression as a stereotype for the UML attribute. This expression has the same syntax as the multiplicity of a role in an association. For example, <<1..*>> would indicate a **lowerBound** of 1 and an **upperBound** of -1 (unbounded). Equal lower and upper bounds can be expressed more simply as, for instance, <<4>>.

Consider the **location** attribute of class **GlobalAddress**, illustrated in Figure 6.7.

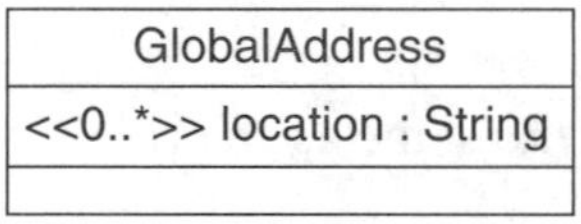

```
+-----------------------------+
|        GlobalAddress        |
+-----------------------------+
| <<0..*>> location : String  |
+-----------------------------+
|                             |
+-----------------------------+
```

Figure 6.7 A multi-valued attribute.

The **EAttribute** in this case is named "location". Once again, its **eType** is the **EString** data type, but in this case, the **lowerBound** and **upperBound** attributes are set explicitly to 0 and -1 (unbounded), respectively. Note that this common case can also be expressed as just <<*>>.

6.3.3 Attributes with a Default Value

We can set the default value of an attribute by specifying an initial value in UML. The initial value is used to set the **defaultValueLiteral** attribute of the corresponding **EAttribute**. Recall from Sections 5.3 and 5.6 that this is the string form of the default value, which then gets converted to a Java object by the appropriate factory for the **eType** of the **EAttribute**. This is the same approach used in deserialization.

The actual string set as the **defaultValueLiteral** depends on whether the initial value is quoted in the UML representation. If not quoted, the value is used unchanged. If it is double-quoted, any escaped characters (e.g., "\n") are interpreted according to the rules for Java string literals. If it is single-quoted, then it should be one character, optionally escaped, which will be interpreted if necessary and then converted to its decimal integer representation.[4]

For example, consider class **Customer**, illustrated in Figure 6.8.

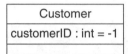

Figure 6.8   Specifying a default value.

Here, the **EAttribute** is named "customerID" and its **eType** is the **EInt** data type, which represents the Java primitive type int. Its **defaultValueLiteral** attribute is set to the string "-1".

6.4   UML Specification for References

Each navigable end of a UML association between two classes is mapped to an **EReference** in the corresponding **EClass**.

- ○ By default, the name of the **EReference** is the same as the role name of the corresponding UML association end.

- ○ The **eType** is the **EClass** corresponding to the UML class at the other end of the association.

- ○ The **lowerBound** and the **upperBound** are derived from the multiplicity of the corresponding UML association end. For example, if the multiplicity is specified as 0..1, the **lowerBound** is set to 0 and the **upperBound** is set to 1. For a multiplicity of 0..*, the **lowerBound** is set to 0 and the **upperBound** to -1 (unbounded).

- ○ If a UML association is navigable in both directions, the **eOpposite**s of the two corresponding **EReference**s refer to each other. If an association can only be navigated in one direction, the **eOpposite** of the corresponding **EReference** is simply null.

---

4 This conversion is consistent with the serialization format for Ecore's default character type, **EChar**.

○ The **containment** attribute is set to true if the corresponding UML association end is a composite, or by-value, aggregate. This is illustrated in a class diagram by a solid diamond on the container side of the association.

○ The **derived** attribute is set to true if the UML association has been tagged as derived.[5]

○ By default, the **transient, volatile,** and **unsettable** attributes are all false, and the **resolveProxies** and **changeable** attributes are true. There is no way to specify these attributes in standard UML.

6.4.1 Bidirectional, Non-Containment References

The name and multiplicity of an **EReference** are derived from the role name and multiplicity of its corresponding UML association end. An **EReference** is contained by the class that is on the opposite end of the line from where its role name and multiplicity appear, whereas its **eType** is the class at the same end as the role and multiplicity. If an association is navigable in both directions, the **eOpposite** reference will be set to the **EReference** representing the other association end. For example, consider the association from the ExtendedPO2 model that is illustrated in Figure 6.9.

Figure 6.9 An association that is navigable in both directions.

This association is bidirectional and therefore maps to two **EReference**s in Ecore:

○ The **EReference** named "customer" that belongs to the **EClass** for "PurchaseOrder". Its **eType** is the **EClass** for "**Customer**", its **lowerBound** and **upperBound** attributes are both 1, and its **containment** attribute is set to false. Its **eOpposite** is the **EReference** named "orders" that belongs to the "Customer" **EClass**.

○ The **EReference** named "orders" that belongs to the "Customer" **EClass**. Its **eType** is the "PurchaseOrder" **EClass**. Its **lowerBound** is 0, its

---

5. In Rose, you can control whether an association is derived via a checkbox on the **Detail** page of its **Association Specification** dialog.

upperBound is -1 (unbounded), and its **containment** is false. Its
eOpposite is the **EReference** named "customer" that belongs to the
"PurchaseOrder" **EClass**.

As you can see, each of the two references has the other as its **eOpposite**.

6.4.2 Containment References

In UML, one end of an association can be designated a composite, or by-value,
aggregate by adding a solid diamond at the opposite end of the line from its role
name. In this case, the **containment** attribute of the corresponding **EReference** is
set to true. This is shown in Figure 6.10.

Figure 6.10   A by-value aggregation.

Here we have a single **EReference** named "orders", which belongs to the
"Supplier" **EClass**. Its **eType** is the **EClass** for "PurchaseOrder". Its **lowerBound**
is 0, its **upperBound** is -1 (unbounded), and its **eOpposite** is null. Its **containment**
attribute is set to true.

6.4.3 Map References

A multiplicity-many containment reference whose target UML class has a stereotype of <<MapEntry>> will be treated specially by the EMF code generator. It
will be implemented using an EMap instead of just an EList. EMap is an EList-
derived interface for a map whose keys and/or values can be **EObjects**. Entries in
an EMap are type-safe and ordered.

The way to specify a map in UML is to model a class that represents a map
entry type. Specifically, you create a UML class that has a <<MapEntry>> stereotype and contains features named "key" and "value", which can be either attributes or references. Any EMF class can then have a containment reference to the
map entry type. For example, consider the class **Index** in Figure 6.11.

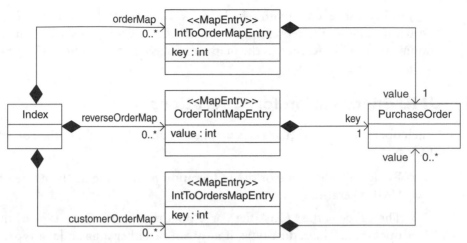

Figure 6.11 UML classes representing map types.

The **EClass** named "Index" has three map-type **EReferences** named "orderMap", "reverseOrderMap", and "customerOrderMap". The **orderMap** reference is a map from integer identifiers to purchase order objects. Its map entry class, **IntToOrderMapEntry,** has an attribute **key** of type int, and a **value** that is a reference to the class of the desired type, **PurchaseOrder.** Conversely, **reverseOrderMap** is a map of objects back to their identifiers. It uses a map entry class, **OrderToIntMapEntry,** whose **key** is a reference to the **PurchaseOrder** class and whose **value** is an int attribute.

The **key** and **value** features can also be multi-valued. The **customerOrderMap** reference is an example. Its map entry class, **IntToOrdersMapEntry,** uses an int attribute **key,** but its **value** is a multiplicity-many reference to a group of purchase orders.

Because either or both of the **key** and **value** features of an EMF map entry can be attributes, it's often more natural to think of the map itself as an attribute of the class that it's contained in. For this reason, a map can alternatively be expressed in UML as an attribute whose type is a UML map entry class. The **details** attribute in the **EAnnotation** class, in Ecore itself, is an example. This class, which we first saw in Section 5.7, is illustrated in Figure 6.12.

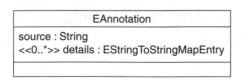

Figure 6.12 A map shown as an attribute.

In this case, even though **details** looks to be defining an **EAttribute**, it's really just an alternative representation in UML. In Ecore, this will map to a containment-type **EReference** to the map entry class, **EStringToStringMapEntry**, just as in the previous examples.

6.5   UML Specification for Operations

Each operation in a UML class is mapped to an **EOperation** in the corresponding **EClass**.

○ By default, the **name** of the **EOperation** is the same as the name of the UML operation.

○ The **eType** is the **EClassifier** corresponding to the return type of the UML operation. The return type, if any, can be either a basic Java type, or a UML class corresponding to an **EEnum**, **EDataType**, or **EClass**. A void operation is modeled as an **EOperation** without an **eType**.

○ By default, the **lowerBound** is 0 and the **upperBound** is 1. A multiplicity expression can also be specified explicitly, as a stereotype on the UML operation. Such a stereotype is handled identically to one on an attribute, as described in Section 6.3.2.[6]

○ The **eParameters** reference is populated with **EParameters** derived from the corresponding parameters of the UML operation. The **name** of each **EParameter** is set to the name of the UML parameter. The **eType** is set to the **EClassifier** corresponding to the UML parameter's type, which can be either a basic Java type, or a UML class corresponding to any **EEnum**, **EDataType**, or **EClass**.

○ The **eExceptions** reference includes the **EClassifiers** corresponding to the exceptions specified for the UML operation.

○ If the UML operation is tagged with semantics, the semantics value is assumed to be a Java implementation for the operation and is recorded in an annotation on the **EOperation**.

○ By default, the **unique** attribute is true; there is no way to specify it in standard UML.

For example, consider the UML operation definition in Figure 6.13.

---

6. Just as the **eType** specifies the return type of an **EOperation**, the multiplicity bounds the number of values that can be returned by the·operation

PurchaseOrder
removeItem(item : SKU) : boolean

Figure 6.13   An operation.

This maps to an **EOperation** named "removeItem". The operation's **eType** is the built-in data type **EBoolean**, which represents the primitve Java type `boolean`. It has a single **EParameter** whose **name** is "item" and whose **eType** is the **EDataType** named "SKU".

We could embed an implementation directly in the model as the semantics of the UML operation. In Rose, this is done in the **Semantics** page of the **Operation Specification** dialog box, as illustrated in Figure 6.14.

Figure 6.14   Operation implementation.

Any semantics value is assumed to be a Java implementation of the operation. This operation body is recorded in the **details** map of a GenModel-sourced annotation on the **EOperation**, where it is keyed by "body". Notice that fully qualified class names can be enclosed between <% and %>, which will cause them to be imported during code generation. See Section 5.7.1 for more information on annotations.

6.6   Documentation

Documentation attached to UML model elements is preserved in Ecore as **EAnnotation**s on the corresponding Ecore model elements.

In UML 1.4, documentation is recorded using a tagged value. Rose provides a **Documentation** field on the **General** page of the specification dialog box for each model element, in which documentation can be entered.

In Ecore, this text is recorded in the **details** map, keyed by "documentation", of a GenModel-sourced **EAnnotation** on the corresponding **EModelElement**. Then, during code generation, it is included in the Javadoc for the corresponding Java construct. See Section 5.7.1 for more information on annotations.

6.7   Ecore Properties in Rational Rose

Rose provides for extensibility by allowing a property file to define additional properties of UML elements, which can then be added and set in user models. To exploit this feature, EMF provides such a file, named *ecore.pty*, which defines all the non-UML Ecore properties, allowing them to be set directly in Rose models.

This property file is located in the *rose/* subdirectory of the `org.eclipse. emf.importer.rose` plug-in, in the EMF Runtime package. You must either manually extract it from the plug-in JAR or import the whole plug-in into your workspace with the **Import** wizard. In Rose, you can then select **Model Properties > Add** from the **Tools** menu, and specify the location of the *ecore.pty* file.

Once added, the additional properties will be accessible on the **Ecore** tab of the specification dialog box for any model element. For example, Figure 6.15 shows the non-UML Ecore properties for an attribute. As pictured, all properties have been left with their default values.

For instance, recall from Section 6.3 that standard UML provides no way to specify a value for the **transient** feature of an **EAttribute** corresponding to a UML attribute. Notice that there is an Ecore property in Figure 6.15, **isTransient**, for that very purpose.

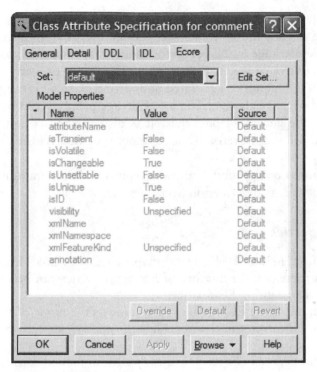

Figure 6.15 Non-UML Ecore properties.

A number of other properties correspond directly to attributes of **EAttribute**. In addition, there are also properties, such as **visibility, xmlName,** and **annotation,** that do not have direct **EAttribute** counterparts. These allow for additional information, not modeled in Ecore directly, to be specified and recorded on the **EAttribute** using **EAnnotation**s.

In the remainder of this chapter, we will describe all of the non-UML Ecore properties for Rose.

6.7.1 Package Properties

As described in Section 6.1, a UML package maps to an **EPackage**. In Rose, Ecore properties can be used to set those attributes of **EPackage** that do not have a UML representation.

By default, the **name** of an **EPackage** is the same as the name of the corresponding UML package. However, the **packageName** property can be used to give it a different name.

The **nsPrefix** and **nsURI** properties are used to assign non-default values to the corresponding **EPackage** attributes.

The **basePackage** and **prefix** properties are special, in that they do not actually set anything directly on the **EPackage**. Rather, they map to attributes of the corresponding **GenPackage** in the generator model that is created along with the Ecore model to control code generation for it. The **prefix** property specifies a prefix to be used in the names of generated supporting classes for the package (e.g., the factory and package classes). The **basePackage** property can be used to add qualification to the generated packages. It is also used in computing the default values for **nsURI** and **nsPrefix**, if they are not specified via the preceding properties.

Finally, the **annotation** property allows arbitrary **EAnnotation**s to be attached to the **EPackage**, as described in Section 6.7.5.

6.7.2 Classifier Properties

As we saw in Section 6.2, a UML class maps to an **EClass**, **EEnum**, or **EDataType**. In all of these cases, a number of Ecore properties can be set on the UML class to affect the resulting **EClassifier**.

By default, the **name** of the **EClassifier** is the same as the name of the corresponding UML class. However, the **classifierName** property can be used to give it a different name.

The **constraints** property can be used to specify a list of named constraints for the **EClassifier**. These are recorded in an Ecore-sourced **EAnnotation**, as described in Section 5.7.1, and can later be used in generating a utility for validating instances of the **EClassifier**. Constraints are discussed in detail in Chapter 18.

The **xmlName** and **xmlContentKind** properties can be used to specialize the XML serialization of instances of the **EClassifier**. An alternate name for the corresponding XML type is specified as the **xmlName**. For an **EClass** only, **xmlContentKind** is used to specify a particular kind of content the corresponding complex type might have. Both properties are recorded in the **details** of an extended metadata **EAnnotation**, keyed by "name" and "kind", respectively. Extended metadata and XML mappings are discussed extensively in Chapters 8 and 9.

Finally, the **annotation** property allows arbitrary **EAnnotation**s to be attached to the **EClassifier**, as we will see in Section 6.7.5.

6.7.3 Structural Feature Properties

As we saw in Sections 6.3 and 6.4, respectively, a UML attribute maps to an **EAttribute**, and each end of a UML association maps to an **EReference**. Because both of these model elements have a common superclass, **EStructuralFeature**, they share many common properties, which we will discuss together.

The Ecore properties for an **EAttribute** are located on the **Ecore** tab of the corresponding **Attribute Specification** dialog box. For the two **EReference**s corresponding to an association, the Ecore properties are located on the **Ecore A** and **Ecore B** tabs of the **Association Specification** dialog box.

By default, the **name** of the **EStructuralFeature** is the same as the name of the corresponding UML attribute or association end. However, the **attributeName** or **referenceName** property can be used to give it a different name.

For either an attribute or an association end, the Ecore properties **isTransient, isVolatile, isChangeable,** and **isUnsettable** can be used to set the **transient, volatile, changeable,** and **unsettable** attributes of the **EStructuralFeature**.

In addition, for an attribute, there are **isUnique** and **isID** properties, which correspond to the **unique** and **iD** attributes of **EAttribute**. For an association end, there is an **isResolveProxies** property, which corresponds to the **resolveProxies** attribute of **EReference**.

There is also a **visibility** property on either an attribute or association end, which can be used to suppress one or more of the accessors associated with the corresponding **EStructuralFeature** from the interface for its containing class. For example, setting the **visibility** to "Read-only" will suppress the generation of the `set()`, `isSet()`, and `unset()` accessors in the interface, assuming the feature was otherwise defined so that such methods would be generated. The methods to be suppressed are noted on the **EStructuralFeature** as **details** of a GenModel-sourced annotation, using the keys "suppressedGetVisibility", "suppressedSetVisibility", "suppressedIsSetVisibility", and "suppressedUnsetVisibility".

The **xmlName, xmlNamespace,** and **xmlFeatureKind** properties can be used to specialize the XML serialization of the **EStructuralFeature**. The **xmlFeatureKind** can specify whether the feature should be serialized in XML as a simple value, an attribute, or an element. An alternate name and namespace for the XML attribute or element can be specified as the **xmlName** and **xmlNamespace**, respectively. All three properties are recorded in the **details** of an extended metadata **EAnnotation**, keyed by "name", "namespace", and "kind". Extended metadata and XML mappings are discussed extensively in Chapters 8 and 9.

Finally, the **annotation** property allows arbitrary **EAnnotation**s to be attached to the **EStructuralFeature**, as described in Section 6.7.5.

6.7.4   *Operation Properties*

As described in Section 6.5, a UML operation maps to an **EOperation**. In Rose, there are three Ecore properties available for specifying non-UML details.

By default, the **name** of an **EOperation** is the same as the name of the corresponding UML operation. However, the **operationName** property can be used to give it a different name. The **isUnique** property corresponds to the **unique** attribute of the **EOperation**. Finally, the **annotation** property allows arbitrary **EAnnotations** to be attached to the **EOperation**, as described in the next section.

6.7.5 Model Element Properties

There is one Ecore model property corresponding to a feature of **EModelElement**. As we have just seen, it is available on UML packages, classes, attributes, association ends, and operations.

The **annotation** property can be used to attach **EAnnotations** to model elements. The following syntax is used for the value:

```
source1 key1a='value1a' key1b='value1b' source2 key2a='value2a' ...
```

This form allows multiple **EAnnotations** to be defined. Each one is identified by the specified **source** attribute, and its **details** map is populated with the associated key–value pairs.

CHAPTER 7

Java Source Code

If you are more familiar with Java programming than you are with modeling tools, you might find that the easiest way to describe your model is to use Java code. In this chapter, we explore the Java source code constructs and the special annotations that are needed to describe an Ecore model.

As you have seen in Chapter 5, an Ecore model is made up of one or more **EPackages**, each of which contains a number of **EClasses**, where each **EClass** has some number of **EAttributes**, **EReferences**, and **EOperations**. An **EPackage** can also contain **EDataTypes** and **EEnums**. If you specify your model using Java source code, the **EClasses** are given as Java interfaces. The **EAttributes**, **EReferences**, and **EOperations** will be inferred from the methods in those interfaces. **EEnums** are specified as Java classes. **EPackages** can also be specified as Java interfaces, although in most cases they do not need to be specified explicitly because they can be inferred from the package statements that are used to define the **EClasses**. Similarly, **EDataTypes** can be specified explicitly, although they can usually be inferred by references to the corresponding Java types.

EMF requires you to annotate your interfaces with specially formatted comments that are used to identify the model elements, and to optionally provide additional information that is not directly expressed in the Java code. These take the form of Javadoc comments that precede the class, interface, or method definitions to which they apply. They are identified by an `@model` tag and have the following syntax:

```
/**
 * @model [ property="value" | property='value' ] ...
 */
```

Each `@model` tag can be followed by several property–value pairs. Different properties are permitted for different model elements, as we will discuss in the following sections. Note that the values must be enclosed in either double quotes or single quotes. One special property, `kind`, can be used on any ambiguous Java construct, in order to specify which model element it is intended to represent.

The Java source code that you specify does not need to be complete. The code only needs to include enough information to describe your model. So, for example, you need to provide a Java interface for each **EClass**, but you do not need to provide an implementation class. Similarly, you need to provide a `get()` method for each attribute and reference, but you do not need to specify any other accessor methods. If other accessor methods are needed, they will be generated by EMF as appropriate.

7.1   Java Specification for Classes

The Java specification for an **EClass** is a Java interface preceded by an `@model` tag that has either no `kind` property or a `kind="class"` property. The **EAttribute**s and **EReference**s that belong to the **EClass** are represented by `get()` methods that are defined in the Java interface. The **EOperation**s that belong to the **EClass** are represented by other methods in the interface.

The **name** attribute of the **EClass** is set to the name of the Java interface.

The **eSuperTypes** reference of the **EClass** is set to include the **EClass**es corresponding to the interfaces listed in the `extends` clause of the interface. Note that **EObject** is the implicit base class of all modeled objects in EMF, and therefore should not be listed in the `extends` clause.

Other properties of the **EClass** can be set using the `@model` properties shown in Table 7.1.[1]

Table 7.1   The `@model` Properties for a Class

Property	Value	Usage
abstract	true|**false**	The abstract attribute of the EClass is set to the specified value.
interface	true|**false**	The interface attribute of the EClass is set to the specified value.

---

1. This is not quite an exhaustive list. There are two more properties that are valid for any model element and are described in Section 7.5. Also, Section 7.2.3 describes how additional properties can be used to directly define structural features on an **EClass**.

For example, you could define the following interface, which would map to an abstract **EClass** named "Address":

```
/**
 * @model abstract="true"
 */
public interface Address
{
  ...
}
```

7.1.1   *Attributes*

An **EAttribute** is specified as an accessor method in the interface corresponding to the **EClass** that contains the attribute. The method must meet the following criteria:

- ○ It is preceded by an @model tag that includes neither a kind nor a parameters property, or that does include a kind="attribute" property.
- ○ The name of the method begins with "get", or the type of the method is boolean and its name begins with "is". The character immediately following the "get" or "is" prefix must be uppercase.
- ○ The method has no arguments.
- ○ The return type of the method does not correspond to an EClass. If the return type is either List or EList, then the type specified with a type property on the @model tag does not correspond to an EClass.

The **name** attribute of the **EAttribute** is derived from the name of the method. Specifically, the prefix (i.e., "get" or "is") is removed from the name of the method and the first character of the resulting name is folded to lowercase.

Generally, the **eType** of the **EAttribute** is set to an **EDataType** corresponding to the return type of the method. However, if this type is List or EList, the @model tag must include a type property, and the **eType** is set to the **EDataType** corresponding to that property's value. In this case, the **EAttribute's upperBound** is set to -1 (unbounded) as well.

Other properties of the **EAttribute** can be set using the @model tag. Table 7.2 identifies the @model properties and values that are used to more fully describe an **EAttribute**.

Table 7.2   The @model Properties for an Attribute

Property	Value	Usage
changeable	**true**|false	The changeable attribute of the EAttribute is set to the specified value.
dataType	*data-type*	The specific EDataType named *data-type* is used as the eType for the EAttribute. If not already modeled, as described in Section 7.3.1, an EDataType is created with the given name.
default or defaultValue	*default-value*	The defaultValueLiteral attribute of the EAttribute is set to the string value identified by *default-value*.
derived	true|**false**	The derived attribute of the EAttribute is set to the specified value.
id	true|**false**	The id attribute of the EAttribute is set to the specified value.
lower or lowerBound	*integer-value*	The lowerBound attribute of the EAttribute is set to *integer-value*. The specified value must be 0 or greater.
many	true|**false**	If true, the upperBound attribute of the EAttribute is set to -1 (unbounded).
ordered	**true**|false	The ordered attribute of the EAttribute is set to the specified value.
required	true|**false**	If true, the lowerBound attribute of the EAttribute is set to 1. Otherwise, it is set to 0.
suppressedGet Visibility	true|**false**	If true, the EAttribute is annotated with a GenModel-sourced EAnnotation that suppresses the get() accessor for the feature in the interface.[2]
suppressedIsSet Visibility	true|**false**	If true, the EAttribute is annotated with a GenModel-sourced EAnnotation that suppresses the isSet() accessor for the feature in the interface.
suppressedSet Visibility	true|**false**	If true, the EAttribute is annotated with a GenModel-sourced EAnnotation that suppresses the set() accessor for the feature in the interface.

---

2. This use of **EAnnotations** was described in Section 5.7.1.

Property	Value	Usage
suppressedUnset Visibility	true|**false**	If true, the EAttribute is annotated with a GenModel-sourced EAnnotation that suppresses the unset() accessor for the feature in the interface.
transient	true|**false**	The transient attribute of the EAttribute is set to the specified value.
type	*type-name*	The eType reference of the EAttribute is set to an EDataType corresponding to the Java *type-name*.
unique	**true**|false	The unique attribute of the EAttribute is set to the specified value.
unsettable	true|**false**	The unsettable attribute of the EAttribute is set to the specified value.
upper or upperBound	*integer-value*	The upperBound attribute of the EAttribute is set to *integer-value*. The specified value must be greater than 0, or -1 (unbounded).
volatile	true|**false**	The volatile attribute of the EAttribute is set to the specified value.

For example, to define the **comment, orderDate, status,** and **totalAmount** attributes of the **PurchaseOrder** class from the ExtendedPO3 model, you could provide the following Java declarations:

```java
/**
 * @model
 */
public interface PurchaseOrder
{
  /**
   * @model
   */
  String getComment();

  /**
   * @model dataType="com.example.epo3.Date"
   */
  Date getOrderDate();

  /**
   * @model
   */
  OrderStatus getStatus();

  /**
   * @model transient="true" changeable="false" volatile="true"
   */
  int getTotalAmount();
}
```

7.1.2   References

An **EReference** is specified as a method in the interface corresponding to the **EClass** that contains the reference. The method must meet the following criteria:

○ It is preceded by an @model tag that includes neither a kind nor a parameters property, or that does include a kind="reference" property.

○ The name of the method begins with "get" followed immediately by an uppercase character.

○ The method has no arguments.

○ The return type of the method corresponds to an EClass. Or, if the return type is List or EList, then the type specified with a type property on the @model tag corresponds to an EClass.

The **name** attribute of the **EReference** is derived from the name of the method. Specifically, the "get" prefix is removed from the name of the method and the first character of the resulting name is folded to lowercase.

Generally, the **eType** of the **EReference** is set to an **EClass** corresponding to the return type of the method. However, if this type is List or EList, the @model tag must include a type property, and the **eType** is set to the **EClass** corresponding to that property's value. In this case, the **EReference**'s **upperBound** is set to -1 (unbounded) as well.

Other properties of the **EReference** can be set using the @model tag. Table 7.3 identifies the @model properties and values that are used to more fully describe an **EReference**.

Table 7.3   The @model Properties for a Reference

Property	Value	Usage
changeable	**true**|false	The changeable attribute of the EReference is set to the specified value.
containment	true|**false**	The containment attribute of the EReference is set to the specified value.
derived	true|**false**	The derived attribute of the EReference is set to the specified value.
lower or lowerBound	*integer-value*	The lowerBound attribute of the EReference is set to *integer-value*. The specified value must be 0 or greater.
many	true|**false**	If true, the upperBound attribute of the EReference is set to -1 (unbounded).

Property	Value	Usage
opposite	*reference-name*	The opposite reference of the EReference is set to the EReference corresponding to the specified *reference-name*. The opposite EReference must belong to the EClass that is identified by the eType of this EReference.
ordered	**true**|false	The ordered attribute of the EReference is set to the specified value.
required	true|**false**	If true, the lowerBound attribute of the EReference is set to 1. Otherwise, it is set to 0.
resolveProxies	true|false	The resolveProxies attribute of the EReference is set to the specified value. The default value is false when containment is true, and true otherwise.
suppressedGet Visibility	true|**false**	If true, the EReference is annotated with a GenModel-sourced EAnnotation that suppresses the get() accessor for the feature in the interface.[3]
suppressedIsSet Visibility	true|**false**	If true, the EReference is annotated with a GenModel-sourced EAnnotation that suppresses the isSet() accessor for the feature in the interface.
suppressedSet Visibility	true|**false**	If true, the EReference is annotated with a GenModel-sourced EAnnotation that suppresses the set() accessor for the feature in the interface.
suppressedUnset Visibility	true|**false**	If true, the EReference is annotated with a GenModel-sourced EAnnotation that suppresses the unset() accessor for the feature in the interface.
transient	true|**false**	The transient attribute of the EReference is set to the specified value.
type	*class-name*	The eType reference of the EReference is set to the EClass corresponding to the Java *class-name*.
unique	**true**|false	The unique attribute of the EReference is set to the specified value.
unsettable	true|**false**	The unsettable attribute of the EReference is set to the specified value.

(continues)

---

3. This use of **EAnnotations** was described in Section 5.7.1.

Table 7.3   The @model Properties for a Reference (continued)

Property	Value	Usage
upper or upperBound	*integer-value*	The upperBound attribute of the EReference is set to *integer-value*. The specified value must be greater than 0, or -1 (unbounded).
volatile	true|**false**	The volatile attribute of the EReference is set to the specified value.

For example, to define the **items** and **previousOrders** references of the **PurchaseOrder** class from the ExtendedPO3 model, you could provide the following Java declarations:

```
/**
 * @model
 */
public interface PurchaseOrder
{
  /**
   * @model type="Item" containment="true"
   */
  EList getItems();

  /**
   * @model
   */
  PurchaseOrder getPreviousOrder();
}
```

7.1.3   Compact Notation for Attributes and References

EAttributes and **EReference**s can also be defined compactly as part of an **EClass** specification. Rather than including an accessor method in the interface for each such feature of the **EClass**, additional properties are added directly to the interface's @model tag.

The features property is used to declare the additional structural features. Its value is a space-separated list of names. One **EAttribute** or **EReference** is created with each name in the list. Additional feature-qualified properties are then used to fully describe these structural features.

A feature-qualified property can be formed from any of the properties listed in Section 7.1.1 or 7.1.2, simply by capitalizing the first letter of its name and prepending the name of the feature to it. The value and usage for each property is unchanged when feature-qualified.

Table 7.4 summarizes how the features and feature-qualified @model properties are used on an **EClass** specification to define features directly.

Table 7.4 The Class @model Properties for Defining Structural Features

Property	Value	Usage
features	*feature-list*	The *feature-list* is a space-separated list of the names of the EAttributes and EReferences to define.
feature-property	*value*	A *feature-property* specifies a property for one of the EAttributes or EReferences. The property name is the concatenation of the desired feature name, from the *feature-list*, above, with any valid property for that feature. The first character of the property should be capitalized. The *value* is simply the desired value for the feature's property.

This technique is generally not recommended, but it becomes necessary if you wish to suppress the get() accessor that would normally be used to define a feature.

For example, suppose that we wanted to declare the **PurchaseOrder** class in the previous section, with the same two references, but that we wanted to suppress the two get() accessors in the interface. The following Java declaration would do that:

```
/**
 * @model features="items previousOrder"
 * itemsMany="true" itemsType="Item" itemsContainment="true"
 * itemsSuppressedGetVisibility="true"
 * previousOrderType="PurchaseOrder"
 * previousOrderSuppressedGetVisibility="true"
 */
public interface PurchaseOrder
{
}
```

7.1.4 Operations

An **EOperation** is specified as a method in the Java interface corresponding to the **EClass** that contains the operation. The method must meet the following criteria:

○ It is preceded by an `@model` tag.

○ The method's name, arguments, and return type do not conform to one of the **EAttribute** or **EReference** patterns, as described in Sections 7.1.1 and 7.1.2.[4]

○ Or, if the method does conform to the EAttribute or EReference pattern, it has been marked as an EOperation in the `@model` tag . This is usually done by including a `kind="operation"` property. A `parameters` property with any value has the same effect, but this approach is not encouraged and is supported only for backward compatibility.

The **name** attribute of the **EOperation** is set to the name of the method.

The **eType** reference of the **EOperation** is the **EClass** or **EDataType** that corresponds to the return type of the Java method. Like for structural features, if this type is `List` or `EList`, the `@model` tag must include a `type` property, and the **eType** is set to the **EDataType** or **EClass** corresponding to that property's value. In this case, the **EOperation's upperBound** is set to -1 (unbounded) as well.

The **eParameters** reference of the **EOperation** is constructed from the arguments of the Java method. Specifically, **EParameters** are constructed for the method where the **name** and **eType** features of each **EParameter** are derived from the name and type of each parameter that appears in the Java method specification. The initialization of these **EParameters** can also be influenced using properties on the method's `@model` tag, as we will soon discuss further.

The **eExceptions** reference of the **EOperation** is populated based on the exceptions listed in the method's `throws` clause. These exceptions are automatically mapped to corresponding modeled **EClasses** and **EDataTypes**. An `exceptions` property can also be added to the `@model` tag to specify by name a particular **EDataType** to be used for each exception.

The **EOperation** can be further described using additional properties on the `@model` tag. Table 7.5 summarizes these properties. Properties that apply to an operation's parameters are not included, as they will be discussed separately.

---

4. For example, consider a method with no arguments and `boolean` return type named `island()`. Such a method would be considered an **EOperation**, but if its name were changed to `isLand()`, it would be considered an **EAttribute**.

Table 7.5   The @model Properties for an Operation

Property	Value	Usage
dataType	*data-type*	The specific EDataType named *data-type* is used as the eType for the EOperation. If not already modeled, as described in Section 7.3.1, an EDataType is created with the given name.
exceptions	*list-of-types*	The *list-of-types* is a space-separated list of names, each specifying the EDataType to be used for the corresponding eException. If not already modeled, as described in Section 7.3.1, each EDataType is created with the given name. To avoid specifying a particular EDataType for the corresponding exception, a "-" character can appear as an item in the list.
lower or lowerBound	*integer-value*	The lowerBound attribute of the EOperation is set to *integer-value*. The specified value must be 0 or greater.
many	true|**false**	If true, the upperBound attribute of the EOperation is set to -1 (unbounded).
ordered	**true**|false	The ordered attribute of the EOperation is set to the specified value.
required	true|**false**	If true, the lowerBound attribute of the EOperation is set to 1. Otherwise, it is set to 0.
type	*type-name*	The eType reference of the EOperation is set to an EDataType or EClass corresponding to the Java *type-name*.
unique	**true**|false	The unique attribute of the EOperation is set to the specified value.
upper or upperBound	*integer-value*	The upperBound attribute of the EOperation is set to *integer-value*. The specified value must be greater than 0, or -1 (unbounded).

For example, including the following methods in the PurchaseOrder interface would declare two **EOperation**s named "isValid" and "computeCodes", and
with **eTypes EBoolean** and **EString**, respectively. The latter operation's
upperBound would be -1.

```
/**
 * @model kind="operation"
 */
boolean isValid();
```

```
/**
 * @model type="String"
 */
List computeCodes();
```

Parameters

As noted earlier, **EParameters** are constructed for the **EOperation** based on the Java method's argument list. Each argument's name is used as the **name** attribute on the corresponding **EParameter**, and each Java type is automatically mapped to a modeled **EClass** or **EDataType** that is used as the **EParameter**'s **eType** by default.

The **EParameters** can be further described with additional, parameter-qualified properties on the method's @model tag. This is analogous to the use of feature-qualified properties on the @model tag for an **EClass** that was described in Section 7.1.3.

A parameter-qualified property is formed from any of the virtual properties for **EParameters**,[5] which are listed in Table 7.6. To do so, the virtual property's first letter is capitalized and the feature's name is prepended to it. The value and usage for each virtual property is unchanged when parameter-qualified.

Table 7.6   The Virtual @model Properties for a Parameter

Property	Value	Usage
dataType	*data-type*	The specific EDataType named *data-type* is used as the eType for the EParameter. If not already modeled, as described in Section 7.3.1, an EDataType is created with the given name.
lower or lowerBound	*integer-value*	The lowerBound attribute of the EParameter is set to *integer-value*. The specified value must be 0 or greater.
many	true|**false**	If true, the upperBound attribute of the EParameter is set to −1 (unbounded).
ordered	**true**|false	The ordered attribute of the EParameter is set to the specified value.
required	true|**false**	If true, the lowerBound attribute of the EParameter is set to 1. Otherwise, it is set to 0.

---

5. The properties are "virtual" because there is no Java construct corresponding to a parameter that carries a Javadoc. Hence, there can be no @model tag specifically for the parameter.

Property	Value	Usage
type	*type-name*	The eType reference of the EParameter is set to an EDataType or EClass corresponding to the Java *type-name*.
unique	**true**|false	The unique attribute of the EParameter is set to the specified value.
upper or upperBound	*integer-value*	The upperBound attribute of the EParameter is set to *integer-value*. The specified value must be greater than 0, or -1 (unbounded).

Table 7.7 identifies the @model properties used on an **EOperation** specification for directly defining its parameters. It summarizes the use of parameter-qualified properties described previously and also includes the parameters property.

Table 7.7   The Operation @model Properties for Defining Parameters

Property	Value	Usage
parameters	*list-of-types*	The *list-of-types* is a space-separated list of names, each specifying the EDataType to be used for the corresponding EParameter. To avoid specifying a particular EDataType for the corresponding parameter, a "-" character can appear as an item in the list.
parameter-property	*value*	A *parameter-property* specifies a property for one of the EParameters. The property name is the concatenation of the desired parameter name with any valid property for that parameter, as listed in Table 7.6. Note that the first character of the property should be capitalized. The *value* is simply the desired value for the parameter's property.

Notice that one or more parameter-qualified dataType properties can convey exactly the same information as the parameters property. The former approach is recommended and, if both are used, takes precedence.

For example, we could add the following method to the PurchaseOrder interface to declare an additional **EOperation** named "removeItem". The item argument's String type would be mapped to an **EDataType** named "SKU".

```
/**
 * @model itemDataType="com.example.epo3.SKU"
 */
boolean removeItem(String item);
```

7.2   Java Specification for Enumerated Types

The Java specification for an **EEnum** is a Java class preceded by an `@model` tag that has either no `kind` property or a `kind="enum"` property.

The **name** attribute of the **EEnum** is set to the name of the Java class. The **eLiterals** reference for the **EEnum** is constructed from the list of **EEnumLiteral**s that are derived from the fields of the Java class, as described next.

7.2.1   Enumeration Literals

Each `int` valued field appearing in a Java class representing an **EEnum** is mapped to an **EEnumLiteral** if it is preceded by an `@model` tag.

If the field has an initial value, that value is used as the **value** of the **EEnumLiteral**.

Normally, the **name** of the **EEnumLiteral** is derived directly from the name of the corresponding field. However, you can add a `name` property to the field's `@model` tag to control the capitalization of the name. To be valid, the value of `name` must expand back to the field name when converted to the conventional naming style for constants, all uppercase with underscores to separate words.

The two `@model` properties applicable to an **EEnumLiteral** are summarized in Table 7.8.

Table 7.8   The `@model` Properties for an Enumeration Literal

Property	Value	Usage
name	*literal-name*	The name of the EEnumLiteral is set to the specified *literal-name*. If not specified, or invalid, the name is automatically derived from the field name.
literal	*literal-literal*	The literal attribute of the EEnumLiteral is set to the specified *literal-literal*.

For example, to define the **OrderStatus** enumerated type from the ExtendedPO3 model, you could declare the following Java class:

```
/**
 * @model
 */
public class OrderStatus
{
  /**
   * @model name="Pending"
```

```
     */
    public static final int PENDING = 0;

    /**
     * @model name="BackOrder" literal="Back Order"
     */
    public static final int BACK_ORDER = 1;

    /**
     * @model name="Complete"
     */
    public static final int COMPLETE = 2;
}
```

7.3 Java Specification for Packages

Normally, you do not need to specify anything to get an **EPackage** because it can be inferred from the classes and enumerated types that appear in the Java package. The only time you might need to explicitly specify a package is when you wish to override some of the package properties.

The Java specification for an **EPackage** is an interface preceded by an `@model` tag with a `kind="package"` property.[6] The interface's name should end with the suffix "Package".[7]

There are various attributes of the **EPackage** that can be specified by including those properties as final static fields in the Java interface. These fields should have type `String` and should be initialized.

- ○ If a field named `eNAME` is specified, the **name** attribute of the **EPackage** is set to the value of the field.

- ○ If a field named `eNS_URI` is specified, the **nsURI** attribute of the **EPackage** is set to the value of the field.

- ○ If a field named `eNS_PREFIX` is specified, the nsPrefix attribute of the EPackage object is set to the value of the field.

For example, you can define the following interface to set the **nsURI** and **nsPrefix** for an **EPackage**:

---

6. In older versions of EMF, no `@model` tag was used on an interface representing an **EPackage**. This pattern is still recognized, but its use is strongly discouraged.

7. When a package is explicitly specified, EMF uses the prefix of the package interface name (i.e., everything before "Package") as the value of the **prefix** attribute of the corresponding **GenPackage** in the generator model, which is created with the Ecore model. If code is generated for the model, this ensures that the generated package interface will replace the existing one.

```
/**
 * @model kind="package"
 */
public interface EPO3Package
{
  String eNS_URI = "http://www.example.com/epo3.ecore";
  String eNS_PREFIX = "epo3";
}
```

Another situation in which it might be necessary to provide a Java specification for an **EPackage** is if you need to define an **EDataType** or a map entry **EClass** explicitly, topics discussed in Sections 7.3.1 and 7.4.1, respectively.

7.3.1   Data Types

EDataTypes can be defined explicitly. However, this is usually unnecessary, as an **EDataType** is automatically created for any Java type used by a structural feature or operation, when one has not been explicitly defined in your model or in Ecore.

There might be some special cases in which you do need to define an **EDataType** explicitly. You might do this if, for example, there is already an existing **EDataType** corresponding to a Java type for which you wish to provide an alternate serialization format. Then, you would need to create a Java interface that represents your **EPackage** and include a `get()` method that accesses the **EDataType**.

To be recognized as explicitly defining an **EDataType**, such a method must meet the following criteria:

○ It is preceded by an `@model` tag.

○ The return type of the method is `EDataType`.

○ The name of the method begins with "get".

The `@model` properties that can be set for an **EDataType** are shown in Table 7.9.

Table 7.9   The `@model` Properties for a Data Type

Property	Value	Usage
instanceClass	*java-type*	The instanceClassName attribute of the EDataType is set to the specified *java-type*. The *java-type* should be a Java primitive type or a fully qualified interface or class name.
serializable	**true**|false	The serializable attribute of the EDataType is set to the specified value.

For example, to define the **Date** data type from the ExtendedPO3 model, you could declare the following method in the `EPOPackage3` interface:

```
/**
 * @model instanceClass="java.util.Date"
 */
EDataType getDate();
```

If you look back at Section 7.1.1 where **Date** is referenced as the type of the **orderDate** attribute, you might notice that the data type's name is prefixed by "com.example.epo3", the name of the Java package that corresponds to the **EPackage** in which **Date** is defined. Such qualification is necessary in any reference to an explicitly defined **EDataType**.

7.4 Java Specification for Maps

EMF provides special support for defining maps that are strongly typed and order preserving. This support requires the creation of a special map entry type. As described in Chapter 5, a map entry is an **EClass** that implements the `Map.Entry` interface and has two features that are named "key" and "value". A containment reference whose target is such an **EClass** will be treated specially by the EMF code generator. It will be implemented using an `EMap`, instead of just an `EList`. Operations and parameters can be map-typed in the same way.

You can define a map entry class in your Java source code either explicitly or implicitly. An explicit definition is made by creating an accessor method for the map entry class in the interface that corresponds to the **EPackage**. An implicit definition is made when a map-typed **EReference**, **EOperation**, or **EParameter** makes use of a map entry type that has not been defined elsewhere. An implicit definition is somewhat simpler but has some limitations.

7.4.1 *Explicit Definition of Map Entry Classes in a Package*

To define a map entry class explicitly, you provide an accessor method for that class in the interface that represents the **EPackage** that contains it.

To be recognized as such, the method must meet the following criteria:

○ It is preceded by an `@model` tag that does not include an `instanceClass` property.

○ The return type of the method is `EClass`.

○ The name of the method begins with "get" followed immediately by an uppercase character.

There is no interface for a map entry, as the class just implements `Map.Entry`. That is the reason for defining it via its accessor in the **EPackage** interface. Still, we need to be able to define the structural features of the class, **key** and **value** in particular. We use the `features` property in combination with feature-qualified properties for this. This is the same technique we saw in Section 7.1.3. The relevant `@model` properties are summarized in Table 7.10.

Table 7.10   The `@model` Properties of a Map Entry Class

Property	Value	Usage
features	*feature-list*	The *feature-list* is a space-separated list of the names of the EAttributes and EReferences to define. If this list is omitted, features named "key" and "value" are assumed.
feature-property	*value*	A *feature-property* specifies a property for one of the EAttributes or EReferences. The property name is the concatenation of the desired feature name, from the *feature-list*, above, with any valid property for that feature, as described in Sections 7.1.1 and 7.1.2. The first character of the property should be capitalized. The *value* is simply the desired value for the feature's property.

For example, the following Java code will define an **EPackage** named "POPackage" that contains two map types:

```java
/**
 * @model kind="package"
 */
public interface POPackage
{
  /**
   * @model features="key value info"
   * keyType="int" keyRequired="true"
   * valueType="PurchaseOrder"
   * valueContainment="true" infoType="String"
   */
  EClass getIntToOrderMapEntry();

  /**
   * @model keyType="int"
   * valueType="PurchaseOrder"
   * valueContainment="true"
   * valueMany="true"
   */
  EClass getIntToOrdersMapEntry();
}
```

The first map entry class is named "IntToOrderMapEntry". It is used to map a single `int` key to a single value, a `PurchaseOrder` object. It also has an additional `String` attribute called "info". The second map entry class, called "IntToOrdersMapEntry", maps an `int` key to a list of `PurchaseOrder` objects.

7.4.2 Definition of Map-Typed References, Operations, and Parameters

EReferences, **EOperations**, and **EParameters** can all have map types. A map-typed **ETypedElement** is defined as usual, as described in Section 7.1.2 or 7.1.4, but with the following additional criteria:

○ The Java type of the method or argument is either `Map` or `EMap`.

○ The `@model` tag includes either a `mapType` or both `keyType` and `valueType` properties.

A typed element defined this way will automatically have its **many** attribute and, if it is an **EReference**, its **containment** attribute, set to true. The `@model` tag that precedes the definition of the typed element can have the properties shown in Table 7.11, in addition to the normal properties for that element.

Table 7.11 Additional `@model` Properties of a Map-Typed Reference, Operation, or Parameter

Property	Value	Usage
keyType	*key-type*	The *key-type* is a Java type used to determine the eType of the key attribute of the EClass that is created to represent the map entry.
mapType	*map-type*	The *map-type* either identifies a map entry EClass that has already been defined or specifies a name that should be given to a new, implicitly defined map entry EClass.
valueType	*value-type*	The *value-type* is a Java type used to determine the eType of the value attribute of the EClass that is created to represent the map entry.

If the `mapType` property is included and its *map-type* identifies a map entry **EClass** that has been explicitly defined in an **EPackage** or implicitly defined as the type of another **EReference**, **EOperation**, or **EParameter**, then that map entry is used as the type of the typed element being defined. The `keyType` and `valueType` properties should not be included in this case.

If the `mapType` property is not included or its *map-type* is not the name of an existing **EClass**, then a map entry class is implicitly defined, and the `keyType` and valueType properties must be included. In this case, the *map-type* is used to name the implicitly defined map entry class. Or, if a mapType property wasn't specified, the class is named using the pattern "*key-type*To*value-type*MapEntry".

The following code defines an **EClass** called "Index" with several map-typed elements: two **EReference**s and one **EOperation** with an **EParameter**:

```
/**
 * @model
 */
public interface Index
{
  /**
   * @model keyType="int" valueType="PurchaseOrder"
   */
  EMap getOrderMap();

  /**
   * @model mapType="IntToOrdersMapEntry"
   */
  EMap getCustomerOrderMap();

  /**
   * @model mapType="IntToOrdersMapEntry"
   * orderMapKeyType="int" orderMapValueType="PurchaseOrder"
   */
  EMap convertOrderMap(EMap orderMap);
}
```

The first method defines an **EReference** called "orderMap" using an implicitly defined map entry **EClass**, which will be given the default name "EIntToPurchaseOrderMapEntry". The second **EReference**, named "customerOrderMap", uses the existing "IntToOrdersMapEntry" map entry class, which was described in the previous section. The third method defines an **EOperation** named "convertOrderMap" that takes the former map type and returns the latter.

7.5   Java Specification for Annotations

As described in Chapter 5, **EAnnotation**s provide an extension mechanism for Ecore. Any **EModelElement** can have **EAnnotation**s attached to it, via its eAnnotations reference, to supply additional arbitrary information about it.

An **EAnnotation** on an **EModelElement** is specified by including an annotation property on the @model tag preceding the Java specification for that **EModelElement**. The annotation and extendedMetaData property, which can both be included in any @model tag, are described in Table 7.12.

Table 7.12 The @model Properties for Defining Annotations

Property	Value	Usage
annotation	*source key1=* '*value1*' ...	An EAnnotation is added to the EModelElement. Its source attribute is set to the specified *source* value. The specified *key*s and *value*s are used to initialize its **details** map.
extended MetaData	*key1*='*value1*' ...	An extended metadata EAnnotation is added to the EModelElement.[8] The specified *key*s and *value*s are used to initialize its **details** map.

For example, in Section 5.7.1, we saw that a GenModel-sourced **EAnnotation** can be used to specify a Java implementation for an **EOperation**. We could specify such an annotation in order to embed the implementation for an operation in the interface that declares it. The following method declaration, if added to the PurchaseOrder interface, would create an **EOperation** called "hasItems" and specify its implementation:

```
/**
 * @model
 * annotation="http://www.eclipse.org/emf/2002/GenModel body='return !getItems().isEmpty();'"
 */
boolean hasItems();
```

Note that property–value pairs, including the annotation property above, must be entered on a single line.

---

8. Extended metadata annotations are discussed at length in Chapters 8 and 9.

CHAPTER 8

Extended Ecore Modeling

Ecore is very much like UML in the way that it represents application data models. Thus, as we have seen, the mapping from UML to Ecore is simple and direct. Moreover, UML, and hence Ecore, was designed to map very cleanly to implementations in object-oriented languages such as Java.

However, in Chapter 4 we also saw that XML Schema's expressive power can result in a less direct mapping to Ecore. In fact, certain schema constructs simply cannot be represented using a traditional UML class diagram approach. Therefore, for EMF to achieve the important goal of unifying UML, Java, and XML, some extended modeling concepts are needed in Ecore.

In this chapter, we'll look at these concepts. We begin with `FeatureMap`, the interface that EMF uses to represent instance data for many of the more advanced schema-derived constructs. Then, we'll discuss how these constructs are described in an Ecore model using extended metadata annotations.

Although these concepts are not necessarily simple, they are necessary to understand the mapping from XML Schema to Ecore, which is the topic of Chapter 9. If they weren't, we would have likely left them for later in the book. Indeed, if you're not immediately interested in understanding how an Ecore model is derived from a schema, you might choose to skip over these two chapters and return to them in the future.

However, even if you never use XML Schema, this material might still be of interest, as you can still use these extended modeling concepts in your models.

8.1   Feature Maps

Before jumping into any details of XML Schema, it would be worth describing one of the general modeling problems that feature maps can be used to solve. This leads us into a discussion of the `FeatureMap` interface.

8.1.1   *Multiple Features and Cross-Feature Order*

Sometimes when we design a model, we are faced with a conflict between maintaining data in a single feature versus dividing it among multiple features. Consider the simple model in Figure 8.1.

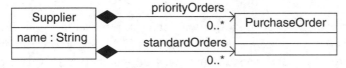

Figure 8.1   Purchase orders maintained by kind.

This is an extension of our purchase order model. We have added a **Supplier** class as a container for purchase orders. We use two containment references, **priorityOrders** and **standardOrders**, to maintain and access the purchase orders according to the importance of the customer.[1]

If, however, we wanted to maintain all of the purchase orders in order—for example, the order in which they arrived—we might instead model this using a single reference, as in Figure 8.2. In this case, we maintain all the purchase orders in a single **orders** list, but we need to add a **kind** attribute to the **PurchaseOrder** class to keep track of the priority or standard status of each purchase order.

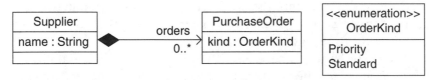

Figure 8.2   Purchase orders maintained in order.

---

1. In this model, it makes sense for **priorityOrders** and **standardOrders** to be containment references. However, feature maps can also be used to maintain order across non-containment references and attributes.

Alternatively, we could define all three references and store each purchase order in two lists: **orders** and either **priorityOrders** or **standardOrders**, depending on its kind.[2] With this approach, it is easier to access just one kind of purchase order, but order is maintained across both.

To avoid the redundant storage and the need to keep multiple lists in sync, this kind of arrangement is most commonly implemented by making some of the references derive from others. For example, the **priorityOrders** and **standardOrders** references could be computed from the **orders** reference, based on the value of the **kind** attribute, as in Figure 8.3.

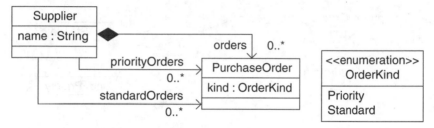

Figure 8.3 Purchase orders maintained in order, with derived features for access by kind.

In this model, the **priorityOrders** and **standardOrders** references would be volatile, transient, non-changeable, and derived. They would be implemented to iterate over and filter the **orders** reference. For example, the `getPriorityOrders()` method would look like this:

```
public EList getPriorityOrders()
{
  ArrayList priorityOrders = new ArrayList();
  for (Iterator i = getOrders().iterator(); i.hasNext(); )
  {
    PurchaseOrder order = (PurchaseOrder)i.next();
    if (order.getKind() == OrderKind.PRIORITY_LITERAL)
    {
      priorityOrders.add(order);
    }
  }
  return new EcoreEList.UnmodifiableEList(this,
                EPOPackage.eINSTANCE.getSupplier_PriorityOrders(),
                priorityOrders.size(), priorityOrders.toArray());
}
```

---

2. Because objects cannot be in two containment references simultaneously, we'd either need to make **orders** or both **priorityOrders** and **standardOrders** non-containment in this case.

With this design, purchase orders are actually contained by the **orders** reference. An order can only be added to or removed from the **priorityOrders** or **standardOrders** reference indirectly, by adding it to or removing it from **orders**, or by changing its **kind**. The two derived lists themselves are not directly modifiable.

An instance of this model is illustrated in Figure 8.4.

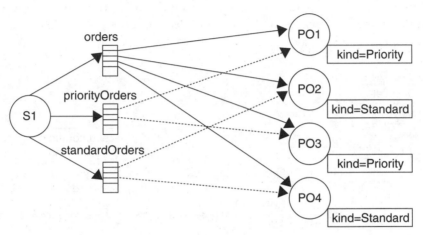

Figure 8.4   Instance of purchase order model with derived features.

A better, but significantly more complicated, solution to this problem would not declare the **priorityOrders** and **standardOrders** references as non-changeable, but instead would realize them using specialized lists that implement the entire `EList` API, including add and remove, by delegating to the **orders** list. For example, an `add()` operation on the **priorityOrders** list would delegate through to `add()` on the **orders** list, and would also set the **kind** of the purchase order to **Priority**. However, because of the complexity of that solution, the read-only approach is generally used.

In Chapter 13, we'll use this pattern again. There, we'll see the ExtendedPO2 model, which also has two references, **pendingOrders** and **shippedOrders**, that are derived from the **orders** reference and computed based on a **status** attribute in the **PurchaseOrder** class. The approach works very well in that example, but is less desirable here. The difference in this example is that, unlike the **status** in ExtendedPO2, the **kind** attribute is unchanging over time. A purchase order's kind is determined immediately when the object is added to the model, and there is never a need to change it later, moving the order from one derived list to the other. In some sense, the kind isn't so much an attribute of the purchase order, as it is one of the supplier.

Ideally, we would like to implement this without the **kind** attribute, or any extra state information, in the purchase order at all. To do that, however, we would need to somehow "tag" the entries in the **orders** list themselves with the equivalent type information, as in Figure 8.5.

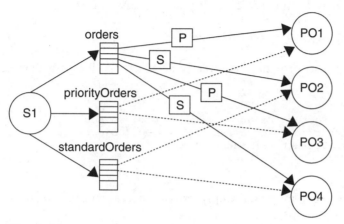

Figure 8.5   Instance of purchase order model with tagged order list entries.

Fortunately, EMF provides a special kind of list for doing this, `FeatureMap`, where each entry is tagged with the feature for a derived list, like **priorityOrders** or **standardOrders**, to which it belongs. Better yet, the EMF code generator understands this pattern, so the implementation can be completely generated, with changeable, derived features that fully implement the `EList` API and are backed by the feature map.

8.1.2   *The FeatureMap Interface*

A `FeatureMap` is simply a specialized `EList`, whose elements are feature–value pairs defined by the `FeatureMap.Entry` interface:

```
public interface FeatureMap extends EList
{
  public interface Entry
  {
    EStructuralFeature getEStructuralFeature();
    Object getValue();
  }

  ...
}
```

A `FeatureMap` will contain only one entry, at most, for a derived, multiplicity-1 feature. It will contain one entry for each individual value of a derived, multiplicity-many feature, rather than just a single list-valued entry. This design allows `FeatureMap` to capture cross-feature order. The `FeatureMap` interface provides a number of convenience accessor methods, one of which can be used to obtain a list view for a derived, multiplicity-many feature:

```
EList list(EStructuralFeature feature);
```

Methods are also provided to directly access the value of a derived, multiplicity-1 feature:

```
Object get(EStructuralFeature feature, boolean resolve);
void set(EStructuralFeature feature, Object object);
boolean isSet(EStructuralFeature feature);
void unset(EStructuralFeature feature);
```

Other convenience methods simply provide access to the feature or value at a specific index in the list:

```
EStructuralFeature getEStructuralFeature(int index);
Object getValue(int index);
Object setValue(int index, Object value);
```

Finally, there are methods to add to the `FeatureMap` directly, without having to first create an `Entry`:

```
boolean add(EStructuralFeature feature, Object value);
void add(int index, EStructuralFeature feature, Object value);

boolean addAll(EStructuralFeature feature, Collection values);
boolean addAll(int index, EStructuralFeature feature,
               Collection values);
```

Thus, `FeatureMap` provides a map-like API for accessing entry values, keyed by a feature—that's why it is named `FeatureMap`, instead of just something like `EntryList`. This API forms the basis for the simple, yet powerful, implementations that are generated for derived features, such as the **priorityOrders** and **standardOrders** references already described above. We'll look closely at the generated code patterns in Section 10.4, but for now, let's see how to define these structures in our models.

8.2   Modeling with Feature Maps

Recall from the previous section that a feature map is just a special type of list whose elements are instances of `FeatureMap.Entry`. In Ecore, `FeatureMap.Entry` is represented by a built-in data type called **EFeatureMapEntry**. Therefore, to represent a feature map, we simply need to model a multiplicity-many attribute whose type is **EFeatureMapEntry**.[3]

8.2.1   UML

Figure 8.6 illustrates our ExtendedPO model, defined using UML. The **priorityOrders** and **standardOrders** references are modeled as usual and marked volatile, transient, and derived. They will be backed by **orders**, a feature map, which we have modeled as a multi-valued attribute of type **EFeatureMapEntry**.[4]

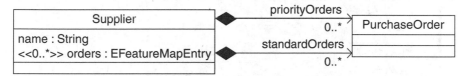

Figure 8.6   FeatureMap-based purchase order model in UML.

Ecore provides no direct way to represent the kind of inter-feature relationships that we have seen in this discussion; however, they can be captured using well-defined annotations. As described in Chapter 5, **EAnnotation**s provide a mechanism for attaching additional information to any Ecore model element.

Indeed, as we will see in Chapter 9, annotations are used extensively to capture extended metadata from XML Schema that cannot be represented directly in Ecore. The EMF runtime framework and code generator know how to interpret these annotations appropriately. Here, we'll use just a small subset.

All of these annotations are recognized by their **source**, which must be set to "http:///org/eclipse/emf/ecore/util/ExtendedMetaData". To indicate that the

---

3. Because `FeatureMap.Entry` is modeled as a data type, and not a class, in Ecore, it can only be the type of an attribute. By contrast, it's worth reemphasizing that feature maps can back both attributes and references. In other words, `Entry.getEStructuralFeature()` can return either an `EAttribute` or an `EReference`.

4. In fact, we could have chosen to represent the feature map as a third reference to **PurchaseOrder**. As long as we include the annotation described later in this section, EMF will recognize such a reference—indeed, a reference to any class—and convert it into an **EFeatureMapEntry**-typed attribute.

orders attribute will combine a group of other features, we use an extended metadata annotation with a single **details** entry: its key is "kind" and its value is "group". Note that there are other feature kinds, which we will see later in this chapter and in Chapter 9.

We must also add annotations to **priorityOrders** and **standardOrders**, to indicate that they are derived from this group attribute. Again, we use an extended metadata annotation with a single **details** entry: its key is "group" and its value is "#orders".

In Rational Rose, we can set these annotations via the **Ecore** page of the **Association Specification** dialog box, as described in Chapter 6. For example, Figure 8.7 shows the annotation property being set on **priorityOrders**.

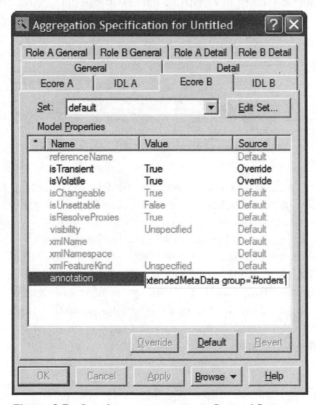

Figure 8.7 Specifying an annotation in Rational Rose.

The value is "http:///org/eclipse/emf/ecore/util/ExtendedMetaData group='#orders'" (the double quotes are not entered). An identical annotation is set on **standardOrders**. For the annotation on **orders**, the value is "http:///org/eclipse/emf/ecore/util/ExtendedMetaData kind='group'".

8.2.2 *Annotated Java*

To model the **orders** feature map using annotated Java, we include the following method in the `Supplier` interface:

```
/**
 * @model extendedMetaData="kind='group'"
 */
FeatureMap getOrders();
```

When converting annotated Java to Ecore, EMF recognizes an accessor method whose return type is `FeatureMap` as representing a multiplicity-many attribute with built-in Ecore type **EFeatureMapEntry**, provided that the method does not have a `dataType` property on its `@model` tag.[5]

In Chapter 7, we learned that an **EAnnotation** can be represented in the `@model` tag with a property of the following form:

```
annotation='source key1="value1" key2="value2" ...'
```

We also saw that there is a more compact form for extended metadata annotations; that is, annotations with a source of "http:///org/eclipse/emf/ecore/util/ExtendedMetaData":

```
extendedMetaData='key1="value1" key2="value2" ...'
```

We use this form to define the same annotation as in the previous section's UML model, indicating that the attribute combines a group of features.

The derived references, **priorityOrders** and **standardOrders**, are modeled as follows:

```
/**
 * @model type="PurchaseOrder" containment="true"
 *        volatile="true" transient="true" derived="true"
```

---

5. A `dataType` property would be used to identify a different data type for the attribute. In this case, `many` would no longer default to `true`. Note that if you specify a `dataType` on any accessor, then you need to specify one on *every* accessor in the model with the same return type. Ecore's default feature map model entry type can be explicitly selected with `dataType="org.eclipse.emf.ecore.EFeatureMapEntry"`.

```
 *           extendedMetaData="group='#orders'"
 */
EList getPriorityOrders();

/**
 * @model type="PurchaseOrder" containment="true"
 *        volatile="true" transient="true" derived="true"
 *        extendedMetaData="group='#orders'"
 */
EList getStandardOrders();
```

As in the UML case, they are defined to be volatile, transient, and derived containment references, and an annotation indicates that they derive from the **orders** group.

8.2.3   XML Schema

As mentioned in this chapter's introduction, the primary purpose of feature maps is to correctly represent structures arising from XML Schema. In fact, the group feature example that we have been discussing is an example of a basic schema structure.

Here is the schema definition for **Supplier**:

```
<xsd:complexType name="Supplier">
  <xsd:sequence>
    <xsd:element name="name" type="xsd:string"/>
    <xsd:choice minOccurs="0" maxOccurs="unbounded"
                ecore:name="orders">
      <xsd:element name="priorityOrders" type="epo:PurchaseOrder"/>
      <xsd:element name="regularOrders" type="epo:PurchaseOrder"/>
    </xsd:choice>
  </xsd:sequence>
</xsd:complexType>
```

A repeating choice model group in XML Schema maps to exactly the same `FeatureMap`-based Ecore representation, including the extended metadata annotations described earlier. The `choice` represents a heterogeneous list of the elements defined within it – the **orders** list in our example. Because XML Schema provides no way to name the choice, itself, EMF introduces the `ecore:name` attribute for that purpose. If we had not specified a name, the feature map attribute would have been given a default name of "group".[6]

Another interesting schema construct that maps to a feature map in Ecore is mixed content. If a complex type has mixed content, elements of that type may

---

6. In case of a conflict, a number would be appended to the default name, resulting in, for example, **group1**.

include simple text, in addition to the sub-elements specified by the type. For example, we could define an `ItemDescription` type like this:

```
<xsd:complexType name="ItemDescription" mixed="true">
  <xsd:sequence>
    <xsd:element name="productName" type="xsd:string"/>
    <xsd:element name="USPrice" type="xsd:decimal"/>
  </xsd:sequence>
</xsd:complexType>
```

This type is meant to represent a free-form description of an item that includes and identifies the product name and price, such as this:

```
Our <productName>apples</productName> are on sale this week
for only $<USPrice>1.29</USPrice> per pound!
```

The `ItemDescription` type maps to a class with an extra feature map attribute, **mixed,** that backs all of the other features in the class. This structure allows values of the class's features to be interspersed with values of two special features, **XMLTypeDocumentRoot.text** and **XMLTypeDocumentRoot.cDATA.** These two features, defined as part of EMF's XMLType model, represent simple text and character data sections in XML.

In addition, XML comments and whitespace can be captured by EMF.[7] Comments are represented by values of a third XML type feature, **XMLTypeDocumentRoot.comment,** in a mixed content feature map. Whitespace is, again, represented by values of **XMLTypeDocumentRoot.text**. In fact, as will be detailed in Section 9.3.5, we can specify that an extra feature map attribute should be created in a class corresponding to a type *without* mixed content, just to allow the comments and whitespace to be captured.

There are more schema constructs, including substitution groups and wild-cards, that map to feature maps in Ecore. Chapter 9 details the complete mapping for all of XML Schema, including these constructs.

---

7. For these to be read into the model from XML instance documents, the `OPTION_USE_LEXICAL_HAN-DLER` resource option must be enabled, as described in Chapter 15.

CHAPTER 9

XML Schema

If you wish to create an object model for manipulating an XML data structure of some type, EMF provides a particularly desirable approach based on XML Schema. EMF can create an Ecore model that corresponds to a schema, allowing you to leverage the code generator, or dynamic EMF, to provide a Java API for manipulating instances of that schema.

At a high level, the mapping to Ecore is quite simple:

○ A schema maps to an **EPackage**.

○ A complex type definition maps to an **EClass**.

○ A simple type definition maps to an **EDataType**.

○ An attribute declaration or element declaration maps to an **EAttribute** if its type maps to an **EDataType**, or to an **EReference** if its type maps to an **EClass**.

From a modeling perspective, however, XML Schema is not as expressive as Ecore. For example, it can't be used to define bidirectional references, or to provide the type of a reference target. To address this, EMF provides a set of extensions to XML Schema in the form of attributes from the Ecore namespace ("http://www.eclipse.org/emf/2002/Ecore"), which can be used to specify this missing information or to customize the mapping in other ways. These attributes are described in the following sections, which correspond to the components to which they apply, and are also summarized in Section 9.10.

Although not expressive enough from a modeling perspective, XML Schema is, at the same time, able to express many details, mostly serialization related, that are not representable in Ecore. Because XML Schema's primary purpose is to define the structure of XML instance documents, instances of the Ecore model should conform to the corresponding schema when they are serialized as XML. EMF records the extra information required to do this on the model using extended metadata **EAnnotations**. Recall from Chapter 8 that the **source** of such an **EAnnotation** is "http:///org/eclipse/emf/ecore/util/ExtendedMetaData". The details of all such annotations are described in this chapter, and their use in customizing the default EMF serialization is discussed in Chapter 15.

One important use of extended metadata **EAnnotations** is to record the original name of an XML Schema component corresponding to an Ecore element whose name is adjusted while mapping to Ecore. Such adjustment is often required because XML Schema naming rules are less restrictive then Java's (and consequently Ecore's). The resulting Ecore names are always valid Java identifiers and conform to the naming conventions outlined in Chapter 6 of the *Java Language Specification* [6]. For example, camel case is used, and **EClassifier** names start with an uppercase letter while **EStructuralFeature** names begin with lowercase.

As we saw briefly in Chapter 8, a number of XML Schema constructs give rise to feature maps in the corresponding Ecore model, where they are used to maintain cross-feature order. Extended metadata annotations are also used capture details about these feature maps, such as what type of construct a feature map represents and, when needed, which other feature's values it can contain.

In the following sections, we'll look at the details of how the various schema components map to Ecore, and how their associated **EAnnotations** are initialized. For each schema component, the corresponding Ecore representation is described along with any attributes and nested content that affect the resulting model. In some situations, the mapping rules, described later, might result in Ecore elements with conflicting names (e.g., two **EAttributes** that are in the same **EClass** and have the same name). In such situations, the second and subsequent elements are made unique by appending a number to the end of their names (e.g., "foo1").

Note that an understanding of XML Schema is assumed in this discussion. Readers who are unfamiliar with this technology should first consult an introductory resource, such as the XML Schema primer. [2]

9.1   Schema

An xsd:schema maps to an **EPackage**. The **name**, **nsURI**, and **nsPrefix** of the **EPackage** depend on whether or not the schema has a targetNamespace attribute.

9.1.1   *Schema without Target Namespace*

An xsd:schema with no targetNamespace maps to an **EPackage** initialized as follows:

○ **nsURI** = the URI of the schema document

○ **nsPrefix** = the last segment of the URI (short file name), excluding the file extension

○ **name** = same as **nsPrefix**

○ **eAnnotations** = an extended metadata **EAnnotation**

The **details** map of the extended metadata **EAnnotation** contains the following entry:

○ **key** = "qualified", **value** = "false"

in resource: *file:/c:/myexample/po.xsd*	EPackage

`<xsd:schema>`
 	
  `...`
 	
`</xsd:schema>`
	name="po"
	nsPrefix="po"
	nsURI="file:/c:/myexample/po.xsd"
	EAnnotation
	    source="…/ExtendedMetaData"
	    details="qualified"→"false"

9.1.2 Schema with Target Namespace

If a schema has a `targetNamespace` attribute, then it is used to initialize the corresponding **EPackage**, as well as to specify the fully qualified Java package name, via the **GenPackage** in the generator model that is created along with the Ecore model to control code generation for it.

In this case, the **EPackage** attributes are set as follows:

○ **nsURI** = the `targetNamespace` value

○ **nsPrefix** = the last segment of the Java package name (derived from the `targetNamespace`)

○ **name** = same as **nsPrefix**

There is no extended metadata **EAnnotation** in this case.

The Java package name, and consequently the **nsPrefix**, is derived from the `targetNamespace` using the following algorithm:

1. Strip the URI scheme and leading slash ("/") characters (e.g., "http://www.example.com/library" → "www.example.com/library").

2. Remove "www" and then reverse the components of the URI authority, if present (e.g., "www.example.com/library" → "com.example/library").

3. Replace slash ("/") characters with dot (".") characters.

4. Split mixed-case names into dot-separated lowercase names.

The **nsPrefix** is then set to the last component of the Java package name.[1] The **basePackage** property in the **GenPackage** is set to the rest of the name.

`<xsd:schema`
    `targetNamespace=`
      `"http://www.example.com/PrimerPO">`
  `...`
`</xsd:schema>`
	EPackage
	  name="po"
	  nsPrefix="po"
	  nsURI="http://www.example.com/PrimerPO"
	  ...
	GenPackage
	  basePackage="com.example.primer"
	  ...

9.1.3 Global Element or Attribute Declaration

If there is one or more global element or attribute declaration in the schema, an **EClass**, representing the document root, is created in the schema's **EPackage**. The name of the document root class is "DocumentRoot" by default.

`<xsd:schema  ... >`
  `<xsd:element ... />`
  `...`
`</xsd:schema>`
	EPackage
	  EClass
	    name="DocumentRoot"
	    ...

A document root class contains one feature for every global attribute or element declaration in the schema (see Sections 9.4.6 and 9.5.7). A single instance of this class is used as the root object of an XML resource (i.e., a conforming XML document). This instance will have exactly one of its element features set: the one corresponding to the global element at the root of the XML document. The features corresponding to global attribute declarations will never be set, but can be used for setting values in attribute wildcard feature maps.

The document root **EClass** looks like one corresponding to a mixed complex type (see Section 9.3.4) including a "mixed" feature, and derived implementations for the other features in the class. This allows it to maintain comments and whitespace that appear in the document, before the root element. A document root class contains two additional features, both string-to-string maps, which are used to record special mappings needed in instance documents. One, named

---

1. A leading underscore is introduced if the **nsURI** would otherwise start with any case variations of "xml", yielding a valid prefix as defined by the Namespaces in XML recommendation. [5]

"xMLNSPrefixMap", records namespace to prefix mappings, and the other, "xSISchemaLocation", records `xsi:schemaLocation` mappings.

The name of a document root class, if there is one, can be changed from the default ("DocumentRoot") by including an `ecore:documentRoot` attribute on the schema.

`<xsd:schema`
    `ecore:documentRoot="PORoot" ... >`
  `<xsd:element ... />`
  `...`
`</xsd:schema>`
	EPackage
	  EClass
	    name="PORoot"
	    ...

9.1.4 Element or Attribute Form Default

Whether qualification of local elements and attributes is required can be globally specified by a pair of attributes, `elementFormDefault` and `attributeFormDefault`, on the schema element, or can be specified separately for each local declaration using the `form` attribute. The value of any of these attributes can be "qualified" or "unqualified", to indicate whether or not locally declared elements and attributes must be qualified in conforming documents.

Neither `elementFormDefault` nor `attributeFormDefault` have any effect on the corresponding **EPackage** or "DocumentRoot" **EClass** (if it exists), but the Ecore model for any corresponding local declarations may include additional information. For details see Sections 9.4.5 and 9.5.6.

`<xsd:schema`
    `elementFormDefault="qualified" ... >`
  `...`
`</xsd:schema>`
	EPackage
	  ...

9.1.5 EMF Extensions

The initialization of an **EPackage** corresponding to a schema can be further customized through the use of additional schema attributes from the Ecore namespace.

An `ecore:nsPrefix` attribute can be used to explicitly set the **nsPrefix** attribute of the **EPackage**.

`<xsd:schema`
    `ecore:nsPrefix="myprefix"  ... >`
  `...`
`</xsd:schema>`
	EPackage
	  nsPrefix="myprefix"
	  ...

An `ecore:package` attribute can be used to specify the fully qualified Java package name corresponding to the schema. It sets both the **name** of the corresponding **EPackage** and the **basePackage** of the **GenPackage** (in the generator model) based on the Java package name, as described in Section 9.1.2.

`<xsd:schema`
`    ecore:package=`
`        "org.basepackage.mypackage" ... >`
`...`
`</xsd:schema>`
	EPackage
	    name="mypackage"
	    ...
	GenPackage
	    basePackage="org.basepackage"
	    ...

Finally, an `ecore:documentRoot` attribute can be used to specify a non-default name for the document root class created in the presence of global element or attribute declarations, as discussed in Section 9.1.3.

9.2 Simple Type Definitions

Each simple type definition in a schema maps to an **EDataType** in the **eClassifiers** list of the schema's corresponding **EPackage**. The **name, instanceClassName,** and **eAnnotations** of the **EDataType** depend on the contents of the type definition.

In some cases, a single simple type actually maps to two **EDataTypes,** where the second represents a wrapper for the first that allows it to be used in certain needed contexts. We'll see these situations in Sections 9.2.1 and 9.2.2.

9.2.1 Restriction

An **EDataType** corresponding to a simple type defined by restriction is initialized as follows:

- **name** = the name of the simple type converted, if necessary, to a proper Java class name
- **instanceClassName** = the **instanceClassName** of the **EDataType** corresponding to the base type
- **eAnnotations** = an extended metadata **EAnnotation**

The **details** map of the extended metadata **EAnnotation** contains the following entries:

- **key** = "name", **value** = the unaltered name of the simple type
- **key** = "baseType", **value** = the restriction's namespace-qualified base type

The restriction's facets, which represent constraints on the base type, are also captured in the **details** map. Each facet produces an additional entry as follows:

- ○ **key** = the name of facet, **value** = the facet's `value`

| ```
<xsd:simpleType name="zipCode">
  <xsd:restriction base="xsd:int">
    <xsd:minInclusive value="10000"/>
    <xsd:maxInclusive value="99999"/>
  </xsd:restriction>
</xsd:simpleType>
``` | **EData Type**<br>    name="ZipCode"<br>    instanceClassName="int"<br>    **EAnnotation**<br>        source=".../ExtendedMetaData"<br>        details="name"→"zipCode",<br>            "baseType"→".../XMLType#int",<br>            "minInclusive"→"10000",<br>            "maxInclusive"→"99999" |

An `ecore:ignore` attribute can be specified on a facet to suppress it in the corresponding **EDataType**.

| ```
<xsd:minInclusive value="10000"
    ecore:ignore="true"/>
``` | *No minInclusive entry in **details** map* |

When the **EDataType** represents a primitive type (i.e., when **instanceClassName** identifies a Java primitive type), a second **EDataType** must be created for the corresponding wrapper class. This is because the simple type may be used as the type of a nillable element (see Section 9.5.4), and a primitive would be unable to represent the `xsi:nill="true"` state. In this case, the wrapper **EDataType** is initialized as follows:

- ○ **name** = the **name** of the primitive **EDataType**, with the suffix "Object" appended
- ○ **instanceClassName** = the wrapper class for the instance class of the primitive **EDataType** (e.g., "java.lang.Integer" for "int")
- ○ **eAnnotations** = an extended metadata **EAnnotation**

The **details** map of the extended metadata **EAnnotation** contains the following entries:

- ○ **key** = "name", **value** = the name of the simple type, with the suffix ":Object" appended
- ○ **key** = "baseType", **value** = the original name of the simple type

`<xsd:simpleType name="zipCode">`
  `<xsd:restriction base="xsd:int">`
    `...`
  `</xsd:restriction>`
`</xsd:simpleType>`
	EDataType name="ZipCode" ...
	EDataType
	    name="ZipCodeObject"
	    instanceClassName="java.lang.Integer"
	    EAnnotation
	        source=".../ExtendedMetaData"
	        details="name"→"zipCode:Object",
	                "baseType"→"zipCode"

The wrapper **EDataType** is only used as the type of an **EAttribute** corresponding to a nillable element, as described in Section 9.5.4. The primitive **EDataType** is used in all other circumstances.

9.2.2   Restriction with Enumeration Facets

A restriction with enumeration facets maps to an **EEnum** and a wrapper **EDataType**. The **EEnum** is initialized as follows:

- ○ **name** = the name of the simple type converted, if necessary, to a proper Java class name
- ○ **eLiterals** = one **EEnumLiteral** for each enumeration facet in the restriction
- ○ **eAnnotations** = an extended metadata **EAnnotation**

Each **EEnumLiteral** has the following attributes:

- ○ **name** = the value of the enumeration facet converted, if necessary, to a valid Java identifier
- ○ **literal** = the unaltered value of the enumeration facet
- ○ **value** = an integer value sequentially assigned, starting at 0

The **details** map of the **EEnum**'s extended metadata **EAnnotation** contains the following entry:

- ○ **key** = "name", **value** = the unaltered name of the simple type

`<xsd:simpleType name="USState">`
  `<xsd:restriction base="xsd:string">`
    `<xsd:enumeration value="A-K"/>`
    `<xsd:enumeration value="A-L"/>`
    `<!-- and so on ... -->`
  `</xsd:restriction>`
`</xsd:simpleType>`
	EEnum
	    name="USState"
	    EEnumLiteral
	        name="AK" **literal=**"A-K" **value=**0
	    EEnumLiteral
	        name="AL" **literal=**"A-L" **value=**1
	    EAnnotation
	        source=".../ExtendedMetaData"
	        details="name"→ "USState"

If the simple type definition includes an `ecore:enum="false"` attribute, the type maps instead to an ordinary **EDataType** as described in Section 9.2.1. If the Java instance class of such an **EDataType** is primitive (e.g., `int`), **EAttributes** of the type will have a default value set (see Sections 9.4.4 and 9.5.5).

An `ecore:name` attribute can be added to an enumeration facet to specify the **name** attribute of the corresponding **EEnumLiteral**.

`<xsd:enumeration value="A-K"`
     `ecore:name="A_K"/>`
	EEnumLiteral
	     name="A_K" ...

Likewise, an `ecore:value` attribute can be used to specify the **value** attribute of an **EEnumLiteral**.

`<xsd:enumeration value="A-K"`
     `ecore:value="100"/>`
	EEnumLiteral
	     value="100" ...

In Ecore, the only valid values of an **EEnum** are its literals; null is not allowed. As a result, **EEnums** have the same limitation as primitive **EDataTypes**: they cannot be used as the type of an attribute corresponding to a nillable element. So, a wrapper **EDataType** is needed for each **EEnum**, for use only in that context. The attributes of the **EDataType** are as follows:

- **name** = the **name** of the **EEnum**, with the suffix "Object" appended
- **instanceClassName** = "org.eclipse.emf.common.util.Enumerator"
- **eAnnotations** = an extended metadata **EAnnotation**

The **details** map of the extended metadata **EAnnotation** contains the following entries:

- **key** = "name", **value** = the name of the simple type, with the suffix ":Object" appended
- **key** = "baseType", **value** = the original name of the simple type

`<xsd:simpleType name="USState">`
  `<xsd:restriction base="xsd:string">`
    `<xsd:enumeration value="A-K"/>`
    `...`
  `</xsd:restriction>`
`</xsd:simpleType>`
	***EEnum name**="USState"* ...
	EDataType
	   name="USStateObject"
	   instanceClassName=
	      "org.eclipse.emf.common.util.Enumerator"
	   EAnnotation
	      source=".../ExtendedMetaData"
	      details="name"→"USState:Object",
	         "baseType"→"USState"

9.2.3 List Type

An **EDataType** corresponding to a list simple type is initialized as follows:

- name = the name of the simple type converted, if necessary, to a proper Java class name **instanceClassName** = "java.util.List"
- eAnnotations = an extended metadata **EAnnotation**

The **details** map of the extended metadata **EAnnotation** contains the following entries:

- key = "name", value = the unaltered name of the simple type
- key = "itemType", value = the itemType of the list

<pre><xsd:simpleType name="nameList">
  <xsd:list itemType="xsd:NCName"/>
</xsd:simpleType></pre>
	EDataType
	    name="NameList"
	    instanceClassName="java.util.List"
	    EAnnotation
	        source=".../ExtendedMetaData"
	        details="name"→"nameList",
	            "itemType"→".../XMLType#NCName"

9.2.4 Union Type

An **EDataType** corresponding to a union simple type is initialized as follows:

- name = the name of the simple type converted, if necessary, to a proper Java class name **instanceClassName** = a common instance class of the members (if there is one) or "java.lang.Object"
- eAnnotations = an extended metadata **EAnnotation**

If the **EDataTypes** corresponding to the union members share a common **instanceClassName**, then the **instanceClassName** of the union's **EDataType** is set to this common value. If they are not all the same, then "java.lang.Object" is used instead.

The **details** map of the extended metadata **EAnnotation** contains the following entries:

- key = "name", value = the unaltered name of the simple type
- key = "memberTypes", value = the space-separated list of memberTypes in the union

```<xsd:simpleType name="zipUnion">```
  ```<xsd:union```
    ```memberTypes="zipCode USState"/>```
```</xsd:simpleType>```
	EDataType
	  name=" ZipUnion"
	  instanceClassName="java.lang.Object"
	  EAnnotation
	    source="…/ExtendedMetaData"
	    details="name"→"zipUnion",
	       "memberTypes"→"zipCode USState"

9.2.5 Anonymous Type

Even when defined anonymously, a simple type still maps to an **EDataType** in the containing package's **eClassifiers** list. If an anonymous simple type is used in an element or attribute declaration, then the corresponding **EDataType's name** is obtained by appending the suffix "Type" to the converted name of that enclosing element or attribute,. The "name" entry in the **details** map of the extended metadata **EAnnotation** has as its value the original name of the enclosing element or attribute, with the suffix "_._type" appended. Any additional entries that would appear in the **details** map for the simple type are unchanged.

```<xsd:element name="myElement">```
  ```<xsd:simpleType>```
    ```...```
  ```</xsd:simpleType>```
```</xsd:element>```
	EDataType
	  name="MyElementType"
	  EAnnotation
	    source="…/ExtendedMetaData"
	    details="name"→"myElement_._type",
	       ...
	  ...

If an anonymous simple type is used as the base type of a restriction, then the corresponding **EDataType's name** is based on the enclosing type's converted name and carries the suffix "Base", instead of "Type". The "name" entry in the **details** map of the extended metadata **EAnnotation** has the suffix "_._base" in this case.

```<xsd:simpleType name="myType">```
  ```<xsd:restriction>```
    ```<xsd:simpleType>```
      ```...```
    ```</xsd:simpleType>```
  ```</xsd:restriction>```
```</xsd:simpleType>```
	EDataType
	  name="MyTypeBase"
	  EAnnotation
	    source="…/ExtendedMetaData"
	    details="name"→"myType_._base", …
	  ...

Similarly, if an anonymous simple type is used as the item type of a list, then the corresponding **EDataType**'s **name** is obtained by appending the suffix "Item" to the enclosing type's converted name. The "name" entry in the **details** map of the extended metadata **EAnnotation** has the suffix "_._item".

`<xsd:simpleType name="myType">`
  `<xsd:list>`
    `<xsd:simpleType>`
      `...`
    `</xsd:simpleType>`
  `</xsd:list>`
`</xsd:simpleType>`
	EDataType
	  name="MyTypeItem"
	  EAnnotation
	    source=".../ExtendedMetaData"
	    details="name"→"myType_._item", ...
	  ...

Finally, if an anonymous simple type is used as a member type of a union, then the corresponding **EDataType**'s **name** is formed from the enclosing type's converted name and the suffix "Member", but in this case, it ends with a number representing the position (starting from 0) of the member in the union. The "name" entry in the **details** map of the extended metadata **EAnnotation** has the suffix "_._member", also qualified with the position number.

`<xsd:simpleType name="myType">`
  `<xsd:union>`
    `<xsd:simpleType>`
      `...`
    `</xsd:simpleType>`
    `...`
  `</xsd:union>`
`</xsd:simpleType>`
	EDataType
	  name="MyTypeMember0"
	  EAnnotation
	    source=".../ExtendedMetaData"
	    details=
	      "name"→"myType_._member0",
	      ...
	  ...

9.2.6   EMF Extensions

In addition to the `ecore:ignore`, `ecore:enum`, `ecore:name`, and `ecore:value` attributes described in Sections 9.2.1 and 9.2.2, there are several attributes from the Ecore namespace that are applicable to simple type declarations in general.

An `ecore:name` attribute can be used to set the **name** of the **EDataType**, for example, if the corresponding simple type is anonymous or if the default name conversion is unacceptable.

| ```
<xsd:simpleType name="stName"
    ecore:name="MyName">
...
</xsd:simpleType>
``` | EDataType<br>  name="MyName"<br>  ... |

An `ecore:instanceClass` attribute can be used to set the **instanceClassName** attribute of the corresponding **EDataType**.

| ```
<xsd:simpleType name="date"
    ecore:instanceClass="java.util.Date">
...
</xsd:simpleType>
``` | EDataType<br>  name="Date"<br>  instanceClassName="java.util.Date"<br>  ... |

The "baseType" (see Section 9.2.1) is not recorded in the **details** map of the extended metadata **EAnnotation** in this case.

An `ecore:serializable` attribute can be used to set the **serializable** attribute of the corresponding **EDataType**.

| ```
<xsd:simpleType name="date"
    ecore:serializable="false">
...
</xsd:simpleType>
``` | EDataType<br>  name="Date"<br>  serializable="false"<br>  ... |

An `ecore:constraints` attribute can be used to declare named constraints by adding an Ecore-sourced **EAnnotation** to the corresponding **EDataType**. Constraints and validation are discussed in depth in Chapter 18.

| ```
<xsd:simpleType name="date"
    ecore:constraints="A B">
...
</xsd:simpleType>
``` | EDataType<br>  name="Date"<br>  EAnnotation<br>    source=" .../emf/2002/Ecore"<br>    details="constraints"→"A B" |

9.3 Complex Type Definitions

Each complex type definition of a schema maps to an **EClass** in the **eClassifiers** list of the schema's corresponding **EPackage**. Such an **EClass** is initialized as follows:

- **name** = the name of the complex type converted, if necessary, to a proper Java class name
- **eAnnotations** = an extended metadata **EAnnotation**

The **details** map of the extended metadata **EAnnotation** contains the following entries:

○ **key** = "name", **value** = the unaltered name of the simple type

○ **key** = "kind", **value** = one of "empty", "simple", "elementOnly", or "mixed"

The value of the "kind" **details** entry depends on the content type of the complex type definition.

``xsd:complexType name="globalAddress">
  <xsd:complexContent>
    ...
  </xsd:complexContent>
</xsd:complexType>```
	EClass
	  name="GlobalAddress"
	  EAnnotation
	    source=".../ExtendedMetaData"
	    details="name"→"globalAddress",
	      "kind"→"elementOnly"

The complex type's attributes, elements, groups, and wildcards map to **EStructuralFeatures** of its corresponding **EClass**. These mappings will be discussed later, in Sections 9.4 through 9.7.

9.3.1 Extension and Restriction

If a complex type is an extension or restriction of another complex type, then the base type's corresponding **EClass** is added to the **eSuperTypes** of the **EClass**.

``xsd:complexType name="globalAddress">
  <xsd:complexContent>
    <xsd:extension base="Address">
      ...
    </xsd:extension>
  </xsd:complexContent>
</xsd:complexType>```
	EClass
	  name="GlobalAddress"
	  eSuperTypes="//Address"
	  ...

In the case of extension, attribute and element declarations within the body of the extension also produce features in the **EClass** as described in the following sections.

The mapping for the contents of a restriction, however, depends on whether or not the `base` type contains any wildcards (i.e., if its definition includes `xsd:any` or `xsd:anyAttribute` elements). If the restricted `base` type contains no wildcards, everything in the restriction body is ignored and the corresponding **EClass** contains no new features. In this case, the subclass is simply provided to restrict the existing features, for example, to constrain their multiplicity or to make their types narrower. Because Ecore does not allow inherited features to be redeclared, such restrictions are not captured in the Ecore representation.

If, on the other hand, the `base` type contains wildcards for which the restricted complex type introduces new elements or attributes, the corresponding derived **EClass** includes features for them.

```
<xsd:complexType name="MyBaseType">             EClass
  <xsd:sequence>                                    name="MyType"
    <xsd:element name="element1" ... />             eSuperTypes="//MyBaseType"
    <xsd:any maxOccurs="unbounded" ... />           ...
  </xsd:sequence>                                 EAttribute
</xsd:complexType>                                  name="element2"
                                                    volatile=true
<xsd:complexType name="MyType">                     transient=true
  <xsd:complexContent>                              derived=true (from "any")
    <xsd:restriction base="MyBaseType">             ...
      <xsd:sequence>
        <xsd:element name="element1" ... />
        <xsd:element name="element2" ... />
      </xsd:sequence>
    </xsd:restriction>
  </xsd:complexContent>
</xsd:complexType>
```

These new features have derived implementations that delegate to the feature map for the `base` type's `xsd:any` or `xsd:anyAttribute` feature (see Section 9.7). This is similar to the way the features of a mixed complex type delegate to a "mixed" feature map, as we will see in Section 9.3.4.

9.3.2 *Simple Content*

A complex type with simple content is defined as an extension or restriction of a simple type. Instead of adding an **eSuperType** to the corresponding **EClass**, a single **EAttribute** is added to its **eAttributes** to represent the simple content. This **EAttribute** is initialized as follows:

○ **name** = "value"

○ **eType** = an **EDataType** corresponding to the simple `base` of the extension or restriction

○ **eAnnotations** = an extended metadata **EAnnotation**

The **details** map of the extended metadata **EAnnotation** on the **EAttribute** contains the following entries:

○ **key** = "name", **value** = ":0"

○ **key** = "kind", **value** = "simple"

The "kind" of the **EClass** is also "simple" in this case.

`<xsd:complexType name="richInt">`
  `<xsd:simpleContent>`
    `<xsd:extension base="xsd:int">`
      `...`
    `</xsd:extension>`
  `</xsd:simpleContent>`
`</xsd:complexType>`
	EClass
	  name="RichInt"
	  EAnnotation
	    source=".../ExtendedMetaData"
	    details="name"→"richInt",
	      "kind"→"simple"
	  EAttribute
	    name="value"
	    eType=".../XMLType#//Int"
	    EAnnotation
	      source=".../ExtendedMetaData"
	      details=
	        "name"→":0", "kind"→"simple"
	  ...

9.3.3 Anonymous Type

If an anonymous complex type is used as the type of an element declaration, then the corresponding **EClass**'s **name** is obtained by appending the suffix "Type" to the enclosing element's converted name. The value of the "name" entry in the **details** map of the extended metadata **EAnnotation** is based on the original, uncoverted name of the enclosing element and carries the suffix "_._type".

`<xsd:element name="myElement">`
  `<xsd:complexType>`
    `...`
  `</xsd:complexType>`
`</xsd:element>`
	EClass
	  name="MyElementType"
	  EAnnotation
	    source=".../ExtendedMetaData"
	    details="name-">"myElement_._type", ...
	  ...

9.3.4 Abstract Type

If a complex type definition includes an `abstract` attribute, it is used to set the **abstract** attribute of the corresponding **EClass**.

`<xsd:complexType abstract="true" ... >`
`...`
`</xsd:complexType>`
	EClass
	    abstract=true
	    ...

9.3.5   Mixed Type

A complex type with mixed content produces a feature map **EAttribute** named "mixed" in the corresponding **EClass**. This **EAttribute** includes the following entries in the **details** map of its extended metadata **EAnnotation**:

- ○ **key** = "name", **value** = ":mixed"
- ○ **key** = "kind", **value** = "elementWildcard"

In this case, the "kind" of the **EClass** is "mixed".

`<xsd:complexType name="MixedType"`
`    mixed="true">`
`...`
`</xsd:complexType>`
	EClass
	    name="MixedType"
	    EAnnotation
	        source="…/ExtendedMetaData"
	        details="name"→"MixedType",
	            "kind"→"mixed"
	    EAttribute
	        name="mixed"
	        eType="…/Ecore#//EFeatureMapEntry"
	        upperBound=-1 *(unbounded)*
	        EAnnotation
	            source="…/ExtendedMetaData"
	            details="name"→":mixed",
	                "kind"→"elementWildcard"
	    ...

The **EAnnotation** specifying the special name ":mixed" identifies the attribute as the mixed feature for the class, of which there can only be one. All other features (**EReferences** and **EAttributes**) mapped from element declarations in the schema are **derived**, with implementations that delegate to the mixed feature map.

`<xsd:complexType name="customersType"`
`    mixed="true">`
`  <xsd:sequence>`
`    <xsd:element name="customer" ... />`
`  </xsd:sequence>`
`</xsd:complexType>`
	EClass **name**=*"CustomersType"* ...
	    EAttribute
	        name="customer"
	        volatile=true
	        transient=true
	        derived=true *(from "mixed")*
	        ...

This structure allows values of the derived references to be mixed with values of the special features **XMLTypeDocumentRoot.text**, **XMLTypeDocumentRoot.cDATA**, and **XMLTypeDocumentRoot.comment**. These features, defined in EMF's XMLType model, represent simple text, character data sections, and XML comments, respectively.[2]

An `ecore:mixed` attribute can be added to a complex type that is not actually mixed in order to produce the same feature-map-based mapping described in this section. The complex type must have complex content and cannot be an extension or restriction of another complex type. This feature is typically used to provide support for adding and accessing comments and whitespace in an XML document,[3] as opposed to real mixed text. Adding any non-whitespace text to instances of such a type would produce an invalid document.

`<xsd:complexType ecore:mixed="true" ... >`
`...`
`</xsd:complexType>`
	EClass ...
	  EAttribute
	    name="mixed"
	    eType=".../Ecore#//EFeatureMapEntry"
	    ...

It is also possible to use a **name** other than "mixed" for the mixed feature. To do so, an `ecore:featureMap` attribute is added to the complex type definition, and the desired name is specified as its value. This works both for real mixed complex types and for other complex types on which the `ecore:mixed` attribute is specified.

`<xsd:complexType mixed="true"`
`    ecore:featureMap="order" ... >`
`...`
`</xsd:complexType>`
	EClass ...
	  EAttribute
	    name="order"
	    eType=".../Ecore#//EFeatureMapEntry"
	    ...

An `ecore:featureMap` attribute can also be specified, without `ecore:mixed`, on a complex type to introduce another, subtly different feature-map-based structure in the corresponding **EClass**. Once again, this is only permitted on a complex type that has complex content and that is not an extension or restriction of another type. In this case, the value of the `ecore:featureMap`

---

2. Beginning in EMF 2.3, processing instructions are also represented using the special feature `XMLTypeDocumentRoot.processingInstruction`.

3. For comments and whitespace to be read from XML documents, the `OPTION_USE_LEXICAL_HANDLER` resource option must be enabled, as described in Chapter 15.

attribute still determines the **name** of the feature map **EAttribute**; however, its **EAnnotation** contains the following **details** entries:

○ **key** = "name", **value** = ":group"

○ **key** = "kind", **value** = "group"

`<xsd:complexType`
    `ecore:featureMap="myMap" ... >`
    `...`
`</xsd:complexType>`
	EClass ...
	    Eattribute
	        name="myMap"
	        eType=".../Ecore#//EFeatureMapEntry"
	        upperBound=-1 *(unbounded)*
	        EAnnotation
	            source=".../ExtendedMetaData"
	            details="name"→":group",
	                "kind"→"group"
	    ...

This structure closely resembles the one used to handle a repeating model group, which is described in Section 9.6.1. All other features mapped from elements in the complex type are still derived from the feature map, as described in that section. The feature map is strictly limited to values of those features, however, and does not allow text, character data or comments, unlike in the case of a mixed type.

9.3.6 EMF Extensions

In addition to the `ecore:mixed` and `ecore:featureMap` attributes described in the previous section, there are several Ecore-namespace attributes that are applicable to complex type declarations in general.

An `ecore:name` attribute can be used to set the **name** of the **EClass**, for example, if the corresponding complex type is anonymous or if the default name conversion is unacceptable.

`<xsd:complexType name="ctName"`
    `ecore:name="MyName"`
    `...`
`</xsd:complexType>`
	EClass
	    name="MyName"
	    ...

An `ecore:instanceClass` attribute can be used to set the **instanceClassName** attribute of the corresponding **EClass**.

`<xsd:complexType`
    `ecore:instanceClass="java.io.Serializable">`
    `...`
`</xsd:complexType>`
	EClass
	instanceClassName="java.io.Serializable"
	...

An `ecore:interface` attribute can be used to set the **interface** attribute of the corresponding **EClass**.

`<xsd:complexType ecore:interface="true">`
    `...`
`</xsd:complexType>`
	EClass
	interface="true"
	...

An `ecore:implements` attribute can be used to specify additional **eSuperTypes** for the corresponding **EClass**. The value of the attribute must be a space-separated list of qualified names, each of which resolves to corresponding complex type.

`<xsd:complexType`
    `ecore:implements="MyOtherType">`
    `...`
`</xsd:complexType>`
	EClass
	eSuperTypes="... //MyOtherType"
	...

An `ecore:constraints` attribute can be used to declare named constraints by adding an Ecore-sourced **EAnnotation** to the corresponding **EClass**. Constraints and validation are discussed in depth in Chapter 18.

`<xsd:complexType ecore:constraints="A B">`
    `...`
`</xsd:complexType>`
	EClass
	EAnnotation
	    source=".../emf/2002/Ecore"
	    details="constraints"→"A B"

9.3.7 Operations

The **EOperation**s of a complex type's corresponding **EClass** can be specified directly in the schema using a specialized appinfo annotation (see Section 9.8.2). To be recognized as defining **EOperation**s, the `xsd:appinfo` element must have the following two attributes: a `source` whose value is "http://www.eclipse.org/emf/2002/Ecore", and an `ecore:key` whose value is "operations".

Each **EOperation** of the **EClass** is represented by an `operation` element within the `xsd:appinfo`. The features of the **EOperation** are specified by attributes and nested elements of the `operation` as follows:

o **name** = the value of the name attribute

o **eType** = an **EDataType** or **EClass** corresponding to the simple or complex type specified as the type attribute, or null if that attribute is absent

o **eParameters** = a list of **EParameters**, one per nested parameter element

o **eExceptions** = a list of **EDataTypes** and **EClass**es corresponding to the space-separated list of simple and complex types in the exceptions attribute

o **lowerBound** = the value of the lowerBound attribute

o **upperBound** = the value of the upperBound attribute

o **ordered** = the value of the ordered attribute

o **unique** = the value of the unique value

o **eAnnotations** = a list of **EAnnotations**, one per nested annotation element

```<xsd:complexType ... >```
  ```<xsd:annotation>```
    ```<xsd:appinfo source=```
      ```"http://www.eclipse.org/emf/2002/Ecore"```
      ```ecore:key="operations">```
    ```<operation name="foo" type="xsd:string"```
      ```lowerBound="1" upperBound="-1"```
      ```exceptions="Exception">```
      ```...```
    ```</operation>```
  ```</xsd:appinfo>```
  ```</xsd:annotation>```
```</xsd:complexType>```
	EClass ...
	  EOperation
	    name="foo"
	    eType=".../XMLType#//String"
	    lowerBound=1
	    upperBound=-1 *(unbounded)*
	    eExceptions="//Exception"
	    ...

Each **EParameter** of the **EOperation** is initialized from the corresponding parameter element as follows:

o **name** = the value of the name attribute

o **eType** = an **EDataType** or **EClass** corresponding to the value of the type attribute

o **lowerBound** = the value of the lowerBound attribute

o **upperBound** = the value of the upperBound attribute

o **ordered** = the value of the ordered attribute

o **unique** = the value of the unique attribute

o **eAnnotations** = list of **EAnnotations**, one per nested annotation element

```
<operation name="foo" ... >          EOperation name="foo" ...
  <parameter name="x"                EParameter
      type="xsd:string"                name="x"
      lowerBound="1"                   eType=".../XMLType#//String"
      upperBound="-1"/>                lowerBound=1
</operation>                           upperBound=-1 (unbounded)
```

If the `operation` element contains a nested `body` element, the corresponding **EOperation** includes an **EAnnotation** with source "http://www.eclipse.org/emf/2002/GenModel" and the following entry in its **details** map:

○ **key** = "body", **value** = the text content of the `body` element

As discussed in Section 5.7.1, this value should be the Java code that implements the **EOperation**. The code generator will make use of it, including it in the generated method.

```
<operation name="foo" ... >          EOperation name="foo" ...
  ...                                EAnnotation
  <body>return x;</body>               source=".../emf/2002/GenModel"
</operation>                           details="body"→"return x;"
```

Arbitrary **EAnnotation**s on an **EOperation** or **EParameter** can be specified by nesting `annotation` elements in the corresponding `operation` or `parameter`.[4] Each **EAnnotation**'s **source** is initialized using the value of the `annotation` element's `source` attribute, and one entry is added to the **details** map for each nested `detail` element as follows:

○ **key** = the value of the `key` attribute, **value** = the content of the `detail` element

```
<operation name="foo" ... >          EOperation name="foo" ...
  <annotation                        EAnnotation
    source="http://www.example.com/A1"/>   source="http://www.example.com/A1"
  <parameter name="x" ... >          EParameter name="x" ...
    <annotation                        EAnnotation
      source="http://www.example.com/A1">    source="http://www.example.com/A1"
    <detail key="key0">someValue</detail>    details="key0"→"someValue",
    <detail key="key1">otherValue</detail>     "key1"→"otherValue"
    </annotation>
  </parameter>
  </annotation>
  ...
</operation>
```

---

4. Elsewhere, schema `xsd:annotations` map directly to **EAnnotations**. See Section 9.8 for details.

9.4   Attribute Declarations

Each schema attribute declaration maps to an **EAttribute** or **EReference** in the **EClass** corresponding to the complex type definition containing the attribute if locally defined, or in the "DocumentRoot" **EClass** if the attribute is global.

An attribute declaration maps to an **EReference** in only a few special cases, which are described in Section 9.4.3. Otherwise, it maps to an **EAttribute** that is initialized as follows:

○ **name** = the name of the attribute converted, if necessary, to a proper Java field name

○ **eType** = an **EDataType** corresponding to the attribute's simple type

○ **lowerBound** = 0 if use="optional" (the default), or 1 if use="required" (see Section 9.4.3)

○ **upperBound** = 1

○ **eAnnotations** = an extended metadata **EAnnotation**

If the type of the attribute is one of the predefined schema types, then the **eType** of the **EAttribute** is set to the corresponding **EDataType** from the XMLType model (see Section 9.9). Otherwise, the **eType** is set to a user-defined **EDataType** created from the simple type as described in Section 9.2.

The **details** map of the extended metadata **EAnnotation** contains the following entries:

○ **key** = "name", **value** = the unaltered name of the attribute

○ **key** = "kind", **value** = "attribute"

`<xsd:attribute name="productName"`
    `type="xsd:string"/>`
	EAttribute
	    name="productName"
	    eType=".../XMLType#//String"
	    lowerBound=0
	    upperBound=1
	    EAnnotation
	        source=".../ExtendedMetaData"
	        details="name"→"productName",
	        "kind"→"attribute"

9.4.1   ID Attribute

An attribute of type xsd:ID, or of any type derived from it, maps to an **EAttribute** whose type is the "ID" **EDataType** from the XMLType model (see Section 9.9). In addition, the **iD** attribute of the **EAttribute** is set to true.

`<xsd:attribute name="id" type="xsd:ID"/>`	**EAttribute**
	  name="id"
	  eType="…/XMLType#//ID"
	  iD=true
	  …

9.4.2   ID Reference or URI Attribute

Attributes of types xsd:IDREF, xsd:IDREFS, and xsd:anyURI, and of types derived from them, usually are intended to represent references to objects defined elsewhere in a document. However, by default, they are handled no differently from attributes of other predefined schema simple types. They simply map to **EAttributes** with **eType** set to the corresponding **EDataType** from the XMLType model (see Section 9.9). Such an **EAttribute** can only record the value of the object identifier appearing in a document, not refer to the object it actually represents.

`<xsd:attribute name="customer"`
`    type="xsd:IDREF"/>`
	EAttribute
	  name="customer"
	  eType="…/XMLType#//IDREF"
	  …

If, however, an attribute of one of these three types also includes an ecore:reference attribute, it maps to an **EReference** instead, capturing the semantic intent of the model. The reference is non-containment (**containment** is false) and its **eType** is set to the **EClass** corresponding to the complex type specified by the ecore:reference attribute. The **upperBound** is set to 1 if the attribute's type is xsd:IDREF or xsd:anyURI, or -1 (unbounded) for xsd:IDREFS. For xsd:IDREF and xsd:IDREFS, which cannot span documents, **resolveProxies** is set to false. For xsd:anyURI, which can span documents, it is set to true.

`<xsd:attribute name="customer"`
`    type="xsd:IDREF"`
`    ecore:reference="Customer"/>`
	EReference
	    name="customer"
	    eType="//Customer"
	    upperBound=1
	    containment=false
	    resolveProxies=false
	    …

`<xsd:attribute name="customers"`
`    type="xsd:IDREFS"`
`    ecore:reference="Customer"/>`
	EReference
	    name="customers"
	    eType="//Customer"
	    upperBound=-1 *(unbounded)*
	    containment=false
	    resolveProxies=false
	    …

`<xsd:attribute name="customer"`
`    type="xsd:anyURI"`
`    ecore:reference="Customer"/>`
	EReference
	    name="customer"
	    eType="//Customer"
	    upperBound=1
	    containment=false
	    resolveProxies=true
	    …

If the relationship is bidirectional, an `ecore:opposite` attribute can be used to specify the attribute or element of the target complex type that corresponds to the reverse (**eOpposite**) **EReference**.

`<xsd:attribute name="customer"`
`    type="xsd:anyURI"`
`    ecore:reference="Customer"`
`    ecore:opposite="orders"/>`
	EReference
	    name="customer"
	    eType="//Customer"
	    upperBound=1
	    containment=false
	    resolveProxies=true
	    eOpposite="//Customer/orders"
	    …

The `ecore:opposite` attribute can be specified on either (or both) sides of the relationship.

9.4.3 Required Attribute

The **lowerBound** of an **EAttribute** or **EReference** corresponding to a required schema attribute is set to 1, instead of the default value of 0.

`<xsd:attribute use="required" ... />`	EAttribute
	    lowerBound=1
	    …

9.4.4 Default Value

Specifying a `default` value on an attribute sets the **defaultValueLiteral** attribute of the corresponding **EAttribute**. The **EAttribute** is also unsettable in this case.

`<xsd:attribute name="message"`
`    type="xsd:string"`
`    default="hello world" ... />`
	EAttribute
	  name="message"
	  eType="…/XMLType#//String"
	  defaultValueLiteral="hello world"
	  unsettable=true
	  …

An attribute declaration without an explicit `default` value also maps to an unsettable **EAttribute** if the type has an intrinsic default value that is non-null (i.e., if the corresponding **eType** is an **EEnum** or an **EDataType** representing a primitive Java type).

`<xsd:attribute name="quantity"`
`    type="xsd:int"/>`
	EAttribute
	  name="quantity"
	  eType="…/XMLType#//Int"
	  unsettable=true
	  …

Section 9.2.2 described how a simple type restriction with enumeration facets can map to an ordinary **EDataType**, instead of an **EEnum**, when `ecore:enum="false"` is specified. If such a simple type maps to a primitive **EDataType** and is used as the type of an attribute, then the resulting **EAttribute** has its default value set, even if no explicit `default` is specified in the attribute declaration. In this case, the **defaultValueLiteral** of the **EAttribute** is set to the first enumeration value of the simple type.

`<xsd:attribute name="oneThreeFive">`
`  <xsd:simpleType ecore:enum="false">`
`    <xsd:restriction base="xsd:int">`
`      <xsd:enumeration value="1"/>`
`      <xsd:enumeration value="3"/>`
`      <xsd:enumeration value="5"/>`
`    </xsd:restriction>`
`  </xsd:simpleType>`
`</xsd:attribute>`
	EDataType
	  name="OneThreeFiveType"
	  instanceClassName="int"
	  …
	EAttribute
	  name="oneThreeFive"
	  eType="//OneThreeFiveType"
	  defaultValueLiteral="1"
	  unsettable=true
	  …

9.4.5 Qualified Attribute

If a local attribute declaration has qualified form, either explicitly declared with a `form="qualified"` attribute or inherited from an `xsd:schema` with `attributeFormDefault="qualified"` (see Section 9.1.7), the **details** map of the extended metadata **EAnnotation** for the corresponding feature contains an additional entry:

○ **key** = "namespace", **value** = "##targetNamespace"

`<xsd:attribute form="qualified" ... />`	EAttribute ... EAnnotation source="…/ExtendedMetaData" details= "namespace"→"##targetNamespace", …

9.4.6 Global Attribute

The **EAttribute** or **EReference** corresponding to a global attribute declaration is added to the package's "DocumentRoot" **EClass** as described in Section 9.1.5, unless it has an `ecore:ignore="true"` attribute, in which case it is ignored. The extended metadata **EAnnotation** on the feature also includes exactly the same "namespace" **details** entry (with value "##targetNamespace") as in the case of a qualified attribute, which was described in Section 9.4.5.

`<xsd:schema ... >`
  `<xsd:attribute name="globalAttribute"`
    `type="xsd:string"/>`
  `...`
`</xsd:schema>`
	EClass name="DocumentRoot" …
	 EAttribute
	  name="globalAttribute"
	  eType="…/XMLType#//String"
	  …
	 EAnnotation
	  source="…/ExtendedMetaData"
	  details=
	   "namespace"→"##targetNamespace",
	   …

9.4.7 Attribute Reference

An attribute reference (i.e., one with a `ref` attribute) maps to an **EAttribute** or **EReference** with a "namespace" entry in the **details** map of its extended metadata **EAnnotation**. If the reference is to a global attribute defined (or included) in the same schema, the value of this entry is "##targetNamespace".

`<xsd:complexType ... >`
  `...`
  `<xsd:attribute ref="globalAttribute"/>`
`</xsd:complexType>`
	EClass ...
	  EAttribute ...
	    EAnnotation
	      source="…/ExtendedMetaData"
	      details=
	        "namespace"→"##targetNamespace",
	        ...

However, if the reference is to a global attribute from a different schema, then the value of the "namespace" entry is set instead to the `targetNamespace` of that schema.

9.4.8   EMF Extensions

The initialization of an **EAttribute** or **EReference** corresponding to a schema attribute can be further customized through the use of several additional attributes from the Ecore namespace. Except as otherwise noted, these extensions are generally applicable to all local and global attribute declarations and attribute references. In cases where one of these attributes is used on both a global attribute declaration and a local reference to it, the value specified on the local attribute reference takes precedence.

The `ecore:reference`, `ecore:opposite`, and `ecore:ignore` attributes, which are not discussed here, have the specific uses outlined in Sections 9.4.2 and 9.4.6.

Name

An `ecore:name` attribute can be used to explicitly set the **name** of the **EAttribute** or **EReference**, if the default name conversion is unacceptable.

`<xsd:attribute name="..."`
  `ecore:name="MyName" ... />`
	EAttribute
	  name="MyName"
	  ...

Default Value

An `ecore:default` attribute can be added to a local attribute declaration to specify the default value of the corresponding **EAttribute**. This would typically be used only if the attribute is required and hence is not permitted to have a schema-specified default.

`<xsd:attribute ecore:default="value" ... />`	**EAttribute** defaultValueLiteral="value" ...

Multiplicity

An `ecore:many` attribute can be used on an attribute of a list simple type to indicate that it should map to a multiplicity-many **EAttribute** with an **eType** corresponding to the list's item type.

`<xsd:attribute type="xsd:IDREFS"` `ecore:many="true" ... />`	**EAttribute** upperBound="-1" eType="…/XMLType#//IDREF" ...

If the list type has an `xsd:maxLength` or `xsd:length` facet, that value is used as the upper bound. If the list has an `xsd:minLength` or `xsd:length` facet, and the attribute is not optional, that value is used as the lower bound. Otherwise, default lower and upper bounds of 0 and -1 apply.

The `ecore:lowerBound` and `ecore:upperBound` attributes can be used to explicitly override the **lowerBound** and **upperBound** of the structural feature corresponding to any attribute declaration or reference, if the default mapping rules don't produce the desired result.

`<xsd:attribute ecore:lowerBound="1" ... />`	**EAttribute** lowerBound="1" ...
`<xsd:attribute ecore:upperBound="10" ... />`	**EAttribute** upperBound="10" ...

When an attribute maps to a multiplicity-many structural feature, `ecore:ordered` and `ecore:unique` attributes can be specified on the declaration or reference to set the feature's **ordered** and **unique** attributes.

`<xsd:attribute ecore:ordered="false" ... />`	**EAttribute** ordered="false" ...
`<xsd:attribute ecore:unique="true" ... />`	**EAttribute** unique="true" ...

Although `ecore:ordered` and `ecore:unique` are allowed on attributes that map to both **EAttributes** and **EReferences**, their usefulness is currently limited, as was described in Section 5.3: basically, only setting **unique** on an **EAttribute** is meaningful.

Behavior

Several boolean attributes of an **EAttribute** or **EReference**, which specify how a feature stores and accesses its values, can be set directly, using Ecore-namespace attributes of the same name. These attributes, which include `ecore:unsettable`, `ecore:changeable`, `ecore:derived`, `ecore:transient`, `ecore:volatile`, and `ecore:resolveProxies`, can be used when the default mapping rules don't produce the desired result.

`<xsd:attribute`
    `ecore:unsettable="true" ... />`
	EAttribute
	    unsettable=“true”
	    ...

`<xsd:attribute`
    `ecore:changeable="true" ... />`
	EAttribute
	    changeable=“true”
	    ...

`<xsd:attribute`
    `ecore:derived="true" ... />`
	∫**EAttribute**
	    derived=“true”
	    ...

`<xsd:attribute`
    `ecore:transient="true" ... />`
	EAttribute
	    transient=“true”
	    ...

`<xsd:attribute`
    `ecore:volatile="true" ... />`
	EAttribute
	    volatile=“true”
	    ...

`<xsd:attribute ecore:reference="..."`
    `ecore:resolveProxies="true" ... />`
	EAttribute
	    resolveProxies=“true”
	    ...

Note that the last of these, `ecore:resolveProxies`, is valid only on an attribute that maps to an **EReference** (see Section 9.4.2).

Accessor Visibility

Four Ecore-namespace attributes, `ecore:suppressedGetVisibility`, `ecore:suppressedSetVisibility`, `ecore:suppressedIsSetVisibility`, and `ecore:suppressedUnsetVisibility`, can be used to add an accessor suppressing GenModel-namespace **EAnnotation** to the structural feature. As described in Section 5.7, such an **EAnnotation** instructs the code generator to suppress one or more of the accessors that would normally appear in the interface generated for the feature's containing class.

`<xsd:attribute`
    `ecore:suppressedGetVisibility="true"`
    `ecore:suppressedSetVisibility="true"`
    `ecore:suppressedIsSetVisibility="true"`
    `ecore:suppressedUnsetVisibility="true"`
    `... />`
	EAttribute
	  ...
	EAnnotation
	  source="…/emf/2002/GenModel"
	  details=
	    "suppressedSetVisibility"→"true",
	    "suppressedGetVisibility"→"true",
	    "suppressedIsSetVisibility"→"true",
	    "suppressedUnsetVisibility"→"true"

9.5   Element Declarations

Each schema element declaration maps to an **EAttribute** or **EReference** in the **EClass** corresponding to the complex type definition containing the element, or in the "DocumentRoot" **EClass** if the element is global.

An element declaration maps to an **EAttribute** if its type is simple (with the exception of the special cases described in Section 9.5.3). Otherwise, if the type is complex, it maps to an **EReference**. In either case, the attributes of the feature are initialized as follows:

- **name** = the `name` of the element converted, if necessary, to a proper Java field name

- **eType** = an **EDataType** or **EClass** corresponding to the element's type

- **lowerBound** = the `minOccurs` value of the element declaration multiplied by the `minOccurs` of any containing model groups, or 0 for a global element or an element nested in an `xsd:choice`

- **upperBound** = the `maxOccurs` value of the element declaration multiplied by the `maxOccurs` of any containing model groups, or -2 (unspecified) for a global element (see Section 9.5.7)

- **eAnnotations** = an extended metadata **EAnnotation**

If the type of the element is one of the predefined schema types, then the **eType** of the corresponding **EAttribute** is set to the corresponding **EDataType** from the XMLType model (see Section 9.9). If the element has a user-defined simple type, the **eType** is set to an **EDataType** created from the simple type as described in Section 9.2.

Otherwise, if the element declaration maps to an **EReference**, the **eType** is set to the **EClass** corresponding to the element's type. The **EReference**'s **containment** attribute is true, except in the cases described in Section 9.5.3.

The **details** map of the extended metadata **EAnnotation** contains the following entries:

○ **key** = "name", **value** = the unaltered name of the element

○ **key** = "kind", **value** = "element"

`<xsd:element name="mySimple"`
`    type="xsd:string"`
`    maxOccurs="unbounded" />`
	EAttribute
	    name="mySimple"
	    eType="…/XMLType#//String"
	    lowerBound=1
	    upperBound=-1 *(unbounded)*
	    EAnnotation
	        source="…/ExtendedMetaData"
	        details="name"→"mySimple",
	        "kind"→"element"

`<xsd:element name="myComplex">`
`  <xsd:complexType … >`
`    …`
`  </xsd:complexType>`
`</xsd:element>`
	EReference
	    name="myComplex"
	    eType="//MyComplexType"
	    lowerBound=1
	    upperBound=1
	    containment=true
	    EAnnotation
	        source="…/ExtendedMetaData"
	        details="name"→"myComplex",
	        "kind"→"element"

9.5.1 AnyType Element

In addition to the **EDataType**s for all the XML Schema predefined simple types (see Section 9.9), the XMLType model also includes an **EClass**, named "AnyType", that corresponds to the xsd:anyType complex type. An element of type xsd:anyType maps to an **EReference**, but not of this type, as you might expect. Instead, the **eType** of the **EReference** is **EObject**, the base class for all EMF objects.

`<xsd:element name="…"`
`    type="xsd:anyType"/>`
	EReference
	    eType="…/Ecore#//EObject"
	    …

Using **EObject** as the type of the reference allows it to take an instance of any EMF object as its value, which is the intended behavior. The purpose of the "AnyType" **EClass** is to handle situations where an instance contains arbitrary XML content. For example, when processing wildcard content in "lax mode" with no metadata available, an instance of the "AnyType" **EClass**, which like every other **EClass** implicitly extends **EObject**, will be used as the value of the feature. Such an instance can represent any arbitrary XML element content including any attributes and mixed text that it might have.

9.5.2 ID Element

Note: The XML Schema specification recommends avoiding the use of xsd:ID as the type of an element declaration.

An element of type `xsd:ID`, or of any type derived from it, maps to an **EAttribute** whose type is the "ID" **EDataType** from the XMLType model (see Section 9.9). In addition, the **iD** attribute of the **EAttribute** is set to true.

`<xsd:element name="..." type="xsd:ID"/>`	**EAttribute** eType="…/XMLType#//ID" iD=true …

9.5.3 ID Reference or URI Element

Note: The XML Schema specification recommends avoiding the use of xsd:IDREF or xsd:IDREFS as the type of an element declaration.

Elements of type `xsd:IDREF` or `xsd:anyURI`, or of any derived simple type, are given the same special treatment as was described for attributes of these types in Section 9.4.2. By default, they are treated as ordinary elements of simple type and mapped to **EAttribute**s. When an `ecore:reference` is specified, they map to **EReference**s, instead.. Unlike attributes, however, elements can be repeated, so the **upperBound** of the **EReference** is not always 1, but is instead set according to the `maxOccurs` attribute of the element declaration.

`<xsd:element name="customer"`
    `type="xsd:anyURI"`
    `maxOccurs="10"`
    `ecore:reference="Customer"/>`
	EReference
	name="customer"
	eType="//Customer"
	upperBound=10
	containment=false
	resolveProxies=true
	…

An ecore:opposite can also be specified to indicate that the relationship described by the element is bidirectional, just like for an attribute.

The xsd:IDREFS case is a little more complicated. This is because the xsd:IDREFS type represents multiple references and can, itself, be repeated (i.e., maxOccurs might be greater than 1). So, in this case the **EReference**'s **containment** attribute is set to true and its **eType** is set to an additional holder **EClass**, instead of to the type specified by the ecore:reference attribute.

`<xsd:element name="customers"`
    `type="xsd:IDREFS"`
    `ecore:reference="Customer"/>`
	EReference
	    name="customers"
	    eType="//CustomersHolder"
	    containment=true
	    …

A holder **EClass**, "CustomersHolder" in this example, is automatically created for every element declaration of type xsd:IDREFS with an ecore:reference attribute specified. This **EClass** is initialized as follows:

○ **name** = the name of the element converted, if necessary, to a proper Java class name, and with the string "Holder" appended

○ **eReferences** = a single, multiplicity-many **EReference**

○ **eAnnotations** = an extended metadata **EAnnotation**

The **details** map of the extended metadata **EAnnotation** for the **EClass** has the following entries:

○ **key** = "name", **value** = the name of the element, with the string ":holder" appended

○ **key** = "kind", **value** = "simple"

The **EReference** in the holder **EClass** is initialized as follows:

○ **name** = "value"

○ **eType** = the **EClass** corresponding to the type specified by the ecore:reference attribute

○ **upperBound** = -1 (unbounded)

○ **containment** = false

○ **resolveProxies** = false

The details map of the extended metadata **EAnnotation** for the "value" **EReference** contains the following:

○ **key** = "name", **value** = ":0"

○ **key** = "kind", **value** = "simple"

`<xsd:element name="customers"`
`    type="xsd:IDREFS"`
`    ecore:reference="Customer"/>`
	EClass
	    name="CustomersHolder"
	    EAnnotation
	        source="…/ExtendedMetaData"
	        details="name"→"customers:holder",
	            "kind"→"simple"
	    …
	    EReference
	        name="value"
	        eType="//Customer"
	        upperBound=-1 *(unbounded)*
	        containment=false
	        resolveProxies=false
	        EAnnotation
	            source="…/ExtendedMetaData"
	            details="name"→":0",
	                "kind"→"simple"
	        …

9.5.4   *Nillable Element*

A `nillable` element with `maxOccurs` equal to 1 maps to an **EAttribute** or **EReference** with **unsettable** set to true.

In the case of an element with simple type, if the type would ordinarily map to a primitive or enumerated type, then a wrapper **EDataType** is used as the **EAttribute**'s **eType**, instead. Recall from Sections 9.2.1 and 9.2.2 that an additional wrapper **EDataType** is produced for each primitive and enumerated type in a schema. In addition, the XMLType model defines wrappers for all of the built-in primitive schema types, as we will see in Section 9.9.

`<xsd:element type="xsd:int"`
`    nillable="true" ... />`
	EAttribute
	    eType="…/XMLType#//IntObject"
	    unsettable=true
	    …

9.5.5 Default Value

When an element maps to an **EAttribute**, specifying a `default` value on the element sets the **EAttribute**'s **defaultValueLiteral**. The **EAttribute** is also unsettable in this case.

`<xsd:element name="message"`
`    type="xsd:string"`
`    default="hello world" ... />`
	EAttribute
	    name="message"
	    eType="…/XMLType#//String"
	    defaultValueLiteral="hello world"
	    unsettable=true
	    …

An element declaration without an explicit `default` value also maps to an unsettable **EAttribute** if the type has an intrinsic default value that is non-null (i.e., if the corresponding **eType** is an **EEnum** or an **EDataType** representing a primitive Java type).

`<xsd:element name="quantity"`
`    type="xsd:int"/>`
	EAttribute
	    name="quantity"
	    eType="…/XMLType#//Int"
	    unsettable=true
	    …

Section 9.2.2 described how a simple type restriction with enumeration facets can map to an ordinary **EDataType**, instead of an **EEnum**, when `ecore:enum="false"` is specified. If such a simple type maps to a primitive **EDataType** and is used as the type of an element, then the resulting **EAttribute** has its default value set, even if no explicit `default` is specified for the element. In this case, the **defaultValueLiteral** of the corresponding **EAttribute** is set to the first enumeration value of the simple type.

`<xsd:element name="oneThreeFive">`
`  <xsd:simpleType ecore:enum="false">`
`   <xsd:restriction base="xsd:int">`
`     <xsd:enumeration value="1"/>`
`     <xsd:enumeration value="3"/>`
`     <xsd:enumeration value="5"/>`
`   </xsd:restriction>`
`  </xsd:simpleType>`
`</xsd:element>`
	EDataType
	    name="OneThreeFiveType"
	    instanceClassName="int"
	    …
	EAttribute
	    name="oneThreeFive"
	    eType="//OneThreeFiveType"
	    defaultValueLiteral="1"
	    unsettable=true
	    …

9.5.6 Qualified Element

If a local element declaration has qualified form, either explicitly declared with a `form="qualified"` attribute or inherited from an `xsd:schema` with `elementFormDefault="qualified"` (see Section 9.1.7), then the **details** map of the extended metadata **EAnnotation** for the corresponding feature contains an additional entry:

○ **key** = "namespace", **value** = "##targetNamespace"

`<xsd:element form="qualified" ... />`	**EReference** ...
	EAnnotation
	  source=".../ExtendedMetaData"
	  details=
	    "namespace"→"##targetNamespace",
	    ...

9.5.7 Global Element

The **EAttribute** or **EReference** corresponding to a global element declaration is added to the package's "DocumentRoot" **EClass** as described in Section 9.1.5, unless it has an `ecore:ignore="true"` attribute, in which case it is ignored. The **upperBound** of the feature is set to -2 (unspecified). The extended metadata **EAnnotation** on the feature also includes exactly the same "namespace" **details** entry (with value "##targetNamespace") as in the case of a qualified element, which was described in Section 9.5.6.

`<xsd:schema ... >`
  `<xsd:element name="address"`
    `type="USAddress"/>`
  `...`
`</xsd:schema>`
	EClass *name="DocumentRoot"* ...
	  EReference
	    name="address"
	    eType="//USAddress"
	    upperBound=-2 *(unspecified)*
	    ...
	    EAnnotation
	      source=".../ExtendedMetaData"
	      details=
	        "namespace"→"##targetNamespace",
	        ...

9.5.8   Element Reference

An element reference (i.e., one with a `ref` attribute) maps to an **EAttribute** or **EReference** with a "namespace" entry in the **details** map of its extended metadata **EAnnotation**. If the reference is to a global element defined (or included) in the same schema, the value of this entry is "##targetNamespace".

<pre><xsd:complexType ...>
  <xsd:sequence>
    <xsd:element ref="address"/>
  </xsd:sequence>
</xsd:complexType></pre>

EClass ...
  EReference ...
    EAnnotation
      source="…/ExtendedMetaData"
      details=
        "namespace"→"##targetNamespace",
        …

However, if the reference is to a global element from a different schema, then the value of the "namespace" entry is set instead to the `targetNamespace` of that schema.

9.5.9   Substitution Group

A `substitutionGroup` attribute in a global element declaration produces an additional entry in the details map of the extended metadata **EAnnotation** of the corresponding **EReference** or **EAttribute**:

○ **key** = "affiliation", **value** = the value of the `substitutionGroup` attribute

<pre><xsd:schema ... >
  <xsd:element name="staffComment"
      substitutionGroup="comment">
    <xsd:complexType>
      ...
    </xsd:complexType>
  </xsd:element>
  ...
  <xsd:element name="comment"
      type="xsd:string"/>
</xsd:schema></pre>

EClass name="DocumentRoot" ...
  EReference
    name="staffComment"
    eType="//StaffCommentType"
    EAnnotation
      source="…/ExtendedMetaData"
      details="affiliation"→"comment",
        …
  …
  EAttribute
    name="comment"
    eType="…/XMLType#//String"
    …

To be in a substitution group, an element must have the same type as the head element (the element named by the `substitutionGroup` attribute) or a type derived from it. In this example, the anonymously defined complex type of the "staffComment" element would extend the "comment" head element's simple string type.

Any reference to a substitution group's head element in a complex type produces an additional feature map **EAttribute** in the corresponding **EClass**, from which the ordinary **EAttribute** or **EReference** derives. By default, the **name** of the feature map **EAttribute** is formed by appending "Group" to the **name** of the ordinary feature. In addition, the extended metadata **EAnnotation** on the feature map **EAttribute** contains the following **details** entries:

○ **key** = "name", **value** = the name of the element, with the suffix ":group" appended

○ **key** = "kind", **value** = "group"

```xsd:complexType name="PurchaseOrder">```
  ```<xsd:sequence>```
    ...
    ```<xsd:element ref="comment"/>```
    ...
  ```</xsd:sequence>```
```</xsd:complexType>```
	EClass name="*PurchaseOrder*" ...
	  EAttribute
	    name="commentGroup"
	    eType=".../Ecore#//EFeatureMapEntry"
	    EAnnotation
	      source=".../ExtendedMetaData"
	      details="name"→"comment:group",
	        "kind"→"group", ...
	  ...
	  EAttribute
	    name="comment"
	    eType=".../XMLType#//String"
	    volatile=true
	    transient=true
	    derived=true *(from "commentGroup")*
	    EAnnotation
	      source=".../ExtendedMetaData"
	      details="name"→"comment",
	        "kind"→"element",
	        "group"→"comment:group", ...
	  ...

This feature-map-based implementation is required to allow instances of the substitution elements to be serialized in an XML document without using an `xsi:type` attribute. The same pattern is also used for a reference to an `abstract` global element, as such an element is prohibited from being used directly, requiring that substitution elements be serialized in its place. The derived feature is also non-changeable in the abstract case.

If the reference to a head or abstract element is nested within a schema component for which a feature map would already be produced (e.g., if the containing complex type is mixed), the resulting feature map **EAttribute** then derives from that other feature map.

It is possible to specify a different **name** for the feature map **EAttribute** as the value of an ecore:featureMap attribute on the head element declaration or reference. Or, if you don't really need the ability to serialize elements from the substitution group, you can disable the feature-map-based implementation by specifying ecore:featureMap="".

`<xsd:element ref="comment"`
`    ecore:featureMap=""/>`
	EAttribute
	    name="comment"
	    eType="…/XMLType#//String"
	    volatile=false
	    …

In fact, even when an element is not the head of a substitution group, an ecore:featureMap attribute can be used to introduce the feature-map-based structure that we have seen in this section.

`<xsd:complexType name="PurchaseOrder">`
  `<xsd:sequence>`
    `...`
    `<xsd:element name="address"`
        `type="USAddress"`
        `ecore:featureMap="addressGroup"/>`
    `...`
  `</xsd:sequence>`
`</xsd:complexType>`
	*EClass **name**="PurchaseOrder"* …
	  EAttribute
	    name="addressGroup"
	    eType="…/Ecore#//EFeatureMapEntry"
	  EAnnotation
	      source="…/ExtendedMetaData"
	      details="name"→"address:group",
	        "kind"→"group", …
	
	    …
	  EReference
	    name="comment"
	    eType="…//USAddress"
	    volatile=true
	    transient=true
	    derived=true *(from "addressGroup")*
	  EAnnotation
	      source="…/ExtendedMetaData"
	      details="name"→"address",
	        "kind"→"element",
	        "group"→"#address:group", …
	
	    …

9.5.10   EMF Extensions

The initialization of an **EAttribute** or **EReference** corresponding to an element can be further customized through the use of several additional attributes from the Ecore namespace. Except as otherwise noted, these extensions are generally applicable to all local and global element declarations and element references. In cases where one of these attributes is used on both a global element declaration and a local reference to it, the value specified on the local element reference takes precedence.

The `ecore:reference`, `ecore:ignore`, and `ecore:featureMap` attributes, which are not discussed here, have the specific uses outlined in Sections 9.5.3, 9.5.7, and 9.5.9.

Name

An `ecore:name` attribute can be used to explicitly set the **name** of the **EAttribute** or **EReference**, if the default name conversion is unacceptable.

`<xsd:element name="..."`
`    ecore:name="MyName" ... />`
	EReference
	  name="MyName"
	  ...

Multiplicity

The `ecore:lowerBound` and `ecore:upperBound` attributes can be used to explicitly override the **lowerBound** and **upperBound** of the structural feature corresponding to any element declaration or reference, if the default mapping rules don't produce the desired result.

`<xsd:element ecore:lowerBound="1" ... />`	**EReference**
	  lowerBound="1"
	  ...

`<xsd:element ecore:upperBound="10" ... />`	**EReference**
	  upperBound="10"
	  ...

When an element maps to a multiplicity-many structural feature, `ecore:ordered` and `ecore:unique` attributes can be specified on the declaration or reference to set the feature's **ordered** and **unique** attributes.

`<xsd:element ecore:ordered="false" ... />`	EAttribute ordered="false" ...
`<xsd:element ecore:unique="true" ... />`	EAttribute unique="true" ...

Although `ecore:ordered` and `ecore:unique` are allowed on elements that map to both **EAttribute**s and **EReferences**, their usefulness is currently limited, as was described in Section 5.3: basically, only setting **unique** on an **EAttribute** is meaningful.

Behavior

Several boolean attributes of an **EAttribute** or **EReference**, which specify how a feature stores and accesses its values, can be set directly, using Ecore-namespace attributes of the same name. These attributes, which include `ecore:unsettable`, `ecore:changeable`, `ecore:derived`, `ecore:transient`, `ecore:volatile`, and `ecore:resolveProxies`, can be used when the default mapping rules don't produce the desired result.

`<xsd:element` `ecore:unsettable="true" ... />`	EReference unsettable="true" ...
`<xsd:element` `ecore:changeable="true" ... />`	EReference changeable="true" ...
`<xsd:element` `ecore:derived="true" ... />`	EReference derived="true" ...
`<xsd:element` `ecore:transient="true" ... />`	EReference transient="true" ...
`<xsd:element` `ecore:volatile="true" ... />`	EReference volatile="true" ...
`<xsd:element` `ecore:resolveProxies="true" ... />`	EReference resolveProxies="true" ...

Note that the last of these, `ecore:resolveProxies`, is only valid on elements that map to **EReferences**, while the rest are valid on all elements.

Opposite

For any element that maps to an **EReference**, an `ecore:opposite` attribute can be used to make the relationship bidirectional and specify an **eOpposite EReference**. If the reference is non-containment (see Section 9.5.3), the `ecore:opposite` attribute identifies an attribute or element declaration in the target complex type, as described in Section 9.4.2. Otherwise, it simply specifies the name of a type-safe container reference to be added automatically to the target **EClass**.

`<xsd:element name="items"`
     `type="Item"`
     `maxOccurs="unbounded"`
     `ecore:opposite="order"/>`
	EReference
	   name="items"
	   eType="//Item"
	   upperBound=-1 *(unbounded)*
	   containment=true
	   eOpposite="//Item/order"
	   ...

Accessor Visibility

Four Ecore-namespace attributes, `ecore:suppressedGetVisibility`, `ecore:suppressedSetVisibility`, `ecore:suppressedIsSetVisibility`, and `ecore:suppressedUnsetVisibility`, can be used to add an accessor suppressing GenModel-namespace **EAnnotation** to the structural feature. As described in Section 5.7, such an **EAnnotation** instructs the code generator to suppress one or more of the accessors that would normally appear in the interface generated for the feature's containing class.

`<xsd:element`
     `ecore:suppressedGetVisibility="true"`
     `ecore:suppressedSetVisibility="true"`
     `ecore:suppressedIsSetVisibility="true"`
     `ecore:suppressedUnsetVisibility="true"`
     `... />`
	EReference
	   ...
	   EAnnotation
	     source="…/emf/2002/GenModel"
	     details=
	       "suppressedSetVisibility"→"true",
	       "suppressedGetVisibility"→"true",
	       "suppressedIsSetVisibility"→"true",
	       "suppressedUnsetVisibility"→"true"

9.6   Model Groups

XML Schema model groups (xsd:sequence, xsd:choice, and xsd:all) with maxOccurs equal to 1 (the default) produce no corresponding elements in the Ecore model. These constructs simply serve to aggregate the elements under them. In Ecore, the **EClass** corresponding to the containing complex type already provides this aggregation function for its features. The only case requiring special treatment is when a model group is allowed to repeat, as described in the following section.

9.6.1   *Repeating Model Group*

A repeating xsd:sequence or xsd:choice model group[5] (one with maxOccurs greater than 1) produces a feature map **EAttribute** in the **EClass** corresponding to the complex type definition containing the group. This is to represent the kind of cross-feature ordering described in Chapter 8. The **EAttribute** is initialized as follows:

○ **name** = "group"

○ **lowerBound** = the minOccurs value of the model group multiplied by the minOccurs of any containing model groups, or 0 if the group is nested in an xsd:choice

○ **upperBound** = the maxOccurs value of the model group multiplied by the maxOccurs of any containing model groups

○ **eAnnotations** = an extended metadata **EAnnotation**

The **details** map of the extended metadata **EAnnotation** contains the following entries:

○ **key** = "name", **value** = the **name** of the **EAttribute**, followed by ":" and its feature ID

○ **key** = "kind", **value** = "group"

<xsd:choice maxOccurs="unbounded"> ... </xsd:choice>	**EAttribute**
	  name="group"
	  eType="…/Ecore#//EFeatureMapEntry"
	  upperBound=-1 *(unbounded)*
	  EAnnotation
	    source="…/ExtendedMetaData"
	    details="name"→"group:0",
	      "kind"→"group"

---

5. A repeating xsd:all model group is not a valid XML Schema construct.

All other **EReferences** and **EAttributes** corresponding to element declarations in the model group have derived implementations that delegate to the feature map:

`<xsd:choice maxOccurs="unbounded">`
  `<xsd:element name="priorityOrders"`
    `type="PurchaseOrder"/>`
  `...`
`</xsd:choice>`
	EAttribute
	  name=" priorityOrders"
	  volatile=true
	  transient=true
	  derived=true *(from "group")*
	  ...
	EAnnotation
	    source="…/ExtendedMetaData"
	    details="group"→"#group:0", …

If the repeating model group is nested within a schema component for which a feature map would already be produced (e.g., if the containing complex type is mixed), the group's corresponding feature map **EAttribute** then derives from that other feature map.

An `ecore:featureMap` attribute can be added to the model group to override the default name of the corresponding feature map **EAttribute**.

`<xsd:choice maxOccurs="unbounded"`
    `ecore:featureMap="choices">`
  `...`
`</xsd:choice>`
	EAttribute
	  name=" choices"
	  eType="…/Ecore#//EFeatureMapEntry"
	  upperBound=-1 *(unbounded)*
	  EAnnotation
	    source="…/ExtendedMetaData"
	    details="name"→"choices:0",
	      "kind"→"group"

Alternatively, if order preservation among the elements in the group is not desired, the feature map implementation can be suppressed by specifying `ecore:featureMap=""`. which produces the ordinary, non-derived implementation pattern for the elements in the group.

`<xsd:choice maxOccurs="unbounded"`
    `ecore:featureMap="">`
  `...`
`</xsd:choice>`
	No feature map attribute

Finally, an `ecore:featureMap` attribute can also be used on a *non-repeating* model group to introduce a feature map implementation. The common use of this is to provide order preservation in an `xsd:all` group. By definition, an xsd:all group is one that places no restriction on the order in which instances of its elements can appear. By default, EMF interprets this as meaning serialization order is irrelevant, so it does not use a feature map to implement the xsd:all group. The other possible interpretation is that the elements can appear in any order, but the order they're in is important and must be maintained. If this is the desired behavior, an ecore:featureMap attribute can be added to override the simpler default mapping and produce a feature map **EAttribute** for the group.

`<xsd:all ecore:featureMap="allGroup">`
  `...`
`</xsd:all>`
	EAttribute
	  name="allGroup"
	  eType=".../Ecore#//EFeatureMapEntry"
	  upperBound=-1 *(unbounded)*
	  EAnnotation
	    source=".../ExtendedMetaData"
	    details="name"→"allGroup:0",
	      "kind"→"group"

9.6.2   Repeating Model Group Reference

The feature map **EAttribute** corresponding to a repeating reference to a model group definition (xsd:group) has its **name** set to that of the model group definition, instead of "group" as described in Section 9.6.1. The name is converted to a proper Java field name if necessary.

`<xsd:group name="content">`
  `<xsd:choice>`
   `...`
  `</xsd:choice>`
`</xsd:group>`
`...`
`<xsd:complexType name="...">`
  `<xsd:group ref="content"`
    `maxOccurs="unbounded"/>`
`</xsd:complexType>`
	EClass name="..."
	  EAttribute
	   name="content"
	   eType=".../Ecore#//EFeatureMapEntry"
	   upperBound=-1 *(unbounded)*
	   EAnnotation
	   source=".../ExtendedMetaData"
	   details="name"→"content:0",
	     "kind"→"group"

An ecore:name attribute can also be added to the group definition to override the **name** of the feature map **EAttribute**.

```
<xsd:group name="content"          EClass name="..."
    ecore:name="orders">             EAttribute
  <xsd:choice>                       name="orders"
    ...                              eType=".../Ecore#//EFeatureMapEntry"
  </xsd:choice>                      upperBound=-1 (unbounded)
</xsd:group>                         EAnnotation
...                                    source=".../ExtendedMetaData"
<xsd:complexType name="...">           details="name"→"orders:0",
  <xsd:group ref="content"               "kind"→"group"
      maxOccurs="unbounded"/>
</xsd:complexType>
```

Note that the same effect could be achieved with an `ecore:featureMap` attribute on the `xsd:choice` itself. If both are specified, the `ecore:featureMap` attribute takes precedence.

9.7 Wildcards

Element and attribute wildcards are represented in Ecore by feature map **EAttributes**, so as to be able to accommodate values of structural features corresponding to any elements and attributes.

9.7.1 Element Wildcard

An element wildcard (`xsd:any`) maps to a feature map **EAttribute** in the **EClass** corresponding to the complex type definition containing the wildcard. The **EAttribute** is initialized as follows:

- **name** = "any"
- **lowerBound** = 0 if the wildcard is nested in an `xsd:choice` model group; otherwise, the value of the `minOccurs` attribute multiplied by the `minOccurs` of any containing model groups
- **upperBound** = the value of the `maxOccurs` attribute multiplied by the `maxOccurs` of any containing model groups
- **eAnnotations** = an extended metadata **EAnnotation**

The case where **upperBound** is 1 is somewhat special. It is still implemented using a feature map, rather than a feature map entry; however, the feature map is permitted to contain just a single entry.

The **details** map of the **EAttribute**'s extended metadata **EAnnotation** contains the following entries:

○ **key** = "name", **value** = ":" followed by the feature ID of the **EAttribute**

○ **key** = "kind", **value** = "elementWildcard"

○ **key** = "wildcards", **value** = the value of the namespace attribute ("##any" by default)

○ **key** = "processing", **value** = the value of the processContents attribute ("strict" by default)

The value of the "processing" entry determines how to handle unrecognized elements when loading an instance document. If it is "strict", then they are not allowed (metadata must be available for all elements). If it is "lax" or "skip", then metadata will be demand created for such elements, and instances of the "AnyType" **EClass** (described in Section 9.5.1) will be used to represent their contents.

`<xsd:any namespace="##other"`
`    maxOccurs="unbounded"/>`
	EAttribute
	    name="any"
	    eType="…/Ecore#//EFeatureMapEntry"
	    lowerBound=1
	    upperBound=-1 *(unbounded)*
	    EAnnotation
	        source="…/ExtendedMetaData"
	        details="name"→":0",
	            "kind"→"elementWildcard",
	            "wildcards"→"##other",
	            "processing"→"strict"

If a wildcard is nested within a schema component for which a feature map would already be produced (e.g., if the containing complex type is mixed), the wildcard's corresponding feature map **EAttribute** then derives from the containing feature map.

9.7.2   Attribute Wildcard

An attribute wildcard (xsd:anyAttribute) also maps to a feature map **EAttribute** in the **EClass** corresponding to the complex type definition containing the wildcard. The **EAttribute** is initialized as follows:

○ **name** = "anyAttribute"

○ **lowerBound** = 0

○ **upperBound** = -1 (unbounded)

○ **eAnnotations** = an extended metadata **EAnnotation**

The **details** map of the extended metadata **EAnnotation** contains the following entries:

- ○ **key** = "name", **value** = ":" followed by the feature ID of the **EAttribute**
- ○ **key** = "kind", **value** = "attributeWildcard"
- ○ **key** = "wildcards", **value** = the value of the `namespace` attribute ("##any" by default)
- ○ **key** = "processing", **value** = the value of the `processContents` attribute ("strict" by default)

The value of the "processing" entry determines how to handle unrecognized attributes when loading an instance document. If it is "strict", then they are not allowed (metadata must be available for all attributes). If it is "lax" or "skip", then metadata will be demand created for such attributes.

`<xsd:anyAttribute processContents="lax"/>`	**EAttribute**
	   name="anyAttribute"
	   eType=".../Ecore#//EFeatureMapEntry"
	   lowerBound=0
	   upperBound=-1 *(unbounded)*
	   EAnnotation
	      source=".../ExtendedMetaData"
	      details="name"→":1",
	            "kind"→"attributeWildcard",
	            "wildcards"→"##any",
	            "processing"→"lax"

If a wildcard is nested within a schema component for which a feature map would already be produced (e.g., if the containing complex type is `mixed`), the wildcard's corresponding feature map **EAttribute** then derives from the containing feature map.

9.7.3 EMF Extensions

There is only one Ecore-namespace attribute applicable to wildcards: `ecore:name`, which can be used to set the **name** of a wildcard **EAttribute** to something other than the default value of "any" or "anyAttribute".

`<xsd:any ecore:name="extension"/>`	**EAttribute**
	   name="extension"
	   eType=".../Ecore#//EFeatureMapEntry"
	   ...

9.8   Annotations

XML Schema annotations map to **EAnnotation**s in Ecore. More specifically, each `xsd:documentation` and `xsd:appinfo` in a schema component's `xsd:annotation` maps to an **EAnnotation** in the **eAnnotations** list of the corresponding Ecore element. Non-schema attributes on schema components are similarly represented as **EAnnotation**s in Ecore.

9.8.1   Documentation

An `xsd:documentation` element in a schema component's `xsd:annotation` maps to a particular GenModel-sourced **EAnnotation**, allowing its contents to be generated into the Javadoc comments of the corresponding Java code. As described in Section 5.7.1, such an **EAnnotation** has as its **source** "http://www.eclipse.org/emf/2002/GenModel". Its **details** map contains a single entry:

o   **key** = "documentation", **value** = the contents of the `xsd:documentation` element

`<xsd:annotation>`
  `<xsd:documentation xml:lang="en">`
    `some information`
  `</xsd:documentation>`
`</xsd:annotation>`
	EAnnotation
	   source="…/emf/2002/GenModel"
	   details=
	      "documentation"→" some information "

A single **EAnnotation** is used to represent all the `xsd:documentation` elements in the `xsd:annotation` on a given schema component, should there be more than one. In this case, the value of the "documentation" entry is simply the concatenation of the individual documentation elements.

`<xsd:annotation>`
  `<xsd:documentation xml:lang="en">`
    `some information`
  `</xsd:documentation>`
  `<xsd:documentation xml:lang="en">`
    `more information`
  `</xsd:documentation>`
`</xsd:annotation>`
	EAnnotation
	   source="…/emf/2002/GenModel"
	   details=
	      "documentation"→" some information
	                          more information "

Note that the contents of each `xsd:documentation` element is stored exactly as is, without removing any line breaks or other whitespace.

9.8.2 *Appinfo*

An xsd:appinfo element in a schema component's xsd:annotation maps to an **EAnnotation** whose **source** is the same as the source attribute of the xsd:appinfo, or null if none is provided. The **EAnnotation**'s **details** map contains a single entry:

 O **key** = "appinfo", **value** = the contents of the xsd:appinfo element

`<xsd:annotation>`
 `<xsd:appinfo source="http://myURI">`
  `<info>hello</info>`
 `</xsd:appinfo>`
`</xsd:annotation>`
	EAnnotation
	 source="http://myURI"
	 details="appinfo"→"\<info>hello\</info>"

Alternatively, an ecore:key attribute can be used to specify an arbitrary key for the **details** entry:

`<xsd:annotation>`
 `<xsd:appinfo source="http://myURI"`
  `ecore:key="info">hello</xsd:appinfo>`
`</xsd:annotation>`
	EAnnotation
	 source="http://myURI"
	 details="info"→"hello"

A single **EAnnotation** is used to represent all the xsd:appinfo elements with a given source on a schema component, should there be more than one. If each such element uses ecore:key to specify a different key, then each value appears in a separate **details** entry. The values of xsd:appinfo elements with the same source and key are concatenated into a single value.

9.8.3 *Ignored Annotation*

An ecore:ignore attribute can be added to an xsd:annotation to suppress the **EAnnotation**s corresponding to all its xsd:documentation and xsd:appinfo children.

`<xsd:annotation ecore:ignore="true">`
 `...`
`</xsd:annotation>`
	*No **EAnnotation***

Alternatively, ecore:ignore can be specified on individual xsd:documentation or xsd:appinfo elements to suppress only their corresponding **EAnnotation**s.

9.8.4 Non-schema Attribute

An attribute from a namespace other than the XML Schema namespace maps to
an **EAnnotation** with **source** set to the the attribute's namespace.[6] The **details**
map of the **EAnnotation** contains a single entry:

○ **key** = the local name of the attribute, **value** = the value of the attribute

`<xsd:element xmlns:x="http://x"`
   `x:a="b" .../>`
	EAttribute ...
	  EAnnotation
	    source="http:///x"
	    details="a"→"b"

9.9 Predefined Schema Simple Types

Each predefined XML Schema simple type maps to a corresponding built-in
EDataType from the special XMLType model. This model defines a single package named "type" with namespace URI "http://www.eclipse.org/emf/2003/
XMLType", which contains these simple type counterparts. Table 9.1 details the
mapping between XML Schema simple types and XMLType **EDataTypes**, including the instance class for each **EDataType**. As pointed out in Section 9.5.4, the
model includes wrapper **EDataTypes** for all the schema primitive types. These are
provided for use in **EAttributes** corresponding to nillable elements.

Table 9.1 Schema Simple Types

Schema Type	EDataType	Instance Class
anySimpleType	AnySimpleType	java.lang.Object
anyURI	AnyURI	java.lang.String
base64Binary	Base64Binary	byte[]
boolean	Boolean	java.lang.boolean
boolean (nillable="true")	BooleanObject	java.lang.Boolean
byte	Byte	byte
byte (nillable="true")	ByteObject	java.lang.Byte

---

6. Since attributes from the Ecore namespace are used specifically to customize the mapping from XML
Schema to Ecore, they are not represented as an **EAnnotation** either.

Schema Type	EDataType	Instance Class
date	Date	java.lang.Object[7]
dateTime	DateTime	java.lang.Object
decimal	Decimal	java.math.BigDecimal
double	Double	double
double (nillable="true")	DoubleObject	java.lang.Double
duration	Duration	java.lang.Object
ENTITIES	ENTITIES	java.util.List
ENTITY	ENTITY	java.lang.String
float	Float	float
float (nillable="true")	FloatObject	java.lang.Float
gDay	GDay	java.lang.Object
gMonth	GMonth	java.lang.Object
gMonthDay	GMonthDay	java.lang.Object
gYear	GYear	java.lang.Object
gYearMonth	GYearMonth	java.lang.Object
hexBinary	HexBinary	byte[]
ID	ID	java.lang.String
IDREF	IDREF	java.lang.String
IDREFS	IDREFS	java.util.List
int	Int	int
int (nillable="true")	IntObject	java.lang.Integer
integer	Integer	java.math.BigInteger
language	Language	java.lang.String
long	Long	long
long (nillable="true")	LongObject	java.lang.Long

(continues)

---

7. Beginning in EMF 2.3, standard Java XML types (from the package `java.xml.datatype`) are used as the instance class for several of these data types. In particular, for **Date, DateTime, GDate, GMonth, GMonthDay, GYear, GYearMonth,** and **Time,** the instance class is `XMLGregorianCalendar`. The instance class of **Duration** is `Duration`. For **NOTATION** and **QName,** the instance class is `QName`. These XML types were introduced in Java 5.0, so they couldn't be used by EMF 2.2, which can run on Java 1.4, or earlier.

Table 9.1   Schema Simple Types (continued)

Schema Type	EDataType	Instance Class
Name	Name	java.lang.String
NCName	NCName	java.lang.String
negativeInteger	NegativeInteger	java.math.BigInteger
NMTOKEN	NMToken	java.lang.String
NMTOKENS	NMTOKENS	java.util.List
nonNegativeInteger	NonNegativeInteger	java.math.BigInteger
nonPositiveInteger	NonPositiveInteger	java.math.BigInteger
normalizedString	NormalizedString	java.lang.String
NOTATION	NOTATION	java.lang.Object
positiveInteger	PositiveInteger	java.math.BigInteger
QName	QName	java.lang.Object
short	Short	short
short (nillable="true")	ShortObject	java.lang.Short
string	String	java.lang.String
time	Time	java.lang.Object
token	Token	java.lang.String
unsignedByte	UnsignedByte	short
unsignedByte (nillable="true")	UnsignedByteObject	java.lang.Short
unsignedInt	UnsignedInt	long
unsignedInt (nillable="true")	UnsignedIntObject	java.lang.Long
unsignedLong	UnsignedLong	java.math.BigInteger
unsignedShort	UnsignedShort	int
unsignedShort (nillable="true")	UnsignedShortObject	java.lang.Integer

9.10   EMF Extensions

As described throughout this chapter, attributes from the Ecore namespace
("http://www.eclipse.org/emf/2002/Ecore") can be added to schema components
to customize the mapping to Ecore. The following attributes are recognized:

o `ecore:changeable` on an attribute or element declaration specifies the value of the **changeable** attribute of the corresponding **EStructuralFeature** (see Sections 9.4.8 and 9.5.10).

o `ecore:constraints` on a simple or complex type definition adds an **EAnnotation** declaring named constraints to the corresponding **EClassifier** (see Sections 9.2.6 and 9.3.6).

o `ecore:default` on an attribute declaration specifies the value of the **defaultValueLiteral** attribute of the corresponding **EAttribute** (see Section 9.4.8).

o `ecore:derived` on an attribute or element declaration specifies the value of the **derived** attribute of the corresponding **EStructuralFeature** (see Sections 9.4.8 and 9.5.10).

o `ecore:documentRoot` on a schema is used to change the name of the document root **EClass** from the default, "DocumentRoot" (see Section 9.1.3).

o `ecore:enum` on a simple type definition with enumeration facets determines whether the type maps to an **EEnum** or to an **EDataType** with the facets recorded in its extended metadata annotation (see Section 9.2.2).

o `ecore:featureMap` on a model group or reference, an element declaration or reference, or a complex type, can be used to force or block the use of a feature map in the corresponding Ecore representation. By default, feature maps are used to implement mixed complex types (see Section 9.3.5), substitution groups and abstract elements (see Section 9.5.9), repeating model groups (see Section 9.6.1), and wildcards (see Section 9.7).

o `ecore:ignore` on a global attribute or element, facet, annotation, documentation or appinfo determines whether the component is excluded from the corresponding Ecore representation (see Sections 9.4.6, 9.5.7, 9.2.1 and 9.8.3).

o `ecore:implements` on a complex type definition specifies additional **eSuperTypes** for the corresponding **EClass** (see Section 9.3.6).

o `ecore:instanceClass` on a simple or complex type definition specifies the **instanceClassName** (i.e., Java class) of the corresponding **EClassifier** (see Sections 9.2.6 and 9.3.6).

o `ecore:interface` on a complex type definition specifies the value of the **interface** attribute of the corresponding **EClass** (see Section 9.3.6).

o `ecore:key` on an `xsd:appinfo` annotation component specifies the key for the corresponding **EAnnotation details** entry (see Section 9.8.2).

○ `ecore:lowerBound` on an attribute or element declaration specifies the value of the **lowerBound** attribute of the corresponding **EStructuralFeature** (see Sections 9.4.8 and 9.5.10).

○ `ecore:many` on an attribute declaration with a list simple type determines whether it maps to a multi-valued **EAttribute** of a type corresponding to the list's item type (see Section 9.4.8).

○ `ecore:mixed` on a complex type definition that is not actually mixed specifies whether to use the feature-map-based Ecore representation for a mixed type anyway (see Section 9.3.5).

○ `ecore:name` on any named schema component or on a wildcard can be used to override the default **name** of the corresponding **ENamedElement** (see Sections 9.2.2, 9.2.6, 9.3.6, 9.4.8, 9.5.10, 9.6.2, and 9.7.3).

○ `ecore:nsPrefix` on a schema specifies the value of the **nsPrefix** attribute of the corresponding **EPackage** (see Section 9.1.5).

○ `ecore:opposite` on an element or attribute declaration that maps to an **EReference** specifies the element or attribute corresponding to the reference's **eOpposite** (see Sections 9.4.2 and 9.5.10).

○ `ecore:ordered` on an attribute or element declaration specifies the value of the **ordered** attribute of the corresponding **EStructuralFeature** (see Sections 9.4.8 and 9.5.10).

○ `ecore:package` on a schema specifies the fully qualified Java package name for the corresponding **EPackage** (see Section 9.1.5).

○ `ecore:reference` on an attribute or element declaration of type `xsd:IDREF`, `xsd:IDREFS`, or `xsd:anyURI` specifies the target type of the corresponding **EReference** (see Sections 9.4.2 and 9.5.3).

○ `ecore:resolveProxies` on an attribute or element declaration specifies the value of the **resolveProxies** attribute of the corresponding **EReference** (see Sections 9.4.8 and 9.5.10).

○ `ecore:serializable` on a simple type definition specifies the **serializable** attribute of the corresponding **EDataType** (see Section 9.2.6).

○ `ecore:suppressedGetVisibility` on an attribute or element declaration adds a GenModel-namespace **EAnnotation** to the corresponding **EStructuralFeature**, specifying that the feature's `get()` accessor should be suppressed (see Sections 9.4.8 and 9.5.10).

○ `ecore:suppressedIsSetVisibility` on an attribute or element declaration adds a GenModel-namespace **EAnnotation** to the corresponding **EStructuralFeature**, specifying that the feature's `isSet()` accessor should be suppressed (see Sections 9.4.8 and 9.5.10).

○ `ecore:suppressedSetVisibility` on an attribute or element declaration adds a GenModel-namespace **EAnnotation** to the corresponding **EStructuralFeature**, specifying that the feature's `set()` accessor should be suppressed (see Sections 9.4.8 and 9.5.10).

○ `ecore:suppressedUnsetVisibility` on an attribute or element declaration adds a GenModel-namespace **EAnnotation** to the corresponding **EStructuralFeature**, specifying that the feature's `unset()` accessor should be suppressed (see Sections 9.4.8 and 9.5.10).

○ `ecore:transient` on an attribute or element declaration specifies the value of the **transient** attribute of the corresponding **EStructuralFeature** (see Sections 9.4.8 and 9.5.10).

○ `ecore:unique` on an attribute or element declaration specifies the value of the **unique** attribute of the corresponding **EStructuralFeature** (see Sections 9.4.8 and 9.5.10).

○ `ecore:unsettable` on an attribute or element declaration specifies the value of the **unsettable** attribute of the corresponding **EStructuralFeature** (see Sections 9.4.8 and 9.5.10).

○ `ecore:upperBound` on an attribute or element declaration specifies the value of the **upperBound** attribute of the corresponding **EStructuralFeature** (see Sections 9.4.8 and 9.5.10).

○ `ecore:value` on an enumeration facet specifies the **value** attribute of the corresponding **EEnumLiteral** (see Section 9.2.2).

○ `ecore:volatile` on an attribute or element declaration specifies the value of the **volatile** attribute of the corresponding **EStructuralFeature** (see Sections 9.4.8 and 9.5.10).

These attributes are described in more detail in the referenced sections.

PART III

Using the EMF Generator

CHAPTER 10

EMF Generator Patterns

Arguably, the most valuable feature of EMF is its ability to generate high-quality implementation code. As a carefully written and well-tested base for application development, generated EMF code both speeds the development process and helps improve software quality. This model code includes type-safe interfaces and efficient implementations for creating, modifying, saving, and loading instances of modeled classes.

This chapter explores the various patterns EMF uses in generating Java code from the elements of a model. We discuss how modeling decisions affect the generated code, and give insights into how to design a model most effectively. To illustrate the code generation patterns, we will begin by drawing on features from the primer purchase order model, PrimerPO. However, as we discuss more advanced features that are not included in this model, we will borrow from the extended versions of it, ExtendedPO, ExtendedPO1, and ExtendedPO2. A summary of all the example models can be found in Appendix B.

As we have seen in the previous part of this book, a model can be specified in several ways. The examples in this chapter are discussed in terms of Ecore and accompanied by UML diagrams that illustrate the model constructs. The same code would be generated if we used annotated Java source or XML Schema to specify an equivalent model.

The code generated to implement an Ecore package is, by default, organized into two Java packages: one contains the set of Java interfaces that together represent the client interface to the model, and the other contains corresponding implementation classes. A third optional utility package can be created containing a switch class and an adapter factory, which can be used to attach adapters to the model classes.

In general, an interface and an implementation class are generated for each class in the model; enumerated types are implemented by a single class. In addition, an interface and an implementation are created for each package, and for the factory that creates instances of the classes defined in it.

In addition to Java code, the EMF generator also produces four other files that support the use of the model code as an Eclipse plug-in. As we described in Chapter 1, two manifest files, *META-INF/MANIFEST.MF* and *plugin.xml*, identify the model plug-in to the platform and declare its interconnections to other plug-ins. A *plugin.properties* file contains translatable strings for use by the plug-in. Finally, a *build.properties* file contains information that is used to guide the process of building the plug-in.

10.1   Modeled Classes

Classes are the essential elements of any EMF model. As we saw in Chapter 5, we model a class in Ecore with an instance of **EClass**. The generated code for a class defines a number of methods that provide access to the attributes and references belonging to the class, as well as methods corresponding to its operations. Details of the generated code depend not only on these structural and behavioral features, but also on the attributes of the **EClass** itself.

10.1.1   Interfaces and Implementation Classes

For each class in a model, the EMF code generator usually produces both a Java interface and an implementation class. Consider the **PurchaseOrder** class in the PrimerPO model. For the moment, let's ignore the attributes and references that belong to it, which leaves us with just the class pictured in Figure 10.1.

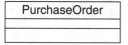

Figure 10.1   A simple model class.

By default, the generated interface for **PurchaseOrder** looks like this:

```
public interface PurchaseOrder extends EObject
{
  ...
}
```

Because the **PurchaseOrder** model class has no explicit base class, the generated PurchaseOrder interface extends the EObject interface. EObject is the

EMF equivalent of `java.lang.Object`; that is, the base of every EMF class. `EObject` and its corresponding implementation class `EObjectImpl` provide a lightweight base for **PurchaseOrder**'s participation in EMF, supporting reflection, notification, and persistence.

The implementation class for **PurchaseOrder** is called `PurchaseOrderImpl`, and it is declared as follows:

```
public class PurchaseOrderImpl extends EObjectImpl
  implements PurchaseOrder
{
  ...
}
```

We will discuss how the use of inheritance affects the interface and class declarations in Section 10.6.

By default, the interfaces for all **EClass**es modeled together in an **EPackage** are generated into the same Java package. The corresponding implementation classes are generated into a subpackage of that package, named `impl`.

10.1.2 Accessor Methods

The code that is generated for a class includes accessor methods that allow us to get and set values for each of the various attributes and references that belong to the class.

Recall that the **PurchaseOrder** class has two simple attributes: **comment** of type **String**, and **orderDate** of type **Date**. Among others, it also has a reference, **items**, to class **Item**. This is illustrated in Figure 10.2.

Figure 10.2 A class with attributes and references.

The generated interface for **PurchaseOrder** looks like this:

```
public interface PurchaseOrder extends EObject
{
  String getComment();
  void setComment(String value);
```

```
   Date getOrderDate();
   void setOrderDate(Date value);
   ...

   EList getItems();
}
```

This interface contains accessor methods that permit access to and modification of the value of each modeled attribute and reference. At a minimum, there is a method that gets the value of the structural feature. Depending on its multiplicity and whether it is changeable and unsettable, you might also see methods that set a value, unset the feature, and check whether a value has been set.

It is also possible to make any structural feature partially or wholly invisible by suppressing one or more of these accessors from the interface. This is done by attaching a GenModel-sourced annotation to the feature, the details of which specify exactly which accessors are to be suppressed. Such annotations, described fully in Section 5.7.1, do not affect the generation of accessors in the implementation class at all.

Each generated implementation class includes implementations of the accessor methods defined in the corresponding interface, plus some other methods required by the EMF's runtime framework. Class `PurchaseOrderImpl` implements the accessors for **comment, orderDate,** and **items:**

```
public class PurchaseOrderImpl extends EObjectImpl
   implements PurchaseOrder
{
   public String getComment() {
      ...
   }

   public void setComment(String newComment) {
      ...
   }

   public Date getOrderDate() {
      ...
   }

   public void setOrderDate(Date newOrderDate) {
      ...
   }

   public EList getItems() {
      ...
   }

   // etc...
}
```

Again, the particular method implementation patterns depend on the definitions of the modeled features. Sections 10.2 and 10.3 describe all the important accessor patterns and how Ecore modeling constructs map to and control them.

10.1.3 Abstract Classes

As in Java, an Ecore class is made abstract to forbid its own instantiation, while allowing other classes to extend it. An abstract class is modeled by an **EClass** with its **abstract** attribute set to true. This is reflected in the generated code in two ways. The first and most obvious impact is that the `class` statement for the implementation class includes the `abstract` keyword. The other is that the generated factory, which we will discuss in Section 10.8, does not include a `create()` method for the class.

10.1.4 Interfaces

Rather than generating implementations for all the classes in a model, it might be desirable to produce only Java interfaces for some of them and let any other classes that inherit from them implement the inherited features themselves. Such an interface-only class is modeled by an **EClass** with its **interface** attribute set to true and no **instanceClass** specified.

If an **instanceClass** is specified, a Java interface will not be generated either. Instead, the class will be considered a proxy for an external interface that already exists, in the same way that data types, which we discuss in Section 10.2.2, are used as proxies for external Java classes. This technique is useful for adding external Java interfaces to a generated interface's `extends` clause, as we see in Section 10.6.3. As an alternative to modeling proxy interfaces explicitly, you can instead specify additional Java interfaces to be extended right in the code with an `@extends` tag, as we will see in Section 10.11.

Like the abstract classes described in the previous section, interfaces cannot be instantiated, so the generator does not include a `create()` method in the factory.

10.2 Attributes

As described previously, the generated interface and implementation class that correspond to an **EClass** include one or more accessor methods for each **EAttribute** that the **EClass** contains. The number and nature of these accessors depend on the type of the attribute, as defined by the **EAttribute**'s **eType**, as well as the values of several of the **EAttribute**'s own attributes. They specify whether an attribute can contain multiple values, what the default value of the attribute will be, whether to provide storage for the attribute's value, whether it can be changed, and whether it can be unset. The following subsections describe how these settings affect the generated code patterns.

10.2.1 Simple Attributes

We describe an attribute as *simple* when it is single-valued and its type is an Ecore-defined data type that corresponds to a basic Java language type like `int`, `boolean`, or `String`.[1] Our purchase order example includes several simple attributes. Let's look at the **comment** attribute in class **PurchaseOrder**, which is illustrated in Figure 10.3.

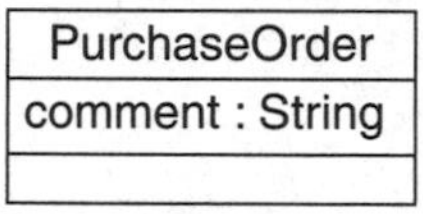

PurchaseOrder
comment : String

Figure 10.3 A simple attribute.

When we generate code for this class, `get()` and `set()` methods for **comment** are included in the `PurchaseOrder` interface:

```
String getComment();
void setComment(String value);
```

Note that the generator departs from this naming pattern only for attributes with `boolean` type. To follow the convention for Java bean properties, the name of the first accessor for such an attribute begins with "is" rather than "get".

We now turn to the implementation of simple attributes. The **comment** attribute is implemented by the following code that is generated in `PurchaseOrderImpl`:

```
protected static final String COMMENT_EDEFAULT = null;
protected String comment = COMMENT_EDEFAULT;

public String getComment()
{
  return comment;
}
```

---

1. These types are modeled in Ecore by **EInt**, **EBoolean**, and **EString**, respectively.

```
public void setComment(String newComment)
{
  String oldComment = comment;
  comment = newComment;
  if (eNotificationRequired())
    eNotify(new ENotificationImpl(this, Notification.SET,
                          PPOPackage.PURCHASE_ORDER__COMMENT,
                          oldComment, comment));
}
```

The generated `get()` method is optimally efficient. It simply returns an appropriately typed instance variable that represents the attribute.

The `set()` method is slightly more complicated. In addition to setting the `comment` instance variable, it needs to send change notification to any observers that might be listening to the object by calling the `eNotify()` method. The notification object, an instance of `ENotificationImpl`, specifies the notifier (`this`), the type of notification (set), the structural feature involved,[2] and the old and new values.

To optimize the case where there are no observers (e.g., in a batch application), the construction of the notification object and the call to `eNotify()` are guarded by an `eNotificationRequired()` test. The default implementation of `eNotificationRequired()` simply checks if there are any adapters[3] attached to the object. Therefore, when EMF objects are used without observers, the call to `eNotificationRequired()` amounts to nothing more than an efficient `null` pointer check. Considering that this can be inlined by a JIT compiler, there is very little overhead for the benefit of being able to participate in the EMF notification framework.

10.2.2 Data Type Attributes

As mentioned previously, all the classes generated from an EMF model, such as `PurchaseOrder` and `Item`, derive from the EMF base class `EObject`. However, models can also refer to Java types that are not `EObjects`.

We have just seen how attributes can use Ecore's built-in data types for Java types like `int` and `String`. However, there are a host of other simple Java classes that could be represented as unstructured data types in Ecore.

---

2. `PPOPackage.PURCHASE_ORDER_COMMENT` is the feature ID for the **comment** attribute. We describe feature IDs, which are defined by the generated package interface, in Section 10.7.1.

3. Recall from Chapter 2 that EMF refers to all observers as adapters because the same `Adapter` interface is used to listen for notifications and to extend the behavior of a type without subclassing it.

For example, it could be useful to represent IP addresses in a network-related model using `java.net.InetAddress`. More commonly, `java.util.Date` is useful for representing dates and times. Whatever the Java type, we must define and use an **EDataType** to represent it in our model.

To illustrate, let's look at the **Date** data type in PrimerPO. In UML, we use a class with the <<datatype>> stereotype to define it, as illustrated in Figure 10.4.

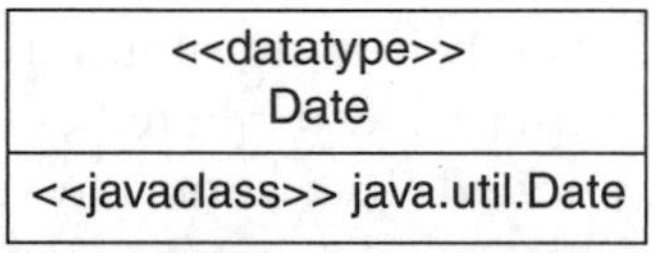

```
+---------------------------------+
|          <<datatype>>           |
|             Date                |
+---------------------------------+
| <<javaclass>> java.util.Date    |
+---------------------------------+
```

Figure 10.4   A data type definition.

A data type is simply a named element in the model that acts as a proxy for the actual Java class, in this case `java.util.Date`. The Java class is specified by the data type's **instanceClass** attribute; it is represented in UML by an attribute with the <<javaclass>> stereotype, whose name is the fully qualified Java class name. Attributes of type **Date**, like the **orderDate** attribute in class **PurchaseOrder**, can then be defined as illustrated in Figure 10.5.

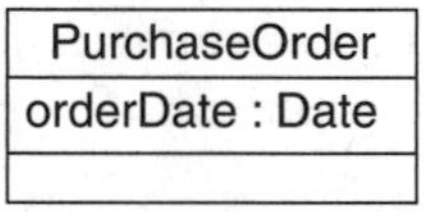

```
+---------------------------+
|       PurchaseOrder       |
+---------------------------+
|    orderDate : Date       |
+---------------------------+
|                           |
+---------------------------+
```

Figure 10.5   An attribute use of a data type.

When we generate code for this class, the accessors for **orderDate** appear like this in the `PurchaseOrder` interface:

```
Date getOrderDate();
void setOrderDate(Date value);
```

As you can see, **orderDate** is treated like any other attribute, and in fact, the generated implementations of these methods are also just like those of simple attributes. As we saw in Chapter 5, all data types, including the Java language types like `int`, `boolean`, and `String`, are modeled in Ecore as instances of **EDataType**. The only special thing about the language types is that their corresponding data types are predefined in the Ecore model, so they don't need to be redefined in every model that uses them.

A data type definition has one other effect on the generated code. Because a data type represents some arbitrary class, a generic serializer and parser, like the default XMI serializer, has no way of knowing how to save the state of an attribute of that type. Should it call `toString()`? That's a reasonable default, but EMF requires more flexibility, so it generates two more methods for every data type that is defined in a modeled package. In our example, they are as follows:

```
/**
 * @generated
 */
public String convertDateToString(EDataType eDataType,
                                    Object instanceValue)
{
  return super.convertToString(eDataType, instanceValue);
}

/**
 * @generated
 */
public Date createDateFromString(EDataType eDataType,
                                  String initialValue)
{
  return (Date)super.createFromString(eDataType, initialValue);
}
```

These methods convert an instance of the data type into a string and back. They are included in the implementation of the factory that is generated for the package to support EMF's standard factory mechanism for the serialization of data type values, which we will discuss in Section 10.8.

As generated, these methods simply delegate to their superclass for default implementations. In the usual case, `convertToString()` just calls `toString()` on the instance, and `createFromString()` tries, using Java reflection, to call a string constructor or, failing that, a static `valueOf()` method. There are a number of special cases that must also be covered by the default implementations, so they are actually somewhat complex and not terribly efficient.

Typically, you should replace these implementations with something more appropriate. For example:

```
/**
 * @generated
 */
public String convertDateToString(EDataType eDataType,
                                    Object instanceValue)
{
  return instanceValue.toString();
}
```

Note that the `@generated` Javadoc comment preceding the method has been removed. As you will see in Section 10.11, this preserves the changes you make to this method should you ever regenerate the code.

If you look closely at the list of Java language types in Section 5.8, you might notice that Ecore already provides an **EDate** data type that can be used to represent `java.util.Date`. So why did we go to the trouble of defining a new data type in our model?

The reason is that Ecore defines **EDate**'s conversion to and from string form in its factory implementation, and we might wish to do this conversion differently. By modeling our own **Date** data type, we are able to implement the preceding two methods and control the conversion exactly. We will look more closely at this topic in Chapter 13.

10.2.3   *Enumerated Type Attributes*

An enumerated type defines an explicit list of values, called literals, that attributes of that type are allowed to assume. Enumerated types are commonly used as the types of attributes that represent status or kind and are implemented in EMF using the Type-safe Enum pattern, described by Joshua Bloch in *Effective Java Programming Language Guide.* [4][4]

ExtendedPO1 introduces an enumerated type attribute called **status** to **PurchaseOrder**, shown in Figure 10.6.

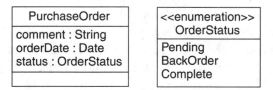

Figure 10.6   The **status** enumerated type attribute.

The following accessors are produced for **status** in the `PurchaseOrder` interface:

```
OrderStatus getStatus();
void setStatus(OrderStatus value);
```

---

4. This pattern is also discussed in the August 7, 2001, edition, of Sun's *JDC Tech Tips*, available at *http://java.sun.com/developer/JDCTechTips/2001/tt0807.html#tip2.*

These generated methods use a type-safe enum class called OrderStatus. This class defines static constants for the enumeration values and other convenience methods like this:

```
public final class OrderStatus extends AbstractEnumerator
{
  public static final int PENDING = 0;
  public static final int BACK_ORDER = 1;
  public static final int COMPLETE = 2;

  public static final OrderStatus PENDING_LITERAL =
          new OrderStatus(PENDING, "Pending", "Pending");
  public static final OrderStatus BACK_ORDER_LITERAL =
          new OrderStatus(BACK_ORDER, "BackOrder", "BackOrder");
  public static final OrderStatus COMPLETE_LITERAL =
          new OrderStatus(COMPLETE, "Complete", "Complete");

  public static OrderStatus get(String literal)
  {
    ...
  }

  public static OrderStatus getByName(String name)
  {
    ...
  }

  public static OrderStatus get(int value)
  {
    ...
  }

  private OrderStatus(int value, String name, String literal)
  {
    super(value, name, literal);
  }
}
```

As shown, the enum class includes static int constants for the enumeration values as well as static constants for the enumeration literal objects. The int constants have the same names as the model's literal names.[5] The literal constants have the same names with _LITERAL appended.

These constants provide convenient access to the literals when, for example, setting the status of a purchase order:

```
po.setStatus(OrderStatus.PENDING_LITERAL);
```

---

5. To conform to proper Java programming style, the static constant names are converted to uppercase if the modeled enumeration literal names are not already uppercase.

Notice that the constructor for OrderStatus is private. Therefore, the only instances of the enum class that will ever exist are the ones used for the static fields PENDING_LITERAL, BACK_ORDER_LITERAL, and COMPLETE_LITERAL. As a result, equality comparisons using equals() are never needed. Literals can always be reliably compared using the simpler and more efficient == operator, like this:

```
po.getStatus() == OrderStatus.PENDING_LITERAL
```

However, when performing repeated comparisons, it is better to use the int value in a switch statement:

```
switch (po.getStatus().value())
{
  case OrderStatus.PENDING:
    // do something...
    break;
  case OrderStatus.BACK_ORDER:
    ...
}
```

For situations in which only the literal string, value, or name is available, the enum class also includes convenient get() and getByName() methods that can be used to retrieve the corresponding literal object.

10.2.4 Multi-valued Attributes

In some cases, it is appropriate for an attribute to hold several values rather than a single one. For example, the ExtendedPO2 model introduces a class to model addresses outside of the United States, called **GlobalAddress**. To accommodate the variety of address formats used globally, this class includes an attribute, called **location**, with a value that is an arbitrary number of strings. In Ecore terms, the **EAttribute** has a **lowerBound** of zero and unbounded **upperBound**. In UML, we indicate the bounds in a stereotype on the attribute, as in Figure 10.7.

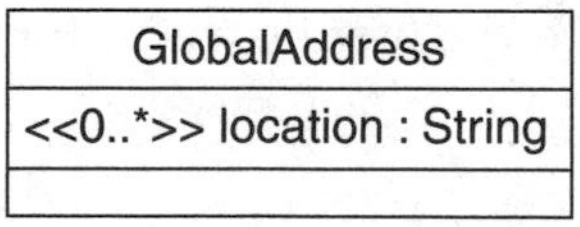

GlobalAddress
<<0..*>> location : String

Figure 10.7 A multi-valued attribute.

The generated `GlobalAddress` interface includes a single `get()` accessor that returns a list:

```
EList getLocation();
```

Notice that this method returns an `EList` as opposed to a `java.util.List`. Actually, the two are almost the same: `EList` is an EMF subclass of `List`, only adding two `move()` methods to the API. From a client perspective, you may consider it a standard Java list.

Some might wonder why EMF lists need to support move directly, when such an operation can be performed using the standard list API by removing an element and then adding it back at a specific location. The reason is that a move can be considered semantically different and, in particular, this difference may impact how an adapter should react to such a change.

The generated implementation in `GlobalAddressImpl` looks like this:

```
protected EList location = null;

public EList getLocation()
{
  if (location == null)
  {
    location = new EDataTypeUniqueEList(String.class, this,
                       EPO2Package.GLOBAL_ADDRESS__LOCATION);
  }
  return location;
}
```

The `EDataTypeUniqueEList` framework utility class implements a list that can contain only elements of the specified type—in this case, `String.class`—and prevents a single value from occurring in it more than once. It also automatically participates in EMF's notification framework, sending change notifications using the supplied feature ID, `EPO2Package.GLOBAL_ADDRESS__LOCA-TION`. We will discuss feature IDs further in Section 10.7.1.

If we did not want to enforce the restriction that each object in the attribute must be unique, we would set the **unique** attribute of the **EAttribute** to false, and `EDataTypeEList` would be used as the `EList` implementation.

An alternate Java realization for multi-valued attributes uses array-typed `get()` and `set()` accessor methods, instead of an `EList`. To use this approach for the previous example, we would need to define the **location** attribute to be single-valued, but of type **StringArray**. We would also need to define this data type as representing the Java type `String[]`. The updated model is illustrated in Figure 10.8.

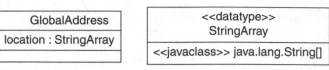

Figure 10.8 An array type attribute.

Based on this model, **location** accessors in the generated `GlobalAddress` interface would look like this:

```
String[] getLocation();
void setLocation(String[] value);
```

Their implementation in `GlobalAddressImpl` would use the standard simple attribute pattern.

Having defined a new data type, we would also need to implement the generated factory's `createFromString()` and `convertToString()` methods to be able to serialize its instances. Note that a string form of this data type would have to be a concatenation of the items in the array, with some sort of delimitation—essentially imposing structure on the serialized form, which should be the job of the resource. This approach also thwarts the notification framework, sending notifications only when the reference to the whole array is changed—when growing the array, for example—and not when items in it are set. For these reasons, the use of the array approach is discouraged for object types like `String`. In general, EMF's normal list-based mechanism for multi-valued attributes is preferable. Array data types are, however, more appropriate for primitive Java types, such as `char[]` or `byte[]`. Indeed, Ecore even provides a built-in **ByteArray** data type for this purpose.

10.2.5   Default Values

All single-valued attributes have well-defined default values. The default value for each attribute appears in the generated code as an appropriately typed, static, final field whose name is constructed by capitalizing the attribute name and appending to it the "_EDEFAULT" suffix.

The default value can always be specified in the model, but if one is not explicitly chosen, EMF automatically picks a value appropriate to the type of the attribute. For Java language types, this is the default defined by Java: `false` for `boolean`, zero for numeric primitive types, and `null` for object types. For an enumerated type, it is the first literal value that it defines.

We already saw an example of this in Section 10.2.1, where the default for the **comment** attribute on the **PurchaseOrder** class was automatically chosen to be `null`. We saw that the `PurchaseOrderImpl` implementation class includes the following:

```
protected static final String COMMENT_EDEFAULT = null;
```

If we want to override this choice, we can update the model to specify an explicit default, as in Figure 10.9.

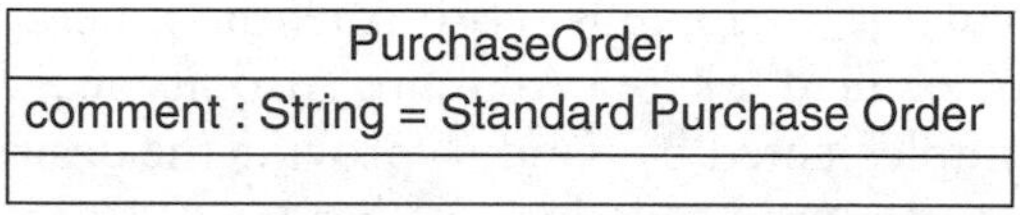

PurchaseOrder
comment : String = Standard Purchase Order

Figure 10.9   An attribute with default value.

Then, the declaration of `COMMENT_EDEFAULT` would look like this:

```
protected static final String COMMENT_EDEFAULT =
   "Standard Purchase Order";
```

For non-string simple attributes, this generated initialization statement constructs an appropriate default primitive value or object from the specified string. For attributes whose type is a user-modeled data type, the initialization statement calls the `createFromString()` method in the appropriate generated factory to perform the string-to-value conversion, as described in Section 10.2.2.

10.2.6   Volatile Attributes

As we have seen, the default implementation for an attribute uses a field to hold its value at runtime. This is because, by default, attributes are non-volatile; a volatile attribute is one for which no storage is set aside at runtime.

In ExtendedPO2, the **PurchaseOrder** class includes an attribute called **totalAmount,** which represents the total value of all the items in the order. The class is illustrated in Figure 10.10.

Notice that **totalAmount** is preceded by a "/", which indicates that the attribute is derived. As discussed in Section 5.3, it is very common for volatile attributes to be derived as well. In this case, no storage is required for **totalAmount** because its value can be calculated by taking the sum of the costs of all the items associated with it. Therefore, we declare the **totalAmount** attribute to be volatile and simply compute it whenever it is needed. This saves storage and avoids the complication of having to update the value every time we add to or remove from the **items** list or modify an **Item** in it.

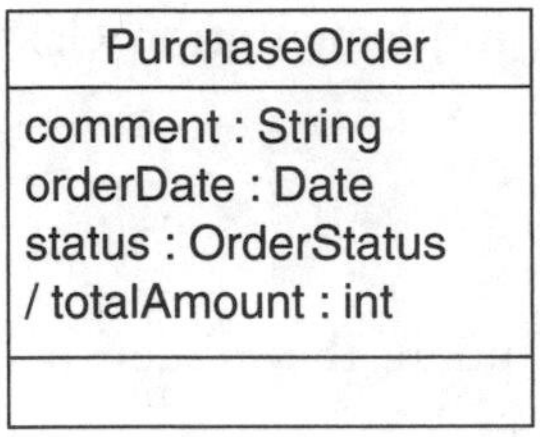

```
┌─────────────────────────────┐
│        PurchaseOrder        │
├─────────────────────────────┤
│ comment : String            │
│ orderDate : Date            │
│ status : OrderStatus        │
│ / totalAmount : int         │
├─────────────────────────────┤
│                             │
└─────────────────────────────┘
```

Figure 10.10   The computable **totalAmount** attribute.

Because the **EAttribute**'s **volatile** attribute is set to true, the generated implementation class does not include a field for **totalAmount**. Also, its accessor methods are stubs that need to be implemented by hand to provide the desired behavior. To indicate that the implementation is missing, the generated stubs throw an `UnsupportedOperationException`. The `getTotalAmount()` method looks like this:

```
/**
 * @generated
 */
public int getTotalAmount()
{
  // TODO: implement this method to return the 'Total Amount'
  // attribute
  // Enusre that you remove the @generated or mark it @generated NOT
  throw new UnsupportedOperationException();
}
```

As the comment indicates, we are now expected to remove or mark the `@generated` tag and replace this implementation with one that does the appropriate calculation. We will discuss the use of `@generated` tags in Section 10.11, and look at the implementation for this attribute in Chapter 13.

10.2.7   Non-Changeable Attributes

By default, every attribute is changeable, which means that its value can be set externally. For single-valued attributes, this means that a `set()` method is generated. We can suppress the generation of this method by setting the **changeable** attribute of an **EAttribute** to false.

Often, volatile attributes should be non-changeable as well. A good example is the **totalAmount** attribute discussed in the previous section. Because its value is computed from the values of several other structural features, it doesn't make much sense to be able to set it explicitly. Therefore, we make it non-changeable, and no `setTotalAmount()` method is generated in either the interface or the implementation class.

Making an attribute non-changeable has an impact on persistence that many people do not initially anticipate. When a resource is loading objects, the resource has no special way to initialize each object; it simply sets the attributes according to what is in the persistent form. However, there is no way to set a non-changeable attribute, so the value of such an attribute cannot be restored. As a result, non-changeable attributes should usually be marked transient, as well, so they are not involved in persistence at all.

A less dramatic alternative to making an attribute non-changeable is simply to suppress its set accessor from the interface, using a GenModel-sourced annotation, as described in Section 5.7.1. With this approach, the `set()` method is still generated in the implementation, and resources can invoke it using EMF reflection.

Note that the values of multi-valued attributes can always be changed using their list interface. Because `set()` methods are never generated for multi-valued attributes, making such an attribute non-changeable has no effect on code generation.

10.2.8 Unsettable Attributes

The set of valid values for an attribute is determined by its type. This set can be limited to a large but finite number of primitive values or a relatively small number of enumerated type literals, or it can include `null` and a conceptually unbounded number of object references.[6]

In any case, it is sometimes desirable to allow attributes to be unset; that is, to have no value set. This state is distinguishable from that of being set to any other value, including the attribute's default value. Such attributes are modeled in Ecore by an **EAttribute** with **unsettable** set to true.

For example, consider the **Item** class in Figure 10.11.

Figure 10.11 The Item class and its attributes.

---

6. In reality, the number of possible objects is limited by the finite amount of memory available.

Suppose that we wish to distinguish between an item that has not yet been shipped and one that could not be shipped because it has been discontinued. We can do this by making **shipDate** unsettable. Before an item has been shipped, its **shipDate** will be unset. If it cannot be shipped, we will set its value to null.

The following additional methods are generated into the Item interface to provide the unsettable functionality of the attribute:

```
void unsetShipDate();
boolean isSetShipDate();
```

The unset() method changes the attribute's value back to its default and marks the attribute as being in the unset state. The isSet() method tests whether the attribute has been set since it was created or last unset.

By default, these methods are implemented in ItemImpl like this:

```
protected boolean shipDateESet = false;

public void unsetShipDate()
{
  Date oldShipDate = shipDate;
  boolean oldShipDateESet = shipDateESet;
  shipDate = SHIP_DATE_EDEFAULT;
  shipDateESet = false;
  if (eNotificationRequired())
    eNotify(new ENotificationImpl(this, Notification.UNSET, ... ,
                                  oldShipDateESet));
}

public boolean isSetShipDate()
{
  return shipDateESet;
}
```

A boolean field is used to keep track of whether the attribute is set. It is tested by the isSet() method and set to false by unset(). The set() pattern is also changed slightly to set this field to true:

```
public void setShipDate(Date newShipDate)
{
  Date oldShipDate = shipDate;
  shipDate = newShipDate;
  boolean oldShipDateESet = shipDateESet;
  shipDateESet = true;
  if (eNotificationRequired())
    eNotify(new ENotificationImpl(this, Notification.SET, ... ,
                                  !oldShipDateESet));
}
```

Notice that unsetting an attribute sends a change notification to any registered listeners in exactly the same manner as setting it. In both of these cases, the `ENotificationImpl` instance is created with an additional constructor argument, indicating whether the "unset state" has changed. The notification's `isTouch()` method is affected by this value.

Multi-valued, unsettable attributes are implemented using subclasses of their usual `EList` implementations that provide `unset()` and `isSet()` methods. Unsetting a multi-valued attribute clears its values and marks it as unset. Adding back any values, or even just calling `clear()` on the list, marks it as set.

Making an attribute unsettable necessarily incurs a storage cost: the size of an instance of the generated class is increased by the extra field that tracks whether the attribute is set. However, this cost can be minimized by enabling the boolean flags pattern described in Section 10.10.1. As we will see, it is often worth using this alternate pattern when dealing with large numbers of unsettable attributes.

10.3   References

As described in Section 10.1.2, the interface and implementation class generated for an **EClass** include at least one accessor method for each of its **EReferences**. The number and nature of these accessors are determined by the **eType** of the reference (i.e., the **EClass** being referenced) as well as the presence or absence of an opposite reference and the values of several of the **EReference**'s own attributes. These attributes specify the multiplicity of the reference, whether the reference represents a containment relationship, and whether it should automatically resolve object proxies. In addition, several additional attributes affect the choice of code patterns for a reference in exactly the same way as for an attribute, including those that determine whether to provide storage for its value, whether it can be changed, and whether it can be unset. The following subsections detail the effects of these settings on the generated code patterns.

10.3.1   One-Way References

In ExtendedPO1, a reference is introduced to link a purchase order to a related previous order. This one-way reference, named **previousOrder**, belongs to the **PurchaseOrder** class, and its type is also **PurchaseOrder**. It is illustrated in Figure 10.12.

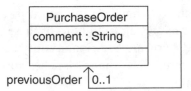

Figure 10.12   A simple one-way reference.

The `PurchaseOrder` interface that is generated for this class includes the following `get()` and `set()` methods:

```
PurchaseOrder getPreviousOrder();
void setPreviousOrder(PurchaseOrder value);
```

Because the **previousOrder** reference is one-way, the implementation of the `setPreviousOrder()` method looks much like the simple `set()` methods for attributes that we saw earlier:

```
protected PurchaseOrder previousOrder = null;

public void setPreviousOrder(PurchaseOrder newPreviousOrder)
{
  PurchaseOrder oldPreviousOrder = previousOrder;
  previousOrder = newPreviousOrder;
  if (eNotificationRequired())
    eNotify(new ENotificationImpl(this, ... ));
}
```

First, notice that there is no static final field specifying a default value—the default value of every reference is `null`.

Beyond that, the only difference from, say, `setComment()` is that the type of the reference is also a modeled class, so we are passing a pointer to another `EObject`.

The implementation of `getPreviousOrder()` is a little more complicated, however, because the previous order might be serialized in a different resource from the referencing order. Because the EMF persistence framework uses a lazy loading scheme, the resource containing the referenced object might not have been loaded when the accessor is first invoked. In such a case, a field like `previousOrder` would refer to a proxy for the object, instead of the object itself. To handle this case, `getPreviousOrder()` is generated like this:

```
public PurchaseOrder getPreviousOrder()
{
  if (previousOrder != null && previousOrder.eIsProxy())
  {
    InternalEObject oldPreviousOrder =
      (InternalEObject)previousOrder;
    previousOrder = (PurchaseOrder)eResolveProxy(oldPreviousOrder);
    if (previousOrder != oldPreviousOrder)
    {
      if (eNotificationRequired()) eNotify(
        new ENotificationImpl(this, Notification.RESOLVE, ...));
    }
  }
  return previousOrder;
}
```

Instead of simply returning the `previousOrder` instance variable, we first call the `EObject`'s `eIsProxy()` method to check if the reference is a proxy, and, if so, call `eResolveProxy()`, which uses the static framework method `EcoreUtil.resolve()` to resolve it. This method attempts to load first the referenced object's document and then the object itself, using the URI specified by the proxy. If successful, it returns the resolved object. If, however, the document fails to load, it just returns the proxy again.[7]

In some circumstances, you might be able to optimize the `get()` method by omitting the code that resolves proxies. This would result in a simpler `get()` method, just like `getComment()`. We will discuss this optimization in Section 10.3.4.

10.3.2 Bidirectional References

In the previous section, we saw how proxy resolution affects the `get()` pattern for one-way references. Now we can look at how the `set()` pattern changes when an association is bidirectional. Consider the bidirectional association between ExtendedPO1's **PurchaseOrder** and **Customer** classes shown in Figure 10.13.

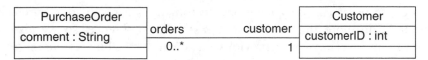

Figure 10.13 A bidirectional association.

---

7. Document loading and proxy resolution are discussed in detail in Chapter 15.

The absence of an arrowhead on either end of the association line indicates its bidirectionality. In Ecore, this is modeled as a reference from **PurchaseOrder** to **Customer** named **customer** and another reference from **Customer** to **PurchaseOrder** named **orders**. These two **EReferences** have each other as their **eOpposite**s.

In the interfaces generated for the two classes, we find the same accessors that we would if these were two independent, one-way references. In `PurchaseOrder`, for example, we find the following:

```
Customer getCustomer();
void setCustomer(Customer value);
```

The implementation of `getCustomer()` in `PurchaseOrderImpl` follows exactly the same pattern as the one-way `getPreviousOrder()` method described in the previous section, but `setCustomer()` looks quite different:

```
public void setCustomer(Customer newCustomer)
{
  if (newCustomer != customer)
  {
    NotificationChain msgs = null;
    if (customer != null)
      msgs =
        ((InternalEObject)customer).eInverseRemove(this, ..., msgs);
    if (newCustomer != null)
      msgs =
        ((InternalEObject)newCustomer).eInverseAdd(this, ..., msgs);
    msgs = basicSetCustomer(newCustomer, msgs);
    if (msgs != null) msgs.dispatch();
  }
  else if (eNotificationRequired()) // send "touch" notification
    eNotify(new ENotificationImpl(this, Notification.SET, ...));
}
```

As you can see, when setting a bidirectional reference like **customer**, the other end of the reference needs to be set as well, by calling `eInverseAdd()`. Notice that the **customer** reference is modeled with multiplicity-1, meaning that a purchase order can only have one customer. As a result, this purchase order cannot be in more than one customer's **orders** reference, so we also need to remove the inverse of any previous customer by calling `eInverseRemove()`. Finally, we set the **customer** reference itself by calling another generated method, `basicSetCustomer()`, which looks like this:

```
public NotificationChain basicSetCustomer(Customer newCustomer,
                                          NotificationChain msgs)
{
  Customer oldCustomer = customer;
  customer = newCustomer;
  if (eNotificationRequired())
  {
    ENotificationImpl notification =
      new ENotificationImpl(this, Notification.SET, ... );
    if (msgs == null) msgs = notification;
    else msgs.add(notification);
  }
  return msgs;
}
```

This method looks very similar to the one-way reference `set()` method, except that the notification gets added to the `msgs` argument, instead of being fired directly. Between the `eInverseAdd()`, the `eInverseRemove()`, and this `basicSet()`, `setCustomer()` can generate three different notifications. In other situations, this could be as many as four. A `NotificationChain` is used to collect all these individual notifications so their firing can be deferred until after all the state changes have been made. Multiple notifications from the same feature of the same object are automatically merged to minimize the number of notifications in the chain. The queued-up notifications are sent by calling `msgs.dispatch()`, as shown previously in the `setCustomer()` method.

You might be wondering why we bother to delegate to a `basicSet()` method at all, when we could just inline the code in the `set()` method. The reason is that it's also needed by the `eInverseAdd()` and `eInverseRemove()` methods, which we will look at in Section 10.7.3.

Finally, notice that if ever we set the reference to its existing value, this implementation will avoid the overhead of performing the reverse remove and add, and of creating a `NotificationChain`. It simply notifies any observers of the "touch," as they would expect.

10.3.3 Multiplicity-Many References

You might have noticed in the previous section's example that the `orders` reference is multiplicity-many, with a lower bound of 0 and no upper bound. In other words, one customer can have many purchase orders. In EMF, a multiplicity-many reference—that is, any reference for which the upper bound is greater than 1—is manipulated using a list API, so only a `get()` method is generated in the interface:

```
EList getOrders();
```

Like the multi-valued attributes that we described in Section 10.2.4, multi-valued references are represented by `EList`, the EMF extension of `java.util.List`. For example, the following code adds a purchase order to a customer's **orders** reference:

```
aCustomer.getOrders().add(aPurchaseOrder);
```

To iterate over a customer's orders, you would do something like this:

```
for (Iterator i = aCustomer.getOrders().iterator(); i.hasNext(); )
{
  PurchaseOrder po = (PurchaseOrder)i.next();
  ...
}
```

As you can see, from a client perspective, the API for manipulating multiplicity-many references is nothing special. However, because the `orders` reference is part of a bidirectional association, we still need to do all the fancy inverse handshaking that we showed for the `setCustomer()` method in the previous section. Looking at the implementation of the `getOrders()` method in `CustomerImpl` shows us how the multiplicity-many case gets handled:

```
protected EList orders = null;

public EList getOrders()
{
  if (orders == null)
  {
    orders =
      new EObjectWithInverseResolvingEList(PurchaseOrder.class,
                          this, EPO1Package.CUSTOMER__ORDERS,
                          EPO1Package.PURCHASE_ORDER__CUSTOMER);
  }
  return orders;
}
```

The `getOrders()` method returns a specialized implementation class, `EObjectWithInverseResolvingEList`, which is constructed with all the information it needs to do the inverse handshaking during add and remove calls. EMF actually provides a number of different `EList` implementation classes,[8] which are used to efficiently implement all the different types of multiplicity-many

---

8. Actually, all the concrete `EList` implementation classes are simple subclasses of one very functional and efficient base implementation class, `EcoreEList`.

structural features. In Section 10.2.4, we saw that `EDataTypeEList` and `EDataTypeUniqueEList` are used for multi-valued attributes. For one-way references, we use `EObjectResolvingEList`. If the reference doesn't need proxy resolution we use `EObjectEList` or `EObjectWithInverseEList`, and so on.

Returning to our example, the list used to implement the **orders** reference is created with two feature ID arguments. `EPO1Package.CUSTOMER__ORDERS` identifies the reference itself and is used in change notifications. The opposite reference is identified by `EPO1Package.PURCHASE_ORDER__CUSTOMER`. It is used in the implementation of `add()`, which calls to `eInverseAdd()` on the `PurchaseOrder`, similar to the way `eInverseAdd()` was called on the `Customer` by `setCustomer()`. We will discuss feature IDs and the reverse handshaking methods further in Section 10.7.

10.3.4 Non–Proxy-Resolving References

In Section 10.3.1, we saw that the implementation of the `get()` method for a reference is slightly more complicated than the implementation of the equivalent method for an attribute. This is true even for a single-valued, one-way reference, such as the **previousOrder** reference of the **PurchaseOrder** class. The reason for this added complexity is that we need to allow for the possibility that the target of a reference is a proxy for an object in a resource that has not been loaded. Extra code is needed to check whether the target object is a proxy, and if so, to resolve it.

If you are sure that the source and target objects of a reference will always reside in the same resource, it is possible to optimize the generated `get()` method by omitting the proxy resolution code. This optimization is made when the **resolveProxies** attribute of an **EReference** is false.

For example, in the ExtendedPO2 model, the **previousOrder** reference is non-proxy-resolving, resulting in the following simple implementation of `getPreviousOrder()`:

```
public PurchaseOrder getPreviousOrder()
{
  return previousOrder;
}
```

A multi-valued, non-proxy-resolving reference uses an `EObjectEList` or `EObjectWithInverseEList` as its `EList` implementation, rather than an `EObjectResolvingEList` or `EObjectWithInverseResolvingEList`. This leads to a slight performance improvement because the implementations of the non-resolving lists, just like the non-resolving `set()` methods, have less overhead.

The decision to disable proxy resolution on any references should be made carefully, based on knowledge of how instance models will be placed in resources for serialization.

10.3.5 Containment References

The **items** reference from **PurchaseOrder** to **Item** is a containment reference, which makes a purchase order a container for items. This is illustrated in Figure 10.14.

Figure 10.14 The **items** containment reference.

A containment reference is indicated by a black diamond on the container end of the association, in this case **PurchaseOrder**. In full, the illustrated association specifies that a **PurchaseOrder** aggregates, by value, 0 or more **Items**. A by-value aggregation association, or containment reference, is modeled in Ecore by an **EReference,** from the container class to the contained class, with its **containment** attribute set to true. Such references are particularly important because they identify the parent or owner of a target instance, which implies the location of the object when persisted. That is to say that objects are persisted in the same document as their container by default.

Here is the generated implementation of the get() method for **items**:

```
protected EList items = null;

public EList getItems()
{
  if (items == null)
  {
    items = new EObjectContainmentEList(Item.class, this, ... );
  }
  return items;
}
```

The default EList implementation for containment references, used here, does not resolve proxies. This is because cross-resource containment support must be explicitly enabled for a model. This is done from within the EMF generator, via a property on the root-level **GenModel** object.[9] The value of the "Containment Proxies" property determines whether any containment references in the model can be proxy resolving. If it is true, then any **EReference** in the model for which **resolveProxies** is true will support cross-resource containment.

For example, if "Containment Proxies" was enabled for the PrimerPO model, the following implementation of `getItems()` would be generated:

```
public EList getItems()
{
  if (items == null)
  {
    items = new EObjectContainmentEList.Resolving(Item.class, ... );
  }
  return items;
}
```

The only difference is that a resolving `EList` implementation is used. The topic of cross-resource containment is explored further in Chapters 13 and 15.

Both `EObjectContainmentEList` and its proxy-resolving subclass `EObjectContainmentEList.Resolving` have an important difference from the other `EList` implementations we have seen so far: they implement the `contains()` method in constant, instead of linear, time. This is particularly important because duplicate entries are not allowed in EMF reference lists, so `contains()` is called during `add()` operations as well.

Because an object can only have one container, adding an object to a containment reference also means removing the object from any container that it is currently in, even if that containment is through a different reference. For example, adding an item to a purchase order's **items** reference might involve removing it from the **items** of some other purchase order. That's no different from any other two-way association with a multiplicity-1 inverse. Imagine, however, that we have another containment reference from **Customer** to **Item** called **consideredItems**. If a given item is in the **consideredItems** reference of some customer when we add it to a purchase order's **items**, then we'd need to remove it from the customer's **consideredItems** association first.

To implement this behavior efficiently, the `EObjectImpl` base class has a field called `eContainer` that it uses to store its container generically. As a result, containment references are always implicitly bidirectional. The following code accesses an **Item**'s containing **PurchaseOrder**:

---

9. GenModel properties are discussed at greater length in Chapter 12.

```
EObject container = item.eContainer();
if (container instanceof PurchaseOrder)
  purchaseOrder = (PurchaseOrder)container;
```

If you want to avoid the downcast, you can change the association to be explicitly bidirectional instead, as in Figure 10.15.

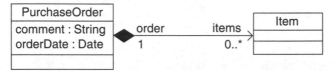

Figure 10.15 An explicitly bidirectional containment association.

Then, EMF will generate a type-safe `get()` method for you in `ItemImpl`:

```
public PurchaseOrder getOrder()
{
  if (eContainerFeatureID != POPackage.ITEM__ORDER) return null;
  return (PurchaseOrder)eContainer;
}
```

This explicit `get()` method uses the `eContainer` field from `EObjectImpl` instead of a generated instance variable, which we have seen is used to implement non-container references such as `getPreviousOrder()`. Also, notice that it verifies that the current containment is, in fact, provided through the **order** feature by testing the `eContainerFeatureID` field, which is also defined and maintained by `EObjectImpl`.

10.3.6 Volatile References

As we saw in Section 10.2.6, volatile attributes have no storage or implementation code generated. You are required to implement a generated stub implementation by hand. The same is true for volatile references. The **pendingOrders** and **shippedOrders** references defined in the ExtendedPO2 model are good examples. They are illustrated in Figure 10.16.

These two references are meant to provide filtered views of the purchase orders according to their **status**, the enumerated type attribute we introduced in Section 10.2.3. The **shippedOrders** reference should include the subset of **orders** whose status is **Complete**, and the **pendingOrders** reference should include those whose status is **Pending**. In fact, we do not need to store these references because the lists can be computed from **orders** when they are accessed. For this reason, we have also marked the two references as derived.

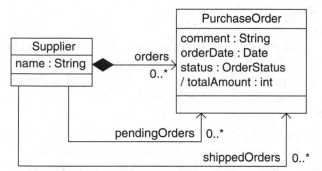

Figure 10.16 The **pendingOrders** and **shippedOrders** volatile references.

The generated implementation for a volatile reference is exactly the same as that for a volatile attribute. It simply throws an UnsupportedOperation-Exception:

```
/**
 * @generated
 */
public EList getPendingOrders()
{
  // TODO: implement this method to return the 'Pending Orders'
  // reference list
  // Ensure that you remove @generated or mark it @generated NOT
  throw new UnsupportedOperationException();
}
```

We'll follow through with this example in Chapter 13, showing how you can implement this method.

10.3.7 Non-Changeable References

We can suppress the generation of the set() method for a reference by setting the **changeable** attribute of the **EReference** to be false. Just as with attributes, it often makes sense to make volatile references non-modifiable as well. Also, as with attributes, the value of a non-changeable reference cannot be restored during a load, so it's often better simply to suppress the set accessor from the interface using a GenModel-sourced annotation instead. Note that a set() method is never generated for a multi-valued reference, so making such a reference non-changeable has no effect on code generation.

10.3.8   Unsettable References

Unsettable references, like their attribute counterparts, support an additional unset state that is distinguishable from that in which any value is set, including the default `null` value. Unsettable multiplicity-1 references are also implemented by `unset()` and `isSet()` methods that are generated in addition to the usual `get()` and `set()` accessors.

For one-way references, the generated `isSet()` and `unset()` implementations use the same patterns that we saw in the discussion of unsettable attributes. For bidirectional references, including implicitly bidirectional containment references, the `unset()` method also needs to do the same kind of inverse handshaking as the `set()` method.

For example, consider the **shipTo** containment reference[10] defined by **PurchaseOrder**, which is shown in Figure 10.17.

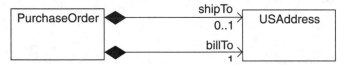

Figure 10.17   PurchaseOrder and its two **USAddress** references.

Suppose that we would like to distinguish between the case where **shipTo** is unset and the case where it is set to null. We could interpret the former case to mean that the order should be shipped to the billing address and the latter to mean that it should be held for pickup.

If **shipTo** is made unsettable, the following implementations are generated by default:

```
protected boolean shipToESet = false;

public void unsetShipTo()
{
  if (shipTo != null)
  {
    NotificationChain msgs = null;
    msgs =
      ((InternalEObject)shipTo).eInverseRemove(this, ... , msgs);
    msgs = basicUnsetShipTo(msgs);
    if (msgs != null) msgs.dispatch();
  }
```

---

10. Recall that containment associations are implicitly bidirectional and therefore require inverse handshaking.

```
    else
    {
      boolean oldShipToESet = shipToESet;
      shipToESet = false;
      if (eNotificationRequired())
        eNotify(new ENotificationImpl(this, ... , oldShipToESet));
    }
}

public boolean isSetShipTo()
{
  return shipToESet;
}
```

As you can see, the unsetShipTo() method uses a pattern similar to the bidirectional set() method pattern described in Section 10.3.2. It is simplified slightly by the fact that unset(), by definition, always sets the value to null. Notice how unset() even delegates to a basicUnsetShipTo() method to do the actual unset, just like a bidirectional set() method delegates to a basicSet() method.

We must also point out that the set() and basicSet() methods are also slightly different for unsettable references. In addition to actually setting the value of the reference, they must also set to true the field that tracks whether the reference has been set.

Finally, a word on multiplicity-many references: like their attribute counterparts, unsettable multiplicity-many references are implemented using subclasses of their usual EList implementations that provide unset() and isSet() methods.

10.3.9 Map References

EMF provides special support for an indexed collection of type-safe key–value pairs via an interface called EMap. Note that EMap is not itself derived from java.util.Map, although it can provide a map view, which is. Instead, it is a special kind of EList—one with items that implement Map.Entry. The items for a particular map type are modeled as a special **EClass**, distinguished by the fact that its **instanceClassName** is set to "java.util.Map$Entry" and by the presence of two structural features: **key** and **value.**

Assume that we want to add a collection of purchase orders to our model. We expect that the collection is going to become large, and we would like to be able to access orders quickly. An approach is captured by the model shown in Figure 10.18.

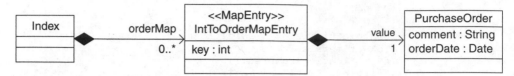

Figure 10.18 A map-type reference.

You might recall this model from Chapter 6. It maps from numeric keys to **PurchaseOrder** values. The keys are new—they do not appear elsewhere in the model—and we will assume that they are non-contiguous.[11]

The following implementation class is generated for **IntToOrderMapEntry**:

```
public class IntToOrderMapEntryImpl extends EObjectImpl
  implements BasicEMap.Entry
{
  protected static final int KEY_EDEFAULT = 0;
  protected int key = KEY_EDEFAULT;
  protected PurchaseOrder value = null;

  ...
}
```

The class extends `EObjectImpl` as usual, but notice that it implements `BasicEMap.Entry`, a simple extension of `Map.Entry` that is used internally for this purpose. No interface is generated.

The implementation mostly follows the usual patterns, with a few important exceptions. Most notably, the usual accessors for **key** and **value** are named `getTypedKey()`, `setTypedKey()`, `getTypedValue()`, and `setTypedValue()`. The ordinary names, `getKey()`, `setKey()`, `getValue()`, and `setValue()`, are used for additional methods that do any casting, wrapping, and unwrapping necessary to connect the generic, `Object`-based `Map.Entry` interface to the type-safe implementation:

```
public Object getKey()
{
  return new Integer(getTypedKey());
}

public void setKey(Object key)
{
  setTypedKey(((Integer)key).intValue());
}
```

---

11. If they were contiguous, we could just use an ordinary multiplicity-many feature and access them by index.

```
public Object getValue()
{
  return getTypedValue();
}

public Object setValue(Object value)
{
  Object oldValue = getValue();
  setTypedValue((PurchaseOrder)value);
  return oldValue;
}
```

Meanwhile, **orderEMap** shows up in **Index** as an `EMap`-typed multiplicity-many containment reference. The following declaration is generated in the `Index` interface:

```
EMap getOrderMap();
```

In the `IndexImpl` implementation class, we find the following:

```
protected EMap orderMap = null;

public EMap getOrderMap()
{
  if (orderMap == null)
  {
    orderMap =
      new EcoreEMap(POMapPackage.Literals.INT_TO_ORDER_MAP_ENTRY,
                    IntToOrderMapEntryImpl.class, this,
                    POMapPackage.INDEX__ORDER_MAP);
  }
  return orderMap;
}
```

The map reference is implemented using `EcoreEMap`, which maintains a containment-like relationship with the `Map.Entry` class and keeps an index, for fast access, based on the **key** structural feature.

By fitting the `Map.Entry` interface on top of a nearly ordinary generated class and maintaining it through a containment-like relationship, we are able to leverage all the usual EMF mechanisms so that everything "just works," including reflection, notification, and persistence. Also, because **key** and **value** are just structural features, their types can be data types or classes, and they can be multiplicity-1 or multiplicity-many. All of the usual patterns do all the usual things under the covers.

10.4   Feature Maps

In Chapter 8, we explored how models can use feature maps to maintain values from multiple features in a single, ordered list. Recall that we introduced the ExtendedPO model, which made use of a feature map, as illustrated in Figure 10.19.

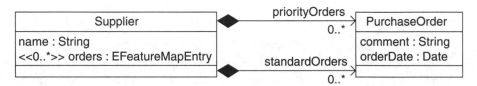

Figure 10.19   A feature map.

The feature map is represented as an attribute, **orders**, of type **EFeatureMapEntry**.[12] It is used to maintain an ordered list across the **priority-Orders** and **standardOrders** references, which are both marked volatile, transient, and derived.

The function of the **order** attribute is expressed by an extended metadata annotation.[13] The annotation has a single **details** entry, whose key is "kind" and value is "group". The relationship between the features is also captured by annotations: **priorityOrders** and **standardOrders** each have an extended metadata annotation. Its single **details** entry, keyed by "group", has a value of "#orders", identifying the feature map that backs the group.

The three features appear in the `Supplier` interface like this:

```
public interface Supplier extends EObject
{
  ...

  FeatureMap getOrders();
  EList getPriorityOrders();
  EList getStandardOrders();
}
```

---

12. A feature map must be an attribute because its type, **EFeatureMapEntry**, is a data type. However, feature maps behave quite differently from ordinary attributes, as they can back references that fully participate in standard EMF mechanisms like containment, bidirectional reference handshaking, and persistence.

13. See Chapter 8 for more information about extended metadata annotations.

In `SupplierImpl`, the `getOrders()` method is implemented using `BasicFeatureMap`, the generic `FeatureMap` implementation:

```
protected FeatureMap orders = null;

public FeatureMap getOrders()
{
  if (orders == null)
  {
    orders = new BasicFeatureMap(this, EPOPackage.SUPPLIER__ORDERS);
  }
  return orders;
}
```

Because of the relationship established by the extended metadata annotations, **preferredOrders** and **standardOrders** are not left unimplemented like ordinary volatile references. Instead, implementations can be generated that simply delegate to the list views provided by the feature map. For example, `getPriorityOrders()` is implemented like this:

```
public EList getPriorityOrders()
{
  return ((FeatureMap)getOrders()).list(
                    EPOPackage.Literals.SUPPLIER__PRIORITY_ORDERS);
}
```

Here, `SUPPLIER__PRIORITY_ORDERS` identifies the derived feature for which to return a list view. As we will see in Section 10.8, it is one of the literal constants from the package interface. This delegating implementation allows us to add, remove, or move purchase orders in any of the three lists, with the others automatically remaining synchronized.

10.5   Operations

Any **EOperation**s contained by an **EClass** correspond to methods in the generated interface and implementation class. EMF provides no means for higher level modeling of operation behavior. If you annotate the operation with a body, written in Java, that code will be included in the generated method. Failing that, empty method bodies will be produced, leaving you to complete the implementations by hand.

As an example, suppose we wish to add an operation to **PurchaseOrder** that removes an item from the order. Without such an operation, an item could still be removed by retrieving the whole list representing the **items** reference, finding the item, and removing it from the list. However, we could also imagine that a **removeItem** operation might conveniently do some additional processing, like checking to see if the removal makes the order complete and, if so, updating its status.[14]

We update the model to include the **removeItem** operation, as illustrated in Figure 10.20.

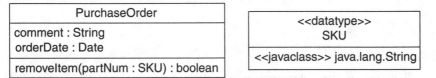

Figure 10.20 Class **PurchaseOrder** with an operation.

This operation has a single **SKU**-typed parameter, identifying the item to be removed by its part number. Its return value indicates whether the removal was successful.

With this addition, the following signature is included in the PurchaseOrder interface:

```
boolean removeItem(String partNum);
```

Recall that the **SKU** data type maps to String, the type used for the generated method's parameter.

The corresponding implementation class includes a stub implementation for the method. To remind you that you need to provide the actual implementation, the generated stub throws an UnsupportedOperationException.

```
/**
 * @generated
 */
public boolean removeItem(String partNum)
{
  // TODO: implement this method
  // Ensure that you remove @generated or mark it @generated NOT
  throw new UnsupportedOperationException();
}
```

---

14. It is also possible to attach this kind of processing directly to the **items** reference by implementing it in an adapter. Section 16.2 discusses adapters in detail.

As always, when you modify this method to provide the appropriate behavior, you should also deal with the `@generated` Javadoc comment that precedes it, as we will discuss in Section 10.11.

If, on the other hand, we'd rather include the Java implementation of the method in the model, we would need to add a GenModel-sourced annotation to the operation. The code is specified as the value of a **details** entry, keyed by "body". For details, see Section 5.7.1. When such an annotation is present, the body is included in the implementation class, in place of the "TODO" comment and `throw` statement.

10.6   Class Inheritance

As we saw in Chapter 5, Ecore supports inheritance by allowing a class to specify any number of other classes as its supertypes. In this section, we explore how inheritance in a model is reflected in the generated code.

10.6.1   *Single Inheritance*

ExtendedPO2 expands the modeling of an address to accommodate those located outside of the United States. It introduces an abstract class, **Address**, as a base for different types of addresses, including **USAddress**. This is illustrated in Figure 10.21.

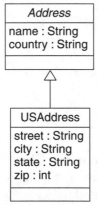

Figure 10.21   Single inheritance.

The EMF generator handles single inheritance as you would expect: the generated interface and implementation class for an **EClass** extend the interface and implementation for its **eSuperType**. Thus, the interface declaration for **USAddress** is as follows:

```
public interface USAddress extends Address
```

The declaration of the implementation class looks like this:

```
public class USAddressImpl extends AddressImpl implements USAddress
```

Note that the interface and class still inherit indirectly from `EObject` and `EObjectImpl`, which remain the bases of `Address` and `AddressImpl`, respectively.

10.6.2 Multiple Inheritance

Like Java itself, EMF supports multiple interface inheritance, but each implementation class can only extend one base. Therefore, when we model multiple inheritance, we need to identify which of the supertypes should be used for the implementation base class. The others will then be treated as mixin interfaces, with their features re-implemented in the derived implementation class.

Consider the example from ExtendedPO2 shown in Figure 10.22.

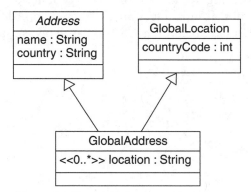

Figure 10.22 Multiple class inheritance.

Here, **GlobalAddress** derives from two classes: **Address** and **GlobalLocation**. We have identified **Address** as the implementation base with an <<extend>> stereotype.[15] When generated, the `GlobalAddress` interface extends the two supertype interfaces:

```
public interface GlobalAddress extends Address, GlobalLocation
```

---

15. Actually, it is the first **EClass** specified by **eSuperType** in the Ecore model that is used as the implementation base class. The UML stereotype is simply needed to indicate that **Address** should be first in that list.

As usual, the `GlobalAddressImpl` class implements this interface and extends the implementation base class. It also includes implementations of the mixed-in `getCountryCode()` and `setCountryCode()` methods:

```
public class GlobalAddressImpl extends AddressImpl
  implements GlobalAddress
{
  public int getCountryCode() {
    ...
  }

  public void setCountryCode(int newValue) {
    ...
  }
}
```

The multiple inheritance also results in the generation of override implementations for `eDerivedStructuralFeatureID()` and `eBaseStructuralFeatureID()`, as we will describe in Section 10.7.4.

10.6.3 *Interface Inheritance and Implementation*

So far, we have not discussed inheritance involving interface-only classes, those modeled by an **EClass** with its **interface** attribute set to true. In fact, such classes are primarily meant to be used in inheritance: they can be specified as supertypes for other interface-only classes, modeling interface inheritance, or for ordinary classes, modeling interface implementation.

Let's illustrate this latter case by modifying the example from the previous section, as in Figure 10.23.

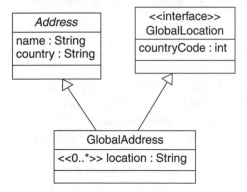

Figure 10.23   Interface inheritance.

If **GlobalLocation** is never going to be instantiated itself, we can make it an interface, suppressing the generation of an implementation class. Because **Address** is now the only supertype with an implementation and, hence, the only option for the implementation base, we can safely remove the <<extend>> stereotype.

Implementing an interface like this involves generating implementations for all of its features. So, the generated `GlobalAddressImpl` class is identical to the one we looked at in the previous section. The only difference here is that no `GlobalLocationImpl` class is generated.

Recall that we can also model non-EMF interfaces, specifying only the name of the Java interface and not any attributes, references, or operations. In the case where such an interface is implemented by a class, the only thing affected is the `extends` clause of the interface generated for the implementing class. Because the model specifies nothing about the external interface, we need to code, by hand, implementations of any methods that it declares.

10.7   Reflective Methods

In addition to the accessor methods that are generated specifically to handle each attribute and reference in a class, the generated Java implementation class includes efficient support for the reflective accessor methods that are declared by the `EObject` interface. Although you are unlikely to ever modify these implementations, you might be interested in knowing how they work if you write code that uses reflection to access structural features.

Such reflective clients can make use of the `eGet()`, `eSet()`, `eIsSet()`, and `eUnset()` methods. In addition, there are several reflective methods defined by another interface, `InternalEObject`, that are generally only used by generated and framework code. This section briefly describes these methods. We will discuss their use further in Section 14.2.

10.7.1   Feature IDs

Before we talk about the various reflective methods, we should understand a little more about feature IDs. We have already come across them several times in this chapter, but we have yet to provide a complete discussion.

Basically, a feature ID is an integer value that uniquely identifies a structural feature within a class. In particular, it is the position of the feature in the list returned by the `getEAllStructuralFeatures()` method of an **EClass**. For easy access, this ID is also generated as a static `int` constant in the interface for the package that contains the class. As we will see in a moment, it is used by the various reflective methods in efficient `switch` statements that select a course of action based on the specified feature.

The assignment of feature IDs occurs when model code is generated. It is quite straightforward for classes that only use single inheritance, but it gets a little more complicated when multiple inheritance is involved. For classes with no supertypes, features are assigned IDs sequentially, beginning with 0. For classes with a single supertype, inherited features have the same ID as in the supertype, and locally defined features are assigned IDs sequentially starting with the next available value.

However, this simple scheme breaks down when a class has more than one supertype, as features inherited from different ones would have conflicting IDs. We handle this problem by offsetting the feature IDs coming from every supertype, except for one. The special supertype whose feature IDs are maintained is the same one that we use as the implementation base, as described in Section 10.6.2. IDs for features inherited from each of the other supertypes are then offset as necessary to ensure uniqueness. Finally, IDs are assigned to locally defined features sequentially, starting with the next available value. As you will soon see, the `eDerivedStructuralFeatureID()` and `eBaseStructuralFeatureID()` methods provide a mapping between a base ID, with no offset, and the corresponding offset value that is used in a particular subclass.

Feature IDs that are negative have a special purpose: they represent container references that have no feature of their own. Recall from Section 10.3.5 that `EObjectImpl` defines two fields, `eContainer` and `eContainerFeatureID`, to generically keep track of an object's container and the feature through which that object is accessed. However, for containment associations that are not bidirectional, there is no container feature to store. In this case, we use the containment feature ID instead, but subtract it from -1 so that we can distinguish it from a real container feature ID, which would be a positive value.[16]

10.7.2 *Reflective Accessors*

`EObject` defines the following reflective accessor methods:

```
public interface EObject extends Notifier
{
  Object eGet(EStructuralFeature feature);
  Object eGet(EStructuralFeature feature, boolean resolve);
  void eSet(EStructuralFeature feature, Object newValue);
  void eUnset(EStructuralFeature feature);
```

---

16. You might think it would be a bit clearer if we just negated the value, but because feature numbering starts at 0, -0 would be indistinguishable from +0.

```
boolean eIsSet(EStructuralFeature feature);
...
}
```

Notice that there is one reflective method corresponding to each of the four basic accessor types that can be generated for a feature, as well as an additional form of eGet(). In each case, the attribute or reference to be accessed is passed as the first argument. The two-argument form of eGet() allows the caller to specify whether proxies, when retrieved as the value of a reference, should be resolved before being returned. The single-argument form always performs such proxy resolution.

Each of these accessors is implemented in BasicEObjectImpl, the superclass of EObjectImpl, which provides the default base for all generated classes. The implementations are all of the same form, similar to this:

```
public Object eGet(EStructuralFeature feature, boolean resolve)
{
  return eGet(eDerivedStructuralFeatureID(eFeature), resolve, true);
}

public void eSet(EStructuralFeature feature, Object newValue)
{
  eSet(eDerivedStructuralFeatureID(eFeature), newValue);
}

public void eUnset(EStructuralFeature feature)
{
  eUnset(eDerivedStructuralFeatureID(eFeature));
}

public boolean eIsSet(EStructuralFeature feature)
{
  return eIsSet(eDerivedStructuralFeatureID(eFeature));
}
```

In fact, we have simplified each of these methods slightly, but the idea is to obtain the ID for the given feature, and call a corresponding method that takes that feature ID. Generated classes then provide efficient implementations of these ID-based methods.

For example, in PrimerPO, PurchaseOrderImpl implements eGet() like this:

```
public Object eGet(int featureID, boolean resolve, boolean coreType)
{
  switch (featureID)
  {
```

```
      case PPOPackage.PURCHASE_ORDER__COMMENT:
        return getComment();
      case PPOPackage.PURCHASE_ORDER__ORDER_DATE:
        return getOrderDate();
      case PPOPackage.PURCHASE_ORDER__SHIP_TO:
        return getShipTo();
      case PPOPackage.PURCHASE_ORDER__BILL_TO:
        return getBillTo();
      case PPOPackage.PURCHASE_ORDER__ITEMS:
        return getItems();
  }
  return super.eGet(featureID, resolve, coreType);
}
```

This method simply delegates to the get() accessors generated for the attributes and references implemented by the class. A switch selects the appropriate accessor for the given feature ID, resulting in just a small, constant-time penalty for using the reflective accessor. For any primitive-typed attributes, the value is wrapped in the appropriate object wrapper before being returned.

If no match is found, super.eGet() is invoked. If the class is modeled using inheritance, each supertype's implementation is responsible for handling the features it introduces. Eventually, a base implementation from BasicEObjectImpl is called to handle any dynamic features that might have been defined.

There are two more details of eGet() to discuss, relating to the two additional arguments: resolve and coreType. Recall from Section 10.3.1 that, by default, references automatically perform proxy resolution when accessed. However, in some situations it is useful to reflectively retrieve the value of a reference without resolving proxies. This is what eGet() does when resolve is false.

Consider again the **previousOrder** reference from ExtendedPO1 that was discussed in Section 10.3.1. The corresponding case in eGet() looks like this:

```
case EPO1Package.PURCHASE_ORDER__PREVIOUS_ORDER:
  if (resolve) return getPreviousOrder();
  return basicGetPreviousOrder();
```

When resolve is true, getPreviousOrder() is called and proxy resolution is automatically performed. However, when resolve is false, basicGetPreviousOrder() is called. This method is generated just for this purpose. It simply returns previousOrder without doing the proxy resolution.

As for the coreType argument, it is applicable only to map and feature map types. It determines whether to return the EMF-specific type, such as EMap, or the corresponding language-type view. For example, consider the **Index** class discussed in Section 10.3.9. The single case in its eGet() implementation, which handles the **orderMap** map feature, looks like this:

```
case PPOPackage.INDEX__ORDER_MAP:
  if (coreType) return getOrderMap();
  else return getOrderMap().map();
```

If `coreType` is `true`, the usual case, `eGet()` simply returns the `EMap` obtained from the generated accessor. Otherwise, it returns the `Map` view. This behavior is needed internally when code has been generated with EMF types suppressed, a topic we will discuss in Section 10.10.2. Because it is not expected that user code should need this API, it is only exposed in the `InternalEObject` interface.

The implementations generated for the other reflective accessors are simpler than `eGet()`. For example, here is how `PurchaseOrderImpl` implements `eSet()` in PrimerPO:

```
public void eSet(int featureID, Object newValue)
{
  switch (featureID)
  {
    case PPOPackage.PURCHASE_ORDER__COMMENT:
      setComment((String)newValue);
      return;
    case PPOPackage.PURCHASE_ORDER__ORDER_DATE:
      setOrderDate((Date)newValue);
      return;
    case PPOPackage.PURCHASE_ORDER__SHIP_TO:
      setShipTo((USAddress)newValue);
      return;
    case PPOPackage.PURCHASE_ORDER__BILL_TO:
      setBillTo((USAddress)newValue);
      return;
    case PPOPackage.PURCHASE_ORDER__ITEMS:
      getItems().clear();
      getItems().addAll((Collection)newValue);
      return;
  }
  super.eSet(featureID, newValue);
}
```

The pattern is much like in `eGet()`, but with no `resolve` or `coreType` to worry about. A `switch` is used to efficiently delegate to the appropriate generated `set()` accessor for the given feature ID. Multiplicity-many features are set by clearing the list and then adding the specified values. As a consequence, setting such a feature to its current value produces the unexpected result of simply clearing the list. Non-changeable features are simply not handled.

The `eUnset()` and `eIsSet()` methods also follow the same switch-based pattern, but features are treated differently based on whether or not they are unsettable. To highlight the difference, let's return to the example from Section 10.3.8, where we modified **PurchaseOrder** by making **shipTo** unsettable. With that change, the following implementations are generated:

```
public void eUnset(int featureID)
{
  switch (featureID)
  {
    ...
    case PPOPackage.PURCHASE_ORDER__SHIP_TO:
      unsetShipTo();
      return;
    case PPOPackage.PURCHASE_ORDER__BILL_TO:
      setBillTo((USAddress)null);
      return;
    ...
  }
  super.eUnset(featureID);
}

public boolean eIsSet(int featureID)
{
  switch (featureID)
  {
    ...
    case PPOPackage.PURCHASE_ORDER__SHIP_TO:
      return isSetShipTo();
    case PPOPackage.PURCHASE_ORDER__BILL_TO:
      return billTo != null;
    ...
  }
  return super.eIsSet(featureID);
}
```

In order to focus on the difference between **shipTo** and **billTo**, we have omitted the cases for the other features. For an unsettable feature like **shipTo**, the two reflective methods simply call their generated `unset()` and `isSet()` counterparts. For a feature like **billTo**, which is not unsettable, the two reflective methods set the feature to its default value and test if it is set to its default value, respectively.

10.7.3   Inverse Handshaking Methods

There are three more reflective methods that can be generated in each implementation class to maintain inverse handshaking: `eInverseAdd()`, `eInverseRemove()`, and `eBasicRemoveFromContainerFeature()`.

The `eInverseAdd()` method is used in bidirectional references to automatically add to or set one end to match an add or set at the opposite end. Thus, it is called from generated `set()` methods, as we saw in Section 10.3.2, and from `EList` implementations for bidirectional references.

As an example, here is the implementation from `PurchaseOrderImpl`. Because PrimerPO includes no bidirectional references, we will look at the version in ExtendedPO2:

```
public NotificationChain eInverseAdd(InternalEObject otherEnd,
                           int featureID, NotificationChain msgs)
{
  switch (featureID)
  {
    case EPO2Package.PURCHASE_ORDER__ITEMS:
      return ((InternalEList)getItems()).basicAdd(otherEnd, msgs);
    case EPO2Package.PURCHASE_ORDER__CUSTOMER:
      if (customer != null)
        msgs = ((InternalEObject)customer).eInverseRemove(this,
                 EPO2Package.CUSTOMER__ORDERS, Customer.class, msgs);
      return basicSetCustomer((Customer)otherEnd, msgs);
  }
  return super.eInverseAdd(otherEnd, featureID, msgs);
}
```

Like the reflective accessors we saw in the previous section, this method switches according to the given feature ID. Here, it selects the proper implementation for adding the inverse reference. If the feature is multiplicity-many, it adds to the reference. Otherwise, it removes the previous value, if necessary, and then sets the reference.

The `eInverseRemove()` method is used in maintaining bidirectional and containment references. It is called to remove from or clear one end of such a reference to match a remove or set at the opposite end.

Here is the implementation from `PurchaseOrderImpl` in ExtendedPO2:

```
public NotificationChain eInverseRemove(InternalEObject otherEnd,
                           int featureID, NotificationChain msgs)
{
  switch (featureID)
  {
    case EPO2Package.PURCHASE_ORDER__ITEMS:
      return ((InternalEList)getItems()).basicRemove(otherEnd,msgs);
    case EPO2Package.PURCHASE_ORDER__BILL_TO:
      return basicSetBillTo(null, msgs);
    case EPO2Package.PURCHASE_ORDER__SHIP_TO:
      return basicSetShipTo(null, msgs);
    case EPO2Package.PURCHASE_ORDER__CUSTOMER:
      return basicSetCustomer(null, msgs);
  }
  return super.eInverseRemove(otherEnd, featureID, msgs)
}
```

It follows a similar pattern to eInverseAdd(), switching on the feature ID, and then removing from a multi-valued reference, or setting a single-valued reference. Notice that both bidirectional and containment references are handled.

Finally, the eBasicRemoveFromContainerFeature() method is used before adding an object to a new container, in order to remove it from its existing container. Unlike eInverseAdd() and eInverseRemove(), this method doesn't take a feature ID as argument, instead acting on the current container feature, which is identified by eContainerFeatureID. For example, here is the implementation from ItemImpl in ExtendedPO2:

```
public NotificationChain eBasicRemoveFromContainerFeature(
                                         NotificationChain msgs)
{
  switch (eContainerFeatureID)
  {
    case EPO2Package.ITEM__ORDER:
      return eInternalContainer().eInverseRemove(this,
                            EPO2Package.PURCHASE_ORDER__ITEMS,
                            PurchaseOrder.class, msgs);
  }
  return super.eBasicRemoveFromContainerFeature(msgs);
}
```

It simply switches on the feature ID, obtains the container object, and invokes eInverseRemove() on it. In this case, there is only one explicit container reference.

Note that the generated forms of eInverseAdd(), eInverseRemove(), and eBasicRemoveFromContainerFeature() are not actually the same forms that we previously saw being invoked, such as by the bidirectional reference setter in Section 10.3.2. In fact, it is only the forms exposed for internal use by InternalEObject that are invoked. Those methods are implemented in BasicEObjectImpl. They simply adjust the feature ID for multiple inheritance, if necessary, and then call the generated, type-specific forms. They also deal with the case of negative feature IDs, which represent container references with no feature of their own. These are handled by removing from or adding to the opposite containment end.

10.7.4 Feature ID Conversion Methods

As discussed in Section 10.7.1, a feature ID uniquely identifies each structural feature within a given class. When a class uses multiple inheritance, the IDs for some of its inherited features are offset from their base values. The mappings from base feature IDs to those appropriate to a given class are defined by `eDerivedStructuralFeatureID()`, and the reverse mappings are defined by `eBaseStructuralFeatureID()`.

`BasicEObjectImpl` provides implementations of these two methods that simply return the feature ID passed in, without offsetting it. Only those classes with more than one supertype require overrides to be generated.

We saw an example of a class from ExtendedPO2 that uses multiple inheritance, **GlobalAddress**, in Section 10.6.2. Here is the `eDerivedStructuralFeatureID()` override that is generated in `GlobalAddressImpl` as a result:

```
public int eDerivedStructuralFeatureID(int baseFeatureID,
                                       Class baseClass)
{
  if (baseClass == GlobalLocation.class)
  {
    switch (baseFeatureID)
    {
      case EPO2Package.GLOBAL_LOCATION__COUNTRY_CODE:
        return EPO2Package.GLOBAL_ADDRESS__COUNTRY_CODE;
      default: return -1;
    }
  }
  return
    super.eDerivedStructuralFeatureID(baseFeatureID, baseClass);
}
```

As you can see, it only needs to adjust the ID for features inherited from mixin classes. In this case, there is only one such feature: **countryCode**, which is defined in **GlobalLocation**. For anything else, the unadjusted value returned by the `BasicEObjectImpl` implementation is appropriate.

The override for `eBaseStructuralFeatureID()` is similar, but with the values reversed:

```
public int eBaseStructuralFeatureID(int derivedFeatureID,
                                    Class baseClass)
{
  if (baseClass == GlobalLocation.class)
  {
    switch (derivedFeatureID)
    {
      case EPO2Package.GLOBAL_ADDRESS__COUNTRY_CODE:
        return EPO2Package.GLOBAL_LOCATION__COUNTRY_CODE;
      default: return -1;
    }
  }
  return
    super.eBaseStructuralFeatureID(derivedFeatureID, baseClass);
}
```

As we have already discussed, eDerivedStructuralFeatureID() is used to obtain the class-relative feature ID that gets passed to all the other, switch-based reflective methods discussed so far.

The other method, eBaseStructuralFeatureID(), is most commonly utilized by adapters in determining the affected feature from a notification. When an object sends a notification, it includes the ID of the feature relative to the class that implements it, not the one that declares it. Of course, the recipient of the notification should not need to know what class is implementing the feature. So, an Adapter, in its notifyChanged() method, wants to obtain the base feature ID. It calls getFeatureID() on the Notification, specifying the class that it is adapting. This method uses eBaseStructuralFeatureID() to adjust the ID before returning it.

10.8 Factories and Packages

So far, we have looked at the interfaces and classes that correspond to the **EClassifier**s contained in an **EPackage**. In addition to these, EMF by default generates two interfaces, along with implementations, corresponding to the **EPackage** itself: a package and a factory.

The package provides some static constants and convenience methods for accessing the metadata for the classifiers defined in the **EPackage**, while the factory, as its name implies, allows for their instantiation.

Although you aren't strictly required to use the package or factory in your application, EMF does strongly encourage the use of the factory for creating instances by making the constructors for modeled classes protected. Thus, client code that resides in another package cannot just use new to create instances directly. You can, however, manually change the visibility of the constructors to public, if that's what you really want.

The factory interface for the primer purchase order model looks like this:

```
public interface PPOFactory extends EFactory
{
  PPOFactory eINSTANCE = com.example.ppo.impl.PPOFactoryImpl.init();

  PurchaseOrder createPurchaseOrder();
  USAddress createUSAddress();
  Item createItem();

  PPOPackage getPPOPackage();
}
```

The base interface for generated factories, EFactory, declares a generic create() method for creating instances of model classes. It also declares generic

createFromString() and convertToString() methods, which convert data
type instances into strings and back.

The generated factory interface adds to this interface a specific create()
method for each instantiable class in the package; that is, for each **EClass** for
which both **abstract** and **interface** are false.

The factory class implements each of these methods simply, by using new to
create an instance of the appropriate class. It implements the generic create()
method with a switch that delegates to these type-specific factory methods. For
example:

```
public class PPOFactoryImpl extends EFactoryImpl
  implements PPOFactory
{
  public EObject create(EClass eClass)
  {
    switch (eClass.getClassifierID())
    {
      case PPOPackage.PURCHASE_ORDER: return createPurchaseOrder();
      case PPOPackage.US_ADDRESS: return createUSAddress();
      case PPOPackage.ITEM: return createItem();
      default:
        throw new IllegalArgumentException("The class '" +
          eClass.getName() + "' is not a valid classifier");
    }
  }

  public PurchaseOrder createPurchaseOrder()
  {
    PurchaseOrderImpl purchaseOrder = new PurchaseOrderImpl();
    return purchaseOrder;
  }

  ...
}
```

Notice that the generic create() method is switching on the classifier ID of
the specified **EClass**. This is a unique integer assigned to each classifier in a package. The concept is analogous to that of feature IDs, which we have discussed,
but without the complications caused by inheritance.

In addition, the implementation includes type-specific versions of
createFromString() and convertToString() for each **EDataType** in the
package, as we saw in Section 10.2.2. It also implements the generic
createFromString() and convertToString() methods by delegating to these
type-specific versions. For example:

```
public Object createFromString(EDataType eDataType,
                               Object instanceValue)
{
  switch (eDataType.getClassifierID())
  {
    case PPOPackage.SKU:
      return createSKUFromString(eDataType, initialValue);
    case PPOPackage.DATE:
      return createDateFromString(eDataType, initialValue);
    default:
      throw new IllegalArgumentException("The datatype '" +
        eDataType.getName() + "' is not a valid classifier");
  }
}
```

The generic `convertToString()` is implemented analogously. Thus, these two methods, exposed by the `EFactory` interface, can be used to convert all data types defined by the package into strings and back. This is the serialization mechanism used by the persistence framework.

Finally, the generated factory interface includes an accessor for its corresponding package, `getPPOPackage()`, and a static constant reference, `eINSTANCE`, to an implementation of the factory.

You might be thinking that it seems strange to see a dependency on the implementation class, right in the interface—it would seem to defeat the purpose of interface–implementation separation. The answer to this concern is that the statically referenced `PPOFactoryImpl` is intended to be the *default* factory implementation, not necessarily the *only* one.[17] The `eINSTANCE` reference is a convenient way to access this default factory, if that's what you're using. Usually, it's all you will need. However, if you want to use a different, specialized factory implementation, then you lose this convenience and will need to locate your factory in some other way.[18]

The generated package interface defines some properties of the package, includes a static constant reference to an implementation of the package, and provides convenient access to all the metadata in the model. For the primer purchase order model, it looks like this:

```
public interface PPOPackage extends EPackage
{
  String eNAME = "ppo";
```

17. You might have noticed earlier that we described the `eINSTANCE` field as a reference to "an implementation," and not "the implementation."

18. This is not to imply that you will be on your own if you need a specialized factory implementation. EMF provides a convenient package registry facility that you can use to locate packages and factories. We discuss it in Section 14.1.2.

```
String eNS_URI = "http://www.example.com/PrimerPO";
String eNS_PREFIX = "ppo";

PPOPackage eINSTANCE = com.example.ppo.impl.PPOPackageImpl.init();

static final int PURCHASE_ORDER = 0;
static final int PURCHASE_ORDER__COMMENT = 0;
static final int PURCHASE_ORDER__ORDER_DATE = 1;
static final int PURCHASE_ORDER__BILL_TO = 2;
static final int PURCHASE_ORDER__SHIP_TO = 3;
static final int PURCHASE_ORDER__ITEMS = 4;
static final int PURCHASE_ORDER_FEATURE_COUNT = 5;
static final int US_ADDRESS = 1;
static final int US_ADDRESS__NAME = 0;
static final int US_ADDRESS__STREET = 1;
...

EClass getPurchaseOrder();
EAttribute getPurchaseOrder_Comment();
EAttribute getPurchaseOrder_OrderDate();
EReference getPurchaseOrder_ShipTo();
...
}
```

As you can see, the generated interface extends the EPackage base interface,
and includes convenient static constants that define values to be used for the
name, nsURI, and **nsPrefix** attributes of the **EPackage.**

Just like the factory, you can access an instance of the generated package
implementation via the eINSTANCE field.

The metadata is available in two forms: as int constants and as instances of
Ecore classes themselves. The int constants are the classifier and feature IDs that
have come up at various points in this chapter. They provide the most efficient
way to pass around meta information and, as we discussed in Section 10.7.4, to
determine which feature has changed when handling notifications. We will discuss EMF adapters in greater detail in Chapter 16.

A generated set of accessors provides direct access to the full metadata: the
Ecore model objects. As discussed in Chapter 5, these objects can be examined
at runtime to dynamically reveal all of the details of the model. They can also be
used with the reflective API, to specify which element of the model should be
operated on.

By default, the generated package interface also includes a nested interface
named Literals, which provides access to these same Ecore objects:

```
interface Literals
{
  EClass PURCHASE_ORDER = eINSTANCE.getPurchaseOrder();
  EAttribute PURCHASE_ORDER__COMMENT =
```

```
    eINSTANCE.getPurchaseOrder_Comment();
  EAttribute PURCHASE_ORDER__ORDER_DATE =
    eINSTANCE.getPurchaseOrder_OrderDate();
  ...
}
```

As you can see, `Literals` simply defines static constants that refer to the metadata from the default package implementation. Accessing the Ecore objects this way is slightly more efficient than using the accessors directly.

The `eINSTANCE` field, through which the default package implementation is accessed, is initialized with the value returned by `PPOPackageImpl.init()`. This static method not only creates and returns an instance of the implementation class, but also programmatically builds the whole Ecore model for the package. This approach is preferred to that of reading the model from its serialized form because it gives better performance and ensures that the model's metadata stays in sync with the classes that realize it.

10.9   Switch Classes and Adapter Factories

By default, the EMF generator also generates two utility classes for each **EPackage**: a switch class and a skeleton adapter factory class. The switch class implements a `switch`-like callback mechanism that is used for dispatching based on a model object's type. The adapter factory is a convenient base for building factories that demand-create type-specific adapters for modeled objects. The switch class is used in the implementation of the adapter factory.

For example, the generated code for the primer purchase order model includes `PPOSwitch` and `PPOAdapterFactory` classes. The switch class looks like this:

```
public class PPOSwitch
{
  protected static PPOPackage modelPackage;

  public Object doSwitch(EObject theEObject)
  {
    return doSwitch(theEObject.eClass(), theEObject);
  }

  protected Object doSwitch(EClass theEClass, EObject theEObject)
  {
    if (theEClass.eContainer() == modelPackage)
    {
      return doSwitch(theEClass.getClassifierID(), theEObject);
    }
    else
    {
```

```
      List eSuperTypes = theEClass.getESuperTypes();
      return eSuperTypes.isEmpty() ? defaultCase(theEObject) :
        doSwitch((EClass)eSuperTypes.get(0), theEObject);
    }
  }

  protected Object doSwitch(int classifierID, EObject theEObject)
  {
    switch (classifierID)
    {
      case PPOPackage.PURCHASE_ORDER: {
        PurchaseOrder purchaseOrder = (PurchaseOrder)theEObject;
        Object result = casePurchaseOrder(purchaseOrder);
        if (result == null) result = defaultCase(theEObject);
        return result;
      }
      case PPOPackage.ITEM: {
        ...
      }
      case PPOPackage.US_ADDRESS: {
        ...
      }
      default: return defaultCase(theEObject);
    }
  }

  ...
}
```

The switch is executed by calling doSwitch(). If the specified EObject is an instance of one of the classes belonging to the package, a switch is entered, based on the classifier ID. This particular model includes no inheritance, but speaking generally, each case walks up the inheritance hierarchy from the actual type of the object to EObject, calling out to a specific case() handler method for each class. It stops when one of these methods returns a non-null value, which doSwitch() then returns.

As generated, each of the handler methods simply returns null. For example:

```
public Object casePurchaseOrder(PurchaseOrder object)
{
  return null;
}
```

Thus, doSwitch() will always fall through all the cases and return null. So, to use the switch class, you will need to subclass it and provide overrides for whichever case() handlers you want to return something.

The switch class also handles the case where the type of the object originally passed to doSwitch() is not actually from the package, but just extends one that is. In this case, the object is simply treated as if it were an instance of the most specific type that is from the package.

Before looking at how the adapter factory uses the switch class, let's briefly discuss what we expect an adapter factory to do. The class declaration gives us a hint:

```
public class PPOAdapterFactory extends AdapterFactoryImpl
{
   ...
}
```

We are subclassing `AdapterFactoryImpl`, which implements `AdapterFactory`. If we look at this interface, we find that the following two methods are the most important to clients:

o `isFactoryForType()` tells the client whether the adapter factory supports a given type. In this context, a type is an arbitrary object for which any significance is imposed by the factory itself.

o `adapt()` takes an object for which an adapter is desired and the type of adapter required. If the object is a `Notifier` and if the factory supports the `type`, it returns an appropriate adapter; otherwise, it returns the object itself.

Now, looking at the base class, we find that `isFactoryForType()` always returns `false`, and that `adapt()` gets the adapters for the `object`, if it is a `Notifier`, and returns the first that is an adapter for the specified `type`. If there is no appropriate adapter, it calls `createAdapter()` to make one. This method just uses `new` to create an instance of `AdapterImpl`.

Thus, an `AdapterFactoryImpl`-based adapter factory really only needs to do two things:

o Override `isFactoryForType()` to determine whether the specified `type` is supported.

o Override `createAdapter()` to create and return an appropriate adapter for a given `target`.

Now, we can look at the whole generated adapter factory pattern to see how it does these things:

```
public class PPOAdapterFactory extends AdapterFactoryImpl
{
   protected static PPOPackage modelPackage;

   public boolean isFactoryForType(Object object)
```

```
  {
    if (object == modelPackage)
    {
      return true;
    }
    if (object instanceof EObject)
    {
      return
        ((EObject)object).eClass().getEPackage() == modelPackage;
    }
    return false;
  }
  ...
}
```

We see that this is an adapter factory for either the EPackage that represents this package or for any EObject that is an instance of a class belonging to it. The createAdapter() method is implemented using the switch class, like this:

```
public Adapter createAdapter(Notifier target)
{
  return (Adapter)modelSwitch.doSwitch((EObject)target);
}

protected PPOSwitch modelSwitch =
  new PPOSwitch()
  {
    public Object casePurchaseOrder(PurchaseOrder object) {
      return createPurchaseOrderAdapter();
    }
    public Object caseItem(Item object) {
      return createItemAdapter();
    }
    public Object caseUSAddress(USAddress object) {
      return createUSAddressAdapter();
    }
    public Object defaultCase(EObject object) {
      return createEObjectAdapter();
    }
  };
```

The switch class is used to select the type of the target; based on that, it calls to a createAdapter() handler method that creates the appropriate adapter. Because this is just a skeleton adapter factory, these handlers all just return null. For example:

```
public Adapter createPurchaseOrderAdapter()
{
  return null;
}
```

So, to use the adapter factory, you will need to subclass it and provide overrides for `createAdapter()` handlers to create and return the desired type-specific adapters.

We will discuss the generated adapter factory and switch classes further in Chapter 16.

10.10   Alternative Generator Patterns

So far in this chapter, we have only looked at the default generator patterns for various Ecore constructs. In fact, EMF's code generator can produce a number of alternative patterns. All such patterns can be enabled from within the EMF generator, via properties on the various elements of a given model. We will discuss all of these GenModel properties in Chapter 12. In this section, we'll look more closely at some of the most interesting alternative patterns. In particular, we will see how different options on the root-level **GenModel** object allow you to select patterns that optimize performance and suppress EMFisms.

10.10.1   *Performance Optimization*

The implementation patterns that we have seen so far are intended to be quite straightforward and obvious. The idea behind their design was to generate the kind of code that users would write by hand.

However, in some circumstances, it is important to tune for performance. In particular, when working with large models, it might be worth sacrificing some of the simplicity of the code to reduce the memory footprint or execution time. Using code generation is especially beneficial in such circumstances, as you can very quickly take advantage of correct implementations that have been proven to improve performance.

That said, you should not expect that these alternative patterns will yield improvements in all cases. Depending on the characteristics of a given model and on how it is intended to be instantiated, one or more of these optimizations might be appropriate. Others might serve only to complicate the code unnecessarily, or might even lead to degraded performance. Armed with an understanding of these patterns, you should be able to determine which, if any, will be appropriate in your application.

Boolean Flags

As we have seen in this chapter, each attribute and reference in a class is stored using an instance variable by default. Moreover, for each unsettable, multiplicity-1 feature, an additional `boolean` field is used to represent whether the feature is set or unset.

In Java, `boolean` values are handled using the same virtual machine instructions as `int` values. As a result, each `boolean` field in a class adds no less than 4 bytes of storage to each instance of that class. For classes with a large number of boolean attributes or unsettable features, each object will waste a significant amount of memory.

For example, consider a class that contains only 16 unsettable, single-valued, boolean attributes. By default, this class would have 32 `boolean` fields, requiring 128 bytes of memory per instance.[19] However, if we could pack each boolean value into a single bit of an `int` field, these attributes could be stored using just 4 bytes. When dealing with large numbers of instances, the memory savings can really add up.

In fact, EMF can generate code that uses this latter pattern, with a single `int` field providing storage for multiple boolean and unsettable features. To do so, simply use the "Boolean Flags Field" GenModel property to specify a name for the field.

For example, imagine that we added two boolean attributes, **processed** and **shipped**, to class **PurchaseOrder**, and made its **shipTo** reference unsettable. This is illustrated in Figure 10.24.

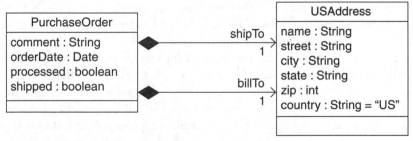

Figure 10.24 Class **PurchaseOrder** with boolean attributes.

If we then set the value of the "Boolean Flags Field" property on our **GenModel** to "flags" and generated the model, we would see the following related code in `PurchaseOrderImpl`:

```
public class PurchaseOrderImpl extends EObjectImpl
    implements PurchaseOrder
{
    protected int flags = 0;
    ...
```

---

19. In fact, there is at least 32 bytes of additional overhead per **EObject**, for storing things like the container, container feature ID, and adapters.

```
protected static final boolean PROCESSED_EDEFAULT = false;
protected static final int PROCESSED_EFLAG = 1 << 0;

protected static final boolean SHIPPED_EDEFAULT = false;
protected static final int SHIPPED_EFLAG = 1 << 1;

protected USAddress shipTo = null;
protected static final int SHIP_TO_ESETFLAG = 1 << 2;
...

public boolean isProcessed()
{
  return (flags & PROCESSED_EFLAG) != 0;
}

public void setProcessed(boolean newProcessed)
{
  boolean oldProcessed = (flags & PROCESSED_EFLAG) != 0;
  if (newProcessed) flags |= PROCESSED_EFLAG;
  else flags &= ~PROCESSED_EFLAG;
  if (eNotificationRequired())
    eNotify(new ENotificationImpl(this, Notification.SET, ...));
}
...
}
```

The `flags` field is used to store the values of **processed** and **shipped**, and to track whether **shipTo** is set or unset. Thus, three `boolean` fields are replaced by a single `int`. The default value constants are static, so they have no per-instance cost. There are also new static bit mask constants. Notice, for example, how `isProcessed()` and `setProcessed()` use the `PROCESSED_EFLAG` mask to access and set the appropriate bit in `flags`. Otherwise, they behave just like ordinary accessor methods. The other accessors are implemented analogously.

Using this pattern does not limit the number of boolean flags that can be accommodated in a single class. When this number exceeds the capacity of a single integer field, additional fields will be introduced.

There is another related GenModel property: "Boolean Flags Reserved Bits". With this property, it is possible to reuse an existing boolean flags field inherited from the base object implementation, such as the protected `eFlags` field in `EObjectImpl`. When the property is changed from its default value of "-1", no flags field is actually generated in classes, and the specified number of bits is reserved for use by the base class. This further reduces the size of generated objects; however it carries some risk. In the future, `EObjectImpl` might begin using additional bits of its flag field, so you might sacrifice future binary compatibility if you choose to reserve too few bits. For this reason, you should avoid setting this property, and just use the pattern already illustrated. However, if you do choose to ignore this recommendation, you are strongly advised to reserve at least 8 bits for EObjectImpl's use.

Virtual Feature Delegation

There is another pattern that EMF can use to try to reduce memory consumption by generating fewer fields on each class. The motivation is the fact that each non-primitive field is a pointer, typically consuming 4 bytes, that is allocated as part of the object, whether or not it ever gets set to refer to another object. By default, one such field is generated for each non-primitive attribute or reference in a class. For very large, sparsely populated models, this results in wasted memory.

The alternative is to store the values of all non-primitive features in a single object array. The advantage here is that the array can be resized dynamically to accommodate values of only the features that have been set. This pattern is enabled by setting the "Feature Delegation" GenModel property to "Virtual".[20] In the PrimerPO model, this would make PurchaseOrderImpl, for instance, look like this:

```
public class PurchaseOrderImpl extends EObjectImpl
  implements PurchaseOrder
{
  protected Object[] eVirtualValues = null;
  protected int eVirtualIndexBits0 = 0;

  protected static final String COMMENT_EDEFAULT = null;
  ...

  public String getComment()
  {
    return (String)eVirtualGet(PPOPackage.PURCHASE_ORDER__COMMENT,
                               COMMENT_EDEFAULT);
  }

  public void setComment(String newComment)
  {
    String comment = newComment;
    Object oldComment =
      eVirtualSet(PPOPackage.PURCHASE_ORDER__COMMENT, comment);
    if (eNotificationRequired())
      eNotify(new ENotificationImpl(this, Notification.SET, ...));
  }
  ...
}
```

---

20. The other possible values for this property are "None", which gives the default pattern that we have already seen, and "Reflective". We discuss the reflective feature delegation pattern in Section 15.5.

Here, the eVirtualValues array provides storage for all the features in **PurchaseOrder**. The eVirtualIndexBits0 field is needed to keep track of which features are actually being stored in the array. Each structural feature, in feature ID order, is represented by a single bit in the field. The bit is set when that field is set to a non-default value, at which point that value must be stored.

Notice that the implementation of getComment(), which would normally just return the value of a generated comment field, is now entirely delegated to eVirtualGet(). This method is part of BasicEObjectImpl, the base implementation for EObjects. It first consults eVirtualIndexBits0, checking for the bit corresponding to the given feature. If that bit is not set, it just returns the given default, in this case COMMENT_EDEFAULT. Otherwise, it counts the number of preceding set bits to determine the feature's index in the eVirtualValues array and returns the value at that index.

Similarly, instead of setting a field, the setComment() method delegates to eVirtualSet(). The code responsible for notification is the same as in the default setter pattern. The eVirtualSet() method is responsible for updating eVirtualIndexBits0 and the eVirtualValues array. Note that setting a feature for the first time involves adding a value to the array, which can necessitate growing the array.

Because the fields for the array and index bits are declared on the generated class, not the base implementation, the following method overrides must also be generated to provide access to these fields:

```
protected Object[] eVirtualValues()
{
  return eVirtualValues;
}

protected void eSetVirtualValues(Object[] newValues)
{
  eVirtualValues = newValues;
}

protected int eVirtualIndexBits(int offset)
{
  switch (offset)
  {
    case 0: return eVirtualIndexBits0;
    default: throw new IndexOutOfBoundsException();
  }
}

protected void eSetVirtualIndexBits(int offset, int newIndexBits)
{
  switch (offset)
  {
```

```
    case 0:
      eVirtualIndexBits0 = newIndexBits;
      break;
    default: throw new IndexOutOfBoundsException();
  }
}
```

These methods are invoked from within eVirtualSet() and eVirtualGet(), described previously. The eVirtualValues() and eSetVirtualValues() methods, which get and set the values array, are very simple and do not require any explanation.

The other two methods, eSetVirutalIndexBits() and eSetVirtualIndexBits(), are slightly more involved. Notice that they switch on an offset argument. The reason is that a single int field contains only 32 bits, each of which can represent one structural feature. When there are more than 32 features, additional fields must be generated. They will be named eVirtualIndexBits1, eVirtualIndexBits2, and so on, as needed. In such cases, these two methods select the appropriate field to get or set, based on an offset calculated from the feature ID.

It is important to know how many non-primitive features need to be defined on a class before the virtual delegation pattern begins to yield memory savings. In fact, once a feature has been set on a given instance, this pattern no longer yields any savings for it, as the array of virtual values will then include the same 4-byte pointer that would have otherwise been allocated as part of the object. Thus, the key consideration is how many *unused* features you would expect on a typical instance.

To weigh the benefits of this pattern, we need to consider the overhead it introduces. For every 32 features, there is a field of index bits, consuming 4 bytes. The array of values typically has an overhead of about 16 bytes. That means that you would need to expect at least five unused features per object just to break even. However, there is an additional complication: because growing the array is an expensive operation, it is not, by default, grown by just one element at a time.[21] As a result, you should expect at least another 8 bytes of overhead in the array, and more as the number of set features increases. Thus, you really shouldn't even consider using the virtual delegation pattern unless you expect most objects to have at least 10 unused, non-primitive features. As the number of such unused features approaches 32, the savings per object should approach 100 bytes.

---

21. The growth factor can be adjusted by overriding eComputeVirtualValuesCapacity().

However, even at that point, you should carefully evaluate the trade-off between memory use and execution time. As we have seen, this pattern makes accessing and, especially, setting features considerably more expensive than the default one. Still, when there are very large numbers of objects in play, the memory savings can absolutely make this pattern worth selecting.

Constant-Time Reflective Methods

In Section 10.7, we saw that the different reflective methods are structured similarly. They all contain a switch, based on the feature ID, with a case for each feature implemented by the class. If the feature ID is not recognized, the superclass's implementation is invoked to handle inherited features.

For example, here is the pattern for eGet():

```
public Object eGet(int featureID, boolean resolve, boolean coreType)
{
  switch (featureID)
  {
    // one case per implemented feature
    ...
  }
  return super.eGet(featureID, resolve, coreType);
}
```

Here, each case invokes a generated accessor. Previously, we said that this pattern adds just a small, constant-time cost to that of the generated accessor. However, that's not quite the whole story.

If the feature being accessed is inherited, the reflective method is invoked on its superclass, and then the same cost is incurred there. If it is inherited from two levels up the hierarchy, there are two additional invocations and switches. Indeed, we should really say that this pattern for reflective methods has linear complexity with respect to inheritance depth.

The alternative would be to generate cases in the reflective methods for all features, whether implemented or inherited. For example:

```
public Object eGet(int featureID, boolean resolve, boolean coreType)
{
  switch (featureID)
  {
    // one case per implemented or inherited feature
    ...
  }
  return eDynamicGet(featureID, resolve, coreType);
}
```

Notice that, with this pattern, unrecognized feature IDs are assumed to represent dynamic features, and `eDynamicGet()` is invoked directly, bypassing any implementations from modeled supertypes. This pattern, which really does offer constant-time performance, is produced when the "Minimal Reflective Methods" GenModel property is set to "false".

While performing better for deep inheritance hierarchies, this pattern does generate duplicative code in all the reflective methods, which results in additional bytecode consuming memory at runtime. So, if your model includes deep inheritance hierarchies and you expect to be reflectively accessing inherited or dynamic features frequently, the constant-time pattern might prove valuable. Otherwise, the default, minimal pattern is probably the better choice.

Moreover, if you are extending classes from another model, this pattern embeds constants from that model in your code. A single addition or removal of an inherited feature will then be a binary incompatible change. Thus, the constant-time pattern is best avoided in this case.

10.10.2 Suppression of EMFisms

One very common use of EMF is to generate model-based APIs. That is, developers working with EMF often wish to expose the code they generate to their own clients. Frequently, there is a tendency to regard EMF as an "implementation detail" that should be hidden from the client, which results in a desire to purge their code of all recognizable "EMFisms."

Not surprisingly, the developers of EMF consider the framework to be solid and well designed, and quite worthy of being exposed to its users' clients. Indeed, a large measure of EMF's appeal is that its own API provides a basis for interoperable model realizations, which can readily be composed and used in generic, EMF-based utilities and frameworks. When EMF's APIs are suppressed, the client gets a simpler API, but one that excludes access to all that power.

So, should EMF be exposed as part of the client API, or treated as an implementation detail? Really, that's a decision that should be left up to the developer using EMF. So, EMF provides a number of generator properties that can be used to suppress the various EMFisms that we have seen so far in this chapter. Ultimately, if you want, you can remove all traces of EMF and produce the simplest possible API.

EObject API

The most immediate and prominent sign of EMF in generated code is that the interfaces representing modeled classes extend `EObject`. This provides easy access to EMF reflection and metadata, and facilitates use with EMF's notification and persistence frameworks. In short, it exposes a lot of API to the client, which might not always be desirable.

To even participate in the framework, it is necessary that all modeled objects implement EObject; however, this need not be exposed to the client. Because generated implementation classes extend EObjectImpl, which already implements EObject, generated interfaces need not state that they implement EObject explicitly.

If we regard the generated interfaces as API and the generated classes as internal implementation, then the client will not see the EObject API. Internally, instances can simply be cast appropriately.

The GenModel property of interest here is "Root Extends Interface". It specifies the base that is to be extended by interfaces generated for modeled classes with no supertypes. By default, it is set to "org.eclipse.emf.ecore.EObject". Simply clear this value to suppress the EObject API from the interfaces.[22]

The PurchaseOrder interface, for instance, would then be generated like this:

```
public interface PurchaseOrder
{
  String getComment();
  void setComment(String value);

  Date getOrderDate();
  void setOrderDate(Date value);
  ...

  EList getItems();
}
```

The only difference from the pattern we saw in Section 10.1.2 is the absence of an extends clause. This leaves just one sure sign that this code was generated by EMF: the EList return type of getItems().

EMF Types

As we saw in Sections 10.2.5 and 10.3.9, EMF uses its own list and map interfaces, EList and EMap, respectively. EList is a simple extension of java.util.List that introduces two move() methods. EMap, on the other hand, does not derive from java.util.Map, but does provide access to a Map-typed view.

---

22. We can also use this property to introduce common behavior instead of to remove it. By specifying any other qualified interface name here, we would ensure that all generated interfaces implement that base. Similarly, the "Root Extends Class" and "Root Implements Interface" properties can be used to introduce common behavior in the implementation. We will discuss these properties further in Chapter 12.

The additional functionality provided by both of these types is needed internally by the framework, but, again, it might not be necessary to expose that functionality to the client.

If the "Suppress EMF Types" GenModel property is set to "true", these types will instead be surfaced as the standard Java `List` and `Map` types. For example, this would change the return type of the preceding `getItems()` accessor to `List`.

One other feature type, which has not yet been discussed, is also affected. A reference that is unconstrained by type is modeled as a reference to **EObject**. This is because, by default, all modeled types implicitly extend **EObject**. As a result, the `get()` accessor for such a reference usually is generated with a return type of `EObject`. However, when EMF types are suppressed, such an accessor simply returns `java.lang.Object`.

EMF Metadata

Once you have decided to remove the reflective `EObject` API from generated interfaces, it no longer makes much sense to generate a package interface. Recall from Section 10.8 that this interface just provides access to the metadata for the model, for use with reflective APIs.

If the "Suppress EMF Metadata" GenModel property is set to "true", no package interface will be generated. Instead, all the static package attributes, classifier and feature IDs, classifier and feature accessors, and literal constants will be generated directly into the package implementation class for internal use.

The factory interface will still be generated, as it provides the recommended means for creating new instances of model classes. However, with metadata suppressed, its declaration is changed slightly. For example:

```
public interface PPOFactory
{
  PPOFactory INSTANCE =
    com.example.ppo.impl.PPOFactoryImpl.eINSTANCE;

  PurchaseOrder createPurchaseOrder();
  USAddress createUSAddress();
  Item createItem();
}
```

First, the factory no longer extends `EFactory`, so generic `create()`, `createFromString()`, and `convertToString()` methods are no longer inherited. Of course, the factory class, `PPOFactoryImpl` in this example, still implements `EFactory`, so these generic methods are still available internally.

Second, the singleton variable is now named `INSTANCE` instead of `eINSTANCE`. Finally, the `getPPOPackage()` method is no longer generated, which makes sense because there is no `PPOPackage` to return.

Interface/Implementation Split

There is one more characteristic of code generated by EMF that isn't desired by all EMF users: the basic pattern of creating an interface and a class for each modeled class. This is quite different from the other EMFisms we have so far discussed in that it is just a design decision favored by EMF, and it does not itself expose the client of generated code to any EMF APIs. Indeed, it's precisely because of this interface/implementation split that we are able to hide such APIs.

As stated in Chapter 2, EMF strongly advocates the use of this design. It's regarded as the best pattern for model-like APIs and is very widely used, both in other Eclipse projects and elsewhere. However, provided your model does not include multiple inheritance, it is possible to select a simpler, class-only pattern.

If you set the "Suppress Interfaces" generator property to "true", no impl package will be generated. A class will be generated in place of each interface discussed so far. That is, for each modeled class, a single Java class will be generated. Its name will be the same as the modeled class name, with no "Impl" suffix. Similarly, a factory class and package class will be generated in place of the default pattern's interfaces.

This pattern has a number of drawbacks compared to the default one, so unless you have a compelling reason for suppressing interfaces, it is not recommended. The basic rationale for the default pattern is that it provides the opportunity to substitute alternate implementations for modeled classes. Of course, with the suppressed interface pattern, this is simply not possible. As already mentioned, multiple inheritance cannot be represented. Finally, this pattern makes it impossible to hide the EMF APIs from your clients, as there are no interfaces in which to suppress EObject.

10.11   Customizing Generated Code

At various points throughout this chapter, we have referred to modifications you must make, by hand, to generated Java code. In particular, you will usually find it necessary to write code for volatile structural features, operations, and data type to string mappings.

If you are going to be modifying generated code by hand, you need to be able to regenerate it without worrying about losing the changes that you have made. Fortunately, the EMF code generator provides a simple mechanism for specifying which elements should be replaced by regenerated versions and which should be left alone.

For example, let's add some new behavior, an isFollowup() method, to our purchase orders. We simply declare the new method in the PurchaseOrder interface:

```
public interface PurchaseOrder ...
{
  boolean isFollowup();
  ...
}
```

Then, we add its implementation to the `PurchaseOrderImpl` class:

```
public class PurchaseOrderImpl ...
{
  public boolean isFollowup()
  {
    return getPreviousOrder() != null;
  }
}
```

The EMF generator won't wipe out this change because it isn't a generated method to begin with. Every interface, class, method, and field generated by EMF includes a Javadoc comment that contains an `@generated` tag, like this:

```
/**
 * ...
 * @generated
 */
public String getComment()
{
  return comment;
}
```

Any method or field in the file that doesn't carry this tag, like `isFollowup()`, will be left untouched whenever we regenerate. In fact, if we want to change the implementation of a generated member, we can do that by removing the `@generated` tag from it:

```
/**
 * ...
 * @̶g̶e̶n̶e̶r̶a̶t̶e̶d̶
 */
public String getComment()
{
  // our custom implementation ...
}
```

Now, because of the missing `@generated` tag, the `getComment()` method is considered to be user code. If we regenerate the model, the generator will detect the collision and discard the generated version of the method.

Another way to indicate to the generator that a method or field that was originally generated has been hand-modified is simply to "dirty" the @generated tag by adding something after it. It is conventional to add the word NOT.

Before discarding a generated method, the generator first checks if there is another generated method in the file with the same name, but with "Gen" appended. If it finds one, it redirects the body of the newly generated version there, instead of just discarding it. For example, if we want to extend the generated getComment() implementation instead of completely discarding it, we can do that by simply renaming it, like this:

```
/**
 *  ...
 * @generated
 */
public String getCommentGen()
{
  return comment;
}
```

We then add our override as a non-generated method. We can make it do whatever we want:

```
public String getComment()
{
  String result = getCommentGen();
  if (result == null)
    result = ... ;
  return result;
}
```

If we regenerate, the generator will detect the collision with our user version of getComment(), but because we also have the @generated version in the class, it will redirect the newly generated implementation to getCommentGen() instead of discarding it.

When we regenerate, the Javadoc comment associated with a generated interface, class, method, or field always replaces the existing comment in the file. However, every generated Javadoc comment includes a section, delimited by <!-- begin-user-doc --> and <!-- end-user-doc -->, where you can enter arbitrary text that will be retained during regeneration.

Unlike on a method, an @generated tag on an interface or class refers only to the declaration itself, and not its contents. Therefore, removing the @generated tag will not actually block the merging of all the type's methods and fields; each will be merged based on the presence or absence of its own @generated tag. If you do wish to block merging of the whole type, including all its members, simply change the @generated tag to @generated NOT. Note that dirtying the tag with any other text is only equivalent to removing the tag; this is the only context where NOT has a special meaning.

There is one more case to consider with regards to merging code. Imagine that you wish to hand-modify a generated interface or class to add a supertype. For example, suppose you wanted to make PurchaseOrder implement java.io.Serializable. Simply adding it to the extends clause would not suffice. Because the interface has an @generated tag by default, the change would be reversed the next time you regenerated the code.

To properly support this kind of change, there is another special Javadoc tag recognized by the EMF code generator: the @extends tag, which is followed by a comma-separated list of interfaces. The generated interface's extends clause will be merged with this list. This allows you to add non-generated supertypes, without removing the @generated tag. For example:

```
/**
 * <!-- begin-user-doc -->
 * A representation of the model object 'Purchase Order'.
 * @extends Serializable
 * <!-- end-user-doc -->
 *
 * ...
 *
 * @model
 * @generated
 */
public interface PurchaseOrder extends EObject, Serializable
{ ...
```

Note that we placed the @extends tag inside the user section of the Javadoc. This ensures that the tag itself will not be removed during merging.

There is also an @implements tag for classes that works exactly the same way, allowing additional interfaces to be added to the class's implements clause.

CHAPTER 11

EMF.Edit Generator Patterns

Attempting to generate an interactive application is a fairly tricky undertaking. In generating a data model implementation, the problem is well defined and well contained: to be useful, the implementation must correctly and efficiently realize the semantics of the model. Its external interfaces need to be well understood by the developer who wishes to use it as a component in the application being built.

By comparison, the problem that EMF.Edit tries to solve is much more open-ended. The code that it generates is meant to be a starting point for the development of an application. Its modification, not just its use, will be necessary.

Thus, EMF.Edit must suggest a design and provide utilities that integrate well with its environment, while offering enough flexibility so that it can be molded into the developer's desired application. After all, there is no way to predict all of the things that you might want your editor to become.

In this chapter, we explore the various patterns employed in generating code for the edit and editor plug-ins for an EMF model, discussing how the generated code functions and how it fits into the overall EMF.Edit design. We see how some details are hidden in generic framework code that uses Ecore's reflective API, and how others are pushed right to the surface to make it easy to modify visible behavior. We also offer suggestions about how these hooks can be used, so that you can start customizing your editor.

As in Chapter 10, we use the primer purchase order model as our example, showing and discussing the code that is generated from it.

Like the EMF.Edit framework itself, generated EMF.Edit code is, by default, divided into two parts: UI-independent code is placed in an edit plug-in, and UI-dependent code is placed in a separate editor plug-in. The UI-independent portion facilitates the viewing and editing of model objects by providing the item providers that we first discussed in Chapter 3. The following types of classes are generated in the edit plug-in:

○ Item provider

○ Item provider adapter factory

○ Plug-in

The UI-dependent portion uses the Eclipse workbench framework, including JFace and SWT, to provide the interface for creating and editing EMF models. The following types of classes are generated in this plug-in:

○ Editor

○ Action bar contributor

○ Wizard

○ Plug-in

In addition to Java code, the generator produces the following content for each of the two EMF.Edit plug-ins:

○ Two manifest files, *META-INF/MANIFEST.MF* and *plugin.xml*

○ A *plugin.properties* file, containing translatable strings

○ A *build.properties* file, containing build settings

○ An *icons/* subdirectory

As we describe the generated code patterns, we also need to make reference to some of these files.

11.1   Item Providers

We introduced item providers in Section 3.2, describing them as adapters that provide the interfaces to support viewing and editing of model objects. At that time, we said they are the most important objects in EMF.Edit, so it's not surprising that we focus heavily on them now. It is the item providers that determine how each type of object will be displayed and how it will respond to editing commands; we need to understand how the generated item provider code does this, and how to modify or add to it effectively.

By default, a different item provider implementation is generated for each class in the Ecore model. The inheritance hierarchy of these classes follows that of the model. Recall from Chapter 10 that, although EMF supports multiple interface inheritance, each class can only extend one implementation base class, and any structural features inherited from other superclasses will be re-implemented in the derived implementation class. The same pattern is followed among item providers: if class B extends class A, then B's item provider class will extend

A's item provider class and will take responsibility for all of the features introduced in B and in any of its mixin interfaces.[1]

In much the same way as implementations for roots in the model's class hierarchy extend `EObjectImpl`, their item providers extend a framework class called `ItemProviderAdapter`. The Template Method design pattern [3] is used extensively in this base class, as it implements most of the default item provider functionality itself, and calls to methods for which overrides are generated to supply details specific to the particular model or class. As we discuss the generated methods, we also have to describe how they fit into the template methods of the base class.

Throughout this section, we look at the item provider that gets generated for the **PurchaseOrder** class, and see how it works with its base class to perform the four item provider roles described in Chapter 3:

1. Implement content and label provider functions.

2. Provide a property source (property descriptors) for EMF objects.

3. Act as a command factory for commands on their associated model object.

4. Forward EMF model change notifications on to viewers.

We begin with the class declaration:

```
public class PurchaseOrderItemProvider extends ItemProviderAdapter
    implements IEditingDomainItemProvider
        IStructuredItemContentProvider,
        ITreeItemContentProvider,
        IItemLabelProvider,
        IItemPropertySource
```

As we've already emphasized, the base class is `ItemProviderAdapter`. We also notice that five interfaces are implemented, corresponding collectively to the item provider roles. In the following subsections, we will discuss the methods that are generated to help implement these interfaces.

11.1.1 *Content and Label Provider*

As we described in Section 3.2.1, item providers support the implementation of content and label providers for the viewers by implementing `ITreeItemContentProvider`, `IStructuredItemContentProvider`, `IItemLabelProvider`, and `ITableItemLabelProvider`.

---

1. Note that we can specify in the generator model that generation of the item provider for any given class should be suppressed, in which case the item provider for its derived class will extend that of its implementation base class.

We begin with ITreeItemContentProvider. Believe it or not, implementing the four methods declared by this interface really comes down to answering the following question: What will we consider to be the children of a given object? This decision is exposed in the generated item provider, as follows:

```
public Collection getChildrenFeatures(Object object)
{
  if (childrenFeatures == null)
  {
    super.getChildrenFeatures(object);
    childrenFeatures.add(
      PPOPackage.Literals.PURCHASE_ORDER__SHIP_TO);
    childrenFeatures.add(
      PPOPackage.Literals.PURCHASE_ORDER__BILL_TO);
    childrenFeatures.add(
      PPOPackage.Literals.PURCHASE_ORDER__ITEMS);
  }
  return childrenFeatures;
}
```

Here we see the answer for purchase orders: a purchase order's children will include all of the objects contained via its **shipTo, billTo,** and **items** references. By default, the set of children of an object includes all objects accessible through its containment references; however, this can be changed via the generator model. Any features can be made to contribute children, determining how getChildrenFeatures() is implemented; the generated code simply adds these features to the childrenFeatures list.

There still remains some distance between deciding which references correspond to an object's children and actually implementing the getParent(), getChildren(), hasChildren(), and getElements() methods declared by the interface. However, given this selection of features and the default assumption that the child relationship corresponds to containment, these methods become generic, straightforward applications of the reflective EObject API. They are implemented by the base class, ItemProviderAdapter, as follows:

○ getParent() returns the container of the object; if the object is not contained but belongs to a resource, it returns that resource.

○ getChildren() iterates over the childrenFeatures list, building and returning a collection of the objects it obtains from those features.

○ hasChildren() returns whether that collection of the objects obtained from the childrenFeatures is non-empty.

○ getElements() simply calls getChildren() and returns its result.

The last of these methods, `getElements()`, is inherited from `IStructuredItemContentProvider`. The only member of that interface, it returns the objects to display as rows in a table, items in a list, or root-level nodes in a tree, for the object given as input to the viewer. Implementing it via `getChildren()` is certainly a reasonable default, but this method is a good candidate for customization, as we will see in Chapter 19.

Moreover, EMF.Edit provides a good deal of flexibility regarding the children and parent of a given object. As mentioned earlier, any structural features can contribute children to the object, including non-containment references, feature maps, and even simple attributes. The implementation of `getChildren()` is sophisticated enough to handle all of these cases.

Because attributes, including feature maps, are generally not **EObject**-typed, we cannot assume that they will yield `Notifiers` for which item provider adapters can be obtained. So, for their values to participate in EMF.Edit, we must use wrappers that directly implement the item provider interfaces.

By default, `getChildren()` automatically creates such wrappers for children contributed by all attributes. These wrappers properly provide labels and properties, and handle commands and notifications, for the values they wrap. The creation of wrappers is performed by `createWrapper()`, which can be overridden to enable or disable wrapping for particular children and to specialize the wrappers that are created. This method consults `isWrappingNeeded()`, allowing wrapping to be vetoed for all the children of a given object. By default, it returns `true` if `getChildrenFeatures()` returns one or more attributes.

In order to ensure that `getChildren()` always returns exactly the same children for a given object, item providers need to cache any wrappers they create. The `isWrappingNeeded()` method has a second function: it controls whether caching is performed. In fact, if this method returns `true`, all children, not just wrappers, are automatically cached.

Wrappers are optional for children contributed by non-containment references. If you are not using wrappers, you will need to override the `ItemProviderAdapter` implementation of `getParent()`, which just returns the container of the object, in the child type's item provider. For instance, if the children reference is bidirectional, with a multiplicity-1 opposite, `getParent()` could be implemented for the child to simply return the value of that opposite reference. If providing a corresponding `getParent()` implementation is impossible or inconvenient, wrappers can be used for the children to yield the correct result. Such wrappers will be created by `createWrapper()` by default only if `isWrappingNeeded()` returns `true`. Note, however, that this is a heavier-weight solution.

Finally, it is also possible to override both `getChildren()` and `getParent()` in your generated item providers to provide an entirely different interpretation. One common pattern is to add an additional set of item providers that offers an alternate view on the model, an idea that we will discuss further in Section 11.3.

We now turn our attention to providing labels: the `IItemLabelProvider` interface includes the `getImage()` and `getText()` methods, which return an icon and a text label, respectively, for a given object. The following implementations are generated in `PurchaseOrderItemProvider`:

```
public String getImage(Object object)
{
  return overlayImage(
    getResourceLocator().getImage("full/obj16/PurchaseOrder"));
}

public Object getText(Object object) {
{
  String label = ((PurchaseOrder)object).getComment();
  return label == null || label.length() == 0 ?
    getString("_UI_PurchaseOrder_type") :
    getString("_UI_PurchaseOrder_type") + " " + label;
}
```

The call to `getResourceLocator()`, which we see here in `getImage()`, returns the object directly responsible for supplying text and image resources—such an object implements the `ResourceLocator` interface. This method is defined in `ItemProviderAdapter` to return the EMF.Edit plug-in class, but an override is generated in `PurchaseOrderItemProvider` as follows:

```
  public ResourceLocator getResourceLocator()
  {
    return PrimerPOEditPlugin.INSTANCE;
  }
```

This returns the generated plug-in class that has access to the text and image resources specific to our purchase order model. This class implements `getImage()` to look for image resources in the *icons/* subdirectory of the plug-in's location and return a reference to the named icon. In this case, it returns a reference to the generated icon representing a purchase order. The call to `overlayImage()`, another method defined by `ItemProviderAdapter`, provides an opportunity for the icon to be decorated with an overlay. It usually does nothing; however, when the object is contained by an object in another resource, an overlay is added to indicate this.[2]

---

2. Cross-resource containment is discussed further in Chapters 10 and 15.

The `getString()` method is implemented in `ItemProviderAdapter` to look up an externalized string for the given key, using the `ResourceLocator` returned by `getResourceLocator()`. Eclipse and EMF use Java's `ResourceBundle` mechanism to supply externalized strings. Each plug-in can include a *plugin.properties* file, which lists key–value pairs, where the values are localized strings. In the preceding `getText()` method, we're looking for the string keyed by "_UI_PurchaseOrder_type", which is generated as follows:

```
_UI_PurchaseOrder_type = Purchase Order
```

The generated property file includes one such string for each class and each feature in the Ecore model.

So, the `getText()` method retrieves a string that gives the type of the object, in this case "Purchase Order". It appends to that the value of one of the object's attributes, in this case, **comment**, and returns the result. The particular attribute to use is selected in the generator model; by default, a single-valued attribute, preferably one whose name is or ends with "name", is chosen.

We have now seen several opportunities to customize the label provider behavior of your item providers. Beyond setting the label attribute for a class in the generator model, you can change the externalized string that identifies the class by editing the property file, and you can replace the generic icon that gets generated for the class. Or, you could just remove the `@generated` tag and then change the implementations of `getImage()` and `getText()`, so that they return something else entirely.

You might have noticed that there was one interface introduced in Section 3.2.1 that is not implemented by `PurchaseOrderItemProvider`: `ITableItemLabelProvider`, which supports label providers for a table viewer. Its two methods, `getColumnImage()` and `getColumnText()`, are not implemented in `ItemProviderAdapter`, either. Instead, the following trick is used in the label provider, which is an instance of class `AdapterFactoryLabelProvider`: if it fails to obtain an adapter that supports `ITableItemLabelProvider`, it tries for `IItemLabelProvider` and just delegates the calls to `getImage()` and `getText()`, dropping the parameter that specifies a column. We see the effect in the **Table** page of the generated editor: each row in the table is populated with one value repeated in each column. You can easily improve on this behavior by changing the item provider to implement `ITableItemLabelProvider`. We'll see exactly how to do this in Section 19.2.2.

11.1.2 Item Property Source

Section 3.2.2 described the rather complex object interactions through which item providers populate a property sheet for an object. Fortunately, the role of the item provider itself is quite simple: it only needs to create and return a list of `ItemPropertyDescriptors`, which, you might recall, get wrapped by `PropertyDescriptors` to implement the `IPropertyDescriptor` interface required by the property sheet.

`PurchaseOrderItemProvider` implements `getPropertyDescriptors()`, one of the three methods of `IItemPropertySource`, with the following generated code:

```
public List getPropertyDescriptors(Object object)
{
  if (itemPropertyDescriptors == null)
  {
    super.getPropertyDescriptors(object);
    addCommentPropertyDescriptor(object);
    addOrderDatePropertyDescriptor(object);
  }
  return itemPropertyDescriptors;
}
```

This method builds up a list of item property descriptors. It calls out to additional generated methods, each of which adds an `ItemPropertyDescriptor` for a feature that is considered to be a property. By default, this includes all attributes and non-containment references, although, once again, we can specify a different choice via the generator model.

The methods that add the `ItemPropertyDescriptors` look like this:

```
protected void addCommentPropertyDescriptor(Object object)
{
  itemPropertyDescriptors.add(
    createItemPropertyDescriptor(
      ((ComposeableAdapterFactory)adapterFactory).
        getRootAdapterFactory(),
      getResourceLocator(),
      getString("_UI_PurchaseOrder_comment_feature"),
      getString("_UI_PropertyDescriptor_description",
                "_UI_PurchaseOrder_comment_feature",
                "_UI_PurchaseOrder_type"),
      PPOPackage.Literals.PURCHASE_ORDER__COMMENT,
      true,
      false,
      false,
      ItemPropertyDescriptor.GENERIC_VALUE_IMAGE,
      null,
      null));
}
```

They call a helper method, createItemPropertyDescriptor(), to create the appropriate descriptor, and everything else is taken care of automatically: the feature value will be accessed via the reflective EObject API, and an editor widget appropriate for its type will be supplied.

The item provider only needs to supply the following information, as parameters to createItemPropertyDescriptor():

○ The adapter factory that created this item provider, or its root, if adapter factory composition is being used[3]

○ The resource locator that can be used to obtain externalized text and icons for model elements

○ The label to be displayed for the property, which is also used as the property's ID

○ The description, which displays in the status bar when the property is selected

○ The feature on which the property is based

○ Whether to allow editing of the property

○ Whether to treat the property value as multi-line text

○ Whether choices for the property value, such as for an enumerated type or reference, should be sorted alphabetically

○ The icon to be displayed with the property

○ The name of a category under which to group the property

○ A set of filter flags that apply to the property

In the generated code, externalized strings are used to supply the label and description. The label is the name of the feature, "Comment", which is retrieved in the same manner as the class name was in getText() earlier. The description is obtained from the three-parameter form of getString() that is defined by the ItemProviderAdapter base class. This method gets externalized strings for its second and third arguments using the single-parameter form, and then substitutes those results into the string retrieved for its first. To be concrete, the generated resource file includes the following:

```
_UI_PropertyDescriptor_description = The {0} of the {1}
```

EMF uses java.text.MessageFormat to perform substitution in externalized strings. Even if you're not already familiar with this mechanism, you can

---

3. We will discuss adapter factory composition in Section 11.2.

probably guess that "{0}" and "{1}" mark where the two substitutions should occur. The resulting string will be "The Comment of the Purchase Order".

By default, whether editing of the property is allowed depends on the feature's **changeable** attribute, but this can be controlled via the generator model.

For attributes, the icon is selected based on the type of the feature. For references, the icon parameter is omitted. In this case, the property descriptor gets an adapter for the referenced object that supports `IItemLabelProvider`, which then supplies the icon via `getImage()`.

The other property descriptor features—including multi-line text, choice sorting, categories, and filter flags—are not used in default generated code. However, they can be enabled via the generator model.

In addition to `getPropertyDescriptors()`, the `IItemPropertySource` interface includes two other methods, both of which are implemented by the base class. The first, `getPropertyDescriptor()`, returns the property descriptor associated with a given ID. It simply calls `getPropertyDescriptors()` and tests the IDs of the resulting descriptors, returning the first one for which it matches. The other, `getEditableValue()`, allows for some transformation of the value to be edited. In general, this is not needed, so the base class implementation just returns the object passed to it, unchanged.

Once again, many opportunities present themselves for customization. While the generator model provides control over which features of a class correspond to editable and non-editable properties, you might also wish to base additional properties on features of other related classes. To do so, you would just need to add code to `getPropertyDescriptors()` to provide the extra property descriptors.

By modifying the calls to the `ItemPropertyDescriptor` constructor, you can control the label, description, and icon for the property. Or, instead of adding `ItemPropertyDescriptors` themselves, you can subclass `ItemPropertyDescriptorDecorator` and override behavior to control, for example, when editing is allowed or how to set up the widget to be used for it. An example in Section 19.2.1 will demonstrate both the inclusion of properties for features of other classes and the use of this decorator pattern.

11.1.3 Command Factory

In Section 3.3, we described EMF.Edit's command framework for model editing, and mentioned that item providers play a role as the command factory by implementing the `IEditingDomainItemProvider` interface. In particular, `createCommand()` is the method that is called to correctly instantiate command objects, based on the information supplied in a `CommandParameter`. The `ItemProviderAdapter` base class provides an implementation of this method, which generically supports all of the EMF.Edit commands listed in Section 3.3.2 that are not handled directly by the editing domain.

The Template Method pattern is used again to offer specialized support to the `createCommand()` implementation. If a class has more than one reference that contributes children, the following method will be generated in its item provider:

```
protected EReference getChildFeature(Object object, Object child)
{
  return super.getChildFeature(object, child);
}
```

This method is called when creating an `AddCommand` or `MoveCommand` when no target feature is supplied. By default, it just invokes the base class implementation, which iterates over the objects returned by `getChildrenFeatures()`, described in Section 11.1.1, and returns the first one whose type is compatible with the given child object. However, if you want to ensure that any or all objects get added to a certain feature, you can modify this method to return it.

There are three additional methods that make up the `IEditingDomainItemProvider` interface. As explained in Section 3.3.3, the editing domain uses `getParent()` to find the object owner to whose item provider `createCommand()` is delegated. It is also required by `DragAndDropCommand`, as is `getChildren()`. Fortunately, these two methods are already implemented to support content providers, as we saw in Section 11.1.1. The interface's last method, `getNewChildDescriptors()`, forms part of the support mechanism for `CreateChildCommand`, which we will discuss in Section 11.1.5.

11.1.4   Change Notification

We described the item provider's final role in Section 3.2.4: it notifies the model's central change notifier of interesting state changes to its associated model object. As a standard EMF adapter for that object, the item provider is notified of all changes via its `notifyChanged()` method.

This method decides whether the notification is important. If so, it decorates it with information describing the extent to which viewers should be updated and forwards the resulting notification.

The following implementation is generated in `PurchaseOrderItem-Provider`:

```
public void notifyChanged(Notification notification)
{
  updateChildren(notification);

  switch (notification.getFeatureID(PurchaseOrder.class))
  {
    case PPOPackage.PURCHASE_ORDER__COMMENT:
    case PPOPackage.PURCHASE_ORDER__ORDER_DATE:
      fireNotifyChanged(new ViewerNotification(
        notification, notification.getNotifier(), false, true));
      return;
    case PPOPackage.PURCHASE_ORDER__SHIP_TO:
    case PPOPackage.PURCHASE_ORDER__BILL_TO:
    case PPOPackage.PURCHASE_ORDER__ITEMS:
      fireNotifyChanged(new ViewerNotification(
        notification, notification.getNotifier(), true, false));
      return;
  }
  super.notifyChanged(notification);
}
```

First, `updateChildren()` is called. If wrapped children are being cached, as described in Section 11.1.1, this method will update the cache to reflect the change to the object.

Notifications will be forwarded by calling `fireNotifyChanged()` for changes to those features corresponding to the generated `case` statements: **comment, orderDate, shipTo, billTo,** and **items.** This set of features for which to provide change notification is specified in the generator model. By default, it includes containment references—recall from Section 11.1.1 that these define the content structure—and attributes. If you change the way the content provider methods work, you will probably need to make corresponding changes here as well.

Each received notification is wrapped in an instance of `ViewerNotification` before `fireNotifyChanged()` is called. This allows the notification to describe the most efficient way in which to update a viewer for the change. The two boolean arguments to the `ViewerNotification` constructor specify whether to update the label of an item and whether to refresh the contents under an item. The preceding argument specifies which item to update or under which to refresh. By default, a change to an attribute will only update the label of the modified item. A change to a containment reference will refresh its contents.

The `ItemProviderAdapter` base class provides the `fireNotifyChanged()` implementation that passes the notification along to the adapter factory, which acts as the model's central change notifier, as well as to its own registered listeners.[4]

11.1.5   Object Creation

One useful feature of EMF.Edit-based editors is object creation support, which we first saw in action in Section 4.4. Both the context-sensitive pop-up menu and the editor-contributed pull-down menu contain **New Child** and **New Sibling** sub-menus, under which appear all of the candidate object types appropriate for the selected object. Figure 11.1 illustrates this for a "Purchase Order" in our model: the possible children are **Ship To US Address**, **Bill To US Address**, and **Item**.

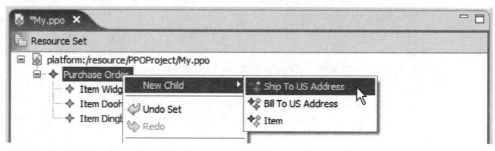

Figure 11.1   Creating a child of a purchase order.

For all other commands, support from item providers is only needed when the command is created, as we saw in Section 11.1.3. However, for `CreateChildCommand`, which provides child and sibling[5] object creation functionality, the item providers play an important part in three roles:

1. Determining candidates for object creation
2. Creating the command
3. Controlling the command's appearance

To understand what these roles mean and why they are required, let's take a top-down look at the object creation support, and compare it with the way in which other commands work.

---

4. The item provider is also an `IChangeNotifier` itself, to support the use of the Decorator pattern [3]: an `ItemProviderDecorator` registers as a listener for the item provider that it decorates, so that it can forward notifications to its own adapter factory.

5. Sibling creation is implemented via a `CreateChildCommand` for which the owner is the selection's parent.

In Section 3.1.1, we described Eclipse's action mechanism, in which operations are carried out by objects that implement the `IAction` interface. Such an object can also control the appearance of the UI element that represents it, such as a menu item, by providing information including its label and icon. EMF.Edit provides several standard actions to perform operations like cut, copy, paste, and delete, which all work in the same way. They are registered to be notified when the selection changes, and they respond to such a notification by creating the command that performs the correct operation on the selected objects. The command's creation may be assisted by the editing domain and the relevant item provider, as we described in Section 3.3.3, and the action's behavior is then delegated to that command. The Eclipse workbench maintains "global actions" for these standard operations that uniformly control their appearance; our command-delegating actions are simply registered as handlers for these global actions.

However, the two actions for object creation, `CreateChildAction` and `CreateSiblingAction`, need to behave somewhat differently. For any given object, we need one action for each candidate we wish to offer for child and sibling creation. This can mean zero, one, or more actions, with each delegating to a `CreateChildCommand` that adds that particular candidate. Therefore, these actions should not be sensitive to selection changes themselves; instead, we need the single object that holds the actions, called the action bar contributor, to respond to selection changes by creating a whole new set of actions for the selected object.

How does the action bar contributor know how many object creation actions to create and how they relate to the different objects that could be created? Not surprisingly, it asks the item providers. The usual pattern is followed, with the request being made of the editing domain:

```
newChildDescriptors = domain.getNewChildDescriptors(object, null);
newSiblingDescriptors = domain.getNewChildDescriptors(null, object);
```

The editing domain simply delegates to the item provider using the familiar adapter factory delegation pattern. For child creation, it adapts on the specified object; for sibling creation, it adapts on the parent of the specified sibling:

```
public Collection getNewChildDescriptors(Object object,
                                         Object sibling)
{
  if (object == null)
  {
    object = getParent(sibling);
  }
  IEditingDomainItemProvider adapter =
```

```
  (IEditingDomainItemProvider)adapterFactory.adapt(
    object, IEditingDomainItemProvider.class);
return editingDomainItemProvider != null ?
  editingDomainItemProvider.getNewChildDescriptors(object, this,
                                                   sibling) :
  Collections.EMPTY_LIST;
}
```

From the point of view of the action bar contributor, the result is just a collection of arbitrary objects, which it uses in constructing a list of corresponding child or sibling creation actions. Each of these actions then creates a CreateChildCommand, with the appropriate child descriptor object, using the usual command creation mechanism as described in Section 3.3.3. When the item provider handles createCommand(), it knows how to interpret the child descriptor object, which it created earlier, to return a command that will add the correct object to the correct place in the model.

The implementation of CreateChildCommand, itself, relies on either SetCommand or AddCommand, depending on whether the child is being created under a multiplicity-1 or multiplicity-many feature. As a subclass of the basic framework CommandWrapper, it delegates to whatever command is returned by its createCommand() method, which is implemented as follows:

```
protected Command createCommand()
{
  if (owner == null || feature == null || child == null)
  {
    return UnexecutableCommand.INSTANCE;
  }

  if (feature.isMany())
  {
    AddCommand.create(domain, owner, feature, child, index);
  }
  else if (owner.eGet(feature) == null)
  {
    return SetCommand.create(domain, owner, feature, child);
  }
  else
  {
    return UnexecutableCommand.INSTANCE;
  }
}
```

Because there are no global actions to control the appearance of the object creation actions, they need to provide their own sensible implementations for methods like getText(), getToolTipText(), and getImage(). The CreateChildCommand implements the CommandActionDelegate interface so that the actions can also delegate these methods to it. It also provides constructor forms that take a helper object, implementing the `CreateChildCommand.Helper` interface, to handle these matters of appearance in a model-specific way. When an item provider creates a `CreateChildCommand`, it passes itself as the helper, so that it ultimately controls the appearance of the action.

We already know how item providers participate in command creation. Now that we have described their other roles in the process of child and sibling creation, let's take a closer look at how the generated code actually fills those roles.

Determining Candidates

Item providers determine which objects can be created as children of an object by implementing the `getNewChildDescriptors()` method of the `IEditingDomainItemProvider` interface. In addition to each possible object itself, this method also needs to specify the reference of the parent object to which it would be added. The parent might be able to accommodate the same type of object under more than one reference; to expose this choice to the user, we need to include the reference in the description of the child to be created. Moreover, if the feature is multiplicity-many, we might wish to specify an index at which the object would be added. To represent these different aspects of each child, we use an instance of `CommandParameter`, which we first met in Section 3.3.2, as the descriptor.

The `ItemProviderAdapter` base class provides an implementation of `getNewChildDescriptors()` that creates a new list and passes it, along with the parent object, to `collectNewChildDescriptors()` to be populated. This method is overridden in the generated item providers. For example, in `PurchaseOrderItemProvider`, the following is generated:

```
protected void collectNewChildDescriptors(
                    Collection newChildDescriptors, Object object)
{
  super.collectNewChildDescriptors(newChildDescriptors, object);

  newChildDescriptors.add(createChildParameter(
    PPOPackage.Literals.PURCHASE_ORDER__SHIP_TO,
    PPOFactory.eINSTANCE.createUSAddress()));
  newChildDescriptors.add(createChildParameter(
    PPOPackage.Literals.PURCHASE_ORDER__BILL_TO,
    PPOFactory.eINSTANCE.createUSAddress()));
  newChildDescriptors.add(createChildParameter(
    PPOPackage.Literals.PURCHASE_ORDER__ITEMS,
    PPOFactory.eINSTANCE.createItem()));
}
```

We use the `createChildParameter()` convenience method, defined by the base class, to create a `CommandParameter` for each parent feature–child object pair, which we add to the collection of descriptors.

By default, only containment references are assumed to contribute candidates for child creation. However, any features can be made to do this via the generator model. The set of child creation features should usually be the same as, or a subset of, the set of features that contribute children, as described in Section 11.1.1. For each child creation feature, one or more statements will be generated to create child descriptors. For a reference, one statement is generated for each non-abstract, type-compatible class in the model. In our case, we have three child creation references—**shipTo**, **billTo**, and **items**—and one compatible class for each.

The list of descriptors that is finally returned to `getNewChild-Descriptors()` will then be modified by the base class implementation as follows: if a sibling object is specified, then for each `CommandParameter` with a multi-valued feature, the index is set so that the new object will be added following the sibling as closely as possible.

Controlling Appearance

As we described earlier, `CreateChildCommand` declares an inner interface, `CreateChildCommand.Helper`, which a delegate can implement to control matters of appearance in a model-specific way. `ItemProviderAdapter` implements this interface and, in `createCreateChildCommand()`, passes itself as an argument to the `CreateChildCommand` constructor.

`ItemProviderAdapter` also provides default implementations for the helper methods. For `getCreateChildText()`, `getCreateChildToolTipText()`, and `getCreateChildDescription()`, externalized strings are retrieved from the generated edit plug-in's *plugin.properties* file, based on the classes and references involved. The `ResourceLocator` mechanism described in Section 11.1.1 is used for this. Similarly, `getCreateChildImage()` returns an appropriate icon from the model plug-in's *icon/* directory. Finally, `getCreateChildResult()` takes the new child object and returns, as the collection of objects that should be considered the command's result,[6] a singleton list of that same object.

A generated item provider can include an override of the `getCreateChildText()` method. The simple string returned by the base class implementation, the name of the class of the child object, is usually sufficient.

---

6. Recall from Section 3.3.1 that the result of a command can be used in compound commands as the input to its following command. In addition, `CreateChildCommand` returns this same result when `getAffectedObjects()` is called after an `execute()` or `redo()`.

However, if a given parent class includes multiple features contributing children that share compatible types, we generate an override that uses the feature names to distinguish among them. For example, in `PurchaseOrderItemProvider`, the following is generated:

```
public String getCreateChildText(Object owner, Object feature,
                                 Object child, Collection selection)
{
  boolean qualify =
    feature == PPOPackage.Literals.PURCHASE_ORDER__SHIP_TO ||
    feature == PPOPackage.Literals.PURCHASE_ORDER__BILL_TO;

  if (qualify)
  {
    return getString("_UI_CreateChild_text2",
      new Object[] { getTypeText(child), getFeatureText(feature),
                     getTypeText(owner) });
  }
  return super.getCreateChildText(owner, feature, child, selection);
}
```

Here, we see that the class name needs to be qualified if the feature is **shipTo** or **billTo**, because they share **USAddress** as their type. We are using the general form of `getString()`, which uses the objects specified in its array argument for the substitutions indicated by the externalized string. The two relevant strings from the generated *plugin.properties* file are as follows:

```
_UI_CreateChild_text = {0}
_UI_CreateChild_text2 = {1} {0}
```

The second, which is used in the generated `getCreateChildText()` override, includes the feature name as qualification. The first, which is used by the base implementation, does not.

Customizing object creation can begin with changing the externalized strings and replacing the generic icons that are used by the `Helper` methods. Beyond that, you can add to or remove from the options offered for children of a particular class by modifying its item provider's implementation of `collectNewChildDescriptors()`. If you wish to create objects in a state other than their default, you can add initialization of the child objects that are included in the descriptors. You could even offer two different children that are instances of the same class, but initialized differently, provided that you override the `Helper` methods to distinguish between them and label them accordingly.

11.2 Item Provider Adapter Factories

To create the item providers for the classes defined in a model, an item provider adapter factory is generated for each modeled package. This class extends the adapter factory utility class generated as part of the model plug-in. The declaration for the item provider adapter factory for our primer purchase order model is as follows:

```
public class PPOItemProviderAdapterFactory extends PPOAdapterFactory
    implements ComposeableAdapterFactory, IChangeNotifier, IDisposable
```

As we described in Chapter 10, implementing an adapter factory essentially involves answering two questions:

○ Which adapter types are supported by the adapter factory? An adapter type can be any arbitrary object; any significance is imposed by an adapter and its factory.

○ If a given target object has no adapter of a given supported type, how should a new adapter be created?

Recall that the generated adapter factory implementation for a package extends the `AdapterFactoryImpl` framework class, overriding the `isFactoryForType()` and `createAdapter()` methods to answer those questions. As we saw in Section 10.9, `PPOAdapterFactory` implements `isFactoryForType()` so that its supported types include the **EPackage** for the model and instances of all classes in that package. Adapter creation is implemented using the generated switch class and the Factory Method pattern [3]. The `createAdapter()` method delegates to type-specific methods, such as `createPurchaseOrderAdapter()`, which are generated for all classes in the package. These factory methods are all implemented to return `null`, with the intention that they will be overridden in subclasses to return the desired adapters.

First, let's look at how the item provider adapter factory overrides the implementation of `isFactoryForType()` to define which types it supports. Returning to the generated `PPOItemProviderAdapterFactory` class, we find the following:

```
protected Collection supportedTypes = new ArrayList();

public PPOItemProviderAdapterFactory()
{
  supportedTypes.add(IEditingDomainItemProvider.class);
  supportedTypes.add(IStructuredItemContentProvider.class);
  supportedTypes.add(ITreeItemContentProvider.class);
  supportedTypes.add(IItemLabelProvider.class);
```

```
    supportedTypes.add(IItemPropertySource.class);
}

...

public boolean isFactoryForType(Object type)
{
  return supportedTypes.contains(type) ||
    super.isFactoryForType(type);
}
```

Notice that we use the implemented item provider interfaces as the supported adapter types. Looking closely at the `isFactoryForType()` method, you might be wondering about the call to the superclass's implementation in the second half of the boolean expression. For some reason, we also want to return true if the type is the **EPackage** for the model, as we described earlier, but we will not be able to explain that reason until the end of this section.

For now, let's return to the factory method overrides that actually create the item provider adapters. One will be included for each generated item provider class, and the form of each will depend on whether the generator model specifies to use the Stateful or Singleton item provider pattern for that class.

As we described in Section 3.2.5, the Stateful pattern involves creating a new item provider, which can carry additional state information for each object in an instance model. In our generated `PPOItemProviderAdapterFactory`, the factory method for stateful purchase order adapters would simply look like this:

```
public Adapter createPurchaseOrderAdapter()
{
  return new PurchaseOrderItemProvider(this);
}
```

If, however, we opted to use the Singleton pattern, a single instance of the item provider would be used for all objects of this type. It could only define behavior, accessing the information stored in the model objects themselves. The following code would be generated, instead:

```
protected PurchaseOrderItemProvider purchaseOrderItemProvider;

public Adapter createPurchaseOrderAdapter()
{
  if (purchaseOrderItemProvider == null)
  {
    purchaseOrderItemProvider =
      new PurchaseOrderItemProvider(this);
  }
  return purchaseOrderItemProvider;
}
```

Note that in both cases, the item provider adapter factory passes itself to the constructor, ensuring that item providers can always find the factories that created them.

Beyond the ordinary EMF adapter factory behavior discussed previously, item provider adapter factories in EMF.Edit have two additional responsibilities:

○ Providing change notification for the model by implementing
  `IChangeNotifier`

○ Supporting composition of the model with others by implementing
  `ComposeableAdapterFactory`

The first of these, which we discussed in Section 3.2.4, simply involves passing along notifications received from this factory's item providers to all registered listeners. Its implementation is delegated to an instance of `ChangeNotifier`, a framework class that provides this functionality:

```
protected IChangeNotifier changeNotifier = new ChangeNotifier();

public void addListener(INotifyChangedListener listener)
{
   changeNotifier.addListener(listener);
}

public void removeListener(INotifyChangedListener listener)
{
   changeNotifier.removeListener(listener);
}

public void fireNotifyChanged(Notification notification)
{
   changeNotifier.fireNotifyChanged(notification);
   ...
}
```

We've omitted part of the `fireNotifyChanged()` method, which we will fill in after some elaboration on the topic of model composition.

EMF.Edit supports editors for objects from more than one package by applying the Composite pattern [3] to the item provider adapter factories for those packages. An instance of the framework class `ComposedAdapterFactory` acts as a single access point for the content and label providers and the editing domain. It maintains a list of adapter factories that implement the `ComposeableAdapterFactory` interface, forwarding its clients' requests to the appropriate adapter factory child and forwarding all of its children's change notifications to its registered listeners.

To allow the item provider adapter factory generated for any package to be reused in this way, the `ComposeableAdapterFactory` interface is always implemented, as follows:

```
protected ComposedAdapterFactory parentAdapterFactory;

public void setParentAdapterFactory(ComposedAdapterFactory parent)
{
   this.parentAdapterFactory = parent;
}

public ComposeableAdapterFactory getRootAdapterFactory()
{
   return parentAdapterFactory == null ?
     this : parentAdapterFactory.getRootAdapterFactory();
}
```

The `setParentAdapterFactory()` method is called by a `ComposedAdapterFactory` when the item provider adapter factory is added to or removed from its list of children. The `parentAdapterFactory` reference is required by `fireNotifyChanged()`. In addition to notifying registered listeners, as we saw previously, it needs to pass the notification up to the parent, if set:

```
public void fireNotifyChanged(Notification notification)
{
   changeNotifier.fireNotifyChanged(notification);
   if (parentAdapterFactory != null)
   {
     parentAdapterFactory.fireNotifyChanged(notification);
   }
}
```

Finally, we can now explain that mysterious call to the superclass's implementation in `isFactoryForType()`. The `ComposedAdapterFactory` needs to be able to select the child adapter factory based on two different criteria: the requested adapter type and the package of the given target object. Thus, it actually invokes this method twice on each of its child adapter factories, selecting one only if it returns `true` both times.

In general, it is not necessary to do any customization of the generated item provider adapter factories by hand. If you wish to provide item providers for classes that are not a part of the model, you can handle them with a separate item provider adapter factory and include both factories in a `ComposedAdapterFactory`.

11.3   Editor

As we now begin to look at the code that depends on the Eclipse workbench UI framework, our approach will change from the previous sections. Rather than aiming for completeness, we focus only on the code that anchors the EMF.Edit mechanisms that we have already seen in this and previous chapters. Although much of the remainder of the generated code would likely serve as a useful example of Eclipse UI programming, we consider that discussion to be outside of the scope of this book.

We start with the editor class itself. This class implements the workbench part through which the user can edit instances of the EMF model. The plug-in's generated *plugin.xml* file registers it as the editor for such documents[7] by declaring an extension to the `org.eclipse.ui.editors` extension point.

The editor is central to the EMF.Edit-based design in that it instantiates most of the important participants that we described in Chapter 3, including the adapter factory, command stack, editing domain, viewers, content providers, and label providers. The generated implementation extends the `MultiPageEditor-Part` workbench abstract base to provide multiple tabbed pages, using one for each of its viewers.

For our purchase order model, the editor's class declaration is as follows:

```
public class PPOEditor extends MultiPageEditorPart implements
   IEditingDomainProvider, ISelectionProvider, IMenuListener ...
```

As an `ISelectionProvider`, the editor passes along notifications when the selection changes in its active viewer. This mechanism is used by the global action handlers to create new commands and by the action bar contributor to create new object creation actions, as described in Section 11.1.5. As an `IMenuListener`, the editor is notified when a pop-up menu is about to show in one of its viewers. It then calls on its action bar contributor to populate this menu with items for the global and object creation actions.

Since the editor uses a single adapter factory, command stack, and editing domain, these are created in the constructor. In the previous section, we discussed composition of adapter factories. The generated editor uses a `ComposedAdapterFactory`, rather than just the model's factory itself, so that its viewers can include objects that are not part of the model:

---

7. That is, it is registered as the editor for files with a filename extension that was chosen by the generator for instances of the model. That extension is just the lowercased package prefix.

```
protected ComposedAdapterFactory adapterFactory;
protected AdapterFactoryEditingDomain editingDomain;

public PPOEditor()
{
  super();
  List factories = new ArrayList();
  factories.add(new ResourceItemProviderAdapterFactory());
  factories.add(new PPOItemProviderAdapterFactory());
  factories.add(new ReflectiveItemProviderAdapterFactory());
  adapterFactory = new ComposedAdapterFactory(factories);
  ...
```

Three adapter factories are explicitly composed here. Of course, the generated PPOItemProviderAdapterFactory is included to create item providers for objects from the purchase order model. The first of the other two adapter factories, ResourceItemProviderAdapterFactory, creates item providers for instances of Resource and ResourceSet, which manage the persistent form of the modeled objects. Thus, the viewers are able to include items representing the resources in which the modeled objects reside.

The last adapter factory, ReflectiveItemProviderAdapterFactory, creates the ReflectiveItemProviders discussed in Chapter 3, which use the reflective EObject API to provide default viewing and editing behavior for arbitrary objects. As such, this adapter factory acts as a fall-back for any object types that are not explicitly supported in the editor. Explicit type support can be added simply by including the generated item provider adapter factory for a given package in the ComposedAdapterFactory, ahead of the ReflectiveItemProvider-AdapterFactory.[8]

After creating the composed adapter factory, the constructor creates a command stack for the editor. It uses the BasicCommandStack implementation from the common command framework, which we discussed in Section 3.3.1, and attaches a listener to it:

```
BasicCommandStack commandStack = new BasicCommandStack();
commandStack.addCommandStackListener(
  new CommandStackListener()
  {
    public void commandStackChanged(final EventObject event)
    {
      getContainer().getDisplay().asyncExec(
```

---

8. It is also possible to globally register adapter factories for inclusion in any ComposedAdapterFactory via the org.eclipse.emf.edit.itemProviderAdapterFactory extension point. Such adapter factories will be consulted after all of the explicitly added ones. Because ReflectiveItemProvider-AdapterFactory can handle any EObject, it must *not* be added to a ComposedAdapterFactory that is to make use of adapter factories registered via the extension point.

```
          new Runnable()
          {
            public void run()
            {
              firePropertyChange(IEditorPart.PROP_DIRTY);
              Command mostRecentCommand =
                ((CommandStack)event.getSource()).
                  getMostRecentCommand();
              if (mostRecentCommand != null)
              {
                setSelectionToViewer(
                  mostRecentCommand.getAffectedObjects());
              }
              if (propertySheetPage != null &&
                  !propertySheetPage.getControl().isDisposed())
              {
                propertySheetPage.refresh();
              }
          }});
  }}}});
  ...
```

Whenever a command is executed, undone, or redone, the property sheet will be updated and the selection changed to whatever the command returns as its affected objects.

Finally, the constructor creates the editing domain, passing it the adapter factory and command stack:

```
  editingDomain = new AdapterFactoryEditingDomain(
    adapterFactory, commandStack, ...);
}
```

During its initialization, the editor's base class invokes `createPages()`, allowing it to supply the controls that should be contained in each tabbed page. This method first calls `createModel()`, to load the model, and then creates the editor's various viewers—each within a pane, which provides a title bar. It also creates an appropriate content and label provider for each viewer, performs any additional initialization that the particular viewer needs, creates a pop-up menu for it, and adds a page for it. The following initialization of the **Selection** page with a simple tree is illustrative:

```
public void createPages()
{
  createModel();
  ...

  ViewerPane viewerPane = ...
```

```
   selectionViewer = (TreeViewer)viewerPane.getViewer();

   selectionViewer.setContentProvider(
     new AdapterFactoryContentProvider(adapterFactory));
   selectionViewer.setLabelProvider(
     new AdapterFactoryLabelProvider(adapterFactory));

   selectionViewer.setInput(editingDomain.getResourceSet());
   viewerPane.setTitle(editingDomain.getResourceSet());
   ...
   createContextMenuFor(selectionViewer);
   int pageIndex = addPage(viewerPane.getControl());

   ...
 }
```

Note that we set the tree's input to the resource set. Recall from Section 11.1.1 that our item providers implement getElements() to return the children of the specified object. Thus, as generated, the resource set is an invisible root. The object actually displayed at the root of the tree will be the singular child of the resource set: the resource corresponding to the file from which the model was loaded.

As the editor class directly defines the appearance and behavior of the application that the user experiences, it offers virtually limitless possibilities for customization. Most likely, you will want to modify the various viewers, perhaps with the exception of the one that we just examined, to make them show something more useful for your model. The example provided in Section 19.2.2 demonstrates such a modification. It is also possible to disable the multi-page editor design via a generator model property, resulting in a createPages() implementation that just creates a single viewer.

In Section 11.1.1, we mentioned the approach of adding an additional set of item providers to provide an alternate view on the model. To do so, you would also need to write an alternate item provider adapter factory to create them, and you would use that adapter factory in creating a viewer's content and label providers.

11.4 Action Bar Contributor

We introduced the action bar contributor in Section 11.1.5 as an object that holds actions. Let's now expand on that brief description. Not only does the action bar contributor define the actions available in a class of editors, but it provides the menu items and toolbar buttons through which these actions are accessed. The action bar to be associated with an editor is named in the extension to the org.eclipse.ui.editors extension point that is declared in the plug-in manifest file.

The action bar contributors that EMF generates extend `EditingDomain-`
`ActionBarContributor`, an EMF.Edit framework class that registers the command-based handlers for global actions, including cut, copy, paste, delete, undo,
and redo. It also populates pop-up menus with items corresponding to these
actions, as we mentioned in the previous section.

For our purchase order model, the action bar contributor's class declaration
is as follows:

```
public class PPOActionBarContributor
  extends EditingDomainActionBarContributor
  implements ISelectionChangedListener
```

It implements `ISelectionChangedListener` so that it can respond to
changes in the selection, as we described in Section 11.1.5. That is, it queries the
appropriate item providers, via the editing domain, for descriptors of the children and siblings that could be created for the selected object:

```
public void selectionChanged(SelectionChangedEvent event)
{
  ...

  Collection newChildDescriptors = null;
  Collection newSiblingDescriptors = null;

  ISelection selection = event.getSelection();
  if (selection instanceof IStructuredSelection &&
      ((IStructuredSelection)selection).size() == 1)
  {
    Object object =
      ((IStructuredSelection)selection).getFirstElement();
    EditingDomain domain =
      ((IEditingDomainProvider)activeEditorPart).getEditingDomain();
    newChildDescriptors =
      domain.getNewChildDescriptors(object, null);
    newSiblingDescriptors =
      domain.getNewChildDescriptors(null, object);
  }
  ...
```

It then creates an action for each descriptor and populates the menus with
corresponding menu items:

```
createChildActions = generateCreateChildActions(
  newChildDescriptors, selection);
createSiblingActions = generateCreateSiblingActions(
  newSiblingDescriptors, selection);
```

```
    if (createChildMenuManager != null)
    {
      populateManager(createChildMenuManager,
                  createChildActions, null);
      createChildMenuManager.update(true);
    }
    if (createSiblingMenuManager != null)
    {
      populateManager(createSiblingMenuManager,
                  createSiblingActions, null);
      createSiblingMenuManager.update(true);
    }
}
```

Note that `createChildMenuManager` and `createSiblingMenuManager` correspond to the **New Child** and **New Sibling** submenus that appear under the editor's pull-down menu. These menus are created in the action bar contributor's `contributeToMenu()` method, which is automatically invoked when the associated editor is loaded. At that time, `contributeToToolBar()` is also called, but our generated action bar contributor adds no buttons to the toolbar. Finally, on the user's right-click, items are added to the pop-up menu in `menuAboutToShow()`. If you wish to add your own actions to an editor, these are the methods that you should modify to make your actions available through the menus or toolbars.

11.5 Wizard

In Section 4.4, we saw the simple two-page wizard that creates an instance of an EMF model. This functionality is provided by a generated class that extends JFace's `Wizard` and is identified in the plug-in's manifest file by an extension to the `org.eclipse.ui.newWizards` extension point.

For our purchase order model, `PPOModelWizard` is generated:

```
public class PPOModelWizard extends Wizard implements INewWizard
```

We will focus on the code that actually instantiates the model, once the **Finish** button has been clicked. In the `performFinish()` method, we find the following:

```
public boolean performFinish()
{
  ...

  ResourceSet resourceSet = new ResourceSetImpl();
  URI fileURI = URI.createPlatformResourceURI(
    modelFile.getFullPath().toString());
```

```
Resource resource = resourceSet.createResource(fileURI);
EObject rootObject = createInitialModel();
if (rootObject != null)
{
  resource.getContents().add(rootObject);
}
Map options = new HashMap();
options.put(XMLResource.OPTION_ENCODING,
            initialObjectCreationPage.getEncoding());
resource.save(options);

...
}
```

Recall that an EMF model's persistent form is managed by a `Resource`. Adding an object to the resource's contents ensures that it, and all of its contents, will be included in that persistent form. Just as we first saw in Section 2.5.2, this code uses the basic framework `ResourceSetImpl` to create a `Resource` that serializes into EMF's default XMI format. The resource's filename, relative to the Eclipse workspace, was set according to the user's selection and must be converted to a platform scheme URI. A single root object is added to the resource, and the resource is saved. The character encoding that was selected by the user is specified as a save option.[9]

The root object is created using the factory, according to the type of model object that the user selected, as follows:

```
EObject createInitialModel()
{
  EClass eClass = (EClass)ppoPackage.getEClassifier(
    initialObjectCreationPage.getInitialObjectName());
  EObject rootObject = ppoFactory.create(eClass);
  return rootObject;
}
```

The wizard also offers many possibilities for customization. For example, you could easily modify `createInitialModel()` to build a more complex model, most likely according to additional information gathered from the user.

11.6 Plug-Ins

One singleton plug-in class is generated for each of the edit and editor plug-ins, as a central provider of text and image resources and logging capabilities to all other classes in the plug-in. We have used these classes to access resources at

---

9. We look at this kind of code in greater depth in Chapter 15, which deals exclusively with persistence.

various points throughout this chapter. Now, we discuss in more detail how they work.

The Eclipse core includes a class that represents a plug-in, `Plugin`. Usually, a plug-in provides a subclass of `Plugin` and identifies this subclass as the `Bundle-Activator` in its *MANIFEST.MF* file. This class is then instantiated when the plug-in is activated. The plug-in's resource bundle, which is populated from its *plugin.properties* file, is accessible through the plug-in class, as are the plug-in's location and the platform's logging facilities. An alternate base for Eclipse plug-in classes, `AbstractUIPlugin`, extends `Plugin` to add utilities that might be useful for UI plug-ins, including an image registry and preference store.

EMF builds on top of Eclipse's plug-in mechanism a more flexible system for providing the needed resources and logging, allowing EMF plug-ins to run within the platform or independently of it. An abstract, common `EMFPlugin` class implements the `ResourceLocator` and `Logger` interfaces. It includes an abstract `getPluginResourceLocator()` method and a `getPluginLogger()` method that just calls `getPluginResourceLocator()`, casting and returning the same result. For the methods belonging to the two implemented interfaces, `EMFPlugin` checks if the corresponding one of these two methods returns a non-`null` result. If so, it delegates to that object. Otherwise, it provides its own default implementations: it looks for a *plugin.properties* file and `icons/` subdirectory at the root of the JAR or classpath directory containing the plug-in class file, and prints log entries to `System.err`. This default behavior is provided for the case where the plug-in is running stand-alone, but it can be overridden.

For the case where the plug-in is running within Eclipse, `EMFPlugin` includes a static member class, `EclipsePlugin`, that subclasses Eclipse's `Plugin` class and implements the resource access and logging methods using the platform facilities.

The generated plug-in class for our purchase order's edit plug-in extends `EMFPlugin` and is a singleton, accessible through its static `INSTANCE` field:

```
public final class PrimerPOEditPlugin extends EMFPlugin
{
  public static final PrimerPOEditPlugin INSTANCE =
    new PrimerPOEditPlugin();
  ...
```

It also contains a private `plugin` field that can hold an instance of its own `Implementation` static member class, a subclass of `EMFPlugin.EclipsePlugin`. This field is set by `Implementation`'s constructor and returned by `getPluginResourceLocator()`:

```
    private static Implementation plugin;

    public ResourceLocator getPluginResourceLocator()
    {
      return plugin;
    }

    public static class Implementation extends EclipsePlugin
    {
      public Implementation()
      {
        super();
        plugin = this;
      }
    }
}
```

It is this `Implementation` class that is identified as the plug-in class in the manifest file. Thus, if Eclipse is running, it is instantiated, the `plugin` field is set to it, `getPluginResourceLocator()` and `getPluginLogger()` will return it, and `EMFPlugin` will use it for resource access and logging.

The class for the editor plug-in works exactly the same way, except its `Implementation` extends `EclipseUIPlugin`, which in turn extends `AbstractUIPlugin`. All of the EMF's runtime framework plug-ins also provide `EMFPlugin`-based plug-in classes.

CHAPTER 12

Running the Generators

Central to EMF's value as a programming tool is its ability to generate high-quality code. Moreover, the EMF code generator is highly configurable, offering the user a great deal of control over the model and editor implementations that it produces. We can affect the choice of generator patterns, as we have seen over the last two chapters, as well as the naming of classes and their organization in packages and plug-ins. If necessary, we can even customize the templates that specify these patterns, giving us total control over each line of generated code.

This chapter describes the code generation tools provided by EMF. It begins with an overview of the code generation process and a summary of the content produced by it. It then discusses, in detail, the Eclipse-based generator GUI and the command-line and Ant generator tools. It concludes by taking a look inside the generator, at the format of the templates that control the content it produces. This final, advanced topic might be of interest to those who wish to customize EMF's standard code generation patterns and to those starting to think about new ways in which the generator could be used to produce custom content of their own design.

12.1 EMF Code Generation

Code generation in EMF is primarily based on an Ecore model. As we have seen throughout the last two chapters, we generate classes that correspond directly to the packages, classes, and enumerated types defined within such a model; the members of these generated classes depend on attributes, references, operations, and enum literals.

As we first explained in Chapter 2, code generation is also affected by additional information that does not constitute part of the data model itself, but instead resides in a generator model made up of decorators for Ecore model objects. A generator model ties together one or more interdependent Ecore models that are to be generated together and also allows access to other referenced Ecore models, for which no new code is to be generated.

A generator model has as its root a **GenModel** object, which has attributes for the generator options that apply globally to the model. It also includes references to two sets of **GenPackage** objects: one set decorates the **EPackage** objects that are the roots of the Ecore models for which code is to be generated, and the other decorates the roots of the referenced Ecore models. Like **GenPackage**, the remaining classes that make up the generator model decorate their correspondingly named Ecore classes and include attributes for their related generator options.

Generating a file is a two-step process. First, content is generated by a template-driven engine called JET, or Java Emitter Templates. Templates express the EMF code patterns in a JSP-like[1] syntax. The engine transforms each template into the source of a Java class that will mix fixed template data with the model-specific results of call backs; it then compiles, dynamically loads, and uses those classes to emit the desired content. Template class call backs are made to the generator model objects, which find the model-specific details either among their own attributes or in the corresponding Ecore model objects. To speed up the generation process, templates can be converted into template classes and compiled ahead of time. We refer to these as *static templates*, while we call the raw JSP-like form *dynamic templates*. In the second step of generation, a source merge utility, called JMerge, merges the emitted content into the pre-existing file, if there is one. Merging of Java files is based on @generated Javadoc tags, as described in Section 10.11. Property files are merged according to their keys; key–value pairs with new keys are added, but existing keys are never replaced. Other files, including images and plug-in manifest files, are neither merged nor replaced; to regenerate these files, they must first be manually deleted or renamed.

EMF uses an extensible generator to drive the code generation process. It knows how to navigate over the objects in the generator model and what content they contribute to each of the four plug-ins: model, edit, editor, and test. The generator creates and invokes the emitters and mergers involved in producing each file. The four generator model classes for which content is generated are **GenModel, GenPackage, GenClass,** and **GenEnum**. As a result, we refer to four code generation units: model, package, class, and enum.

Tables 12.1 through 12.4 summarize the content that can be produced for each of these units in the four generated EMF plug-ins. Table 12.1 shows the content for the model plug-in. This includes the plug-in manifest files; properties

---

1 JavaServer Pages (JSP) is a server technology for generating dynamic Web content. For more information, see *http://java.sun.com/products/jsp/*.

files; and all of the interfaces and classes corresponding to the Ecore packages, classes, and enums that we described in Chapter 10.

Table 12.1   Generated Model Content

Unit	Description	File Name	Subpkg.	Opt.
Model	Plug-in class			Y
	OSGi manifest	META-INF/MANIFEST.MF		Y
	Plug-in manifest	plugin.xml		N
	Translation file	plugin.properties		N
	Build properties file	build.properties		N
Package	Package interface	*Prefix*Package.java		N
	Package class	*Prefix*PackageImpl.java	impl	N
	Factory interface	*Prefix*Factory.java		N
	Factory class	*Prefix*FactoryImpl.java	impl	N
	Switch	*Prefix*Switch.java	util	Y
	Adapter factory	*Prefix*AdapterFactory.java	util	Y
	Validator	*Prefix*Validator.java	util	Y
	XML processor	*Prefix*XMLProcessor.java	util	Y
	Resource factory	*Prefix*ResourceFactoryImpl.java	util	Y
	Resource	*Prefix*ResourceImpl.java	util	Y
Class	Interface	*Name*.java		N
	Class	*Name*Impl.java	impl	N
Enum	Enum	*Name*.java		N

The names of generated classes and interfaces generally depend on the names of the corresponding Ecore model objects; for packages, these names depend instead on the **prefix** attribute that is specified in the generator model. The Java package in which all of these classes and interfaces reside has the same name as the Ecore package. The Java packages can be made subpackages of a **basePackage**, also an attribute in the generator model. We will see how to modify the prefix and base package in Section 12.3. Implementation and utility code resides by default in a further `impl` or `util` subpackage, as indicated by the fourth column in the table. The final column specifies whether the creation of each piece of content is optional.

There are two artifacts listed in Table 12.1 that have not been mentioned previously: the validator and the XML processor. The former is described in detail in Chapter 18. The latter is a utility class that provides a convenient API for working with XML files that conform to the schema described by the Ecore model.

As we described in Chapter 11, the generated code in the edit and editor plug-ins requires plug-in classes to provide text and image resources and logging capabilities. Although the generated code for the model plug-in does not require such support, you might want to have a plug-in class available for use by your additional, handwritten model code. This is why the table includes such a class, but with no file name: it can be generated but, by default, it is not.

Table 12.2 summarizes the UI-independent portion of the editor code and its related content, which is generated in the edit plug-in.

Table 12.2   Generated Edit Content

Unit	Description	File Name
Model	Plug-in class	*ModelName*EditPlugin.java
	OSGi manifest	META-INF/MANIFEST.MF
	Plug-in manifest	plugin.xml
	Translation file	plugin.properties
	Build properties file	build.properties
Package	Adapter factory	*Prefix*ItemProviderAdapterFactory.java
Class	Item provider	*Name*ItemProvider.java

The generated classes reside by default in a `provider` subpackage of the corresponding model package. If the model contains more than one package, the first will be selected, by default, to hold the single plug-in class. However, this default can be changed, along with the name of the class itself, as we will see in Section 12.3.

In addition to the content listed in the table, various sample icons are generated to represent the classes and the object creation actions; these are all placed in the *icons/* subdirectory of the project.

Table 12.3 summarizes the UI-dependent portion of the editor code and its related content, which is generated in the editor plug-in.

Table 12.3 Generated Editor Content

Unit	Description	File Name
Model	Plug-in class	*ModelName*EditorPlugin.java
	Plug-in manifest	plugin.xml
	Translation file	plugin.properties
	Build properties file	build.properties
Package	Editor	*Prefix*Editor.java
	Advisor	*Prefix*Advisor.java
	Action bar contributor	*Prefix*ActionBarContributor.java
	Wizard	*Prefix*ModelWizard

The generated classes reside by default in a `presentation` subpackage of the corresponding model package. Again, the plug-in class goes with the first package by default, and a sample icon for the wizard is created and placed in the *icons/* project subdirectory.

There is also one class listed in Table 12.3 that we have not seen yet: the advisor. This class is only created when generating an RCP application, a topic discussed in Chapter 20.

Table 12.4 summarizes the JUnit tests and stand-alone examples that are generated for the model in the test plug-in.

Table 12.4 Generated Test Content

Unit	Description	File Name
Model	Test suite	*Prefix*AllTests.java
	Plug-in manifest	plugin.xml
	Translation file	plugin.properties
	Build properties file	build.properties
Package	Test suite	*Prefix*Tests.java
	Example	*Prefix*Example.java
Class	Test case	*Prefix*Test

The generated tests are located by default in a `tests` subpackage of the corresponding model package. The first package contains a model test suite capable of invoking the suites generated for each package, which in turn execute all the test cases created for the modeled classes. Each test case class provides the scaffolding required by JUnit[2] to define test cases for the corresponding modeled class. The intent is for you to write test methods that exercise the behaviors that you have implemented yourself. To this end, the generated test case class declares a test method for each operation and for each volatile feature and derived feature defined by the model. These methods are marked with TODO comments to remind you to provide their implementations.

We have already mentioned that the four generated plug-ins can be combined into three, two, or even just one. In particular, the following combinations are supported:

- ○ Model and edit
- ○ Model and test
- ○ Edit and editor
- ○ Model, edit, and editor
- ○ Model, edit, editor, and test

When plug-ins are combined, no conflicting model-level contents are generated. Instead, they are also combined appropriately and included as part of the editor plug-in, if it is among those combined, or the edit plug-in, otherwise.

12.2   The Generator UI

The EMF generator is typically operated through an Eclipse-based GUI, which we first saw in Chapter 4. It is, itself, an EMF.Edit-based editor, registered to handle resources with a *.genmodel* extension. As a result, it is opened by double-clicking on any such file in the Navigator or Package Explorer view.

The generator's interface is quite simple: it consists of a single tree viewer, showing the objects in the loaded generator model: the model, packages, classes, structural features, operations, enums, enum literals, and data types. Figure 12.1 shows the generator with a "Supplier" model loaded. We won't look closely at this model, called ExtendedPO3, until Chapter 13; however, it is a good example as it references a package from an independent model that could be generated separately. Notice the different icon for "EPO3", indicating that it is such a referenced package.

---

2. JUnit is a widely used open source framework for writing unit tests using Java, and is fully supported by Eclipse. For further information on JUnit see *http://www.junit.org/*.

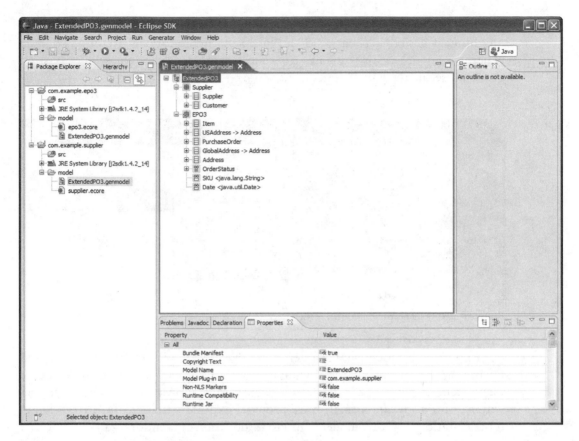

Figure 12.1   EMF generator with "Supplier" model loaded.

The generator interface allows us to do a few things:

1. Reload the generator and underlying Ecore models from their original source.

2. Export the model using a contributed model exporter.

3. Toggle the display of generator model annotations.

4. Modify the generator model attributes.

5. Generate code.

To reload the models, we simply select **Reload...** from the **Generator** pull-down menu, which is illustrated in Figure 12.2. This launches the same wizard that was used to create the Ecore and generator models initially. We can then step through the wizard, reviewing the selections we made at that time and changing anything, if desired. When we click **Finish,** the Ecore models are updated. The generator model is also updated to reflect structural changes, while existing attribute settings are maintained.

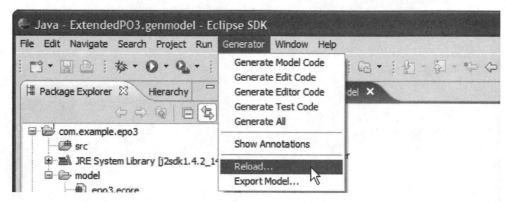

Figure 12.2   Generator pull-down menu.

Exporting a model simply refers to converting the information represented by the *.ecore* and *.genmodel* files into another format. The **Export Model...** menu item in Figure 12.2 displays a wizard that allows you to select a model exporter for a specific format. EMF provides exporters that create XML Schema representations of the model. Different projects or vendors can exploit the `org.eclipse.emf.exporter.modelExporter-Descriptors` extension point to contribute additional exporters.

As mentioned in Chapter 5, you can add information to Ecore elements using **EAnnotations.** The generator model provides an analogous capability in the form of **GenAnnotations.** Usually these annotations are not meant for direct consumption by the user, so they are not displayed in the generator by default. In the rare case that you do want to see or edit them, you can toggle their display by selecting **Show Annotations** from the **Generator** pull-down menu. When they are displayed, the context-sensitive menu for the tree elements will include an **Annotate** action that can be used to create **GenAnnotation**s.

As different objects are selected in the generator's tree viewer, their attributes are displayed in the Properties view. These properties give us the ability to control what code is generated, how it is organized, and what patterns are used in it;

we discuss them in detail in the following section. It is worth noting that the attributes of any objects under a referenced package, like "EPO3", cannot be edited. To change them, you need to edit the referenced generator model directly.

Code is generated by selecting an object from the generator model, right-clicking, and selecting **Generate Model Code, Generate Edit Code, Generate Editor Code, Generate Test Code,** or **Generate All** from the pop-up menu, as illustrated in Figure 12.3.

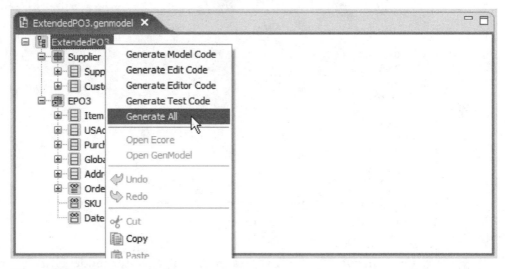

Figure 12.3   Generator pop-up menu.

These actions are also available from the **Generator** pull-down menu. The code and other content generated correspond to the selected object, its parents, and all of its children, as specified by Tables 12.1, 12.2, 12.3, and 12.4. So, for example, when the root-level model object is selected, **Generate All** generates all four plug-ins completely. If, however, a single class is selected, the code corresponding to other classes and enums in the model is not generated.

Some or all of these menu items might be disabled based on the type or state of the selected object. For example, there is never any content to be generated for a feature or a data type. Also, you cannot generate any content at all unless a destination directory is specified on the generator model object, as we will see in Section 12.3.1. Moreover, nothing can ever be generated for referenced packages.

12.3 Generator Model Properties

We now return to the generator model properties. In this section, we describe the properties of each type of object in the generator model, explaining their impact on the code to be generated. These properties are grouped into various categories, as shown in Figure 12.4.

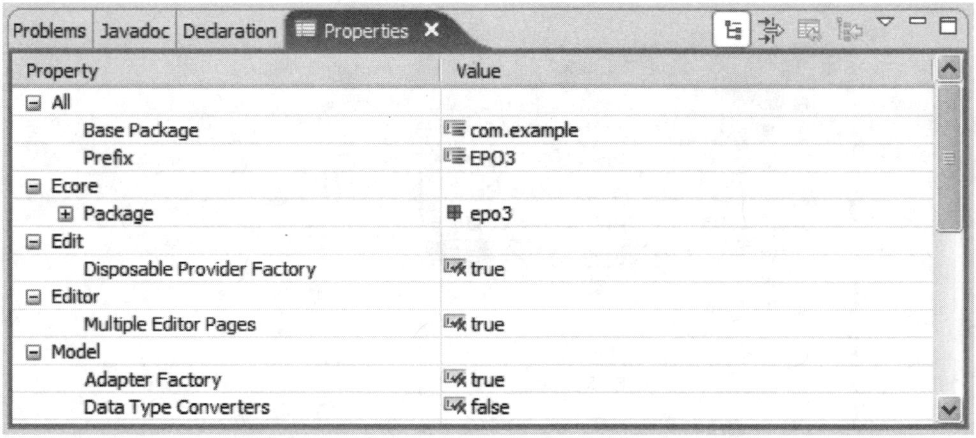

Figure 12.4 Generator model properties.

One category, "Ecore", is present for all generator model elements that decorate Ecore model elements—that is, all but the **GenModel** object itself and any **GenAnnotation**s. This category provides a nested, read-only view of the Ecore object.

The remaining properties are all editable. They are described, grouped by category, in the following sections. For quick reference when using the generator UI, a brief description is also displayed in the status bar for each property, as it is selected in Eclipse's Properties view.

12.3.1 Model Object Properties

The model object has properties that determine the naming and contents of files corresponding to the model generation unit, that apply to all code produced for the generator model, and that offer control over the low-level operation of the code generator.

All

This category contains properties that affect common naming and code patterns across the plug-ins.

Bundle Manifest—When OSGi was adopted as the underlying infra-structure for plug-in activation and management in Eclipse, developers had to start dealing with the OSGi manifest file. You can use this property to decide whether you want the manifest to be generated or not. Setting it to false implies that the *plugin.xml* file is generated with all the runtime information for the plug-in, which, since Eclipse 3.0, is no longer recommended.

Copyright Text—All generated Java source files include a static string `copyright` field initialized to this value. If it is empty, as by default, no such field is generated.

Model Name—The names of the generated plug-ins are formed from this value. These names are declared in the manifest files, as the value of the `Bundle-Name` property.

Model Plug-In ID—Eclipse uses a unique string to identify each of its registered plug-ins. The plug-in declares this string in its manifest file, as the value of the `Bundle-SymbolicName` property. The "Model Plug-In ID" property determines the identifier to be declared for each generated plug-in. The model plug-in uses this value exactly. If edit and editor plug-ins are generated, ".edit" and ".editor" are appended to form their identifiers. By default, this value is set to the project name, as per the PDE convention. To ensure uniqueness, the recommended convention is to begin plug-in identifiers, and hence project names, with a reversed domain name.

Non-NLS Markers—Eclipse's Java compiler has the ability to flag non-externalized strings as a warning or error, to facilitate enablement of National Language Support (NLS). EMF-generated code does not use hard-coded strings for messages that the user will see; however, string literals do appear frequently, for example, as keys for lookup of externalized strings in a property file. This property controls whether to include comments that mark those literals as non-translatable, so that the compiler will not flag them.

Runtime Compatibility—With the adoption of OSGi, the behavior of the plug-in activation in Eclipse 3.0 has changed a bit. To ensure backward compatibility of plug-ins created with previous versions of Eclipse, the platform has made available a runtime compatibility layer that is exposed when a plug-in requires `org.eclipse.core.runtime.compatibility`. This option was provided to aid in migrating to Eclipse 3.0 and should not be used in general.

Runtime Jar—Each plug-in declares in its manifest file where to find the compiled class files that make up its runtime. Typically these class files are included either directly at the root of the plug-in or in a JAR file inside of it. By default, this property's value is false, corresponding to the former approach.[3] If it is set to true, the latter approach is taken, and the plug-in ID is used as the name of the JAR file.

Model

This category contains properties that affect naming and code patterns used in the model project.

Array Accessors—Setting this property to true causes EMF to generate bean-like array accessors for many-valued features, along with the regular `List` accessors. These additional getters and setters allow an application to manipulate the referenced objects directly through arrays. This can arguably improve performance, but bypasses important mechanisms such as change notification.

Containment Proxies—This property controls whether the **resolveProxies** attribute of each containment **EReference** is taken into consideration when generating code. If both this property and the **resolveProxies** attribute are true, the reference will support cross-resource containment. This topic is discussed further in Section 13.8.2.

Feature Delegation—This property defines which delegation pattern should be implemented by the feature accessor methods. The possible values are:

○ None—No delegation pattern is used, hence the accessors read from and write to instance variables. This is the default value.

○ Reflective—The feature accessors invoke the reflective eGet() and eSet() methods and the generator does not create instance variables to store the value of the features. By default, this option causes your generated code to use EMF's dynamic infrastructure, but it can also be used to implement a custom storage strategy, as explained in Section 15.6.

---

3. If you are deploying your plug-in as a JARed plug-in, rather than as a directory, it is recommended that you include the class files at its root. Having a runtime JAR nested inside a JARed plug-in is considerably less efficient and less flexible.

○   Virtual—Instead of using separate variables to store the value of non-primitive features, all of the feature accessors read from and write into a single, dynamically allocated array. This option can help reduce the memory usage for models that are sparsely populated; it is further discussed in Section 10.10.1.

Generate Schema—EMF can generate an XML Schema that defines the serialized form of the model, if enabled via this property. This option has been kept for backward compatibility only. Instead of using it, you should invoke **Export Model...** from the **Generator** pull-down menu, which produces a higher quality XML Schema.

Minimal Reflective Methods—This property controls whether the implementation of the reflective accessor methods for a class (`eGet()`, `eSet()`, etc.) delegate the handling of inherited structural features to their superclass's implementation. Disabling this property can improve performance, especially when dealing with deep inheritance hierarchies. However, it not only increases the size of the subclasses but also requires them to be regenerated whenever their superclasses are changed. See Section 10.10.1 for more details.

Model Directory—This property controls the location, relative to the workspace root, into which model code is generated. Note that the first segment of this path corresponds to the project name, and the remainder of the path specifies the subdirectory under the project's base at which the source tree is rooted. Of course, further subdirectories will be created according to the package structure of the generated code. Model code cannot be generated while this value is empty.

Model Plug-In Class—This property specifies the qualified class name of the singleton plug-in class for the model. As we explained in Section 12.1, you might wish to generate such a class, analogous to those required in the edit and editor plug-ins, to provide resources and logging capabilities for use by any additional model code you write. If so, specify a package and class name here. By default, this value is empty and no plug-in class is generated.

Model Plug-In Variables—This property allows you to enter a comma-separated list of plug-in IDs that are added to the dependency list of the model plug-in. Optionally, when not developing a plug-in (i.e., when no "Model Plug-In ID" has been set), it is possible to define Java Classpath variables, using the following syntax: *variable-name=plug-in-id*. Such variables are then included in the project's class path.

Suppress Containment—Setting this property to true causes the generator to suppress all the code that implements containment semantics, essentially ignoring the value of the **containment** attribute for all references in the model. For example, an object would not be removed from its container when added to a different containment tree. Note that containment is an important concept in modeling, and suppressing it is not recommended.

Suppress EMF Metadata—This property specifies whether to generate package interfaces that provide public access to the Ecore metadata for the model. Because the package classes are always generated, all the normal features of EMF are still available to any code that is not restricted to the API defined by the interfaces. The generated factory interface is also affected by this property. See Section 10.10.2 for details.

Suppress EMF Model Tags—Controls whether @model tags are included in the Javadoc of generated code. Usually, the model can be re-created from just the generated code, but only if these tags are included.

Suppress Interfaces—This property controls whether each modeled class is generated as an interface and implementation or as an implementation only. The split interface/implementation pattern usually provides better isolation between API and implementation details, also allowing multiple inheritance in Java. An implementation-only approach might reduce the size of the code and avoid the performance cost of interface casts, but has been proven to limit the evolution of APIs.

Suppress Notifications—Setting this property to true causes the generator to suppress all code implementing change notification. This reduces the size of each class and makes the setting of structural features slightly faster because it eliminates the need to check if notifications are required. On the other hand, these benefits arguably do not justify sacrificing the capabilities that notifications can bring to your application: rich UI feedback, adapter-based behavioral extensions, and many others.

Model Class Defaults

This category contains properties that affect the signature of the interface and implementation generated for each class in the model.

Root Extends Class—This property can be used to change the base class of all implementations generated for modeled classes. More precisely, it specifies the qualified name of a class that will be extended by the generated implementations of root classes; that is, classes for which no supertypes are modeled. This is convenient, for example, when you require the modeled classes in your application to implement a non-modeled interface, which can be specified using the "Root Extends Interface" property discussed next. The default value of this property is `org.eclipse.emf.ecore.impl.EObjectImpl`. Most commonly, the class specified here would extend this default implementation, adding the required additional behavior. Or, it could extend `BasicEObjectImpl` to specialize the allocated storage characteristics as well. Alternatively, this property can be set to one of the subclasses of `EObjectImpl` already provided by EMF, to tweak performance and memory characteristics of modeled objects. For example, `org.eclipse.emf.ecore.impl.FlatEObjectImpl` is tuned to perform best as the base of classes with no dynamic features. By contrast, `org.eclipse.emf.ecore.impl.DynamicEObjectImpl` is optimized for dynamically implemented features, which occur in generated code when the "Feature Delegation" property is set to "Reflective".

Root Extends Interface—This property is similar to the previous one, but it specifies the qualified name of an interface to be extended by the interfaces generated for the model's root classes. The value of this property is `org.eclipse.emf.ecore.EObject` by default, and can be changed to anything, or even cleared. See Section 10.10.2 for more details.

Root Implements Interface—This property can be used to specify an interface to be implemented by all implementations generated for classes in your model. Unlike the previous two properties, this one can only be used in a very specific context: when at least one class of your model extends a class from another model and these models have different root base classes; that is, they define different values for the "Root Extends Class" property. As we have seen, that property can be used to ensure that all modeled classes share some common behavior fully implemented by their root base class. When some classes extend classes based on a different root base class, that behavior must instead be mixed into their generated implementations via an interface. This interface, which must also be implemented by the root base class of your model, is specified as the value of this property, "Root Implements Interface". If this is a modeled interface, you can use the technique described in Section 10.5 to include Java implementations of its methods as body annotations. The generator will then include this code in all classes for which it mixes in the interface.

Static Packages—If the interface specified in the "Root Implements Interface" property is modeled and is not in the model being generated, you must use this property to specify the namespace URI of its package.

Model Feature Defaults

This category contains properties that can be used to customize implementation details for the features defined in modeled classes.

Boolean Flags Field—Normally each boolean attribute and the unset state of each single-valued unsettable feature is stored in its own boolean field. If a value is specified for this property, the generator will use an alternative pattern in which these boolean values are stored as the bits of integer fields, reducing the amount of memory required to store them. These fields are named based on the value of this property. All the bitwise logic required for this implementation is included in the generated getters and setters. For more information, refer to Section 10.10.1.

Boolean Flags Reserved Bits—Setting this property causes your generated code to reuse an existing boolean flags field of the class specified by the "Root Extends Class" property. If changed from its default value of -1, this property specifies the number of bits reserved for the use of that class. In this case, the value of the previous property identifies the field to reuse. In particular, if you would like to reuse the `eFlags` field defined in `EObjectImpl`, you must set the value of this property to at least 8, as the framework reserves the right to make use of this number of bits. For more information, refer to Section 10.10.1.

The following three properties allow you to define an API to hide feature maps from your public interfaces, surfacing their capabilities through other interfaces. The first two of these properties must be used together and the third is optional.

Feature Map Wrapper Class—This property specifies the qualified name of the class that serves as the wrapper for feature maps. It must define a constructor that takes a `FeatureMap` as its argument, and a `featureMap()` method that returns the wrapped feature map.

Feature Map Wrapper Interface—This property's value is the qualified name of the interface that is surfaced in the generated API. This interface must be implemented by the class specified as the "Feature Map Wrapper Class" property.

Feature Map Wrapper Internal Interface—This property specifies an interface that is used internally to refer to instances of the wrapper class. If specified, this interface must be implemented by the class specified as the "Feature Map Wrapper Class" and declare the `featureMap()` method that is used to access the wrapped feature map.

Suppress EMF Types—Setting this property to true causes the generator to use Java's standard collection and object types for features and operations. So, for example, the generated getters for multiplicity-many features would return `java.util.List` instead of EMF's `EList`. One disadvantage of this particular change is that your application would not be able to use the `move()` methods declared on `EList`, which carries the consequences described in Section 10.2.4.

Suppress Unsettable—This property controls whether `unset()` and `isSet()` methods are generated for features marked as unsettable.

Edit

This category contains properties that affect naming and code patterns for the edit project.

Creation Commands—Support for child and sibling creation is optionally included in the generated code according to this value. Specifically, disabling creation commands suppresses generation of code in the item providers and action bar contributors, as described in Sections 11.1.5 and 11.4, respectively, and of supporting text and image resources.

Creation Icons—This property specifies whether the icons for object creation actions should be generated. If generated, they are located in the *icons/full/ctools16* directory of the edit plug-in.

Edit Directory—This property controls the location, relative to the workspace root, into which edit code is generated. It can be the same as the model directory, in which case the model and its edit support are combined into the same plug-in. Edit code cannot be generated while this property is empty.

Edit Plug-In Class—This property specifies the qualified class name of the singleton plug-in class for the model's edit support. Code for the edit plug-in cannot be generated while this value is empty, unless this plug-in is combined with the model or editor plug-in, or both, in which case only one plug-in class needs to be specified among them.

Editor

This category contains properties that affect naming and code patterns for the editor project.

Editor Directory—This property controls the location, relative to the workspace root, into which editor code is generated. It can be the same as the edit directory, to include the editor and edit support in the same plug-in. If it is also the same as the model directory, all three pieces are combined in a single plug-in. Editor code cannot be generated while this value is empty.

Editor Plug-In Class—This property specifies the qualified class name of the singleton plug-in class for the model's editor. Code for the editor plug-in cannot be generated while this value is empty, unless this plug-in is combined with the edit and, optionally, model plug-ins, in which case only one plug-in class needs to be specified among them.

Rich Client Platform—This property controls whether the generated editor plug-in targets the full Eclipse IDE or an RCP configuration. Section 20.1 details what an RCP application is and the impact of this option on your code.

Tests

This category contains properties that affect naming and code patterns for the test project.

Tests Directory—This property controls the location, relative to the workspace root, into which test code is generated. The test code cannot be generated when this property is empty.

Test Suite Class—This property specifies the qualified class name of the JUnit test suite that can be used to run all the test cases generated for your model. No suite class is generated for the model if no value is specified here.

Templates & Merge

This category contains properties that affect the basic operation of the JET and JMerge engines.

Code Formatting—This property controls whether Eclipse's code formatter is invoked on the generated classes and interfaces. Eclipse provides very flexible formatting for Java code. You can customize the default settings, and even import and export your customizations as formatter profiles. To do so, choose **Preferences...** from the **Window** menu and select the "Formatter" preference page located under the "Java/Code Style" category.

Dynamic Templates—As discussed in Section 12.1, code generation can be based on dynamic or static templates. EMF ships with dynamic and static forms of its templates, and this property determines which form to use. If you switch to dynamic templates, any changes you make to them are reflected in the generated code.

Facade Helper Class—This property specifies the qualified class name of the facade helper that is used during code generation. A facade helper object defines how the merge tool reads Java code and should only be changed in the rare case that the parser API used by the default helper is not suitable or available.

Force Overwrite—This property specifies whether the generator should attempt to overwrite read-only files. By default, it is set to false and any existing, read-only files are left unchanged.

Redirection Pattern—Generator output can be redirected to alternate filenames according to the value of this property. If not empty, it acts as the pattern used to form such filenames, where "{0}" is replaced by the usual filename. So, for example, a value of "{0}.test" will cause the generator to append a *.test* extension to each output filename.

Template Directory—This property specifies the location, relative to the workspace root, in which to look for custom dynamic templates. EMF's templates are found in the *templates/* subdirectory of the `org.eclipse.emf.codegen.ecore` plug-in. To modify them, copy part or all of the contents of this directory, maintaining the subdirectory structure, to another location, and specify it as the value of this property. Modifications to any templates that are found in this directory are picked up by the generator; if any are missing, the ordinary templates are used instead.

Update Classpath—This property specifies whether the generator should, every time code is generated, add entries to each project's class path for its framework and generated EMF dependencies. If false, the class path will only be updated when projects are automatically created.

12.3.2   Package Properties

The following properties affect code generation for each package defined in the model.

All

This category contains properties that affect naming and code patterns common across the plug-ins.

Base Package—If this value is not empty, it is used as the package of which all generated packages are made subpackages. This is the preferred way to generate code with globally unique package names, rather than modeling empty, nested packages.

Prefix—The names of the package-related classes are formed from this value, as specified by Table 12.1. Also, the extension for resources containing instances of this model is the lowercased form of this value.

Model

This category contains properties that affect the code patterns used in the model project.

Adapter Factory—This property determines whether to generate the switch and adapter factory classes, described in Section 10.9, as part of the model plug-in. If the edit plug-in is to be generated, this value should be true, as its item provider adapter factory extends this adapter factory.

Data Type Converters—This property controls whether the methods to convert data types to and from strings are added to the package interface. This option should be used if there is a need to provide these conversions as part of the application's API.

Initialize By Loading—This property controls whether the metadata for a package is initialized by generated code in the package implementation class or is loaded dynamically from an *.ecore* file. This capability is automatically enabled by default for larger models, so as to avoid generating methods in the package implementation class that exceed Java's 64Kb size limit.

Literals Interface—This property controls whether the nested Literals interface is included in the generated package interface. Literals provides fast, static access to the package's metadata and is discussed in greater detail in Section 10.8. This property is enabled by default.

Resource Type—This property specifies whether to create a customizable resource and resource factory implementation for the package and, if so, which base class the resource should extend. The following values are possible:

- o None—No specialized implementations are created and no resource factory registration is declared.
- o Basic—The resource extends the most basic framework base class, ResourceImpl. This implementation is not complete: several methods must be re-implemented or exceptions will be thrown on loading and saving.
- o XML—The resource extends XMLResourceImpl to provide XML serialization and deserialization.

○ XMI—The resource extends `XMIResourceImpl`, the default EMF resource that specializes the XML serialization and deserialization to conform to the XMI specification.

For all values but the first, the custom resource factory is registered to be used for resources containing instances of the package, as determined from their filename extension. This is accomplished by declaring, in the *plugin.xml* file, an extension to the `org.eclipse.emf.ecore.extension_parser` extension point. For more information on resource factory registration, see Section 15.2.4.

Package Suffixes

The package suffix properties define the last segment of the Java packages into which the various types of classes are generated. Table 12.5 lists the types of classes represented by the properties, along with their default values. After working with EMF for even a short while, you will certainly recognize these default package names.

Table 12.5 Package Suffix Properties

Property	Type of Generated Class	Default
Implementation	Model implementation classes	impl
Interface	Model interfaces and enumerations	
Metadata	Package and factory classes	
Presentation	Editor and wizard	presentation
Provider	Item providers	provider
Tests	JUnit tests and stand-alone example	tests
Utility	Switch, validator, resource, and adapter factory	util

Edit

The property in this category affects a code pattern in the edit project.

Disposable Provider Factory—This property specifies whether the item provider adapter factory is able to dispose the item providers it creates. It is true by default to provide a simple adapter disposal mechanism, which is, for example, automatically invoked when closing a generated editor. In general, this pattern is recommended for any scenario in which the life span of an instance of your model might be longer than that of the adapters used to view and edit it.

Editor

This category contains one property that affects a code pattern in the editor project.

Multiple Editor Pages—Setting this property to true causes the generated editor for the package to have only a single page, which presents the model in a tree view. By default it is false, causing additional pages to be generated. These pages illustrate how a model can be visualized using different Eclipse widgets, and can serve as a starting point for customization of the editor, as we will see in Chapter 19.

Tests

This category contains one property that affects the artifacts generated in the tests project.

Generate Example Class—This property controls whether an example class is generated together with the tests for your model. This class is a simple but complete example of an application that runs outside the Eclipse environment, and it demonstrates how to load and validate instances of your model. For further details on how to deploy EMF applications in a stand-alone environment, see Section 20.2.

12.3.3 Class Properties

The following properties affect code generation for each class defined in the model.

Model

This category contains one property that affects a code pattern in the model project.

Dynamic—This property controls whether or not to generate a specific Java type for the modeled class. If it is set to false, instances of the class are created and manipulated as if they were defined using dynamic EMF. However, the package will still provide access to the metadata for the class, and the factory will still include a method to create instances of it. See Chapter 14 for more on dynamic EMF.

Edit

This category contains properties that affect code patterns for the edit project.

Image—This property determines whether to generate an icon file to represent instances of the class.

Label Feature—This property indicates which of the class's single-valued attributes is used in the `getText()` method of its item provider adapter, as described in Section 11.1.1.

Provider Type—This property determines whether to generate an item provider for this class and, if so, which of the patterns described in Section 11.2—Singleton or Stateful—should be used by its adapter factory to create it.

12.3.4 Feature Properties

The following properties affect code generation for each feature defined in modeled classes.

Edit

This category contains properties that affect code patterns for the edit project.

Children—This property specifies whether objects referenced via this feature are to be considered children. As explained in Section 11.1.1, this value affects the `getChildrenReferences()` implementation generated in the item provider for the feature's containing class. By default, it is true for all containment references and feature map attributes, and false for all other features.

Create Child—This property controls whether children can be created under the feature. As described in Section 11.1.5, this value affects the `collectNewChildDescriptors()` implementation generated in the item provider for the feature's containing class. By default, it is true for all containment references and feature map attributes, and false for all other features.

Notify—This property determines whether notifications for this feature are to be forwarded to the model's central change notifier. This is reflected in the implementation of `notifyChanged()` generated in the item provider for the feature's containing class, as described in Section 11.1.4.

Property Type—This property specifies whether a property descriptor should be contributed for this feature, resulting in an entry in the property sheet, and whether it should be editable or read-only. This affects the implementation of `getPropertyDescriptors()` generated in the item provider for the feature's containing class, as described in Section 11.1.2.

The following five properties are only applicable to features that are being exposed as properties; that is, those for which "Property Type" is set to either editable or read-only.

Property Category—This property can be used to specify a property category for the feature. If a modeled class has many features presented as properties, it is often convenient to group these properties in categories. This can simplify the use of the generated editor.

Property Description—This property can be used to briefly describe the feature. This text will be displayed in Eclipse's status bar when the property representing the feature is selected.

Property Filter Flags—This property can be used to provide flags, which the property sheet can then use to filter the feature's display. The only flag currently recognized in Eclipse's Properties view is "org.eclipse.ui.views. properties.expert". Properties marked with this flag will not be displayed unless **Show Advanced Properties** is selected in the view's drop-down menu.

Property Multiline—This property controls whether the feature should be edited as multi-line text.

Property Short Choices—Features that can only assume a limited set of values, such as enumerations, are usually represented by properties that are edited by selecting a value from a list. Setting this property to true causes this list to be sorted in alphabetical order.

12.4   The Command-Line Generator Tools

For those who love to script, command-line interfaces to the EMF generator are provided as an alternative to the integrated Eclipse UI. There are also utilities for building Ecore and generator models from a Rational Rose class model and XML Schema.

Because the generator has dependencies on non-UI Eclipse facilities, including resource management and Java parsing, we run it under the platform, but without launching the workbench interface. We call this a *headless* invocation.

The following subsection gives some background on headless invocation. After that, we will take a look at the four command-line tools: Rose2GenModel,

XSD2GenModel, Ecore2GenModel, and Generator. The first three of these tools are referred as *model importer applications*. They are responsible for converting different forms of models to the *.ecore* and *.genmodel* artifacts used by EMF. The fourth tool, Generator, is then used to generate code from these artifacts.

12.4.1 Headless Invocation

The familiar *eclipse* or *eclipse.exe* executable simply starts up a Java Virtual Machine and executes a launcher application. This launcher initializes the platform and then, by default, starts the IDE. We can instruct it to start another Eclipse application instead—Rose2GenModel, for example—via a command-line option.

The command line in our examples will always start like this:

```
> eclipse -noSplash -data C:\temp\emf-ws
    -application ...
```

For the sake of readability only, we will continue to wrap command lines as just shown.

The "-application" launcher option is followed by the ID for the application to run. Application IDs are defined in *plugin.xml* files; each is associated with a class that implements the IPlatformRunnable interface.

The "-data" option specifies a location for the workspace. The workspace is not of particular interest to us in this context, as our utilities will map projects to whatever locations are appropriate. However, if we do not specify a location for the workspace, it will automatically be created in the current working directory and workspace metadata will be stored in it. Things break down if that directory is, or is under, one of the directories to which we try to map a project. So, just to be safe, we specify a location under the system-wide temporary directory. We consider this to be transient data, and we must delete it between headless invocations. If we fail to do so, mysterious errors might result when a project that already exists should be mapped to a new location.

The "-noSplash" option suppresses the Eclipse splash screen, which normally would be presented when executing the preceding command line in a console window in a graphical environment. This option is not required to run the EMF applications, but avoids loading UI plug-ins and probably reduces execution time.

On Windows, the preceding command line works, but the application's output does not appear in the console in which it is executed. In fact, by default, it does not appear anywhere. Because you will probably want to see what the application is doing, you should add two more options to the command line, before "-application": "-console" and "-noExit". The former option brings up a second console window that displays the application's output. This console can also be used to interact with the OSGi runtime, but we will not be making use of this capability. The latter option, "-noExit", ensures that the second console window stays open after the application exits. When you finish with the application's output, you can enter "close" to dismiss the console.

Eclipse 3.3 has made it easier to access an application's output in Windows. Instead of adding extra options to your command line and dealing with more than one console window, you can simply invoke a different executable, *eclipsec.exe*. This executable directs the output to the console from which the application was launched, exhibiting the same behavior as *eclipse* on other platforms.

Non-Windows users need to slightly modify the preceding command line as follows:

```
$ ./eclipse –noSplash -data /tmp/emf-ws
    -application ...
```

In general, both UNIX and Windows path separators ("/" and "\") are accepted. For the sake of brevity and consistency, we will continue to show command lines in the Windows style, and leave it to users of other platforms to make the required simple substitutions mentally.

12.4.2 *Rose2GenModel*

Rose2GenModel provides a command-line interface for building Ecore and generator models from a Rose class model. Because it serves the same role as the EMF Model Wizard, which we discussed in Chapter 4, we will demonstrate it using the same example model: the primer purchase order, which is defined in *PrimerPO.mdl*.

In the simplest case, it is invoked as follows:

```
> eclipse –noSplash -data C:\temp\emf-ws
    -application org.eclipse.emf.importer.rose.Rose2GenModel
    PrimerPO.mdl
```

Here, we just pass Rose2GenModel the name of the Rose file, which we assume is located in the current working directory. An Ecore model called *ppo.ecore* is created for the single root package in the Rose model. A generator model called *PrimerPO.genmodel* is then created to decorate it. Had there been more than one root package in the Rose model, one Ecore model would have been created for each and the generator model would have, by default, decorated all of them. As created, the generator model is suitable for generating the model plug-in only, as no target directories are specified for the edit, editor, and test plug-ins. If you look at the generator model, you will notice that the **GenModel** element contains no **editDirectory, editorDirectory,** or **testsDirectory** attribute. Also, you might notice that the value of **modelDirectory** is the absolute path to the current working directory, while the values we have seen before were simpler locations relative to the workspace root. This different value is specially encoded to allow the generator to correctly map the target project to its actual target directory. By default, this is just the current working directory, but we'll see how to change that in the next example.

Suppose that we want to re-create the familiar four plug-in pattern for code generation with the CLI tools and, further, that we wish to have those four project directories be subdirectories of some arbitrary directory on our file system. If the Rose model resides in that directory, we simply change to it and issue the following command:

```
> eclipse –noSplash –data C:\temp\emf-ws
    -application org.eclipse.emf.importer.rose.Rose2GenModel
    PrimerPO.mdl com.example.ppo\model\PrimerPO.genmodel
    -modelProject com.example.ppo src
    -editProject com.example.ppo.edit src
    -editorProject com.example.ppo.editor src
    -testsProject com.example.ppo.tests src
```

Here, we have included an optional argument following the Rose file name, which specifies the pathname to use for the created generator model. We have also used the "-modelProject", "-editProject", "-editorProject", and "-testsProject" options to specify targets for each of the four plug-ins. Each of these options is followed by two additional arguments: first the directory to which the project should map, and then the target directory, relative to that, for generated code.

Rose2GenModel can take several more options, which we have not demonstrated. The most important ones offer control over which Ecore models the generator model should include and reference. The "-package" option, which can be repeated, is followed by the name of an Ecore package to include. This name can then, optionally, be followed by four additional arguments specifying the namespace prefix, namespace URI, base package name, and prefix for the package. These values are ignored if any of them are specified in the Rose model itself.[4]

If the Rose model includes packages for which Ecore models have already been created, you can use the "-refGenModel" option to reference them via their generator models. This option is followed by the path to the existing generator model. If this model includes additional packages that are not relevant, you can select particular packages by listing their namespace URIs after the generator model path. This option can be repeated to reference packages from more than one generator model.

The "-pathMap" option allows us to specify a mapping for any path map symbols that are used in the Rose file. It is followed by one or more symbol–directory argument pairs. The "-templatePath", "-modelPluginID", and "-copyright" options correspond directly to the "Template Directory", "Model Plug-in ID", and "Copyright Text" properties described in Section 12.3.1. Each is followed by a single argument, the value to which the appropriate generator model attribute should be set.

If the command-line options are not sufficient to customize the code generation to your needs, you can initially use the generator UI to create and configure a generator model. Then, every time you modify the Rose model, you can invoke the Rose2GenModel application, simply specifying the path to the customized *.genmodel* file and the option "-reload". This will ensure that your settings are preserved while the Ecore model is updated.

A summary of Rose2Ecore's arguments and options is displayed by invoking it with no arguments at all:

```
> eclipse -console -noExit -noSplash -data C:\temp\emf-ws
     -application org.eclipse.emf.importer.rose.Rose2GenModel
```

The "-console" and "-noExit" options are used in this command line for the reasons discussed in Section 12.4.1. As a reminder, they are only needed on Windows and even there, under Eclipse 3.3 or later, can be avoided by invoking the *eclipsec.exe* executable.

---

4. Section 4.2.2 described how to set them in Rose.

12.4.3   XSD2GenModel

Similar to the Rose2GenModel application, XSD2GenModel builds Ecore and generator models for XML Schemas. This headless application can be invoked using the following command:

```
> eclipse –noSplash -data C:\temp\emf-ws
     -application org.eclipse.xsd.ecore.importer.XSD2GenModel
     PrimerPO.xsd
```

Unlike for Rose2GenModel, you can specify multiple schema files when invoking XSD2GenModel. These schemas, along with any others they import, will all be processed and, by default, converted to Ecore packages and included in the resulting generator model. To include only a subset of the schemas, you can use the "-packages" option, followed by a list of namespace URIs. You can also use the "-packageMap" option to specify qualified names for the packages, in the form of a list of namespace URI–qualified package name pairs. XSD2GenModel also supports the "-refGenModel" option for referencing existing packages, as described in the previous section.

Indeed, XSD2GenModel shares most options with Rose2GenModel, with the exception of "-pathMap" and "-package". The following command lists all the arguments and options of XSD2GenModel:

```
> eclipse –console –noExit –noSplash -data C:\temp\emf-ws
     -application org.eclipse.xsd.ecore.importer.XSD2GenModel
```

Again, the "-console" and "–noExit" options are used in this command line on Windows for the reasons discussed in Section 12.4.1.

12.4.4   Ecore2GenModel

This application builds Ecore and generator models for an existing Ecore model. The following command illustrates its most typical use:

```
> eclipse –noSplash -data C:\temp\emf-ws
     -application org.eclipse.emf.importer.ecore.Ecore2GenModel
     PrimerPO.ecore
```

This simply produces a *PrimerPO.genmodel* file that decorates the specified Ecore model. In general, more than one *.ecore* file can be specified, and they can be followed by the pathname of the *.genmodel* file to create. Any Ecore model that is not in the same directory as this *.genmodel* file will be copied into it, and it is these copies to which the generator model refers.

It is possible to restrict which **EPackage**s are used as input by this application. You can identify each package to include by specifying the "-package" option followed by its namespace URI. Optionally, this URI can be followed by two arguments specifying the "Base Package" and "Prefix" generator properties for the package. These properties are described in Section 12.3.2.

All the options available for XSD2Genmodel can be applied to this application, with the exception of "-packageMap" and "-packages". Also, like the previous applications, Ecore2GenModel can be invoked without any arguments to display its usage instructions.

12.4.5 *Generator*

Generator provides a command-line interface for generating code from a generator model and one or more Ecore models, which are typically created by one of the model importer applications.

Each of the previous sections included a simple example where we created a basic generator model and Ecore model for the primer purchase order. The following command generates code based on the model:

```
> eclipse —noSplash -data C:\temp\emf-ws
    -application org.eclipse.emf.codegen.ecore.Generator
    PrimerPO.genmodel
```

In this most basic form, we simply specify the generator model. Because we did not do anything special to specify a location when we created the model, the project directory is mapped to the same directory, and generated code is not placed in any further subdirectory. Rather, the package corresponding to our outermost package, *com/*, shows up in the current working directory. By default, only the model plug-in is generated.

We can explicitly specify which plug-ins to generate with the "-model", "-edit", "-editor", and "-test" options. In the second example of Section 12.4.2, we created a generator model and an Ecore model that would support generation of all four plug-ins and provide the familiar project and directory structure for generated content. Here is the corresponding generator command, to be executed from the same location:

```
> eclipse ñnoSplash -data C:\temp\emf-ws
    -application org.eclipse.emf.codegen.ecore.Generator
    -model -edit -editor -tests
    com.example.ppo\model\PrimerPO.genmodel
```

The generator provides several more simple option flags, which correspond to generator model attributes described in Section 12.3. Dynamic templates are used if "-dynamicTemplates" is specified; recall that the template directory can be set by the model importer application. To attempt to force overwriting of existing, read-only files, use "-forceOverwrite". Alternately, to facilitate comparisons of existing and generated content, specify "-diff" and the generator will use a redirection pattern of ".{0}.new" for the generated files, instead of merging them into the existing versions. To generate an XML Schema along with the model plug-in, use the "-generateSchema" option. To include non-NLS markers in generated code, specify "-nonNLSMarkers". To disable Eclipse's auto-build, which can speed up code generation, specify "-autoBuild false".

Finally, the CLI-based generator can use a generator model that was created by the EMF Model Wizard, instead of one from a model importer application. Recall that such a model has, as its values for the **modelDirectory**, **editDirectory**, **editorDirectory**, and **testsDirectory** attributes, workspace-based locations in which the first segment specifies a project name, and the remainder specifies a subdirectory under that project. In this case, we need to provide a final command-line argument, the actual location to which the project should map, because it is not encoded in the attribute itself. Assuming that we are in the parent of that directory and that the generator model is in the *model/* subdirectory of it, we would use the following command to generate the model plug-in code from the generator model that we created back in Section 4.2.2:

```
> eclipse -noSplash -data C:\temp\emf-ws
    -application org.eclipse.emf.codegen.ecore.Generator
    com.example.ppo\model\PrimerPO.genmodel com.example.ppo
```

Once again, a usage summary can be displayed by invoking the generator with no arguments at all:

```
> eclipse -console -noExit -noSplash -data C:\temp\emf-ws
    -application org.eclipse.emf.codegen.ecore.Generator
```

The "-console" and "-noExit" options are used in this command line on Windows for the reasons discussed in Section 12.4.1.

12.5 The Generator Ant Tasks

Although headless applications can be easily employed in a build process, Ant[5] has become the build technology of choice in the Java world. In general terms,

---

5. Ant (*http://ant.apache.org/*) is an open-source Java and XML-based build process, developed at Apache.

when a project is built using Ant, a runtime executes the operations described in an XML file. This file is usually referred to as an *Ant script* and the operations as *tasks*. The Ant runtime provides several predefined tasks such as `copy`, `move`, and `javac` for the most common operations, and also an API for the creation of custom tasks for specific domains.

EMF provides three such tasks: `emf.Rose2Java`, `emf.XSD2Java`, and `emf.Ecore2Java`. Before jumping into their details, let's first examine some considerations that apply to all of them.

Due to the platform dependencies mentioned in Section 12.4, it is necessary to use the Ant Runner provided by Eclipse to execute an Ant script that invokes the EMF tasks. Because the runner is just another Eclipse application, the command we will use to run such a script is:

```
> eclipse -noSplash -data C:\temp\emf-ant
    -application org.eclipse.ant.core.antRunner
    -buildfile build.xml
```

This executes the Ant script named *build.xml*, located in the current working directory. In fact, this is the default script file name that is used when no "-buildfile" option is specified.

It is also possible to run an Ant script that uses an EMF task via the Eclipse UI. This can be done by right-clicking a script and selecting **Run As > Ant Script…**. On the **JRE** tab of the dialog box that appears, ensure that the **Run in the same JRE as the workspace** option is selected.

There a few helpful side effects of using Eclipse to run your Ant scripts. One of them, which might come as a pleasant surprise to experienced Ant users, is that you do not need to use `taskdef` to invoke the EMF tasks in your scripts. The Eclipse Ant runner allows the provider of a task to register it via an extension point, making it immediately available to any script. Moreover, the Eclipse platform also provides tasks to manipulate workspace resources and other artifacts, making them available through the same mechanism. These tasks are fully documented in the Eclipse help system.

Perhaps the most convincing reason to use the EMF Ant tasks instead of the headless applications is the potential for performance improvement. Whereas using the applications requires that Eclipse be started each time a model is created or code is generated, the tasks allow you to perform many of these operations in one script, and hence within a single Eclipse invocation. For example, if your build creates ten models and generates code for them, then switching over to the EMF tasks can reduce the build time by 80 percent.

12.5.1   emf.Rose2Java

This task can build Ecore and generator models from a Rose class model, as well as generate code from them. Actually, this is a departure from the design of the headless applications: whereas each of these two transformations is performed by an application, the emf.Rose2Java task can perform one or both of them in a single step.

This is a snippet of an Ant script that builds the models and generates code for *PrimerPO.mdl*:

```
<emf.Rose2Java
    model="c:/emf/PrimerPO.mdl"
    genModel="c:/emf/ppo/model/PrimerPO.genmodel"
    modelProject="c:/emf/ppo"
    modelProjectFragmentPath="src">
  <arg line="-package ppo"/>
</emf.Rose2Java>
```

Table 12.6 lists the attributes for the emf.Rose2Java task.

Table 12.6   emf.Rose2Java Attributes

Attribute	Description	Opt.
model	The Rose model file.	N
genModel	The generator model file to be created or reloaded.	N
reconcileGenModel	If the generator model specified via the preceding attribute already exists, this attribute determines how it should be handled. The possible values are: overwrite – replaces the existing generator model file (default). keep – leaves the existing generator model unchanged. reload – reloads the generator model to reflect changes in the specification.	Y
modelProject	The directory under which the model code will be generated.	Y
modelProject-FragmentPath	The relative path of the source folder in the model project.	Y
modelPluginID	The ID for the generated model plug-in.	Y
generateJavaCode	Boolean value indicating whether any code should be generated. This should be set to false when you only want to create or update the Ecore and generator models.	Y

(continues)

Table 12.6   emf.Rose2Java Attributes (continued)

Attribute	Description	Opt.
`generateModelProject`	The model project will only be generated if this attribute is set to `true` and the `modelProject` attribute above is specified. Its default value is `true`.	Y
`generateEditProject`	The edit project will only be generated if this attribute is set to `true` and the edit project directory and fragment path are specified using the `arg` element described after this table. Its default value is `true`.	Y
`generateEditorProject`	The editor project will only be generated if this attribute is set to `true` and if the editor project directory and fragment path are specified using the `arg` element described after this table. Its default value is `true`.	Y
`templatePath`	The directory where your customized JET templates are located.	Y
`autoBuild`	Boolean value that enables Eclipse's auto-build. If not specified, the current workspace's setting will not be changed.	Y
`copyright`	If used, all generated Java source files will include a static string `copyright` field initialized to the value of this attribute.	Y

In addition to using the attributes listed in Table 12.6, you can also declare an `arg` element under the `Rose2Java` element. If you look closely at the example at the beginning of this section, you might recognize the "-package" option used there as one of the Rose2GenModel application's options, described in Section 12.4.2. Each EMF task is implemented as a wrapper over the appropriate model importer application and the generator application. Any option specified via the `arg` element is transferred, as is, to the model importer application, providing access to the options that are not explicitly exposed as attributes of the task.

12.5.2   emf.XSD2Java

Similar to the previous task, `emf.XSD2Java` can build Ecore and generator models and generate Java code, but it uses XML Schema as the original model form. Here's an example:

```
<emf.XSD2Java genModel="c:/emf/po/model/CustomPO.genmodel"
    modelProject="c:/emf/po"
    modelProjectFragmentPath="src">
  <arg line="-packages http://www.example.com/CustomPO"/>
  <model uri="http://www.example.com/common.xsd"/>
  <model file="c:/emf/CustomPO.xsd"/>
</emf.XSD2Java>
```

emf.XSD2Java supports all the attributes listed for emf.Rose2Java, and delegates the options specified via the arg element to the XSD2GenModel application. Because a model is often described in multiple XML Schema files, this task also provides an alternative way of specifying the location of these files. As you can see from the preceding example, instead of using the model attribute on emf.XSD2Java, the pathname or the URI of each file is specified in a model element.

12.5.3   emf.Ecore2Java

This task can generate Ecore and generator models for existing Ecore models and also generate code. It behaves completely analogously to other tasks we have seen. This is how it would be used in an Ant script:

```
<emf.Ecore2Java genModel="c:/emf/po/model/CustomPO.genmodel"
    modelProject="c:/emf/po"
    modelProjectFragmentPath="src">
  <arg line="-package http://www.example.com/CustomPO"/>
  <model uri="http://www.example.com/common.ecore"/>
  <model file="c:/emf/CustomPO.ecore"/>
</emf.Ecore2Java>
```

12.6   The Template Format

In this chapter, we have explained that EMF code generation is template based and that additions and modifications can be made to the templates and picked up by the generator on the fly. However, for this information to be useful, we really need to understand the template format itself.

As previously mentioned, JET templates are based on the powerful JavaServer Pages (JSP) syntax. In fact, the template engine was built using code from Tomcat, the Apache Software Foundation's (*http://www.apache.org/*) Servlet and JSP implementation.

Template files primarily contain fixed content that is meant to be output exactly as it appears.[6] Mixed in with this text are a number of JSP-like tags that are evaluated and interpreted by the template engine in various ways. The different types of tags are summarized in Table 12.7.

Table 12.7   JET Template Tags

Type	Syntax	Description
JET directive	`<%@ jet attributes %>`	Declares the start of a template
Include directive	`<%@ include file="URI" [fail=silent|alternative]%>`	Includes another template
Start directive	`<%@ start %>`	Starts an alternative block for a preceding include directive
End directive	`<%@ end %>`	Ends an alternative block begun by a start directive
Expression	`<%= expression %>`	Substitutes in expression result
Scriptlet	`<% code %>`	Executes the code fragment

Based on JSP Reference Card (*http://java.sun.com/products/jsp/syntax/1.2/card12.pdf*).

Notice that these tags constitute only a subset of those available in JSP. In particular, neither declarations nor comments are supported. Let us now look at a simple template that illustrates the typical use of these tags.

12.6.1   *An Example Template*

Imagine that we want to generate an additional package containing a validator for each Ecore class. For the sake of simplicity, our template will just define an interface that includes a single method to validate each of its structural features. This method takes a single parameter of the correct type for the feature and returns a `boolean` value indicating whether the feature validated successfully. Our validator interface extends an imaginary `EMFValidator` framework base class that might, for example, declare a generic, reflective `eValidate()` method.

The template, which we call *Validator.javajet*, is defined as follows:

---

6. You might have noticed that by default the EMF generator changes indentation, replacing tabs with spaces, and inserts line breaks before braces. This is not done by JET, but rather during the subsequent merge step, You can ensure that your formatting preferences are applied to the generated code using the "Code Formatting" property described in Section 12.3.1.

```
<%@ jet
    imports="java.util.* org.eclipse.emf.codegen.ecore.genmodel.*"%>
<%@ include file="../Header.javajetinc"%>
<%GenClass genClass = (GenClass)argument;
  GenPackage genPackage = genClass.getGenPackage();%>

package <%=genPackage.getInterfacePackageName()%>.validation;
import org.eclipse.emf.validation.EMFValidator;

public interface <%=genClass.getInterfaceName()%>Validator
  extends EMFValidator
{
<%for (Iterator i=genClass.getGenFeatures().iterator();
       i.hasNext();) {
  GenFeature f = (GenFeature)i.next();%>
<%if (f.isChangeable()) {%>
    boolean validate<%=f.getCapName()%>(<%=f.getType()%> value);
<%}%>
<%}%>
}
```

The fixed content is shown in bold here to make it stand out more clearly from the directives, expressions, and scriptlets.

The template begins with a JET directive, which provides information about the class into which it will be transformed. Here, we are not referring to the class that will eventually be generated, but the intermediate class, mentioned in Section 12.1, that will be created and used to emit that content. Imports for this template class are expressed as the value of the JET directive's `imports` attribute.

Next, we have an include directive. This causes the engine to process the specified template, inserting the result into its output. In this case, we include a standard header that we intend to be used for copyright information or anything else desired at the top of each generated file.

Following this is the template's first scriptlet. Templates are able to refer to a special variable called `argument`, which is used to provide arbitrary input to the template. When the EMF generator invokes a template, it supplies a generator model element as the value of this variable. Throughout the template, this element provides the required details of the object for which code is being generated. Because we generate one validator interface for each Ecore class, we expect that `argument` will be a `GenClass`. The first scriptlet casts this object appropriately and obtains its `GenPackage` for convenience.

Next, we see some fixed content with details left to be filled in as the results of expressions. For example, in the `package` line, we will insert the name of the model interface package that is obtained from the `GenPackage` object.

Repeated and conditional inclusion of content is provided using normal Java control structures contained in scriptlets. We see a `for` loop that iterates over the class's structural features and an `if` statement that ensures that the feature is changeable.

To understand the effects of these code segments, it is helpful to consider the class into which the template is transformed. The template's fixed content appears in this class as a series of string literals. A single `StringBuffer` is created, and the string literals and the results of expressions are appended to it in sequence. The contents of the scriptlets are interspersed among the `append()` calls, as they appear in the template. For example, let's look at how the following lines would be transformed:

```
<%if (f.isChangeable()) {%>
    boolean validate<%=f.getCapName()%>(<%=f.getType()%> value);
<%}%>
```

The corresponding portion of the template class would look something like this:

```
if (f.isChangeable()) {
  stringBuffer.append("boolean validate");
  stringBuffer.append(f.getCapName());
  stringBuffer.append("(");
  stringBuffer.append(f.getType());
  stringBuffer.append("value);");
}
```

Thus, you can think of the transformation from template to template class as something like turning the template inside out. The code contained in the scriptlets is actually used to control the flow through the `append()` statements.

If we wanted to use this template to generate validator interfaces for our primer purchase order model, we could hook it up to the generator via the `org.eclipse.emf.codegen.ecore.generatorAdapters` extension point.[7] Then, the validator generated for the **PurchaseOrder** class would look like this:

```
/**
 * <copyright>
 * </copyright>
 *
 * %W%
 * @version %I% %H%
 */
```

---

7. One of EMF's example plug-ins, `org.eclipse.emf.examples.generator.validator`, shows exactly how to hook up a template like this one.

```
package com.example.ppo.validation;
import org.eclipse.emf.validation.EMFValidator;

public interface PurchaseOrderValidator
  extends EMFValidator
{
  boolean validateComment(java.lang.String value);
  boolean validateOrderDate(java.util.Date value);
  boolean validateShipTo(com.example.ppo.USAddress value);
  boolean validateBillTo(com.example.ppo.USAddress value);
  boolean validateItems(org.eclipse.emf.common.util.EList value);
}
```

Notice that this code would be a little more readable if we could drop the object qualification from each of the parameter types and insert the necessary `import` statements instead. Fortunately, EMF provides an import manager mechanism that can help us to do this. You can see it in use throughout the templates that ship with EMF.

12.6.2   Template Extensibility

There are two more forms of the `include` directive that we have not yet discussed, although they were summarized in Table 12.7. They provide a mechanism for fine-grained customization of templates. In our discussion of dynamic templates, we have already seen how EMF templates can be customized; however, so far that has always required a "clone and own" approach for whole templates. This is not always ideal, as templates continue to evolve. After making even a small modification to one portion of a larger template, you'll then need to keep your copy up to date with all the subsequent changes to the original.

Often, a better alternative is to design a template for extensibility. This is done by defining insertion and override points, which are expressed in JET as optional includes and includes with alternatives, respectively. By default, the file specified in an `include` directive must be available when the template is transformed. If it does not exist or, for that matter, cannot be read, the JET engine will throw an exception. However, a `fail` attribute can be added to change this behavior.

An `include` directive with `fail="silent"` simply suppresses the exception if the specified file is not available. For example:

```
<%@ include file="Insertion.javajetinc" fail="silent"%>
```

Assuming no *Insertion.javajetinc* template is provided, this produces no content by default. However, it allows for arbitrary output to be inserted dynamically simply by creating such a file.

An `include` directive with `fail="alternative"` also throws no exception if the specified file is not available. In addition, it provides alternative content to be included in that case. For example:

```
<%@ include file="Override.javajetinc" fail="alternative"%>
<%@ start %>
// Fallback code...
<%@ end %>
```

If no *Override.javajetinc* template is provided, the content between the `start` and `end` directives is output by default. However, that content can be replaced dynamically simply by creating an *Override.javajetinc*.

Optional includes and includes with alternatives are used quite extensively in the templates that ship with EMF. Thus, when generating code using dynamic templates, you're able to modify the default generation patterns with particular insertions and replacements, simply by adding the appropriate templates to your template directory. You can also use this mechanism in your own templates to provide for this kind of extensibility.

A word of caution is needed here: the functionality provided by the `include` directive really is just equivalent to copying and pasting the text of the included file into the base. There is no scoping to isolate your changes and no API-style guarantees. As such, you should never assume that your insertions and overrides will work against a changed base template without testing. For example, something as simple as a variable declaration in a scriptlet can be broken if a variable of the same name is later introduced into the base.

CHAPTER 13

Example—Implementing a Model and Editor

Now that you are familiar with the capabilities of the EMF generator, it's time to look at a more elaborate example. In this chapter we generate the ExtendedPO2 model, which includes some common real-world features that require special treatment when generating with EMF. They include:

1. References that do not require proxy resolution.

2. Volatile attributes and references.

3. Custom data types.

4. References with a restricted set of valid targets.

We show how these features can be implemented using a combination of generator control options and custom implementation in the generated classes. We then consider an alternative design, ExtendedPO3, which uses multiple packages to implement the same model. We look at some of the pros and cons of splitting the model into multiple packages and consider the issues it brings to the table. Finally, we show how the editor generated from ExtendedPO3 can be used to concurrently edit multiple instance documents with cross-document references between them.

13.1 Getting Started

The ExtendedPO2 model is shown in Figure 13.1. We have already looked at some aspects of this model in previous chapters, but we will now consider all of the details that need to be addressed when completing its implementation.

As you can see, the ExtendedPO2 model is a superset of the PrimerPO model, which we introduced in Chapter 4. Like PrimerPO, this model includes a

PurchaseOrder class that aggregates items and addresses, but in this model the addresses need not be in the United States (i.e., instances of class **USAddress**). An abstract base class, **Address,** is used as the target of the **shipTo** and **billTo** references. Class **USAddress** extends **Address** and contains the typical U.S. address components (street, city, state, and zip code). Another concrete class, **GlobalAddress,** is used to represent addresses anywhere else in the world. Notice how we use a single multi-valued string attribute (**location**) to represent the address components in this case.

Class **PurchaseOrder** has two new features that were not in the PrimerPO model: **previousOrder** and **totalAmount.** The **previousOrder** reference will be used to identify a previous purchase order associated with the same customer, if there is one. The **totalAmount** attribute is, as you'd expect, the total cost of the order, that is, the sum of the individual item amounts.

The ExtendedPO2 model includes two more classes: **Supplier** and **Customer.** Class **Supplier** acts as the root container for both purchase orders and customers. Notice that in addition to the containment (black diamond) association from **Supplier** to **PurchaseOrder** (i.e., **orders**), there are two more references, **pendingOrders** and **shippedOrders,** between them. These two references will be used to locate the subsets of **orders** whose **status** attributes are **Pending** and **Complete,** respectively.

Because **pendingOrders** and **shippedOrders** are simple-to-compute subsets of the **orders** feature, we've defined them to be derived, transient, volatile, and non-changeable. This is not obvious from the UML diagram in Figure 13.1 because, as discussed in Chapter 6, these are extended non-UML properties of the model that are specified separately. In the corresponding Ecore model they look like this:

```
<eClassifiers xsi:type="ecore:EClass" name="Supplier">
  ...
  <eStructuralFeatures xsi:type:"ecore:EReference"
     name="pendingOrders" upperBound="-1" eType="#//PurchaseOrder"
     changeable="false" volatile="true" transient="true"
     derived="true" resolveProxies="false"/>
  < eStructuralFeatures xsi:type:"ecore:EReference"
     name="shippedOrders" upperBound="-1" eType="#//PurchaseOrder"
     changeable="false" volatile="true" transient="true"
     derived="true" resolveProxies="false"/>
  ...
</eClassifiers>
```

In addition to these two references, there is one other derived feature in this model. The **totalAmount** attribute, in class **PurchaseOrder,** can be computed from the individual item amounts and therefore we have declared it to be derived, transient, volatile, and non-changeable as well.

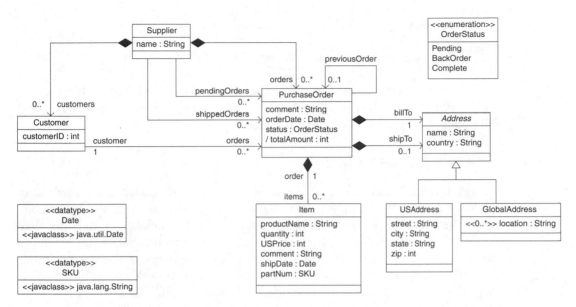

Figure 13.1   The ExtendedPO2 model.

Class **Customer** is used to represent a supplier's customers. Each purchase order of a supplier is associated with exactly one customer. A customer, however, can have many purchase orders, as indicated by the bidirectional one-to-many association between **Customer** and **PurchaseOrder**. A single supplier is intended to aggregate purchase orders and their corresponding customers. Because we will not enable cross-resource containment in the model, we are assured that all associated purchase orders and customers will reside in the same resource. Therefore, we have optimized both ends of the association to not resolve proxies.[1]

```
<eClassifiers xsi:type="ecore:EClass" name="PurchaseOrder">
  <eStructuralFeatures xsi:type:"ecore:EReference" name="customer"
      lowerBound="1" eType="#//Customer" resolveProxies="false"
      eOpposite="#//Customer/orders"/>
    ...
</eClassifiers>
<eClassifiers xsi:type="ecore:EClass" name="Customer">
  <eStructuralFeatures xsi:type:"ecore:EReference" name="orders"
      upperBound="-1" eType="#//PurchaseOrder"
  resolveProxies="false"
```

---

1. This is a very minor optimization that, arguably, isn't worth the loss of flexibility in the model. As we will see later in this chapter, other changes we make in the model will require that we revisit this decision.

```
        eOpposite="#//PurchaseOrder/customer"/>
  ...
</eClassifiers>
```

For the same reason, we have also set **resolveProxies** to false for the **previousOrder** reference of class **PurchaseOrder** and for the **pendingOrders** and **shippedOrders** references of class **Supplier**.

13.2   Generating the Model

We begin with a definition of the model specified in UML. As described in Section 4.2.2, the next step is to convert it to Ecore, so that we can generate code for it. Because the ExtendedPO2 model is a single package model, just like PrimerPO, there's nothing new to be said about how to do that. You simply use the **New Project** wizard to create the project and the Ecore and generator models, and then generate the code as described in Chapter 4. You can also experiment with some of the options described in Chapter 12 if, for example, you want to generate the code into a single plug-in instead of the usual three.

After generating this model and editor, you will not be able to simply run it without further work. If you try, you'll notice that the editor will not function properly. The problem is that, unlike the PrimerPO model from Chapter 4, the ExtendedPO2 model, as generated, is not completely implemented.

13.3   Implementing Volatile Features

Before we can run our generated ExtendedPO2 model editor, we first need to implement its volatile features: the **totalAmount** attribute in class **PurchaseOrder,** and the **pendingOrders** and **shippedOrders** references in class **Supplier**. Otherwise the model will throw exceptions whenever they are accessed. In class `PurchaseOrderImpl`, for example, the `getTotalAmount()` method has the following generated implementation:

```
/**
 * @generated
 */
public int getTotalAmount()
{
  // TODO: implement this method to return the 'Total Amount'
  // attribute
  throw new UnsupportedOperationException();
}
```

The exception-throwing implementation was generated as a placeholder for the implementation that, by declaring the feature volatile, we have implicitly agreed to provide by hand.

Before we change the generated implementation, we first need to remove the `@generated` tag from the method comment. Instead of actually deleting it, we will simply add NOT after the `@generated` tag. This works because the generator considers any change from the simple tag that it generated (alone on the line), to indicate removal of the tag. This approach makes it easy for us to keep track of the generated methods that we've taken over and modified.

Here's what our implementation looks like:

```
/**
 * @generated NOT
 */
public int getTotalAmount()
{
    // TODO: implement this method to return the 'Total Amount'
    // attribute
    throw new UnsupportedOperationException();
    int totalAmount = 0;
    for (Iterator iter = getItems().iterator(); iter.hasNext(); )
    {
        Item item = (Item)iter.next();
        totalAmount += item.getUSPrice() * item.getQuantity();
    }
    return totalAmount;
}
```

As you can see, we simply iterate through the purchase order items and sum up the products of each individual item's price multiplied by its quantity.

Our other two volatile features, **pendingOrders** and **shippedOrders**, have similar implementations; they are both filtered subsets of the **orders** feature. We implement the `getPendingOrders()` method in class `SupplierImpl` by simply iterating through the **orders** reference, collecting orders that have a **Pending** value for the **status** attribute:

```
/**
 * @generated NOT
 */
public EList getPendingOrders()
{
    List pendingOrders = new ArrayList();
    for (Iterator iter = getOrders().iterator(); iter.hasNext(); )
    {
        PurchaseOrder order = (PurchaseOrder)iter.next();
        if (order.getStatus() == OrderStatus.PENDING_LITERAL)
        {
```

```
        pendingOrders.add(order);
      }
   }
   return new EcoreEList.UnmodifiableEList(this,
            EPO2Package.Literals.SUPPLIER__PENDING_ORDERS,
            pendingOrders.size(), pendingOrders.toArray());
}
```

Notice how we use the EMF collection class `EcoreEList.UnmodifiableEList` to return the pending orders. Although we use a simple `java.util.ArrayList` to collect the required subset of features, we cannot return this list directly. Like all multiplicity-many feature implementations in EMF, `getPendingOrders()` needs to return an `EList`, not just a `java.util.List`. You might recall from Chapter 10 that the EMF interface `EList` is essentially the same as `java.util.List` (it extends from it), only with the addition of the `move()` API, which all multi-valued EMF features support.[2]

Another reason for using `EcoreEList.UnmodifiableEList` here is that the **pendingOrders** feature is declared in the model as non-changeable. By using `EcoreEList.UnmodifiableEList`, we ensure that any client attempt at modifying the returned collection will cause an exception to be thrown.

Ultimately, this simple approach prevents indirect modification of the **orders** reference through **pendingOrders**. However, we have not done anything to ensure that a list returned by `getPendingOrders()` is kept up to date with subsequent changes to **orders**. The intent is that client code would not cache this result, but instead invoke the method whenever the list is required. If this limitation was not acceptable for the application, we could, for example, implement **pendingOrders** with a wrapper that would provide a filtered view over the **orders** list.

We implement the `getShippedOrders()` method in class `SupplierImpl` similarly, only there we look for orders where the **status** is **Complete**, instead of **Pending**:

```
/**
 * @generated NOT
 */
public EList getShippedOrders()
{
  List shippedOrders = new ArrayList();
  for (Iterator iter = getOrders().iterator(); iter.hasNext(); )
  {
    PurchaseOrder order = (PurchaseOrder)iter.next();
```

---

2. In addition to being an `EList` implementation, `EcoreEList.UnmodifiableEList` also implements the `InternalEList` and `EStructuralFeature.Setting.Internal` interfaces, which are also required of multi-valued feature implementations.

```
      if (order.getStatus() == OrderStatus.COMPLETE_LITERAL)
      {
        shippedOrders.add(order);
      }
    }
    return new EcoreEList.UnmodifiableEList(this,
                    EPO2Package.Literals.SUPPLIER__SHIPPED_ORDERS,
                    shippedOrders.size(), shippedOrders.toArray());
  }
```

13.4   Implementing Data Types

Now that we've implemented the volatile features, we can turn our attention to our custom data types: **Date** and **SKU**. In Chapter 10, we explained how each custom data type in a model produces a pair of methods in the generated factory implementation class that are responsible for converting the data type to and from `String`. The default implementations of the two conversion methods for our **Date** data type look like this in class `EPO2FactoryImpl`:

```
/**
 * @generated
 */
public Date createDateFromString(EDataType eDataType,
                                 String initialValue)
{
  return (Date)super.createFromString(eDataType, initialValue);
}

/**
 * @generated
 */
public String convertDateToString(EDataType eDataType,
                                  Object instanceValue)
{
  return super.convertToString(eDataType, instanceValue);
}
```

Like the method generated for any other data type, the implementation of `createDateFromString()` simply calls `super.createFromString()`, which attempts to instantiate the data type generically, based on the supplied `String`-typed `initialValue`. This base implementation provides special support for certain types and, for the rest, just uses Java reflection to invoke a constructor or a static `valueOf()` method. The generated `convertDateToString()` method also calls super, which generically converts the typed `instanceValue` to a corresponding string. Usually, this is done simply by calling `toString()`, but again special support is provided for certain types.

The generic base implementations of the two data type conversion methods handle many, but not all, Java types. Moreover, these implementations are not terribly efficient and might not even produce the particular string representation that you desire. As a result, you will usually find it makes sense to provide a custom implementation of the generated conversion methods.

The generic approach does support java.util.Date, which is the Java type represented by our **Date** data type. However, the string representation it produces is a little more verbose than we would like. We wish to record only simple dates in our sample application, without times or time zone qualification. For example, we would prefer to see a date like "2007.09.30" instead of something like "2007-09-30T00:00:00.000-0400".[3] Thus, we opt to implement our own custom string conversion method implementations.

Here is our modified convertDateToString() method in class EPO2FactoryImpl:

```
/**
 * @generated NOT
 */
public String convertDateToString(EDataType eDataType,
                                  Object instanceValue)
{
    return super.convertToString(eDataType, instanceValue);
    if (instanceValue == null) return null;
    SimpleDateFormat format = new SimpleDateFormat("yyyy.MM.dd");
    return format.format((Date)instanceValue);
}
```

As you can see, we use the convenient Java date formatting class, SimpleDateFormat (from the java.text package), to do the work for us. We also use the same convenient class to implement the corresponding createDateFromString() method:

```
/**
 * @generated NOT
 */
public Date createDateFromString(EDataType eDataType,
                                 String initialValue)
{
    return (Date)super.createFromString(eDataType, initialValue);
    if (initialValue == null) return null;

    SimpleDateFormat format = new SimpleDateFormat("yyyy.MM.dd");
    ParsePosition position = new ParsePosition(0);
    Date result = format.parse(initialValue, position);
```

---

3. Unsurprisingly, this default string representation is the one used by Ecore's built-in **EDate** data type. We chose to define our own **Date** type expressly so we could provide a different string representation.

```
  if (position.getIndex() == 0)
  {
    throw new IllegalArgumentException(
      "Date must be of format yyyy.MM.dd");
  }
  return result;
}
```

This method is necessarily a bit more complicated, as it is used to handle arbitrary string input. We use `SimpleDateFormat` to parse the `initialValue` string and, if it is able to extract a date, return the result. If no date is found at the beginning of the string, indicated by no change in the parse position index, we throw an exception. The exception will be well handled by the framework. If a generated editor tries to load a file with an invalid date, the exception will be converted to an EMF diagnostic, which will be displayed in a **Problems** page, as illustrated in Figure 13.2.

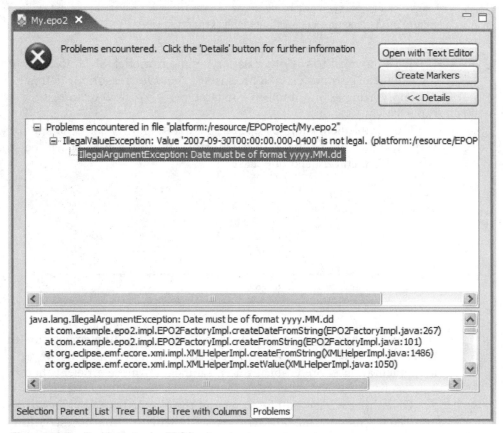

Figure 13.2   Problems in the EPO2 editor.

As the user edits a date in the Properties view, the same conversion is performed. If this method throws an exception, it will be used to generate an error message, and the editor will not accept the value. This is illustrated in Figure 13.3.

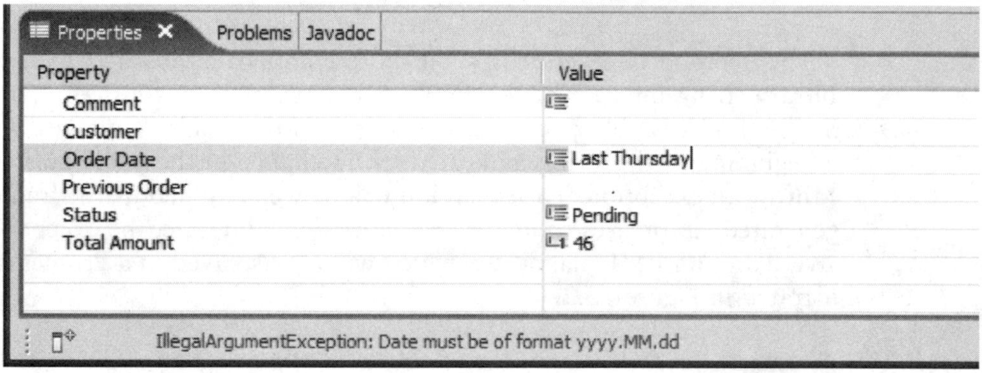

Figure 13.3   Entering an invalid date in the Properties view.

Let's move on to the other data type in our model: **SKU**. Recall from Section 13.1 that the instance class of **SKU** is `String`. Our reason for defining it, instead of simply using Ecore's built-in **EString** type, is to allow us to restrict its possible range of values.

Our implementation of `convertSKUToString()` in `EPO2FactoryImpl` is very straightforward. Because we already know that a **SKU** will be stored as a string, this method need only cast it:

```
/**
 * @generated NOT
 */
public String convertSKUToString(EDataType eDataType,
                                 Object instanceValue)
{
    return super.convertToString(eDataType, instanceValue);
    return (String)instanceValue;
}
```

This produces the same result as the generic base implementation that would be invoked if we had left the generated code untouched. However, the direct implementation is preferable as it is significantly more efficient than the generic approach.

Given that we would like to restrict the allowed string values of a **SKU**, one approach might be to try to implement that restriction in the `createSKUFromString()` method:

```
/**
 * @generated NOT
 */
public String createSKUFromString(EDataType eDataType,
                                  String initialValue)
{
  return (String)super.createFromString(eDataType, initialValue);
  if (initialValue == null) return null;

  if (Pattern.matches("\\d{3}-[A-Z]{2}", initialValue))
  {
    return initialValue;
  }
  throw new IllegalArgumentException(
    "SKU must match the pattern \\d{3}-[A-Z]{2}");
}
```

This implementation checks whether the string matches a regular expression. Strings that do, such as "123-AB", are returned. In other cases, an exception is thrown.

At first glance, this might seem similar to the `createDateFromString()` implementation, which can also throw an exception when the string input is invalid. However, there is a subtle but important distinction: `createDateFromString()` parses the string as leniently as possible, only throwing an exception when it is unable to extract a date. It rejects only strings that cannot be converted to any `Date`; it does not restrict which instances of `Date` are considered valid. EMF provides a validation framework that should be used for this latter purpose.

If we do not try to do this kind of validation here, the implementation of `createSKUFromString()` turns out to be trivial:

```
/**
 * @generated NOT
 */
public String createSKUFromString(EDataType eDataType,
                                  String initialValue)
{
  return (String)super.createFromString(eDataType, initialValue);
  return initialValue;
}
```

The validity restriction should be implemented using the validation framework by adding a constraint to the data type, as we discuss in Chapter 18. This is a cleaner and more flexible approach than adding validation directly to the factory.

13.5   Running the ExtendedPO2 Editor

Now that we've implemented the volatile features and data types, we can run the generated ExtendedPO2 editor to edit instances of the model. You can create an instance document using the EPO2 Model wizard, in the same way as described in Section 4.4 for the PPO model. If you create an instance document choosing a **Supplier** as the root object, you can then use the EPO2 editor to populate a complete model as shown in Figure 13.4.

While creating and initializing the model, notice how the volatile features **pendingOrders**, **shippedOrders**, and **totalAmount** are automatically updated as expected when you change the other features that affect them. Notice also how the data types, **SKU** and **Date**, affect the display and editing of the **partNum** and **shipDate** attributes in the property sheet.

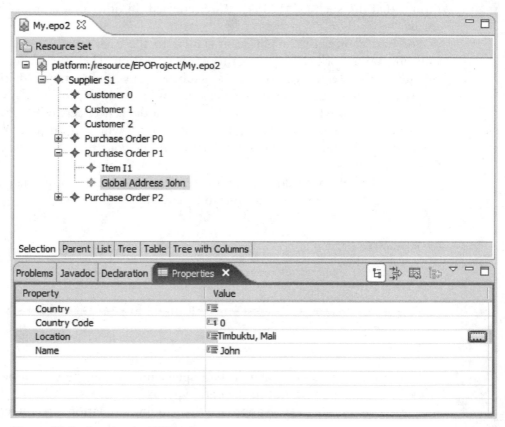

Figure 13.4   Running the EPO2 editor.

If you look in the properties sheet at a multi-valued attribute or reference, like **pendingOrders** of class **Supplier,** you'll see how they are displayed as a comma-separated list of values. When a global address is selected, notice that the property value cell for the editable multi-valued **location** attribute has a button on its far right side. Pressing that button will launch the dialog box shown in Figure 13.5. As you can see, you can use this dialog box to add, remove, and reorder strings in the **location**.

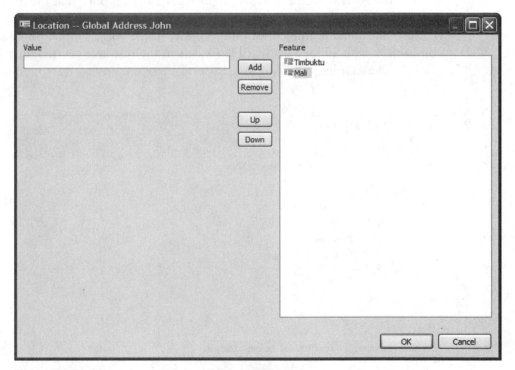

Figure 13.5   Editing the multi-valued "Location" property.

13.6   Restricting Reference Targets

Recall that class **PurchaseOrder** includes a **previousOrder** reference, which is intended to be used to identify a previous purchase order associated with the same customer, if there is one. The relevant portion of the model is shown in Figure 13.6.

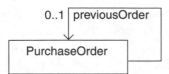

Figure 13.6 **PurchaseOrder** and its **previousOrder** reference.

We can set the previous order of a given order (e.g., P1) using the property sheet in the generated editor, as shown in Figure 13.7. Notice that the drop-down combo box includes every purchase order in the model, even P1 itself. This is because the default implementation in the framework simply populates the combo box with all type-compatible objects in the resource set (i.e., instances of class **PurchaseOrder**, including subclasses if there are any).

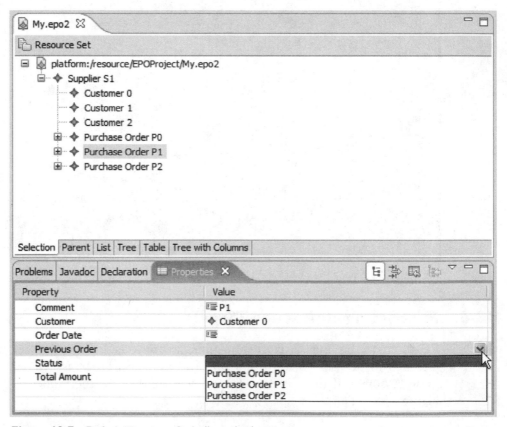

Figure 13.7 Default "Previous Order" combo box items.

Because the previous order is supposed to reference a different order, and one associated with the same customer, we should ideally filter the orders in the combo box to give the user a list that only includes valid targets from which to choose. We can easily do this by overriding the getChoiceOfValues() method (in class ItemPropertyDescriptor) for the **previousOrder** property descriptor. The easiest way to do it is by creating an anonymous ItemPropertyDescriptor subclass in the addPreviousOrderPropertyDescriptor() method in class PurchaseOrderItemProvider, like this:

```
/**
 * @generated NOT
 */
protected void addPreviousOrderPropertyDescriptor(Object object)
{
  itemPropertyDescriptors.add(
    createItemPropertyDescriptor(
    new ItemPropertyDescriptor(
      ((ComposeableAdapterFactory)adapterFactory).
        getRootAdapterFactory(),
      getString("_UI_PurchaseOrder_previousOrder_feature"),
      getString("_UI_PropertyDescriptor_description",
                "_UI_PurchaseOrder_previousOrder_feature",
                "_UI_PurchaseOrder_type"),
      EPO2Package.Literals.PURCHASE_ORDER__PREVIOUS_ORDER,
      true, false, true, null, null, null)
    {
      public Collection getChoiceOfValues(Object object)
      {
        PurchaseOrder order = (PurchaseOrder)object;
        Customer customer = order.getCustomer();
        List result = new ArrayList();
        result.add(null);
        if (customer != null)
        {
          result.addAll(customer.getOrders());
          result.remove(order);
        }
        return result;
      }
    });
}
```

Recall from Chapter 11 that this method is generated to create an item property descriptor and add it to the list returned by the item provider. As generated, it calls a helper method, createItemPropertyDescriptor(), which actually creates an instance of ItemPropertyDescriptor. This pattern makes it easy to change the type of descriptor being produced for all properties of a class, as the creation of all the descriptors is delegated to a single method that can be overridden. However, because we only wish to adjust the descriptors created for one property, we simply change `addPreviousOrderPropertyDescriptor()` to instantiate our anonymous subclass of `ItemPropertyDescriptor` directly.

As you can see, we've implemented the `getChoiceOfValues()` method by navigating to the selected order's customer and then returning all the customer's purchase orders, excluding the selected one.[4] The value `null` is also included, allowing the user to indicate that an order is the first by a given customer. If we run the editor again, we'll see that the list of available targets for the previous order is now filtered appropriately. For example, assuming that purchase orders P0 and P1 in Figure 13.7 are associated with customer 0, but P2 is not, then the combo box will now only include P0, as shown in Figure 13.8. As expected, the invalid targets, P1 and P3, are no longer among the available choices.

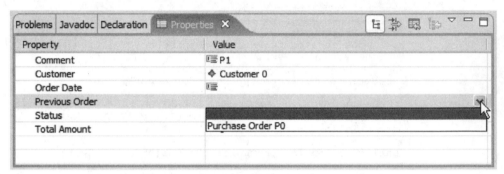

Figure 13.8   Filtered previous order combo box items.

13.7   Splitting the Model into Multiple Packages

As models get larger, it is often desirable to split them into multiple packages. For example, the ExtendedPO3 model is another variation of the purchase order model, similar to ExtendedPO2, only with the classes split into two packages: **epo3** and **supplier**. The **epo3** package includes class **PurchaseOrder** and its component classes (**Item** and the three address classes) as shown in Figure 13.9.

The remaining classes from ExtendedPO2's single **epo2** package are, in ExtendedPO3, located in a separate **supplier** package. This package is illustrated in Figure 13.10. If you look closely at the association between class **Customer** and class **PurchaseOrder**, you'll notice that we've changed it to be one-way instead of bidirectional as it was in ExtendedPO2. This illustrates a subtle issue

---

4. If we wanted to get fancier yet, we could take **orderDate** into account as well.

that arises when separating a model into multiple packages: cyclical dependencies. When we separated the model into two packages, we had the option either to layer the package dependencies as we did (here, we made the **epo3** package have no knowledge of its use by the **supplier** package), or to simply separate them for organizational purposes but leave them interdependent.

By changing the model to make all the associations between the packages one-way from **supplier** to **epo3**, we give ourselves the option of generating the **epo3** package alone in a plug-in project and then later generating the **supplier** package as an extension of **epo3**. If we had kept the two-way dependencies between the packages, we would have no choice but to generate them together in a single plug-in. This is an extremely important consideration when designing large models with more than one package.

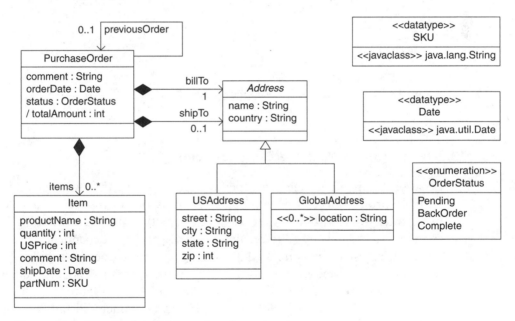

Figure 13.9 The ExtendedPO3 **epo3** package.

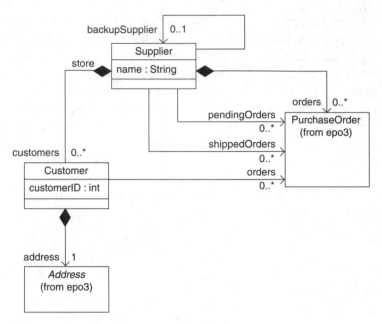

Figure 13.10   The ExtendedPO3 **supplier** package.

13.7.1   Resolving Package Dependencies

Because the **epo3** package is independent, let's assume that we decided to create an EMF project for just the **epo3** package using one of the techniques described in Chapter 4. Now, if we want to extend it with a project containing only the **supplier** package, we need to resolve the cross-package dependency first.

If we're using the annotated Java approach to define the **supplier** package, then we need to establish the existing plug-in that contains **epo3** as a dependency of the new one. We can do this via the Plug-in Manifest editor, as illustrated in Figure 13.11. If we do not do this, importing the model will fail because of the unresolved references to the classes in **epo3**. Once the dependency is set, we can then simply proceed as described in Section 4.2.1.

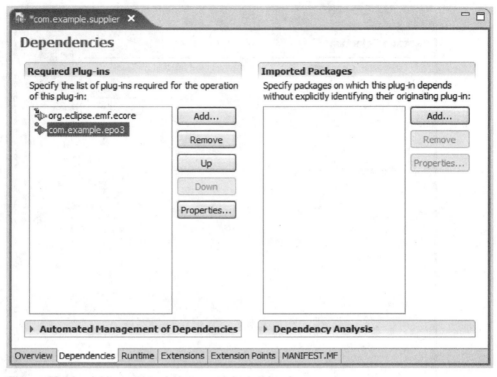

Figure 13.11 Adding required projects to the build path.

If instead we want to create the **supplier** package from Rational Rose, XML Schema, or from Ecore directly, then we need to resolve the package dependency on the last page of the EMF Project or EMF Model wizard. For example, in Figure 13.12, we are creating a new project from the *ExtendedPO3.mdl* Rose model. We elect to generate only the **supplier** package, so on the last page of the wizard, we select only "com.example.supplier". Notice that the **Finish** button is disabled because of the unresolved references to the **epo3** package.

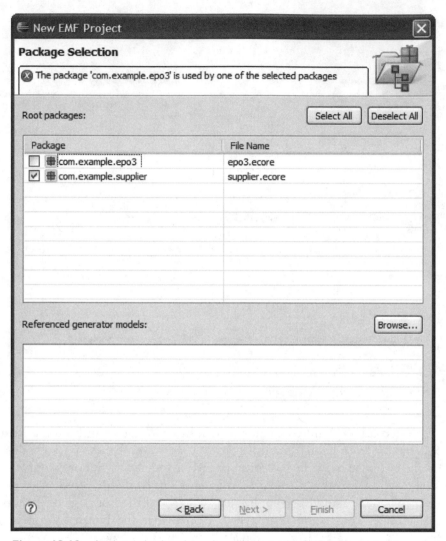

Figure 13.12   An unresolved package dependency in the EMF Project wizard.

To proceed, we click the **Browse...** button to display a file selection dialog box, from which we select the existing generator model containing the package that we wish to reference. The model shows in the **Referenced generator models** table. If we select the "com.example.epo3" package in that table, the error message disappears and the **Finish** button is enabled, as in Figure 13.13. We can then proceed to generate the model in the usual way.

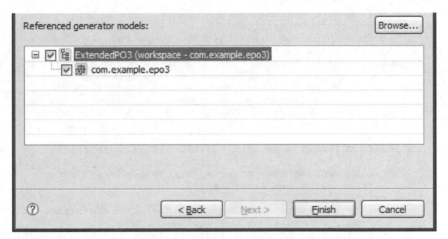

Figure 13.13   Locating a referenced model using the EMF Project wizard.

13.7.2   *Restricting Reference Targets Revisited*

As we described previously, to implement the two ExtendedPO3 packages in separate projects we needed to change the model to remove the bidirectional association between class **Customer** and class **PurchaseOrder**. You might have noticed that this small design change breaks the implementation we provided in Section 13.6 for filtering the choices in the "Previous Order" combo box. We were using the `getCustomer()` method to navigate to the selected order's customer, which we then used to locate the valid orders. Now that we've made the association one-way, from **Customer** to **PurchaseOrder**, we do not have the `getCustomer()` method on interface `PurchaseOrder` any more. Without it, we need to find another way of locating the customer.

EMF includes a number of convenient utility classes, one of which can be used to help with this problem. The class `EcoreUtil.UsageCrossReferencer` can be used to find incoming references, or usages, of an object. We will use it to find the customer whose **order** feature references the selected purchase order, after which we can proceed to populate the purchase order list as in the previous example. Here's our new version of the getChoiceOfValues() method.

```java
/**
 * @generated NOT
 */
protected void addPreviousOrderPropertyDescriptor(Object object) {
  itemPropertyDescriptors.add(
    createItemPropertyDescriptor(
    new ItemPropertyDescriptor(
      ((ComposeableAdapterFactory)adapterFactory).
        getRootAdapterFactory(),
      getString("_UI_PurchaseOrder_previousOrder_feature"),
      getString("_UI_PropertyDescriptor_description",
                "_UI_PurchaseOrder_previousOrder_feature",
                "_UI_PurchaseOrder_type"),
      EPO3Package.Literals.PURCHASE_ORDER__PREVIOUS_ORDER,
      true, false, true, null, null, null)
    {
      public Collection getChoiceOfValues(Object object)
      {
        final PurchaseOrder order = (PurchaseOrder)object;
        List result = new ArrayList();
        result.add(null);
        Collection settings = EcoreUtil.UsageCrossReferencer.find(
          order, order.eResource().getResourceSet());
        for (Iterator iter = settings.iterator(); iter.hasNext();)
        {
          EStructuralFeature.Setting setting =
            (EStructuralFeature.Setting)iter.next();

          if (setting.getEStructuralFeature() ==
              SupplierPackage.Literals.CUSTOMER__ORDERS)
          {
            Customer customer = (Customer)setting.getEObject();
            result.addAll(customer.getOrders());
            result.remove(order);
            break;
          }
        }
        return result;
      }
    });
}
```

As you can see, we first call the static find() method on class UsageCrossReferencer to locate the incoming references to the selected order. Notice how we pass two arguments to the cross-referencer, order and order.eResource().getResourceSet(). The first argument is the object of which we want to find usages, which in our example is the selected purchase order. The second argument is the scope in which to search.

Like all cross-referencers, a UsageCrossReferencer searches for particular instances of references within a given scope. An instance of a reference can be uniquely identified in terms of the reference itself and the object holding that particular instance. In EMF, this is known as a *setting* and is represented by the interface EStructuralFeature.Setting, which looks like this:

```
interface EStructuralFeature
{
  ...
  interface Setting
  {
    EObject getEObject();
    EStructuralFeature getEStructuralFeature();
    object get(boolean resolve);
    void set(Object newValue);
    boolean isSet();
    void unset();
  }
}
```

Notice that a setting allows you to access and manipulate its value. This makes it useful in several places in EMF, particularly for the dynamic EObject implementation.

The cross-referencer returns the result of its search as a collection of settings. So, to find our order's customer we proceed to iterate through these settings, searching for the first one with the right feature, SupplierPackage.Literals. CUSTOMER__ORDERS.[5] Once we find the right setting, we simply retrieve the referencing customer by calling the getEObject() method on the setting, and then continue with the implementation as before.

There are actually four different variants of the UsageCrossReferencer.find() method:

```
public static Collection find(EObject eObjectOfInterest,
                              EObject eObject)

public static Collection find(EObject eObjectOfInterest,
                              Resource resource)

public static Collection find(EObject eObjectOfInterest,
                              ResourceSet resourceSet)

public static Collection find(EObject eObjectOfInterest,
                              Collection emfObjectsToSearch)
```

---

5. Notice how we're assuming that there will only be one customer referencing a given purchase order, even though this is no longer enforced by the model, as it was in ExtendedPO2. If we want to guarantee this, we would need to add some filtering for valid targets of the **orders** feature of class **Customer**, to exclude purchase orders that are already associated with a customer.

The first version allows you to search for referencing objects within the containment tree rooted by the specified eObject. The second and third allow you to widen the search to the contents of a resource or an entire resource set, respectively. The final version lets you provide a heterogeneous list of context roots (EObjects, Resources, or ResourceSets), all of which will be searched.

You might be wondering why we used the resource set version in our example. If we know that the previous order is always limited to other orders owned by the same supplier, then we could have narrowed the search to the current order's supplier, like this:

```
Collection references = EcoreUtil.UsageCrossReferencer.find(
    order, order.eContainer());
```

This would run faster but would not allow us to find customers from a different supplier. We designed it with the wide search in anticipation of the changes we're going to make in the following sections, but for now suffice to say that either approach would have worked equally well.

13.8 Editing Multiple Resources Concurrently

Another helpful feature of EMF that we can exploit in our extended purchase order application is its support for references between objects in different resources. By persisting related objects in separate resources, we can reduce the size of the resulting documents. When dealing with very large numbers of objects, this approach can dramatically benefit performance, too, as EMF's use of automatically resolving proxies helps to ensure that resources are only loaded when they are needed.

In this section we will see what needs to be done to support cross-document references in our model, and how the generated editor can be used to instantiate the model across multiple resources.

13.8.1 Cross-Document Non-Containment References

Another design change we made in the ExtendedPO3 model, which you might have noticed already, was to add another association on class **Supplier**. This addition is shown in Figure 13.14.

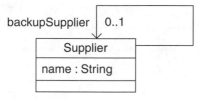

Figure 13.14 Adding an association on **Supplier**.

We added the **backupSupplier** reference to the model to represent another supplier that a given supplier might use to service orders for its customers. We made the **resolveProxies** property true for this reference so that we can serialize a supplier and its backup into different resources if we want to. Because of this design change, we need to reconsider our decision from Section 13.1 to declare several other references in the model as non-proxy resolving. Specifically, now that a customer's order might be filled by a backup supplier in a different resource, the **orders** reference from class **Customer** to **PurchaseOrder** and the **previousOrder** reference of class **PurchaseOrder** must now also be made to resolve proxies. We can no longer optimize these references.

With these changes we now have a version of the purchase order model that supports multiple cooperating suppliers in potentially more than one resource. But, now that we've enabled this capability in the model, how do we make use of it? Our generated editor only edits a single resource containing a single root object, right? Well, not exactly.

One thing that you've probably noticed by now is that the viewers in a generated EMF editor always display the resource at the top, instead of the root object(s) in the resource. For example, in Figure 13.15, the resource *platform:/resource/EPOProject/My.supplier* appears as the root of the tree viewer. Nested under it is the supplier S0, the root object in that resource. Although this default behavior can be easily changed, and we will show how in Chapter 19, it does give us the ability to use the default generated editor to work with resources that have cross-document references.

For example, assume we have created another resource, named *My_backup.supplier*, containing just a single supplier named "S1." We can then open that other resource in the same editor by selecting **Load Resource...** from the **Supplier Editor** pull-down menu. The dialog box illustrated in Figure 13.16 displays. We can use the **Browse Workspace...** button to select the file, and the corresponding URI will be filled in.

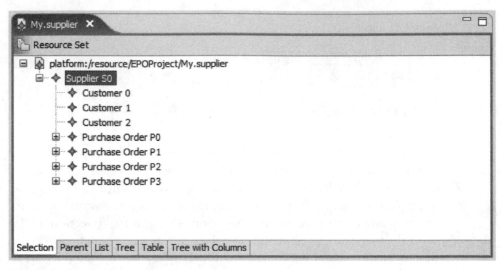

Figure 13.15   Editing a single resource.

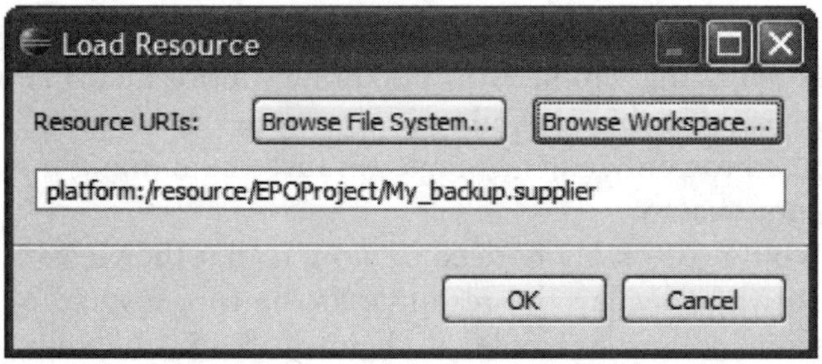

Figure 13.16   Loading an additional resource.

On hitting **OK**, the resource will be loaded into the editor, as illustrated in Figure 13.17. We can then set the **backupSupplier** for S0 to be S1, from the second resource.

We then save and close the editor, and look at *My.supplier* in a text editor to see what has happened:

```
<supplier:Supplier xmi:version="2.0" ... name="S0">
  ...
  <backupSupplier href="My_backup.supplier#/"/>
</supplier:Supplier>
```

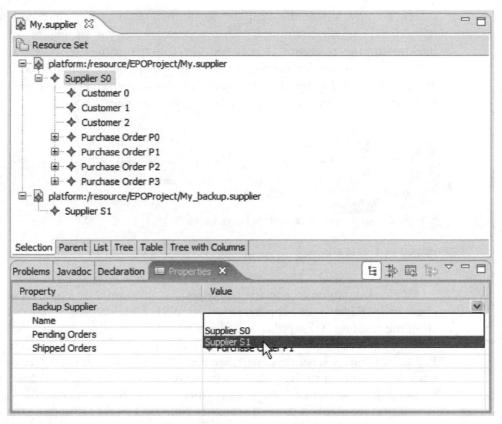

Figure 13.17   Setting a cross-document reference.

As we will discuss further in Chapter 15, the cross-document reference is serialized using an `href` attribute. Its value is a relative URI identifying the target object in another resource. The URI's fragment, "/", identifies the single root object in a resource, in this case supplier S1.

If we close the text editor and again open *My.supplier* with the generated Supplier editor, the tree viewer will once again display only the supplier S0 under its resource, as shown in Figure 13.18. Notice that the second resource, *My_backup.supplier*, is not yet showing.

Figure 13.18   Editing a resource with cross-document references.

If we now select the supplier S0 in this viewer, the referenced resource, *My_backup.supplier*, will then also appear as shown in Figure 13.19. The **backupSupplier** reference is accessed for the first time when the supplier is selected and it is needed for display in the property sheet. As described in Chapter 10, the generated getter for this reference then uses `EcoreUtil.resolve()` to lazily load the referenced resource, *My_backup.supplier*.

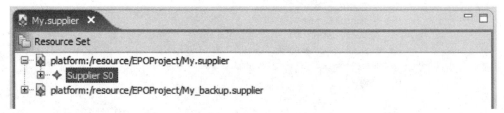

Figure 13.19   Lazy loading to resolve cross-document references.

We can continue to edit the resources. For example, we could drag the purchase order P2 between suppliers, from S0 to S1. Note that this removes the object from the resource *My.supplier* and places it into the resource *My_backup.supplier*, where S1 already resides. If there are any customers of S0 whose **orders** included P2, as in Figure 13.20, these will now become cross-document references. Think back for a moment to the design decision we made in Section 13.7.2 while implementing the `getChoiceOfValues()` method for the **previousOrder** property. Recall that we invoked `UsageCrossReferencer.find()`, specifying the resource set as the context in which to search. We can now see why. If we had instead used the resource or supplier as the context, it would be impossible to set the **previousOrder** reference of P2 to any other orders associated with customer 1, as they would have been excluded from the search. The resource set is a container for all of the resources that have been loaded into the editor, and as such it is the broadest context available.

If we save again, the editor in fact saves both resources loaded into its resource set. If it only saved the changes to *My.supplier*, the purchase order P2 would be lost altogether.

As we've now seen, generated EMF editors provide out-of-box support for cross-document references. However, it is also possible to enhance that support. For example, we could certainly make it easier to create a backup supplier in a second resource.

The approach we will take is to modify the Supplier wizard: when the user creates a supplier, it will automatically create a backup supplier in another resource at the same time. This is a pretty simple enhancement, and it has the added benefit of illustrating what is happening under the covers with cross-document references.

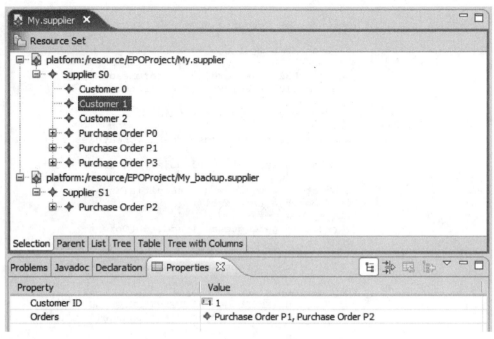

Figure 13.20   Concurrently editing two supplier resources.

We change the `performFinish()` method in class `SupplierModelWizard`, like this:

```
/**
 * @generated NOT
 */
public boolean performFinish()
{
  try
  {
    // Remember the file.
    //
    final IFile modelFile = getModelFile();

    // Do the work within an operation.
    //
    WorkspaceModifyOperation operation =
      new WorkspaceModifyOperation()
      {
        protected void execute(IProgressMonitor progressMonitor)
        {
          try
          {
            // Create a resource set
```

```
    //
    ResourceSet resourceSet = new ResourceSetImpl();

    // Get the URI of the model file.
    //
    URI fileURI = URI.createPlatformResourceURI(
      modelFile.getFullPath().toString());

    // Create a resource for this file.
    //
    Resource resource = resourceSet.createResource(fileURI);

    // Add the initial model object to the contents.
    //
    EObject rootObject = createInitialModel();
    if (rootObject != null)
    {
      resource.getContents().add(rootObject);
    }

    // Save the contents of the resource to the file system.
    //
    Map options = new HashMap();
    options.put(XMLResource.OPTION_ENCODING,
                initialObjectCreationPage.getEncoding());

    if (rootObject instanceof Supplier)
    {
      // Create and save a backup for a supplier.
      //
      Supplier supplier = (Supplier)rootObject;
      Supplier supplier2 =
        SupplierFactory.eINSTANCE.createSupplier();
      supplier.setBackupSupplier(supplier2);

      IPath path =
        modelFile.getFullPath().removeFileExtension();
      URI uri = URI.createPlatformResourceURI(
        path + "_backup.supplier");
      Resource resource2 = resourceSet.createResource(uri);
      resource2.getContents().add(supplier2);
      resource2.save(options);
    }

    resource.save(options);
  }
  ...
}
```

As generated, the wizard allows the user to specify which class defined by the model should be instantiated and placed into the resource. The createInitialModel() method reads the user's selection, and creates the correct object. We have added code that checks whether this object is an instance of

Supplier. If so, we create another supplier, and make it the backup for the first supplier. We then create a second resource with a filename derived from the first, place the backup supplier into it, and serialize it. The first resource is then serialized as usual, but because its supplier's **backupSupplier** refers to a supplier in another resource, we end up with a cross-document reference, as described earlier in this section.

13.8.2 Cross-Document Containment References

The support for cross-document non-containment references that we saw in the previous section provides a good deal of control over how to split related objects across multiple resources. However, it might not be sufficient in all circumstances.

In EMF models, it is the containment references that are often most significant, as they define the closest types of relationships between objects. If you are dealing with models that describe deep trees of containment, or even with instances that populate shallower containment hierarchies with large numbers of objects, you might benefit from using cross-document containment.

In our example, we might find that a single supplier fills many large purchase orders and maintains a substantial customer list. The individual orders are largely independent of each other, so we might decide to persist each order in its own resource. This approach leaves the simple structure of the model intact, but allows each order to be loaded and edited individually in contexts where that makes sense.

The ExtendedPO3 model includes a few small changes that enable this behavior. To this point, we have only considered proxy resolution on non-containment references in our purchase order model, but as discussed in Section 10.3.5, containment references can resolve proxies, too, allowing them to cross documents. By default, proxy resolution is disabled for all containment references to maintain backward compatibility with earlier versions of EMF that did not support it. Because we will be enabling it on this model, each containment reference must be considered and its **resolveProxies** attribute set appropriately.

We decided that the **orders** reference, from class **Supplier** to **PurchaseOrder**, will be the only proxy-resolving containment reference in the model. Because the default value of **resolveProxies** is true, all the other containment references must be set explicitly to be non-proxy resolving. Also, the derived, non-containment references **pendingOrders** and **shippedOrders** are made to resolve proxies, as they will now be able to refer to orders contained by a given supplier but persisted in a different resource from it.

Having made these changes in the model, we now enable containment proxies in the EMF generator, as illustrated in Figure 13.21.

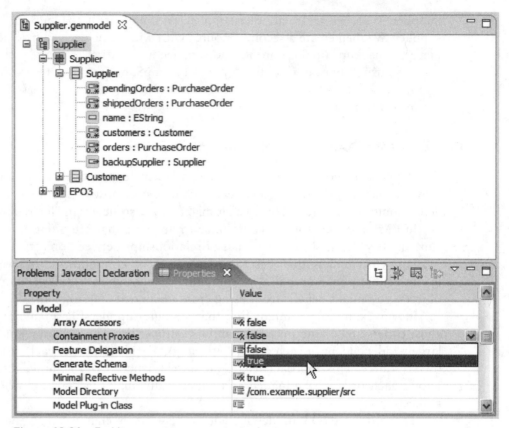

Figure 13.21   Enabling containment proxies in the generator.

We then regenerate the code, so that we can begin working with the generated editor's out-of-box support for cross-document containment. We begin with the same simple version of the *My.supplier* resource that we created in the previous section, and we will move a purchase order into a separate resource from its supplier.

For example, we can right-click P0 and select **Control...** from the pop-up menu, as illustrated in Figure 13.22.

The dialog box shown in Figure 13.23 is displayed. We click the **Browse Workspace...** button, select our *EPOProject* project, enter the filename *PO.epo3*, and the corresponding URI is filled in.

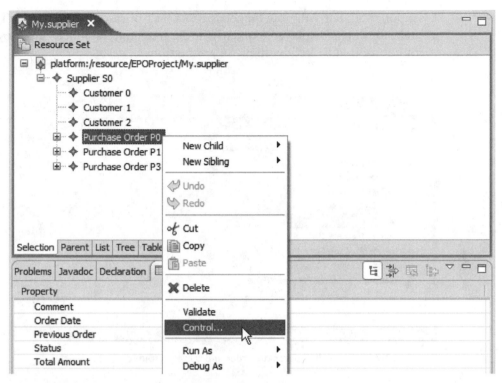

Figure 13.22   Controlling a purchase order.

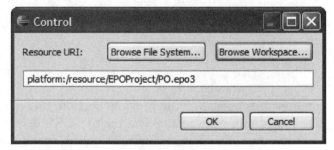

Figure 13.23   Specifying a resource URI.

After we click **OK**, the new resource is created and displayed in the editor, as illustrated in Figure 13.24. At first glance, it appears that the resource is empty; however, its icon has been annotated with a target symbol. Correspondingly, the icon for the purchase order we controlled, PO, has been annotated with an arrow. This reflects the situation we have created: PO is still logically contained by supplier S0, but will now be persisted as part of resource *PO.epo3*. The logical relationship is displayed explicitly in the tree, and its underlying cross-document nature is indicated by the icon annotations.

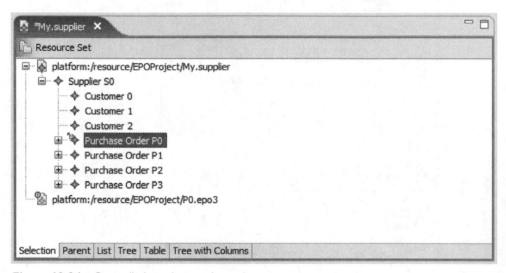

Figure 13.24   Controlled purchase order and target resource.

If we now save, the new resource will be created. In the original resource, *My.supplier*, the cross-document containment reference looks like this:

```
<supplier:Supplier xmi:version="2.0" ... name="S0">
  ...
  <orders href="P0.epo3#/"/>
  ...
```

Like the non-containment reference of the previous section, this reference is serialized using an `href` attribute, whose value is a relative URI identifying the target object in the new resource. The new resource, *PO.epo3*, looks like this:

```
<epo3:PurchaseOrder xmi:version="2.0" ... comment="P0">
  <items productName="I0" quantity="10" USPrice="2"/>
</epo3:PurchaseOrder>
```

Notice that no explicit reference back to *My.supplier* is serialized. In this model, the **orders** reference is not bidirectional, but even if it was, the opposite reference would be transient by default. This allows *PO.epo3* to be loaded completely independently. However, when *My.supplier* is loaded and the proxy is resolved, the implicitly bidirectional nature of the containment reference is reestablished in memory.

Once an object has been placed in a resource other than its container's, establishing a cross-document reference, the **Control...** item on its pop-up menu is replaced by **Uncontrol**. This allows us to return the object to its container's resource.

We finish this discussion with another look under the covers at cross-document containment. We can further enhance the Supplier wizard so that when a user creates a supplier, a contained purchase order is automatically created in another resource. As in the previous section, we add to the the `performFinish()` method in class `SupplierModelWizard`:

```
...
if (rootObject instanceof Supplier)
{
  // Create and save a backup for a supplier.
  //
  ...

  // Create and save a purchase order for a supplier.
  //
  PurchaseOrder order = EPO3Factory.eINSTANCE.createPurchaseOrder();
  supplier.getOrders().add(order);

  uri = URI.createPlatformResourceURI(path + ".epo3");
  Resource resource3 = resourceSet.createResource(uri);
  resource3.getContents().add(order);
  resource3.save(options);
}

resource.save(options);
...
```

Here, we are adding some more initialization when the user chooses to create an instance of **Supplier**. We create an instance of **PurchaseOrder** and add it to the supplier's **orders** reference. We then create a new resource, add the order to it, and save it. Because proxy resolution is enabled for the **orders** containment reference, the object is not removed from its container when we add it to the resource.

With this final change, our example is complete. If you managed to follow along and successfully implement the example, you can now consider yourself a bona fide EMF novice. After having read this much of the book, you might have been hoping that you had advanced further than the "lowly" level of novice. Well, the next part of the book covers several more advanced topics and provides examples to help you advance to the intermediate level or, dare we say it, become an EMF expert.

PART IV

Programming with EMF

CHAPTER 14

Exploiting Metadata

So far, we've talked a great deal about how EMF can produce an Ecore model from various different sources and how it can then generate code from that model. EMF is, however, not just a generator tool; it's also a powerful runtime framework. In the remaining chapters of this book, we discuss the functionality provided by the runtime framework and how to effectively program with it. To begin, this chapter focuses on the use of EMF metadata at runtime.

Ecore is, itself, an EMF model. From it, an implementation has been generated, with an API like that generated from any other model. The Java package `org.eclipse.emf.ecore` contains interfaces corresponding to each of the classes modeled in Ecore, with generated getters and setters for all of the attributes and references detailed in Chapter 5. The metadata for any EMF object is expressed using this Ecore implementation. This information is always available at runtime, so we can use the Ecore API to query the structure of the model, and use the reflective `EObject` API to generically access and manipulate data in its instances. Moreover, we can dynamically define a model at runtime, just by instantiating Ecore.

In this chapter, we look closely at the metadata exposed by EMF objects and see how it is exploited by the reflection and dynamic EMF mechanisms.

14.1 Packages

As we saw in Chapter 10, EMF generates a package interface that provides easy access to the metadata for the types defined in that package. Recall that this interface extends the generic Ecore interface `EPackage`, defining specific constants and accessors for the modeled classifiers and features.

As we will now see, this generated interface is only a convenience: everything that it provides access to is also available using generic methods in the base interface. For example, interface EPO2Package, which is generated from the ExtendedPO2 model, provides a convenience method for accessing the **PurchaseOrder** class. We can use it like this:

```
EClass poClass = epo2Package.getPurchaseOrder();
```

Without the generated class, we would simply retrieve the class by using the getEClassifier() method from the EPackage interface, like this:

```
EClass poClass = (EClass)epo2Package.getEClassifier("PurchaseOrder");
```

We can similarly access the attributes, references, and everything else provided by the generated package. The generated methods are easier to use and more efficient, but otherwise offer nothing new. The EPackage interface also gives us the ability to work with objects generically. Other parts of the EMF runtime rely on this capability, and you might also find it to be useful in certain types of applications.

14.1.1 Accessing Package Metadata Generically

Let's look at a simple example that shows more use of the generic Ecore API. It walks through a complete package, printing the names of all its classifiers, along with their contents. For each **EClass**, we'll print the names of its attributes and references. For an **EEnum**, we'll display the names of its literals, whereas for any other **EDataType**, we'll just print the instance class name. Here is the method:

```
public static void print(EPackage ePackage)
{
  for (Iterator iter = ePackage.getEClassifiers().iterator();
       iter.hasNext(); )
  {
    EClassifier classifier = (EClassifier)iter.next();
    System.out.println(classifier.getName());
    System.out.print("  ");

    if (classifier instanceof EClass)
    {
      EClass eClass = (EClass)classifier;
      for (Iterator ai = eClass.getEAttributes().iterator();
           ai.hasNext(); )
      {
        EAttribute attribute = (EAttribute)ai.next();
        System.out.print(attribute.getName() + " ");
      }
      if (!eClass.getEAttributes().isEmpty() &&
          !eClass.getEReferences().isEmpty())
```

```
          {
            System.out.println();
            System.out.print("  ");
          }
          for (Iterator ri = eClass.getEReferences().iterator();
               ri.hasNext(); )
          {
            EReference reference = (EReference)ri.next();
            System.out.print(reference.getName() + " ");
          }
        }
        else if (classifier instanceof EEnum)
        {
          EEnum eEnum = (EEnum)classifier;
          for (Iterator ei = eEnum.getELiterals().iterator();
               ei.hasNext(); )
          {
            EEnumLiteral literal = (EEnumLiteral)ei.next();
            System.out.print(literal.getName() + " ");
          }
        }
        else if (classifier instanceof EDataType)
        {
          EDataType eDataType = (EDataType)classifier;
          System.out.print(eDataType.getInstanceClassName());
        }
        System.out.println();
      }
}
```

As you can see, we simply iterate through the set of classifiers, check the type of each, and act accordingly. If we were to call this method with the package from ExtendedPO2, EPO2Package.eINSTANCE, it would produce the following output:

```
Item
  productName quantity USPrice comment shipDate partNum
  order
USAddress
  street city state zip
PurchaseOrder
  comment orderDate status totalAmount
  items billTo shipTo customer previousOrder
Address
  name country
Supplier
  name
  customers orders pendingOrders shippedOrders
Customer
  customerID
  orders
GlobalAddress
```

```
    location
GlobalLocation
  countryCode
OrderStatus
  Pending BackOrder Complete
SKU
  java.lang.String
Date
  java.util.Date
```

You can use the `EPackage` interface to access all of the metadata in a model, whether it is a generated package, like EPO2Package in this example, or a dynamically created one. Note, however, that you should never attempt to modify the metadata describing a generated package. It is available for inspection only.

We'll see how metadata can be used to work with objects reflectively in Section 14.2 and discuss dynamic EMF in Section 14.3.

14.1.2   Locating Packages

Given the important role that packages play in obtaining metadata about EMF objects, the next topic we need to address is how to find packages. Specifically, we need to understand how to locate a particular instance of `EPackage`.

You might recall from Chapter 2 that an **EPackage** is the root object in a serialized Ecore model:

```
<?xml version="1.0" encoding="UTF-8"?>
<ecore:EPackage xmi:version="2.0" xmlns:xmi=... xmlns:xsi=...
    xmlns:ecore="http://www.eclipse.org/emf/2002/Ecore"
    name="epo2" nsURI="http://www.example.com/epo2.ecore"
    nsPrefix="epo2">
  <eClassifiers xsi:type="ecore:EClass" name="PurchaseOrder">
  ...
```

So, to access a package, we could simply retrieve it from a serialized form:

```
ResourceSet resourceSet = new ResourceSetImpl();
URI fileURI = URI.createFileURI(".../ExtendedPO2.ecore");
Resource resource = resourceSet.getResource(fileURI, true);
EPackage epo2Package = (EPackage)resource.getContents().get(0);
```

Here, we are using EMF's persistence framework to load an XMI serialization from the named *ExtendedPO2.ecore* file. The corresponding model is built in memory and accessed as the contents of a resource. We will discuss this kind of code in greater detail in Chapter 15.

Loading a serialized form of the model is a valid way to obtain metadata at runtime. Indeed, it is a common way initially to create the model in memory. However, it is not something we want to do every time we need to access a piece of metadata. Reading from the disk, parsing XML, and constructing the whole model are very expensive operations, so we should aim to do them only once for a given model.

Moreover, it does not make much sense to have multiple bits of metadata floating around representing, for example, the same class, as could happen if we load the same resource multiple times. We might wish to be able to check whether two EMF objects are instances of the same class. If we can assume that there is only a single copy of each piece of metadata in the system, then this can be done simply by asking each object for its class and checking whether they reference the same `EClass` instance.

The other source of metadata that we have seen so far is the generated package implementation, which programmatically builds a model and exposes it via the corresponding generated interface. So, we need a facility to provide access to the packages that contain the metadata describing all the data in our system, no matter how those packages were initialized. The package registry fills this need. You will find the interfaces for this registry nested in the `EPackage` interface:

```
public interface EPackage extends ENamedElement
{
  public interface Registry extends Map
  {
    EPackage getEPackage(String nsURI);
    EFactory getEFactory(String nsURI);
    Registry INSTANCE = EPackageRegistryImpl.createGlobalRegistry();
  }

  public interface Descriptor
  {
    EPackage getEPackage();
    EFactory getEFactory();
  }

  ...
```

Interface `EPackage.Registry` simply provides mappings between namespace URIs and packages. Given a namespace URI, which uniquely identifies a package, a registry allows you to obtain the corresponding `EPackage` instance. Notice that there is a default, global package registry, available via the `INSTANCE` field of the nested `Registry` interface. However, this need not be the only package registry used. In fact, in Section 15.2.5 we'll see that the usual configuration is to have multiple context-specific registries that delegate to the single global registry as a fallback when they cannot find a package locally.

A package registry is populated using the `java.util.Map` API. When manually putting entries in the map, you must use a `String`-typed namespace URI as the key and an `EPackage` as the value. However, you should always retrieve a package using the typed `getEPackage()` method.

Some of the registry map's values may be instances of `EPackage.Descriptor`, which are created under the covers during plug-in initialization. Descriptors provide for early registration of generated packages, deferring the loading of each package until it is actually used. If you've ever looked at the generated *plugin.xml* file in an EMF model plug-in, you might have noticed that it includes one or more extensions that look something like this:

```
<extension point="org.eclipse.emf.ecore.generated_package">
  <package
    uri = "http://www.example.com/epo2.ecore"
    class = "com.example.epo2.EPO2Package" ... />
</extension>
```

During plug-in initialization, this will cause an `EPackage.Descriptor` for the `EPO2Package` to be added to the global package registry. Later, when the package is needed, the registry's `getEPackage()` method is called. From the given namespace URI, this method obtains the corresponding descriptor and, in turn, calls `getEPackage()` on it, automatically creating and initializing the `EPackage` instance, and then updating the registry to refer directly to this new package. This is why you should never retrieve a package directly from the map, but rather use the registry's typed `getEPackage()` method.

Generated packages are not always registered using the extension-based deferred loading mechanism. For example, when EMF is run stand-alone, this mechanism is not available. In this case, generated packages are usually registered during their construction. This simply occurs when a package instance is first accessed via its interface. For example:

```
EPO2Package epo2Package = EPO2Package.eINSTANCE;
```

As a side effect of accessing the `EPO2Package` instance, the package is registered in the global registry.

There are two other usual mechanisms for registering packages, `URIConverters` and `xsi:schemaLocation`, which are used with models for which no code is generated. With these approaches, which we will discuss in Chapter 15, packages are loaded from their serialized form and registered automatically, as a side effect of loading instance documents that require them. A context-specific package registry is used for such registrations.

Once a package is registered, it is easy to access it wherever it's needed: just call the `getEPackage()` method on the appropriate `EPackage.Registry`. For example, here is a very simple method that uses the global package registry to obtain a particular `EClassifier` based on its name and its package's namespace URI. Because each package should have a globally unique namespace URI and each classifier's name must be unique in its package, this is really enough information to identify any classifier in EMF.

```
public static EClassifier getEClassifier(String nsURI, String name)
{
  EPackage ePackage = EPackage.Registry.INSTANCE.getEPackage(nsURI);
  return ePackage == null ? null : ePackage.getEClassifier(name);
}
```

For example, we can use this method to obtain a particular class from the ExtendedPO2 model like this:

```
EClassifier poClass = getEClassifier(
  "http://www.example.com/epo2.ecore","PurchaseOrder"));
```

Looking back at the `EPackage.Registry` interface, you'll notice that it also includes a `getEFactory()` method, which obtains the factory for a registered package. You might recall from Chapter 5 that an **EPackage** always has an associated **EFactory** that can be used to instantiate the classifiers defined in the package. The `getEFactory()` method can act as a shortcut for obtaining a package and calling `getEFactoryInstance()` on it. More important, it's also a hook for a package descriptor to register a factory override for the package.

The *plugin.xml* file for a plug-in can register an override for a package's default factory implementation using an extension like this:

```
<extension point="org.eclipse.emf.ecore.factory_override">
  <factory
      uri="http://www.example.com/epo2.ecore"
      class="com.example.epo2.extension.impl.MyEPO2FactoryImpl"/>
</extension>
```

Note that only one factory override can be declared for a given package and that the specified factory class must implement the generated factory interface. The significance of factories is discussed further in the following section.

14.2   Reflection

EMF provides a reflective API that allows your programs to examine the metadata for the objects they're working with and to access and manipulate data generically. EMF reflection is similar to Java reflection, but it operates at a slightly higher level. Whereas you might use Java reflection to invoke a method or set the value of a field directly, EMF reflection deals explicitly with attributes and references, providing a means to invoke exactly the same kind of accessors that are generated for each modeled structural feature. Like Java, EMF also provides a generic facility for instantiating classes.

14.2.1   Creating Objects

EMF objects are created using factories. As we have seen, each modeled **EPackage** has a corresponding **EFactory** that is responsible for instantiating the classes defined in the package. When we generate code for a package, we get a factory interface, EPO2Factory for example, with a specific method for creating an instance of each class. We can use the factory to create an object like this:

```
PurchaseOrder order = epo2Factory.createPurchaseOrder();
```

Generated factories also extend the base factory interface, EFactory, inheriting the generic create() method, which can be used to create objects reflectively. This method takes an EClass, to specify which class should be instantiated:

```
EClass poClass = ...
EFactory epo2factory = poClass.getEPackage().getEFactoryInstance();
EObject order = epo2factory.create(poClass);
```

Notice that to create an object, all we need is an EClass. From it, we can easily obtain its containing package and the corresponding factory. In fact, as a convenience, we can use an EMF utility method to do this for us:

```
EObject order = EcoreUtil.create(poClass);
```

So, how do we get an EClass to use in object creation? Ultimately, it will come from a package. Depending on how the model was obtained and how you are using it, you might access it in different ways. For a simple example, let's build on what we learned in the previous section about accessing packages from a registry. We can retrieve a package based on a namespace URI, and then get a named class from the package. Then, we can instantiate that class reflectively:

```
public static EObject createEObject(String nsURI, String name)
{
  EPackage ePackage = EPackage.Registry.INSTANCE.getEPackage(nsURI);
  EClass eClass = (EClass)ePackage.getEClassifier(name);
  return ePackage.getEFactoryInstance().create(eClass);
}
```

Note that this method assumes that the namespace URI and class name are valid, and will throw an exception if they're not. We can now create an instance of class **PurchaseOrder** like this:

```
EObject order = createEObject("http://www.example.com/epo2.ecore",
                             "PurchaseOrder");
```

This is actually very similar to what EMF's XML resource implementation does during a load when it has to create objects based on a namespace-qualified type name.

Reflective object creation always leaves us with an instance of EObject, EMF's highly functional base interface for modeled objects. As we will see in the next section, we can use this interface to retrieve the metadata for the object and access its features generically.

14.2.2 Interrogating and Modifying Objects

Now that we know how to examine metadata and create objects, all we need is a way to access the attributes and references reflectively. We do this using the reflective EObject API.

Our usual point of access to the metadata is EObject's eClass() method, which, unsurprisingly, returns the EClass that describes the object. We can then use that metadata together with the reflective eGet(), eSet(), eIsSet(), and eUnset() methods to access and set the values of the object's attributes and references. Each of these methods takes an EStructuralFeature identifying the feature that is to be accessed.

For example, here is a simple method that prints names and values of all the attributes of an arbitrary object:

```
public static void printAttributeValues(EObject object)
{
  EClass eClass = object.eClass();
  System.out.println(eClass.getName());
  for (Iterator iter = eClass.getEAllAttributes().iterator();
       iter.hasNext(); )
  {
```

```
    EAttribute attribute = (EAttribute)iter.next();
    Object value = object.eGet(attribute);
    System.out.print("  " + attribute.getName() + ": " + value);
    if (object.eIsSet(attribute))
    {
      System.out.println();
    }
    else
    {
      System.out.println(" (default)");
    }
  }
}
```

We start by accessing the `EClass` of the object we wish to interrogate. Notice that to retrieve the class's attributes, we use the `getEAllAttributes()` method, which returns *all* of the attributes, including the ones defined in base classes. For each attribute, we call the reflective `eGet()` method to retrieve its value. We also call `eIsSet()` to decide whether to append the extra informational string "(default)" to the printed value. For an instance of **Item**, the output might look like this:

```
Item
  productName: Tire
  quantity: 4
  USPrice: 50
  comment: null (default)
  shipDate: null (default)
  partNum: 622-RT
```

You might be wondering why we are calling `eIsSet()` on attributes that were not defined as unsettable and, indeed, what the method even does in this case. Recall that marking a feature unsettable means that it can be in an unset state, which is distinguishable from being set to any value, including null or its default value. Unsurprisingly, `eIsSet()` is used to check that such features are not in the unset state, and `unset()` is used to put them in that state.

However, these two reflective methods can also be used with features that are not unsettable. In this case, `eIsSet()` simply returns `true` if the feature's value is not its default, and `unset()` sets it back to its default value. So, in the preceding example, `eIsSet()` returns `false` for **command** and **shipDate**, which are set to their default value, null.

Now, let's look at an example where we actually modify data. This method changes the price of an item generically. Actually, it has no particular knowledge of the **Item** class; it simply looks for an integer-typed feature named "USPrice", defined in the class of whatever object it receives. If it finds one, it gets the current value and reduces it by 10 percent:

```
public static void adjustPrice(EObject object)
{
  EStructuralFeature feature =
    object.eClass().getEStructuralFeature("USPrice");
  if (feature != null &&
      feature.getEType() == EcorePackage.Literals.EINT)
  {
    int price = ((Integer)object.eGet(feature)).intValue();
    object.eSet(feature, new Integer(price * 9 / 10));
  }
}
```

Ecore's **EInt** data type represents the primitive Java type `int`, so it is interesting to note that we still have to use the `Integer` wrapper class with `eGet()` and `eSet()`. This is just a natural consequence of using generic code with Java's split primitive/object type system, and it applies to all the primitive types.

Navigating references among objects is similar to retrieving attribute values, except that you know the type of the value will always be `EObject`. There are also some additional methods of `EObject` that can help. For example, if you wanted to find the container of an object, you might be inclined to write a method like `findContainer()`, which iterates through all of the object's references, checks `isContainer()` on each, and returns the first non-null value:

```
public static EObject findContainer(EObject object)
{
  for (Iterator i = object.eClass().getEAllReferences().iterator();
       i.hasNext(); )
  {
    EReference reference = (EReference)i.next();
    if (reference.isContainer())
    {
      EObject value = (EObject)object.eGet(reference);
      if (value != null)
      {
        return value;
      }
    }
  }
  return null;
}
```

However, this doesn't actually work if no opposite is modeled for the containment reference that is in use, which is most often the case. Fortunately, an `EObject` always knows its container, and makes it available via the eContainer() method. If this method returns null, the object is not contained.

Similarly, you might want to obtain all of the objects contained by a given object. In this case, it would actually work to manually iterate through all of its references, check isContainment() on each, and accumulate all of their values. However, there's a more convenient way to do this using the EObject API: just call eContents(), which returns a single, read-only list view over all the object's containment references. Similarly, eCrossReferences() returns a read-only view over the object's non-containment references.

We can use eContents() to build on our price adjustment example:

```
public static void adjustPrices(EObject object)
{
  adjustPrice(object);
  for (Iterator i = object.eContents().iterator(); i.hasNext(); )
  {
    adjustPrices((EObject)i.next());
  }
}
```

This method applies the adjustment to all objects within a tree of containment. It recursively visits the given object and all of its contents, invoking adjustPrice() on each object. We can even eliminate the recursion if we use eAllContents(), which returns a single iterator over the whole containment tree under the object:

```
public static void adjustPrices(EObject object)
{
  adjustPrice(object);
  for (Iterator i = object.eAllContents(); i.hasNext(); )
  {
    adjustPrice((EObject)i.next());  // No recursion!
  }
}
```

Specifically eAllContents() returns an instance of TreeIterator, an EMF extension of java.util.Iterator that adds a prune() method to the interface. Calling prune(), while iterating, causes the following next() call to skip over children of the current node, if there are any. In this example, however, we are simply treating the tree iterator just like an ordinary iterator, walking the entire structure.

Let's look at one final reflection example, which uses the EObject API together with generic object creation and more extensive examination of

metadata. Here is a method that ensures that a given object's references are minimally populated to conform to its model:

```
public static void populateReferences(EObject object)
{
  EClass eClass = object.eClass();
  for (Iterator iter = eClass.getEAllReferences().iterator();
       iter.hasNext(); )
  {
    EReference ref = (EReference)iter.next();
    EClass type = getInstantiableClass(ref.getEReferenceType());
    if (type != null && ref.isChangeable() && ref.isRequired())
    {
      if (ref.isMany())
      {
        EList list = (EList)object.eGet(ref);
        while (list.size() < ref.getLowerBound())
        {
          list.add(EcoreUtil.create(type));
        }
      }
      else if (object.eGet(ref) == null)
      {
        object.eSet(ref, EcoreUtil.create(type));
      }
    }
  }
}
```

The method retrieves the class for the given object, from which it obtains
the list of all the references it needs to consider, including any inherited ones.
For each reference, it calls `getInstantiableClass()`, which attempts to
obtain a concrete, type-compatible `EClass`. If it finds such a class and if the reference is both changeable and required, then it can instantiate the class to populate the reference. For a multiplicity-many reference, new instances are repeatedly created and added until the lower bound is satisfied. For a multiplicity-one
reference, only one object is created and added if the reference is not already set.
In either case, any new objects are created using the `EcoreUtil.create()`
convenience method.

The `getInstantiableClass()` method is used to handle the fact that only
concrete classes can be instantiated. Given a concrete class, it simply returns that
same class. If the given class is abstract, it must search in some context for a concrete subclass:

```
private static EClass getInstantiableClass(EClass target)
{
  if (!target.isAbstract()) return target;
```

```
List classifiers = target.getEPackage().getEClassifiers();
for (Iterator iter = classifiers.iterator(); iter.hasNext(); )
{
  Object o = iter.next();
  if (o instanceof EClass)
  {
    EClass eClass = (EClass)o;
    if (!eClass.isAbstract() && target.isSuperTypeOf(eClass))
    {
      return eClass;
    }
  }
}
return null;
}
```

The simple approach taken here is to look at the other classes defined in the same package. The first concrete subclass encountered is returned. More elaborate tactics, like looking in subpackages or other packages in the registry, would be possible. However, our simple approach is sufficient for self-contained packages.

If we pass a new, uninitialized **PurchaseOrder** to populateReferences(), it will set the **customer** reference to a new instance of **Customer**, and set **billTo** to a new instance of **USAddress**. Notice that **billTo**'s type is actually the abstract class **Address**, and a concrete subclass is being correctly selected. All of **PurchaseOrder**'s other references have a lower bound of 0, so none of them are populated. If we were to change the lower bound of **items**, for instance, and regenerate the model, the multiplicity-many path in populateReferences() would be exercised, and one or more **Item**s would be created, depending on what value we had chosen for the lower bound.

It would not be difficult to build on this example to ensure that a complete model instance is fully populated. This would simply be a matter of repeatedly processing objects by calling populateReferences() and then adding all other accessible objects to the set being processed. For example, you might imagine this being done as part of pre- or post-processing of arbitrary data to ensure that it conforms to a given schema.

14.3 Dynamic EMF

As we've seen throughout this book, both the EMF generator and the code it generates are based on and leverage the Ecore metamodel. So far, we've mainly focused on the use of EMF to generate code for a model. In this chapter, we've been using metadata and reflective APIs to deal generically with objects, but those objects have been instances of the classes we have already generated. We have not really considered the situation where an application simply wants to share data without the need for a generated type-safe API. The reflective EMF API is sometimes all one really needs.

EMF provides a dynamic implementation of the reflective `EObject` API that behaves exactly like EMF's generated type-specific classes. Not surprisingly, generated code is more efficient than the dynamic implementation, using less memory and providing faster access to your data. However, if you do not need to provide a type-safe API or modify the default behaviors, the dynamic implementation is worth considering, as it allows models to be more freely shared and to be evolved without maintenance of generated classes. This is the normal trade-off between dynamic and static implementations.

One possible way to get the performance benefit of code generation and the flexibility of dynamic EMF is to invoke the code generator at runtime and then dynamically load the generated classes. This would involve significantly more startup cost and require access to the EMF and JDT development-time plug-ins at runtime, but it would provide performance improvements over the dynamic implementation. This approach is analogous to the way a JIT compiler can be used to boost the performance of a Java program.

For pure runtime uses, the development tool prerequisite of the dynamic generation approach is often problematic. Also, because the topic of programmatic generator invocation is beyond the scope of this book, let's instead assume that we have a scenario in which it is impractical or otherwise undesirable to generate our model. So, we use EMF in a purely dynamic way.

For this example, we'll return to our first purchase order model, SimplePO, from Chapter 2. As a reminder, Figure 14.1 shows what it looks like in UML.

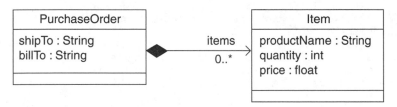

Figure 14.1 The SimplePO model.

Rather than importing the model into EMF and generating code for it, we use the Ecore API to build the model programmatically and then create instances of it dynamically. We are using this simplified version of the model just to keep the example compact. Here's how we create the Ecore model in memory:

```
EcoreFactory ecoreFactory = EcoreFactory.eINSTANCE;

EClass purchaseOrderClass = ecoreFactory.createEClass();
purchaseOrderClass.setName("PurchaseOrder");

EAttribute shipTo = ecoreFactory.createEAttribute();
shipTo.setName("shipTo");
shipTo.setEType(EcorePackage.Literals.ESTRING);
purchaseOrderClass.getEStructuralFeatures().add(shipTo);
EAttribute billTo = ecoreFactory.createEAttribute();
billTo.setName("billTo");
billTo.setEType(EcorePackage.Literals.ESTRING);
purchaseOrderClass.getEStructuralFeatures().add(billTo);

EClass itemClass = ecoreFactory.createEClass();
itemClass.setName("Item");

EAttribute productName = ecoreFactory.createEAttribute();
productName.setName("productName");
productName.setEType(EcorePackage.Literals.ESTRING);
itemClass.getEStructuralFeatures().add(productName);
EAttribute quantity = ecoreFactory.createEAttribute();
quantity.setName("quantity");
quantity.setEType(EcorePackage.Literals.EINT);
itemClass.getEStructuralFeatures().add(quantity);
EAttribute price = ecoreFactory.createEAttribute();
price.setName("price");
price.setEType(EcorePackage.Literals.EFLOAT);
itemClass.getEStructuralFeatures().add(price);

EReference items = ecoreFactory.createEReference();
items.setName("items");
items.setEType(itemClass);
items.setUpperBound(ETypedElement.UNBOUNDED_MULTIPLICITY);
items.setContainment(true);
purchaseOrderClass.getEStructuralFeatures().add(items);

EPackage poPackage = ecoreFactory.createEPackage();
poPackage.setName("po");
poPackage.setNsPrefix("po");
poPackage.setNsURI("http://www.example.com/SimplePO");
poPackage.getEClassifiers().add(purchaseOrderClass);
poPackage.getEClassifiers().add(itemClass);
```

As you can see, we're using the singleton `EcoreFactory` to instantiate the necessary Ecore objects. First, we create and initialize an `EClass` for **PurchaseOrder**. Next, we create `EAttributes` representing the **shipTo** and **billTo** attributes, and add them to the class's `eStructuralFeatures()` list. Notice that we have used the **EString** data type from Ecore as the type of these attributes. Ecore types are accessed most simply via the constants in the `EcorePackage.Literals` interface.

We then repeat the process for **Item,** creating the class and its attributes. An `EReference` is created to represent the **items** reference. Notice that its type is the **Item** class and that it is defined as a containment reference with unbounded multiplicity.

Finally, we create and initialize an `EPackage` for the model and add the two classes to it. The name, namespace prefix, and namespace URI for the package are all specified as required.

Now that we have built up the model in memory, we can immediately obtain a factory and use it to create dynamic instances of the modeled classes. For example, the following code creates a purchase order containing one item:

```
EFactory poFactory = poPackage.getEFactoryInstance();

EObject purchaseOrder = poFactory.create(purchaseOrderClass);
purchaseOrder.eSet(shipTo, "123 Maple Street");

EObject item = poFactory.create(itemClass);
item.eSet(productName, "Apples");
item.eSet(quantity, new Integer(12));
item.eSet(price, new Float(0.50));
((EList)purchaseOrder.eGet(items)).add(item);
```

Notice that we access the factory by calling the `getEFactoryInstance()` method on our package. If the **po** package had been generated, this method would return the corresponding generated factory. Because there is no generated factory, an instance of the generic implementation, `EFactoryImpl`, is returned instead. Once we have the factory, we simply create and initialize the instances using the reflective `EFactory` and `EObject` APIs.

Because we did not generate any classes for the model, the objects created by the factory will be instances of class `DynamicEObjectImpl`. Like the generated classes described in Chapter 10, this class extends `EObjectImpl`, which actually provides dynamic capabilities for all `EObjects`. `DynamicEObjectImpl` just tweaks the storage used by the implementation to be optimal for the fully dynamic case. Overrides in generated classes prevent the dynamic portions of `EObjectImpl` from being exercised for the features that have been implemented in generated code.

Even when using dynamic EMF, once we begin instantiating the model, it is no longer safe to change it. We can only examine the model elements to inform and control the use of their instances, just as we have previously been doing with generated models. For performance reasons, the dynamic `EObjectImpl` implementation allocates storage for each modeled attribute and reference when it is instantiated, making it impossible for new features to be added after the fact.

You can, however, define a new class that extends a class that has already been instantiated and add additional features there.

It is also possible to create dynamic classes that extend those with generated implementations. The dynamic factory, `EFactoryImpl`, implements the `create()` method something like this:

```
public EObject create(EClass eClass)
{
  for (List eSuperTypes = eClass.getESuperTypes();
       !eSuperTypes.isEmpty(); )
  {
    EClass eSuperType = (EClass)eSuperTypes.get(0);
    if (eSuperType.getInstanceClass() != null)
    {
      EObject result =
        eSuperType.getEPackage().getEFactoryInstance().create(
                                                  eSuperType);
      ((InternalEObject)result).eSetClass(eClass);
      return result;
    }
    eSuperTypes = eSuperType.getESuperTypes();
  }
  return basicCreate(eClass);
}
```

Rather than immediately creating an instance of `DynamicEObjectImpl`, this method first looks for a generated supertype of the given class that can be instantiated. It does this by walking up the chain of implementation supertypes, looking for one whose instance class has been specified. If such a class is found, the appropriate factory is used to instantiate it. However, the `eSetClass()` method is called to tell the implementation that it must actually represent the given dynamic subclass. It will then dynamically handle any features with no generated implementation. It is only if there is no generated supertype that `basicCreate()` is called, which instantiates `DynamicEObjectImpl`.

This capability allows you to mix generated and dynamic features in a single object, taking advantage of both the performance of generated code and the flexibility of dynamic EMF.

All `EObjects`, whether generated, dynamic, or these generated–dynamic hybrids, support exactly the same reflective APIs. They can therefore be freely mixed and used with all reflection-based generic EMF utilities and frameworks, including the persistence framework, change recorders, the validation framework, and EMF.Edit. The persistence framework also supports dynamic EMF directly by automatically demand-loading serialized models to provide needed dynamic implementations for arbitrary instances. We'll look at this topic in Section 15.3.4.

14.4   Extended Metadata

In Chapter 8, we looked at how Ecore model elements can be annotated with extended metadata specifying, among other things, how to interpret feature map based features and derive other features from them. The annotations could be set and read directly, but for convenience, EMF provides an interface, ExtendedMetaData, that assists in recording, accessing, and interpreting this information. This interface is useful both for querying metadata when working with instance data reflectively and for defining dynamic models.

ExtendedMetaData is not, strictly speaking, part of the Ecore metamodel. Rather, it is a utility interface that assists us in working with it. So, we won't see an instance of ExtendedMetaData for each class or attribute. Rather, we'll use a single instance, and pass Ecore elements to each method that we invoke. Typically, we can just use the default instance, available as ExtendedMetaData.INSTANCE:

```
public interface ExtendedMetaData
{
   ...
   String getName(EClassifier eClassifier);
   void setName(EClassifier eClassifier, String name);
   ...
   ExtendedMetaData INSTANCE = new BasicExtendedMetaData();
}
```

An instance of ExtendedMetaData uses a package registry to obtain metadata for the model elements on which it operates. The default instance simply uses the global package registry, EPackage.Registry.INSTANCE, which we discussed in Section 14.1.2. When working with another, context-specific registry, you will need to construct and use another instance of BasicExtendedMetaData, passing that package registry to its constructor.

In Chapter 9, we examined all of the extended metadata annotation details that correspond to different schema constructs. Not surprisingly, the methods defined by ExtendedMetaData relate very closely to those annotation details, presenting a schema-friendly view of Ecore models. They're used extensively by the XML Schema model importer to record the details of the schema, and, optionally, by the XML resource implementations to serialize models into conformant instance documents. So, they are best understood in terms of the corresponding schema constructs.

For example, a number of the methods deal with naming and identification. As we saw in Chapter 9, XML Schema's naming rules and conventions diverge from those for Java and, as a result, for EMF. When importing a model from a schema, EMF will use only valid, conventional names for the resulting Ecore model elements. The original names are stored on extended metadata annotations via the `setName()` methods. They can then be retrieved easily with the corresponding `getName()` methods. There are also methods for specifying whether a package corresponds to a schema whose target namespace is the null namespace, and for associating a feature with another package by namespace, which allows Ecore to represent a reference to another schema's globally declared attribute or element.

Let's take a look at an example of how the `ExtendedMetaData` interface can be used in defining a dynamic model. We return to the ExtendedPO model,[1] which we discussed in Chapter 8. As a reminder, it used a feature map called **orders** to maintain order across two derived references, **priorityOrders** and **standardOrders**. The situation is illustrated in Figure 14.2.

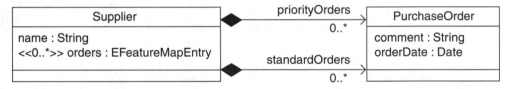

Figure 14.2   The FeatureMap-based ExtendedPO model in UML.

To indicate that the **orders** attribute will combine a group of other features, it needs an extended metadata annotation with a single **details** entry: its key is "kind" and its value is "group." We must also add annotations to **priorityOrders** and **standardOrders,** to indicate that they are derived from this group attribute. Again, an extended metadata annotation with a single **details** entry is used: its key is "group" and its value is "#orders."

Let's start defining the package programmatically, from the top down:

```
EPackage epoPackage = ecoreFactory.createEPackage();
epoPackage.setName("epo");
epoPackage.setNsPrefix("epo");
epoPackage.setNsURI("http://www.example.com/ExtendedPO");
```

---

1. It is purely coincidental that the names of this model (ExtendedPO) and the interface we are illustrating with it (`ExtendedMetaData`) both start with "Extended."

```
EClass supplierClass = ecoreFactory.createEClass();
epoPackage.getEClassifiers().add(supplierClass);
supplierClass.setName("Supplier");

EAttribute name = ecoreFactory.createEAttribute();
supplierClass.getEStructuralFeatures().add(name);
name.setName("name");
name.setEType(EcorePackage.Literals.ESTRING);
```

This looks very similar to the example we saw in the previous section, as we are just using the Ecore API to create and initialize a package, the **Supplier** class, and its simple attribute. However, notice that, as model elements are created, we are immediately adding them to their containers. This approach is necessary when working with ExtendedMetaData, as computing values for use in extended metadata annotations sometimes involves navigating among model elements. We will see an example of this in a moment. The code for defining the **PurchaseOrder** class is so similar to the preceding code that we do not list it here.

We can now add the **orders** attribute like this:

```
EClass purchaseOrderClass = ...

EAttribute orders = ecoreFactory.createEAttribute();
supplierClass.getEStructuralFeatures().add(orders);
orders.setName("orders");
orders.setUpperBound(ETypedElement.UNBOUNDED_MULTIPLICITY);
orders.setEType(EcorePackage.Literals.EFEATURE_MAP_ENTRY);
ExtendedMetaData.INSTANCE.setFeatureKind(
  orders, ExtendedMetaData.GROUP_FEATURE);
```

This code creates the attribute, adds it to the containing class, and does the usual sort of initialization. Notice that we're using the **EFeatureMapEntry** data type, defined in the Ecore package, as the type. Finally, it invokes setFeatureKind() on the default extended metadata instance, passing the attribute and a constant representing the desired kind, ExtendedMetaData.GROUP_FEATURE. This method adds an extended metadata annotation with a "kind" details entry to the specified feature.

Instead of using the ExtendedMetaData interface, we could have achieved the same result by replacing the last line of the previous example with code that adds the underlying annotation explicitly, like this:

```
EAnnotation annotation = ecoreFactory.createEAnnotation();
annotation.setSource(
  "http:///org/eclipse/emf/ecore/util/ExtendedMetaData");
annotation.getDetails().put("kind", "group");
orders.getEAnnotations().add(annotation);
```

Using `ExtendedMetaData.setFeatureKind()` shields us from the details of how a feature's kind is modeled with an annotation on that feature. As mentioned previously, `ExtendedMetaData` is just a convenient API that allows clients to work with these special annotations while simply thinking of them as additional, extended features of Ecore.

The two derived references, **priorityOrders** and **standardOrders** are defined as follows:

```
EReference priorityOrders = ecoreFactory.createEReference();
supplierClass.getEStructuralFeatures().add(priorityOrders);
priorityOrders.setName("priorityOrders");
priorityOrders.setUpperBound(ETypedElement.UNBOUNDED_MULTIPLICITY);
priorityOrders.setEType(purchaseOrderClass);
priorityOrders.setVolatile(true);
priorityOrders.setTransient(true);
priorityOrders.setDerived(true);
ExtendedMetaData.INSTANCE.setGroup(priorityOrders, orders);

EReference standardOrders = ecoreFactory.createEReference();
supplierClass.getEStructuralFeatures().add(standardOrders);
standardOrders.setName("standardOrders");
standardOrders.setUpperBound(ETypedElement.UNBOUNDED_MULTIPLICITY);
standardOrders.setEType(purchaseOrderClass);
standardOrders.setVolatile(true);
standardOrders.setTransient(true);
standardOrders.setDerived(true);
ExtendedMetaData.INSTANCE.setGroup(standardOrders, orders);
```

For each reference, we set the type to the other class, `purchaseOrderClass`, mark the reference as volatile, transient, and derived, and call `setGroup()` on the default extended metadata instance to specify that the reference will delegate to the `orders` group feature. Again, this method adds the needed extended metadata annotation to the reference. The annotation contains a details entry keyed by "group", identifying the group feature from which the reference derives. In this case, the name of the group feature is sufficient to identify it, but in other contexts, it must be qualified with a namespace URI. So, to compute the correct value, `setGroup()` must actually navigate up to the package containing the features. If it was unable to reach a package, it would just throw an exception. This is the reason we built the model from the top down, adding each model element to its container as we went.

Having defined the feature map and its two derived references, we could now instantiate the **Supplier** class and begin adding **PurchaseOrder**s to it. The three features would exhibit the same delegating behavior as if we had generated a model implementation from a UML, annotated Java, or XML Schema definition, as described in Chapter 8.

As we have just seen, the `ExtendedMetaData` interface provides a convenient means for annotating dynamic Ecore models with extended metadata. This interface is similarly useful for accessing such annotations on any Ecore model, whether dynamic or generated. Moreover, as we will see in Section 15.3.5, it can also be used to specify how a model should be serialized in a given context, without adding anything to the model at all.

CHAPTER 15

Persistence

EMF includes a powerful framework for model persistence. Out of the box, it supports XML serialization via a highly customizable resource implementation. Specialized versions are also provided to support the XML Metadata Interchange (XMI) 2.0 standard, which is used as the canonical representation of Ecore, and to serialize Ecore as Essential MOF (EMOF), facilitating interoperability with various modeling tools.

However, EMF does not require that persistence be XML-based or even stream based. The framework provides an API that is flexible enough to support any kind of storage, and even to persist objects across different kinds of storage, with references among them.

In Chapter 2, we introduced the persistence framework and saw how EMF objects can easily be loaded and saved via resources. In this chapter, we'll look more closely at the framework API and examine the XML-based resource implementations that EMF provides. We will also discuss `EStore`, an alternate mechanism for persistence, which allows active objects to be directly backed by external storage.

15.1 Overview of the Persistence Framework

The basic unit of persistence in EMF is called a *resource*. Simply put, a resource is a container for one or more objects that are to be persisted together, along with their contents.

EMF objects are persisted via the `Resource` interface, by adding them to the resource's list of contents, and then calling the `save()` method on it. For example:

```
PurchaseOrder po = ...
Resource resource = ...
resource.getContents().add(po);
resource.save(null);
```

Here, `purchaseOrder` is added to the contents of `resource`, which is then saved. If `purchaseOrder` contains any other objects, for instance, a list of items, they will be persisted along with it in the same resource by default. If it references any other object via a non-containment reference, it is our responsibility to ensure that the other object is contained in a resource: it could be added directly to the same resource or to another one, or it could be directly or indirectly contained by an object that is already in a resource. Otherwise, the dangling reference will be discarded when the resource is persisted.

The argument to `save()`, a `Map`, will be non-null if we want to specify some options to be used in the save operation. We'll look at the options supported by EMF's XML resources in Section 15.3.3.

The opposite operation, recreating active objects in memory from their persistent form, is done similarly. In this case, the `load()` method is used, and then the objects are accessed from the resource's contents list:

```
Resource resource = ...
resource.load(null);
PurchaseOrder po = (PurchaseOrder)resource.getContents().get(0);
```

We look more closely at the `Resource` interface in Section 15.2.3.

The preceding code fragments raise at least a couple more questions: where the XML serialization is being written to or read from, and how we even obtained the resource in the first place.

To manage references between objects in different resources, EMF's persistence framework includes another interface, called `ResourceSet`, which acts as a container for resources. The `getResources()` method returns the list of resources in a set. Generally, a resource is created via a resource set, either explicitly or automatically as part of a demand load. For example:

```
ResourceSet resourceSet = new ResourceSetImpl();
URI uri = URI.createURI("file:/c:/data/out.epo2");
Resource resource = resourceSet.createResource(uri);
```

Here, we create a resource set,[1] on which we then invoke `createResource()` to create a resource explicitly. We pass this method a

---

1. EMF provides no factory for resource sets. It is up to the user to instantiate an appropriate implementation. `ResourceSetImpl` is a functional, flexible implementation and should usually suffice. However, it can be extended and customized if necessary.

Uniform Resource Identifier (URI), which is assigned to the resource, to identify it within the resource set. Later, when we call `save()` or `load()`, the resource can use this URI to determine where to write to or read from. Here, we have used a simple file-scheme URI to directly specify a location in the local file system. We'll discuss other supported URI types in Section 15.2.1.

The URI passed to `createResource()` serves another purpose, too. A resource set maintains a registry of resource factories. To create a resource, it consults this registry to obtain an appropriate factory based on the specified URI. It is this factory that actually creates the resource and, as a result, determines how objects are to be persisted.

The registry is used to select a resource factory based on either the scheme or the file extension of the URI. We can register EMF's default XMI resource factory against the *.epo2* file extension as follows:

```
resourceSet.getResourceFactoryRegistry().getExtensionToFactoryMap().
  put("epo2", new XMIResourceFactoryImpl());
```

When using a generated model under Eclipse, this registration is not necessary, as a similar registration is done automatically via an extension specified in the model plug-in's manifest file.[2] However, when running stand-alone, this registration must be made explicitly. Otherwise, `createResource()` will be unable to create a resource and will return `null`. We'll look more closely at `Resource`'s nested `Factory` and `Registry` interfaces in Section 15.2.4 and at `ResourceSet` in Section 15.2.5.

We now have enough of an understanding of the persistence framework to write a simple, yet functional, program to save a purchase order:

```
PurchaseOrder po = createPurchaseOrder();
ResourceSet resourceSet = new ResourceSetImpl();
resourceSet.getResourceFactoryRegistry().getExtensionToFactoryMap().
  put("epo2", new XMIResourceFactoryImpl());

URI uri = URI.createURI("file:/c:/data/out.epo2");
Resource resource = resourceSet.createResource(uri);
resource.getContents().add(po);
try
{
  resource.save(null);
  System.out.println("saved");
}
catch (IOException e)
{
```

---

2. Similar, but not identical. We'll see the registration that actually occurs for this case in Section 15.2.4.

```
    System.out.println("failed to write " + uri);
}
```

Here, `createPurchaseOrder()` returns the purchase order that we wish to persist. We will not look at its implementation; we'll just assume that it creates an instance of **PurchaseOrder** and adds a couple of **Items** to it. The resulting serialization in *out.epo2* looks like this:

```
<?xml version="1.0" encoding="ASCII"?>
<epo2:PurchaseOrder xmi:version="2.0"
    xmlns:xmi="http://www.omg.org/XMI"
    xmlns:epo2="http://www.example.com/epo2.ecore"
    comment="rush order">
  <items productName="apple" quantity="10" partNum="3313"/>
  <items productName="orange" quantity="10" partNum="9145"/>
</epo2:PurchaseOrder>
```

Notice that `Resource.save()` throws an `IOException` if it cannot write out the file.

The equivalent program to load the purchase order from its persistent form looks like this:

```
EPO2Package epo2Package = EPO2Package.eINSTANCE;
ResourceSet resourceSet = new ResourceSetImpl();
resourceSet.getResourceFactoryRegistry().getExtensionToFactoryMap().
  put("epo2", new XMIResourceFactoryImpl());

URI uri = URI.createURI("file:/c:/data/out.epo2");
Resource resource = resourceSet.createResource(uri);
try
{
  resource.load(null);
  PurchaseOrder po = (PurchaseOrder)resource.getContents().get(0);
  System.out.println("loaded: " + po);
}
catch (IOException e)
{
  System.out.println("failed to read " + uri);
}
```

The first line, which accesses the package for the purchase order model, registers the package as a side effect. As discussed in Section 14.1.2, generated packages automatically register themselves in the global package registry when accessed for the first time. The resource depends on being able to find a registered package to reflectively instantiate the classes it describes. However, like the resource factory registration, this explicit registration step is only required when running stand-alone, as it is done automatically via an extension point under Eclipse. We further discuss stand-alone applications in Chapter 20.

This overview touched on the most important parts of EMF's persistence framework. In the next section, we take a closer look at the interfaces we've just introduced.

15.2   The EMF Persistence API

EMF's persistence framework is centered on four fundamental interfaces: `Resource`, `ResourceSet`, `Resource.Factory`, and `URIConverter`. In this section, we describe each of these interfaces, pointing out the most important aspects of their design and describing the behavior of their base implementations and how they can be extended.

However, before we begin to describe these interfaces, we should understand a few details about URIs, which serve a crucial role in the persistence framework.

15.2.1   URI

EMF uses URIs extensively in its persistence framework. As we saw in Section 15.1, URIs are used to uniquely identify resources. EMF also uses URIs to reference objects within resources and to identify packages. URI is an open-ended standard for identifying and locating data of various types. The data could be some file in a file system or on the Internet, an object in a file, or in a database of some kind, or any other type of data you might imagine.

A URI is a string composed of three fundamental parts: a *scheme*, a *scheme-specific part*, and an optional *fragment*. EMF includes a URI implementation class, `org.eclipse.emf.common.util.URI`, which offers convenient ways of working with and manipulating a URI and its parts.

The URI scheme identifies the protocol used to access the resource. Some common ones are "file", to directly identify the location of files, and "jar", to identify files archived within a JAR file. In Eclipse, we use "platform" for URIs that identify resources in Eclipse-specific locations, such as the workspace or external plug-ins in the running workbench.

The scheme is the first part of the URI, separated from the rest by the ":" character. For example, *platform:/resource/data/po.xml* is a platform-scheme URI.

The scheme-specific part includes everything between the scheme and the fragment. In general, its format and interpretation depend entirely on the scheme. However, the schemes that EMF concerns itself with tend to use a common hierarchical format for this part. This format can include an *authority*, a *device*, and any number of *segments*. An authority, if included, is separated from the scheme by "//". It generally specifies a host in a networked environment. The device, if included, is preceded by "/". Finally, the segments, if any, are also preceded and separated from each other by "/". Together, the device and segments constitute a local path to a resource's location. For example, here is a file-scheme URI with no authority, a device, and three segments: *file:/c:/dir1/dir2/myfile.xml*.[3]

The platform scheme mentioned earlier also uses the hierarchical format for its scheme-specific part. A platform URI has no authority or device, but assigns special significance to the first segment of the path. For example, it can be "resource" to identify a resource in the workspace or "plugin" to identify one in an external plug-in. The remainder of the path is then a workspace or plug-in path, beginning with a project name or plug-in ID, respectively.[4]

The URI fragment identifies a part of the contents of the resource specified by the scheme and scheme-specific part. It is separated from the rest of the URI by the "#" character. For example, the URI *file:/c:/dir1/dir2/myfile.xml#loc* identifies something in *myfile.xml*, which would be located using the fragment "loc". As we'll see in the next section, EMF uses URIs with fragments to reference **EObjects** in resources.

Instances of URI are generally created by parsing a string. A factory method, `createURI()`, takes a complete URI string, and convenience factories `createFileURI()` and `createPlatformResourceURI()` are provided to convert file paths and workspace paths into URIs.[5]

Unfortunately, EMF's URI class predates the appearance of a standard `java.net.URI` implementation in Java 1.4. Although the two representations are not type-compatible, interchange is possible simply by calling `toString()` on either form and then using the other to re-parse the resulting string.

For more details on URI syntax, refer to the Internet Engineering Task Force RFC 3986, *Uniform Resource Identifier (URI): Generic Syntax*, available at *http://www.ietf.org/rfc/rfc3986.txt*.

---

3. You might have seen slightly different file-scheme URIs before, like *file:///c:/dir1/dir2/myfile.xml*,. Because of the additional "//", this URI specifies an empty string as its authority, whereas the other specifies no authority at all. Both refer to the same resource, but when compared as URIs, they are different.

4. As we will see later in this chapter, EMF provides facilities that assign meaning to platform resource URIs even in stand-alone applications.

5. In fact, there are multiple forms of URI.createURI() and URI.createPlatformResourceURI(). The multi-argument forms provide support for automatic encoding of any characters, such as spaces, that are disallowed in a URI. Generally, it is highly advisable to enable such automatic encoding. The single-argument form of createURI() should be used only to parse literally defined strings that are known to contain no such disallowed characters. Using the single argument form of createPlatformResourceURI() is discouraged altogether.

15.2.2 URIConverter

The URIConverter interface is used by the framework to *normalize* URIs: to convert one URI into another, which is then used to access a resource. It can be used to provide mappings from namespace URIs (for example, *http://www.example.com/epo2.ecore*) to URIs representing physical URIs, or to redirect old or alias URI references to a different location.

A URI converter maintains a set of URI to URI mappings, which can be specified by clients. The normalize() method is used to convert a URI to its normalized form, based on any mappings that might apply. For example, we could use a URI converter to map an **EPackage**'s namespace URI to a physical resource, like this:

```
URIConverter converter = new URIConverterImpl();

URI uri1 = URI.createURI("http://www.example.com/epo2.ecore");
URI uri2 = URI.createURI("platform:/resource/models/epo2.ecore");
converter.getURIMap().put(uri1, uri2);

URI normalized = converter.normalize(uri1);
System.out.println(normalized);
```

If we run this program, it will output the following:

```
platform:/resource/models/epo2.ecore
```

As you can see, if normalize() finds the logical URI as a key in the URIConverter's URI map, it simply returns the associated value. If an **EPackage** with namespace URI *http://www.example.com/epo2.ecore* is serialized in the workspace as */models/epo2.ecore*, this mapping allows the framework to automatically read in this metadata as needed, when loading an instance of the model. We'll look more closely at how this occurs in Section 15.3.2.

URI mappings that end with "/" can be used to replace just a URI prefix within any number of related URIs. For example, we could make the following registration:

```
converter.getURIMap().put(
  createURI("http://www.example.com/"),
  createURI("platform:/resource/models/"));
```

Then, for example, a URI like *http://www.example.com/old/order.ecore* would normalize into *platform:/resource/models/old/order.ecore*. The normalization of the *epo2.ecore* namespace URI from the previous example would be unchanged.

The `normalize()` method is also recursive; if the output of a mapping matches the input to another, it will be normalized again.

In addition to normalizing URIs, a URI converter is also used to create input and output streams for a URI. The `createInputStream()` and `createOutputStream()` methods normalize a specified URI, by calling the `normalize()` method, and then immediately open a stream on it. The default URI converter implementation, `URICoverterImpl`, provides direct support for the file and platform resource URIs, whether running inside or outside of Eclipse. Other common schemes are supported by converting the URI to a `java.net.URL`. Subclasses might also override the stream creation methods to add direct support for any other schemes.

As we'll see in the next two sections, URI converters are used primarily by resource sets to locate resources and by resources to open streams for saving or loading.

15.2.3 Resource

As outlined in Section 15.1, a resource is the basic unit of persistence in EMF. Although resources interact directly with **EObjects**, the `Resource` interface does not actually represent a modeled class itself, unlike the various Ecore interfaces that were generated from the metamodel described in Chapter 5. However, it behaves like one in a couple of significant ways:

```
public interface Resource extends Notifier
{
  int RESOURCE__RESOURCE_SET = 0;
  int RESOURCE__URI = 1;
  int RESOURCE__CONTENTS = 2;
  ...

  ResourceSet getResourceSet();
  URI getURI();
  void setURI(URI uri);
  EList getContents();
  ...
}
```

First, resources are notifiers: adapters can be attached to a resource, and it will send them notifications when it is changed. As you can see, the interface defines constants for "virtual features", such as **resourceSet**, **URI**, and **contents**, which are used in the notifications.[6]

---

6. The notification's `getFeatureID()` method will return the constant identifying the changed virtual feature. Its `getFeature()` method will simply return `null`.

Second, the list returned by `getContents()`, which represents the contents of the resource, behaves very much like a modeled, bidirectional reference for which the opposite reference is implemented by the `eResource()` method in `EObject`. Again, this relationship is not actually modeled, but conceptually, the situation looks like Figure 15.1.

Figure 15.1   Conceptual model of resource contents.

It is worth reinforcing that, while the **contents** virtual feature has the expected `getContents()` accessor, the name of its opposite's accessor, `eResource()`, is decidedly unconventional. This is because it instead follows the pattern used by all other methods in `EObject`, chosen to avoid clashing with the names of accessors that will be generated in modeled subclasses. It is also worth noting that there is no corresponding set method for `eResource()`, so this virtual feature can only be set from the `Resource` end, by adding an object to the contents list.

As we mentioned in Section 15.1, a resource implicitly includes by default the entire tree of objects contained by each object in its contents list. This is reflected in the following special behavior of the `eResource()` method: it always returns the resource with which the object will be persisted. Thus, it only returns `null` if neither the object itself nor any other in its complete chain of containers resides in a resource's contents list.

The **contents** virtual feature behaves like an ordinary bidirectional feature whose opposite is multiplicity-one. That is to say that, if an object already resides in the contents of one resource, adding it to another will automatically remove it from the first.

Moreover, it exhibits containment semantics, but only with respect to modeled containment references that are not proxy resolving. In other words, if an object already resides in any modeled, non-proxy-resolving containment reference, adding it to the contents of a resource will automatically remove it from its container. Recall from Chapter 10 that containment references are not proxy resolving by default. Thus, it is this behavior that prevents cross-resource containment by default: an object can only be placed directly in a container object or directly in a resource's contents, but not both.

It is only when proxy resolution is enabled on a containment reference that the container and contained objects can reside in different resources. In this situation, adding an object to a resource's contents does not automatically remove it from its existing container. Note that this behavior is only available beginning in EMF 2.2. Also, when generating a model, containment proxies must be enabled explicitly for the whole model, or else all containment references will be considered non-proxy-resolving, completely disabling cross-resource containment. We saw this in Section 13.8.2, when we enabled the "Containment Proxies" property in the generator model for ExtendedPO3. Because proxy resolution is enabled by default for references but was previously ignored for containment references, this extra step is required for compatibility with older versions of EMF.

Previous to EMF 2.2, you could always be sure that the resource of an **EObject** in a containment tree would also be the resource of its container. Enabling cross-resource containment breaks this assumption, which could impact existing applications. For example, saving an object's resource does not guarantee that its contents are saved.

A resource is usually contained by a resource set, which is accessible via getResourceSet(). The resource is uniquely identified in the set by a URI. The URI is typically specified when the resource is created, but can also be accessed and set with getURI() and setURI(). The URI usually determines where the persistent form of the resource will be stored.

Save and Load

As we've seen, the save() and load() methods copy a resource from its active, in-memory form to persistent storage and vice versa. There are two forms of each:

```
void save(Map options) throws IOException;
void load(Map options) throws IOException;

void save(OutputStream outputStream, Map options) throws IOException;
void load(InputStream inputStream, Map options) throws IOException;
```

EMF provides a base class for resources, ResourceImpl, that implements each single-parameter method by obtaining a URIConverter from the resource set, which it uses to open an output or input stream for the resource's URI, and passing this stream to the corresponding two-parameter method. It is then the role of a particular subclass to provide meaningful, storage-specific save and load implementations.

You might think that this interface implies that EMF resources are inherently stream-based. Although such resources are most common in EMF, non-stream-based resources, such as one backed by a relational database, can also be implemented. In these cases, the stream versions of load() and save() can be handled in one of two ways:

1. Throw UnsupportedOperationException. This will be the default behavior if you subclass ResourceImpl and override only the single-argument version of save().

2. Treat them as "Save As" and "Open With" operations. By extending XMLResourceImpl, you can inherit, for free, the ability to produce an XML serialization of any resource, regardless of its ordinary persistent form.

When faced with errors in the persistent form, load() should perform as complete a load as is possible. Errors and warnings are accumulated as instances of Resource.Diagnostic and made available after the load is finished via getErrors() and getWarnings().

Resources can be unloaded by calling the unload() method. Unloading turns all the objects in the resource into proxies, which will result in a demand-reload of the resource (by EcoreUtil.resolve()) the next time one of these objects is accessed via cross-reference from another resource. This allows you to bring a resource up to date if, for example, the underlying file has changed since it was last loaded. The isLoaded() method indicates whether the resource is currently loaded.

A resource can track any changes to its complete contents and return, via isModified(), whether anything has changed since its last save or load. By default, this feature is disabled, as its implementation is expensive and ill-suited for use with undoable commands, as an undo would look like a change. When appropriate, setTrackingModification() can be used to enable it.

Options

As the signatures of the save() and load() methods show, each can also be passed options, in the form of a Map containing name–value pairs. The options recognized by a resource are, for the most part, implementation specific. However, the Resource interface does define string constants for a couple of option names that any implementation might wish to support. This support is actually provided by the save() and load() implementations in ResourceImpl, so subclasses inherit them for free.

We will look at these options now and at the longer list of options supported by EMF's XML resources in Section 15.3.3. For each option, the appropriate value type will be specified, and the option will be identified as applicable to save, load, or both.

OPTION_CIPHER   (URIConverter.Cipher, Save/Load)

This option can be used to encrypt and decrypt the stream data produced by and consumed by the two-argument save() and load() methods. By default, no encryption is performed; however, this option can be used to specify an implementation of the URIConverter.Cipher interface that will then be used to encrypt the stream. Such an implementation should wrap the stream to perform the desired type of encryption and also gets an opportunity to take action before the stream is closed. EMF provides a default Cipher implementation, CryptoCipherImpl, that provides Data Encryption Standard (DES) encryption based on the Java platform cryptography support.[7]

OPTION_ZIP   (Boolean, Save/Load)

This option can be enabled, by specifying a value of Boolean.TRUE, to apply ZIP compression automatically to the steam data produced by the two-argument form of save() and, likewise, to unzip the stream data in the corresponding load() method.

URI Fragments

Each object within a resource is uniquely identified by a URI fragment, which can be appended to the resource's URI to locate the object within the resource set. By default, resources based on ResourceImpl use an XPath-like fragment path to locate objects. For example, assume we have a resource that contains an instance of class **PurchaseOrder**, which in turn contains a set of items under it. The fragment path "//@items.0" would identify the first instance of **Item** instance under the **PurchaseOrder**. For the remaining items, we would use the paths "//@items.1", "//@items.2", and so on. If the **PurchaseOrder** instance was itself contained by a **Supplier**, for example, then the path would include another level: "//@orders.0/@items.2", for example.

These fragments provide an alternative means to obtain a particular object from the contents of a resource, rather than having to manually navigate through the tree. The Resource interface defines a getEObject() method, which retrieves an object given its fragment path:

```
Resource resource = ...
Item item = (Item)resource.getEObject("//@orders.0/@items.2");
```

---

7. Beginning in EMF 2.3, this implementation has been renamed to DESCipherImpl and is superseded by the new AESCipherImpl, which uses the stronger Advanced Encryption Standard (AES) cryptography algorithm.

The reverse operation, determining the fragment path for a given object, is performed by getURIFragment():

```
Item item = ...
String fragment = resource.getURIFragment(item);
```

These two methods are implemented in ResourceImpl by delegating to the objects on the path, allowing type-specific customization of fragment paths via the generated classes. The implementation of getEObject() simply breaks the fragment path into its "/" separated components, and then iteratively calls the eObjectForURIFragmentSegment()   method   on   interface InternalEObject. In each call, this method locates and returns the next object in the path, based on the path component that identifies it.

The getURIFragment() method works in a similar way to produce a fragment path for a given object. Starting from the object, it uses the EObject.eContainer() method to walk up through its containers toward the root object that is in the resource's contents. For each container along the path, it calls eURIFragmentSegment(), also defined on InternalEObject, which computes and returns the fragment component for that step.

All generated implementation classes inherit generic implementations of eObjectForURIFragmentSegment() and eURIFragmentSegment() from EObjectImpl. These produce and consume the fragment path segments, based on feature name and index, seen earlier. However, they can be overridden to produce fragment paths that are more readable and robust.[8] For example, if a model has unique, hierarchically named objects, the index-based default syntax can be replaced with a name-based lookup. In fact, Ecore is such a model: it overrides the two fragment methods in class EModelElementImpl. Recall that the simple purchase order model, which we introduced in Chapter 2, has an XMI serialization that looks something like this:

```
<?xml version="1.0" encoding="UTF-8"?>
<ecore:EPackage xmi:version="2.0" ... name="po" ... >
  <eClassifiers xsi:type="ecore:EClass" name="PurchaseOrder">
    <eStructuralFeatures xsi:type="ecore:EReference" name="items"
        upperBound="-1" eType="#//Item" containment="true"/>
    ...
  </eClassifiers>
  <eClassifiers xsi:type="ecore:EClass" name="Item">
    ...
  </eClassifiers>
</ecore:EPackage>
```

---

8. As we'll see in Section 15.3.1, URI fragments appear in EMF's XML serialization to identify the target of a reference, including when the reference is in another document. So, if the fragments are index-based, simply reordering objects within the target document can break any references to it.

Notice that the **eType** of the items reference is serialized as the URI "#//Item". This name-based fragment results from Ecore's override of eURIFragmentSegment(). Had the default implementation not been overridden, it would have produced "//@eClassifiers.1" instead.

One other thing to notice is that all of the fragment paths we've seen start with "//". Given our description of the algorithm, you might have expected the previous example path, for example, to be "#/po/Item", instead of just "#//Item". The reason it isn't so is because getURIFragment() provides different handling for the first segment, in particular, optimizing the typical case where there is only a single root object in the resource. Because there are not multiple features in which the root objects can appear, this first segment in the fragment is handled differently, by another pair of methods on the resource, getURIFragmentRootSegment() and getEObjectForURIFragmentRootSegment(). The default behavior is to use just the index of the object in the contents list, or the empty string ("") if there is only a single object in the contents. You could override both of these methods if, for example, you wanted to change the root segment lookup to be name-based instead of index-based.

Instead of using the default fragment path, it is possible to use a unique ID stored directly on the model object as the fragment that identifies it in a resource. We often refer to this as an *intrinsic ID*. Recall from Chapter 5 that one of the **EAttribute**s in an **EClass** can be designated as the ID via its boolean **iD** attribute. This should only be done when the value of that attribute can be used to uniquely identify instances of the class within a resource. If an object has an ID attribute, the implementation of getURIFragment() in ResourceImpl simply returns the value of that attribute. The implementation of getEObject() actually handles this case by first checking whether the fragment it has been passed begins with a "/". If it does, it handles the fragment path as described previously; if not, it simply iterates over all of the contents of the resource and returns the one whose ID attribute matches the given fragment.[9]

15.2.4   *Resource.Factory and Resource.Factory.Registry*

Nested in the Resource interface is a Factory interface, which defines how resources are created:

```
public interface Resource extends Notifier
{
  ...

  interface Factory
```

---

9. This is an expensive operation. A cache can be used to improve performance, as described in Section 15.5.2.

```
  {
    Resource createResource(URI uri);

    interface Descriptor
    {
      Factory createFactory();
    }

    interface Registry
    {
      Factory getFactory(URI uri);
      Map getProtocolToFactoryMap();
      Map getExtensionToFactoryMap();

      String DEFAULT_EXTENSION = "*";
      Registry INSTANCE = new ResourceFactoryRegistryImpl();
    }
  }
}
```

As the interface suggests, a resource factory simply knows how to create one type of resource. By using an appropriate resource factory, you can determine the persistent form to be produced and consumed.

Nested within `Factory` is a `Registry` interface, which provides the mechanism for selecting an appropriate resource factory, based on aspects of a specified URI. A resource factory registry maintains two maps, in which we can register resource factories. Those maps are then consulted by the `getFactory()` method to obtain an appropriate factory for the given URI.

The default implementation, `ResourceFactoryRegistryImpl`, follows these steps to obtain a resource factory:

1. Check the map returned by `getProtocolToFactoryMap()`, using the scheme of the URI as the key.

2. If nothing was found, check the map returned by `getExtensionToFactoryMap()`, using the file extension of the URI as the key.

3. If still nothing was found, check for a default in the map returned by `getExtensionToFactoryMap()`, by using `DEFAULT_EXTENSION` (the wildcard character, "*") as the key.

4. If no match could be found, call the protected `delegatedGetFactory()` method. By default, this does nothing, but can be overridden to look elsewhere.

In Section 15.1, we saw that a resource set maintains a resource factory registry, which it consults to obtain a factory whenever it needs to create a resource.

In addition, there is a global registry available as `Resource.Factory.Registry.INSTANCE`, in which we can make registrations that affect all resource sets in the system. The registry implementation used in a default resource set overrides `delegatedGetFactory()` to delegate to the global registry. So, the global registry will be consulted only if an appropriate factory is not found locally for the URI's scheme, for its file extension, or as a default.

We also mentioned in Section 15.1 that, when running under Eclipse, resource factories can be registered automatically via Eclipse's extension point mechanism. Such registrations are made in the global registry.

The plug-in manifest file for the `org.eclipse.emf.ecore.xmi` plug-in contains the following extension:

```
<extension point="org.eclipse.emf.ecore.extension_parser">
  <parser type="*"
      class="org.eclipse.emf.ecore.xmi.impl.XMIResourceFactoryImpl"/>
</extension>
```

This registers the `XMIResourceFactoryImpl` resource factory implementation as the default. This is why we describe EMF's XMI serialization as the default persistence format and why, in Section 15.1, we said no explicit registration was required when running under Eclipse.

If you create your own resource implementation class, you'll need to create a factory for it and then register it, in a similar way, in your own plug-in. For example, assume that you have created your own resource implementation class, `EPO2ResourceImpl`, which you want to use to persist *.epo2* resources. To do so, you would need to create a resource factory as follows:

```
public class EPO2ResourceFactoryImpl implements Resource.Factory
{
  public Resource createResource(URI uri)
  {
    return new EPO2ResourceImpl(uri);
  }
}
```

Then, you could add the following extension to your *plugin.xml* file:

```
<extension point="org.eclipse.emf.ecore.extension_parser">
  <parser type="epo2"
      class="com.example.epo2.util.EPO2ResourceFactoryImpl"/>
</extension>
```

Indeed, this is exactly what is done for you when "Basic", "XML", or "XMI" is selected as the "Resource Type" for a package in the generator, as described in Section 12.3.2. It is particularly important when starting with a model described via XML Schema, as a default XMI resource will be unable to read or write a serialization that conforms to the schema. If this registration is not done or if you try to load a resource that doesn't have the appropriate file extension, `Resource.load()` will throw a `ClassNotFoundException`. For stand-alone applications, you would need to make the following equivalent registration in your code:

```
Resource.Factory.Registry.INSTANCE.getExtensionToFactoryMap().put(
    "epo2", new EPO2ResourceFactoryImpl());
```

Although equivalent, there is one minor difference between these last two resource factory registrations. In the latter, explicit registration, a new instance of the factory is created and registered directly in one of the registry's maps. However, in the former extension-based registration, a `Descriptor` is actually registered instead.

`Descriptor`, another nested interface in `Resource.Factory`, simply provides an extra level of indirection in creating resource factories. After completing the four steps enumerated previously, if the registry obtains a descriptor, instead of a resource factory, it will call `createFactory()` on it and return the result. This capability allows EMF to defer loading the specialized resource factory class until it is actually needed. This is important for extension-based registration, which occurs at platform start-up.[10]

15.2.5 ResourceSet

`ResourceSet` is the highest level interface in the persistence API, acting as the container for resources, so as to allow for references among them. It provides access to these resources, defining a context for objects from a model or a set of related models. In addition, it maintains a URI converter, resource factory registry, and package registry for its own use and for the use of its resources.

Like `Resource`, `ResourceSet` does not represent a modeled class, but it implements the `Notifier` interface:

---

10. This is analogous to how `EPackage.Descriptor` provides for deferred loading of packages when extension-based registration is used, as described in Section 14.1.2.

```
public interface ResourceSet extends Notifier
{
  int RESOURCE_SET__RESOURCES = 0;
  EList getResources();
  ...
}
```

The list of resources returned by getResource() constitutes its only virtual feature, and behaves like a containment reference. In other words, a resource can only be in one resource set at a time.

ResourceSet provides the user-level interface for creating new resources. In Section 15.1, we used the simplest method for this purpose, createResource(), which delegates to a resource factory returned by the set's resource factory registry. Recall that this registry, returned by getResourceFactoryRegistry(), delegates to the global resource factory registry when it fails to locate an appropriate resource factory itself. The createResource() method simply creates a resource in memory and adds it to the resource set, making no effort to load from or write to a persistent representation. It also doesn't check whether the set already contains a resource with the given URI before blindly creating one, which could possibly put the set in an invalid state.

A more powerful method, getResource(), first normalizes the given URI, checks if any resource in the resource set has a matching normalized URI, and, if so, returns the existing resource. This resource, if not already loaded, will be demand-loaded if the second, boolean argument to the method is true. If an existing resource is not found and the second argument is true, the resource will be both demand-created and demand-loaded.[11] URIs are normalized using the URI converter returned by getURIConverter(), and demand-loading is done using the options specified in the map returned by getLoadOptions().

So, the last example in Section 15.1 could be simplified. After setting up the resource set and creating the URI, two lines are sufficient to create the resource, load it, and access the object in it:

```
...
Resource resource = resourceSet.getResource(uri, true);
PurchaseOrder po = (PurchaseOrder)resource.getContents().get(0);
System.out.println("loaded: " + po);
```

---

11. Note that the *persistent* form of the resource will *not* be demand-created. If the demand-load fails because the persistent form cannot be found, getResource() throws an exception.

Another convenience method on `ResourceSet`, `getEObject()`, allows us to simplify even further, replacing the two lines that get the resource and retrieve the object from it with a single statement:

```
...
PurchaseOrder po =
  (PurchaseOrder)resourceSet.getEObject(uri.appendFragment("/"),true);
...
```

The `getEObject()` method simply invokes `getResource()` to obtain the resource, demand-creating and demand-loading it if necessary, and then uses the fragment of the specified URI to locate and return an object within that resource.

In Section 14.1.2, we discussed package registries, which provide a means for locating metadata describing any particular package. You might recall from that section that there is a global package registry, `EPackage.Registry.INSTANCE`, in which generated packages are registered automatically, either via an extension during plug-in initialization, or at the time the package implementation is constructed. That section also suggested that, in other situations, a context-specific package registry is more appropriate.

In fact, it is the resource set that provides such a context. `ResourceSet` defines a `getPackageRegistry()` method, which returns a local registry. This local package registry delegates to the global registry only when it fails to find a package locally. Thus, packages that have been retrieved from resources loaded into a given resource set can be registered without polluting the global registry. It is even possible to override a global registration just by locally registering a different package against the same namespace URI. Automatic loading and registration of packages will be discussed further in Section 15.3.2.

The main purpose of the resource set is to support references between objects in different resources. In particular, they are critical to demand-loading and proxy resolution. For example, consider a resource that serializes as follows:

```
<?xml version="1.0" encoding="ASCII"?>
<epo2:Supplier ... >
  <orders>
    <previousOrder href="sample.epo2#//@orders.1"/>
  </orders>
</epo2:Supplier>
```

We can see that the **Supplier** in this resource contains a **PurchaseOrder** referencing another **PurchaseOrder** that is serialized with another **Supplier**, in another resource. The cross-document reference is represented by the `href` attribute, whose value is a URI that identifies the target of the reference in the other resource.

When this resource is loaded, a proxy is created as the target of the **previousOrder** reference, specifying the URI of the actual object (e.g., *platform:/resource/project/sample.epo2#//@orders.1*). If we attempt to access the purchase order's previous order, by calling getPreviousOrder(), EcoreUtil.resolve() is invoked to resolve the proxy.[12] This method attempts to navigate up through the resource to the resource set and, if there is one, uses getEObject() to return the object referenced by the proxy URI, demand-creating and demand-loading its containing resource as necessary. If the resource is not in a resource set, the proxy simply fails to resolve and is returned unchanged.

15.3   XML Resources

EMF's base interface for XML-based resources, XMLResource, extends Resource to add several methods relevant to this form of persistence. The base implementation, XMLResourceImpl, which can be used to serialize any EMF data as XML, is highly flexible. The format of the XML that it produces and consumes, as well as its performance characteristics, can be controlled in a number of ways, as we'll see in this section.

We begin by discussing the default serialization format provided by this implementation, and then look at the many save and load options that it supports. We also describe how extended metadata can be used to customize the serialization format. Finally, we discuss a few other features of the implementation, including its support for default options, extrinsic IDs, and DOM conversion.

15.3.1   Default Serialization Format

To illustrate XMLResourceImpl's default output format, we'll begin by creating a single object and saving it, like this:

```
USAddress address = EPO2Factory.eINSTANCE.createUSAddress();
URI uri = URI.createPlatformResourceURI("/project/out.xml", true);
Resource resource = new XMLResourceImpl(uri);
resource.getContents().add(address);
resource.save(null);
```

---

12. Actually, we intentionally disabled proxy resolution on **PurchaseOrder.previousOrder** in ExtendedPO2, making the design decision that related orders must belong to the same supplier. However, for this example, let's assume we hadn't, and that the proxy-resolving code had been generated in the accessor.

We create an instance of the **USAddress** class, add it to the contents of an XML resource, and save the resource. Note that we are explicitly instantiating XMLResourceImpl here, just for the sake of illustration. In a practice, you should always create resources through the ResourceSet interface, as described in Section 15.2.5.

The resulting serialization, in *out.xml*, looks like this:

```
<?xml version="1.0" encoding="ASCII"?>
<epo2:USAddress xmlns:epo2="http://www.example.com/epo2.ecore"/>
```

First, you'll notice that the encoding specified in the XML declaration is ASCII. This is the default, but it's not an especially good default. You will most often want to use a Unicode encoding like UTF-8. We will see how an option can be used to select a different encoding in Section 15.3.3.

Following the XML declaration, you can see that the single **USAddress** has been serialized as an element, using a namespace. The namespace prefix ("epo2") and corresponding URI ("http://www.example.com/epo2.ecore") come from the **nsPrefix** and **nsURI** attributes of the **EPackage** for the model. Notice that the namespace declaration appears as an attribute of the USAddress element itself. In general, namespace declarations are added to the root element of the document. In this example, there is only one object in the resource, so it corresponds to the root element to which the namespace declaration is added. In general, the resource can contain objects from more than one package, in which case, the root element will include one namespace declaration for each such package. We'll soon see how EMF uses this namespace information when deserializing XML documents.

The name of the object's class is also used as the name of the element. This is only the case for objects appearing directly in the resource's contents.

The attributes and content of the element depend on the attributes and references of the corresponding EMF object. You might recall that class **USAddress** defines four simple attributes: **street, city, state,** and **zip**. If you're wondering why they didn't appear in the serialization, it's because they haven't been set. By default, the XMLResourceImpl serializer only includes attributes and references that are set (i.e., those for which the reflective EObject.eIsSet() method returns true). This approach minimizes the size of the XML file by including only the minimum amount of information needed to restore the state of the object at load time.

Multiplicity-1 Attributes

A single-valued attribute is serialized as an XML attribute. For example, if we had set **street**, **city**, and **zip** in the previous example, the serialization of the **USAddress** would have looked like this:

```
<epo2:USAddress xmlns:epo2="http://www.example.com/epo2.ecore"
    street="123 Main Street" city="Anytown" zip="81101"/>
```

As you can see, each attribute of the object is recorded as an XML attribute. The value of the attribute is converted to a string by the `convertToString()` method on the factory associated with the attribute's type. In this example, all three attributes have built-in Ecore types, so the `EcoreFactory` is used.[13]

Notice also that the **state** attribute, which we haven't changed from its default value, is not included in the serialization again.

Multiplicity-Many Attributes

Each value of a multi-valued attribute is serialized as a nested XML element. For example, we could create an instance of **GlobalAddress** and add three values to the multiplicity-many **location** attribute. The serialization would look like this:

```
<epo2:GlobalAddress ... >
  <location>GPO Box 9000</location>
  <location>Sydney, NSW</location>
  <location>2001</location>
</epo2:GlobalAddress>
```

Notice that each value is serialized in its own element, named for the attribute.

Containment References

A contained object is serialized by default as an XML element nested within the element corresponding to its container. The name of the element is that of the reference, not the object's class. For example, suppose we create a **Supplier**, containing a **Customer** and a **PurchaseOrder**:

```
Supplier supplier = EPO2Factory.eINSTANCE.createSupplier();
supplier.setName("Market Farms");
```

---

13. Both **street** and **city** are of type **EString**, for which no conversion is needed. For **zip**, of type **EInt**, the conversion is implemented by a simple invocation of `toString()`.

```
Customer customer = EPO2Factory.eINSTANCE.createCustomer();
customer.setCustomerID(1);
supplier.getCustomers().add(customer);

PurchaseOrder order = EPO2Factory.eINSTANCE.createPurchaseOrder();
order.setComment("rush order");
supplier.getOrders().add(order);
```

Serialized, the model would look like this:

```
<epo2:Supplier ... name="Market Farms">
  <customers customerID="1"/>
  <orders comment="rush order"/>
</epo2:Supplier>
```

Each contained object is serialized as an element whose name specifies the reference through which it is contained. In this example, the type of each object is exactly the type of the reference, so no type information needs to be serialized.

Non-Containment References

By default, a non-containment reference is serialized as an XML attribute whose value is the URI fragment that identifies the referenced object. For example, in the preceding example, we could set the **customer** reference on the **PurchaseOrder** to refer to the **Customer**:

```
order.setCustomer(customer);
```

Because the association is bidirectional, the **PurchaseOrder** is automatically added to the opposite reference, **orders**. The serialization would then look like this:

```
<epo2:Supplier ... name="Market Farms">
  <customers customerID="1" orders="//@orders.0"/>
  <orders comment="rush order" customer="//@customers.0"/>
</epo2:Supplier>
```

Notice the `orders` and `customers` attributes representing the two opposite cross-references. Their values are URI fragment paths, of the form described in Section 15.2.3.

Recall, also from that section, that it is also possible to use intrinsic IDs, instead of fragment paths, to identify objects. This is done by selecting one attribute in the model as the ID attribute. Then, the value of that attribute will be serialized to identify the object in references. For example, if we were using

customerID as the ID attribute for **Customer,** the `orders` element would look like this:

```
<orders comment="rush order" customer="1"/>
```

When using intrinsic IDs in an XML resource, it is important to ensure that the ID attribute values serialize as valid XML IDs, as defined by the XML Schema recommendation [7]. That is, they should be non-colonized names (NCNames).

Because **PurchaseOrder** has no attribute suitable for use as an ID, the opposite reference in this example, **orders,** must still be serialized as a fragment path. The two forms of fragment can coexist in a single resource without any problem.

Cross-Document References

Now, let's consider the case of a reference between documents. By default, this is serialized as an XML element with an `href` attribute, whose value is a URI that identifies the object in the other resource. This is the case for both non-containment and containment references. Continuing from the previous examples, suppose we created another **Supplier** and **PurchaseOrder,** and set the latter's **previousOrder** to the existing **PurchaseOrder:**[14]

```
...
Supplier supplier2 = EPO2Factory.eINSTANCE.createSupplier();
supplier2.setName("Valley Produce");

PurchaseOrder order2 = EPO2Factory.eINSTANCE.createPurchaseOrder();
order2.setComment("hand deliver");
order2.setPreviousOrder(order);
supplier2.getOrders().add(order2);
```

We could then serialize the two resources as follows:

```
ResourceSet rs = new ResourceSetImpl();
rs.getResourceFactoryRegistry().getExtensionToFactoryMap().put(
  Resource.Factory.Registry.DEFAULT_EXTENSION,
  new XMLResourceFactoryImpl());

URI uri = URI.createPlatformResourceURI("/project/sup1.xml", true);
Resource resource = rs.createResource(uri);
resource.getContents().add(supplier);
```

---

14. As in the example in Section 15.2.5, we assume that proxy resolution was not disabled on **PurchaseOrder.previousOrder** in ExtendedPO2. If it was disabled, after loading the model, the proxy would never resolve, and we wouldn't end up with the correct original form.

```
resource.save(null);

URI uri2 = URI.createPlatformResourceURI("/project/sup2.xml", true);
Resource resource2 = rs.createResource(uri2);
resource2.getContents().add(supplier2);
resource2.save(null);
```

Serialized, the second resource would look like this:

```
<epo2:Supplier ... name="Valley Produce" >
  <orders comment="hand deliver">
    <previousOrder href="sup1.xml#//@orders.0"/>
  </orders>
</epo2:Supplier>
```

Notice the `previousOrder` element, representing the cross-document reference, and the `href` attribute that specifies its target. The value of this attribute, "sup1.xml#//@orders.0", is the URI of the first resource, relative to that of the second resource, with a fragment that, like in the previous section, identifies the object in its resource. In the case of a multiplicity-many, non-containment reference that represents a mix of same- and cross-resource references, all the values are serialized using the cross-document form described in this section. In this case, the URI used for a same-resource reference consists of just "#" followed by the appropriate fragment.

Notice that we waited and saved both resources at the end, after all the objects had been added to them. If we had tried to save the first resource before adding the referenced object to the second resource, the serializer would not have been able to determine the `href` value and would have thrown an exception. This is something to keep in mind whenever saving resources with references between them.

Another important issue regarding cross-document references is whether the URI in the `href` will be relative or absolute. Relative references are usually preferred because they allow you to move both resources to a different absolute location, without breaking their connection. When loaded, a relative URI is resolved against the URI of the containing resource, in exactly the same way that a Web browser resolves a reference in an HTML file before requesting the linked document.

In the preceding example, a relative cross-document reference was used in the serialization. This is what we wanted, but the reason why it happened might not be obvious. When we created the two resources, we did so using *absolute* URIs – that is, URIs with schemes. We did that specifically so that any references between the documents would be relative. The XML serializer attempts to deresolve, or make relative, a target URI against the base URI of the source document only if both URIs are absolute. If they are not, it simply serializes the target's URI as is.

For this reason, it is always a very good idea to use absolute URIs when creating or loading resources. In this example, we used platform resource URIs, which we discussed in Section 15.2.1. We can make this example run in a stand-alone context by using the map returned by `EcorePlugin`. `getPlatformResourceMap()` to associate the simple project name, *project*, with a directory in the physical file system. This map is used by the default `URIConverter` implementation, when running stand-alone, to open streams for such URIs. This approach lets us work with absolute URIs, without having to include long, brittle file system paths in each one.

References to Subclasses

Sometimes, the type of an object cannot be determined just from the feature. In such cases, it is necessary to explicitly specify the type in the serialization. An XML attribute called `xsi:type` is used for this purpose.

For example, if we add a **USAddress** to the **billTo** reference of a **PurchaseOrder**, the serialization will look like this:

```
<epo2:PurchaseOrder
    xmlns:xsi="http://www.w3.org/2001/XMLSchema-instance"
    xmlns:epo2="http://www.example.com/epo2.ecore"
    comment="rush order">
  <billTo xsi:type="epo2:USAddress" street="123 Main Street"/>
</epo2:PurchaseOrder>
```

Recall that the type of **billTo** was the abstract class **Address**. As a result, the concrete subclass used, **USAddress**, must be serialized.

Notice that the type of the object is namespace-qualified, to identify what package it comes from. The `xsi` namespace prefix of the `type` attribute, itself, corresponds to the XML Schema instance namespace, defined by the XML Schema recommendation [8] for use in any XML document.

15.3.2   Deserialization

The `XMLResourceImpl` loader uses SAX (the Simple API for XML) to provide its load support. As a document is parsed, SAX events are used to build the EMF objects in memory. By comparison, using DOM (the Document Object Model) would construct an intermediary model, consuming more memory and taking longer to run. That said, there is value in being able to access the DOM tree corresponding to an EMF model, so `XMLResourceImpl` provides that capability, as we'll see in Section 15.3.6.

During a load, namespace URIs are read from namespace declarations and used to locate the corresponding Ecore packages. This usually just involves querying a package registry, a local registry if the loading resource is in a resource set, or the global registry otherwise. However, when no matching package has been registered, the loader automatically uses the namespace URI to load one into the resource set. In general, it simply attempts to load from that URI directly and, if that yields an EMF resource containing an instance of **EPackage**, registers the package locally. This all works because a serialized Ecore model is just an instance of another model, the Ecore metamodel, so it can be loaded just like any other EMF data.

Note that any mappings in the resource set's URI converter will be applied automatically when the Ecore resource is loaded. That is why mappings from namespace URIs to physical resources can be programmatically registered in the URI converter, as illustrated in Section 15.2.2.

There is also another, more dynamic, way to map namespace URIs to physical resource URIs for automatic loading of package metadata. It is based on the standard XML mechanism for locating metadata, the `xsi:schemaLocation` attribute. In this case, the instance document itself specifies these mappings as space-separated URI pairs. The loader then replaces any matching namespace URI by the corresponding resource URI before attempting to load it. We will see an example of `xsi:schemaLocation` use in Section 15.3.4.

Once the loader has a package, it can obtain the corresponding factory for creating EMF objects. A factory obtained from a generated package registered in the global package registry will supply instances of generated classes. If, on the other hand, a package was loaded from its serialized form, its factory will simply instantiate the dynamic `EObject` implementation.

For each XML attribute and element encountered, the corresponding Ecore construct is located by name within the appropriate package. EMF objects are created and initialized using the reflective `EObject` API. For example, when an attribute is processed, the loader obtains the Ecore feature whose name matches that of the XML attribute. If the feature is an **EAttribute**, it uses the corresponding factory to convert the string value into an object and sets the value of the attribute appropriately. If the feature is an **EReference**, it uses the attribute value, a fragment path or ID, to obtain the corresponding **EObject**. If the object has not been created yet, it stores the value and defers setting the reference value until after the parsing is complete.

When the loader processes a cross-document reference, it creates a proxy for the object. Loading of the target document is delayed until the referenced object is actually accessed, as was discussed in Section 15.2.5. Note that even a same-document reference serialized using a URI will be represented by a proxy object, unless the reference is bidirectional.

The loader continues working even after it encounters an XML element or attribute that it cannot process correctly. This way, it loads as much of the data as possible, even if there are errors. After loading, you can look in the resource's errors and warnings lists to see any problems that might have occurred.

15.3.3 Options

As we saw in Section 15.2.3, you can pass options to the `save()` and `load()` methods to customize their behavior. Recall that these options are specified as a `Map`, where each key is a string identifying the particular option. This section summarizes the various kinds of options supported by XML resources, giving the value type for each. Each option is also identified as being applicable to save or load, or both, and described. The option names correspond to string constants defined on the `XMLResource` interface.

Model-Serialization Mapping Options

The following options affect the mapping between a model and the serialization of its instances.

OPTION_ANY_TYPE   (EClass, Save/Load)

EMF's XMLType model provides an **AnyType** class that corresponds to the XML Schema `anyType` and is used by default to represent arbitrary XML content. When working with models that were created from an XML Schema, this option can be used to specify an alternate Ecore mapping for `anyType`. The value, an `EClass`, must identify a modeled class that extends the default **AnyType** class. Note that this option can only be used together with the OPTION_ANY_SIMPLE_TYPE option.

OPTION_ANY_SIMPLE_TYPE   (EClass, Save/Load)

EMF's XMLType model provides a **SimpleAnyType** class that corresponds to the XML Schema `anyType` and is used by default to represent arbitrary XML content in a data type context. When working with models that were created from an XML Schema, this option can be used to specify an alternate Ecore mapping. The value, an `EClass`, must identify a modeled class that extends the default **SimpleAnyType** class. Note that this option can only be used together with the OPTION_ANY_TYPE option.

OPTION_DOM_USE_NAMESPACES_IN_SCOPE   (Boolean, Load)

When loading from a DOM element node, this option should be enabled to ensure that the loader builds a complete collection of namespace declarations by visiting all parents of the node. This option is not necessary when loading from a document node. Loading from DOM is discussed in Section 15.3.6.

OPTION_EXTENDED_META_DATA   (Boolean or ExtendedMetaData, Save/Load)

This option is used to tailor XML serialization. If your model was defined using XML Schema, you must use this option to save and load instances of it. If Boolean.TRUE is specified as the value, a default ExtendedMetaData implementation is used to handle any extended metadata annotations defined on the Ecore model. As detailed in Chapters 8 and 9, these annotations can specify, for example, how features are to be represented in the serialization and with what name. Alternatively, a specialized ExtendedMetaData implementation can be specified. This mechanism, which is meant to supersede OPTION_XML_MAP, is discussed further in Section 15.3.5.

OPTION_KEEP_DEFAULT_CONTENT   (Boolean, Save)

By default, if a feature is not set, according to the reflective eIsSet() method, it will not be serialized explicitly. This option can be enabled, with a value of Boolean.TRUE, to serialize attributes even when not set. Because null cannot be serialized, this option only affects attributes with non-null default values (the default value of a reference is always null).

OPTION_LAX_FEATURE_PROCESSING   (Boolean, Load)

When loading an instance of a model that was created from an XML Schema, this option can be enabled to relax the rules used for matching XML attributes and elements to Ecore features. This allows a feature that was originally defined as an element to be read from an attribute and vice versa. It also allows a name with no namespace to match the same name defined with a namespace and vice versa.

OPTION_RECORD_ANY_TYPE_NAMESPACE_DECLARATIONS   (Boolean, Load)

When loading an instance of a model that was created from an XML Schema, the namespace declarations in the document are normally stored in the **xMLNSPrefixMap** attribute of the **DocumentRoot**.[15] If the instance is serialized

---

15. As described in Section 9.1.3, a **DocumentRoot** instance is used as the root object in an XML resource to produce a schema-compliant serialization. This class is created when converting a schema to Ecore and contains one feature for each global element and attribute declaration in the schema.

again, all of these declarations will then appear on the root element of the document. This option can be enabled to maintain the location of namespace declarations in the instance, but only for elements that were declared in the schema as `anyType` wildcards. Prefix-to-URI mappings for the namespaces are recorded as entries in the **AnyType**'s **anyAttribute** feature map, where the entry feature is demand-created for the prefix name and the value is the URI. When the instance is serialized again, these declarations will then appear in their original locations.

OPTION_RECORD_UNKNOWN_FEATURE   (Boolean, Load)

This option can be used to record values of invalid features during a load. By default, if an element or attribute is encountered for which a corresponding feature cannot be located, it will be treated as an error—a `FeatureNotFoundException` will be recorded. However, if this option is enabled, an **AnyType** will be demand-created and instantiated to represent the open content. The resulting objects and their metadata are stored as **EObject-AnyType** mappings and available via `XMLResource.getEObjectTo-ExtensionMap()`.

OPTION_SAVE_TYPE_INFORMATION   (Boolean, Save)

By default, an `xsi:type` attribute can be included in a cross-document reference, but only if it is to an instance of an abstract class. If this option is set to `Boolean.TRUE`, then `xsi:type` will also be used to identify a subclass of a non-abstract type in a cross-document reference. Then, when the referencing resource is loaded, exactly the correct type of proxy will be created.

OPTION_USE_ENCODED_ATTRIBUTE_STYLE   (Boolean, Save/Load)

This option affects how EMF serializes and loads references. If this option is set to `Boolean.TRUE` when saving, then non-containment references, whether local or cross-document, are always serialized as URIs in XML attributes. Recall from Section 15.3.1 that by default, a cross-file reference is serialized using an element with an `href` attribute, whereas a local reference is serialized as an attribute containing a fragment path. This option affects both patterns.

In the previous section, we saw that a customer's **orders** reference to a purchase order in the same resource is serialized like this by default:

```
<customers customerID="1" orders="//@orders.0"/>
```

With `OPTION_USE_ENCODED_ATTRIBUTE_STYLE` enabled, it is serialized like this instead:

```
<customers customerID="1" orders="#//@orders.0"/>
```

Can you see the subtle difference? The leading "#" character indicates that we're now using a URI instead of a simple fragment path to reference the purchase order. For a cross-document reference, the difference is less subtle. As a cross-document reference, **orders** would be serialized like this by default:

```
<customers customerID="1">
  <orders href="supplier3.xml#//@orders.0"/>
</customers>
```

Using the encoded attribute style, it looks like this:

```
<customers customerID="1" orders="supplier3.xml#//@orders.0"/>
```

Notice that with this option, the cross-document reference is now encoded in exactly the same way as the reference to an object in the same resource.

Because this option forces all same-document references to be serialized using URIs, you should probably never use it with models that include any non-proxy-resolving references. On load, these same-document references, unless bidirectional, would be represented by proxies, which would then never automatically resolve.[16]

This option can be enabled on a load to indicate that `href` attributes should not be interpreted as cross-document references but, instead, be treated just like any other attribute. This is necessary when reading an instance of a model that actually contains a structural feature named **href**. However, in the absence of such a feature, a serialization produced using the `OPTION_USE_ENCODED_ATTRIBUTE_STYLE` option can be loaded without it. Note also that cross-document containment references cannot be loaded using this option, as they are always serialized using an `href` attribute.

`OPTION_USE_LEXICAL_HANDLER`   (`Boolean`, Load)

This option can be enabled to use a lexical handler to preserve comments and CDATA in mixed text processing. In Section 8.2.3, we saw that these artifacts can be recorded as entries in a feature map attribute. However, for that to work, this option must be enabled.

`OPTION_XML_OPTIONS`   (`XMLOptions`, Load)

This option is used to control a set of advanced features for handling instance data without corresponding metadata. These features include using **AnyType** to repre-

---

16. Models created from XML Schema are exempt from this advice. Different handling in the presence of extended metadata ensures that IDREF attributes are serialized correctly even when this option is enabled, as it is in the default resource factory implementations generated for such models.

sent arbitrary unrecognized XML, as well as demand-loading XML Schemas, including those identified via an xsi:schemaLocation attribute, and converting them into dynamic Ecore on the fly. The individual options are configured via an instance of XMLOptionsImpl, which is then supplied as the value of the OPTION_XML_OPTIONS option. All of these features are disabled by default.

OPTION_XML_MAP   (XMLResource.XMLMap, Save/Load)

This was the mechanism used to specify a mapping from Ecore to XML prior to EMF 2.0. Although still supported, this approach to tailoring XML serialization is no longer recommended. The more powerful OPTION_EXTENDED_META_DATA supersedes it.

Serialization Tweaks

The following options make small changes to the document that results from saving an XML resource. They affect such aspects of the serialization as encoding, formatting, and escaping.

OPTION_DECLARE_XML   (Boolean, Save)

This option can be set to Boolean.FALSE to prevent the serializer from writing an XML declaration at the beginning of the document. However, you need to be careful when you do this because it's illegal for the declaration to be absent if the character encoding is anything other than UTF-8. One reason you might want to suppress the declaration is if you're writing into the middle of an output stream that already includes an XML declaration.

OPTION_ENCODING   (String, Save)

This option can be used to specify a character encoding for the serialization. As an alternative to this option, you can change the encoding via the setEncoding() method on XMLResource. The default encoding is "ASCII". However, for most applications, you should specify a Unicode encoding, such as "UTF-8" or "UTF-16".

OPTION_FORMATTED   (Boolean, Save)

This option can be used to disable the default line breaking and indentation. This results in a smaller and faster, although less human-readable, serialization.

OPTION_LINE_WIDTH   (Integer, Save)

This option can be used to set a line width, beyond which lines will be broken. You can use this option to make the serialization more readable.

OPTION_SAVE_DOCTYPE   (Boolean, Save)

This option can be enabled to include a DOCTYPE declaration in the serialization. EMF provides no direct support for DTDs, but if you have defined one that the serialization will conform to, this option can be used to reference it. The system and public identifiers to be used can be specified via the setDoctypeInfo() method on XMLResource.

OPTION_SCHEMA_LOCATION   (Boolean, Save)

This option can be enabled to produce an xsi:schemaLocation attribute in the root element, to specify the locations of the persisted resources that contain the **EPackages** needed to load the document. This approach is an alternative to pre-registration of packages, allowing metadata to be located and loaded automatically, based only on information in the instance document. It is only appropriate when the metadata will be available at load time in persistent form at a known location. We'll discuss this approach further in Section 15.3.4.

OPTION_SCHEMA_LOCATION_IMPLEMENTATION   (Boolean, Save)

Like the previous option, this can be enabled to produce an xsi:schemaLocation attribute in the root element. However, this option is appropriate for use with generated packages, as the attribute will refer to a generated package interface, through which the metadata can be initialized and accessed.

OPTION_SKIP_ESCAPE   (Boolean, Save)

This option can be set to Boolean.TRUE to tell the serializer not to encode the characters "<", ">", and "&" using the predefined entities "<", ">", and "&". You can use this option to reduce the save time, but you should only set it if you know, for sure, that your attribute values do not contain characters that need to be treated specially in XML; otherwise, you won't be able to reload the document.

OPTION_SKIP_ESCAPE_URI   (Boolean, Save)

This option can be used to enable escaping within URIs. By default, even when escaping is enabled (see OPTION_SKIP_ESCAPE), it is not performed within URIs. Setting this option to Boolean.FALSE enables escaping in URIs, too.

OPTION_XML_VERSION   (String, Save)

This option can be used to specify the XML version to be included in the XML declaration. By default, "1.0" is used.

Performance

The following options can be used to improve the performance of the save or load operation, by decreasing either the running time of the operation or the amount of memory it uses.

OPTION_CONFIGURATION_CACHE   (Boolean, Save)

This option can be enabled to cache and reuse generic data in repeated save operations, avoiding the cost of reinitializing the data.

OPTION_DEFER_ATTACHMENT   (Boolean, Load)

This option can be enabled to defer adding a root object to the resource's contents until after the whole tree of objects has been built under it. By default, the resource is populated from the root down, with each object being added to its container as the corresponding element is encountered. In some situations, resources have to perform computation whenever an object is attached, so this default strategy can be very expensive. Enabling this option reduces that cost.

OPTION_DEFER_IDREF_RESOLUTION   (Boolean, Load)

This option can be enabled to defer resolving references within a resource until the whole document has been parsed. The default strategy is to try to resolve each reference as it is encountered and then, at the end, resolve any ones that failed. This wastes time looking up forward references that do not exist yet, which, if you're using intrinsic IDs, can involve iterating over every object in the resource.

OPTION_FLUSH_THRESHOLD   (Integer, Save)

This option can be used to specify a maximum number of characters to allow in the output stream before flushing it. This reduces the memory used in serializing a large file, but it is slower than the default behavior.

OPTION_USE_CACHED_LOOKUP_TABLE   (List, Save)

This option can be used to cache information about the structure of the model being serialized. A list is provided as the value of this option, and it is used as a placeholder for this cached data. Exactly how the list is used for caching is considered an implementation detail. When possible, the same placeholder list should be shared among resources that serialize instances of the same model; however, it must not be shared across threads.

OPTION_USE_DEPRECATED_METHODS   (Boolean, Load)

This option can be used to take advantage of recent refactorings in the loader implementation. By default, the old, deprecated methods are used to preserve backward compatibility for derived implementations. This option can be set to `Boolean.FALSE` to use the new methods, instead. Note that they require the use of a namespace-aware SAX parser, which is not created by default. Thus, this option should only be used in conjunction with `OPTION_PARSER_POOL`, as the default parser pool does create namespace-aware parsers.

`OPTION_USE_FILE_BUFFER`   (`Boolean`, Save)

This option can be enabled to accumulate output during serialization in a temporary file, rather than an in-memory buffer. This reduces the memory used in serializing a large file, but it is slower than the default behavior.

`OPTION_USE_PARSER_POOL`   (`XMLParserPool`, Load)

This option can be used to provide a parser pool, from which `SAXParser` instances are created and reused. `XMLParserPool` defines a simple interface for obtaining and releasing parsers based on their features and properties. Specifying a parser pool, such as an instance of the default implementation, `XMLParserPoolImpl`, can improve performance dramatically when a resource performs repeated loads. A single parser pool can also be shared among multiple resources.

`OPTION_USE_XML_NAME_TO_FEATURE_MAP`   (`Map`, Load)

This option can be used to share the cache of mappings between qualified XML names and corresponding Ecore features across invocations of `load()`, or even among resources. It can take some time to determine these associations, as they can be affected by `ExtendedMetaData` or an `XMLMap`, so they are cached during a load. If you use this option to specify the same map for several loads, that instance will be used as the cache, improving the performance for all but the first. You can share a single map among multiple resources, unless they load different models with conflicting qualified names or are used in different threads.

Underlying Parser Control

`OPTION_PARSER_FEATURES`   (`Map`, Load)

This option can be used to tailor parsing by specifying features that are to be set on created parsers. Parser features are identified by a URI string and are boolean-valued. A number of standard SAX features are defined, and specific parser implementations are allowed to define their own. The standard features and properties are specified by the SAX package Javadoc (see *http://www.saxproject.org/apidoc/org/xml/sax/package-summary.html*). The features recognized by the Apache Xerces parser, for example, are described in its *Parser Features* document (see *http://xerces.apache.org/xerces2-j/features.html*). Please consult your parser's documentation for details.

OPTION_PARSER_PROPERTIES   (Map, Load)

This option can be used to tailor parsing by specifying properties that are to be set on created parsers. Parser properties are identified by a URI string and can have arbitrary object values. As with features, a number of standard SAX properties are specified, and parser implementations can define additional ones. For example, the properties recognized by the Apache Xerces parser are described in its *Parser Properties* document (see *http://xerces.apache.org/xerces2-j/properties.html*). Please consult your parser's documentation for details.

Miscellaneous Behavior

The following options control aspects of an XML resource's behavior during a save or load operation, changing the way it interacts with the application.

OPTION_DISABLE_NOTIFY   (Boolean, Load)

This option can be used to disable notifications during a load. If you've modified your factory or constructor to add adapters to your objects immediately on creation, notification to those adapters can significantly increase the time it takes to load a document. This option can be used to reduce the load time in this situation. Notifications will be re-enabled at the end of the load operation.

OPTION_PROCESS_DANGLING_HREF   (String, Save)

This option can be used to select the action to be taken during serialization when a referenced object is not in a resource. One of three values can be specified: "THROW", "RECORD", or "DISCARD". XMLResource defines a constant for each of these values. If the value is "THROW", the default, and referenced objects without resources are encountered, the serializer will discard the bad references, save the rest of the model, and then throw an exception at the end. For "RECORD", the serializer will do the same, except it will add the exception to the resource's error list, instead of throwing it. For "DISCARD", it will silently discard the bad references without informing the application in any way.

OPTION_RESOURCE_HANDLER   (ResourceHandler, Save/Load)

This option can be used to register a ResourceHandler, which will then be invoked to provide arbitrary pre- and post-processing of the resource or stream when saving and loading. The specified handler should extend BasicResourceHandler.

15.3.4 Dynamic EMF

In Chapter 14, we saw how a model can be programmatically defined and then instantiated immediately using the EMF's dynamic `EObject` implementation. At that time, we claimed that all `EObjects`, whether generated or dynamic, can be freely mixed and used interchangeably in EMF. Now, we will see that this is most certainly true with respect to persistence, and we will also see how the XML resource implementation provides additional support for some of the more interesting scenarios in which dynamic EMF can be used.

In Section 14.3, we used the Ecore API to define the SimplePO model at runtime. We then obtained a factory from the **po** package and used it to instantiate the model dynamically. The code in this section builds on that example.

To begin, we simply serialize the instance using exactly the same approach that we have discussed throughout this chapter.

```
EPackage poPackage = ...
EObject purchaseOrder = ...

ResourceSet rs = new ResourceSetImpl();
rs.getResourceFactoryRegistry().getExtensionToFactoryMap().put(
  "xml", new XMLResourceFactoryImpl());

Resource resource = rs.createResource(
  URI.createPlatformResourceURI("/project/po.xml", true));
resource.getContents().add(purchaseOrder);
resource.save(null);
```

First, we create a resource set and register the default XML resource factory against the *.xml* extension in the resource set's local registry. Then, we simply create a resource, add the purchase order instance to it, and call `save()` on it. Notice that the type of `purchaseOrder` is just `EObject`, as we have not generated an interface to represent the modeled **PurchaseOrder** class. This difference does not change how the resource behaves, however. The resulting *po.xml* file looks just as you would expect:

```
<?xml version="1.0" encoding="ASCII"?>
<po:PurchaseOrder xmlns:po="http://www.example.com/SimplePO"
    shipTo="123 Maple Street">
  <items productName="Apples" quantity="12" price="0.5"/>
</po:PurchaseOrder>
```

Now that we've serialized an instance of our dynamic model, you might be wondering how to read it back. The only potential issue is how to make the package metadata available to the resource during the load. In this example, we could just manually register the package in the resource set's package registry:

```
ResourceSet rs = new ResourceSetImpl();
rs.getPackageRegistry().put(poPackage.getNsURI(), poPackage);
```

Then, we could continue to load the document as follows:

```
rs.getResourceFactoryRegistry().getExtensionToFactoryMap().put(
  "xml", new XMLResourceFactoryImpl());

Resource resource = rs.getResource(
  URI.createPlatformResourceURI("/project/po.xml", true), true);
EObject purchaseOrder = (EObject)resource.getContents().get(0);
```

This is no different from what we have done previously with generated models. The question of package registration becomes an issue only when we start to think about where the package referenced by poPackage might come from in practice. In this example, it was built up by the code we saw in Section 14.3. Of course, we needed this model to instantiate it and save the instance. But what about on the load side? Do we need to rerun the code that builds the model before we can load the instance?

For generated packages, that's exactly how things work: when the INSTANCE field in the generated package interface is accessed, it calls the package implementation's init() method, which builds up all the metadata and adds the package to the registry. However, when working with dynamic packages, some more flexibility is desirable.

One interesting type of application would be able to consume and operate on arbitrary data, automatically reading in the corresponding models as necessary. The models would inform the handling of the data, which would be performed using the reflective EObject API. The application could provide a batch processing service, or even offer an interactive UI that is dynamically assembled based on the model. Fortunately, EMF's XML resource implementation provides direct support for such an application.

EMF reuses the xsi:schemaLocation attribute defined by XML Schema recommendation [8] to provide this support. This attribute is allowed in any XML document to help locate the schema definitions associated with namespaces used in the document. In the context of EMF serializations, the "schema" is actually a serialized Ecore model.[17] That model will then be loaded and the package it contains will be registered in the resource set's local package registry, as described in Section 15.3.2. This all happens automatically at load time, as

---

17. It is also possible, with the OPTIONS_XML_OPTIONS load option, to automatically load XML Schemas and convert them to Ecore on the fly. This approach, although less common, is used by resources created via the GenericXMLResourceFactoryImpl, which is described in Section 15.4.2.

needed, if an `xsi:schemaLocation` attribute is present in the serialization. So, what do we need to do at save time to produce this attribute?

It's actually very simple. First, we change our example so that, before saving the instance, we actually save the Ecore model itself:

```
ResourceSet rs = new ResourceSetImpl();
rs.getResourceFactoryRegistry().getExtensionToFactoryMap().put(
  "xml", new XMLResourceFactoryImpl());
rs.getResourceFactoryRegistry().getExtensionToFactoryMap().put(
  "ecore", new EcoreResourceFactoryImpl());

Resource ecoreResource = rs.createResource(
  URI.createPlatformResourceURI("/project/po.ecore", true));
ecoreResource.getContents().add(poPackage);
ecoreResource.save(null);
```

Notice that we have also registered the Ecore resource factory implementation in the local resource factory registry. This registration ensures that we will use a slightly specialized version of the XMI resource implementation for saving and loading *.ecore* files, as we will discuss in Section 15.4.4. When running under Eclipse, this registration is not necessary.

We have then created a resource, placed the package into it, and saved it. Next, we save the instance itself, using the `OPTION_SCHEMA_LOCATION` option:

```
Resource resuource = rs.createResource(
  URI.createPlatformResourceURI("/project/po2.xml", true));
resource.getContents().add(purchaseOrder);

Map options = new HashMap();
options.put(XMLResource.OPTION_SCHEMA_LOCATION, Boolean.TRUE);
resource.save(options);
```

If we look at the resulting serialization in *po2.xml*, we see only a small difference from what was produced before:

```
<?xml version="1.0" encoding="ASCII"?>
<po:PurchaseOrder
    xmlns:xsi="http://www.w3.org/2001/XMLSchema-instance"
    xmlns:po="http://www.example.com/SimplePO"
    xsi:schemaLocation="http://www.example.com/SimplePO po.ecore"
    shipTo="123 Maple Street">
  <items productName="Apples" quantity="12" price="0.5"/>
</po:PurchaseOrder>
```

Two additional attributes are now present on the `PurchaseOrder` element: the `xsi` namespace declaration and the `xsi:schemaLocation` attribute that we wanted. The value of this attribute specifies a mapping between a namespace URI and the URI of a resource that contains the package with that namespace. In general, more namespace-to-resource URI mappings can be specified in an `xsi:schemaLocation` value as additional space-separated URI pairs. In this case, the namespace of our **po** package is mapped to the relative URI *po.ecore*. This instructs the loader that it should look in the same location as the instance document for a file called *po.ecore*, which will contain the needed metadata. The relative URI was computed automatically for us because we specified absolute URIs for both resources, as described in Section 15.3.1.

Now, with the Ecore model available and referenced by the `xsi:schemaLocation` attribute, the instance document can be loaded without any pre-registration of a package. More generally, the model need not even be serialized at the same time as the instance. For example, the model could be available from a fixed location on the Web. As long the package is in a resource with the correct HTTP-scheme URI when the instance is serialized, that URI will be used in the `xsi:schemaLocation`.[18]

15.3.5 *Extended Metadata*

In Chapters 8 and 9, we discussed quite extensively how a model derived from an XML Schema is annotated with Ecore annotations, which are used to tailor the serialization of instances of the model, so as to conform to the schema. In Chapter 14, we looked at the `ExtendedMetaData` interface, through which these annotations are handled, and we've seen that it provides a general-purpose mechanism for tailoring the mapping between models and their XML serialization. In this section, we'll see a complete example that defines extended metadata through that interface, and uses it to produce a customized serialization.

Once again, we will work with the ExtendedPO2 model, but let's say we would like to produce serializations that look a little different from the default. We'll build a small purchase order instance with a couple of items, and we would like it to be saved like this:

```xml
<?xml version="1.0" encoding="ASCII"?>
<order>
  <item productName="apple" quantity="10"/>
  <item productName="orange" quantity="20"/>
  <comment>rush order</comment>
</order>
```

---

18. Note that if the namespace URI and resource URI are the same, an `xsi:schemaLocation` attribute is not needed because, in the absence of the attribute, the loader tries to retrieve required metadata directly from the namespace URI. In this case, specifying the `OPTION_SCHEMA_LOCATION` save option has no effect.

This is actually quite different from the default serialization:

```xml
<?xml version="1.0" encoding="ASCII"?>
<epo2:PurchaseOrder xmlns:epo2="http://www.example.com/epo2.ecore"
    comment="rush order">
  <items productName="apple" quantity="10"/>
  <items productName="orange" quantity="20"/>
</epo2:PurchaseOrder>
```

Notice the following customizations:

o The name of the root element is order, instead of the default, PurchaseOrder.

o The root element is not namespace-qualified.

o The name of the nested elements is item, not items. This looks a little nicer as XML, as each element represents a single item.

o The comment for the purchase order is represented as an element, instead of as an attribute.

To achieve this, we can create extended metadata annotations for the **epo2** package as follows:

```java
final ExtendedMetaData ext = new BasicExtendedMetaData(
  ExtendedMetaData.ANNOTATION_URI,
  EPackage.Registry.INSTANCE, new HashMap());

ext.setQualified(EPO2Package.eINSTANCE, false);
ext.setName(EPO2Package.Literals.PURCHASE_ORDER, "order");
ext.setName(EPO2Package.Literals.PURCHASE_ORDER__ITEMS, "item");
ext.setFeatureKind(EPO2Package.Literals.PURCHASE_ORDER__COMMENT,
                ExtendedMetaData.ELEMENT_FEATURE);
```

There are a few things to note here. First, we're working with a generated model, and dynamically modifying such a model is not allowed. The default ExtendedMetaData instance, which we have used in previous examples, directly annotates the model elements and is therefore inappropriate in this scenario. Instead, we instantiate BasicExtendedMetaData, passing to the constructor the URI for extended metadata, the global package registry, and an empty map.

The first argument to the constructor, the extended metadata URI, will be used by the BasicExtendedMetaData instance as the source URI on the annotations it consults and creates. We have the flexibility to specify any URI for this purpose, but because we are just using standard extended metadata annotations here, we can simply use the standard URI, available as ExtendedMetaData.ANNOTATION_URI.

The second argument, a package registry, is used to locate packages, when needed, based on their namespace URIs. For now, this is not important, but when extended metadata is used for loading a model, an appropriate registry must be specified.

The third argument, a new `HashMap`, is the most important one and, in fact, the reason we didn't just use the default `ExtendedMetaData` instance. When we pass a map to the `BasicExtendedMetaData`'s constructor, that map will be used to record and obtain its annotations. By storing annotations off to the side, instead of directly on the model elements, we are able to tailor the serialization format for an existing model that we cannot change. We just have to be sure to specify the same instance when saving and loading.

In the more common case of specifying some default sterilization customizations for a model that should always be applied, we would usually define the extended metadata in the model's original form—UML, Java, or XML Schema—as described in Chapter 8. Or, for a dynamically defined Ecore model, we would take a similar approach as in this example, but we would just use `ExtendedMetaData.INSTANCE` to annotate the model directly.

Returning to the example, after instantiating the `ExtendedMetaData` instance, we use it to specify that the **epo2** package will be identified by the null namespace by calling `setQualified()`. That prevents the root-level element from being namespace qualified. Then we use `setName()` to set different names to use when serializing the **PurchaseOrder** class and its **items** attribute. Recall that the root element will be named for the object's class, but that nested elements and attributes will be named for the corresponding structural features. Finally, we use `setFeatureKind()` to specify that the **comment** attribute should be represented as an XML element.

Next, we can instantiate the model in the usual way:

```
PurchaseOrder order = EPO2Factory.eINSTANCE.createPurchaseOrder();
order.setComment("rush order");

Item item1 = EPO2Factory.eINSTANCE.createItem();
item1.setProductName("apple");
item1.setQuantity(10);
order.getItems().add(item1);

Item item2 = EPO2Factory.eINSTANCE.createItem();
item2.setProductName("orange");
item2.setQuantity(20);
order.getItems().add(item2);
```

Finally, we save the instance, like this:

```
ResourceSet rs = new ResourceSetImpl();
rs.getResourceFactoryRegistry().getExtensionToFactoryMap().put(
  "xml", new XMLResourceFactoryImpl());

Resource resource = rs.createResource(
  URI.createPlatformResourceURI("/project/tailored.xml", true));
resource.getContents().add(order);

Map options = new HashMap();
options.put(XMLResource.OPTION_EXTENDED_META_DATA, ext);
resource.save(options);
```

Here, we create a resource set, as usual, and register
XMLResourceFactoryImpl locally. This ensures that XMLResourceImpl will
be used to save the purchase order. Then, we obtain a resource from the resource
set. When we call save(), we pass it a map enabling the OPTION_EXTEND-
ED_META_DATA option and specifying the ExtendedMetaData instance created
earlier. This ensures that the desired serialization is produced.

When we want to load it again, we must be sure to use the same option to
specify the same ExtendedMetaData; otherwise, the resource will not be able
to recognize the package, class, or features for which it has tailored the serialization. As we'll see in the next section, there's actually a way to do this automatically, ensuring that the correct extended metadata is used by default.

Had we been writing the annotations through to the model elements, instead
of recording them in a particular BasicExtendedMetaData instance, we could
have simply used Boolean.TRUE as the value of
OPTION_EXTENDED_META_DATA. In that case, the resource would check if it is
in a resource set and, if so, create an ordinary instance of
BasicExtendedMetaData that uses that resource set's local package registry to
obtain packages.[19] Otherwise, the default ExtendedMetaData instance, which
just consults the global package registry, would be used. In either case, the
ExtendedMetaData would read the annotations directly from the model.

15.3.6 Other Features

EMF's XML resource implementation provides several other features and conveniences, which we will look at in this section. These features are exposed by
methods on the XMLResource interface.

---

19. Recall that by default, a resource set's local package registry delegates to the global package registry
when it fails to find a package locally.

Default Options

In some cases, we might want to use certain options by default for saving or loading a particular resource, or a particular type of resource. For example, in the previous section, we remarked that, having used extended metadata to tailor the serialization of a purchase order, we would need to use it again on loading. In fact, we'd like to use it consistently on both operations.

For situations like this, `XMLResource` offers two methods, `getDefaultSaveOptions()` and `getDefaultLoadOptions()`, which return maps that, as the names suggest, represent the default options for the two operations. It's typical to set default options in a resource factory immediately after creating the resource.

For example, in the previous example, we could have initialized the resource factory registry like this:

```
ResourceSet rs = new ResourceSetImpl();
rs.getResourceFactoryRegistry().getExtensionToFactoryMap().put("xml",
  new ResourceFactoryImpl()
  {
    public Resource createResource(URI uri)
    {
      XMLResource resource = new XMLResourceImpl(uri);
      String option = XMLResource.OPTION_EXTENDED_META_DATA;
      resource.getDefaultSaveOptions().put(option, ext);
      resource.getDefaultLoadOptions().put(option, ext);
      return resource;
    }
  });
```

This registers a specialized resource factory against the *.xml* file extension. This factory creates an ordinary `XMLResourceImpl`, but initializes it with `OPTION_EXTENDED_META_DATA` as a default save and load option. With this change, it is no longer necessary to specify the option explicitly to `save()` or `load()`.

Extrinsic IDs

We've already seen how EMF resources automatically support two different mechanisms for identifying and locating objects: fragment paths, based on feature names and indexes, and intrinsic IDs, based on the value of an attribute. `XMLResources` support another mechanism, *extrinsic IDs*, where unique object IDs are stored, external to the corresponding objects, by the resource. Such IDs are useful when they really do not constitute part of the object's modeled state.

The `setID()` method records a mapping between an object in the resource and the unique ID that identifies it. The `getID()` method returns the ID for an object, and `getEObject()` returns the object with a given ID. In fact, `XMLResourceImpl` stores these mappings from both directions, so both `get` methods work in constant-time.

If an extrinsic ID has been assigned to an object, it will be recorded as the value of an additional attribute, named `id`, on the XML element that represents the object in the serialization. References to that object will be identified by just the ID. Extrinsic IDs can be mixed freely with intrinsic IDs and fragment paths in a single resource.

You are free to assign any kind of ID you want, although each ID must be unique within the resource. Moreover, like intrinsic IDs, extrinsic IDs will not resolve unless they are valid XML IDs, as defined by the XML Schema recommendation [7]. That is, they must be non-colonized names (`NCNames`).

`EcoreUtil` provides a `generateUUID()` utility method, which generates and returns a universally unique identifier that can be used as an extrinsic ID. As a convenience, you can subclass `XMLResourceImpl` and override `useUUIDs()` to return `true`, and the resource will automatically generate and record UUIDs for objects as they are attached to it.[20] UUIDs will be remembered even after the objects are detached from the resource, to be reused if the objects are reattached.

DOM Conversion

Throughout this book, we have seen several ways in which EMF acts as a unifying technology. `XMLResource` provides another one: it can load from and save to DOM directly.[21] This allows you to more easily integrate EMF applications with other XML technologies. For example, you could convert data from an XML resource into a DOM tree, then use TrAX (the Transformations API for XML) to transform it into an XHTML report or a Scalable Vector Graphics (SVG) image. Or, you could evaluate XPath queries against the tree as a convenient way to obtain certain nodes and their corresponding EMF objects.

We can obtain a DOM tree for an XML resource like this:

```
Supplier supplier = createSupplier();

ResourceSet rs = new ResourceSetImpl();
rs.getResourceFactoryRegistry().getExtensionToFactoryMap().put(
  "xml", new XMLResourceFactoryImpl());
```

---

20. "Attached" refers not just to being added directly to a resource's contents, but also to being added anywhere within a tree of contained objects beneath it.

21. As you might know, the Document Object Model (DOM) is an XML API, in which a tree of nodes is built in memory, representing the elements, attributes, text, and other XML components in a document. The nodes can then be traversed and modified directly by the client. DOM is specified by a number of W3C recommendations (see *http://www.w3.org/DOM/DOMTR*).

```
XMLResource resource = (XMLResource)rs.createResource(
  URI.createPlatformResourceURI("/project/sample.xml", true));

resource.getContents().add(supplier);

Map options = new HashMap();
options.put(XMLResource.OPTION_KEEP_DEFAULT_CONTENT, Boolean.TRUE);
Document document = resource.save(null, options, null);
DOMHelper helper = resource.getDOMHelper();
```

We are assuming that the `createSupplier()` method just builds a sample instance of the ExtendedPO2 model, consisting of a **Supplier** containing some **Customers**, **PurchaseOrders**, and **Items**. We've chosen a URI with which to create the resource, but because we never actually persist the model, its only significance is in determining what resource implementation gets created.

We add the supplier to the resource's contents, and then we invoke the three-argument form of `XMLResource.save()` to create the DOM tree. A node representing the complete document is returned. We use an option, `OPTION_KEEP_DEFAULT_CONTENT`, to ensure that nodes are created in the DOM tree to represent all of the data in the instance, including default values.

We also obtain an instance of `DOMHelper` from the resource. This interface provides a way to obtain the original EMF constructs from the corresponding DOM nodes.

Now, as an example of what we can do with this DOM tree and helper, let's use an XPath query to obtain a particular subset of purchase order items from the model. We'll use the Xalan-Java, from the Apache Software Foundation,[22] to evaluate the query:

```
String query = "//items[@USPrice > 10]";
NodeList nodes = XPathAPI.selectNodeList(document, query);
for (int i = 0, len = nodes.getLength(); i < len; i++)
{
  Node node = nodes.item(i);
  Item item = (Item)helper.getValue(node);
  // do something with each item...
}
```

We've used a simple query that will match all `items` elements having a `USPrice` attribute whose value is greater than 10.[23]

---

22. We use Xalan because the Java platform did not include a standard API for XPath before version 5.0. Some Java distributions bundle Xalan, but if yours doesn't, you'll need to install it from *http://xml.apache.org/xalan-j/* to run this example.

23. All of the details of XPath syntax can be found in the W3C Recommendation (see *http://www.w3.org/TR/xpath*).

`XPathAPI.selectNodeList()` is a convenient API provided by Xalan for evaluating a query, though it's not terribly efficient for evaluating the same query repeatedly. We pass to it a context node and the query, and the matching nodes are returned.

We iterate through the list of nodes, and for each one, we use the `DOMHelper` supplied by the resource to obtain the corresponding EMF object. Based on our knowledge of the model and its serialization, we know that each `items` element corresponds to an instance of **Item**. So, we can safely cast each value to `Item`, and process it in some way.

One important point to keep in mind when working with EMF and DOM is that the tree produced by an `XMLResource` is not kept in synch with the EMF representation. If, for instance, you were to add a new order to the supplier, you would need to call `save()` again to obtain a new DOM tree.

15.4   EMF Resource and Resource Factory Implementations

EMF provides several XML-based resource and resource factory implementations. Recall that a resource is responsible for persisting the objects that it contains, and that a resource factory is used to create and configure one type of resource. So, ultimately, it is the resource factory that determines the persistent form to be produced and consumed for the URI types against which it is registered.

In this section we will look at the resource and resource factory implementations that are included in EMF. We'll describe how and when they can be used and, when appropriate, how they differ from the base XML resource implementation.

In Section 15.2.4, we saw that, when running under Eclipse, the extension point mechanism is used to automatically register certain resource factories in the global registry, defining some default persistence formats. In this section, we'll see exactly which default resource factories are used for what. You can manually perform these registrations, as described in Section 15.2.4, to provide the same environment for stand-alone applications.

15.4.1   *Base XML*

`XMLResourceImpl` is the highly flexible base implementation for XML resources that we examined in the previous section. `XMLResourceFactoryImpl` creates vanilla instances of this resource implementation, with no customization and no additional default options set. Because it is unusual to use this implementation without some configuration or customization, `XMLResourceFactoryImpl` is not automatically registered in the global registry.

15.4.2   Generic XML

GenericXMLResourceFactoryImpl also creates instances of XMLResourceImpl, but configures them to support saving and loading of schema-conformant documents. In particular, default options are set on the resource to use extended metadata, to record an xsi:schemaLocation attribute, to use the encoded attribute style for references, and to enable a lexical handler for recording comments and CDATA sections. The resource is also set to use UTF-8 encoding and to limit the line width at 80 characters.

In addition, OPTION_XML_OPTIONS is used to enable extended support by default for loading instance data in the absence of corresponding Ecore metadata. Any resources identified by an xsi:schemaLocation attribute will be handled as XML Schemas, being demand-loaded and automatically converted to Ecore for dynamic instantiation.[24] Any unrecognized XML will also be loaded, using instances of **AnyType** to represent arbitrary XML element structure.

GenericXMLResourceFactoryImpl is not automatically registered in the global registry; however, it is often a good choice for registration against the *.xml* extension, especially when working with models defined using XML Schema.

15.4.3   XMI

XMIResourceImpl extends XMLResourceImpl to support the XML Metadata Interchange (XMI) 2.0 standard. The way that EMF maps a model to an "ordinary" XML serialization is already heavily inspired by XMI, so there really isn't a big difference between the two formats.

The following serialization highlights the differences:

```
<?xml version="1.0" encoding="ASCII"?>
<xmi:XMI xmi:version="2.0" xmlns:xmi="http://www.omg.org/XMI"
    xmlns:epo2="http://www.example.com/epo2.ecore">
  <epo2:PurchaseOrder xmi:id="_xNSb8KfZEdm0dNl1iq3EdQ"
      comment="rush order">
    <items xmi:id="_xO0F8KfZEdm0dNl1iq3EdQ" productName="apple"/>
  </epo2:PurchaseOrder>
  <epo2:PurchaseOrder xmi:id="_xO0F8afZEdm0dNl1iq3EdQ"
      comment="special promotion"
      previousOrder="_xNSb8KfZEdm0dNl1iq3EdQ">
    <items xmi:id="_xO0F8qfZEdm0dNl1iq3EdQ" productName="orange"/>
  </epo2:PurchaseOrder>
</xmi:XMI>
```

---

24. Note that this is different from the default handling described in Section 15.3.4, in which xsi:schemaLocation attributes are assumed to identify serialized Ecore models directly.

Notice that there is an additional namespace declaration on the root element, introducing the namespace for XMI, which is to be identified by the xmi prefix. The root element in an XMI serialization always includes a version attribute, from that namespace, to identify which version of XMI is being used.

Probably the most noticeable characteristic of the previous serialization is the additional xmi:XMI element at the root. This element was introduced by XMIResourceImpl because two objects were added directly to the resource's contents list. A well-formed XML document must contain exactly one root element, so XMI defines this element to handle the case where multiple top-level objects need to be represented. We've never done this with an ordinary XMLResourceImpl for good reason: it would simply persist the first object in the resource, ignoring the rest.

The last remaining difference is small: an extrinsic ID is specified by xmi:id, instead of an unqualified id attribute. Because XMI defines this attribute for this purpose, XMIResourceImpl makes use of it.

Note that, in this example, we are using automatically generated UUIDs. We have enabled them using the approach suggested in Section 15.3.6. We have registered a resource factory that creates instances of a simple subclass of XMIResourceImpl, in which useUUIDs() is overridden to return true:

```
ResourceSet rs = new ResourceSetImpl();
rs.getResourceFactoryRegistry().getExtensionToFactoryMap().put(
  Resource.Factory.Registry.DEFAULT_EXTENSION,
  new ResourceFactoryImpl()
  {
    public Resource createResource(URI uri)
    {
      return new XMIResourceImpl(uri)
      {
        protected boolean useUUIDs() { return true; }
      };
    }
  });
```

It is quite common to see UUIDs being used in XMI, although the specification does not require them. EMF's base XMIResource implementation doesn't use them because the default, index-based fragment paths are generally more efficient.

There is an interface for XMI resources, XMIResource, which defines one additional option key: OPTION_USE_XMI_TYPE takes a Boolean value, and is applicable only to save(). If it is enabled, an xmi:type attribute will be used to identify the type of a reference, where necessary, instead of xsi:type.

When running under Eclipse, XMIResourceFactoryImpl is registered as the default resource factory in the global registry. In other words, XMI is the default persistence format, to be used when there is no other specific one registered against a particular URI scheme or file extension.

15.4.4   Ecore

EcoreResourceFactoryImpl is a simple resource factory implementation that creates instances of the ordinary XMIResourceImpl, then sets their encoding to UTF-8 and enables certain default options. In particular, the encoded attribute style is used for references, and the line width is set to 80.

This resource factory is registered in the global registry against the *.ecore* and *.genmodel* file extensions. In other words, it defines the conventional format for serializing Ecore and generator models. Note, however, that a default XMIResourceImpl can still load such a serialization.

15.4.5   EMOF

As described in Section 2.6.2, MOF was split into two pieces in its version 2.0. EMOF is the new, lightweight core of the metamodel that quite closely resembles Ecore. EMOF is defined in the *Meta Object Facility (MOF) Core Specification* (see *http://www.omg.org/technology/documents/formal/MOF_Core.htm*).

Because the two models are so similar, EMF is able to support EMOF directly as an alternate XMI serialization of Ecore. EMOFResourceImpl extends XMIResourceImpl, providing this special support.

The conversion from Ecore to EMOF is very straightforward, mostly consisting of renaming classes and features. For example, here is how the SimplePO model looks when serialized by EMOFResourceImpl:

```
<?xml version="1.0" encoding="UTF-8"?>
<emof:Package xmi:version="2.0"
    xmlns:xmi="http://www.omg.org/XMI"
    xmlns:emof="http://schema.omg.org/spec/mof/2.0/emof.xmi"
    xmi:id="po" name="po" uri="http://www.example.com/SimplePO">
  <ownedType xmi:type="emof:Class" xmi:id="po.PurchaseOrder"
      name="PurchaseOrder">
    <ownedAttribute xmi:id="po.PurchaseOrder.shipTo" name="shipTo">
      <type xmi:type="emof:PrimitiveType"
          href="http://schema.omg.org/spec/mof/2.0/emof.xmi#String"/>
    </ownedAttribute>
    <ownedAttribute xmi:id="po.PurchaseOrder.billTo" name="billTo">
      <type xmi:type="emof:PrimitiveType"
          href="http://schema.omg.org/spec/mof/2.0/emof.xmi#String"/>
    </ownedAttribute>
    <ownedAttribute xmi:id="po.PurchaseOrder.items" name="items"
        upper="*" type="po.Item" isComposite="true"/>
  </ownedType>
```

```
<ownedType xmi:type="emof:Class" xmi:id="po.Item" name="Item">
  <ownedAttribute xmi:id="po.Item.productName" name="productName">
    <type xmi:type="emof:PrimitiveType"
        href="http://schema.omg.org/spec/mof/2.0/emof.xmi#String"/>
  </ownedAttribute>
  <ownedAttribute xmi:id="po.Item.quantity" name="quantity">
    <type xmi:type="emof:PrimitiveType"
        href="http://schema.omg.org/spec/mof/2.0/emof.xmi#Integer"/>
  </ownedAttribute>
  <ownedAttribute xmi:id="po.Item.price" name="price">
    <type xmi:type="emof:PrimitiveType"
        href=
        "http://www.eclipse.org/emf/2002/Ecore.emof#ecore.EFloat"/>
  </ownedAttribute>
</ownedType>
<xmi:Extension extender="http://www.eclipse.org/emf/2002/Ecore">
  <nsPrefix>po</nsPrefix>
</xmi:Extension>
</emof:Package>
```

If you compare this to the direct XMI serialization of the same model in Section 2.3.3, you'll probably see the correspondences between the two metamodels. Note, however, that Ecore includes a few features without EMOF equivalents. These are recorded in the EMOF serialization using `xmi:Extension` elements, to provide complete support for round tripping. Similarly, the one EMOF construct without an Ecore equivalent, **Tag**, is represented in Ecore using an **EAnnotation**.

`EMOFResourceFactoryImpl` creates properly initialized instances of `EMOFResourceImpl` for EMOF persistence. It is registered in the global factory registry against the *.emof* file extension. This provides transparent support for saving and loading EMOF files in Ecore editors, such as the sample editor included with EMF.

15.4.6   *Generated*

Recall from Section 12.3.2 that a resource implementation and resource factory implementation will be generated with every package that has its "Resource Type" property set to "Basic", "XML", or "XMI" in the generator. The resource implementation is a trivial subclass of `ResourceImpl`, `XMLResourceImpl`, or `XMIResourceImpl`, acting as a placeholder where you can complete or specialize the implementation. The generated resource factory implementation extends `ResourceFactoryImpl`, overriding `createResource()` to instantiate the resource implementation. If the model was created from an XML Schema, default options will be set on the resource to use extended metadata, to record an `xsi:schemaLocation` attribute, to use the encoded attribute style for references, and to enable a lexical handler for recording comments and CDATA sections. You can modify this method to set other default options for your custom resource.

This resource factory implementation is registered in the global registry against a file extension formed for the model by lowercasing the package prefix. For schema-based models, in order to save and load conforming documents, you must ensure that resources are being obtained from this generated factory or from another factory that enables extended metadata, such as the generic XML resource factory described in Section 15.4.2.

15.5 Performance Considerations

Operations involving persistent storage are naturally quite time-consuming, and XML isn't the simplest format to compose or parse. Fortunately, we can benefit from today's parsers, which, after years of development, are quite efficient. Nonetheless, persistence is an area in which attention to performance can be very well rewarded. With that in mind, as EMF evolves, it continues to add features to help improve performance. In this section, we'll look at some of these features.

15.5.1 Recommended XML Resource Options

As we saw in Section 15.3.3, resources based on XMLResourceImpl recognize a number of performance options, several of which are strongly recommended for regular use. For saving, the following two performance options are recommended:

○ OPTION_CONFIGURATION_CACHE

○ OPTION_USE_CACHED_LOOKUP_TABLE

These options are described in Section 15.3.3.

There is one other option, OPTION_FORMATTED, which you might want to use to improve the performance of saving and, subsequently, loading the resulting document. Disabling this option (setting it to Boolean.FALSE) won't affect the structure of the document, but whitespace and line breaks will be omitted. This means fewer bytes have to be written and read, but the serialization will be less human-readable.

For loading, the following five performance options are recommended:

○ OPTION_DEFER_ATTACHMENT

○ OPTION_DEFER_IDREF_RESOLUTION

○ OPTION_USE_DEPRECATED_METHODS

○ OPTION_USE_PARSER_POOL

○ OPTION_USE_XML_NAME_TO_FEATURE_MAP

For example, the following resource factory implementation creates XMI resources with all of the recommended options enabled by default:

```
public class PerformantXMIResourceFactoryImpl
  extends ResourceFactoryImpl
{
  private List lookupTable = new ArrayList();
  private XMLParserPool parserPool = new XMLParserPoolImpl();
  private Map nameToFeatureMap = new HashMap();

  public Resource createResource(URI uri)
  {
    XMIResource resource = new XMIResourceImpl(uri);

    Map saveOptions = resource.getDefaultSaveOptions();
    saveOptions.put(XMLResource.OPTION_CONFIGURATION_CACHE,
                 Boolean.TRUE);
    saveOptions.put(XMLResource.OPTION_USE_CACHED_LOOKUP_TABLE,
                 lookupTable);

    Map loadOptions = resource.getDefaultLoadOptions();
    loadOptions.put(XMLResource.OPTION_DEFER_ATTACHMENT,
                 Boolean.TRUE);
    loadOptions.put(XMLResource.OPTION_DEFER_IDREF_RESOLUTION,
                 Boolean.TRUE);
    loadOptions.put(XMLResource.OPTION_USE_DEPRECATED_METHODS,
                 Boolean.TRUE);
    loadOptions.put(XMLResource.OPTION_USE_PARSER_POOL, parserPool);
    loadOptions.put(XMLResource.OPTION_USE_XML_NAME_TO_FEATURE_MAP,
                 nameToFeatureMap);
    return resource;
  }
}
```

For simplicity, the lookup table, parser pool, and name-feature map are shared among all resources created by an instance of this factory. Note, however, that the lookup table and name-feature map are not thread-safe, so if the factory is going to be used across multiple threads, they would need to be created within `ThreadLocals`. You must also be careful never to share the name-feature map among resources that will load instances of different models with conflicting qualified names.

15.5.2 *Caching Intrinsic IDs*

As discussed at the end of Section 15.2.3, one attribute in a class can be designated as the ID attribute, meaning that the value of that attribute will be used as the URI fragment that uniquely identifies instances of the class within a resource. Unfortunately, locating an object by its intrinsic ID is very slow: the resource must iterate over all of the objects it contains, looking at that attribute on each one.

Usually, the ID attribute of an object shouldn't change during the time that object is contained in a resource. So, `ResourceImpl` provides a mechanism for caching the mapping of intrinsic IDs to objects. The cache is enabled as follows:

```
((ResourceImpl)resource).setIntrinsicIDToEObjectMap(new HashMap());
```

When the resource needs to locate an object by ID, this map, if non-null, will first be consulted. If the given ID is not found in the map, it will iterate over all of the objects, as usual, and if it finds the one it's looking for, the mapping will be recorded. The next time, that object will be quickly located. Mappings will also be recorded as objects are attached to the resource, so it's a good idea to initialize the map immediately after creating the resource.

The `setIntrinsicIDToEObjectMap()` method is "hidden away" on the implementation, not exposed on the `Resource` interface, because using it requires that you assume responsibility for maintaining the integrity of the cache. In particular, if the value of an object's ID attribute is changed, you must update the map accordingly. Entries will be automatically removed only as objects are detached from the resource.

15.5.3 Caching Resource URIs

Locating a resource in a resource set by its URI can also be a fairly expensive operation. It involves iterating over all of the resources in the set, normalizing each one, and comparing it to the normalized target URI. Failing that, other means can be used, including looking in the package registry.

So, if there are many resources in the set or if they require normalization, it can be useful to record the mappings from URIs to resources as they are computed. `ResourceSetImpl` provides another caching mechanism for this, which is enabled as follows:

```
((ResourceSetImpl)resourceSet).setURIResourceMap(new HashMap());
```

This map is used analogously to the intrinsic ID cache discussed in the previous section. If non-null, the map is consulted by the resource set before it tries to locate a resource. It is also populated as the URI-resource mappings are computed.

Again, this method appears only on the implementation class because, when using it, you must take responsibility for ensuring the map is in a consistent state. For example, if you change the URI of a resource in the set, you must update the map as well. Entries will be automatically removed as resources are removed from the set.

15.6 Custom Storage for Active Objects

A somewhat hidden, but very powerful, feature of EMF provides the ability to completely change the storage implementation of the **EObjects** in your model. Using this feature, the in-memory storage of active objects is replaced by an external backing store. This store could be implemented with a relational database, so that the EMF APIs "read through" and "write through" active objects to persistent storage. When using this mechanism, EMF's resource-based persistence framework, although still available, is usually not needed.

As we've seen in previous chapters, the usual in-memory storage of an **EObject**'s features is in one of two places:

1. In instance variables of the generated classes, if the model is generated.

2. In the default base implementation of EObject, if the feature or model is dynamic.

For the moment, let's consider the dynamic case only. In this case, the in-memory data storage is in a dynamically allocated array maintained by the default EObject implementation class, EObjectImpl. An alternative EObject implementation class, EStoreEObjectImpl, allocates no storage, but instead implements the reflective methods, for example, eGet(), by delegation to another object, usually a singleton, that implements an interface named EStore.

The EStore interface and the methods to associate a store implementation with an **EObject** are provided in the InternalEObject interface. They look something like this:

```
public interface InternalEObject extends EObject
{
  ...
  EStore eStore();
  void eSetStore(EStore store);

  public interface EStore
  {
    int NO_INDEX = -1;
    Object get(InternalEObject object, EStructuralFeature feature,
            int index);
    Object set(InternalEObject object, EStructuralFeature feature,
            int index, Object value);
    boolean isSet(InternalEObject object,
            EStructuralFeature feature);
    void unset(InternalEObject object, EStructuralFeature feature);
```

```
    boolean isEmpty(InternalEObject object,
                    EStructuralFeature feature);
    int size(InternalEObject object, EStructuralFeature feature);
    boolean contains(InternalEObject object,
                    EStructuralFeature feature, Object value);
    int indexOf(InternalEObject object, EStructuralFeature feature,
                Object value);
    int lastIndexOf(InternalEObject object,
                    EStructuralFeature feature, Object value);
    void add(InternalEObject object, EStructuralFeature feature,
            int index, Object value);
    Object remove(InternalEObject object, EStructuralFeature feature,
                    int index);
    Object move(InternalEObject object, EStructuralFeature feature,
                int targetIndex, int sourceIndex);
    void clear(InternalEObject object, EStructuralFeature feature);
    Object[] toArray(InternalEObject object,
                    EStructuralFeature feature);
    Object[] toArray(InternalEObject object,
                    EStructuralFeature feature, Object[] array);
    int hashCode(InternalEObject object, EStructuralFeature feature);

    InternalEObject getContainer(InternalEObject object);
    EStructuralFeature getContainingFeature(InternalEObject object);
    EObject create(EClass eClass);
  }
}
```

As you can see, the `eStore()` and `eSetStore()` methods are used to get and set the store implementation associated with an **EObject**. In EMF's default implementation base class, `EObjectImpl`, the `eSetStore()` method simply throws `UnsupportedOperationException`, but this implementation is overridden in `EStoreEObjectImpl` to set the store that it will use.

If you now look at the `EStore` interface, you can see that it includes a complete set of methods for managing the storage of single and multi-valued **EStructuralFeature**s. As you might have guessed, `EStoreEObjectImpl` uses the first four `EStore` methods, `get()`, `set()`, `isSet()`, and `unset()`, to implement the `EObject` methods `eGet()`, `eSet()`, `eIsSet()`, and `eUnset()`, respectively.

The second group of methods in the `EStore` interface is used to implement multi-valued features. Class `EStoreEObjectImpl` uses an `EStore`-specific `EList` implementation class to implement such features. This `EList` class delegates its implementation to these `EStore` methods, for example, `List.add()` delegates to `EStore.add()`.

The last group of methods in `EStore` is used to implement the `EObject` methods `eContainer()` and `eContainingFeature()`, and finally, to provide a convenient factory method for creating instances of `EStoreEObjectImpl` that use that store for their implementation.

15.6.1 Using an EStore

A user who wants to override the storage implementation for a model must implement the `EStore` interface. A typical implementation would look something like this:

```
public class MyEStore implements InternalEObject.EStore
{
  Object get(InternalEObject object, EStructuralFeature feature,
             int index)
  {
    // retrieve the value of "feature" for the specified "object"
    Object result = ...
    return result;
  }

  Object set(InternalEObject object, EStructuralFeature feature,
             int index, Object value)
  {
    // set the "feature" of the specified ìobjectî to the specified
    // "value"
    ...
  }

  // implementation of remaining EStore methods
  ...

  public static EStore INSTANCE = new MyEStore();
}
```

We'll leave it as an exercise for the reader to actually implement these methods.[25] They would typically be implemented to manage the data in some "real" back-end store, for example, a relational database.

Given an `EStore` implementation, we need to "hook up" the store with the objects that should use it. To do this, we must set the store of each object immediately after it has been created (i.e., before we start to set any of its features). If our model is dynamic, we can do this by simply using the create method on our store to create the instances:

```
EObject someObject = MyStore.INSTANCE.create(someEClass);
```

Alternatively, we can create, and then use, a specialized factory class that overrides the `EFactory.create()` method, something like this:

---

25. Note that there is a test class provided with EMF, `EStoreEObjectImpl.EStoreImpl`, that uses a `HashMap` to implement the `EStore` interface.

```
public MyFactory extends EFactoryImpl
{
  public EObject create(EClass eClass)
  {
    InternalEObject newObject =
      (InternalEObject)super.create(eClass);
    newObject.eSetStore(MyEStore.INSTANCE);
  }

  ...

}
```

Either way, we now have everything we need to create objects that use our custom storage implementation. We've completely replaced the default implementation provided by the EMF base class, EObjectImpl, but only if the model is a dynamic one. If the model is generated, there is still more to do.

15.6.2   EStore and Generated Classes

As we've seen, an instance of the EStore interface can be used to change the implementation of the EObject reflective methods. Recall from Chapter 10, however, that generated EMF classes normally override the reflective methods to simply call the generated type-safe methods. For example, Section 10.7.2 showed how class PurchaseOrderImpl, from the PrimerPO model, would include a generated eGet() method that looks something like this:

```
public Object eGet(int featureID, boolean resolve, Boolean coreType)
{
  switch (featureID)
  {
    case PPOPackage.PURCHASE_ORDER__COMMENT:
      return getComment();
    case PPOPackage.PURCHASE_ORDER__ORDER_DATE:
      return getOrderDate();
            ...
  }
  return super.eGet(featureID, resolve, coreType);
}
```

As you can see, this pattern overrides the use of the EStore for any features with generated implementations.

From an implementation perspective, setting a store and generating code constitutes using contradictory features. The store provides an EStore-based storage implementation, while the generated implementation classes provide their own. However, the use of generated type-safe interfaces along with a store is not contradictory.

To support this feature, EMF provides a code generator option, "Feature Delegation", which can be set to "Reflective" to generate type-safe interfaces with implementations that do not provide their own storage.[26] Instead, the feature accessors delegate to the reflective methods. For example, the generated `get()` method for a simple feature will simply call the reflective `eGet()` method, instead of returning an instance variable as described in Section 10.3. The `getComment()` method in class `PurchaseOrderImpl` will look like this:

```
public String getComment()
{
  return
    (String)eGet(PPOPackage.Literals.PURCHASE_ORDER__COMMENT, true);
}
```

The other generated methods, `set()`, `isSet()`, and `unset()`, follow similar patterns.

When the reflective delegation pattern is used, there are also no overrides for the reflective methods, like `eGet()`, generated in the implementation class. All of the generated type-safe methods will therefore default to the base implementation that, if store-based, will then delegate to the associated store.

To complete the picture, however, we still need to do two things:

1. Change the base of our generated implementation class to be `EStoreEObjectImpl`.

2. Set the store in the generated factory class.

For the first, we can simply set the "Root Extends Class" generator property (see Section 12.3.1) to "org.eclipse.emf.ecore.impl.EStoreEObjectImpl". The second is done in a similar way to the dynamic factory override suggested in the previous section. However, we will incorporate the standard EMF pattern for customizing the implementation of methods in a generated class discussed in Section 10.11:

```
/**
 * @generated
 */
public class MyModelFactoryImpl extends ...
{
```

---

26. We saw virtual delegation, the other non-default feature delegation pattern available via this generator option, in Section 10.10.1. The option was also discussed in Section 12.3.1.

```
/**
 * @generated
 */
public EObject createGen(EClass eClass)
{
  ...
}

public EObject create(EClass eClass)
{
   InternalEObject newObject = (InternalEObject)createGen(eClass);
   newObject.eSetStore(MyEStore.INSTANCE);
}

...
}
```

As you can see, here we simply renamed the create() method in our generated FactoryImpl class to createGen(), and then implemented the create() method to call it and then set the store on the resulting object.

With these changes in place, our generated type-safe model will now use the custom store, MyStore, for its implementation.

CHAPTER 16

Client Programming Toolbox

The availability of metadata and the notification framework, as we've already seen in previous chapters, are responsible for a great deal of the power offered to applications running on the EMF runtime. One of their particularly important benefits is to enable the creation of generic, reusable tools for working with EMF objects. This chapter takes a peek inside the toolbox that no developer using EMF should be without. It examines many of the tools already provided by the framework, and also discusses how to reuse and adapt them to most effectively write your own.

One class that will come up often is `EcoreUtil`. This class consists only of static utility methods and other nested classes, so it should never be instantiated or extended. In it, you'll find a wealth of handy tools. In fact, if you ever find that you're thinking about writing a generic EMF utility of some kind, you should probably look in `EcoreUtil` first, as there's a reasonably good chance it already exists.

We will use the ExtendedPO2 model for the examples in this chapter, except for those in Section 16.3, for which we'll use ExtendedPO3.

16.1 Tree Iterators and Switches

In Chapters 2 and 10 we saw that EMF can optionally generate an adapter factory and corresponding switch class for a model package. We described how the adapter factory uses the switch class in its implementation to dispatch to an appropriate `create()` method based on the type of object being adapted. You might be wondering what else the switch class is good for. Let's look at a simple example.

In this example, we're going to use the generated EPO2Switch class to implement a simple Visitor-like [3] pattern for visiting a purchase order model instance. We'll start by creating an anonymous visitor class, like this:

```
EPO2Switch visitor = new EPO2Switch()
{
  public Object caseItem(Item object)
  {
    System.out.println("visiting Item: " + object.getProductName());
    return Boolean.TRUE;
  }
  public Object caseUSAddress(USAddress object)
  {
    System.out.println("visiting USAddress: " + object.getName());
    return Boolean.TRUE;
  }
  public Object casePurchaseOrder(PurchaseOrder object)
  {
    System.out.println("visiting PurchaseOrder: " +
                       object.getComment());
    return Boolean.TRUE;
  }
  public Object caseSupplier(Supplier object)
  {
    System.out.println("visiting Supplier: " + object.getName());
    return Boolean.TRUE;
  }
  public Object caseCustomer(Customer object)
  {
    System.out.println("visiting Customer: " +
                       object.getCustomerID());
    return Boolean.TRUE;
  }
  public Object caseGlobalAddress(GlobalAddress object)
  {
    System.out.println("visiting GlobalAddress: " +
                       object.getName());
    return Boolean.TRUE;
  }
  public Object defaultCase(EObject object)
  {
    System.out.println("visiting Unknown object: " + object);
    return Boolean.TRUE;
  }
};
```

As you might recall from Section 10.9, the generated EPO2Switch class includes a doSwitch() method that efficiently switches based on the type of the given object. It then passes that object to an appropriate type-specific handler method. As generated, these methods—caseItem(), caseUSAddress(), and so on—simply return null. Here we've created a subclass of EPO2Switch, overriding each case() method to print a string indicating that it has been visited. In a more useful example, we would use each case() method to perform some action on the object.

Notice that all of our overrides return the constant Boolean.TRUE. We just selected this value arbitrarily: the exact return value is irrelevant, as long as it is not null. The reason for this is that the generated doSwitch() method doesn't just call a single case() method for each class. Indeed, if the selected case() method returns null, it then walks up the hierarchy of supertypes, calling their corresponding case() methods. This stops only when one of them indicates that the case has been handled by returning a non-null result. The defaultCase() method is finally called if no type-specific case() method handles the case. It is also invoked directly for any object whose type is not from the switch's package. So, as our override illustrates, it acts as a kind of catch-all case of last resort.

Now that we've created a visitor class, we need some objects to visit. Let's assume we have a purchase order instance document, *sample.epo2*, that contains the following:

```
<epo2:Supplier xmi:version="2.0" ... name="S1">
  <customers orders="//@orders.0 //@orders.1"/>
  <customers customerID="1"/>
  <customers customerID="2" orders="//@orders.2"/>
  <orders comment="P0" orderDate="2007.10.01"
      status="Complete" customer="//@customers.0">
    <items productName="I2" quantity="5" USPrice="10"/>
    <items productName="I3" quantity="6" USPrice="20"/>
    <items productName="I4" quantity="7" USPrice="30"/>
  </orders>
  <orders comment="P1" customer="//@customers.0">
    <items productName="I1" quantity="1" USPrice="5"/>
  </orders>
  <orders comment="P2" customer="//@customers.2">
    <items productName="I1" quantity="2" USPrice="5"/>
  </orders>
</epo2:Supplier>
```

If we load this document, we can then use the EcoreUtil.getAllContents() method to obtain an iterator over its full contents:

```
ResourceSet resourceSet = new ResourceSetImpl();
URI uri = URI.createPlatformResourceURI("/project/sample.epo2");
Resource resource = resourceSet.getResource(uri, true);

for (Iterator iter = EcoreUtil.getAllContents(resource, true);
```

```
        iter.hasNext(); )
{
  EObject eObject = (EObject)iter.next();
  visitor.doSwitch(eObject);
}
```

We simply use the iterator to walk over the contents and call
visitor.doSwitch() for each node in the tree. The doSwitch() method subsequently calls out to the appropriate case() method, based on the type of
object encountered. If we run this program, it produces the following output:

```
visiting Supplier: S1
visiting Customer: 0
visiting Customer: 1
visiting Customer: 2
visiting PurchaseOrder: P0
visiting Item: I2
visiting Item: I3
visiting Item: I4
visiting PurchaseOrder: P1
visiting Item: I1
visiting PurchaseOrder: P2
visiting Item: I1
```

As you can see, the iterator returned by EcoreUtil.getAllContents()
performs a depth-first traversal of the containment structure of the model.
Although we haven't yet used it as such, this iterator is actually a tree iterator. As
mentioned in Chapter 14, EMF defines a TreeIterator interface that extends
java.util.Iterator, adding a prune() method. Calling prune() while iterating causes the following next() call to skip over any children of the current
node. We can use this capability to write efficient visitors that skip over entire
subtrees that aren't of interest. Consider the following modification to the loop
in our example:

```
for (TreeIterator iter = EcoreUtil.getAllContents(resource, true);
     iter.hasNext(); )
{
  EObject eObject = (EObject)iter.next();
  if (visitor.doSwitch(eObject) == Boolean.FALSE)
  {
    iter.prune();
  }
}
```

This allows the switch to signal that a prune should be performed by returning Boolean.FALSE. If, for example, we decide that we do not want to go any

deeper in the tree than purchase orders (i.e., if we want to skip all items and addresses), we can simply change the `casePurchaseOrder()` method in the switch like this:

```
public Object casePurchaseOrder(PurchaseOrder object)
{
   System.out.println("visiting PurchaseOrder: " +
                      object.getComment());
   return Boolean.TRUE
   return Boolean.FALSE;
}
```

There are several different forms of the `getAllContents()` utility method in `EcoreUtil`:

```
getAllContents(EObject eObject, boolean resolve)
getAllContents(Resource resource, boolean resolve)
getAllContents(ResourceSet resourceSet, boolean resolve)
getAllContents(Collection emfObjects, boolean resolve)
getAllContents(Collection emfObjects)
```

Notice that there are forms that take a single **EObject**, a resource, and a resource set. The last two forms take a collection that can include any mix of the three. The iterators that they return actually yield the objects in the specified collection, along with their contents. By contrast, the first three forms return iterators that strictly yield the contents of the given object. In this section, we have been using the second form, passing in a resource and getting back an iterator over all of the **EObjects** in it.

All but the last of these methods also take a second argument, specifying whether the iterator should automatically resolve proxies. This is only relevant in the case of cross-resource containment, which is not in play in this particular example. We have chosen to pass `true` quite arbitrarily, only because a resolving iterator is a more generally useful utility. Note that the last form of the method, which does not take a second argument, never resolves proxies.

`EcoreUtil` also includes several forms of the closely related `getAllProperContents()` method:

```
getAllProperContents(EObject eObject, boolean resolve)
getAllProperContents(Resource resource, boolean resolve)
getAllProperContents(ResourceSet resourceSet, boolean resolve)
getAllProperContents(Collection emfObjects, boolean resolve)
```

The tree iterators returned by these methods do not follow cross-resource containment references, skipping over any objects that are not in the same resource as their container. Again, the different forms of the method take different types of input, and they all accept a second argument specifying whether the resulting iterator should automatically resolve proxies. Note that it doesn't usually make sense to obtain a non-resolving iterator over the proper contents of a resource, unless you know that all the contents have already been visited and any proxies resolved. This is because an unresolved containment proxy actually appears to be in the same resource as its container, so it will be included among the objects yielded by the iterator. The only benefit to not resolving proxies is a slight performance increase.

16.2 Adapters

EMF adapters are what other programming frameworks call observers. We call them adapters because, in addition to merely observing changes, they also allow you to extend the behavior of objects without subclassing.

16.2.1 Object Adapting

Let's consider a trivial adapter whose job is to keep track of the number of changes being made to instances of classes in the purchase order model. To be specific, we're going to define three static counters to keep track of changes to instances of classes **PurchaseOrder**, **Item**, and **Address**, and then use adapters to increment the appropriate counter in response to change notifications from the objects. We're going to look at three different ways of doing this:

1. Attaching an adapter to each object by simply adding it to their eAdapters lists.

2. Using a simple adapter factory adapt() call to attach the same adapter to the objects.

3. Using the generated purchase order adapter factory to attach type-specific adapters to the objects.

Although this example is quite trivial, it should give you a sense of how these three approaches compare, and why you might choose one over the others.

For the first approach, we start by defining a generic adapter class, like this:

```
public class ChangeCounterAdapter extends AdapterImpl
{
  public static int purchaseOrderCount;
```

```
  public static int itemCount;
  public static int addressCount;

  public void notifyChanged(Notification notification)
  {
    if (notification.getNotifier() instanceof PurchaseOrder)
      ++purchaseOrderCount;
    else if (notification.getNotifier() instanceof Item)
      ++itemCount;
    else if (notification.getNotifier() instanceof Address)
      ++addressCount;
  }
}
```

Here we've created a simple subclass of the framework's adapter implementation base class AdapterImpl. We've implemented the notifyChanged() method to check what type of object is sending the notification and then, based on that, to increment the appropriate one of three counters. Because static fields are used for these counters, we consider a ChangeCounterAdapter to be stateless and, as we will soon see, a single instance can be used to adapt multiple objects.

Notice that we use the getNotifier() method, on the notification argument, to access the affected object. In addition to getNotifier(), the Notification interface includes methods for retrieving the notification (event) type, the feature (or just the feature's ID) that has changed, and the old and new values of the changed feature, among other things. For example, if we wanted to ignore "touch" notifications (i.e., non-state-changing events), we could have checked the isTouch() method, like this:

```
  public void notifyChanged(Notification notification)
  {
    if (notification.isTouch()) return;
    if (notification.getNotifier() instanceof PurchaseOrder)
      . . .
  }
```

Now that we have defined our adapter, we need to add one to an instance of the purchase order model. Here's a simple program that does that:

```
ChangeCounterAdapter adapter = new ChangeCounterAdapter();

USAddress address = EPO2Factory.eINSTANCE.createUSAddress();
address.eAdapters().add(adapter);
address.setName("123 Maple Street");

Item item = EPO2Factory.eINSTANCE.createItem();
item.eAdapters().add(adapter);
```

```
item.setProductName("Apples");
item.setQuantity(20);

PurchaseOrder purchaseOrder =
    EPO2Factory.eINSTANCE.createPurchaseOrder();
purchaseOrder.eAdapters().add(adapter);
purchaseOrder.setBillTo(address);
purchaseOrder.getItems().add(item);

System.out.println("PurchaseOrder changes: " +
                ChangeCounterAdapter.purchaseOrderCount);
System.out.println("Item changes: " +
                ChangeCounterAdapter.itemCount);
System.out.println("Address changes: " +
                ChangeCounterAdapter.addressCount);
```

As you can see, we're using a single adapter to compute the number of changes that occur while instantiating a purchase order, an item, and an address. As we said it would, our first approach simply attaches the adapter to each object by adding directly to the eAdapters list; that is, by calling eAdapters().add(). We create the adapter and then attach it to the objects immediately after they are created.

If we run this program, each time an attribute or reference of any of the three created (and adapted) objects is set, the adapter will receive a change notification and increment the appropriate counter. In case you're interested, the program produces the following output:

```
PurchaseOrder changes: 2
Item changes: 3
Address changes: 1
```

Notice that the item, perhaps unexpectedly, has sent a third notification when it was added to the purchase order because of the bidirectional reference between the two.

Now let's move on to our second approach of using an adapter factory instead of adding directly to the eAdapters lists. The idea behind this approach is to introduce a factory that has responsibility for creating, attaching, and managing adapters for the client code. We can use the same adapter class, ChangeCounterAdapter, but we'll need to add one more method to it:

```
public class ChangeCounterAdapter extends AdapterImpl
{
    public static int purchaseOrderCount;
    public static int itemCount;
    public static int addressCount;
```

```
public void notifyChanged(Notification notification)
{
  if (notification.getNotifier() instanceof PurchaseOrder)
    ++purchaseOrderCount;
  else if (notification.getNotifier() instanceof Item)
    ++itemCount;
  else if (notification.getNotifier() instanceof Address)
    ++addressCount;
}

public boolean isAdapterForType(Object type)
{
  return type == ChangeCounterAdapter.class;
}
}
```

The isAdapterForType() method will be used by adapter factories when checking if an adapter of a specified type is already attached to an object. Remember that adapter factories are used to attach adapters, which usually represent some kind, or "type," of behavioral extensions to the object. This method, then, allows the adapter to declare what type of behavior it provides. In our example, we're using the class ChangeCounterAdapter.class to represent the adapter's type.[1]

Now that the adapter knows its type, we need an adapter factory capable of adapting objects with adapters of this type. We can create such an adapter factory like this:

```
public class ChangeCounterAdapterFactory extends AdapterFactoryImpl
{
  protected static final ChangeCounterAdapter ADAPTER =
    new ChangeCounterAdapter();

  protected Adapter createAdapter(Notifier target)
  {
    return ADAPTER;
  }

  public boolean isFactoryForType(Object type)
  {
    return type == ChangeCounterAdapter.class;
  }
}
```

---

1. Notice that you can use anything you want as an adapter type; it is represented by a java.lang.Object. The two most commonly used types are java.lang.Class and java.lang.String.

We are subclassing the framework base class `AdapterFactoryImpl`, which provides most of the implementation. Most importantly, its `adapt(Notifier target, Object type)` method is the one that a client calls whenever it needs to obtain an adapter. It searches through the given target object's `eAdapters` list, calling `isAdapterForType()` on each adapter. If there is an existing adapter that returns `true`, it is returned. Otherwise, `createAdapter()` is called to obtain an appropriate adapter, which is then attached to the target and returned to the client.

So, the first thing we needed to do was implement `createAdapter()`. Because we still have a stateless adapter implementation that supports all of the objects we're adapting, we can again just use a single instance of `ChangeCounterAdapter`. Thus, `createAdapter()` is implemented to simply return that instance.

The other method we have implemented, `isFactoryForType()`, is similarly straightforward. In general, this method should return `true` for all of the "types" of the adapters the factory creates. In other words, `isFactoryForType()` should return `true` for a given type if the adapter factory can create an adapter whose `isAdapterForType()` returns `true` for it.[2] In this example, we're only using this adapter factory for our single adapter type, so it has the same implementation as the adapter's `isAdapterForType()` method, returning `true` only for the type `ChangeCounterAdapter.class`.

Using the adapter factory approach, we would now change the test program to attach the adapters like this:

```
AdapterFactory adapterFactory = new ChangeCounterAdapterFactory();

USAddress address = EPO2Factory.eINSTANCE.createUSAddress();
adapterFactory.adapt(address, ChangeCounterAdapter.class);
address.setName("123 Maple Street");

Item item = EPO2Factory.eINSTANCE.createItem();
adapterFactory.adapt(item, ChangeCounterAdapter.class);
item.setProductName("Apples");
item.setQuantity(20);

PurchaseOrder purchaseOrder =
  EPO2Factory.eINSTANCE.createPurchaseOrder();
adapterFactory.adapt(purchaseOrder, ChangeCounterAdapter.class);
purchaseOrder.setBillTo(address);
purchaseOrder.getItems().add(item);
```

---

2. The `isFactoryForType()` method is typically used when we need to select a factory to create an adapter of a specific type. We'll see an example of this in the next section.

```
System.out.println("PurchaseOrder changes: " +
                    ChangeCounterAdapter.purchaseOrderCount);
...
```

Running this program produces exactly the same output as before. The difference in doing it this way is that our test program no longer needs to create and keep any relevant adapters. Instead, it repeatedly calls the adapt() method on the adapter factory, specifying each object to adapt and the type of adapter it needs. In our simple example, this approach doesn't really add much value. That is because we're only using a single stateless adapter for all our objects, and we are just adding it to each object and never accessing it again. Using adapter factories would, however, prove advantageous if we wanted to use multiple adapters of different types and pass the (adapted) objects around, retrieving existing adapters at various points in the code as needed.

Now that we're using an adapter factory, let's move on to our third, and final, approach: using type-specific adapters. To do this we'll create another adapter factory, but this time it will subclass the generated EPO2AdapterFactory, like this:

```
public class TypedChangeCounterAdapterFactory
    extends EPO2AdapterFactory
{
  protected static Adapter purchaseOrderAdapter;
  protected static Adapter itemAdapter;
  protected static Adapter addressAdapter;

  public Adapter createPurchaseOrderAdapter()
  {
    if (purchaseOrderAdapter == null)
    {
      purchaseOrderAdapter = new ChangeCounterAdapter()
      {
        public void notifyChanged(Notification notification) {
          ++purchaseOrderCount;
        }
      };
    }
    return purchaseOrderAdapter;
  }

  public Adapter createItemAdapter()
  {
    if (itemAdapter == null)
    {
      itemAdapter = new ChangeCounterAdapter()
      {
        public void notifyChanged(Notification notification) {
          ++itemCount;
```

```
      }
    };
  }
  return itemAdapter;
}

public Adapter createAddressAdapter()
{
  if (addressAdapter == null)
  {
    addressAdapter = new ChangeCounterAdapter()
    {
      public void notifyChanged(Notification notification) {
        ++addressCount;
      }
    };
  }
  return addressAdapter;
}

public boolean isFactoryForType(Object type)
{
  return type == ChangeCounterAdapter.class;
}
}
```

The primary difference from the previous implementation is that instead of implementing the single `createAdapter()` method, here we implement specific create methods for each type of adapter. You might recall from Chapter 10 that a generated adapter factory, such as our base class `EPO2AdapterFactory`, implements the `createAdapter()` method by delegating to type-specific `create()` methods, which by default return `null`. A derived class, like ours, can then simply override the appropriate methods to return type-specific adapters. Notice that in our case, we simply use anonymous subclasses of the generic `ChangeCounterAdapter`, each of which overrides the `notifyChanged()` method to increment the appropriate counter. This clearly illustrates the benefit of the typed adapter approach: no `instanceof` checking. We now have a pure object-oriented implementation.

The base adapter factory is implemented using the generated switch class. Because it uses a constant-time `switch` statement to select the appropriate type-specific `create()` method, this approach also scales better, should we wish to add support for more classes. As explained in Section 16.1, the switch class also has explicit support for class inheritance, which is why we are able to override `createAddressAdapter()` and provide a single adapter for all instances of the abstract **Address** class.

Now that we have a different adapter implementation for each supported class, clearly we can no longer use a single instance as the adapter for every object. However, because the adapters are still stateless, we do not need to create a new one for each object being adapted, either. The middle ground we have chosen is very common for stateless adapters: a single, static adapter instance is being shared among objects of the same type. We are supporting three classes, so we can have up to three shared adapters, and we're deferring creating them until they are actually needed.

In spite of the fact that we have now significantly changed the implementation and management of our adapters, the impact on our client code will be minimal. All we need to do is switch to the new adapter factory:

```
AdapterFactory adapterFactory =
   new TypedChangeCounterAdapterFactory();

USAddress address = EPO2Factory.eINSTANCE.createUSAddress();
adapterFactory.adapt(address, ChangeCounterAdapter.class);
address.setName("123 Maple Street");
...
```

This robustness is another important benefit of using adapter factories.

16.2.2 Behavioral Extensions

Now that we've looked at three ways of adding an adapter, we can see how they compare. The first approach was, in fact, the simplest for our trivial example of adding a single observer to an object. That approach, however, would not be particularly useful if we wanted our adapter to actually provide some kind of extended behavior to the object, instead of simply counting change events. Let's consider a slightly different example, which does involve a behavioral extension.

Let's assume that instead of having static counters to keep track of changes to "types of objects," we want to keep track of the changes at the instance level. Imagine as well that we want to "extend" the interface of the objects in the purchase order model (without subclassing) with the following methods:

```
public interface InstanceChangeCounter
{
   public int getCount();
   public boolean isMoreActive(EObject otherObject);
}
```

The method `getCount()` will return the number of changes that have occurred in the object, and `isMoreActive()` will return `true` if the object has changed more than the specified `otherObject` argument.

Here's an adapter and corresponding adapter factory that implement this extension:

```
public class InstanceChangeCounterAdapter extends AdapterImpl
  implements InstanceChangeCounter
{
  protected int count;

  public int getCount()
  {
    return count;
  }

  public boolean isMoreActive(EObject otherObject)
  {
    InstanceChangeCounter otherAdapter = (InstanceChangeCounter)
      InstanceChangeCounterAdapterFactory.INSTANCE.adapt(
                        otherObject, InstanceChangeCounter.class);
    return otherAdapter == null || otherAdapter.getCount() < count;
  }

  public void notifyChanged(Notification notification)
  {
    ++count;
  }

  public boolean isAdapterForType(Object type)
  {
    return type == InstanceChangeCounter.class;
  }
}

public class InstanceChangeCounterAdapterFactory
  extends AdapterFactoryImpl
{
  public boolean isFactoryForType(Object type)
  {
    return type == InstanceChangeCounter.class;
  }

  protected Adapter createAdapter(Notifier target)
  {
    return new InstanceChangeCounterAdapter();
  }

  public static final AdapterFactory INSTANCE =
    new InstanceChangeCounterAdapterFactory();
}
```

As you can see, the adapter factory uses the same approach as ChangeCounterAdapterFactory from the previous section: because we're using a single adapter implementation for all objects, our adapter factory just extends

AdapterFactoryImpl. The major difference, however, is that createAdapter() creates and returns a new instance of the now stateful adapter each time it is called; we cannot use a singleton now that we have an instance variable, count, in the adapter.

As for the adapter class itself, it has a fairly straightforward implementation. The isMoreActive() method is the most interesting. Notice how it uses the adapter factory to access the adapter that provides the InstanceChangeCounter interface for the otherObject argument, in order to do its comparison. The adapter is acting as a client of the extended behavior in its own implementation. We're able to access the adapter factory from this method because we have made a singleton instance available as the static INSTANCE field in class InstanceChangeCounterAdapterFactory. An even more flexible alternative would have been to add a field to InstanceChangeCounterAdapter so that each adapter could record and use the adapter factory that created it.

To test this extension, we can use the same set of objects as in the previous example:

```
AdapterFactory adapterFactory =
   InstanceChangeCounterAdapterFactory.INSTANCE;

USAddress address = EPO2Factory.eINSTANCE.createUSAddress();
adapterFactory.adapt(address, InstanceChangeCounter.class);
address.setName("123 Maple Street");

Item item = EPO2Factory.eINSTANCE.createItem();
adapterFactory.adapt(item, InstanceChangeCounter.class);
item.setProductName("Apples");
item.setQuantity(20);

PurchaseOrder purchaseOrder =
   EPO2Factory.eINSTANCE.createPurchaseOrder();
adapterFactory.adapt(purchaseOrder, InstanceChangeCounter.class);
purchaseOrder.setBillTo(address);
purchaseOrder.getItems().add(item);

InstanceChangeCounter poChangeCounter = (InstanceChangeCounter)
   adapterFactory.adapt(purchaseOrder, InstanceChangeCounter.class);

System.out.println("purchase order changes: " +
                   poChangeCounter.getCount());
System.out.println("  more than item: " +
                   poChangeCounter.isMoreActive(item));
System.out.println("  more than address: " +
                   poChangeCounter.isMoreActive(address));
```

If we run this program, it produces the following output:

```
purchase order changes: 2
  more than item: false
  more than address: true
```

All of the examples that we've looked at so far needed the adapters to be created immediately after their targets were instantiated, so that they would start counting events at that point. In general, however, adapters don't need to be active from the point of creation of their targets, hence they are often lazily created when they're first needed. We've already mentioned that this is one of the advantages of using an adapter factory to access adapters. The first client that needs to access an adapter implementing some extended interface will also create the adapter (transparently) when calling `adapt()` on the adapter factory.

Before a client can adapt an object, it needs to have access to an adapter factory of the appropriate type. In this simple example, we have just used a singleton adapter factory, but this approach is not always flexible enough. Often, you will find that whatever is using the adapter factory provides a natural context for it. For example, as we've already seen in Chapter 11, in EMF.Edit, an editor maintains the adapter factories that back its viewing and editing capabilities.

Sometimes, however, the application provides no obvious context for adapter factories. To help with this situation, resource sets can provide such a context, by maintaining a list of registered adapter factories that can be used to adapt objects in any resource of the set. An adapter factory can be registered with a resource set using the `getAdapterFactories()` method on the `ResourceSet` interface:

```
ResourceSet resourceSet = ...
resourceSet.getAdapterFactories().add(
  new InstanceChangeCounterAdapterFactory());
```

The `EcoreUtil.getRegisteredAdapter()` method can then be used to adapt objects using the registered adapter factory, like this:

```
Adapter adapter = EcoreUtil.getRegisteredAdapter(
  purchaseOrder, InstanceChangeCounter.class);
```

The `getRegisteredAdapter()` method first checks if the given target object already has an adapter of the requested type. If not, it navigates from the object to its resource and then its resource set, from which it retrieves the list of registered adapter factories. It then iterates through the registered adapter factories, searching for one where `isFactoryForType()` returns `true`. If it finds one, it uses that factory to create the adapter.

This approach might suffice in some situations, but it has some clear limitations. As you can see, it requires that objects be added to a resource in a resource set before they can be adapted. It is also somewhat inflexible, in that it can only provide one adapter factory for any given type of adapter, which all clients must use.

16.2.3 Content Adapters

In all of the examples we have seen so far, we have needed to attach an adapter to each object that we wished to observe or extend. Whether we did this directly by adding to the object's `eAdapters` list or simply requested an adapter for the object from an adapter factory, our test programs have always had to explicitly state their interest in each target object.

In some situations, however, we might need to observe changes from all the objects in a content tree. It would be very convenient to be able to attach an adapter to a single object, resource, or resource set, and then to receive notifications from its complete contents. Fortunately, EMF provides a special kind of adapter for exactly this purpose: the content adapter.

When attached to an object, a content adapter recursively attaches itself to the complete object tree beneath it, as well. As objects are added and removed beneath the adapted objects, the adapter responds to the notifications, automatically attaching and detaching itself to provide full coverage of the content tree.

A content adapter is implemented simply by subclassing `EContentAdapter`, instead of `AdapterImpl`. For example, here's a variation on our change counter adapter that counts the changes made to a complete content tree:

```
public static class ChangeCounterContentAdapter
  extends EContentAdapter
{
  protected int count;

  public int getCount()
  {
    return count;
  }

  public void notifyChanged(Notification notification)
  {
    super.notifyChanged(notification);
    ++count;
  }
}
```

One important detail to note is that the `notifyChanged()` override must call `super.notifyChanged()` to invoke the `EContentAdapter` implementation of the method, as it is what causes adapters to be attached and detached as contents are added and removed.[3] After this, we can make our override do anything; in this simple example, we're just incrementing the change counter.

We can test the content adapter with a slightly modified version of our test program:

```
ChangeCounterContentAdapter adapter =
  new ChangeCounterContentAdapter();

PurchaseOrder purchaseOrder =
  EPO2Factory.eINSTANCE.createPurchaseOrder();
purchaseOrder.eAdapters().add(adapter);

USAddress address = EPO2Factory.eINSTANCE.createUSAddress();
purchaseOrder.setBillTo(address);
address.setName("123 Maple Street");

Item item = EPO2Factory.eINSTANCE.createItem();
purchaseOrder.getItems().add(item);
item.setProductName("Apples");
item.setQuantity(20);

System.out.println("Total changes to purchase order: " +
                   adapter.getCount());
```

Here we have simply attached one instance of the adapter to the purchase order object. As the address and item are added to it, the adapter begins receiving notifications from them. Running this program will produce the following output:

```
Total changes to purchase order: 5
```

Interestingly, if we compare this to the total number of notifications counted in the previous examples, we notice that the content adapter has recorded one fewer. The reason for this is that when **Item.order** is automatically set, as a result of adding the item to the purchase order, the content adapter is not yet aware that the item is part of the contents tree. It is only after the bidirectional hand-shaking is complete that the notifications are sent. So, the adapter receives a notification of the change to the purchase order, and responds by attaching itself to the item. However, this is too late for the adapter to receive a notification of the corresponding change to the item.

---

3. Likewise, an override of `setTarget()` or `unsetTarget()` must also invoke the corresponding `EContentAdapter` implementation.

16.2.4 Observing Generated Classes

When writing adapters that target generated classes, there are two optimizations that you should try to take advantage of. The first has to do with determining what feature has changed, the second with accessing the old and new values of a feature with a primitive type.

Let's assume that we've created an adapter for observing instances of class **PurchaseOrder**. Assume as well that in our observer, we need to figure out what feature has changed before handling the event. To do this, we could write something like this:

```
public void notifyChanged(Notification notification)
{
  Object feature = notification.getFeature();
  if (feature == EPO2Package.Literals.PURCHASE_ORDER__ITEMS)
    // do something ...
  else if (feature == EPO2Package.Literals.PURCHASE_ORDER__BILL_TO)
    // do something ...
  else ...
}
```

Although this will work, it's not the most efficient way to do it. You might recall from Chapter 10 that generated `set()` methods use feature IDs, as opposed to feature objects, when constructing the notification. As a result, the feature itself is never actually accessed unless, like we just did, the `getFeature()` method is called (i.e., it is retrieved lazily).

A better alternative is to use the feature ID itself:

```
public void notifyChanged(Notification notification)
{
  switch (notification.getFeatureID(PurchaseOrder.class))
  {
    case EPO2Package.PURCHASE_ORDER__ITEMS:
      // do something ...
    case EPO2Package.PURCHASE_ORDER__BILL_TO:
      // do something ...
    case ...
  }
}
```

The `getFeatureID()` method simply returns the feature ID that the notification was constructed with—possibly corrected, in the case of multiple inheritance—for the expected class supplied to the method (`PurchaseOrder.class` in this case). We described in Section 10.7.4 how this correction, if necessary, is also done quite efficiently. Using the feature ID also has the more evident benefit of allowing you to replace the (possibly lengthy) string of `if...else if...` clauses with a single, efficient `switch` statement.

Now let's look at the second opportunity for optimization, available when observing an attribute of primitive type. Let's imagine that we're observing changes to the **quantity** attribute of class **Item**, and that we're interested in comparing the old and new values whenever it changes. We could do this as follows:

```
public void notifyChanged(Notification notification)
{
  switch (notification.getFeatureID(Item.class))
  {
    case EPO2Package.US_ITEM__QUANTITY:
      if (((Integer)notification.getOldValue()).intValue() >
          ((Integer)notification.getNewValue()).intValue())
        // do something ...
  }
}
```

However, for features of primitive type, the `Notification` interface provides a set of convenient type-specific value accessors, which we can use instead. In our case, we can access the **quantity** attribute's old and new `int` values like this:

```
public void notifyChanged(Notification notification)
{
  switch (notification.getFeatureID(Item.class))
  {
    case EPO2Package.ITEM__QUANTITY:
      if (notification.getOldIntValue() >
          notification.getNewIntValue())
        // do something ...
  }
}
```

In addition to the convenience aspect, this approach also has a significant performance implication if the class we're observing is a generated one. When a generated `set()` method for a primitive-typed attribute constructs its notification, it passes the old and new values as primitives. If we later access them using the appropriate type-specific `getValue()` method (e.g., `getOldIntValue()`), the notification will simply return the value with which it was constructed. If, instead, we call the generic `getValue()` method (e.g., `getOldValue()`), then the notification will need to first construct an appropriate Java wrapper object (`java.lang.Integer` in this case) before returning it.

16.3   Cross-Referencers

When working with EMF models, one often needs to search in a resource, or possibly an entire resource set, for objects that have references that meet certain criteria. For example, when deleting an object you might want to search for other objects that have one-way references to it so you can clean them up. Another common example is searching a resource for objects that have unresolvable references (i.e., broken proxies). EMF provides a utility called a cross-referencer to help with these kinds of things.

16.3.1   Basic Cross-Referencers

You might recall that, in Chapter 13, we already used one type of cross referencer, `EcoreUtil.UsageCrossReferencer`, to find the customer associated with a given purchase order from the ExtendedPO3 model. In that model, the **orders** reference from class **Customer** to class **PurchaseOrder** is one-way, as illustrated in Figure 16.1. We had to use the cross-referencer because we couldn't simply navigate to the customer.

Figure 16.1   One-way reference.

We started by using the cross-referencer's static `find()` method to retrieve all of the references to a particular purchase order, `order`, from any other object in the resource set:

```
Collection settings = EcoreUtil.UsageCrossReferencer.find(
  order, order.eResource().getResourceSet());
```

The cross-referencer returned a collection of `EStructuralFeature.Settings`, representing all of the incoming references. Because we were really only interested in the customer reference, we then needed to iterate through the collection to find it:

```
for (Iterator iter = settings.iterator(); iter.hasNext(); )
{
  EStructuralFeature.Setting setting =
    (EStructuralFeature.Setting)iter.next();
  if (setting.getEStructuralFeature() ==
```

```
    SupplierPackage.Literals.CUSTOMER__ORDERS)
  {
    Customer customer = (Customer)setting.getEObject();
    ...
  }
}
```

We needed to do this because we chose to use the cross-referencer's default implementation. If instead we created a subclass of UsageCrossReferencer, we could have customized the search to match our more specific criteria. For example, the following anonymous subclass would do the trick:

```
Collection settings =
  new EcoreUtil.UsageCrossReferencer(
    order.eResource().getResourceSet())
  {
    protected boolean crossReference(EObject eObject,
                                     EReference eReference,
                                     EObject referencedObj)
    {
      return super.crossReference(eObject, eReference, referencedObj)
        && eReference == SupplierPackage.Literals.CUSTOMER__ORDERS;
    }

    public Collection findUsage(EObject eObject)
    {
      return super.findUsage(eObject);
    }
  }.findUsage(order);
```

Class UsageCrossReference, like every other cross-referencer in EcoreUtil, works by iterating through the content tree rooted at the object, resource, or resource set passed to its constructor (the resource set, in this case). For each object encountered, it retrieves all of its cross-references (i.e., non-containment references) by calling eCrossReferences() from the EObject interface. For each cross-reference retrieved, it then calls its protected crossReference() method, passing the object that owns the reference (eObject), the reference itself (eReference), and the target of the reference (referencedObj). Every cross-reference for which the crossReference() method returns true is then added to the result set. In our example, we simply override the crossReference() method to restrict the cases in which it returns true. The base implementation in UsageCrossReferencer returns true only when the cross-referenced object is the specified object (in this case, the purchase order we pass to findUsage()), and we add the additional condition that the reference must be **orders**.

Because we've created a subclass of `UsageCrossReferencer`, we can't simply call the static `find()` method to invoke the search as before; we need to call the `findUsage()` method instead. Notice how we also needed to override the `findUsage()` method in our subclass. This was simply to make it public. It is protected in the base class because there, calling the static `find()` method is the proper way to do it.

By subclassing a cross-referencer, we also have an opportunity to speed up the search by reducing the number of objects being checked. In our example, where we are only interested in references from customers, there is no need to search for referencing objects in the containment tree below a purchase order. The only possible children of a purchase order are items and address objects, never customers. We can stop the cross-referencer from going further by overriding the `containment()` method like this:

```
Collection references =
  new EcoreUtil.UsageCrossReferencer(
    order.eResource().getResourceSet())
  {
    protected boolean crossReference(EObject eObject,
                                     EReference eReference,
                                     EObject referencedObj)
    {
      return super.crossReference(eObject, eReference, referencedObj)
        && eReference == SupplierPackage.Literals.CUSTOMER__ORDERS;
    }

    protected boolean containment(EObject eObject)
    {
      return !(eObject instanceof PurchaseOrder);
    }

    public Collection findUsage(EObject eObject)
    {
      return super.findUsage(eObject);
    }

  }.findUsage(order);
```

This causes the cross-referencer to completely ignore the cross-references and the children of any purchase order it encounters.

In addition to `UsageCrossReferencer`, class `EcoreUtil` includes several other cross-referencer classes. They all work essentially the same way, only with different built-in search criteria. Another particularly useful one is `UnresolvedProxyCrossReferencer`, which finds broken (unresolvable) references in a resource or resource set. It can be used in cleaning up after another (referenced) resource is deleted or moved, for example:

```
Map proxies =
  EcoreUtil.UnresolvedProxyCrossReferencer.find(resource);
for (Iterator iter = proxies.entrySet().iterator(); iter.hasNext();)
{
  Map.Entry entry = (Map.Entry)iter.next();
  EObject proxy = (EObject)entry.getKey();
  Collection settings = (Collection)entry.getValue();
  ...
}
```

As you can see, the `find()` method of `UnresolvedProxyCrossReferencer` returns a `Map`, unlike `UsageCrossReferencer.find()`, which returns a collection of settings. In fact, the returned map is quite special: it is the cross-referencer itself. That is to say that any cross-referencer is an instance of `java.util.Map`, in which each entry's key is a target object (an unresolvable proxy, in this case) and value is the collection of settings referencing that target. It is usual, when searching for references to more than a single object, for the cross-referencer to return itself as the result of `find()`.

16.3.2   Cross-Reference Adapters

The basic cross-referencers defined in `EcoreUtil` all walk the entire content tree each time they are invoked. Depending on the number of objects in play, this can be an expensive operation. As a result, cross-referencers are not well suited to repeated invocation on a changing set of objects.

EMF does, however, provide an adapter, `ECrossReferenceAdapter`, designed for exactly this use. Like a content adapter, a cross-reference adapter attaches itself to all the objects in a content tree and then responds to notifications to maintain complete coverage as objects are added to and removed from that tree. It also uses the notifications to keep a cross-referencer up to date with the changing objects.

For example, we can attach a cross-reference adapter to a resource set like this:

```
ECrossReferenceAdapter adapter = new ECrossReferenceAdapter();
resourceSet.eAdapters().add(adapter);
```

As the adapter is recursively added to every object in the resource set, its cross-referencer is used to record all of the one-way, non-derived cross-references into each object. Then, we can easily obtain this collection for any particular object. For example, to get the references into a purchase order:

```
PurchaseOrder order = ...
Collection settings =
  adapter.getNonNavigableInverseReferences(order);
```

The getNonNavigableInverseReferences() method returns a collection of settings, just like the UsageCrossReferencer.find() method we saw at the beginning of the previous section. The collection includes settings representing all of the recorded references, so if we were interested in only one particular type of reference, we would still need to filter that list. We'll see an easy way to do that in the next example. The important thing about the adapter approach is that, as we add or remove references to the purchase order, the cross-referencer is updated automatically, so that calling getNonNavigableInverseReferences() will never cause another walk over the whole content tree.

To put it another way, the cross-reference adapter simply maintains all of the inverse reference values for references with no modeled opposite. In fact, we can use this capability to write a simple utility method that efficiently obtains the inverse of any reference:

```
public static Iterator getInverse(EReference reference,
                                  EObject object, Notifier context)
{
  if (context == null)
  {
    context = getContext(object);
  }

  ECrossReferenceAdapter adapter =
    ECrossReferenceAdapter.getCrossReferenceAdapter(context);
  if (adapter == null)
  {
    adapter = new ECrossReferenceAdapter();
    context.eAdapters().add(adapter);
  }
  return
    new EcoreUtil.FilteredSettingsIterator(
      adapter.getInverseReferences(object, true), reference, null)
    {
      protected Object yield(Setting setting)
      {
        return setting.getEObject();
      }
    };

public static Notifier getContext(EObject object)
{
  EObject root = EcoreUtil.getRootContainer(object);
  Resource resource = root.eResource();
  if (resource != null)
```

```
  {
    ResourceSet resourceSet = resource.getResourceSet();
    return resourceSet != null ? (Notifier)resourceSet : resource;
  }
  return root;
}
```

Our `getInverse()` method will return an iterator over the inverse values of the specified `reference`, whether or not it has a modeled opposite, for the given `object`.

The optional `context` defines the root of the content tree that we will be monitoring. If no context is specified, we invoke `getContext()` to obtain the broadest one possible. So, specifying a context only serves to improve the performance of our utility.

Once we have a context, we call the `getCrossReferenceAdapter()` method from `ECrossReferenceAdapter`, which simply tries to obtain an existing cross-reference adapter from it. If there is no such adapter, we create and attach one. Subsequent calls to `getInverse()` will use this same adapter.

With the adapter in place, we call `getInverseReferences()` on it, to obtain the full collection of references into the specified object. Unlike `getNonNavigableInverseReferences()`, this method supplements the list of settings it returns to include bidirectional and container references that are read directly from the object.[4]

Now we have a collection of settings representing all of the references into the specified object. However, we're only interested in those corresponding to a single reference, and we would like to expose the objects directly, not via settings. Rather than copying the whole collection, filtering it as we go, we wrap it in an instance of the convenience class `EcoreUtil.FilteredSettingsIterator`. This class is designed for exactly this purpose: exposing a filtered view over a collection of settings. Note that we pass in the reference of interest and we override the `yield()` method to surface the **EObjects** directly.

We can now use this method to uniformly obtain the inverse value of any reference, whether the model defines an opposite or not. For example:

```
PurchaseOrder order = ...
Iterator iter = getInverse(SupplierPackage.Literals.CUSTOMER__ORDERS,
                           order, null));
while (iter.hasNext())
{
```

---

4. We could have made our utility more efficient by providing special handling for such references before even attaching any adapters, and then we would have just used `getNonNavigableInverse-References()` again.

```
EObject object = (EObject)iter.next();
        ...
}
```

Using a cross-reference adapter still has drawbacks compared to actually modeling bidirectional references, however. Unsurprisingly, recording the inverse values in a map on an adapter is less memory efficient than simply storing them right on the objects. Also, modeling the references allows you to express constraints that will be automatically enforced by the implementation. For example, the multiplicity constraint that we placed on **orders**'s opposite reference in ExtendedPO2 is not enforced here.

16.4 Copying Objects

EMF provides a powerful facility for creating copies of **EObjects**, as part of the `EcoreUtil` class. As we will see, this copy facility is simple to use in its basic form, but it is also highly customizable. Knowing how to customize the copy algorithm can be useful whenever you need to create new objects based on a set of existing objects. Also, as a side effect, understanding its implementation provides an opportunity to improve your knowledge of EMF's reflection API.

Let's start by looking at the following example:

```
PurchaseOrder po1 = ...
PurchaseOrder po2 = ...
PurchaseOrder po1Copy = (PurchaseOrder)EcoreUtil.copy(po1);
PurchaseOrder po2Copy = (PurchaseOrder)EcoreUtil.copy(po2);
```

The objects `po1Copy` and `po2Copy` are copies of `po1` and `po2`, respectively. We could have written the same code using the `copyAll()` method, which we can almost think of as an overload of `copy()`. It takes a collection of the objects to be copied and returns a collection of the copies.

But what does it mean to copy an object? In general terms, it means to create an instance of the same type of a given object and to set each attribute of the new object to the value of the corresponding attribute of the original object. It also involves repeating this very same process on every object contained by the original object. In our example, `po1Copy` has the same number of items as `po1`. Indeed, each item in `po1Copy` is an exact copy of the equivalent item in `po1`.

Up to this point, the copy facility is probably doing exactly what one would expect. Things become a little more interesting when the objects being copied have non-containment references, as illustrated in the following example:

```
PurchaseOrder po1 = ...
PurchaseOrder po2 = ...
po1.setPreviousOrder(po2);
PurchaseOrder po1Copy = (PurchaseOrder)EcoreUtil.copy(po1);
PurchaseOrder po2Copy = (PurchaseOrder)EcoreUtil.copy(po2);
```

In the first example, every **EObject** accessible to the copy method was actually copied. Here, when copying po1, the object referred to by the non-contained reference, po2, is not copied: both po1Copy and po1 have po2 as their previous order. The fact that po2 is copied as well, in the last line, does not influence how po1 is copied.

However, using copyAll() to create po1Copy and po2Copy would produce a different result:

```
PurchaseOrder po1 = ...
PurchaseOrder po2 = ...
po1.setPreviousOrder(po2);
Collection orders = Arrays.asList(new PurchaseOrder[] {po1, po2});
Collection copies = EcoreUtil.copyAll(pos);
```

By putting the original objects in a collection and calling copyAll(), we tell the copy facility that they should be copied as a unit, so any references within that unit become references within the resulting copied objects. In this example, po1Copy refers to po2Copy as its previous order.

You might not be happy with the results produced by the default implementation of the copy facility. For example, you could prefer copyAll() to behave just as a simplified way of copying several objects, without redirecting the non-containment references. Or you could want to exclude a few objects from the copy, or even convert them to a different type of object. The good news is that the implementation of the copy facility was designed to be extremely flexible and easily customized to suit the specific needs of an application. We will now delve into its implementation details.

This is the code for the copy() method in EcoreUtil:

```
public static EObject copy(EObject eObject)
{
  Copier copier = new Copier();
  EObject result = copier.copy(eObject);
  copier.copyReferences();
  return result;
}
```

As you see, all this method does is instantiate a new `EcoreUtil.Copier` and execute its `copy()` and `copyReferences()` methods. The other copy-related static method in `EcoreUtil`, `copyAll()`, is almost identical to `EcoreUtil.copy()`. The difference is that it calls the copier's `copyAll()` method instead of its `copy()` method.

The copier object is a map (i.e., class `Copier` extends `java.util.Map`), in which each entry has an original object as its key and the corresponding copy as its value. The entries are created as the copy is performed. This is the code for the `Copier.copy()` method, which implements the main copy algorithm for each object:

```
public EObject copy(EObject eObject)
{
  EObject copyEObject = createCopy(eObject);
  put(eObject, copyEObject);
  EClass eClass = eObject.eClass();
  for (int i = 0, s = eClass.getFeatureCount(); i < s; ++i)
  {
    EStructuralFeature eStructuralFeature =
      eClass.getEStructuralFeature(i);
    if (eStructuralFeature.isChangeable() &&
        !eStructuralFeature.isDerived())
    {
      if (eStructuralFeature instanceof EAttribute)
        copyAttribute((EAttribute)eStructuralFeature,
                      eObject, copyEObject);
      else
      {
        EReference eReference = (EReference)eStructuralFeature;
        if (eReference.isContainment())
          copyContainment(eReference, eObject, copyEObject);
      }
    }
  }

  copyProxyURI(eObject, copyEObject);

  return copyEObject;
}
```

The argument to this method is the original object to be copied. Its first step is to create an instance of the same class as the original object. To do this, it invokes `Copier.createCopy()`, which in turn uses `EcoreUtil.create()` to reflectively instantiate the **EClass** returned by `Copier.getTarget(EClass)`. Here's our first extensibility point. By simply overriding `getTarget()`, you can easily change the type of instance that is created as the copy of an object. This can be really handy in cases where you are reusing the `Copier` implementation to create a slightly modified version of the objects being copied. After the copy is instantiated, the copier records the mapping from the original object to this copy.

The next step is to iterate through all the structural features of the original object's **EClass** and copy the attributes and containment references that are changeable and non-derived. The copying of each feature is delegated to `copyAttribute()` or `copyContainment()`.

The `copyAttribute()` method handles the copying of multi-valued and single-valued attributes. The value of an attribute for the original object is obtained via EMF's reflective method `eGet()`. On the copied object, instead of using the **EAttribute** argument directly in setting the value, `copyAttribute()` uses the **EStructuralFeature** returned by `getTarget(EStructuralFeature)`. This is analogous to the `getTarget(EClass)` method explained before: it is an extensibility point that can be used when you are changing the default behavior of the `Copier`. One important thing to note about the process of copying attributes is that the values themselves are not copied. So if an **EObject** has a mutable object as the value of a non-primitive attribute, that mutable object can be changed by code that is interacting with either the original or the copied **EObject**.

The `copyAttribute()` method also partially handles attributes that are feature maps. As discussed in Chapter 8, a feature map is a list of feature–value pairs that is used to maintain a cross-feature ordering of values. At this point in the copy process, it is not yet possible to copy the feature map itself as it might include values of non-containment references. The values of such references in the copied objects may end up being either original or copied objects; thus, we cannot begin to set these references until after the complete set of copied objects has been created. For now, `copyAttribute()` can only invoke the copier's `copy()` method for each object contained via the feature map, recursively copying these objects.

The `copyContainment()` method is fairly straightforward. It deals only with multi-valued and single-valued containment references, invoking either `copyAll()` or `copy()` to recursively copy the contained objects. Like `copyAttribute()`, it delegates to `getTarget(EStructuralFeature)` the task of deciding which structural feature of the copied object corresponds to the original object's feature, passed in as an argument. That feature is then set to the result of the recursive copy.

Back to the `Copier.copy()` method, there is one final step to be described. Before returning the copied object, the method invokes `copyProxyURI()`. This method checks whether the original object is a proxy, and, if it is, sets the proxy URI of the copied object accordingly. This ensures not only that both the original and copied objects are proxies, but also that they will resolve to the same object.

As we saw when we discussed the static `EcoreUtil.copy()` and `EcoreUtil.copyAll()` methods, the copy process happens in two phases. First, as we've just examined, the original objects are copied, along with their containment trees. Then, after that, the non-containment references are copied, as a result of invoking `copyReferences()`. When this method is executed, the `copier` object already has a set of map entries that ties original objects to copied objects. For each of these entries, the structural features of the original object are analyzed. The ones that are both changeable and non-derived, and either feature maps or cross-references, are then properly handled by the method. In particular, each reference is passed to the `copyReference()` method, which is responsible for actually setting its value in the copied object. Like all the other `Copier` methods that set values on copied objects, `copyReference()` delegates to `getTarget(EStructuralFeature)` the decision of which feature to use. Note that `copyReference()` is also the method that decides whether to use the actual object referenced by the original object or an existing copy.

An interesting point to notice is that one can easily override any of the copy methods to implement, for example, a copier that doesn't copy specific objects or features. The following code shows how simple it is to prevent the **shipTo** attribute, for example, from being copied:

```
EcoreUtil.Copier myCopier = new EcoreUtil.Copier()
{
  protected void copyContainment(EReference eReference,
                                 EObject eObject,
                                 EObject copyEObject)
  {
    if (eReference != EPO2Package.Literals.PURCHASE_ORDER__SHIP_TO)
      super.copyContainment(eReference, eObject, copyEObject);
  }
};

PurchaseOrder po1 = ...
PurchaseOrder po2 = ...
Collection orders = Arrays.asList(new PurchaseOrder[] { po1, po2 });
myCopier.copyAll(orders);
myCopier.copyReferences();
PurchaseOrder po1Copy = (PurchaseOrder)myCopier.get(po1);
```

This example also shows how you can exploit the fact that the copier is a map: you can use the `get()` method to retrieve the copy of a specific object.

16.5   Comparing Objects

The last tool we will look at, also provided by `EcoreUtil`, is a facility for comparing the structure of two **EObject**s. The following example shows how to use it:

```
PurchaseOrder po1 = ...
PurchaseOrder po2 = ...
po1.setPreviousOrder(po2);
PurchaseOrder po1Copy = (PurchaseOrder)EcoreUtil.copy(po1);
PurchaseOrder po2Copy = (PurchaseOrder)EcoreUtil.copy(po2);
System.out.println(EcoreUtil.equals(po1, po1Copy));
System.out.println(EcoreUtil.equals(po2, po2Copy));
po1Copy.setPreviousOrder(po2Copy);
System.out.println(EcoreUtil.equals(po1, po1Copy));
```

In this example, `po1` and `po1Copy`, and `po2` and `po2Copy` are reported as equal by every invocation of `EcoreUtil.equals()`. This happens even after we modify `po1Copy` to have `po2Copy` as its previous order. Although this might surprise you, the algorithm is doing exactly what it was designed to do: check whether the objects are structurally equal or, put differently, whether their topologies are the same. Even after the change, both `po1` and `po1Copy` have previous purchase orders that are structurally equal; hence, they remain structurally equal themselves.

Two objects are considered structurally equal if they are of the same type, and if, for each feature, their `isSet` states are the same and their values are also structurally equal. For attributes in particular, the values must be equal according to Java equality.

The design of the `equals()` method is analogous to that of the copy facility described in the previous section. So here again you can customize the algorithm to produce the results your application requires. For example, in the case where a specific subset of attributes uniquely identifies each object, you could tweak the algorithm to compare only those attributes.

Like `EcoreUtil`'s `copy()` and `copyAll()` methods, the `equals()` method is merely a simplified way of invoking methods of a specific utility class. It instantiates an `EqualityHelper` and returns the result of its `equals()` method:

```
public static boolean equals(EObject eObject1, EObject eObject2)
{
  EqualityHelper equalityHelper = new EqualityHelper();
  return equalityHelper.equals(eObject1, eObject2);
}
```

An equality helper is a map (i.e., class `EqualityHelper` extends `java.util.Map`), in which each entry associates a pair of objects that are considered structurally equal. This map is valid and complete only when the `equals()` method returns `true`. If we had instantiated the `EqualityHelper` ourselves in the example at the beginning of this section, we could then write the following code:

```
PurchaseOrder po1 = (PurchaseOrder)equalityHelper.get(po1Copy);
PurchaseOrder po1Copy = (PurchaseOrder)equalityHelper.get(po1);
```

As you can see, the map can be consulted to obtain the peer of any object after a successful comparison. Note that the map has been populated with two entries for each pair of objects, allowing you to find the association from either direction.

CHAPTER 17

The Change Model

As we've seen in previous chapters, there are many possible kinds of EMF models. Application-specific models like the various purchase order models we've looked at in this book; Ecore, the metamodel for all EMF models; and the generator model, used to implement the EMF code generator, are all examples of EMF models. Another useful generic model provided by EMF is the change model, a model for representing changes, or deltas, to an instance of any other EMF model. In this chapter, we'll look at the design of the change model and at how you can use it to represent and make changes to objects, or to record changes as they're being made, enabling you to later roll them back (i.e., undo them).

17.1 Describing a Change

Let's assume that we have a simple purchase order instance document, *My.epo2*, containing a single purchase order with a couple of items:

```
<epo2:PurchaseOrder ... >
  <items productName="Apples" quantity="10" USPrice="45"/>
  <items productName="Oranges" quantity="5" USPrice="50"/>
</epo2:PurchaseOrder>
```

Now consider another version of this document that contains a simple change; the value of the **quantity** attribute of the "Apples" item is changed from 10 to 12:

```
<epo2:PurchaseOrder ... >
  <items productName="Apples" quantity="12" USPrice="45"/>
  <items productName="Oranges" quantity="5" USPrice="50"/>
</epo2:PurchaseOrder>
```

The purpose of the change model is to allow us to describe a change like this. A serialized instance of the model representing this change would look something like this:

```
<change:ChangeDescription ... >
  <objectChanges>
    <key href="My.epo2#//@items.0"/>
    <value featureName="quantity" dataValue="12"/>
  </objectChanges>
</change:ChangeDescription>
```

As you can see, our change is represented by an instance of class **ChangeDescription**, the contents of which describe the details of the change. **ChangeDescription** is, in fact, the central component of the change model. It is used to describe arbitrary changes to one or more features of any number of objects. The main classes of the change model are shown in Figure 17.1.

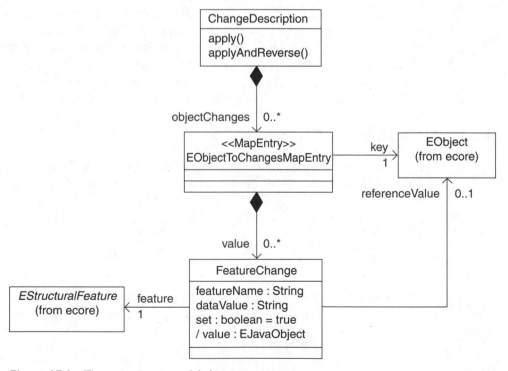

Figure 17.1   The main change model classes.

A **ChangeDescription** uses a map, **objectChanges**, to maintain the collection of objects being changed, along with the changing features of those objects. Entries in the map (**EObjectToChangesMapEntry**) are keyed by the **EObject** being changed, and have as value a list of **FeatureChange** instances, one for each changing feature of the corresponding object. In our example, the change description contains just a single entry for the "Apples" item (i.e., key "My.epo2#//@items.0") with a single value (for the **quantity** feature).

Notice that class **FeatureChange** contains both a **featureName** attribute and a **feature** reference. You might have noticed that in our serialized change description, **featureName** is the persistent version (i.e., `featureName="quantity"` appears in the XML). The **feature** reference, on the other hand, is transient and volatile in the model. It is derived from the **featureName** by calling the `getEStructuralFeature()` method on the changed **EObject**'s class. This approach simplifies the persistent form of the model, serializing just the feature name ("quantity") instead of the much longer URI of the corresponding **EStructuralFeature** ("http://www.example.com/epo2.ecore#//Item/quantity").

A similar story applies to the three value features: **value**, **dataValue**, and **referenceValue**. In this case, the **value** attribute is derived from either the **dataValue** attribute or the **referenceValue** reference, depending on the type of the corresponding feature; **dataValue** is used for the persistent form if the feature is an **EAttribute**, whereas **referenceValue** is used if it is an **EReference**. In our example, **dataValue** is, as expected, the persistent form (i.e., the XML says `dataValue="12"`) because the **quantity** feature is an **EAttribute**.

17.1.1 *Applying a Change Description*

Given an instance of the change model that describes our change, we can use it to make the change by invoking the **apply** operation on the **ChangeDescription**. Assuming our example change description is contained in the file *ChangeQuantity.change*, we can load and apply the change as follows:

```
// load the change resource
ResourceSet resourceSet = new ResourceSetImpl();
URI changeURI =
  URI.createPlatformResourceURI("/project/ChangeQuantity.change");
Resource changeResource = resourceSet.getResource(changeURI, true);

// get the change description (root object) from the change resource
ChangeDescription change =
  (ChangeDescription)changeResource.getContents().get(0);

// apply the change
change.apply();
```

The original purchase order is demand-loaded from *My.epo2* during `apply()`. If we now save that resource, we'll see that the quantity attribute has, in fact, been changed to 12 as expected:

```
<epo2:PurchaseOrder ... >
  <items productName="Apples" quantity="12" USPrice="45"/>
  <items productName="Oranges" quantity="5" USPrice="50"/>
</epo2:PurchaseOrder>
```

After calling the `apply()` method, the change description itself is also changed. The reason for this is that after applying a change, the description is no longer meaningful, as the referenced objects (just the single "Apples" item in this example) are already in the new, changed state. Therefore the `apply()` method has the added effect of clearing the change description. If we save *ChangeQuantity.change* again, it will look something like this:

```
<change:ChangeDescription ... />
```

Class **ChangeDescription** also provides another operation for applying the change. The **applyAndReverse** operation will, like **apply**, apply the change, but in this case the change description will be modified to describe the reverse set of changes, instead of being cleared. Let's change our previous example to call `applyAndReverse()`:

```
...
ChangeDescription change =
  (ChangeDescription)changeResource.getContents().get(0);

// apply the change
change.applyAndReverse();
```

This will have the exact same effect on the purchase order document, *My.epo2* (**quantity** will be changed from 10 to 12), but the change description, *QuantityChange.change*, will now look like this:

```
<change:ChangeDescription ... >
  <objectChanges>
    <key href="My.epo2#//@items.0"/>
    <value featureName="quantity" dataValue="10"/>
  </objectChanges>
</change:ChangeDescription>
```

In this simple example, the only change is to the **dataValue** attribute in the **FeatureChange**. It is now set to 10 because this represents the original value that we would need to change the **quantity** to, in order to reverse (undo) the applied change. If we now call `apply()` or `applyAndReverse()` again, the purchase order will revert to its original state:

```
<epo2:PurchaseOrder ... >
  <items productName="Apples" quantity="10" USPrice="45"/>
  <items productName="Oranges" quantity="5" USPrice="50"/>
</epo2:PurchaseOrder>
```

Notice that calling `applyAndReverse()` repeatedly provides a convenient undo/redo capability for a change description.

17.1.2 Changing Multi-Valued Features

So far, we've only looked at changes to single-valued features. As a matter of fact, the value features (**dataValue** and **referenceValue**) in class **FeatureChange** are only capable of representing single data values. For the multi-valued case, these features are not even used. For simplicity, we didn't show it in Figure 17.1, but class **FeatureChange** also includes a containment reference, **listChanges**, to another class in the change model, **ListChange**. This is illustrated in Figure 17.2.

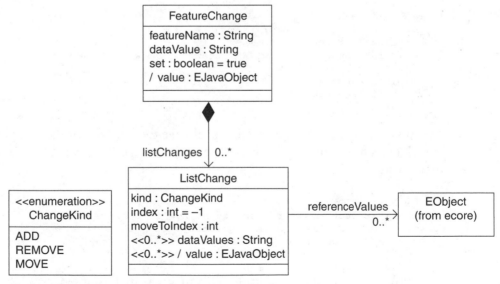

Figure 17.2 Changes to multi-valued features (lists).

In the case of a multi-valued feature, **ListChanges** are used to represent addition to, removal from, or movement within the specified feature's list. The change indicated by the **kind** attribute (enumeration **ChangeKind**) is made at the position in the list indicated by the **index** attribute. For the same reason, described earlier, that class **FeatureChange** provides three features (**value**, **dataValue**, and **referenceValue**) to represent the changed value for single-valued features, **ListChange** includes the **values**, **dataValues**, and **referenceValues** features to represent the values to add to, remove from, or move within a multi-valued feature list. The **values** feature must always be set when the **kind** attribute is **ADD**. For **MOVE** or **REMOVE**, however, it is only needed if more than one value is being changed; otherwise, the **index** alone is sufficient to identify the changed value. Another attribute, **moveToIndex**, is only used when the **kind** is **MOVE** to indicate, as you might expect, the position to which to move the object(s).

The following change description adds a second change to our previous example. It includes a **ListChange** to move the object in the purchase order's **items** feature at position 1 (i.e., the "Oranges" item) to position 0:

```
<change:ChangeDescription ... >
  <objectChanges>
    <key href="My.epo2#//@items.0"/>
    <value featureName="quantity" dataValue="12"/>
  </objectChanges>
  <objectChanges>
    <key href="My.epo2#/"/>
    <value featureName="items">
      <listChanges kind="MOVE" index="1" moveToIndex="0"/>
    </value>
  </objectChanges>
</change:ChangeDescription>
```

If we apply this change, it will still change the **quantity** of the "Apples" item to 12 as before, but it will also move the "Oranges" item to the front of the **items** list:

```
<epo2:PurchaseOrder ... >
  <items productName="Oranges" quantity="5" USPrice="50"/>
  <items productName="Apples" quantity="12" USPrice="45"/>
</epo2:PurchaseOrder>
```

Now let's consider an addition. To add a new item to the purchase order, we use a **ListChange** with **kind** equal to **ADD**. We can add a new "Peaches" item to the beginning of the list (i.e., at index 0) as follows:

```
<change:ChangeDescription ... >
  <objectChanges>
    <key href="My.epo2#//@items.0"/>
    <value featureName="quantity" dataValue="12"/>
  </objectChanges>
  <objectChanges>
    <key href="My.epo2#/"/>
    <value featureName="items">
      <listChanges kind="MOVE" index="1" moveToIndex="0"/>
      <listChanges kind="ADD" index="0"
        referenceValues="//@objectsToAttach.0"/>
    </value>
  </objectChanges>
  <objectsToAttach xsi:type="epo2:Item" productName="Peaches"
    quantity="50" USPrice="60"/>
</change:ChangeDescription>
```

Notice that we've simply added another **ListChange** to the **listChanges** for the **items** reference of the purchase order, as opposed to adding to the **value** list or **objectChanges** map. All the **ListChange**s associated with a specific feature of a given object (the **items** feature of the root purchase order, "My.epo2#/" in this example) are grouped together under a single **FeatureChange** entry for the feature.

Because we're adding a new "Peaches" item, which doesn't already exist in the purchase order, the change description needs to contain it. Class **ChangeDescription** includes another containment reference for this purpose. In fact, **ChangeDescription** actually includes two more references, as shown in Figure 17.3.

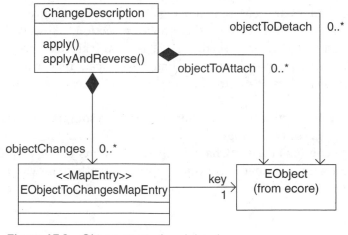

Figure 17.3 Objects to attach and detach.

As we've seen in our example, the change description uses the **objectsToAttach** reference to contain new objects that are not already contained in the instance itself, but will be once the change is applied. The other reference, **objectsToDetach** is used to identify the list of objects that are already contained in the instance, but will no longer be once the change has been applied. It's essentially the opposite of **objectsToAttach.** Unlike **objectsToAttach,** it is not a containment reference, because the objects to be detached are already contained elsewhere. In fact, **objectsToDetach** is actually transient, and derived from the **FeatureChange**s in the change description. It simply serves as a convenient identification of the objects that will be orphaned after the change is made.

If we proceed to apply our latest change description, we will have the following purchase order:

```
<epo2:PurchaseOrder ... >
  <items productName="Peaches" quantity="50" USPrice="60"/>
  <items productName="Oranges" quantity="5" USPrice="50"/>
  <items productName="Apples" quantity="12" USPrice="45"/>
</epo2:PurchaseOrder>
```

The **quantity** value change and the reordering of the "Apples" and "Oranges" items have been applied as in the previous example, and our new "Peaches" item has also been added at the beginning of the list.

17.1.3 Changing Resources

A change description can also specify changes to the root objects in a resource's contents list (i.e., in the list returned by the `Resource.getContents()` method). These changes are represented using class **ListChange**, just like the list-based feature changes described in the previous section. However, because `Resource` is not a modeled class, there is no structural feature corresponding to its contents, and consequently no **FeatureChange** for it can appear in the change description. Another class, **ResourceChange** is used instead, as illustrated in Figure 17.4.

Class **ChangeDescription** uses another reference, **resourceChanges,** to contain a list of **ResourceChange**s, one for each changed resource. A **ResourceChange** contains the **ListChange**s for the contents list of the associated resource. For example, a change description representing the removal of the top-level purchase order from our *My.epo2* resource would look something like this:

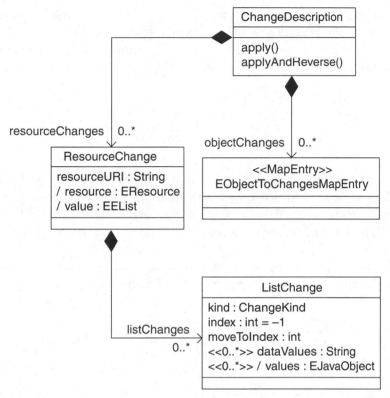

Figure 17.4 Changes to a resource's contents list.

```
<change:ChangeDescription ... >
  <resourceChanges resourceURI="platform:/resource/project/My.epo2">
    <listChanges kind="REMOVE" index="0"/>
  </resourceChanges>
</change:ChangeDescription>
```

As you can see, a **ResourceChange** is very similar to a **FeatureChange** for a many-valued feature, only it identifies a resource (using the **resourceURI** attribute), instead of an object and a feature of that object's class.

17.2 **Change Recording**

Included in EMF with the change model is a very powerful adapter class, `ChangeRecorder`, which can be used to monitor a set of objects and build a change description based on the notifications they send. It attaches to all the objects in one or more content trees, recording all changes made to them.

The `ChangeRecorder.beginRecording()` method can be used to attach an existing change recorder to objects, which it then begins monitoring. More commonly, however, one of four convenient `ChangeRecorder` constructors is used to create the recorder and then immediately start monitoring objects:

```
public ChangeRecorder(EObject rootObject)
public ChangeRecorder(Resource resource)
public ChangeRecorder(ResourceSet resourceSet)
public ChangeRecorder(Collection rootObjects)
```

The first constructor monitors the containment tree rooted by the specified object. The second and third monitor the contents of a resource and an entire resource set, respectively. The last one lets you provide an arbitrary list of roots (any combination of `EObjects`, `Resources`, and `ResourceSets`), all of which will be monitored.

Let's use a change recorder to monitor some changes that we make to our purchase order instance document from the previous section:

```
// load the purchase order
ResourceSet resourceSet = new ResourceSetImpl();
URI uri = URI.createPlatformResourceURI("/project/My.epo2");
Resource resource = resourceSet.getResource(uri, true);
PurchaseOrder order = (PurchaseOrder)resource.getContents().get(0);

// start recording
ChangeRecorder recorder = new ChangeRecorder(resource);

// change the purchase order
Item item = (Item)order.getItems().get(0);
item.setQuantity(40);
order.getItems().add(EPO2Factory.eINSTANCE.createItem());

// stop recording
ChangeDescription description = recorder.endRecording();
```

As you can see, the program loads our familiar *My.epo2* purchase order document, changes the quantity of the "Apples" item to 40, adds a new item to the end of the list of items, and finally ends the recording. If we run this program, the change description returned by the `endRecording()` method will look like this:

```
<change:ChangeDescription ... >
  <objectChanges>
    <key href="My.epo2#//@items.0"/>
    <value featureName="quantity" dataValue="10"/>
```

```
    </objectChanges>
    <objectChanges>
      <key href="My.epo2#/"/>
      <value featureName="items">
        <listChanges kind="REMOVE" index="2"/>
      </value>
    </objectChanges>
  </change:ChangeDescription>
```

As expected, it includes two **objectChange** entries, one for each of the two changes we made. Notice, however, that the changes are in the form of a reverse delta (i.e., the changes needed to roll back to the starting state). The first change sets the **quantity** of the "Apples" item ("My.epo2#//@items.0") back to its original value of 10. The second change, to the **items** feature of the purchase order, removes the third entry ("My.epo2#//@items.2") that we added in the program. Given that the objects have already changed, this reverse delta is the most meaningful change description that the recorder could produce. Calling applyAndReverse() on the change description would reverse the changes and modify the change description to describe exactly the changes we originally made.

It is worth noting that a change recorder does not necessarily record every change made. Multiple changes involving the same feature of the same object can be discarded or merged, as long as the result still describes how to return the objects to their original state. As a consequence of this, when you apply the change description produced by a change recorder, any other observers attached to the objects might actually see fewer changes in the reverse delta than were originally made.

17.2.1   *Transaction Atomicity and Rollback*

Sometimes when working with EMF objects, several changes need to be made as an atomic operation; either all or none of them should succeed. If an error occurs during any single change, the objects must be rolled back to their initial state.

As you might have guessed, a change recorder can be used to provide a powerful transaction rollback mechanism for EMF. The change recorder can monitor all of the changes that are made over some period of time. At any point, the endRecording() method can be called to obtain a description of the changes required to return the affected objects to their original state. Invoking apply() on it produces the desired rollback effect.

The following example uses a change recorder at the resource set level to provide complete rollback of all changes if any exceptions are thrown while modifying the resources in it:

```
// start the transaction
ResourceSet resourceSet = new ResourceSetImpl();
ChangeRecorder recorder = new ChangeRecorder(resourceSet);

try
{
  // perform arbitrary manipulation
  ...
}
catch(Exception e)
{
  // error, rollback all changes
  recorder.endRecording().apply();
}
```

When recording at the resource set level (as in this example), the apply() method will roll back changes made to all resources in the set, even ones that were demand-loaded. One thing to keep in mind, however, is that it will not roll back the creation or deletion of files in the file system. For example, it will roll back all changes made to newly created files, but it will not delete the files themselves. This is because the change model isn't intended to manage resources, just object changes within those resources. If you want that additional resource deletion behavior, you'll need to implement it yourself. The change model certainly simplifies the problem by handling everything else.

CHAPTER 18

The Validation Framework

One problem we have not yet addressed is how we can define what constitutes a valid state for objects modeled in EMF. As we will see in this chapter, you can declare, right in your model, constraints and invariants to be verified when a validation is performed against the instances of your classes. Also, we'll detail how the code generated by EMF is affected by these new elements and how you can invoke validation either from your code or through the generated editors.

18.1 Constraints and Invariants

EMF's notion of constraints and invariants is inspired by their definition in UML. There, a constraint is a statement that must be valid at some point in time, whereas an invariant is an assertion that should always be true. For example, a method's precondition is definitely a constraint because it is a restriction that must be satisfied immediately before the method is executed. On the other hand, as an example, an invariant might state that an attribute that represents the age of a person must never assume a value less than zero, regardless of the moment this value is consulted.

In EMF, a class or data type can carry an Ecore annotation[1] representing one or more constraints. Each constraint corresponds to an assertion about the state of an instance of that classifier when validation is invoked. Using the PrimerPO example, suppose we wish to define the following two constraints on the class **Item**:

○ The quantity ordered of an item must be greater than zero.

○ An item's ship date must be later than the date of its order.

---

1. Ecore annotations are discussed in Section 5.7.

If we defined the model using annotated Java, then we could add the following annotation to the header of the `Item` interface (the annotation must be written in a single line):

```
/**
 * @model annotation="http://www.eclipse.org/emf/2002/Ecore constraints='NonNegativeQuantity ValidShipDate'"
 */
public interface Item
{
  ...
}
```

If the model was expressed as an XML Schema, we could declare the constraints as follows:

```
<xsd:complexType name="Item"
    ecore:constraints="NonNegativeQuantity ValidShipDate">
  ...
</xsd:complexType>
```

Note that `constraints` is one of the attributes defined in the Ecore namespace ("http://www.eclipse.org/emf/2002/Ecore"), which are used to represent Ecore model elements that otherwise couldn't be expressed directly in XML Schema.

In a Rose class diagram, we could simply set the **constraints** field in the **Ecore** page of the Class Specification dialog box, as illustrated in Figure 18.1.[2]

Although the annotation mechanism is really handy to specify constraints, it is not adequate for invariants. An invariant is a very strong statement about the object it is defined for, and because of that, it should be easily accessible to any code that manipulates the object. With this in mind, EMF represents invariants as operations of the class. An invariant operation has some special properties: its type is **EBoolean**, to indicate whether the invariant is satisfied, and it has two parameters, of types **EDiagnosticChain** and **EMap**.[3] The former is used by the validation framework to aggregate the results of the validation of constraints and invariants, whereas the latter caches information that needs to be accessed in different steps of the validation process. We'll look at these types more closely in the next section. Note that because operations cannot be defined on data types in Ecore, it is not possible to declare invariants on them.

---

2. The same effect could also be achieved by setting the **annotation** field to "http://www.eclipse.org/emf/ 2002/Ecore constraints='NonNegativeQuantity ValidShipDate'".

3. In the generated method these three types correspond to `boolean`, `DiagnosticChain`, and `Map`.

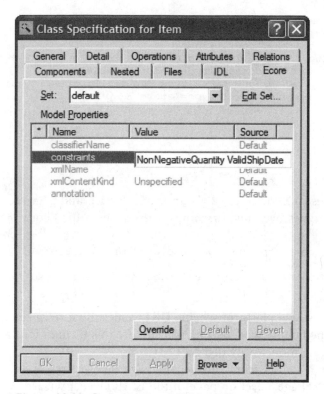

Figure 18.1   Constraints modeled in UML.

Back to the PrimerPO example, a possible invariant for a **USAddress** could assert that the **state** attribute is not empty if "US" is the specified **country**. For models defined as annotated Java, we would write this as follows:

```
/**
 * @model
 */
public interface USAddress
{
  ...
  /**
   * @model
   */
  boolean hasUSState(DiagnosticChain diagnostics, Map context);
}
```

Operations can be represented in XML Schema by a special Ecore appinfo annotation, as detailed in Section 9.3.7. This mechanism is used to declare an invariant as follows:

```
<xsd:complexType name="USAddress"
  <xsd:annotation>
    <xsd:appinfo ecore:key="operations"
        source="http://www.eclipse.org/emf/2002/Ecore">
      <operation name="hasUSState" type="ecore:EBoolean">
        <parameter name="diagnostics" type="ecore:EDiagnosticChain"/>
        <parameter name="context" type="ecore:EMap"/>
      </operation>
    </xsd:appinfo>
  </xsd:annotation>
  ...
</xsd:complexType>
```

For the references to `EBoolean`, `EDiagnosticChain`, and `EMap` to resolve to the desired Ecore types, we must first import the schema for Ecore:

```
<xsd:import namespace="http://www.eclipse.org/emf/2002/Ecore"
    schemaLocation=
      "platform:/plugin/org.eclipse.emf.ecore/model/Ecore.xsd"/>
```

Note that we're using a platform scheme URI to identify a resource within a plug-in installed in the Eclipse workbench. You can use this form of URI any time you need to reference a model provided by EMF.

When we create a model from this schema, we need to resolve the Ecore dependency on the **Package Selection** page of the EMF Project wizard. We do so simply by selecting "Ecore (external – org.eclipse.emf.ecore)" from the **Referenced generator models** table.

In UML, the **hasUSState** invariant is modeled as an operation with <<inv>> stereotype,[4] as in Figure 18.2.

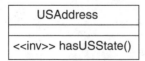

Figure 18.2   Invariant modeled in UML.

However you have chosen to express your model originally, it is always possible to add constraints and invariants directly to the Ecore model. Figure 18.3

---

4. Instead of using the stereotype, we could set the return and parameter types of the method as we did in the annotated Java file.

shows the model opened in the sample Ecore editor, where the invariant and constraint are represented directly as an operation and an annotation, respectively.[5]

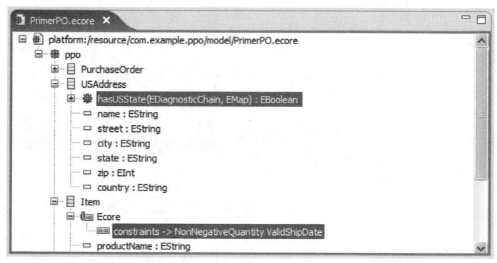

Figure 18.3   Invariant and constraints in the PrimerPO Ecore model.

18.2   Effects on Generated Code

The introduction of constraints and invariants in a model results in some changes in the generated code. Certainly the most obvious is the creation of a method for each operation that represents an invariant. Another change, less obvious yet more important for the validation framework, is the introduction of a new class in the *util* package: the package's validator class. In this section we will use these new elements as the starting point to present the details behind validations in EMF.

The **hasUSState** invariant declared in the previous section is implemented by the generator in the USAddressImpl class as follows:

```
public boolean hasUSState(DiagnosticChain diagnostics, Map context)
{
  // TODO: implement this method
  // -> specify the condition that violates the invariant
  // -> verify the details of the diagnostic, including severity
```

5. Although the Ecore editor just shows the last segment of the annotation's source, you must enter its full value: "http://www.eclipse.org/emf/2002/Ecore".

```
  //    and message
  // Ensure that you remove @generated or mark it @generated NOT
  if (false)
  {
    if (diagnostics != null)
    {
      diagnostics.add(
        new BasicDiagnostic(
          Diagnostic.ERROR,
          PPOValidator.DIAGNOSTIC_SOURCE,
          PPOValidator.US_ADDRESS__HAS_US_STATE,
          EcorePlugin.INSTANCE.getString(
            "_UI_GenericInvariant_diagnostic",
            new Object[] {
              "hasUSState",
              EObjectValidator.getObjectLabel(this, context)}),
          new Object [] { this }));
    }
    return false;
  }
  return true;
}
```

This method has to be hand modified, as stated in its comments. First, you must replace the word `false` in the first `if` clause with the condition that violates the invariant, which for this example could be:

```
if ("US".equals(getCountry()) && getState() == null)
```

We need to specify this condition here, in the Java code, because Ecore provides no way to represent it in the model.

Second, you might want to customize the details of the result produced when the validation fails. This result is called a *diagnostic* and is represented by an instance of the `Diagnostic` interface, such as the `BasicDiagnostic` used by default in the generated code. The arguments used when constructing this object are summarized in Table 18.1.

To provide complete feedback from the validation, you should ensure that the values for the arguments described in Table 18.1 are accurate. Note that the generated code computes a generic value for `message`, which includes the invariant name and a label for the object being validated. You should usually define a more specific, descriptive message for each invariant. In either case, the message does need to properly identify the object being validated. Analyzing the generated code, we can see that it delegates this task to the convenience method `getObjectLabel()` implemented in `EObjectValidator` as follows:

```
public static String getObjectLabel(EObject eObject, Map context)
{
```

Table 18.1 Basic Diagnostic Constructor Arguments

Argument	Type	Description
severity	int	Summarizes the outcome of the validation. This can be one of the following: Diagnostic.OK, Diagnostic.INFO, Diagnostic.WARNING, Diagnostic.ERROR, or Diagnostic.CANCEL. OK indicates the validation is successful; INFO, WARNING, and ERROR are applicable when the constraint or invariant is violated; and CANCEL is used to signal that a validation was interrupted (we discuss later the concept of chains of diagnostics, which can be interrupted).
source	String	Identifies where the constraint or invariant is defined. As generated, the model plug-in ID, which is the value of the validator class's DIAGNOSTIC_SOURCE constant, is used. This value usually need not be changed.
code	int	Identifies the particular reason for the validation's failure. Applications might want to define diagnostic codes that uniquely identify errors from a given source. The validation framework does not make use of this value, however.
message	String	Describes the outcome of the validation. The default implementation generated by EMF uses an externalized string to create a message with the name of the constraint or invariant and the label of the object being validated.
data	Object[]	References objects that are relevant to the diagnostic, such as the instance against which the validation is being performed.

```
if (context != null)
{
  SubstitutionLabelProvider substitutionlabelProvider =
    (SubstitutionLabelProvider)context.get(
      SubstitutionLabelProvider.class);
  if (substitutionlabelProvider != null)
  {
    return substitutionlabelProvider.getObjectLabel(eObject);
  }
}
return EcoreUtil.getIdentification(eObject);
}
```

Here you can see one of the usages for the context map. The code invoking the validation can add to the map an instance of the EValidator. SubstitutionLabelProvider interface to be queried for the label of the object. This design allows you to create a wrapper for the label provider you are using for the UI, ensuring that a given instance will be consistently labeled across your application.[6] If there is no such object in the map, the method returns a unique identifier for the object, as defined by `EcoreUtil.getIdentification()`. Of course, you can replace or complement this algorithm to better suit the requirements of your application. If that's the case, you might also want to customize the `EObjectValidator` methods `getFeatureLabel()` and `getValueLabel()`. They are to structural features and data types what `getObjectLabel()` is to classes.

The last comment to be made about the default implementation of the `hasUSState()` method is related to this line:

```
diagnostics.add(new BasicDiagnostic(...));
```

The `diagnostics` object implements the `DiagnosticChain` interface, and can be used to group all the diagnostics produced by the validation of different constraints and invariants. As we'll see in the next section, the data available in a chain of diagnostics provides very rich feedback to the user if properly presented.

Let's turn our attention to the package's validator class, the other difference you'll see when code is generated for a model with constraints and invariants. This class plays a very important role in the validation framework. Besides defining the constants to help identify what a `diagnostic` describes, it is where all the constraints defined on classes and data types in the package are implemented. As with invariants, each constraint corresponds to a method that requires your attention to work properly. For example, this is the implementation for the **ValidShipDate** constraint generated in `com.example.ppo.util.PPOValidator`:

```
public boolean validateItem_ValidShipDate(
  Item item, DiagnosticChain diagnostics, Map context)
{
  // TODO implement the constraint
  // -> specify the condition that violates the constraint
  // -> verify the diagnostic details, including severity, code,
  //    and message
  // Ensure that you remove @generated or mark it @generated NOT
  if (false)
  {
    if (diagnostics != null)
    {
      diagnostics.add(
```

---

6. That is exactly what is done behind the scenes in generated EMF editors.

```
          new BasicDiagnostic(
            Diagnostic.ERROR,
            DIAGNOSTIC_SOURCE,
            0,
            EcorePlugin.INSTANCE.getString(
              "_UI_GenericConstraint_diagnostic",
              new Object[] {
                "ValidShipDate",
                getObjectLabel(item, context) }),
            new Object[] { item }));
      }
    return false;
  }
  return true;
}
```

Again it is necessary to set the condition in the first `if` clause and to ensure that the instantiated `BasicDiagnostic` has the right information. For the preceding example, we could check if the item is in a purchase order and if the order and ship date are correct as follows:

```
public boolean validateItem_ValidShipDate(
    Item item, DiagnosticChain diagnostics, Map context)
{
  if (item.eContainer() instanceof PurchaseOrder)
  {
    Date orderDate =
      ((PurchaseOrder)item.eContainer()).getOrderDate();
    Date shipDate = item.getShipDate();

    if (orderDate != null && shipDate != null &&
        shipDate.before(orderDate))}
    {
      if (diagnostics != null)
      {
        diagnostics.add(new BasicDiagnostic(
          ...
```

We might also need to customize the diagnostic that gets produced. All of the previous comments about initializing the diagnostic and computing the object's label are also applicable here.

18.3   Invoking Validation

With the constraints and invariants fully implemented, you can take advantage of them in your application by validating your objects at important moments or at the user's discretion. For example, before actually placing a purchase order, you might want to verify that all objects in the order are in a valid state. A first attempt at a method that performs this validation might look like this:

```
// First implementation of the validateObject() method
public static boolean validateObject(PurchaseOrder order)
{
  if (!order.getBillTo().hasUSState(null, null) &&
      !order.getShipTo().hasUSState(null, null))
  {
    return false;
  }

  PPOValidator validator = PPOValidator.INSTANCE;
  for (Iterator i = order.getItems().iterator(); i.hasNext();)
  {
    Item item = (Item)i.next();
    if (!validator.validateItem_NonNegativeQuantity(item, null, null)
        && !validator.validateItem_ValidShipDate(item, null, null))
    {
      return false;
    }
  }
  return true;
}
```

This definitely fulfills the requirement of validating the purchase order, but it has a serious design flaw: it has to be manually updated to reflect any future changes to the model. New constraints and invariants, or even structural changes to the model, will easily make this method useless. A better implementation might be as follows:

```
// Second implementation of the validateObject() method
public static boolean validateObject(PurchaseOrder order)
{
  PPOValidator validator = PPOValidator.INSTANCE;

  if (!validator.validatePurchaseOrder(order, null, null))
  {
    return false;
  }
  if (!validator.validateUSAddress(order.getBillTo(), null, null))
  {
    return false;
  }
  if (!validator.validateUSAddress(order.getShipTo(), null, null))
  {
    return false;
  }

  for (Iterator i = order.getItems().iterator(); i.hasNext();)
  {
```

```
        if (!validator.validateItem((Item)i.next(), null, null))
        {
          return false;
        }
      }
    }
    return true;
  }
```

Whenever the package's validator class is generated, it will include a validate method for each class defined in the package. Here, we are invoking these methods, which are guaranteed to call out to all the constraints and invariants defined on the corresponding classes.

This solves the problem of hard-coding the explicit calls to the methods implementing the constraints and invariants, but it does not strengthen the algorithm to support other changes to the model. Because models do have a tendency to evolve, we could try another more generic implementation:

```
// Third implementation of the validateObject() method
public static boolean validateObject(EObject eObject)
{
  EValidator validator =
    EValidator.Registry.INSTANCE.getEValidator(
      eObject.eClass().getEPackage());
  if (validator != null)
  {
    if (!validator.validate(eObject, null, null))
    {
      return false;
    }

    for (Iterator i = eObject.eAllContents(); i.hasNext();)
    {
      if (!validator.validate((EObject)i.next(), null, null))
      {
        return false;
      }
    }
  }
  return true;
}
```

This implementation exposes the EValidator interface, which we have not mentioned until now. An EValidator is an object responsible for performing validation; as you might guess, PPOValidator, like any other generated package's validator class, implements this interface.

Also, right at the beginning of the method, you can see yet another global registry used in EMF. When a generated package is being initialized, it registers its default validator in the `EValidator.Registry`, which then can be queried by any code that needs to validate an object.

So, is this version of the algorithm the best implementation? It certainly addresses all the problems we've mentioned, but it still leaves a hole that we wouldn't notice in the PrimerPO example. It does not handle the scenario in which an object contains objects from different packages. To be as general as possible, we would have to ensure that we are using the appropriate validator for each object in the containment tree; that is, the validator registered for the package in which the object's class is defined.

As you can see, there are lots of details to be considered when writing a method to validate constraints and invariants. With that in mind, EMF's validation framework includes a helper class called `Diagnostician` that is the recommended entry point for validation. With this class, we can easily write the final version of the `validateObject()` method we've been evolving in this section:

```
// Fourth implementation of the validateObject() method
public static boolean validateObject(EObject eObject)
{
   Diagnostic diagnostic = Diagnostician.INSTANCE.validate(eObject);
   return diagnostic.getSeverity() == Diagnostic.OK;
}
```

The `Diagnostician` class provides several methods to start a validation, of which we've selected the simplest. The others allow you to specify, for example, the context and the diagnostic chain to use in the validation. `Diagnostician` also provides methods to verify if a given value violates any constraint defined for a data type. These methods can be really handy in some scenarios. For example, if you know there are several adapters listening to changes in your model, you can use one of these methods to validate a value before actually modifying an attribute of a class.

One interesting side effect of using a `Diagnostician` is that you can easily compute the result of the evaluation based on a diagnostic, instead of simply forwarding a `boolean` return value. This allows you not only to decide which severity represents a failure, but also to expose the information collected about the constraints and invariants that were not satisfied. As an example, if you were interested only in errors and warnings, you could replace the last line of the preceding implementation with this:

```
...
if (diagnostic.getSeverity() == Diagnostic.ERROR ||
    diagnostic.getSeverity() == Diagnostic.WARNING)
{
  System.err.println(diagnostic.getMessage());
  for (Iterator i=diagnostic.getChildren().iterator(); i.hasNext();)
  {
```

```
                  Diagnostic childDiagnostic = (Diagnostic)i.next();
                  switch (childDiagnostic.getSeverity())
                  {
                    case Diagnostic.ERROR:
                    case Diagnostic.WARNING:
                      System.err.println("\t" + childDiagnostic.getMessage());
                  }
              }
              return false;
        }
        return true;
```

Generated editors already provide a **Validate** action, which uses a diagnostician to perform full validation of the object selected in the editor. To use this UI to validate the constraints and invariant we've defined in this chapter, you need to generate edit and editor plug-ins for the PrimerPO model and start a new Eclipse instance to run them. In this second workbench, create a purchase order instance that violates the constraints and invariant, as detailed in Table 18.2.

Table 18.2 Purchase Order Instance Details

Type	Property	Value
Purchase Order	Order Date	2007-06-01
Item	Ship Date	2007-00-01
Item	Quantity	-2
US Address	State	Empty (null)

After initializing the objects, select the purchase order and choose **Validate** from either the menu bar, illustrated in Figure 18.4, or the context-sensitive menu.

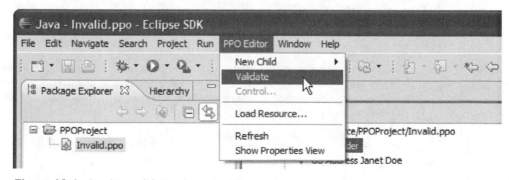

Figure 18.4 Invoking validation from the UI.

The diagnostics created during the validation process are presented in an error dialog box. All of the individual diagnostic messages are available to the user, as shown in Figure 18.5.

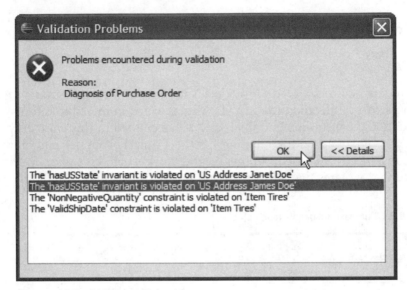

Figure 18.5　Validation dialog box.

If the user selects one of the diagnostics in the dialog box before clicking **OK**, the object that has caused that specific violation will be selected in the editor. Another free goody is the inclusion of markers for these diagnostics in Eclipse's Problems view, as shown in Figure 18.6.

Problems ✕　Javadoc	Declaration	Properties		
4 errors, 0 warnings, 0 infos				
Description ▲			Resource	Path
⊟ ☷ Errors (4 items)				
✖ The 'hasUSState' invariant is violated on 'US Address James Doe'			Invalid.ppo	PPOProject
✖ The 'hasUSState' invariant is violated on 'US Address Janet Doe'			Invalid.ppo	PPOProject
✖ The 'NonNegativeQuantity' constraint is violated on 'Item Tires'			Invalid.ppo	PPOProject
✖ The 'ValidShipDate' constraint is violated on 'Item Tires'			Invalid.ppo	PPOProject

Figure 18.6　Diagnostics in Eclipse's Problems view.

Another way of triggering validation in the UI is to use the Properties view to set the value of an attribute whose type has a constraint. For example, we could define the pattern-based constraint for the **SKU** data type mentioned in Section 13.4. After regenerating the model and adding the code to implement the constraint, you could restart the runtime workspace and try to set the **partNumber** of an **Item** to "a product". Behind the scenes, your input would be validated as you entered it. Because the value is invalid, you wouldn't be able to complete the change and the error message produced by the validation framework would be displayed in the status bar.

18.4 Basic EObject Constraints

All of the implementations of `validateObject()` in the previous section, except for the first, do a little more work than you might expect. Recall that, instead of directly calling the methods generated for each constraint, they make use of the validate methods for each type. As a "free bonus", these methods validate some intrinsic constraints, along with the ones we've defined. For example, reading the generated code for the method `PPOValidator.validateItem()`, which is executed directly in the second implementation of `validateObject()` and through the framework in the last two, you will see that the following constraints are being validated:

○ The actual multiplicities of the attributes and references match the bounds defined in the model.[7]

○ Any constraints on the data types of the attributes are respected.

○ Any cross-referenced objects are contained in resources.

○ Every referenced proxy resolves properly.

○ The object is uniquely identified in the resource by the ID attribute, if one is defined in the model.

The methods that validate these intrinsic constraints are inherited from `EObjectValidator`, which is the base for all generated package validator classes. It is also used directly for types from packages that do not have their own specialized validators.

Any diagnostic created when one of these constraints fails has `EObjectValidator.DIAGNOSTIC_SOURCE` as its source. This allows you to identify it in the diagnostic children list, which can be useful if you don't want to consider these constraints in computing the final validation status.

---

7. This is the only place in EMF where the exact bounds of the multiplicity are significant, beyond determining whether the feature is single-valued or multi-valued.

18.5   XML Schema Constraints

When your model is defined as an XML Schema, you are able to specify constraints on the values of data types by adding facets to simple type restrictions. EMF knows how to interpret the restrictions and how to convert them to annotations representing Ecore constraints. You can mix these built-in schema-based constraints with your own named constraints that are defined as described in Section 18.1.

Although we haven't highlighted them yet, we can find a couple of examples in the PrimerPO schema that we introduced in Chapter 4:

```xsd
<xsd:complexType name="Item">
  <xsd:sequence>
    ...
    <xsd:element name="quantity">
      <xsd:simpleType>
        <xsd:restriction base="xsd:positiveInteger">
          <xsd:maxInclusive value="100"/>
        </xsd:restriction>
      </xsd:simpleType>
    </xsd:element>
    ...
  </xsd:sequence>
  <xsd:attribute name="partNum" type="ppo:SKU" use="required"/>
</xsd:complexType>

<xsd:simpleType name="SKU">
  <xsd:restriction base="xsd:string">
    <xsd:pattern value="\d{3}-[A-Z]{2}"/>
  </xsd:restriction>
</xsd:simpleType>
```

We start by looking at the SKU simple type, which is used as the type of the partNum attribute. SKU is declared to be a restriction on the string built-in schema type. The pattern facet constrains the type to only allow values that match the given regular expression. When this simple type is converted to Ecore, the extended metadata annotation on the resulting **SKU** data type records the constraint, as described in Section 9.2.1. Then, when code is generated, a complete validateSKU_Pattern() method is included in the PPOValidator class. With no hand-coding required, the constraint will be validated for all instances of **SKU**—in this case, for the **partNum** of each **Item**.

The other simple type in the preceding snippet is defined anonymously for quantity: it is a restriction on the built-in positiveInteger type. This type is already constrained to allow only values of 0 or greater, and the additional maxInclusive facet further restricts it to 100 or less. When this is converted to

Ecore, a **QuantityType** data type is created and used as the type of **Item**'s **quantity** attribute. The data type's extended metadata annotation records the base type and the constraint, causing code to be generated into PPOValidator to validate that values do, indeed, fall within these specified bounds.

In Section 18.1, we implemented a similar restriction with a "NonNegativeQuantity" named constraint on the class **Item**. However, we then actually had to express the constraint using Java code, by implementing a method in the validator. When using XML Schema to define a model, you should take advantage of simple type restrictions to define constraints whenever possible, letting the generator do all of the implementation for you.

CHAPTER 19

EMF.Edit Programming

By now, you probably have a fairly good understanding of EMF and what you can do with it. You also know how EMF.Edit and its code generator let you quickly create viewers and editors for your EMF models. We've talked about how the framework is also designed to allow you to easily customize your views and editors, but we haven't really seen how that works yet.

The best way to show how easily EMF.Edit behavior can be customized is by looking at some examples. The following sections include several examples, each of which implements one or more common kinds of customization. Through the examples, we'll also introduce some of EMF.Edit's convenience classes that help make these kinds of customizations easier to implement.

19.1 Overriding Commands

In Chapter 3, we explained how modifications to modeled objects in EMF.Edit are made using commands. In an EMF.Edit-based editor, all the menu actions, property sheet changes, and even drag-and-drop, are implemented this way. By constructing commands using an editing domain, instead of simply using the Java `new` operator, the framework provides a convenient way for you to override the behavior of any editing command on your model; you can override the `createCommand()` method to return your own specialized implementation class.

We described in Section 3.3.3 how the default editing domain, `AdapterFactoryEditingDomain`, delegates the `createCommand()` method to the item provider of the primary object involved in the command (the command owner). We also mentioned how EMF.Edit's item provider base class, `ItemProviderAdapter`, implements the `createCommand()` method for all the generic EMF.Edit commands (`AddCommand`, `RemoveCommand`, etc.) described in Section 3.3.2, but we did not elaborate. Let's take it from there.

`ItemProviderAdapter` implements `createCommand()` by dispatching the creation of each of the standard (built-in) commands to command-specific convenience methods, something like this:

```
public Command createCommand(final Object object,
                             final EditingDomain domain,
                             Class commandClass,
                             CommandParameter cmdParam)
{
  ...
  if (commandClass == RemoveCommand.class)
    return createRemoveCommand(domain, cmdParam.getEOwner(),
      cmdParam.getEStructuralFeature(), cmdParam.getCollection());
  else if (commandClass == AddCommand.class)
    return createAddCommand(domain, cmdParam.getEOwner(), ...);
  else ...
}
```

The default implementation of each of these convenience methods simply returns a new instance of the appropriate command. For example, the `createRemoveCommand()` method in class `ItemProviderAdapter` looks pretty much like this:

```
protected Command createRemoveCommand(EditingDomain domain,
                                      EObject owner,
                                      EStructuralFeature feature,
                                      Collection collection)
{
  return new RemoveCommand(domain, owner, feature, collection);
}
```

With this design, you can customize any predefined EMF.Edit command by simply overriding its command-specific `create()` method; you don't need to override `createCommand()` itself unless you're adding a new type of command. Notice how, before calling the `create()` methods, the arguments for the various commands are first extracted from the generic `commandParameter` argument. The `create()` methods have the same signature as their corresponding command constructors, making them a most convenient override point.[1]

---

1. Actually, each command-specific `create()` method handles the case where the `feature` is an instance of `EReference` specially, further delegating to another, deprecated form of the method. This is because, originally, `ItemProviderAdapter` only provided command support for references and so the `create()` method signatures all included an `EReference` argument. When support was added for attributes, the new `create()` methods were added, but the originals had to be retained and invoked for references, to continue to support existing overrides. New code should only ever override the newer, `EStructuralFeature` forms, such as the `createRemoveCommand()` method shown earlier.

The first example we will look at involves customizing the purchase order application to support volume discounting. For the purpose of this example, any of the model versions that we've introduced previously will do, so we might as well use the simplest one, SimplePO, which was first introduced back in Chapter 2.

Recall that a purchase order item included, among other things, **price** and **quantity** attributes, as illustrated in Figure 19.1.

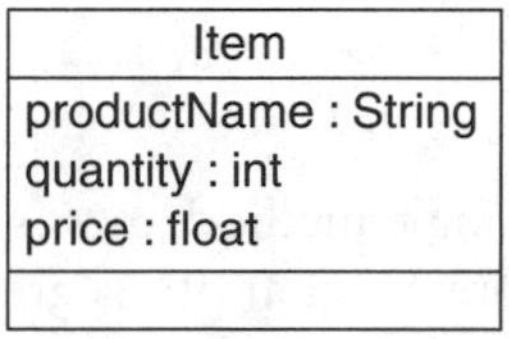

Item
productName : String quantity : int price : float

Figure 19.1   Purchase order item attributes.

In our example application we are going to provide a 10 percent price discount for item quantities of 10 or more, and we will implement this "volume discounting" by overriding the SetCommand. We need to implement the following special behavior:

1. When we set the quantity to a value greater than or equal to 10 and the previous quantity is less than 10, then we will also reduce the price by 10 percent.

2. When we set the quantity to a value less than 10 and the previous quan-tity is greater than or equal to 10, then we will increase the price (i.e., remove the 10 percent discount).

3. If we set the price while the quantity is greater than or equal to 10, then we will reduce the price by 10 percent before setting it.

Because we're changing the behavior when setting either the **price** or **quantity**, we need to customize the SetCommand for both attributes. We do this using two command subclasses, SetPriceCommand and SetQuantityCommand.

SetPriceCommand is a trivial subclass of the generic SetCommand that looks like this:

```
public class SetPriceCommand extends SetCommand
{
  public SetPriceCommand(EditingDomain domain, EObject owner,
                   EStructuralFeature feature, Object value)
  {
```

```
      super(domain, owner, feature, value);
    }

    public void doExecute()
    {
      Item item = (Item)owner;
      if (item.getQuantity() >= 10)
      {
        double newPrice = ((Float)value).floatValue() * 0.9;
        value = new Float(newPrice);
      }
      super.doExecute();
    }
}
```

As you can see, all we need to do is override a single method, doExecute(),[2]
to reduce the value (i.e., the price being set) if the item's quantity is greater than
or equal to 10. Because we're changing the actual value instance variable during doExecute(), the undo() and redo() methods will work without change.
Notice how we downcast the owner and value instance variables (from the base
class, SetCommand) to Item and Float, respectively. We can safely do this
because we will only be using this command for setting the **price** attribute on
purchase order items. We'll see how we arrange for this soon, but first let's take
a look at our other command subclass, SetQuantityCommand:

```
public class SetQuantityCommand extends CompoundCommand
{
  protected Item item;
  protected Object value;
  protected EditingDomain domain;

  public SetQuantityCommand(EditingDomain domain, Item item,
                            EStructuralFeature feature, Object value)
  {
    super(0);
    this.item = item;
    this.value = value;
    this.domain = domain;
    append(new SetCommand(domain, item, feature, value));
  }

  public void execute()
  {
    int oldQuantity = item.getQuantity();
    super.execute();
```

---

2. If you're wondering why we override the doExecute() method, instead of just execute(), it is
because the generic SetCommand, like all the EMF.Edit generic commands, is a subclass of
AbstractOverrideableCommand, which introduces this pattern as described in Chapter 3.

```
    int quantity = ((Integer)value).intValue();
    if (oldQuantity < 10 && quantity >= 10 ||
        oldQuantity >= 10 && quantity < 10)
    {
      double newPrice = quantity >= 10 ?
        item.getPrice() * 0.9 : item.getPrice() / 0.9;
      appendAndExecute(
        new SetCommand(domain, item, POPackage.Literals.ITEM__PRICE,
                       new Float(newPrice)));
    }
  }
}
```

The `SetQuantityCommand` is also quite simple, but notice how it is a subclass of `CompoundCommand` instead of `SetCommand`. EMF.Edit never relies on particular concrete command classes; it only ever deals with commands using the base interface `Command`. Even the return type of the `createSetCommand()` method in `ItemProviderAdapter` is `Command`; not `SetCommand`. This gives us a great deal of flexibility when overriding commands. As long as we implement the correct command semantics, we can use any implementation class we wish.

As you can see, the purpose of the `CompoundCommand` is to aggregate a `SetCommand` for the quantity, with possibly another one for setting the price. In the constructor, we create a "real" `SetCommand` for the quantity and append it to the empty compound command (i.e., `this`) by calling `append()`. Notice that we also record the `item`, `value`, and `domain` in instance variables, so that we can use them during `execute()` where we will need to determine if a change in price is also needed.

The `execute()` method works by first calling `super.execute()` to execute the actual `SetCommand` for the quantity. Next it performs the necessary checks to determine if a price increase or decrease is also required and if so, it calls the `CompoundCommand`'s `appendAndExecute()` method to append, and immediately execute, another `SetCommand` for the price.

Notice that with this compound command approach, we didn't need to override any other methods. By optionally appending the second `SetCommand` to the compound command during `execute()` this way, the default `undo()` and `redo()` methods (from class `CompoundCommand`) will simply call the corresponding methods on the one or two actual `SetCommands` that were executed.

Now that we have both our command override classes, all we need to do is plug them into the framework. Assuming we are using generated item providers, we can simply override the `createSetCommand()` method in class `ItemItemProvider` (i.e., the item provider for class **Item**) like this:

```
protected Command createSetCommand(EditingDomain domain,
                                   EObject owner,
                                   EStructuralFeature feature,
                                   Object value)
{
  if (feature == POPackage.Literals.ITEM__PRICE)
  {
    return new SetPriceCommand(domain, owner, feature, value);
  }
  else if (feature == POPackage.Literals.ITEM__QUANTITY)
  {
    return new SetQuantityCommand(domain, (Item)owner,
                                  feature, value);
  }
  return super.createSetCommand(domain, owner, feature, value);
}
```

The first check ensures that whenever a SetCommand is created for the **price** feature of a purchase order item (class **Item**), our SetPriceCommand will be used instead of the default implementation. The second check ensures that our SetQuantityCommand will be used whenever setting the **quantity** attribute. Any other feature will be set using the default SetCommand, which is constructed by calling super.createSetCommand().

Now that we've made these changes, you might be wondering what the visible effect will be. As we mentioned previously, property sheet changes in an EMF.Edit editor are implemented using SetCommand, so you can use the property sheet of the EMF.Edit generated editor to try out the new commands.

For example, if you run the purchase order editor and select an item with a quantity less than 10, the property sheet will look something like Figure 19.2.

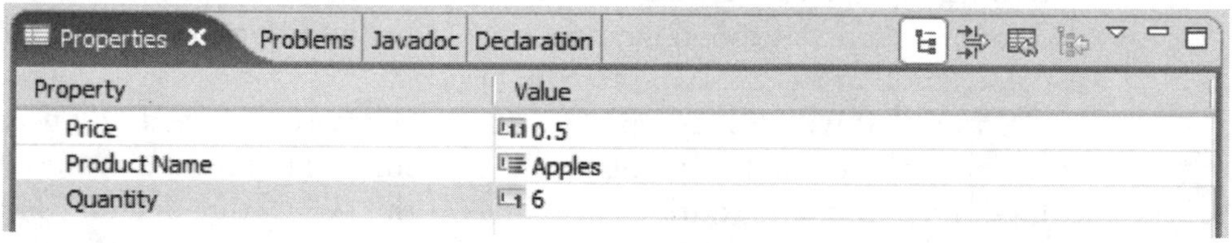

Figure 19.2 Property Sheet view for a purchase order item.

If you now change the "Quantity" to a value greater than 10 and press Enter, you'll see that the "Price" will now be reduced by 10 percent, as shown in Figure 19.3. You can also invoke the undo and redo actions, and you'll see that both attributes will be updated for them as well.

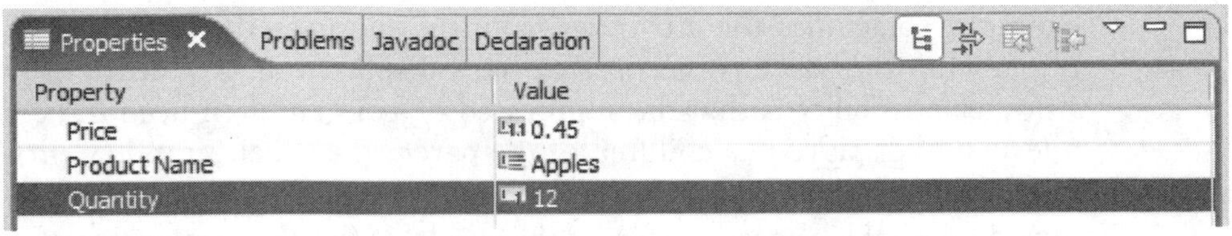

Figure 19.3   Volume discounting in action.

As you can see, overriding standard commands in EMF.Edit is really quite simple. The design we chose, using `CompoundCommand` as the base of `SetQuantityCommand`, is not the only way of doing this, but it is the simplest; it involves the minimum number of method overrides. If, instead, you try to do it by subclassing `SetCommand` (and maintaining the second `SetCommand` in an instance variable), for example, you'll see that's also simple enough, but it will require trivial overrides of the `undo()` and `redo()` methods as well.

19.2   Customizing Views

Whether you use a reflective item provider or generated ones, the views that EMF.Edit provides by default correspond very closely to the structure of the model. However, the structure that we want to display in a view is often quite different from that of the model. We've seen in Chapters 12 and 13 how you can use options in the generator model to control the EMF.Edit behavior (e.g., the references considered to be children, the features displayed in the property sheet, etc.). Now, we will consider some more significant changes that require hand-coding to implement.

In the following sections we'll look at three examples that change the view structure. In the first example, we'll modify the purchase order editor to suppress some of the model objects from the view. In the second example, we'll show how to modify the generated editor to use the list and table viewers to display more interesting data than they do by default. The final example will enhance the generated views by introducing additional (non-modeled) intermediate objects into the view structure.

19.2.1   *Suppressing Model Objects*

One of the most common customizations to an EMF.Edit generated editor involves suppressing some of the model objects from the view. In Chapters 11 and 12, we saw how, by setting the "Children" property to false in the generator model, we can avoid displaying some or all of the children of an object. Unfortunately, that's usually not the end of the story. Most of the time, information from the suppressed objects still needs to be displayed somewhere. For example, sometimes the attributes from the suppressed child should be used in the label of the parent object, or perhaps displayed as properties of the parent. Another possibility is that the suppressed object's children need to be pushed up a level and displayed as children of the parent (i.e., their grandparent).

This example is based on the PrimerPO model from Chapter 4. One of the most undesirable characteristics of this model (from the perspective of EMF.Edit's default behavior) is that class **PurchaseOrder** includes containment references for items as well as addresses (**billTo** and **shipTo**), as shown in Figure 19.4.

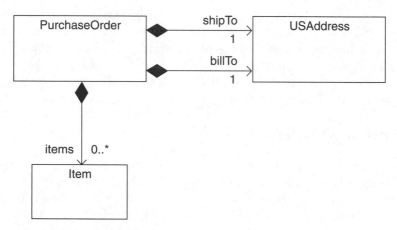

Figure 19.4 Model with multiple containment references.

As a result, the default purchase order editor displays both items and address as the children of a purchase order, as shown in Figure 19.5. To set the actual **shipTo** (or **billTo**) attributes (i.e., **name**, **street**, **city**, etc.) in the property sheet, you would first need to select the appropriate address in the tree view, for example. Notice that by default it isn't even clear which of the two addresses is the **shipTo** and which is the **billTo**.

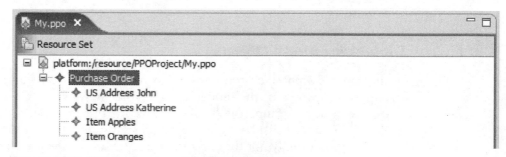

Figure 19.5 Default tree view of the PrimerPO model.

Although usable, this is clearly not the best way to display the model. A better approach, which we will implement in this example, is to suppress the addresses and only show the items as children, as shown in Figure 19.6. Notice that this view also has another change: we suppressed the root object (i.e., the resource *My.ppo*) and made the purchase order itself the root. This is another common example where suppression makes sense, because this editor will only ever be editing a single resource at a time.

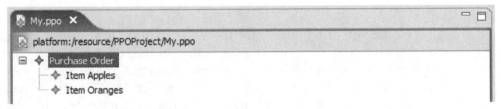

Figure 19.6   Improved purchase order tree view.

Now that we'll be suppressing the **billTo** and **shipTo** addresses, we need to figure out how the user will set their attributes. Making them additional properties of the purchase order would make sense because they can be seen as just the components of two compound attributes anyway. In this example, we will make the property sheet display them as categorized attributes of the purchase order as shown in Figure 19.7.

Property	Value
☐ Bill To	
City	SomeCity
Country	US
Name	Katherine
State	SomeState
Street	123 Maple Street
Zip	12345
☐ Misc	
☐ Ship To	

Figure 19.7   Customized purchase order property sheet.

Now that we've figured out how we want the purchase order editor to look, let's get to it. The first thing we will change is actually the simplest; suppressing the root object (the resource) from the tree view. The root object of the tree viewer (**Selection** tab) is set by a call to the viewer's `setInput()` method, made from the generated editor's `createPages()` method:

```
public void createPages()
{
  ...
  selectionViewer.setInput(editingDomain.getResourceSet());
  viewerPane.setTitle(editingDomain.getResourceSet());
  ...
}
```

Notice that it sets the input to be the resource set, not the resource. You might recall from Chapter 11 that this is because the tree viewer's input is an invisible root, whose children (the single resource, *My.ppo*, in this case) are the actual displayed roots. So, to change the displayed root to be the purchase order, instead of the resource, all we need to do is set the input and title (because we want the pane title to also reflect this change) to the resource, like this:

```
/**
 * @generated NOT
 */
public void createPages()
{
  ...
  selectionViewer.setInput(editingDomain.getResourceSet());
  viewerPane.setTitle(editingDomain.getResourceSet());
  ResourceSet resourceSet = editingDomain.getResourceSet();
  Resource resource = (Resource)resourceSet.getResources().get(0);
  selectionViewer.setInput(resource);
  viewerPane.setTitle(resource);
  ...
}
```

Since we know there is only one resource in the resource set, we simply get the first resource from the set by calling `get(0)`. Then we use it as the input and title for the view.

Because we're changing a generated method here, we also need to remove the `@generated` tag from the method comment. Notice that instead of actually deleting it, we did this by adding NOT after the `@generated` tag, as described in Chapter 10, so that we can easily keep track of which generated methods we've modified.

Now that we've eliminated the resource, the next job is to suppress the two addresses, **shipTo** and **billTo**. The best way to do this is by simply setting the "Children" and "Create Child" properties to "false" on the two features in the generator model, and then regenerating the `PurchaseOrderItemProvider`.

Once we do that, the generated `getChildrenFeatures()` method should only include the **items** reference:

```
public Collection getChildrenFeatures(Object object)
{
  if (childrenFeatures == null)
  {
    super.getChildrenFeatures(object);
    childrenFeatures.add(
      PPOPackage.Literals.PURCHASE_ORDER__SHIP_TO);
    childrenFeatures.add(
      PPOPackage.Literals.PURCHASE_ORDER__BILL_TO);
    childrenFeatures.add(PPOPackage.Literals.PURCHASE_ORDER__ITEMS);
  }
  return childrenFeatures;
}
```

This change eliminates the addresses from the view, as they are no longer considered children of the purchase order. A similar change appears in `collectNewChildDescriptors()`, eliminating **New Child** menu items for the addresses.

So far, so good. Now we just need to add the address properties to the purchase order. We can do that by overriding the generated `getPropertyDescriptors()` method in class `PurchaseOrderItemProvider` like this:

```
public List getPropertyDescriptors(Object object)
{
  if (itemPropertyDescriptors == null)
  {
    getPropertyDescriptorsGen(object);

    addAddressPropertyDescriptors(
      ((PurchaseOrder)object).getShipTo(),
      getString("_UI_PurchaseOrder_shipTo_feature"));
    addAddressPropertyDescriptors(
      ((PurchaseOrder)object).getBillTo(),
      getString("_UI_PurchaseOrder_billTo_feature"));
  }
  return itemPropertyDescriptors;
}
```

Here we first call the generated version, which we've renamed `getPropertyDescriptorsGen()`, to add the normal purchase order properties, and then we use a convenience method, `addAddressPropertyDescriptors()`, to also add the **shipTo** and **billTo** properties. The `addAddressProperty-Descriptors()` method looks like this:

```
public void addAddressPropertyDescriptors(USAddress address,
                                          final String addressFeature)
{
  USAddressItemProvider addressItemProvider =
    (USAddressItemProvider)adapterFactory.adapt(
      address, IItemPropertySource.class);
  List descriptors =
    addressItemProvider.getPropertyDescriptors(address);

  for (Iterator iter = descriptors.iterator(); iter.hasNext(); )
  {
    ItemPropertyDescriptor descriptor =
      (ItemPropertyDescriptor)iter.next();
    itemPropertyDescriptors.add(
      new ItemPropertyDescriptorDecorator(address, descriptor)
      {
        public String getCategory(Object thisObject)
        {
          return addressFeature;
        }

        public String getId(Object thisObject)
        {
          return addressFeature + getDisplayName(thisObject);
        }
      });
  }
}
```

As you can see, all this method does is delegate to the appropriate address's item provider to get the required property descriptors. Notice how, instead of directly adding the descriptors to its list, it uses the EMF.Edit helper class `ItemPropertyDescriptorDecorator` to override the `getCategory()` and `getId()` methods. It needs to override `getCategory()` to achieve the grouping shown in Figure 19.7. The `getId()` override is needed because every property must be uniquely identified, and since we're using the `USAddressItemProvider`'s properties twice (for **shipTo** and then again for **billTo**), they will otherwise conflict.

That's all there is to it; the two addresses have been suppressed and their properties merged with those of the purchase order. There are, however, a couple of other minor changes that we should make in support of this change. First, when one of the `USAddress`'s properties is changed, using the `SetCommand`, we would like to make it appear (in the UI) as if the purchase order, which is pretending to own it, has changed instead of the invisible **billTo** or **shipTo** address. We can easily do this by overriding the `createSetCommand()` method in `USAddressItemProvider` like this:

```
protected Command createSetCommand(EditingDomain domain,
                                   EObject owner,
                                   EStructuralFeature feature,
                                   Object value)
{
  return
    new SetCommand(domain, owner, feature, value)
    {
      public Collection doGetAffectedObjects()
      {
        return Collections.singleton(owner.eContainer());
      }
    };
}
```

Here we use a simple anonymous subclass of SetCommand to override the doGetAffectedObjects() method to return the eContainer() (i.e., the purchase order) of the command owner, which will be either the **shipTo** or **billTo** address. This way the purchase order will be selected whenever an address property is set. Without this change, nothing would appear to be selected because the affected object (the address) is nowhere visible.

The final change we make for this example relates to the creation of the **USAddress** objects. Notice how the changes we made in createSetCommand() and addAddressPropertyDescriptors() blindly assume that addresses are associated with purchase orders; the associations between them are assumed to never return null. If we wanted to do lazy creation of the addresses, we could add guards in our methods to handle the null case appropriately, but to keep the example as simple as possible we decided instead to simply guarantee that a purchase order and its two addresses will always exist as a group. We accomplished this by simply modifying the createInitialModel() method in PPOModelWizard like this:

```
/**
 * @generated NOT
 */
EObject createInitialModel()
{
  PurchaseOrder rootObject = ppoFactory.createPurchaseOrder();
  rootObject.setShipTo(ppoFactory.createUSAddress());
  rootObject.setBillTo(ppoFactory.createUSAddress());
  return rootObject;
}
```

By modifying the createInitialModel() method this way, we've removed the ability for the user to select a root object in the wizard. Because of this, we should also remove the initial object creation page from the wizard by modifying the addPages() method as we did in the final example of Chapter 13.

19.2.2   Using List and Table Viewers

Now that you are familiar with EMF.Edit and the kind of editor that it generates, you've probably noticed that the standard tree viewer (**Selection** tab) is the only one that is more than marginally interesting. The other tabs (**Parent, List,** etc.) are not providing any additional information. They're all displaying the same relationships, but in a slightly different way.

This is fine for the generated views, which are only intended to illustrate how other viewers work with EMF.Edit, but for a real model editor, like the purchase order editor, there are other more interesting uses for these viewers.

In this example, we are going to modify the generated purchase order editor's **List** and **Table** views to display more interesting information. This example is based on the ExtendedPO1 model, which includes an association between customers and purchase orders, as illustrated in Figure 19.8.

Customer		PurchaseOrder
customerID : int	customer ...... orders	comment : String
	1 ...... 0..*	orderDate : Date

Figure 19.8   Model showing association between customers and purchase orders.

We're going to change the generated editor's list view so that whenever a customer is selected (e.g., in the outline view), the list will display that customer's purchase orders, as shown in Figure 19.9.

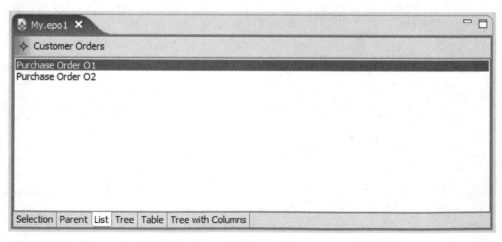

Figure 19.9   Customer orders list view.

To accomplish this, we'll use EMF.Edit's `ItemProvider` convenience class, a customizable item provider implementation for providers that are not also EMF adapters. You might recall from Chapter 11 (and the previous example) that the object passed to a tree viewer (i.e., to the `setInput()` method) is not actually displayed. Instead, the `getElements()` method on the content provider is called to retrieve the root objects for the viewer. This is actually true for all JFace viewers, including our list viewer. The object that we pass to the `setInput()` method of the list viewer will only be used to retrieve the actual list of objects to display; it will not be displayed itself. So, to produce our desired list of purchase orders, all we need to do is create an instance of class `ItemProvider` that will return the required purchase orders when the `getElements()` method, from interface `IStructuredContentProvider`, is called. We do it like this in class `EPO1Editor`:

```
/**
 * @generated NOT
 */
public void handleContentOutlineSelection(ISelection selection)
{
  if (currentViewerPane != null && !selection.isEmpty() &&
      selection instanceof IStructuredSelection)
  {
    Iterator selectedElements =
      ((IStructuredSelection)selection).iterator();
    if (selectedElements.hasNext())
    {
      Object selectedElement = selectedElements.next();
      if (currentViewerPane.getViewer() == selectionViewer)
      { ... }
      else if (currentViewerPane.getViewer() == listViewer)
      {
        Collection customerOrders =
          selectedElement instanceof Customer ?
            ((Customer)selectedElement).getOrders() :
            Collections.EMPTY_LIST;

        ItemProvider listRoot =  new ItemProvider(
          "Customer Orders",
          ExtendedPO1EditPlugin.INSTANCE.getImage(
            "full/obj16/PurchaseOrder"),
          customerOrders);
        listViewer.setInput(listRoot);
        currentViewerPane.setTitle(listRoot);
      }
      else
      { ... }
    }
  }
}
```

As you can see, we modify the `handleContentOutlineSelection()` method, which is called whenever the selection changes. If the current selection is a customer, then we get its associated purchase orders by calling the `getOrders()` method, create an instance of class `ItemProvider` using them, and then pass it to the `setInput()` and `setTitle()` method of the list viewer. Now, whenever we select a customer in the ExtendedPO1 editor, the list viewer will display the customer's orders as we intended.

Now that we have a more useful list viewer, let's look at enhancing the table viewer. You might have noticed that the table viewer, as generated, isn't particularly interesting; it displays the same thing in each of its two columns. We're going to change it to instead display the complete list of purchase orders in the first column (column 0) and each order's associated customer in the second (column 1). Our modified view is shown in Figure 19.10.

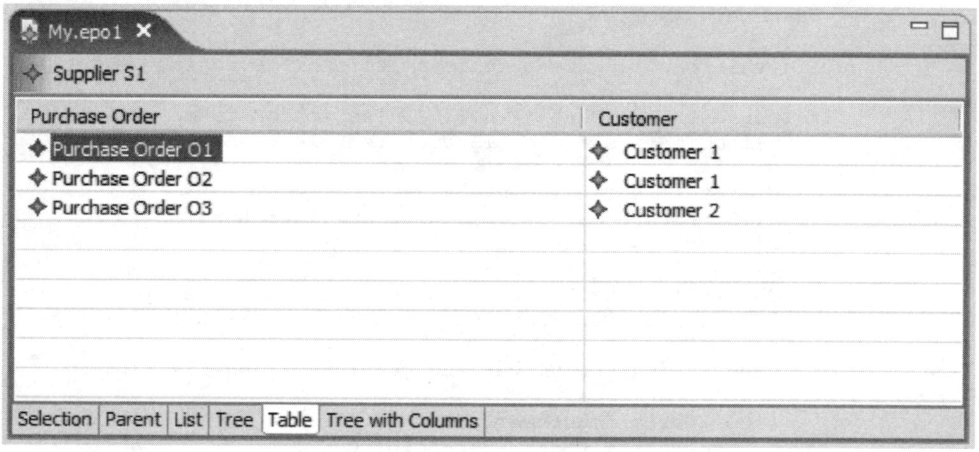

Figure 19.10 Purchase order table view.

In Chapter 3, we mentioned how EMF.Edit's generic content and label provider classes, `AdapterFactoryContentProvider` and `AdapterFactory-LabelProvider`, implement the JFace provider interfaces by delegating to item providers. We described how their implementations delegate to corresponding interfaces on an item provider. As we saw in Chapter 11, the generated item providers (and the reflective one, for that matter) implement all of the required item provider interfaces except one: `ITableItemLabelProvider`. To properly support a table viewer, we will need to mix it in and implement it ourselves.

We explained in Chapter 11 that the generated table viewer works because `AdapterFactoryLabelProvider`'s implementation of the JFace interface

`ITableLabelProvider` first checks if the `ITableItemLabelProvider` interface is supported by the item provider and if not, it delegates to the `IItemLabelProvider` interface instead. If you look at the two interfaces, you'll notice that the only difference is that the `getText()` and `getImage()` methods in the table version include a column index argument, whereas the ordinary label provider interface does not. As a result, any table viewer based on the default item providers will only be able to retrieve one label per row, so if there is more than one column in the table, they will all display the same thing.

Now that we want to put something more interesting in the table viewer, what we need to do is add the `ITableItemLabelProvider` interface to the implements list of class `PurchaseOrderItemProvider`, like this:

```
/**
 * This is the item provider adapter for a PurchaseOrder object.
 * <!-- begin-user-doc -->
 * @implements ITableItemLabelProvider
 * <!-- end-user-doc -->
 * @generated
 */
public class PurchaseOrderItemProvider
  extends ItemProviderAdapter
  implements
    IEditingDomainItemProvider,
    IStructuredItemContentProvider,
    ITreeItemContentProvider,
    IItemLabelProvider,
    IItemPropertySource,
    ITableItemLabelProvider
{ ...
```

Notice that we have also added an `@implements` tag to the user section of the Javadoc. As described in Section 10.11, this ensures that the additional interface will be retained when we regenerate the class.

Next, we simply implement the `getColumnText()` method to return the associated customer's text for column 1, like this:

```
public String getColumnText(Object object, int columnIndex)
{
  if (columnIndex == 0) return getText(object);
  Customer customer = ((PurchaseOrder)object).getCustomer();
  if (customer == null) return "";

  IItemLabelProvider itemLabelProvider =
    (IItemLabelProvider)adapterFactory.adapt(
      customer, IItemLabelProvider.class);
  return itemLabelProvider.getText(customer);
}
```

Notice that for column 0, we retrieve the label by simply calling the IItemLabelProvider.getText() method on the same item provider (i.e., the method that previously was called for all columns). For column 1, we first need to adapt the customer before we call getText() on its label provider.

We implement the getColumnImage() method similarly:

```
public Object getColumnImage(Object object, int columnIndex)
{
  if (columnIndex == 0) return getImage(object);
  Customer customer = ((PurchaseOrder)object).getCustomer();
  if (customer == null)
    return getResourceLocator().getImage("full/obj16/Customer");

  IItemLabelProvider itemLabelProvider =
    (IItemLabelProvider)adapterFactory.adapt(
      customer, IItemLabelProvider.class);
  return itemLabelProvider.getImage(customer);
}
```

Finally, we need to add one more supported type to the constructor of the item provider adapter factory, like this:

```
/**
 * This constructs an instance.
 * <!-- begin-user-doc -->
 * <!-- end-user-doc -->
 * @generated NOT
 */
public EPO1ItemProviderAdapterFactory()
{
  supportedTypes.add(IStructuredItemContentProvider.class);
  supportedTypes.add(ITreeItemContentProvider.class);
  supportedTypes.add(IItemPropertySource.class);
  supportedTypes.add(IEditingDomainItemProvider.class);
  supportedTypes.add(IItemLabelProvider.class);
  supportedTypes.add(ITableItemLabelProvider.class);
}
```

With these changes in place, a table viewer, when populated with a list of purchase orders, can display each purchase order with its associated customer as desired. So, to finish our enhancement, we now need to populate our generated editor's table viewer with a set of purchase orders.

By default, the contents of the generated table viewer are selection driven; it displays the children of the current selection in the outline view. We're going to change it so that the content is the complete set of purchase orders, regardless of the current selection. We'll also change *its* selection to match the outline view's selection. Notice that this is how the generated tree viewer on the **Selection** page works.

To make our change, we first need to override the `createPages()` method in class `EPO1Editor` to populate the table viewer with the list of purchase orders. There are several ways that we could do this (including using class `ItemProvider` as we did for the **List** view) but the simplest approach is to subclass the `AdapterFactoryContentProvider` that we use for the table viewer in the generated editor. While we're doing this, we'll also change the viewer's column headings. Here's our modified version of the generated `createPages()` method:

```
/**
 * @generated NOT
 */
public void createPages()
{
  ...
  TableColumn objectColumn = new TableColumn(table, SWT.NONE);
  layout.addColumnData(new ColumnWeightData(3, 100, true));
  objectColumn.setText(getString("_UI_ObjectColumn_label"));
  objectColumn.setText("Purchase Order");
  objectColumn.setResizable(true);

  TableColumn selfColumn = new TableColumn(table, SWT.NONE);
  layout.addColumnData(new ColumnWeightData(2, 100, true));
  selfColumn.setText(getString("_UI_SelfColumn_label"));
  selfColumn.setText("Customer");
  selfColumn.setResizable(true);

  tableViewer.setColumnProperties(new String [] {"a", "b"});
  tableViewer.setContentProvider(
    new AdapterFactoryContentProvider(adapterFactory)
    {
      public Object [] getElements(Object object)
      {
        return ((Supplier)object).getOrders().toArray();
      }
      public void notifyChanged(Notification notification)
      {
        super.notifyChanged(new ViewerNotification(notification));
      }
    });
  tableViewer.setLabelProvider(
    new AdapterFactoryLabelProvider(adapterFactory));

  Resource resource =
    (Resource)editingDomain.getResourceSet().getResources().get(0);
  Object rootObject = resource.getContents().get(0);
  if (rootObject instanceof Supplier)
  {
    tableViewer.setInput(rootObject);
```

```
    viewerPane.setTitle(rootObject);
  }

  createContextMenuFor(tableViewer);
  ...
}
```

As you can see, in addition to changing the two table column headings (text), we've overridden the `AdapterFactoryContentProvider` `getElements()` method to only return purchase orders (i.e., the value of the **orders** feature on class **Supplier**) and the `notifyChanged()` method to only pass on changes to the **orders** feature. Notice how we assume that the only object that will ever be passed to the `getElements()` method will be an instance of class **Supplier**. We can do this because we've also added the call to `setInput()` to guarantee it. We've made sure that the root object is an instance of class **Supplier**, before calling `setInput()`. If it's not, we'll simply leave the table view empty.

We have also implemented `notifyChanged()` to ensure that the table viewer will be updated after every change notification. In Section 11.1.4, we described how item providers can wrap model change notifications in `ViewerNotifications` that describe how to update viewers in response to the changes. Here, we are always creating and passing along a notification that completely refreshes the viewer. We could make things a little more efficient by first checking the notification's feature, and only updating the viewer when **PurchaseOrder.comment**, **PurchaseOrder.customer**, **Customer.customerID**, or **Supplier.orders** is changed. However, the approach we have taken is the simplest. In either case, we also need to ensure that `CustomerItemProvider`'s `notifyChanged()` method will forward **customer** change notifications to the adapter factory, as it doesn't by default. We can do this via the generator model. We simply set the "Notification" property on the feature to "true" and regenerate the code.

We need to make one more change to prevent the table viewer's input from being changed to reflect the current selection. We do this by changing the `handleContentOutlineSelection()` method like this:

```
public void handleContentOutlineSelection(ISelection selection)
{
  ...
      if (currentViewerPane.getViewer() == selectionViewer ||
          currentViewerPane.getViewer() == tableViewer)
      {
        ArrayList selectionList = new ArrayList();
        selectionList.add(selectedElement);
        while (selectedElements.hasNext())
        {
```

```
              selectionList.add(selectedElements.next());
          }

          // Set the selection to the widget.
          //
          selectionViewer.setSelection(
            new StructuredSelection(selectionList));
          currentViewerPane.getViewer().setSelection(
            new StructuredSelection(selectionList));
      }
    ...
}
```

Notice that, as we said earlier, we're changing the selection behavior for the table viewer to be the same as it is for the viewer on the **Selection** page (selectionViewer).

19.2.3 Adding Non-Model Intermediary View Objects

Another common EMF.Edit customization involves introducing non-model view objects between an object and its children. Model classes often include more than one containment reference, but sometimes the default item provider implementation, which displays them as one flat heterogeneous list of children, is not desirable. Unlike our solution for the **shipTo** and **billTo** references in Section 19.2.1, suppressing some of them is often not an option. Grouping them, using intermediary objects in the view, is a good alternative in this situation. The ExtendedPO1 model is a good example.

Recall that in the ExtendedPO1 model, class **Supplier** includes two kinds of children, customers and purchase orders, as illustrated in Figure 19.11.

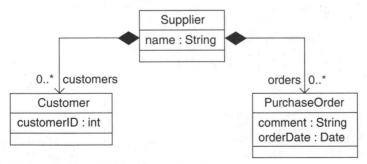

Figure 19.11 Children of class Supplier.

Instead of suppressing one or the other, we'd like both associations to be displayed as children, but in this example, we will introduce "Orders" and

"Customers" nodes into the view to separate the two categories of children, as shown in Figure 19.12.

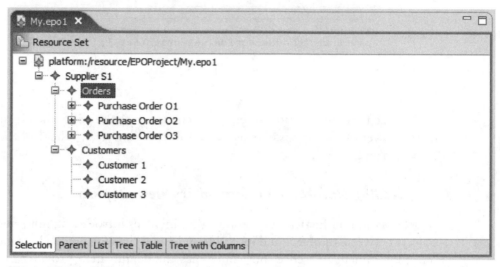

Figure 19.12   Adding non-modeled nodes in a view.

Adding such objects in a view is really quite simple, although there is some extra work involved to keep all the commands (especially drag-and-drop) working properly. Even so, it's still not that hard, as we'll see next.

As you might have guessed, the first change we need to make is to override the getChildren() method in the item provider for class **Supplier**. Assuming generated item providers, we can simply add the following to class Supplier-ItemProvider:

```
protected List children = null;

public Collection getChildren(Object object)
{
  if (children == null)
  {
    Supplier supplier = (Supplier)object;
    children = new ArrayList();
    children.add(new OrdersItemProvider(adapterFactory, supplier));
    children.add(new CustomersItemProvider(adapterFactory,
                                           supplier));
  }
  return children;
}
```

Here we're overriding the getChildren() method to return instances of two item provider classes, OrdersItemProvider and CustomersItemProvider, which we will implement by hand. Recall from Chapter 3 that the getChildren() method is supposed to return objects from the model, not item providers. The item providers are usually retrieved from these returned objects when the content and label providers call the adapt() method on the adapter factory. In our example, however, there are no "Orders" or "Customers" model classes, so we simply return item providers instead. This all hangs together because of the default implementation of adapt() (in class AdapterFactoryImpl):

```
public Object adapt(Object target, Object type)
{
  if (target instanceof Notifier)
  {
    return adapt((Notifier)target, type);
  }
  else
  {
    return resolve(target, type);
  }
}

protected Object resolve(Object object, Object type)
{
  return object;
}
```

Notice that if the object being adapted is not an EMF object (a Notifier), it simply returns the object itself. With this design, an item provider—like **Supplier**—that wants to add non-model objects to a view can simply return instances of any class that implements the required item provider interfaces itself. This is the secret to displaying a mixture of EMF (modeled) and non-modeled objects in the same view.

Before we move on to look at the implementation of our two new item provider classes, there is one more thing worth mentioning about SupplierItemProvider. Notice in the preceding code fragment that we also added an instance variable, children, to maintain the children collection. As a result, we must regenerate the supplier item provider using the Stateful pattern (instead of the usually preferred Singleton pattern), which we described in Chapter 11.

Let's move on and look at our new item providers. Actually, they both use exactly the same pattern so we really just need to look at one of them to understand the design. We choose OrdersItemProvider for no particular reason:

```
public class OrdersItemProvider
  extends TransientSupplierItemProvider
{
  public OrdersItemProvider(AdapterFactory adapterFactory,
                            Supplier supplier)
  {
    super(adapterFactory, supplier);
  }

  public Collection getChildrenFeatures(Object object)
  {
    if (childrenFeatures == null)
    {
      super.getChildrenFeatures(object);
      childrenFeatures.add(EPO1Package.Literals.SUPPLIER__ORDERS);
    }
    return childrenFeatures;
  }

  public String getText(Object object)
  {
    return "Orders";
  }

  protected void collectNewChildDescriptors(
    Collection newChildDescriptors, Object object)
  {
    super.collectNewChildDescriptors(newChildDescriptors, object);
    newChildDescriptors.add(createChildParameter(
        EPO1Package.Literals.SUPPLIER__ORDERS,
        EPO1Factory.eINSTANCE.createPurchaseOrder()));
  }

}
```

Notice how it looks very similar to a generated item provider. In fact, if you compare these methods with the generated ones in class SupplierItemProvider, you'll notice that they're implementing the **orders**-specific subset of each method. For example, getChildrenFeatures() looks like this in SupplierItemProvider:

```
public Collection getChildrenFeatures(Object object)
{
  if (childrenFeatures == null)
  {
    super.getChildrenFeatures(object);
    childrenFeatures.add(EPO1Package.Literals.SUPPLIER__CUSTOMERS);
    childrenFeatures.add(EPO1Package.Literals.SUPPLIER__ORDERS);
  }
  return childrenFeatures;
}
```

As you can see, the difference is the elimination of the **customers** part, which makes perfect sense because this is the "Orders" node, which shouldn't know anything about the **customers** reference.

You might have noticed that some of the methods in class `OrdersItemProvider`, like `getChildrenFeatures()`, are template methods from class `ItemProviderAdapter`, as described in Chapter 11. You might also recall from Chapters 3 and 11 how class `ItemProviderAdapter` is used as the convenient base class for item providers that are adapters for EMF model objects. This might seem surprising, because we already pointed out how there are no modeled classes for "Orders" or "Customers". So what model objects are they adapting?

If you think about it, although not the "official" item providers for class **Supplier**, `CustomersItemProvider` and `OrdersItemProvider` can really be thought of as providers of a subset of a supplier. Much of their implementation works in the usual way using the supplier model object. Also, registering them as observers of the supplier is necessary if they need to respond to or forward its change notifications. So, the bottom line is that we simply have three item providers attached to the supplier model object; the first (i.e., `SupplierItemProvider`) is the real item provider for the supplier, whereas the other two are simply attached as an implementation convenience.

You might have noticed that the base class of `OrdersItemProvider` is not actually `ItemProviderAdapter`, but instead another class, `TransientSupplierItemProvider`. `TransientSupplierItemProvider` is another hand-coded convenient base class, which contains a few methods that are shared by `OrdersItemProvider` and `CustomersItemProvider`. It is, itself, a typical subclass of `ItemProviderAdapter` that mixes in the standard item provider interfaces:

```
public class TransientSupplierItemProvider
  extends ItemProviderAdapter
  implements
    IEditingDomainItemProvider,
    IStructuredItemContentProvider,
    ITreeItemContentProvider,
    IItemLabelProvider,
    IItemPropertySource
{ ...
```

Because the "Orders" and "Customers" item providers are not created in the usual way (i.e., by calling `adapt()` for the supplier), their constructors explicitly add them to the `eAdapters` list like this:

```
public TransientSupplierItemProvider(AdapterFactory adapterFactory,
                                      Supplier supplier)
{
  super(adapterFactory);
  supplier.eAdapters().add(this);
}
```

Most of the other methods in `TransientSupplierItemProvider` are simple method overrides that substitute arguments before calling the super version of the same method. For example, `getChildren()` looks like this:

```
public Collection getChildren(Object object)
{
  return super.getChildren(target);
}
```

Notice how the `object` argument is replaced with the target of the adapter. When `getChildren()` is called, the `object` argument will be the item provider itself, because the transient item providers are masquerading as model objects as well. The `target` instance variable comes from the adapter base class `AdapterImpl`, and in this case will be the supplier to which the adapter was attached; it is the real EMF model object from which the children will be retrieved.

The `getParent()` method is simply overridden to return the `target`, like this:

```
public Object getParent(Object object)
{
  return target;
}
```

Now that we've changed `SupplierItemProvider` to return our transient item providers as its children, and our transient providers are implemented to return the supplier as their parent and the **orders** or **customers** as their children, we need to make one more parent change. The `getParent()` methods in `PurchaseOrderItemProvider` and `CustomerItemProvider` need to return the appropriate transient item provider. We use exactly the same pattern in both classes. In `PurchaseOrderItemProvider`, for example, it looks like this:

```
public Object getParent(Object object)
{
  Object supplier = super.getParent(object);
  SupplierItemProvider supplierItemProvider =
```

```
(SupplierItemProvider)adapterFactory.adapt(
  supplier, IEditingDomainItemProvider.class);

return supplierItemProvider != null ?
  supplierItemProvider.getOrders() : null;
}
```

Notice how in the non-null case it calls the getOrders() method on the supplier item provider. By adding two convenience methods, getOrders() and getCustomers(), on the supplier item provider we avoid adding state to PurchaseOrderItemProvider and CustomerItemProvider and can continue to use the Singleton pattern for them. The getOrders() method in class SupplierItemProvider is very simple and looks like this:

```
public Object getOrders()
{
  return children.get(0);
}
```

As you might expect, getCustomers() is the same only it returns children.get(1) and it is used for the implementation of getParent() in class CustomerItemProvider.

Now that we've overridden all the applicable getChildren() and getParent() methods, we can run the ExtendedPO1 editor and the tree view will look as shown in Figure 19.12. There are however, still a few details that we need to address unless we want to disable command execution entirely (e.g., by simply overriding the createCommand() method to return UnexecutableCommand.INSTANCE). Because fixing them isn't really that hard, and we're trying to learn about the framework anyway, we'll just bite the bullet and fix all the problems.

The first problem that we need to address is that the (generated) SupplierItemProvider adds new child descriptors for purchase orders and customers to itself. We don't want the CreateChildCommand to be enabled on the supplier node (i.e., we should only be adding new purchase orders to the "Orders" node and new customers to the "Customers" node). In the generator, we disable the "Create Child" property on the **customers** and **orders** features of **Supplier**. After regenerating the code, the collectNewChildDescriptors() method in SupplierItemProvider will be fixed:

```
protected void collectNewChildDescriptors(
  Collection newChildDescriptors, Object object)
{
  super.collectNewChildDescriptors(newChildDescriptors, object);
}
```

The second problem that we need to address is the same problem that we handled in Section 19.2.1 when we suppressed the **USAddress** objects from the view, but then needed to override the `getAffectedObjects()` method on commands involving them, to return the purchase order instead. In this case, it is not the `SetCommand`, but rather `AddCommand` and `RemoveCommand` that have this problem.

After removing a purchase order or customer from a supplier, we want the affected object (i.e., the selection) to be the appropriate transient node, instead of the supplier. We also want this to be the case if we undo an add command. To make it work in all cases (remember that `AddCommand` and `RemoveCommand` are primitive commands used for a lot of things, including drag-and-drop) we need to override `AddCommand` and `RemoveCommand` in both the `Transient-ItemProvider` and `SupplierItemProvider` to switch the affected objects. In `SupplierItemProvider`, we do it like this:

```
protected Command createRemoveCommand(EditingDomain domain,
                                      EObject owner,
                                      EStructuralFeature feature,
                                      Collection collection)
{
  return createWrappedCommand(
    super.createRemoveCommand(domain, owner, feature, collection),
    owner, feature);
}

protected Command createAddCommand(EditingDomain domain,
                                   EObject owner,
                                   EStructuralFeature feature,
                                   Collection collection,
                                   int index)
{
  return createWrappedCommand(
    super.createAddCommand(domain, owner, feature, collection,
                           index),
    owner, feature);
}

protected Command createWrappedCommand(Command command,
  final EObject owner, final EStructuralFeature feature)
{
  if (feature == EPO1Package.Literals.SUPPLIER__ORDERS ||
      feature == EPO1Package.Literals.SUPPLIER__CUSTOMERS)
  {
    return
      new CommandWrapper(command)
      {
        public Collection getAffectedObjects()
        {
          Collection affected = super.getAffectedObjects();
```

```
          if (affected.contains(owner))
          {
            affected = Collections.singleton(
              feature == EP01Package.Literals.SUPPLIER__ORDERS ?
                getOrders() : getCustomers());
          }
          return affected;
        }
      };
  }
  return command;
}
```

As you can see, for the **orders** and **customers** features, we create an anonymous command subclass that overrides the `getAffectedObjects()` method to return the appropriate transient item provider whenever the "real" affected object is the `owner` (i.e., the supplier). Notice how we used the EMF.Edit convenience class `CommandWrapper` so that we could handle both the `AddCommand` and `RemoveCommand` cases with a single implementation.

As mentioned previously, we need to also include this affected object correction code in class `TransientItemProvider`. There, however, the `createWrappedCommand()` method can be a little simpler:

```
protected Command createWrappedCommand(Command command,
                                       final EObject owner)
{
  return
    new CommandWrapper(command)
    {
      public Collection getAffectedObjects()
      {
        Collection affected = super.getAffectedObjects();
        if (affected.contains(owner))
        {
          affected = Collections.singleton(
            TransientSupplierItemProvider.this);
        }
        return affected;
      }
    };
}
```

Notice that here we do not need to check which feature we're dealing with, because each of our two transient classes only supports one feature (i.e., `OrdersItemProvider` only supports the **orders** feature and `CustomersItemProvider` only supports **customers**).

We're on the final stretch now. With the changes we've made so far, only one more questionable behavior will remain, involving drag-and-drop. With our current implementation, you can drag a purchase order and drop it on the "Customers" node, or drag a customer and drop it on the "Orders" node. The effect will be to add the object to the end of the other list. It won't corrupt the model, but it certainly doesn't seem right from the user's perspective. This happens because, as we've seen, class `TransientItemProvider` implements most of its methods by effectively redirecting them to the adapter's `target` (supplier). This is also the case for the `createCommand()` method, so add commands on either the "Orders" or "Customers" node are simply converted to add commands on the supplier, which then enable the drop, regardless of the user's actual chosen drop target.

To prevent this final problem from occurring, we need to override the `createDragAndDropCommand()` method in our two transient item providers to disallow dropping of the wrong kind of object. In `OrdersItemProvider`, we need to make sure that only purchase orders are being dropped, and in `CustomersItemProvider`, there should only be customers. Here's how we do it in `OrdersItemProvider`:

```
protected Command createDragAndDropCommand(EditingDomain domain,
                  Object owner, float location, int operations,
                  int operation, Collection collection)
{
  if (new AddCommand(domain, (EObject)owner,
                  EPO1Package.Literals.SUPPLIER__ORDERS,
                  collection).canExecute())
  {
    return super.createDragAndDropCommand(
      domain, owner, location, operations, operation, collection);
  }
  return UnexecutableCommand.INSTANCE;
}
```

Notice how we decided to use an `AddCommand` as a convenient way to verify that all the objects in the collection of drop items are purchase orders (i.e., the correct target type for the **orders** feature); the `AddCommand`'s enablement check is exactly this. If the `canExecute()` method returns `false`, then some or all of the objects being dropped are not purchase orders, so we simply disable the drag-and-drop command by returning `UnexecutableCommand.INSTANCE`. Now all we need to do is add the same override in `CustomersItemProvider`, only using the **customers** feature instead of the **orders** feature in the `AddCommand`, and we're done. The ExtendedPO1 editor will now correctly implement all of the commands.

There is still one minor issue that needs to be addressed: the disposal of our transient item providers. By default, adapter factories provide a disposal mechanism for their item providers that is used when a generated editor is closed. An adapter factory keeps a reference to each item provider that it creates. It can then provide a `dispose()` method that, in turn, invokes `dispose()` on each of its item providers. This is important if you wish to have model objects that stay in memory longer than the editor for them. Each object maintains a list of its adapters, so we need the `dispose()` method as an opportunity to remove each item provider from its notifier's list.

However, because we have manually registered the transient item providers as adapters on the supplier, the item provider adapter factory will not automatically dispose them. As a result, we must do so manually to avoid introducing a potential memory leak. The simplest way is to add the following override of `dispose()` to `SupplierItemProvider`:

```
public void dispose()
{
  super.dispose();
  if (children != null)
  {
    ((IDisposable)children.get(0)).dispose();
    ((IDisposable)children.get(1)).dispose();
  }
}
```

This implementation invokes `dispose()` directly on the two transient item providers. In general, you should always directly dispose of any item providers that you create without using the generated item provider adapter factory.

As you can see, there were quite a few details that we needed to address to get this example working, but each particular problem had a fairly simple solution. The total amount of code that we needed to add was only about 150 lines, but only because we knew how to use the framework effectively. Now that we've painstakingly walked through this example, you should be all set to attack your own customization problems and come up with short and elegant implementations for them as well.

CHAPTER 20

Outside of the Eclipse IDE

Throughout this book, a great deal of the discussion about EMF has been focused on its use in developing Eclipse components. This chapter expands your horizons for applying EMF by detailing how you can use it in Eclipse Rich Client Platform (RCP) and stand-alone applications.

Most of EMF's features are completely independent of Eclipse, allowing them to be used on any platform that supports Java, without any Eclipse classes in the class path. In fact, EMF's only real dependencies on Eclipse are in its UI elements and code generation tools.

20.1 Rich Client Platform

Imagine a lightweight version of Eclipse, one that you could use as a framework to develop anything from an e-mail client to a game, without the burden of IDE features. Imagine if your applications could exploit any or all of Eclipse's powerful general-purpose facilities:

- ○ SWT to create fast and user friendly interfaces.
- ○ The plug-in mechanism to help you define and clearly identify the boundaries of your components.
- ○ The help system to deliver first-class user assistance.
- ○ The update manager to deploy new versions of your code.

If you are screaming "Yes! Yes!", or at least thinking "that would be nice," welcome to the world of RCP. RCP consists of just the minimal set of plug-ins needed to build a rich client application: the Eclipse runtime, SWT, JFace, and the generic Workbench. IDE-specific components, such as the workspace resource model, team support, and the IDE UI, are excluded. In an RCP application, you have the freedom to define which menus, views, and perspectives are presented to your users. You can also selectively include any other Eclipse components that might be applicable to your application, including the standard

Outline and Property views, the help system, the update manager, and the welcome page. Since its debut, RCP has allowed Eclipse to be used as a framework for almost any type of application. Obviously, EMF couldn't be left out of this.

20.1.1   RCP and EMF

EMF could minimally support RCP simply by avoiding using classes that are not available in a basic RCP environment, which would allow you to use a generated model implementation and its edit support in custom applications. However, EMF can actually go far beyond this, generating a complete RCP application tailored to your model. This application provides a workbench-based UI, which offers menus and editors to create and manipulate instances of the classes you've defined. As always, behind the scenes, the UI elements are making calls to EMF APIs such as the commands defined in EMF.Edit.

To generate an RCP application for one of our models, we simply need to change the "Rich Client Platform" property under the "Editor" category in the generator to "true". For this example, we'll use our most basic purchase order model, SimplePO, as illustrated in Figure 20.1.

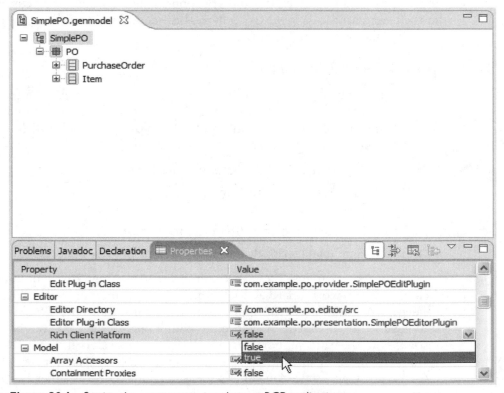

Figure 20.1   Setting the generator to produce an RCP application.

After saving the .*gemodel* file and generating the code, you will be able to run the RCP application. Before jumping into it though, it is important to point out that the value of the RCP property affects the contents of the generated *plug-in.xml* and *META-INF/MANIFEST.MF* files in the editor plug-in. If you are regenerating over an existing plug-in, you will need to delete these files because EMF cannot merge changes into them. Note that the model, edit, and test plug-ins are not affected at all by the RCP property.

20.1.2 Launching an RCP Application

Although you could run the generated RCP application from the command line, at this point it is probably better to use Eclipse to launch it. This is the simplest approach and, for example, it allows you to benefit from Eclipse's debug capabilities if something goes wrong. Before we can run the application, we'll need to create an appropriate Eclipse application launch configuration. In the Java perspective, select **Run...** from the toolbar drop-down, as illustrated in Figure 20.2.

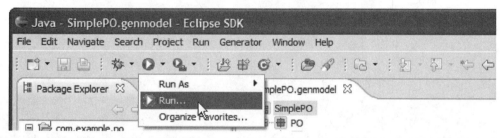

Figure 20.2   The **Run...** toolbar drop-down.

Create a new "Eclipse Application" configuration, as shown in Figure 20.3.

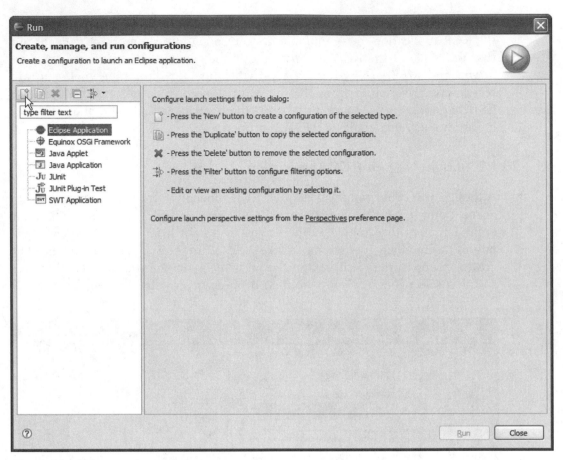

Figure 20.3   Creating the configuration.

Give the configuration a name, such as "SimplePO." On the **Main** tab, illustrated in Figure 20.4, select the **Clear workspace data before launching** check box. Unlike the Eclipse IDE, our generated RCP application doesn't use the workspace to persist user data. As a result, its workspace directory will only contain a *.metadata* directory that stores workbench layout settings for the application. There's no reason to maintain these settings during development; moreover, clearing them reduces the chance of running into conflicts as the UI evolves.

To make the configuration launch the generated RCP application, instead of the Eclipse IDE, select **Run an application** and choose "com.example.po.editor.SimplePOEditorAdvisorApplication" as the application ID.

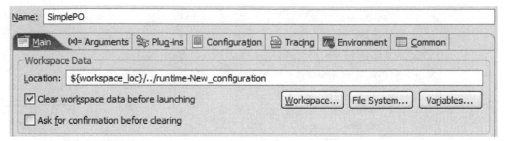

Figure 20.4   Launch configuration **Main** tab.

Switch to the **Arguments** tab and specify the program argument "-consoleLog", as shown in Figure 20.5. This tells Eclipse to echo any log output to the Console view, which can be handy for debugging.

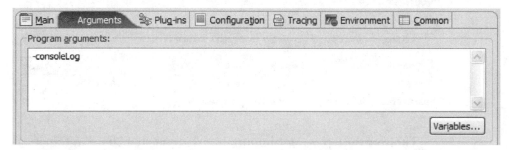

Figure 20.5   Adding a program argument to the configuration.

The **Plug-ins** tab is where we'll define which plug-ins will be available when executing the application. We'll select the minimum set of dependencies:

1. Select the **Choose plug-ins and fragments to launch from the list** option.

2. Click **Deselect All**.

3. Under "Workspace Plug-ins", select the editor plug-in: "com.example.po.editor (1.0.0)" in this case.

4. Unselect the **Include optional dependencies when computing required plug-ins** option.

5. Click **Add Required Plug-ins**, as illustrated in Figure 20.6.

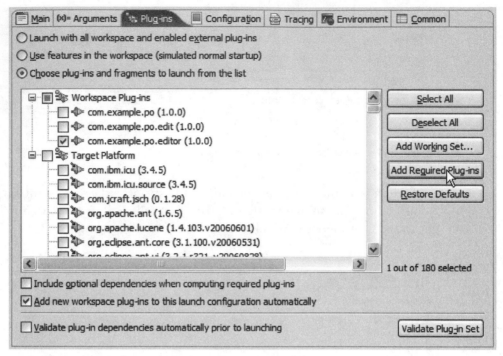

Figure 20.6   Selecting the appropriate plug-ins.

The fourth step is very important. Without it, Eclipse automatically selects all optional dependencies, which, for EMF, includes resource and IDE plug-ins that are not actually used by the RCP application. During development, the testing environment should be as similar as possible to the eventual deployment configuration. Therefore, you should exclude these superfluous plug-ins, which could otherwise compromise the effectiveness of your tests.

To reduce its startup time, Eclipse caches some information about the active set of plug-ins in the *eclipse/configuration* directory. Although this is a very nice trick to enhance the user experience, it can cause some annoying problems related to plug-in activation during development, which can be time-consuming to diagnose. To avoid such problems, switch to the **Configuration** tab and select the **Clear configuration area before launching** option. Click **Apply** to save the configuration. Finally, click **Run**, as shown in Figure 20.7.

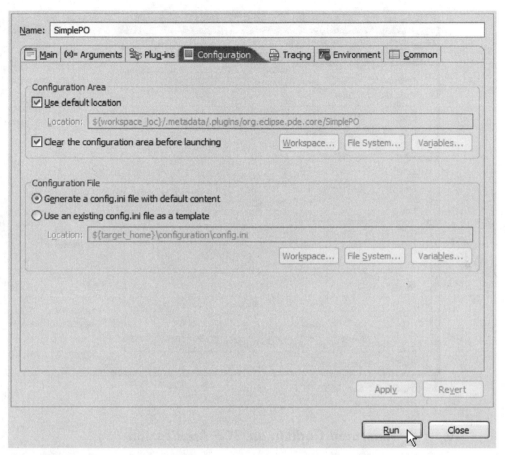

Figure 20.7   Completing the launch configuration.

You should now see a "small" Eclipse workbench running an application that is able to create, save, load, and manipulate instances of the purchase order model, as illustrated in Figure 20.8. Feel free to experiment with it. When you are done, we will delve into some details of the application that might be of interest as you continue to work with RCP.

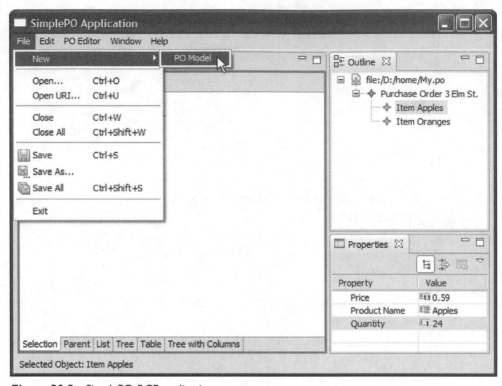

Figure 20.8 SimplePO RCP application.

20.1.3 Generated Code in an RCP Application

As mentioned earlier, the differences that result from targeting RCP for code generation are limited to the editor plug-in. If you inspect the contents of our newly generated editor plug-in for SimplePO, you will notice a couple of new elements in the *plugin.xml* manifest file and a new class called `SimplePOEditorAdvisor`. There are a couple of other minor differences that we will leave for you to explore.

In the manifest file, the most important difference is the declaration of an Eclipse application as follows:

```
<extension point="org.eclipse.core.runtime.applications"
  id="SimplePOEditorAdvisorApplication">
 <application>
  <run class=
    "com.example.po.presentation.SimplePOEditorAdvisor$Application">
  </run>
 </application>
</extension>
```

An *application* is a very important concept for the Eclipse platform, allowing a plug-in to specify an entry point for execution following platform initialization. The application is run via the platform launcher by specifying the declared extension ID. For example:

```
> eclipse -application
    com.example.po.editor.SimplePOEditorAdvisorApplication
```

The other important artifact in the generated RCP application is the class `SimplePOEditorAdvisor`. This is the place where the workbench is configured, defining the appearance of the application. Table 20.1 describes the advisor's inner classes, which do most of the work for it.

Table 20.1   Inner Classes of the Editor Advisor

Class	Description
Application	Implements the `run()` method required by the Eclipse `IPlatformRunnable` interface, which is the first method executed when the application is started.
Perspective	Defines the initial layout of the application. As generated, the perspective is created with the Outline and Property views appearing to the right of the editor area.
WindowAdvisor and WindowActionBarAdvisor	Configure the workbench window and its menu bar, setting the window size, setting the title, and creating several pull-down menus.
AboutAction, OpenAction, and OpenURIAction	Implement the **About...**, **Open...**, and **Open URI...** menu items. The first simply displays a sample About message, and the latter two provide suitable dialog boxes for loading resources in the absence of a workspace.

Note that the inner perspective and action classes are all registered independently of the application in the *plugin.xml* file.

Finally, it is worth highlighting one additional issue related to implementing an EMF editor in an RCP application, where we must assume the workspace is not available. The usual input to an IDE-based editor is of type `FileEditorInput`, which is based on the `IFile` workspace resource API. If you look at the generated `openEditor()` method in `SimplePOEditorAdvisor`, you'll see that in an RCP-based editor, EMF uses `URIEditorInput`, a simple wrapper for `URI`, instead.

20.1.4 Deploying an RCP Application

Once an RCP application is complete, there is one more required step before it can easily be distributed: it must be wrapped in fancy wrapping paper to produce what is known as a *product*. Fortunately, the Eclipse Plug-in Development Environment (PDE) provides specific wizards and editors to help you accomplish this task in little more than a few clicks.

The first step is to create a *Product Configuration* for the RCP application. This configuration describes every aspect of the application, from technical details, including the list of required plug-ins and the application arguments, to deployment information like the icon and splash screen image. To create this file, open the **New > Other...** wizard, expand "Plug-in Development", and select "Product Configuration". You will be pleased to see that the launch configuration created in Section 20.1.2 can be reused here. After specifying the location and name of the *.product* file to create, you can simply select the "SimplePO" RCP launch configuration to feed in most of the details needed to run the application as a product.

Once the wizard has completed, the product configuration file is created and opened in its editor. You can then fill in any remaining details to customize the launching and branding of your application. When complete, click "Eclipse Product export wizard" on the **Overview** tab to package and export the product.

20.2 Stand-Alone Applications

There are many types of applications that don't fit well in an Eclipse shell: server-side components, applets, Swing GUI applications, and the list could go on and on. From an Eclipse point of view, these are called stand-alone applications. To EMF, they are just more Java code that can exploit its features.

All of EMF's runtime facilities are available to stand-alone applications. Although support for generating code outside Eclipse is limited, any application can use a generated or dynamic model and benefit from EMF's support for rich metadata, notification, change recording, validation, persistence, and so forth. In this section, we will discuss some important details of stand-alone application development, as we build a small program to save and load instances of the SimplePO model.

Faced with the task of writing such a program, you could easily assemble some of the code snippets from Chapter 2 into the following, which creates and saves a purchase order:

```
public class POApplication
{
```

```
public static void savePurchaseOrder() throws IOException
{
  PurchaseOrder aPurchaseOrder =
    POFactory.eINSTANCE.createPurchaseOrder();
  aPurchaseOrder.setBillTo("123 Maple Street");

  Item aItem = POFactory.eINSTANCE.createItem();
  aItem.setProductName("Apples");
  aItem.setQuantity(12);
  aItem.setPrice(0.50f);
  aPurchaseOrder.getItems().add(aItem);

  ResourceSet rs = new ResourceSetImpl();
  URI fileURI =
    URI.createFileURI(new File("mypo.xml").getAbsolutePath());
  Resource poResource = rs.createResource(fileURI);
  poResource.getContents().add(aPurchaseOrder);
  poResource.save(null);

  System.out.println("\nAfter saving:");
  System.out.println("PurchaseOrder - Bill To:" +
                      aPurchaseOrder.getBillTo());
  System.out.println("Item - Product:" + aItem.getProductName() +
                     " Quantity:" + aItem.getQuantity() +
                     " Price:" + aItem.getPrice());
  }
}
```

After creating a `main()` method that invokes `savePurchaseOrder()`, you feel ready to run the stand-alone application. However, you realize that there is one very important question that needs to be answered first: what classes must be added to the class path?

20.2.1 Adding EMF to the Class Path

Throughout this book, we have often referred to plug-ins, but we have not talked about how they are actually deployed in Eclipse. In general, and for EMF in particular, the content of a plug-in is provided as a single JAR file that gets installed into the *plugins/* directory of an Eclipse install location. In a stand-alone context, these plug-in JAR files can simply be added to the class path. So which EMF JAR files should you add? One simple answer might be, "all of them."

Bloating your class path this way solves the problem when all you want is to run a simple test. On the other hand, this might not be appropriate if your goal is, for example, to pack the EMF JAR files with your application and deploy it to a server where it will be invoked by a Web service. In this scenario, you probably will be looking for ways to reduce the size of your application and wouldn't want to ship unnecessary binaries.

The key thing is to identify which features of EMF you are using in your application. After doing this, you can look for the EMF plug-in JAR files that provide these features, as listed in Table 20.2.

Table 20.2   Features Provided by EMF JAR Files

Feature	Required JAR File(s)
Core runtime: Ecore, reflective API, dynamic EMF, and validation framework	*org.eclipse.emf.common_<version>.jar* *org.eclipse.emf.ecore_<version>.jar*
XML/XMI persistence	*org.eclipse.emf.xmi_<version>.jar* plus core runtime JARs
EMF.Edit	*org.eclipse.emf.edit_<version>.jar* plus core runtime JARs
Change model	*org.eclipse.emf.change_<version>.jar* plus core runtime JARs
Service Data Objects (SDO)[1]	*org.eclipse.emf.commonj.sdo_<version>.jar* *org.eclipse.emf.ecore.sdo_<version>.jar* plus all core runtime, change model, and XML/XMI persistence JARs
Ecore to XML persistence mapping	*org.eclipse.emf.mapping.ecore2xml_<version>.jar* plus all core runtime and XML/XMI persistence JARs
XML Schema Infoset model	*org.eclipse.xsd_<version>.jar* plus core runtime JARs

The corresponding **.edit_<version>.jar* files provide the command and item provider support for Ecore, the change model, SDO, and the XML Schema Infoset model. You can include them in the class path if needed. The full picture of JAR dependencies is shown in Figure 20.9, a UML component diagram in which, for each JAR, an arrow points to the other JARs it requires.

---

1. We have not discussed SDO, Ecore to XML persistence mapping, or the XML Schema Infoset model in this book.

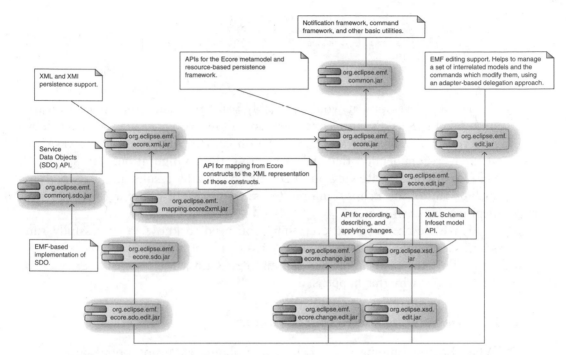

Figure 20.9 Plug-in JAR files and dependencies.

Although you can use a plug-in JAR file like any other JAR file, you should pay attention to one important detail: the EMF plug-in JAR files are actually OSGi bundles, as described in Chapter 1. In practice, this means that they specify OSGi directives in their manifest file, which will be respected if they are deployed to an OSGi environment.[2] These directives can specify a start-up class, plug-in dependencies, and packages that are exported, and they can affect how your application runs. If you are not deploying to an OSGi environment, you need not worry about this.

Returning to our example, let's assume you JAR up the generated SimplePO model implementation, along with `POApplication`, into *SimplePO.jar* and place it in the same location as the EMF plug-ins. Then, you would need to use a command line like this to start the application:[3]

---

2. Eclipse is an obvious example of an OSGi environment, but other runtimes, including some application servers, also fall into this category.

3. This assumes you're using EMF 2.2.5, the latest 2.2 release at the time of this book's writing. For other releases, the version numbers in the JAR filenames will be different.

```
> java -classpath org.eclipse.emf.common_2.2.2.v200808252119.jar;
    org.eclipse.emf.ecore_2.2.4.v200808252119.jar;
    org.eclipse.emf.ecore.xmi_2.2.5.v200808252119.jar;
    SimplePO.jar
    POApplication
```

During development, you'll probably want to launch the application from within Eclipse, as it's more convenient and allows you to make use of the debugger. You can do so with a Java application launch configuration. However, it is strongly recommended that, when creating the configuration, you specify the class path yourself. Relying on "PDE magic" usually results in a class path that includes all of the Eclipse runtime JARs, which might not match your eventual deployment environment.

Have we now covered everything you need to know to successfully run a stand-alone application? The answer is no. If you execute the preceding command line, the application will fail and exit with a `NullPointerException`. Let's look at why this happens.

20.2.2   Registering the Resource Factory

When EMF is running under Eclipse, the plug-in extension point mechanism is used to perform registrations required at runtime. This is true for the Eclipse IDE, as well as in RCP and headless applications. Because a stand-alone application is completely unaware of plug-ins, you'll have to roll up your sleeves and add some extra code to do this work.

In the `savePurchaseOrder()` method, you are asking the resource set to obtain a resource that knows how to save and load .*xml* files without first specifying how such a resource can be created. In EMF terms, you need to register a `ResourceFactory`:

```
...
ResourceSet rs = new ResourceSetImpl();
rs.getResourceFactoryRegistry().getExtensionToFactoryMap().put(
  "xml", new XMLResourceFactoryImpl());
...
```

Now, the resource set knows that the resource for any file with extension .*xml* has to be created by the registered `XMLResourceFactoryImpl`. By choosing an implementation of `Resource.Factory`, you determine the persistence format used for files with that extension. Note that if you are working with a model created from an XML Schema, you should probably register the resource factory that EMF generates together with the model implementation.

That way, the extended metadata annotations on the model are used to ensure that persisted resources conform to the schema.[4]

Note that you could have chosen to register the resource factory for any file extension not explicitly registered, by specifying `Resource.Factory.Registry.DEFAULT_EXTENSION` instead of `"xml"` as the registry key. You could have also registered the resource factory globally instead of locally to the instantiated `ResourceSet`:[5]

```
Resource.Factory.Registry.INSTANCE.getExtensionToFactoryMap().put(
  "xml", new XMLResourceFactoryImpl());
```

Now that you've registered the resource factory and sorted out the class path, you can use the `POApplication` to save the objects it creates. But how about loading? Again, referring to the snippets in Chapter 2, you could write the following method to load the purchase order back from the file:

```
public static void loadPurchaseOrder()
{
  ResourceSet rs = new ResourceSetImpl();
  rs.getResourceFactoryRegistry().getExtensionToFactoryMap().put(
    "xml", new XMLResourceFactoryImpl());
  URI fileURI =
    URI.createFileURI(new File("mypo.xml").getAbsolutePath());
  Resource poResource = rs.getResource(fileURI, true);

  PurchaseOrder aPurchaseOrder =
    (PurchaseOrder)poResource.getContents().get(0);
  Item aItem = (Item)aPurchaseOrder.getItems().get(0);

  System.out.println("\nAfter loading:");
  System.out.println("PurchaseOrder - Bill To:" +
                     aPurchaseOrder.getBillTo());
  System.out.println("Item - Product:" + aItem.getProductName() +
                     "  Quantity:" + aItem.getQuantity() +
                     "  Price:" + aItem.getPrice());
}
```

After adding a call to this method to your `main()`, immediately following the call to `savePurchaseOrder()`, your application will be able to successfully save and load a purchase order as intended.

---

4. The same is true for `GenericXMLResourceFactoryImpl`, an implementation provided by the framework and described in Section 15.4.2.

5. The differences between local and global registration are explained in Section 15.2.4.

What would happen if, after running the application, you commented out the call to `savePurchaseOrder()`? Because the file was already created and was not deleted, everything should work, right? Actually, no. As we will see, there is one more registration required.

20.2.4 *Registering the Package*

Comparing the save and load methods closely, we can see a very important difference between them. Whereas the former makes explicit calls to the generated factory, `POFactory`, to instantiate the objects, the latter assumes that the resource loading mechanism is able to figure out how to create the instances. And that's the catch: to properly instantiate objects from files, EMF needs to be able to access their **EPackage**s. Like resource factories, packages are registered automatically under Eclipse but require explicit registration in a stand-alone application.

Registering an **EPackage** is really simple when you are working with generated models. In our example, adding the following line to the beginning of `loadPurchaseOrder()` does the trick:

```
POPackage poPackage = POPackage.eINSTANCE;
```

Accessing the `eINSTANCE` field causes the `POPackage` to be registered automatically in the global package registry.

But why did you need to register the package? When you load a resource, the first thing encountered in the file is the name of a class, qualified by a namespace URI. This namespace URI is there to uniquely identify the **EPackage** in which the class is defined. After reading the namespace URI value, the loader consults a registry to retrieve the package associated with that value. From the package, it then obtains the right factory to instantiate the named class. So, in a stand-alone application, you need the preceding line of code to establish this association in the global package registry. In fact, you'll need to register any package that you wish to load instances of, including those defined in models provided by EMF, such as the change model. The one exception is Ecore itself, which never needs to be registered explicitly.[6]

Finally, the stand-alone application is complete! Accessing the package is a safe way to ensure that it gets registered. Even if you add back the call to the

---

6. Package registration is discussed in more detail in Section 14.1.2 and throughout Chapter 15. In particular, Section 15.2.5 discusses the difference between global and local package registration, and Sections 15.3.2 and 15.3.4 detail the situations in which dynamic packages are registered automatically.

`savePurchaseOrder()` method, everything will still work—accessing the package in `loadPurchaseOrder()` simply has no effect in that case.

As mentioned in Chapter 12, EMF will, by default, generate a stand-alone example as part of the test project for a model. Like the `POApplication` we developed in this chapter, the example saves and loads instances of the model from which it was generated. In addition, it uses EMF's validation framework, seen in Chapter 18, to diagnose any problems in the loaded objects. You can use this example as a starting point for developing your own stand-alone applications or, if you run into unexpected troubles, as a means to validate your runtime environment.

CHAPTER 21

EMF 2.3 and 2.4

During the preparation of this book, EMF has evolved through a couple of new versions. The previous chapters were based on EMF 2.2. Although that version is not dramatically different from the very latest, 2.4, there have nevertheless been a few notable changes introduced since then. This chapter provides an overview of the new features in EMF 2.3 and 2.4, and explains the motivation behind some of them.

21.1 Java 5.0 Support

The most noteworthy changes to EMF after the 2.2 release were to introduce support for two important Java 5.0 features, enumerations and generics. These features have great potential to increase the quality of Java applications as they improve type checking at compile time, which will help developers avoid mistakes.

A significant challenge in supporting these features was to continue to provide backward compatibility and to ensure that users could continue to generate code that runs on an older version of Java. Because the runtime in EMF 2.3 and later exploits Java 5.0 language features, it cannot run on older versions of Java. Thus, it is necessary, beginning in 2.3, that EMF be able to generate code that runs on the EMF 2.2 runtime. As such, a new generator model property was added to those described in Section 12.3.1. It appears on the root, model object, under the category "All" (see Figure 21.1).

Compliance Level—This property defines which version of the Java language should be adopted by generated code. When it is set to 1.4, the patterns described in Chapter 10 are used. Setting it to 5.0 or greater tells the generator that the code is expected to exploit newer features of the language, which are described in this section. When moving existing models to EMF 2.3 or later, the compliance level defaults to 1.4; however, for new models, this property is set automatically based on the compiler workbench preferences in Eclipse.

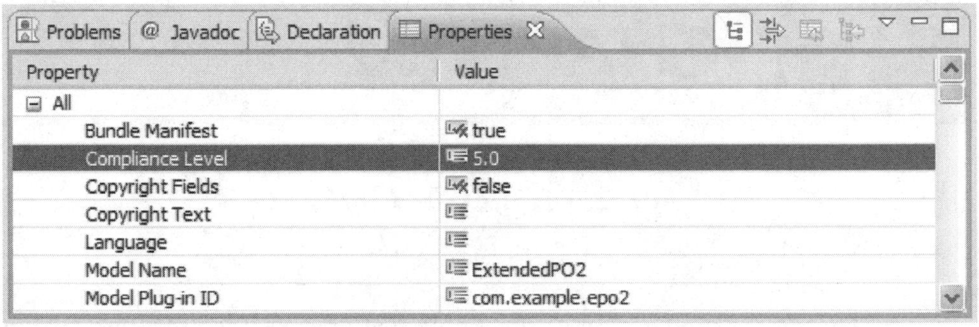

Figure 21.1 The "Compliance Level" generator model property.

21.1.1 *Enumerations*

In previous versions of EMF, enumerated types were implemented using the well known Type-safe Enum pattern described in Section 10.2.3. Given that Java 5.0 provides language support for enumerated types via the enum keyword, the latest versions of EMF have been enhanced to support it as well.

Enumerated Type Generator Pattern

Because EMF's previous approach was based on the Type-safe Enum Pattern and because Java 5 enums are simply special classes, the new pattern for enumerated types is not significantly different from the one shown in Section 10.2.3. Let's regenerate the **OrderStatus** enumerated type from that section, this time with the "Compliance Level" set to 5.0:

```
public enum OrderStatus implements Enumerator
{
  PENDING(0, "Pending", "Pending"),
  BACK_ORDER(1, "BackOrder", "BackOrder"),
  COMPLETE(2, "Complete", "Complete");

  public static final int PENDING_VALUE = 0;
  public static final int BACK_ORDER_VALUE = 1;
  public static final int COMPLETE_VALUE = 2;

  public static OrderStatus get(String literal)
  {
    ...
  }
```

```
      public static OrderStatus getByName(String name)
      {
        ...
      }

      public static OrderStatus get(int value)
      {
        ...
      }

      private final int value;
      private final String name;
      private final String literal;

      private OrderStatus(int value, String name, String literal)
      {
        this.value = value;
        this.name = name;
        this.literal = literal;
      }

      public int getValue()
      {
        return value;
      }

      public String getName()
      {
        return name;
      }

      public String getLiteral()
      {
        return literal;
      }

      @Override
      public String toString()
      {
        return literal;
      }
    }
```

As you can see, OrderStatus follows a pattern that is similar to the old one, including all the same convenience methods, but it is now generated as an enum instead of a class. The most significant difference is that the basic enumeration names (PENDING, BACK_ORDER, and COMPLETE) are now used for the enumeration literals themselves, instead of for the int constants as in the old pattern. Previously, the literals were given longer, mangled names (PENDING_LITERAL, BACK_ORDER_LITERAL, and COMPLETE_LITERAL), whereas now the int constants are the mangled ones (PENDING_VALUE, BACK_ORDER_VALUE, and COMPLETE_VALUE).

The int constants were previously given the short names to facilitate their most common use, in a switch statement. In Java 5.0, enumeration literals are now handled specially within the Java runtime and can themselves be used in switch statements, so the generator pattern has been changed to use the more straightforward names.

Unfortunately, this new pattern is not backward compatible with the one used in EMF 2.2. To allow for easy migration of existing applications to newer versions of EMF, the "Type Safe Enum Compatible" property was introduced. It can be used to instruct the generator to use a backward compatible naming pattern, as illustrated in Figure 21.2.

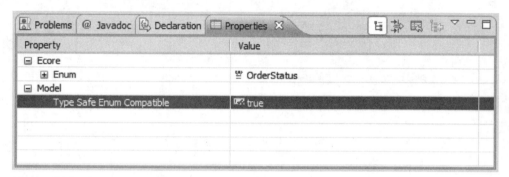

Figure 21.2 Backward compatible enumerated types.

Setting this property to true and regenerating OrderStatus produces the following:

```
public enum OrderStatus implements Enumerator
{
    PENDING_LITERAL(0, "Pending", "Pending"),
    BACK_ORDER_LITERAL(1, "BackOrder", "BackOrder"),
    COMPLETE_LITERAL(2, "Complete", "Complete");

    public static final int PENDING = 0;
    public static final int BACK_ORDER = 1;
    public static final int COMPLETE = 2;

    ...
}
```

Notice that the new Java 5.0 enum-based pattern is still used, but with the old naming conventions.[1]

One more characteristic of the Java 5.0 enumeration pattern, which you may have already noticed, is worth highlighting. In the old pattern, shown in Section 10.2.3, the class extends the EMF base class `AbstractEnumerator`, which provides the implementation for the methods in interface `Enumerator`. These methods are required for integration with dynamic EMF, but because Java 5.0 enums are not allowed to have a base class (they implicitly extend `java.lang.Enum`), the `Enumerator` method implementations must instead be generated into the enum itself in the new pattern. This is unfortunate, although, as you can see from the listing above, it's not really a significant amount of code.

Java Specification for Enumerated Types

Section 7.2 described how an **EENum** can be defined starting from a Java class declaration. As you might expect, in EMF 2.3 and beyond you can do the same thing using a Java 5.0 enum instead. For example, the **OrderStatus** enumerated type from the ExtendedPO3 model, can be defined like this:

```
/**
 * @model
 */
public enum OrderStatus
{
  /**
   * @model value="0" name="Pending"
   */
  PENDING,

  /**
   * @model value="1" name="BackOrder" literal="Back Order"
   */
  BACK_ORDER,

  /**
   * @model value="2" name="Complete"
   */
  COMPLETE
}
```

---

1. If you want to revert completely to the old `class`-based pattern, you'll need to set the "Compliance Level" generator model property to 1.4. This should only be necessary if you plan to run with an older JRE, since the new `enum`-based pattern is binary compatible when the "Type Safe Enum Compatible" property is enabled.

As you can see, this provides exactly the same information as the example in Section 7.2.1, only using a Java enum instead of a class. Notice that this syntax introduces an additional property (`value`) that can be used on the `@model` tags to specify the **value** of each **EEnumLiteral**. If no `value` is specified, the position of the literal in the enum is used by default.

21.1.2 Generics

Generics have had a major impact on how Java programs are written since they were introduced in version 5.0. Most significant is the parameterization of collections, which provides type safety for elements and makes possible the new simpler collection iteration syntax (`for` loop) of Java 5.0. Beyond collections, developers can also use Java generics to parameterize their own classes and interfaces, enabling another dimension of flexibility and reuse. Since version 2.3, all of these same benefits can also be exploited in EMF.

Generics in Collections

One of the most common uses of generics in Java is to parameterize the element type in a collection (e.g., a `List`, `Set`, `Map`, etc.). For that reason, the suitability of generics to EMF is nowhere more evident than in its list-based Java representation of multiplicity-many features.

Our very first example of a model, back in Section 2.1, began by looking at a simple `PurchaseOrder` interface, which included the following:

```
List getItems(); // List of Item
```

As you can see, the definition of the multiplicity-many **items** reference used a comment to document the type of the feature (**Item**), a glaringly obvious example of where Java generics would serve both this purpose and provide type safety in the API.[2] Given the availability of Java 5.0 generics, the list return type of a multiplicity-many feature's `get()` method is now parameterized with the feature type:

```
List<Item> getItems();
```

This is probably the most significant impact of generics on a typical EMF user. When a model is generated with the "Compliance Level" generator model

---

2. Concretely, this means that when using annotated Java to define a model, the type of a multiplicity-many feature no longer needs to be specified in the `@model` tag, as it is already captured in the parameterized return type.

property set to 5.0 or greater, generics will be used to implement all of the many-valued features. In this example, the generated `getItems()` implementation is essentially the same as described in Section 10.3.5, only with the addition of the `Item` type argument:

```
protected EList<Item> items = null;

public EList<Item> getItems()
{
  if (items == null)
  {
    items = new EObjectContainmentEList<Item>(Item.class, this, ... );
  }
  return items;
}
```

Notice that the `EList` implementation class, `EObjectContainment-EList`, is also parameterized now. As you might imagine, this is the case for the entire hierarchy of `EList` classes in EMF.

Moreover, if you look at the implementation of Ecore in EMF version 2.3 and beyond, you'll notice that the Ecore metamodel itself has been regenerated for Java 5.0. It now uses generics for all of its features. For example, `EClass.getEAttributes()` now returns `EList<EAttribute>`, instead of just the raw type `EList`. Generic types have also been adopted in non-generated EMF APIs, such as `ResourceSet.getResources()` and `Resource.getContents()`, which now return `EList<Resource>` and `EList<EObject>`, respectively.

Modeling with Generics

Beyond leveraging generics in the Java interfaces and implementations generated from models, as described in the previous section, EMF actually lets you use generics in modeling your classes. The Ecore metamodel was extended to allow you to specify formal type parameters on **EClassifiers** and **EOperations** and to use generic types in **ETypedElements**, **EClass** supertypes, and **EOperation** exceptions. Basically anything you can do with generics in Java, you can now also model in Ecore. Figure 21.3 shows the new additions to Ecore that are used to model generics.

As you can see, two new classes, **ETypeParameter** and **EGenericType**, have been added to Ecore to represent generics. These constructs also have been carefully designed to allow backward compatibility with the previous version of Ecore. For that, generic types provide a raw type view, similar to that in Java 5.0 itself.

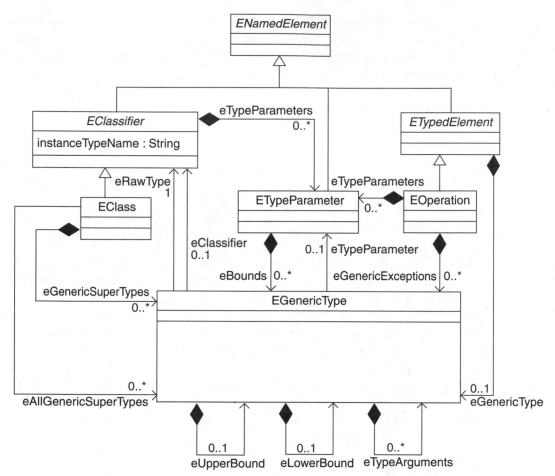

Figure 21.3   Representing generics in the Ecore metamodel.

Rather than explaining all the details of how generics are represented in the Ecore metamodel, let's look right at an example of how you can use generics in your own model. In Section 13.1 we introduced the version of class **PurchaseOrder** from ExtendedPO2. You might recall that one of the purposes of this model was to introduce a base class, **Address,** from which we derived two different kinds of addresses, as illustrated in Figure 21.4.

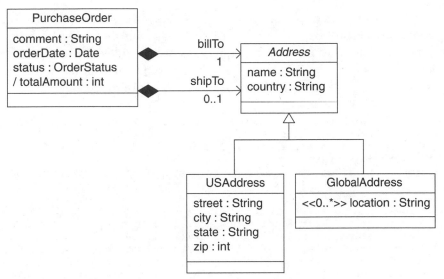

Figure 21.4 Addresses in ExtendedPO2.

In this model, both the **billTo** and **shipTo** references are to the abstract class **Address**, which, when instantiated, would be either a **USAddress** or a **GlobalAddress**. Notice that this model, as designed, allows the two addresses to be of different types. For example, the **billTo** address could be an instance of **USAddress**, while the **shipTo** address is a **GlobalAddress**. As you'd expect, the Java representation of these two references looks like this:

```
Address getBillTo();
void setBillTo(Address value);

Address getShipTo();
void setShipTo(Address value);
```

Let's say that we would like to change this model to require that both addresses be of the same type: either both **USAddress** or both **GlobalAddress**. Java generics are well suited to this kind of problem, which we could solve by parameterizing the `PurchaseOrder` interface and using the type parameter (instead of `Address`) in the signatures of the feature accessor methods:

```
public interface PurchaseOrder<A extends Address>
{
  A getBillTo();
  void setBillTo(A value);

  A getShipTo();
  void setShipTo(A value);
  ...
}
```

With this version of the `PurchaseOrder` interface, the **billTo** and **shipTo** addresses can still be any subclass of `Address`, but they must both be the same subclass. This kind of thing can quite easily be modeled using the new generic support in Ecore. Since there is no familiar graphical notation for generics, here is the XMI serialization of the corresponding Ecore model:

```
<eClassifiers xsi:type="ecore:EClass" name="PurchaseOrder">
  <eTypeParameters name="A">
    <eBounds eClassifier="#//Address"/>
  </eTypeParameters>
  <eStructuralFeatures xsi:type="ecore:EReference" name="items"
      upperBound="-1" eType="#//Item" containment="true"
      eOpposite="#//Item/order"/>
  ...
  <eStructuralFeatures xsi:type="ecore:EReference" name="billTo"
      containment="true" resolveProxies="false">
    <eGenericType eTypeParameter="#//PurchaseOrder/A"/>
  </eStructuralFeatures>
  <eStructuralFeatures xsi:type="ecore:EReference" name="shipTo"
      containment="true" resolveProxies="false">
    <eGenericType eTypeParameter="#//PurchaseOrder/A"/>
  </eStructuralFeatures>
  ...
</eClassifiers>
```

Relating this back to Figure 21.3, we can see how the new elements of the Ecore metamodel are used in this example. The **PurchaseOrder EClass** contains a single **ETypeParameter** via **eTypeParameters,** named "A". The **eBounds** reference on that **ETypeParameter** represents the type bound specified in Java as "extends Address". Notice that the value of this reference is always an **EGenericType,** whether the corresponding Java type is parameterized or not. In fact, every usage of a type in an Ecore model is now represented by a contained **EGenericType.** In the case of an ordinary, non-parameterized type, such as this one, only its **eClassifier** reference is set, identifying the appropriate **EClassifier.**

Interestingly, the existing features in the class look exactly the same in the Ecore serialization as they would have in EMF 2.2. For example, the type of the **items** reference is still represented by the value of **eType.** However, if you actually loaded this model and looked at the objects in memory, you would discover that there is really an instance of **EGenericType** contained by the **EReference** via **eGenericType.** Again, because it represents an ordinary type, this **EGenericType** has only its **eClassifier** reference set, in this case to the **EClass** named "Item". **ETypedElement.eType** is now a derived feature that, in this simple case, identifies the very same **EClassifier.** The implementation of Ecore contains special logic to ensure that this extra complexity is suppressed in the serialization, so models that don't take advantage of generics remain interchangeable with older versions of EMF.

The new references in our example, **billTo** and **shipTo**, make use of the type parameter, **A**, which is modeled as an **EGenericType** with its **eTypedParameter** reference set to that **ETypedParameter**. In this case, the serialization explicitly shows the **EGenericType**.

EGenericType is also used to model the two generic constructs not illustrated in this example, parameterized and wildcard types. For a parameterized type, the **eClassifier** reference is set to an **EClassifier** containing one or more **ETypeParameters**, and **eTypeArguments** is used to contain the **EGenericTypes** representing the corresponding actual type arguments. For a wildcard type, only the **eUpperBound** or **eLowerBound** reference is set. An excellent way to explore these constructs is by experimenting with the sample Ecore editor. Be sure the **Sample Ecore Editor > Show Generics** menu item is enabled.

UML Specification for Generics

As we mentioned in Chapter 6, some of the features of certain Ecore model elements have no equivalent representation in UML. Generics fall into this category, so we need to define some extended notation for them. One could easily imagine several ways of describing the generic **PurchaseOrder** model using a UML diagram. One way of doing it, but certainly not the only way, is as shown in Figure 21.5. This is, in fact, the notation recognized by the EMF model importer that provides out-of-box support for UML models created in Rational Rose.

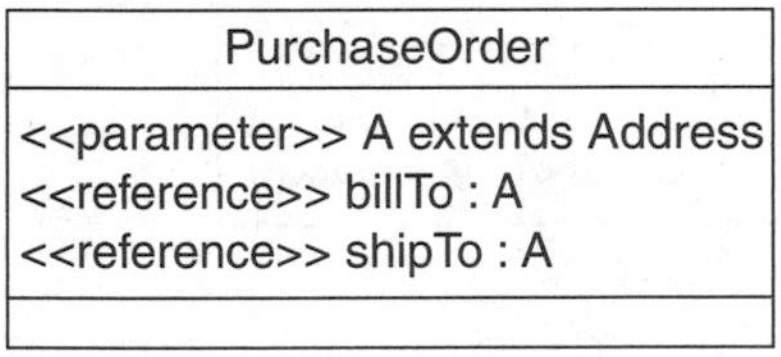

```
┌─────────────────────────────────┐
│         PurchaseOrder           │
├─────────────────────────────────┤
│ <<parameter>> A extends Address │
│ <<reference>> billTo : A        │
│ <<reference>> shipTo : A        │
├─────────────────────────────────┤
│                                 │
└─────────────────────────────────┘
```

Figure 21.5 Rational Rose representation of a generic **EClass**.

In a Rose model, an attribute with the stereotype <<parameter>> declares a formal type parameter of the containing class. The name of the attribute gives the name and bound of the parameter, exactly as they would appear between the angle brackets of the corresponding Java interface. The references **billTo** and **shipTo** are declared using UML attributes with the stereotype <<reference>>, instead of the usual UML association notation seen in Figure 21.4. This is necessary because there is no UML class corresponding to the type of the feature, the type parameter **A**, to which a line could be drawn.

One could imagine a different, conceptual UML notation, as illustrated in Figure 21.6, that allows references to be represented as associations by specifying the type parameter using a class. The class, which would have a <<parameter>> stereotype, could then be used as the target of the **billTo** and **shipTo** references. A dashed line, which in UML typically depicts a dependency on a class, could be used to associate the type parameter with the **PurchaseOrder** class.

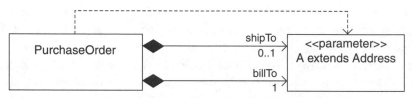

Figure 21.6   Conceptual UML representation of a generic **EClass**.

Whether this, or any other, notation can be used to represent generics depends on the UML tool from which the model is imported into EMF. This particular notation is not supported by EMF's Rose model importer. Users of other tools should refer to their documentation for the correct notation to use.

As mentioned previously, EMF allows generics anywhere they can be used in Java. Figure 21.7 illustrates several more examples, using the supported Rational Rose notation.

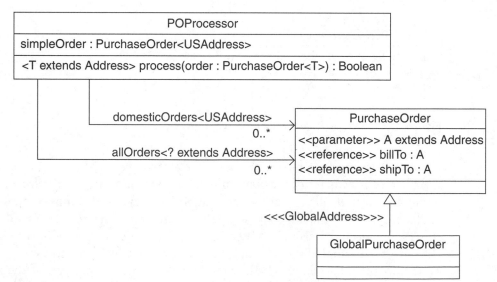

Figure 21.7   Generics in features, operations, and class inheritance.

Class **POProcessor** includes four uses of generics in its features and operations:

1. **simpleOrder**, a reference to a parameterized type declared as a UML attribute. Its type is specified using the normal Java generic syntax: PurchaseOrder<USAddress>. A <<reference>> stereotype is not needed in this case because the type is unambiguously recognizable as a class.

2. **domesticOrders**, another parameterized type reference, declared using the UML association notation. In this case, the type argument, **USAddress**, is appended to the feature name: domesticOrders<USAddress>.

3. **allOrders**, a reference with a wildcard type, which uses the same approach, specifying the wildcard bound with the feature name: allOrders<? extends Address>.

4. **process**, a generic operation declared, as in Java, with the generic parameter, <T extends Address>, preceding the operation signature that uses it. Here, the type parameter is actually recorded as part of the UML operation name, but when the model is converted to Ecore, it is translated into the correct structure.

GlobalPurchaseOrder is a subclass of the generic **PurchaseOrder** base class. The <<<GlobalAddress>>> stereotype specifies **GlobalAddress** as the actual type to be bound to the base class's type parameter **A**.

Java Specification for Generics

Since the modeling of generics in Ecore follows Java's generics design so closely, there is not much EMF-specific about the Java specification. The Ecore representation of generic types in the model is fully specified by the Java types that appear in the code.

The generic **PurchaseOrder** class in our running example, with its **billTo** and **shipTo** references, can be declared in Java as follows:

```
/**
 * @model
 */
public interface PurchaseOrder<A extends Address>
{
  /**
   * @model containment="true"
   */
  A getBillTo();

  /**
   * @model containment="true"
   */
```

```
    A getShipTo();

    ...
}
```

The **POProcessor** class, which uses generics in its features and operations, is specified in Java as follows:

```
/**
 * @model
 */
public interface POProcessor
{
    /**
     * @model containment="true"
     */
    PurchaseOrder<USAddress> getSimpleOrder();

    /**
     * @model
     */
    EList<PurchaseOrder<USAddress>> getDomesticOrders();

    /**
     * @model
     */
    EList<PurchaseOrder<? extends Address>> getAllOrders();

    /**
     * @model
     */
    <T extends Address> Boolean process(PurchaseOrder<T> order);
}
```

Finally, class **GlobalPurchaseOrder**, which extends a generic type to bind its type parameter, looks like this:

```
/**
 * @model
 */
public interface GlobalPurchaseOrder
    extends PurchaseOrder<GlobalAddress>
{
}
```

XML Schema Specification for Generics

Like UML, XML Schema provides no standard representation for generic type information, and therefore needs to be augmented. A particular Ecore-sourced appinfo annotation is used to define type parameters on a complex type. For example, the generic parameter **A**, for our **PurchaseOrder**, would look like this in a schema:

```
<xsd:complexType name="PurchaseOrder">
  <xsd:annotation>
    <xsd:appinfo source="http://www.eclipse.org/emf/2002/Ecore"
        ecore:key="typeParameters">
      <typeParameter bounds="epo2:Address" name="A"/>
    </xsd:appinfo>
  </xsd:annotation>
  ...
</xsd:complexType>
```

As you can see, the `xsd:appinfo` has two attributes: a `source` whose value is "http://www.eclipse.org/emf/2002/Ecore", and an `ecore:key` whose value is "typeParameters". It contains a `typeParameter` element for each parameter of the type.

Features that use the type parameter, like **billTo** and **shipTo** in our example, are represented by an element declaration with an `ecore:type` attribute as follows:

```
<xsd:complexType name="PurchaseOrder">
  ...
  <xsd:sequence>
    <xsd:element name="billTo" type="epo2:Address" minOccurs="0"
        ecore:type="A"/>
    <xsd:element name="shipTo" type="epo2:Address" minOccurs="0"
        ecore:type="A"/>
  ...
  </xsd:sequence>
  ...
</xsd:complexType>
```

The schema `type`, which is not generics-aware, refers simply to the type parameter's bound, **Address**.

The XML Schema representations for the **POProcessor** and **GlobalPurchaseOrder** classes provide a few more examples of Ecore generics in XML Schema. The generic **process** operation shows how a `typeParameter` element can be used to define a type parameter, in much the same way as it was for a class:

```
<xsd:complexType name="POProcessor">
  <xsd:annotation>
    <xsd:appinfo source="http://www.eclipse.org/emf/2002/Ecore"
        ecore:key="operations">
```

```
        <operation name="process" type="ecore:EBooleanObject">
          <typeParameter name="T" bounds="epo2:Address"/>
          <parameter name="order" type="epo2:PurchaseOrder{T}"/>
        </operation>
      </xsd:appinfo>
    </xsd:annotation>
    ...
</xsd:complexType>
```

Notice the special syntax used here to represent the generic type of the **order** parameter. It is essentially the same as the Java generics syntax, only using "{" and "}" in place of "<" and ">".[3] This is, in fact, the same syntax that we use in the ecore:type of an attribute or element if it corresponds to a feature with a parameterized type, like the **simpleOrder** reference in **POProcessor**, for example:

```
<xsd:element name="simpleOrder" type="epo2:PurchaseOrder"
  minOccurs="0" ecore:type="epo2:PurchaseOrder{epo2:USAddress}"/>
```

Finally, let's take a look at how we represent a subclass of a generic class, like **GlobalPurchaseOrder**:

```
<xsd:complexType name="GlobalPurchaseOrder"
      ecore:extends="epo2:PurchaseOrder{epo2:GlobalAddress}">
  <xsd:complexContent>
    <xsd:extension base="epo2:PurchaseOrder"/>
  </xsd:complexContent>
</xsd:complexType>
```

As usual, the complex type specifies its base type in the xsd:extension, but an ecore:extends attribute is also needed on the complex type to specify type arguments. This attribute uses the same Java-like type syntax as ecore:type.

21.2 EMF Persistence Enhancements

EMF 2.4 provides several notable enhancements to the persistence APIs that were the subject of Section 15.2. Most of these changes were motivated by the growing popularity of the REpresentational State Transfer (REST) style of programming.[4] Although previous versions of EMF already supported most of the main principles of REST, there were two notable violations:

---

3. Angle brackets could not be used in this context; they would have to appear as XML entities.

4. REST proposes a number of network architecture principles for scalable distributed systems. For more information, see *http://en.wikipedia.org/wiki/Representational_State_Transfer*.

1. EMF has always provided CREATE, READ, and UPDATE operations on resources, but there was no API for the remaining CRUD operation, DELETE.

2. EMF relied on the structure of a URI (that is, the scheme or file extension) to identify the type of a resource, instead of looking at its content.

EMF version 2.4 addresses these shortcomings by introducing API for resource deletion and providing mechanisms for identifying resources based on their content type. We'll discuss these and a few other changes in the following sections.

21.2.1 Resource Deletion

A resource can now be deleted by calling the `delete()` method on the `Resource` interface:

```
public interface Resource ...
{
  ...
  void delete(Map<?, ?> options) throws IOException;
}
```

This method delegates to a URI converter the task of deleting the state associated with the resource's URI (e.g., by deleting the underlying file in the file system). It then unloads the resource, converting all of its contents to proxies. Finally, the resource is removed from its resource set, if it is in one.

To handle the delegation from `Resource.delete()`, a similar `delete()` method has also been added to the `URIConverter` interface, along with another related method, `exists()`:

```
public interface URIConverter
{
  ...
  boolean exists(URI uri, Map<?, ?> options);
  void delete(URI uri, Map<?, ?> options) throws IOException;
}
```

The `exists()` method can be used to test whether there is any state associated with a specified URI. This is generally more efficient than fetching an input stream, which could also fail due to insufficient permission, for example. The `delete()` method simply deletes the state associated with a URI. Although both methods are commonly called on URIConverter directly, `delete()` is most often called indirectly via `Resource.delete()`.

21.2.2   Content Types

A content type is a universally unique string identifying a specific kind of resource content. For example, we could use "com.example.epo2" as the identifier for files containing instances of the ExtendedPO2 model serialized as XMI. We could then configure EMF and the Eclipse platform to handle this content type as we wish. For example, we might register an EMF resource factory and an Eclipse editor against it. In the past, we would have just used a file extension for this, but recognizing content types as a more abstract concept provides additional flexibility. In the simplest case, a single file extension can be associated with several different content types. More generally, we can recognize types of content from a variety of sources, without any regard for file name patterns or even for whether the content is stored in files at all.

Previously, when we identified content strictly by file extension, we could do so simply by looking at the URI of a resource. A content type may also be partly or even completely inferred from the form of a URI, but that is often insufficient. Usually, you actually need to look into the contents associated with the URI to conclusively determine its content type. To support this in EMF, the URIConverter interface has been expanded to include the following two new methods:

```
Map<String, ?> contentDescription(URI uri, Map<?, ?> options)
  throws IOException;
EList<ContentHandler> getContentHandlers();
```

The contentDescription() method can be invoked to obtain a description of the contents associated with a specified URI. It returns a map of properties describing the contents, which is typically determined by reading from and analyzing an input stream for the URI. This analysis is done by a configurable list of content handlers returned by the getContentHandlers() method.

The ContentHandler interface includes two methods, contentDescription() and canHandle(), both of which are used by URI converters to implement their own contentDescription() method:

```
public interface ContentHandler
{
  boolean canHandle(URI uri);

  String OPTION_REQUESTED_PROPERTIES = "REQUESTED_PROPERTIES";

  Map<String, ?> contentDescription(URI uri, InputStream inputStream,
      Map<?, ?> options, Map<Object, Object> context)
    throws IOException;
  ...
}
```

The URI converter creates an input stream along with an empty context (which caches state to reduce duplicate computation costs) and simply delegates the `contentDescription()` call to each content handler for which `canHandle()` returns `true`. The result is a map in which the values of properties, such as byte order or character set, are keyed by strings that identify them. The `OPTION_REQUESTED_PROPERTIES` option can be passed to `contentDescription()` in the `options` map to request specific properties. Two properties, however, are always computed: validity and content type. Constants identifying these properties are defined in the `ContentHandler` interface:

```
String CONTENT_TYPE_PROPERTY = "org.eclipse.emf.ecore:contentType";
String VALIDITY_PROPERTY = "org.eclipse.emf.ecore:validity";
```

The value of the content type property is a content type string recognized by the particular content handler. The value of the validity property is an enum, `Validity`, that indicates whether the content is valid, invalid, or indeterminate:

```
enum Validity { INVALID, INDETERMINATE, VALID }
```

Having possibly invoked `contentDescription()` on several content handlers, the URI converter uses the validity to decide which content description to return. It returns the first valid description or, failing that, the first indeterminate one. Only if all content handlers return invalid descriptions does the URI converter return an invalid result. In this case, the content type property is not included in the returned description.

Content handlers are maintained in a registry (`ContentHandler.Registry`), which can be populated via the `org.eclipse.emf.ecore.content_handler` extension point. Handlers are registered with an associated priority, from which a sorted list view is computed and used by the default `URIConverter` implementation to initialize the list that its `getContentHandlers()` method returns.

A single default content handler is registered by EMF. It works by delegating to the Eclipse platform's content type catalog, bridging the gap between EMF and platform content types. Thus, it turns out that the most common way to define an EMF content type is simply to extend the platform's `org.eclipse.core.contenttype.contentTypes` extension point:

```
<extension point="org.eclipse.core.contenttype.contentTypes">
  <content-type base-type="org.eclipse.emf.ecore.xmi"
      file-extensions="epo2"
      id="com.example.epo2"
      name="ExtendedPO2 File"
```

```
      priority="normal">
    <describer class="...RootXMLContentHandlerImpl$Describer">
      <parameter name="namespace"
          value="http://www.example.com/epo2.ecore"/>
      <parameter name="kind" value="xmi"/>
    </describer>
  </content-type>
</extension>
```

The describer is what actually analyzes the input stream and determines the validity, type, and other properties of the contents. In this case, we're using an implementation provided by EMF, `RootXMLContentHandlerImpl$Describer`, to test for XMI files in which the root element has a namespace corresponding to the **epo2** package. This kind of content type registration can be automatically generated into the model's *plugin.xml* file. To do so, ensure that the "Content Type Identifier" generator model property (on the package, under the "Model" category) is set to the desired content type string. Because the string is used as an ID in the extension, it should be of the dotted form shown in this example.

The added flexibility provided by content types comes with a considerable performance cost. Opening an input stream and reading from it is very expensive, and often the old mechanism based on file extensions is sufficient. As a result, content type registrations are not generated by default.

In Section 15.2.4, we looked at how a resource set uses a resource factory registry to create the correct type of resource for a given URI. In particular, we saw that the registry chooses a factory that is registered against the scheme or file extension of the URI. Similarly, in EMF 2.4, resource factories can also be registered against content types. The `Resource.Factory.Registry` interface includes the following new methods to support this:

```
interface Registry
{
  ...
  Map<String, Object> getContentTypeToFactoryMap();
  Factory getFactory(URI uri, String contentType);
}
```

Registration can be performed programmatically by adding to the map returned by `getContentTypeToFactoryMap()`, or, in the global registry, declaratively via the `org.eclipse.emf.ecore.content_parser` extension point.

The new, two-argument form of `getFactory()` takes a content type, which is then considered in selecting the appropriate resource factory. For backward compatibility, the registry first consults the old scheme and file extension registrations and, only if the specified URI matches neither, looks for a resource factory registered against the given content type.[5] If no exact matches are found, the factory for the default file extension or, failing that, content type is returned. Note that if no content type is specified (i.e., if the `contentType` argument is `null`), the registry simply skips the step where it looks for a matching content type registration. If, however, the special value `ContentHandler.UNSPECI-FIED_CONTENT_TYPE` is specified, the registry tries to obtain the content type from the URI converter, by calling the `contentDescription()` method described previously.

There is also a corresponding new method on the `ResourceSet` interface:

```
public interface ResourceSet ...
{
  ...
  Resource createResource(URI uri, String contentType);
}
```

This method simply uses the new form of `getFactory()` to obtain the resource factory that then creates a resource, allowing the specified content type to be considered in the process. This new form is also now used by the existing `getResource()` method when performing demand loading. It specifies `ContentHandler.UNSPECIFIED_CONTENT_TYPE` so that the content type is automatically obtained from the resource. This makes sense in this context, as the resource should already exist if it is being demand-loaded.

21.2.3 Other Enhancements

With the enhancements described in the previous two sections, we may begin to view EMF's persistence API as a unifying API for working with various different types of underlying resource-based storage. Whether resources are persisted in the Eclipse workspace, on a local file system, or elsewhere on the network and accessed via HTTP, EMF applications can use the same `Resource` and `URIConverter` interfaces to interact with them.

Looking at those underlying storage mechanisms, we may notice that there are a couple of additional common resource operations that EMF could support: retrieving time stamps and accessing attributes. We also may wonder how the

---

5. It is also possible to make content type registrations take precedence over old scheme and file extension registrations in contexts where backwards compatibility isn't an issue. To do so, copy the map returned by the global resource factory registry's `getContentTypeToFactoryMap()` method into that of the resource set's local registry. This works because attempts to match all types of registrations are made locally before delegating to the global registry.

framework could be extended to add support for additional underlying storage mechanisms. In this section, we will look at the remaining enhancements in the persistence API that address these issues.

Time Stamps

Section 15.2.3 discussed several "virtual features" of the `Resource` interface, embodied by feature ID constants and accessor methods. A new one, **timestamp**, was added in EMF 2.4:

```
public interface Resource extends Notifier
{
  ...
  int RESOURCE__TIME_STAMP = 8;
  long getTimeStamp();
  void setTimeStamp(long timeStamp);
}
```

The `getTimeStamp()` method can be used to retrieve the time stamp on the resource, for example, to help implement optimistic concurrency or to detect external changes. Although the time stamp can be set explicitly, by calling `setTimeStamp()`, it is typically updated as a side effect of loading or saving the resource. When loading, it is set to the time stamp of the resource when the input stream is opened. When saving, it's set to the time stamp when the output stream is closed. When populating a new resource, it's set to the time at which the first object is added.

In support of this feature, new forms of `createInputStream()` and `createOutputStream()`, each with an `options` argument, were added to `URIConverter`:

```
public interface URIConverter
{
  ...
  String OPTION_RESPONSE = "RESPONSE";
  String RESPONSE_TIME_STAMP_PROPERTY = "TIME_STAMP";

  InputStream createInputStream(URI uri, Map<?, ?> options)
    throws IOException;
  OutputStream createOutputStream(URI uri, Map<?, ?> options)
    throws IOException;
}
```

These new methods allow for arbitrary options to be passed to a `URIConverter`. In particular, `OPTION_RESPONSE` can be used to pass in a map to be populated with the values of certain properties. If RESPONSE_TIME_ STAMP_PROPERTY is specified as a key in the OPTION_RESPONSE map, the time stamp of the resource, at the moment the stream is created, will be filled in as the corresponding value. It is this feature that is used to set the time stamp in the resource on loading and saving.

Resource Attributes

Two new methods in the URIConverter interface allow users to get and set the values of various attributes associated with the state represented by a URI:

```
public interface URIConverter
{
  ...
  String ATTRIBUTE_TIME_STAMP = "timeStamp";
  long NULL_TIME_STAMP = -1;
  String ATTRIBUTE_LENGTH = "length";
  String ATTRIBUTE_READ_ONLY = "readOnly";
  String ATTRIBUTE_EXECUTABLE = "executable";
  String ATTRIBUTE_ARCHIVE = "archive";
  String ATTRIBUTE_HIDDEN = "hidden";
  String ATTRIBUTE_DIRECTORY = "directory";

  String OPTION_REQUESTED_ATTRIBUTES = "requestedAttributes";

  Map<String, ?> getAttributes(URI uri, Map<?, ?> options);

  void setAttributes(URI uri, Map<String, ?> attributes,
                     Map<?, ?> options) throws IOException;
}
```

The getAttributes() method can be used to retrieve one or more attribute name-value pairs associated with the specified URI. The corresponding setAttributes() method is used to set attribute values. Notice that URIConverter also defines constants (with the prefix ATTRIBUTE_) for a number of standard attributes. You can make a resource read-only, for examples, as follows:

```
Map<String, Object> attributes = new HashMap<String, Object>();
attributes.put(URIConverter.ATTRIBUTE_READ_ONLY, Boolean.TRUE);
myResource.getResourceSet().getURIConverter().setAttributes(
  myResource.getURI(), attributes, null);
```

Another constant in URIConverter, OPTION_REQUESTED_ATTRIBUTES, can be passed to getAttributes(), via the options argument, to specify that only a subset of attributes should be retrieved. For example, you can read the length and read-only attributes of a resource like this:

```
Set<String> requested = new HashSet<String>();
requested.add(URIConverter.ATTRIBUTE_LENGTH);
requested.add(URIConverter.ATTRIBUTE_READ_ONLY);
Map<String, Set<String>> opt = new HashMap<String, Set<String>();
opt.put(URIConverter.OPTION_REQUESTED_ATTRIBUTES, requested);
Map<String, ?> attributes = myResource.getResourceSet().
    getURIConverter().getAttriubtes(myResource.getURI(), opt);
```

If `OPTION_REQUESTED_ATTRIBUTES` is not specified, all the available attributes are returned.

URI Handlers

In previous versions of EMF, customizing the behavior of a URI converter usually required a customized subclass. Unfortunately, sometimes two different customizations were needed in the same context (resource set), but given the lack of multiple inheritance in Java, there was no simple way to combine them into a single URI converter. To alleviate this problem, EMF 2.4 has introduced a new interface, `URIHandler`, and provided a new default `URIConverter` implementation, `ExtensibleURIConverterImpl`, that delegates its method implementations to URI handlers.

The `URIHandler` interface includes the full complement of URI converter methods, plus a `canHandle()` method, which is used to indicate whether a handler is applicable for a given URI:

```
public interface URIHandler
{
  boolean canHandle(URI uri);

  InputStream createInputStream(URI uri, Map<?, ?> options)
    throws IOException;
  OutputStream createOutputStream(URI uri, Map<?, ?> options)
    throws IOException;
  boolean exists(URI uri, Map<?, ?> options);
  void delete(URI uri, Map<?, ?> options) throws IOException;
  ...
}
```

A number of default URI handlers are provided by the framework to support the Eclipse workspace, the file system, the Eclipse file system (EFS),[6] nested

---

6. EFS is a file system abstraction layer for arbitrary resources, allowing them to be used in the platform resource model. An EFS file system provides support for resources identified by a particular URI scheme. That support is comparable to what a URI handler provides in EMF, so it is leveraged in this design.

archives, and arbitrary URLs. These default handlers are made available via the DEFAULT_HANDLERS constant in the URIHandler interface:

```
List<URIHandler> DEFAULT_HANDLERS = Collections.unmodifiableList(
  Arrays.asList(new URIHander[]
  {
    new PlatformResourceURIHandlerImpl(),
    new FileURIHandlerImpl(),
    new EFSURIHandlerImpl(),
    new ArchiveURIHandlerImpl(),
    new URIHandlerImpl()
  }));
```

Two new methods have been added to the URIConverter interface, in support of URI handler delegation:

```
public interface URIConverter
{
  ...
  EList<URIHandler> getURIHandlers();
  URIHandler getURIHandler(URI uri);
}
```

The getURIHandlers() method returns a configurable list of URI handlers, initially populated with URIHandler.DEFAULT_HANDLERS. The getURIHandler() method determines the appropriate handler for the specified URI, by calling canHandle() on each handler in the list.

In Section 15.2.2, we mentioned the previous default URIConverter implementation class, URIConverterImpl, which has now been deprecated. Users should now use (and subclass if necessary) ExtensibleURIConverterImpl, which provides all the same functionality and more. Given the new configurable URI handler design, the need for custom URIConverter subclasses has been dramatically reduced. Users will now typically customize the URI converter behavior by creating a custom URI handler, and adding it to the converter's list of handlers.

21.3 Other New Features

In addition to changes in support of Java 5.0 and the EMF persistence API changes, there have also been a few smaller features added to EMF since version 2.2. This sections gives brief overviews of them.

21.3.1   Ecore Validation

As of version 2.3, EMF includes a validator for Ecore, `EcoreValidator`. This is a typical EMF validator, built on the validation framework described in Chapter 18. Thus, it can be invoked programmatically, as described in Section 18.3, by any tool that needs to validate Ecore models.

The sample Ecore model editor provides a simple UI for validating models. The validator is invoked by selecting a model element (usually the **EPackage**) and selecting **Validate** from either the context-sensitive menu or the **Sample Ecore Editor** pull-down menu. For example, Figure 21.8 shows the **epo2** package in *ExtendedPO2.ecore* being validated.

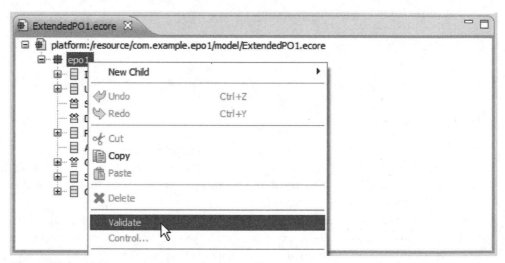

Figure 21.8   Validating a package in the sample Ecore editor.

Once the validator has run, a dialog box appears to report any problems that were found in the model.

One common source of frustration caused by invalid Ecore models occurs when using the EMF code generator. Invalid models can cause the generator to produce bad code or even fail. To avoid this problem, the Ecore validator is now invoked automatically when you load a model in the generator. If there's a problem with the model, a **Problems** page, illustrated in Figure 21.9, is displayed. Although it is still possible to switch to the familiar **Generator** page,[7]

---

7. In some cases, like when an XML file is not well formed, only the **Problems** page is shown in an editor. This means you actually need to address the issues before continuing so that the objects can be loaded and displayed.

this alerts you that you should to fix the model before generating frustratingly incorrect code.

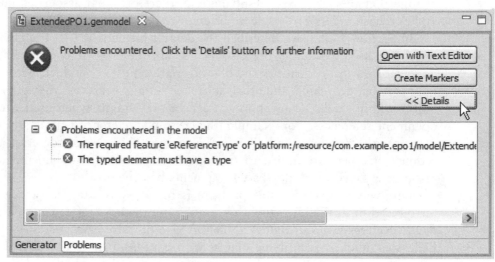

Figure 21.9   The generator's **Problems** page.

21.3.2 Reference Keys

Consider class **Customer** in the ExtendedPO2 model. As we described in Section 13.1, this class is used to represent a supplier's customers, and there is a bidirectional reference between it and **PurchaseOrder**, associating orders with the customers that placed them. Figure 21.10 illustrates the relevant parts of the model.

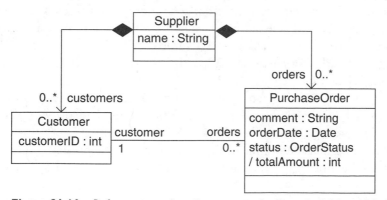

Figure 21.10   References to class Customer in the ExtendedPO2 model.

We modeled both cross-references, **customer** and **orders**, as non-proxy-resolving, assuming that only customers and purchase orders belonging to the same supplier could be associated. However, for the sake of this discussion, let's assume that they are proxy-resolving and, therefore, that associated customers and purchase orders can reside in different resources.

In Section 15.2.3, we described the default format for URI fragment paths, which are used to identify objects when serializing cross references. Each component of the path identifies the object, relative to its container, with the containment feature name and, for multiplicity-many features, the index of the object within the list. This approach can be very fragile when used with cross-document references. For example, the **customer** reference here is serialized by default with a fragment path like "//@customers.0" or "//@customers.1". If preceding customers are added to or removed from their supplier and just that resource is saved, the index-based fragments become invalid.

One way of avoiding this problem is to take advantage of a new feature introduced in EMF 2.3, reference keys. We use the **keys** reference on a containment **EReference** in our model to identify one or more **EAttribute**s of the target **EClass** as uniquely identifying objects within an instance of that **EReference**. In our example, we can use the **customerID** attribute as they key for the **Suppliers.customers** reference. As XMI, **Supplier** looks like this:

```
<eClassifiers xsi:type="ecore:EClass" name="Supplier">
  <eStructuralFeatures xsi:type="ecore:EAttribute" name="name" ... />
  <eStructuralFeatures xsi:type="ecore:EReference" name="customers"
      upperBound="-1" eType="#//Customer" containment="true"
      eKeys="#//Customer/customerID"/>
  ...
</eClassifiers>
```

By doing this, we ensure that cross-references to customers are serialized using the specified key. For example, let's assume that the third **Customer** in the **Supplier.customers** list has a **customerID** value of 777. Instead of using the fragile index-based path "//@customers.2", cross–references to that object look like "//@customers[customerID='777']".[8]

Even prior to EMF 2.3, you could avoid relying on brittle, position-based path segments by using ID-based fragments that uniquely identify objects within a resource. However, as described in Sections 15.2.3 and 15.3.6, this approach incurs its own costs and complications. Reference keys represent a happy medium, offering the most important advantages of the two original approaches.

---

8. If there is more than one **eKeys** attribute for an **EReference**, the corresponding fragment path segment has the following generalized form: "@featurename[key1='value1',key2='value2']".

In addition to providing this more robust cross-reference format, defining **eKeys** also has another advantage. As mentioned previously, the **eKeys** are attributes that should "uniquely identify" the objects within a reference. The EMF validator for the model can be used to check and enforce this constraint in instances.

21.3.3   *Annotated Java Model Importer*

Section 12.4 described in detail the three model importer applications available in EMF 2.2: Rose2GenModel, XSD2GenModel, and Ecore2GenModel. We saw how each application is invoked in Eclipse's headless mode to create or to update Ecore and generator models. Section 12.5 described how to do the same thing using the EMF Ant tasks and discussed the potential benefits of this approach.

Of the four model sources supported out-of-box by EMF, annotated Java is the only one that didn't have a model importer application and Ant task before EMF 2.3. The reason for such negligence was that this model source requires a more complicated setup than the others: the files it uses as input (i.e., the annotated Java interfaces) have to be located in an Eclipse Java project, properly registered in a workspace. This way, EMF can make use of the facilities provided by JDT to figure out the code's dependencies, and to locate and parse the interfaces in order to extract the model they convey.

Even with such complications, users have expressed the need to bring EMF's support for annotated Java to the same level as the other model sources. This section describes the application and Ant task introduced in EMF 2.3 to bridge this gap.

The Eclipse headless application for annotated Java is Java2GenModel. The following command illustrates its most typical use:

```
> eclipse –noSplash –data C:\emf\workspace
    -application org.eclipse.emf.importer.java.Java2GenModel
    /com.example.ppo/model/PrimerPO.genmodel
    -modelProject /com.example.ppo
```

The first two lines of this command are explained in Section 12.4. You should consult that section if you are not familiar with Eclipse headless applications. Notice, however, that rather than regarding the workspace location as transient data, as we did with the other model importer applications, we are specifying the location of a real workspace containing the Java project we want to analyze.

The first argument to the Java2GenModel application is the absolute path in the workspace of the generator model to be created or updated. If this model doesn't exist, the "-modelProject" option is required and must indicate the project containing the annotated Java files.

A summary of all arguments and options supported by this application is displayed when it is invoked without any arguments. They are identical to the ones used with Ecore2GenModel and are detailed in Chapter 12.

The Ant task to use with annotated Java is emf.Java2Java. It supports most of the attributes described for emf.Ecore2Java in Section 12.5.3. The few differences result from to the additional complication in setup mentioned previously. The model and modelProjectFragmentPath attributes are not supported by the new task. In addition, the location of the generator model must be specified as a workspace path via the genModelPath attribute. The genModel attribute, which is used for the same purpose by the other tasks, also is not supported.

This Ant script snipet shows how the new task can be used:

```
<emf.Java2Java
    genModelPath="/com.example.ppo/model/PrimerPO.genmodel"
    modelProject="c:/emf/workspace/com.example.ppo">
  <arg line="-package http://www.example.com/PrimerPO"/>
</emf.Java2Java>
```

21.4   Resource Options

In Sections 15.2.3 and 15.3.3, we looked at all the save and load options supported by EMF's resource implementations as of version 2.2. Unsurprisingly, a number of new options have been added since then. This section describes these new options.

One new option has been added to the generic Resource interface, and it is supported by the base ResourceImpl implementation.

OPTION_SAVE_ONLY_IF_CHANGED   (String, Save)

This option can be used to specify that the resource should be saved only if it would be different from what already exists. If there is existing content corresponding to the resource's URI, the new content is redirected into a temporary buffer and the two versions are compared byte-wise. The existing content is only updated if the two are different. This option can be given one of two values: "FILE_BUFFER" or "MEMORY_BUFFER", indicating whether the temporary buffer for the new content should be on disk or in memory. Resource defines a constant for each of these values.

21.4.1   *XMLResource Options*

There are several new XMLResource options available, joining those that we saw in Section 15.3.3.

OPTION_ELEMENT_HANDLER   (XMLResource.ElementHandler, Save)

This option can be used to specify an XMLResource.ElementHandler for deducing the feature used to serialize a specific type of value. This option is particularly useful when feature maps for substitution groups have been suppressed, in which case it may be desirable to deduce substitution group element names during serialization. An instance of the default implementation, ElementHandlerImpl, can be used for this purpose.

OPTION_ESCAPE_USING_CDATA   (Boolean, Save)

If this option is enabled, element content that needs escaping and does not contain the sequence of characters "]]>" will be serialized in a CDATA section. By default, disallowed characters are represented as XML entities, instead.

OPTION_LAX_WILDCARD_PROCESSING   (Boolean, Load)

This option can be set to Boolean.TRUE to force all wildcards to be handled as if they explicitly specified lax processing, demand creating metadata for unrecognized elements.

OPTION_RESOURCE_ENTITY_HANDLER
              (XMLResource.ResouceEntityHandler, Save/Load)

This option causes XML entities to be used in place of URIs in cross-document references. This allows all such references to be determined just by parsing the entity declarations, and can reduce the size of the serialization if a long file name is repeated frequently. The specified XMLResource.ResourceEntityHandler maintains the mapping between entity names and URI values during save and load. An instance of the default implementation, ResourceEntityHandlerImpl, can be used for this purpose.

OPTION_ROOT_OBJECTS   (List<EObject>, Save)

This option can be used to save only the subtree starting with the specified **EObjects**. These objects must all be contained, directly or indirectly, by the resource.

OPTION_SUPPRESS_DOCUMENT_ROOT   (Boolean, Load)

When OPTION_EXTENDED_META_DATA is also used, setting this option to Boolean.TRUE directs the loader to suppress the document root from the resource contents (document root classes were discussed in Section 9.1.3). If a resource is loaded with this option, it should probably then be saved with `OPTION_ELEMENT_HANDLER`, which will deduce an appropriate root element for the resulting serialization.

`OPTION_URI_HANDLER`   (XMLResource.URIHandler, Save/Load)

This option can be used to specify an `XMLResource.URIHandler` that controls how URIs are resolved during load and deresolved during save.[9] A basic implementation, `URIHandlerImpl`, is provided as a base for custom handlers.

21.5 Generator Model Properties

A number of new properties have been added to the generator model since EMF 2.2, allowing more control for the user and offering new patterns for the generated code.

21.5.1 Model Object Properties

The majority of the new properties appear on the model object. These properties are in addition to those described in Section 12.3.1.

All

Compliance Level—This property specifies the JDK compliance level for the generated Java code. A value of 1.4 ensures that generated code is compatible with Java 1.4. A value of 5.0 allows generated code to exploit generics, as well as language features including enums, for-each loops, and annotations like `@Override`. See Section 21.1 for more details.

Copyright Fields—This boolean property controls whether the value of the "Copyright Text" property should be used to produce a static `copyright` field in each generated source file. In EMF 2.2 and before, that property's value was always used to generate such a field, but beginning in EMF 2.3, it is used only in a Javadoc comment by default.

Language—This property can be set to a two-letter ISO language code, in order to specify that that language, instead of the system default, should be used in

---

9. Note that this nested interface is not the same as the `URIHandler` interface described in Section 21.2.3

converting strings to upper and lower case. For example, to always use English, specify "en" here. This is important for locales where the uppercase version of "i" is not "I", in particular.

Runtime Version—This property specifies the version of EMF on which the generated code will run. It can be used to select an older version of EMF, to ensure that the code does not depend on any newer features of EMF. Note that, if this property is set to 2.2, the "Compliance Level" must be 1.4.

Edit

Color Providers—An `IItemColorProvider` interface (`ITableItem-ColorProvider`, for tables), similar to `IItemLabelProvider`, was introduced in EMF 2.4 to provide colors for items. This option controls whether or not generated item providers provide this support. A value of true ensures that the item providers extend `IItemColorProvider`, the item provider adapter factory lists it as a supported interface, and the registration of that factory declares this support.

Edit Plugin ID—This property specifies the unique string that identifies the edit plug-in to Eclipse. By default, ".edit" is appended to the "Model Plug-in ID" to form this value.

Edit Plugin Variables—The property allows you to enter a comma-separated list of plug-in IDs to be included in the edit plug-in's classpath, optionally specifying classpath variable names (as *variable-name=plug-in-id*).

Font Providers—An `IItemFontProvider` interface (`ITableItemFontProvider`, for tables), similar to `IItemLabelProvider`, was introduced in EMF 2.4 to provide fonts for items. This option controls whether or not generated item providers provide this support. A value of true ensures that the item providers extend `IItemFontProvider`, the item provider adapter factory lists it as a supported interface, and the registration of that factory declares this support.

Optimized Has Children—Setting this property to true causes item providers to use an optimized `hasChildren()` implementation that does not access more children values than necessary.

Provider Root Extends Class—This property can be used to change the base class of all generated item providers. More precisely, it specifies the qualified name of a class that will be extended by item providers for root classes (i.e., classes for which no supertypes are modeled).

Table Providers—This property specifies whether generated item providers should support providing column labels. A value of true ensures that the item providers extend `ITableItemLabelProvider`, that the item provider adapter factory lists it as a supported interface, and that the registration of that factory declares this support. `ITableItemFont-Provider` and `ITableItemColorProvider` might also be supported, depending on the "Font Providers" and "Color Providers" properties.

Editor

Creation Submenus—This property determines whether to organize qualified child creation actions into submenus. In the case where an object can have children of the same type via more than one of its features, setting this property to true results in a submenu per feature.

Editor Plugin ID—This property specifies the unique string that identifies the editor plug-in to Eclipse. By default, ".editor" is appended to the "Model Plugin ID" to form this value.

Editor Plugin Variables—This property allows you to enter a comma-separated list of plug-in IDs to be included in the editor plug-in's classpath, optionally specifying classpath variable names (as *variable-name=plug-in-id*).

Model

Binary Compatible Reflective Methods—This property determines whether to generate slower reflective accessor implementations that remain binary compatible even when features are added to base classes defined in other models. If this property is true, offset-correcting code is generated to ensure that these accessors (`eGet()`, `eSet()`, etc.) dispatch to the correct cases even if the number of features in the base class has changed since compile time.

Suppress GenModel Annotations—This property can be used to suppress generation-related annotations, such as those that record documentation and operation bodies, from the package metadata. A value of true ensures that the generated package implementation does not include any GenModel-sourced **EAnnotations** in the model it builds at runtime.

Model Class Defaults

Public Constructors—Setting this property to true causes generated model classes to have public, rather than protected, constructors.

Model Feature Defaults

Packed Enums—This property determines whether enumerated type attributes should be packed into the boolean flags bit field. Setting it to true and specifying a "Boolean Flags Field" results in any such feature being encoded in the minimum required number of bits.

Templates & Merge

Template Plugin Variables—This property allows you to enter a comma-separated list of plug-in IDs to be included in the *.JETEmitter* project's classpath, optionally specifying classpath variable names (as *variable-name=plug-in-id*). This is needed when using dynamic templates with dependencies beyond those of EMF's base templates.

Tests

Tests Plugin ID—This property specifies the unique string that identifies the tests plug-in to Eclipse. By default, ".tests" is appended to the "Model Plug-in ID" to form this value.

Tests Plugin Variables—This property allows you to enter a comma-separated list of plug-in IDs to be included in the tests plug-in's classpath, optionally specifying classpath variable names (as *variable-name= plug-in-id*).

21.5.2 Package Properties

Four new generator model properties appear on packages in the model. These properties are in addition to those described in Section 12.3.2.

Edit

Child Creation Extenders—This property specifies whether the generated item provider adapter factory should include child creation extenders. If classes in the package extend classes from another model with "Extensible Provider Factory" enabled, then enabling this property allows the package to contribute children for its derived types. See *http://ed-merks.blogspot. com/2008/01/creating-children-you-didnt-know.html* for details.

Extensible Provider Factory—This property specifies whether the generated item provider adapter factory should support extensible child creation.

Model

Content Type Identifier—This property can be used to define a content type for serialized instances of the model. If a value is specified for the property, a content type declaration and a corresponding resource factory registration are generated in the *plugin.xml*, as discussed in Section 21.2.2. The content type identifier is also exposed for programmatic use via a static eCONTENT_TYPE field generated in the package interface.

File Extensions—This property specifies the file extension against which to register the model's resource factory, or the file extensions for its content type. If a "Content Type Identifier" is specified, a comma separated list is permitted (e.g. "epo2,xmi") and the content type registration will apply to all of those extensions.

Editor

Generate Model Wizard—This property specifies whether the wizard class described in Section 11.5 is generated. Note that in Eclipse, wizards are registered in a *plugin.xml* file. Because EMF does not update this file automatically, if you change the value of this property, you will need to delete the existing file or edit it manually.

21.5.3 Enum Properties

A single generator model property is now available on enums. Prior to EMF 2.3, there were no such properties.

Model

Type Safe Enum Compatible—This property specifies whether to use the backward compatible naming pattern for Java 5.0 enums, as described in Section 21.1.1.

APPENDIX A

UML Notation

UML class diagrams are the most concise way of describing EMF models. We use UML diagrams throughout the book to depict examples and to illustrate various EMF concepts. EMF uses only a subset of the complete UML notation along with some conventions of its own. Here we provide a quick summary of the subset UML notation used in the book. For a complete description of the mapping of UML to EMF, refer to Chapter 6.

Classes and Interfaces

Figure A.1 shows the UML notation for concrete and abstract classes and for interfaces. All three are denoted by a box containing three compartments, with the class or interface name in the top one. Concrete class names are displayed in regular font and the names of abstract classes are *italicized*. An interface name is also in regular font, but preceded by the stereotype <<interface>>.

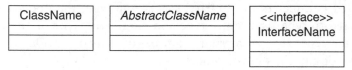

Figure A.1 Classes and interfaces.

A UML class, abstract or concrete, is used to represent an EMF class, not just a Java class. An EMF class maps to both a Java interface and a corresponding implementation class as described in Chapter 10. A UML/EMF interface, on the other hand, maps to just a Java interface with no corresponding implementation class.

The second and third compartments of a UML class or interface include its attributes and operations, respectively. Figure A.2 shows a class containing three attributes and two operations. Attributes represent the data elements that comprise the class.

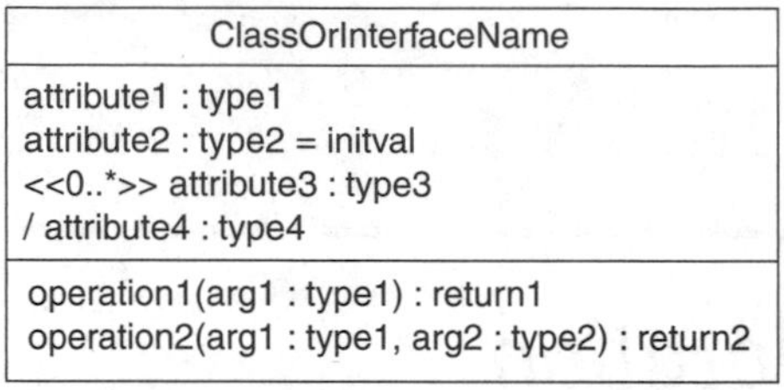

ClassOrInterfaceName
attribute1 : type1 attribute2 : type2 = initval <<0..*>> attribute3 : type3 / attribute4 : type4
operation1(arg1 : type1) : return1 operation2(arg1 : type1, arg2 : type2) : return2

Figure A.2 Attributes and operations.

In a UML class, an attribute appears as a name followed by a colon (:) and then its type. The type of an attribute can be any Java primitive type (`boolean`, `int`, `long`, and so on), a basic Java data type from the `java.lang` package (`Boolean`, `Integer`, `Long`, `String`, and so on), or the name of a user-defined enumeration or data type as we'll describe next. An attribute declaration (like **attribute2**, in our example) can also optionally be followed by an equal sign (=) and then an initial value suitable for the type of the attribute. An attribute can also be preceded by a stereotype that indicates that the attribute is not a single value, but instead a list of values. For example, the stereotype on **attribute3** indicates an unbounded multiplicity. Multiplicity-many associations are much more common than multiplicity-many attributes. We'll describe multiplicities further in "Class Relationships" on page 655. An attribute, like **attribute4**, can also be preceded by a slash (/) to indicate that it is derived.

The operations in the bottom compartment of the UML class are declared in a similar way to attributes, only with the addition of a list of zero or more comma-separated parameters inside parentheses following the operation name and before the return type. The return type and parameter types of an operation can be any of the types that an attribute can be, described previously, but also can be the name of any class in the model.

Enumerations and Data Types

As stated earlier, the type of an attribute can be an enumeration or user-defined data type. Figure A.3 shows the UML notation for defining such types. Both are represented as UML classes, but with only two compartments instead of three.[1]

---

1. By convention, we suppress the third (operation) compartment because it would always be empty anyway.

As with classes and interfaces, the top compartment contains the name of the type, but in these cases, preceded by the stereotype <<enumeration>> or <<datatype>>.

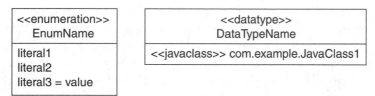

Figure A.3 Enumerations and data types.

In an enumeration declaration, the second compartment (that is, the attribute compartment of the UML class) contains the set of names of the enumeration's literals. A literal name can optionally be followed by an equal sign (=) and then its corresponding integer value. Literals without an explicit supplied value are automatically assigned sequential values starting from zero.

The second compartment of a data type contains a single entry (attribute) that is the fully qualified name of an arbitrary Java class that represents the type. The name must also be preceded by the stereotype <<javaclass>>.

Class Relationships

An inheritance relationship in UML is represented by a line between the classes with a triangle pointing to the superclass. Figure A.4 shows two examples of a subclass (**ClassB**), one involving single inheritance, the other multiple.

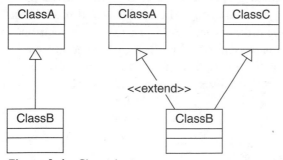

Figure A.4 Class inheritance.

Although EMF supports multiple inheritance, Java only supports single-implementation inheritance. Therefore, in the case of multiple inheritance, the

<<extend>> stereotype is used to indicate which of the multiple superclasses is to be used as the base class for the corresponding Java implementation class. The others only involve interface inheritance in Java and their implementations are replicated in the subclass.

A one-way association, or reference, between two classes is depicted in UML by a line with an arrowhead on the target end. Figure A.5 shows three examples of one-way references from a source class, **ClassA**, to a target **ClassB**. At the target end appears the name of the reference (often referred to as the role name), and its multiplicity. The multiplicity is typically of the form *lower..upper*, where *lower* represents the lower bound and *upper* represents the upper bound, although the single value 1 is often used as a short form for 1..1. An upper bound value of * represents unlimited multiplicity.

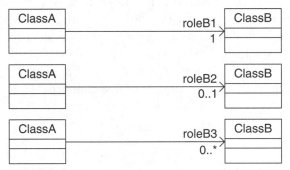

Figure A.5   One-way associations.

The difference between **roleB1** and **roleB2** in Figure A.5 is that **roleB1** (whose lower bound is implicitly 1) is declared to be required, whereas **roleB2** is declared as optional; it might or might not be set in a valid model instance.

Associations can also be bidirectional. A bidirectional association is the same as two one-way associations in opposite directions, only the inverse is automatically updated when either end is set. As shown in Figure A.6, a bidirectional association is represented in UML by a line between the classes with no arrowhead on either end.

Figure A.6   Bidirectional associations.

The last, and arguably the most important, kind of association that EMF is concerned with is referred to as containment or by-value aggregation. As shown in Figure A.7, a containment reference is indicated by a black diamond on the source (that is, the container) end of the association. Containment associations imply physical location and ownership. Instances of **ClassB** in our example are owned by and persisted with an instance of **ClassA**.

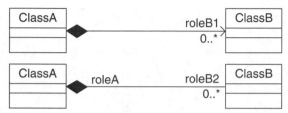

Figure A.7 Containment associations.

Just like other associations, a containment association can be one-way or bidirectional.[2] The multiplicity of the container end of a containment association need not be specified. It is implicitly, and can only be, 1; an object can only exist in one container.

---

2. In fact, all containment references are implicitly bidirectional in EMF; any EMF object can generically access its container. The benefit of a bidirectional containment association is that its access can be type-safe, and that notification will be provided for the contained object when its container changes.

APPENDIX B

Summary of Example Models

The code fragments and examples used throughout this book are based on six main models. These models, SimplePO, PrimerPO, ExtendedPO, ExtendedPO1, ExtendedPO2, and ExtendedPO3, define the data for purchase order management applications, each one progressively more complicated than the last. The models are shown here, along with a brief description of how each builds on the one before it. The first two models are provided in four forms: UML, XML Schema, annotated Java interfaces, and Ecore/XMI. For the more complicated extended models, we only show the most concise form: UML. Note that all of these models, along with the rest of the example code used throughout this book, can also be downloaded from the book's Web site at *http://www.informit.com/ title/9780321331885.*

SimplePO

This is the first and simplest example in the book. It includes two classes, **PurchaseOrder** and **Item**, with a containment association between them. The SimplePO model is used in Chapters 2 and 3 to introduce EMF. It also shows up in examples illustrating dynamic EMF (Sections 14.3 and 15.3.4), the EMOF resource factory (Section 15.4.5), and command specialization (Section 19.1). In addition, all of the RCP and stand-alone examples in Chapter 20 are based on it. Figure B.1 illustrates the model in UML.

Figure B.1   The SimplePO model.

In the form of an XML Schema, the SimplePO model looks like this:

SimplePO.xsd:

```xml
<?xml version="1.0" encoding="UTF-8"?>
<xsd:schema xmlns:xsd="http://www.w3.org/2001/XMLSchema"
            xmlns:po="http://www.example.com/SimplePO"
            targetNamespace="http://www.example.com/SimplePO">
  <xsd:complexType name="PurchaseOrder">
    <xsd:sequence>
      <xsd:element name="shipTo" type="xsd:string"/>
      <xsd:element name="billTo" type="xsd:string"/>
      <xsd:element name="items"  type="po:Item"
                   minOccurs="0" maxOccurs="unbounded"/>
    </xsd:sequence>
  </xsd:complexType>

  <xsd:complexType name="Item">
    <xsd:sequence>
      <xsd:element name="productName" type="xsd:string"/>
      <xsd:element name="quantity" type="xsd:int"/>
      <xsd:element name="price" type="xsd:float"/>
    </xsd:sequence>
  </xsd:complexType>
</xsd:schema>
```

Using annotated Java, the SimplePO model can be described with two Java source files: *PurchaseOrder.java* and *Item.java*.

PurchaseOrder.java:

```java
package com.example.po;

import org.eclipse.emf.common.util.EList;

/**
 * @model
 */
public interface PurchaseOrder
{
  /**
   * @model
   */
  String getShipTo();

  /**
   * @model
   */
  String getBillTo();

  /**
   * @model type="Item" containment="true"
   */
  EList getItems();
}
```

Item.java:

```java
package com.example.po;

/**
 * @model
 */
public interface Item
{
   /**
    * @model
    */
   String getProductName();

   /**
    * @model
    */
   int getQuantity();

   /**
    * @model
    */
   float getPrice();
}
```

The Ecore model for SimplePO looks like this when serialized as XMI:

SimplePO.ecore:

```xml
<?xml version="1.0" encoding="UTF-8"?>
<ecore:EPackage xmi:version="2.0" xmlns:xmi="http://www.omg.org/XMI"
    xmlns:xsi="http://www.w3.org/2001/XMLSchema-instance"
    xmlns:ecore="http://www.eclipse.org/emf/2002/Ecore" name="po"
    nsURI="http://www.example.com/SimplePO" nsPrefix="po">
  <eClassifiers xsi:type="ecore:EClass" name="PurchaseOrder">
    <eStructuralFeatures xsi:type="ecore:EAttribute" name="shipTo"
        eType="ecore:EDataType
              http://www.eclipse.org/emf/2002/Ecore#//EString"/>
    <eStructuralFeatures xsi:type="ecore:EAttribute" name="billTo"
        eType="ecore:EDataType
              http://www.eclipse.org/emf/2002/Ecore#//EString"/>
    <eStructuralFeatures xsi:type="ecore:EReference" name="items"
        upperBound="-1" eType="#//Item" containment="true"/>
  </eClassifiers>
  <eClassifiers xsi:type="ecore:EClass" name="Item">
    <eStructuralFeatures xsi:type="ecore:EAttribute"
        name="productName"
        eType="ecore:EDataType
              http://www.eclipse.org/emf/2002/Ecore#//EString"/>
    <eStructuralFeatures xsi:type="ecore:EAttribute" name="quantity"
        eType="ecore:EDataType
              http://www.eclipse.org/emf/2002/Ecore#//EInt"/>
    <eStructuralFeatures xsi:type="ecore:EAttribute" name="price"
        eType="ecore:EDataType
              http://www.eclipse.org/emf/2002/Ecore#//EFloat"/>
```

```
    </eClassifiers>
</ecore:EPackage>
```

PrimerPO

The PrimerPO model builds on the SimplePO model, making it closely resemble the purchase order example used in the XML Schema primer [2]. It adds some new features to the **PurchaseOrder** and **Item** classes, a new class **USAddress**, and two data types, **Date** and **SKU**. The PrimerPO model is introduced in Chapter 4. It's also used as the main example for illustrating code generator patterns in Chapters 10 and 11. In addition, it is the basis for all validation examples in Chapter 18, and for examples showing how to use custom storage for generated models (Section 15.6) and how to suppress objects from generated views (Section 19.2.1). Figure B.2 illustrates the model.

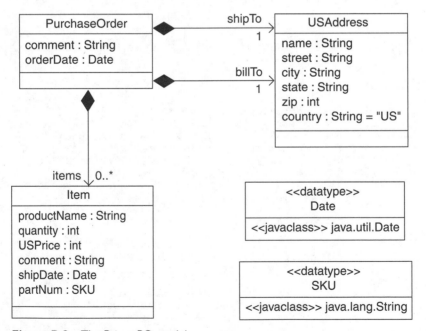

Figure B.2   The PrimerPO model.

In the form of an XML Schema, the PrimerPO model looks like this:

PrimerPO.xsd:

```xml
<?xml version="1.0" encoding="UTF-8"?>
<xsd:schema xmlns:xsd="http://www.w3.org/2001/XMLSchema"
            xmlns:ecore="http://www.eclipse.org/emf/2002/Ecore"
            xmlns:ppo="http://www.example.com/PrimerPO"
            targetNamespace="http://www.example.com/PrimerPO"
            ecore:package="com.example.ppo" ecore:nsPrefix="ppo">
  <xsd:element name="order" type="ppo:PurchaseOrder"/>
  <xsd:element name="comment" type="xsd:string"/>

  <xsd:complexType name="PurchaseOrder">
    <xsd:sequence>
      <xsd:element name="shipTo" minOccurs="0"
                   type="ppo:USAddress"/>
      <xsd:element name="billTo" type="ppo:USAddress"/>
      <xsd:element ref="ppo:comment" minOccurs="0"/>
      <xsd:element name="items" type="ppo:Item"
                   minOccurs="0" maxOccurs="unbounded"/>
    </xsd:sequence>
    <xsd:attribute name="orderDate" type="xsd:date"/>
  </xsd:complexType>

  <xsd:complexType name="USAddress">
    <xsd:sequence>
      <xsd:element name="name"   type="xsd:string"/>
      <xsd:element name="street" type="xsd:string"/>
      <xsd:element name="city"   type="xsd:string"/>
      <xsd:element name="state"  type="xsd:string"/>
      <xsd:element name="zip"    type="xsd:decimal"/>
    </xsd:sequence>
    <xsd:attribute name="country" type="xsd:NMTOKEN" fixed="US"/>
  </xsd:complexType>

  <xsd:complexType name="Item">
    <xsd:sequence>
      <xsd:element name="productName" type="xsd:string"/>
      <xsd:element name="quantity">
        <xsd:simpleType>
          <xsd:restriction base="xsd:positiveInteger">
            <xsd:maxExclusive value="100"/>
          </xsd:restriction>
        </xsd:simpleType>
      </xsd:element>
      <xsd:element name="USPrice" type="xsd:decimal"/>
      <xsd:element ref="ppo:comment" minOccurs="0"/>
      <xsd:element name="shipDate" type="xsd:date" minOccurs="0"/>
    </xsd:sequence>
    <xsd:attribute name="partNum" type="ppo:SKU" use="required"/>
  </xsd:complexType>
```

```
<xsd:simpleType name="SKU">
  <xsd:restriction base="xsd:string">
    <xsd:pattern value="\d{3}-[A-Z]{2}"/>
  </xsd:restriction>
</xsd:simpleType>
</xsd:schema>
```

Using annotated Java, the PrimerPO model can be described with four Java source files: *PurchaseOrder.java*, *Item.java*, *USAddress.java*, and *PPOPackage.java*.

PurchaseOrder.java:

```java
package com.example.ppo;

import java.util.Date;
import java.util.List;

/**
 * @model
 */
public interface PurchaseOrder
{
  /**
   * @model
   */
  String getComment();

  /**
   * @model dataType="com.example.ppo.Date"
   */
  Date getOrderDate();

  /**
   * @model containment="true" required="true"
   */
  USAddress getShipTo();

  /**
   * @model containment="true" required="true"
   */
  USAddress getBillTo();

  /**
   * @model type="Item" containment="true"
   */
  List getItems();
}
```

Item.java:

```
package com.example.ppo;

import java.util.Date;

/**
 * @model
 */
public interface Item
{
  /**
   * @model
   */
  String getProductName();

  /**
   * @model
   */
  int getQuantity();

  /**
   * @model
   */
  int getUSPrice();

  /**
   * @model
   */
  String getComment();

  /**
   * @model dataType="com.example.ppo.Date"
   */
  Date getShipDate();

  /**
   * @model dataType="com.example.ppo.SKU"
   */
  String getPartNum();
}
```

USAddress.java:

```
package com.example.ppo;

/**
 * @model
 */
public interface USAddress
{
  /**
```

```
 * @model
 */
String getName();

/**
 * @model
 */
String getStreet();

/**
 * @model
 */
String getCity();

/**
 * @model
 */
String getState();

/**
 * @model
 */
int getZip();

/**
 * @model default="US" changeable="false"
 */
String getCountry();
}
```

PPOPackage.java:

```
package com.example.ppo;

/**
 * @model kind="package"
 */
public interface PPOPackage
{
  String eNS_URI = "http://www.example.com/PrimerPO";
  String eNS_PREFIX = "ppo";
}
```

The Ecore model for PrimerPO looks like this when serialized as XMI:

PrimerPO.ecore:

```
<?xml version="1.0" encoding="UTF-8"?>
<ecore:EPackage xmi:version="2.0" xmlns:xmi="http://www.omg.org/XMI"
    xmlns:xsi="http://www.w3.org/2001/XMLSchema-instance"
    xmlns:ecore="http://www.eclipse.org/emf/2002/Ecore" name="ppo"
    nsURI="http://www.example.com/PrimerPO" nsPrefix="ppo">
```

```
        <eClassifiers xsi:type="ecore:EClass" name="PurchaseOrder">
          <eStructuralFeatures xsi:type="ecore:EAttribute" name="comment"
              eType="ecore:EDataType
                    http://www.eclipse.org/emf/2002/Ecore#//EString"/>
          <eStructuralFeatures xsi:type="ecore:EAttribute"
              name="orderDate" eType="#//Date"/>
          <eStructuralFeatures xsi:type="ecore:EReference" name="shipTo"
              lowerBound="1" eType="#//USAddress" containment="true"/>
          <eStructuralFeatures xsi:type="ecore:EReference" name="billTo"
              lowerBound="1" eType="#//USAddress" containment="true"/>
          <eStructuralFeatures xsi:type="ecore:EReference" name="items"
              upperBound="-1" eType="#//Item" containment="true"/>
        </eClassifiers>
        <eClassifiers xsi:type="ecore:EClass" name="USAddress">
          <eStructuralFeatures xsi:type="ecore:EAttribute" name="name"
              eType="ecore:EDataType
                    http://www.eclipse.org/emf/2002/Ecore#//EString"/>
          <eStructuralFeatures xsi:type="ecore:EAttribute" name="street"
              eType="ecore:EDataType
                    http://www.eclipse.org/emf/2002/Ecore#//EString"/>
          <eStructuralFeatures xsi:type="ecore:EAttribute" name="city"
              eType="ecore:EDataType
                    http://www.eclipse.org/emf/2002/Ecore#//EString"/>
          <eStructuralFeatures xsi:type="ecore:EAttribute" name="state"
              eType="ecore:EDataType
                    http://www.eclipse.org/emf/2002/Ecore#//EString"/>
          <eStructuralFeatures xsi:type="ecore:EAttribute" name="zip"
              eType="ecore:EDataType
                    http://www.eclipse.org/emf/2002/Ecore#//EInt"/>
          <eStructuralFeatures xsi:type="ecore:EAttribute" name="country"
              eType="ecore:EDataType
                    http://www.eclipse.org/emf/2002/Ecore#//EString"
              changeable="false" defaultValueLiteral="US"/>
        </eClassifiers>
        <eClassifiers xsi:type="ecore:EClass" name="Item">
          <eStructuralFeatures xsi:type="ecore:EAttribute"
              name="productName"
              eType="ecore:EDataType
                    http://www.eclipse.org/emf/2002/Ecore#//EString"/>
          <eStructuralFeatures xsi:type="ecore:EAttribute" name="quantity"
              eType="ecore:EDataType
                    http://www.eclipse.org/emf/2002/Ecore#//EInt"/>
          <eStructuralFeatures xsi:type="ecore:EAttribute" name="USPrice"
              eType="ecore:EDataType
                    http://www.eclipse.org/emf/2002/Ecore#//EInt"/>
          <eStructuralFeatures xsi:type="ecore:EAttribute" name="comment"
              eType="ecore:EDataType
                    http://www.eclipse.org/emf/2002/Ecore#//EString"/>
          <eStructuralFeatures xsi:type="ecore:EAttribute" name="shipDate"
              eType="#//Date"/>
          <eStructuralFeatures xsi:type="ecore:EAttribute" name="partNum"
              eType="#//SKU"/>
        </eClassifiers>
        <eClassifiers xsi:type="ecore:EDataType" name="SKU"
            instanceClassName="java.lang.String"/>
        <eClassifiers xsi:type="ecore:EDataType" name="Date"
            instanceClassName="java.util.Date"/>
      </ecore:EPackage>
```

ExtendedPO

This model extends PrimerPO, adding class **Supplier,** as a container for two lists of purchase orders. The **priorityOrders** and **standardOrders** references are backed by a feature map, **orders,** which maintains cross-feature order between them. ExtendedPO is the basis for the discussion of extended Ecore modeling features in Chapter 8 and is used again as a generator pattern example in Chapter 10. Figure B.3 illustrates the model in UML.

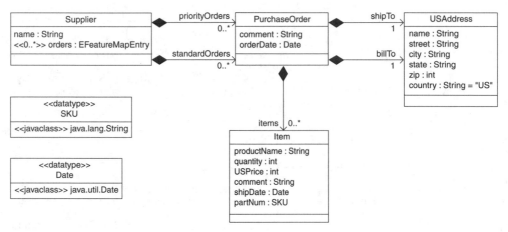

Figure B.3   The ExtendedPO model.

The **priorityOrders** and **standardOrders** references are modeled with non-default values for certain non-UML Ecore properties: **volatile, transient,** and **derived** are all true for both references. In addition, the inter-feature relationships in ExtendedPO are represented by extended metadata annotations, as summarized in Table B.1.

Table B.1   ExtendedPO Annotations

Feature	Annotation
Supplier.orders	http:///org/eclipse/emf/ecore/util/ExtendedMetaData kind='group'
Supplier.priorityOrders	http:///org/eclipse/emf/ecore/util/ExtendedMetaData group='#orders'
Supplier.standardOrders	http:///org/eclipse/emf/ecore/util/ExtendedMetaData group='#orders'

ExtendedPO1

This model also builds on PrimerPO, though somewhat differently from ExtendedPO. It adds class **Customer** into the picture, along with a simplified **Supplier** class, as a container for both purchase orders and customers. It also adds a new one-way reference, **previousOrder,** and an enumeration type **OrderStatus**. It's the last of the example models that can be generated and run without any hand modification. Elements of the ExtendedPO1 model are used for some of the examples of generator patterns in Chapter 10 and Section 21.1.1. Two examples of view customization (Sections 19.2.2 and 19.2.3) are also based on it. The model is illustrated in Figure B.4.

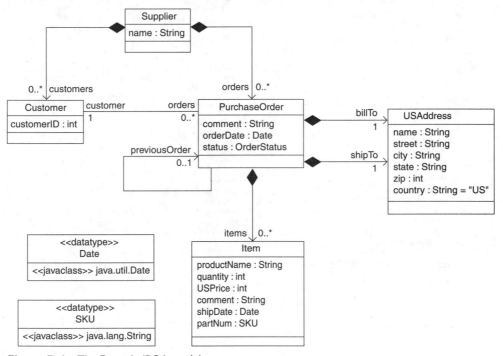

Figure B.4   The ExtendedPO1 model.

ExtendedPO2

This model builds further on ExtendedPO1, adding an abstract class, **Address,** which **USAddress** and another new class, **GlobalAddress,** extend. A second base class, **GlobalLocation,** of class **GlobalAddress** is added to illustrate multiple inheritance. Two new volatile references, **pendingOrders** and **shippedOrders,** are added to class **Supplier,** and the volatile **totalAmount** attribute is added to class **PurchaseOrder.** The ExtendedPO2 model is introduced in Chapter 13, and is the subject of most of the examples in that chapter, as well as Chapters 14 and 16. It also appears in extended metadata (Section 15.3.5) and DOM conversion (Section 15.3.6) examples. Finally, it is the basis for the discussion of modeling with generics (Section 21.1.2), where it is enhanced with some generic types. The model is shown in Figure B.5.

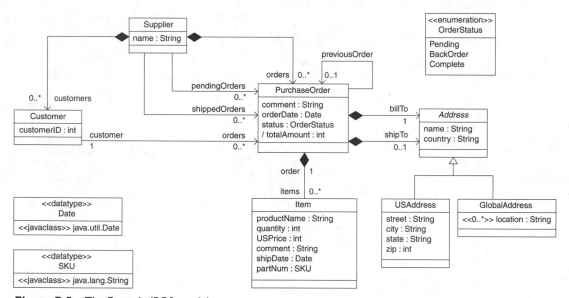

Figure B.5   The ExtendedPO2 model.

Some of the features in the ExtendedPO2 model have non-default values for certain non-UML Ecore properties. They are summarized in Table B.2.

Table B.2 ExtendedPO2 Model Properties

Feature	derived	volatile	transient	changeable	resolveProxies
Supplier.pendingOrders	true	true	true	false	false
Supplier.shippedOrders	true	true	true	false	false
PurchaseOrder.totalAmount	true	true	true	false	
PurchaseOrder.previousOrder					false
PurchaseOrder.customer					false
Customer.orders					false

ExtendedPO3

The ExtendedPO3 model is essentially the same model as ExtendedPO2, but split into two separate packages, **epo3** and **supplier**. Like ExtendedPO2, it is introduced in Chapter 13. It is also used for the cross-referencer examples of Section 16.3. Figure B.6 illustrates the **epo3** package.

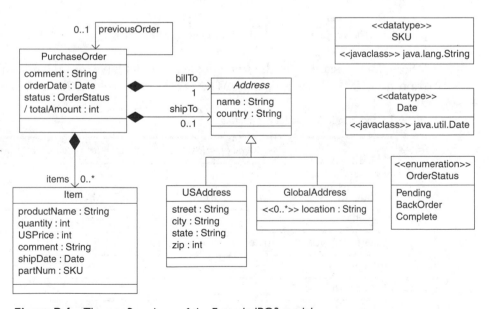

Figure B.6 The **epo3** package of the ExtendedPO3 model.

The rest of the ExtendedPO3 model is in the **supplier** package. It is shown in Figure B.7.

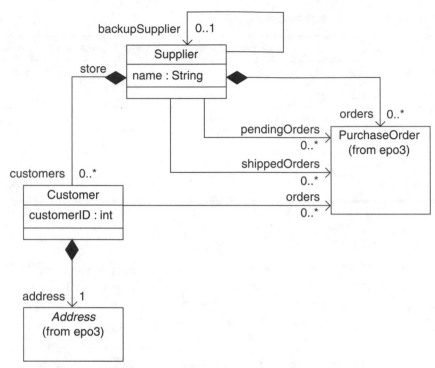

Figure B.7   The **supplier** package of the ExtendedPO3 model.

Some of the features in the ExtendedPO3 model have non-default values for certain non-UML Ecore properties. They are summarized in Table B.3.

Table B.3   ExtendedPO3 Model Properties

Feature	*derived*	*volatile*	*transient*	*changeable*	*resolveProxies*
Supplier.customers					false
Supplier.pendingOrders	true	true	true	false	
Supplier.shippedOrders	true	true	true	false	
PurchaseOrder.totalAmount	true	true	true	false	
PurchaseOrder.items					false
PurchaseOrder.billTo					false
PurchaseOrder.shipTo					false
Customer.store					false
Customer.address					false

Note that all the containment and container references except **Supplier.orders** are explicitly defined to be non-proxy-resolving in this version of the model. In Section 13.8, the model is generated with containment proxies enabled, allowing purchase orders to be persisted in different resources from their containing supplier.

Index

A

AbstractOverrideableCommand class, 61
abstract property (EClass class), 146
abstract types
    AbstractCommand class, 56
    XML Schema complex type definitions, 194
accessing
    metadata in packages, 420-422
    packages, 422
    resource sets, 64-65
accessors
    reflective, 279-283
        eGet(), 280-282
        eIsSet(), 282
        eSet(), 282
        eUnset(), 282
    generated, 241-243
    visibility attribute, 209, 221
action bar contributor, 45
    generated class, 67, 334-336
    object creation support, 322
actions, 8, 44-45
    code generation, 94-95, 349
adapt() method, 30, 293, 508, 513, 518
    default implmentation, 589
    EMF.Edit, 48, 63, 589
AdapterFactoryContentProvider class, 47, 52
AdapterFactoryEditingDomain class, 51, 62
AdapterFactoryLabelProvider class, 47
Adapter Factory property, 360
adapters, 29, 508
    adding to objects, 508-515
        adapter factories, 510-513
        eAdapters lists, 508-510
        type-specific adapters, 513-515
    as behavior extensions, 30
    behavioral extensions, 515-519
    content, 519-520
    cross-referencers, 526-529
    EContentAdapter class, 31
    ECrossReferenceAdapter, 526
    factories, 30-31
        adding adapters to objects, 510-513
        EMF.Edit Item providers, 327-330
        generated classes, 291-295
    generated classes, observing, 521-522
    as simple observers, 29

AddCommand class, 59-60
adding
    adapters to objects, 508-515
        adapter factories, 510-513
        eAdapters lists, 508-510
        type-specific adapters, 513-515
    JAR files to class paths, 609-612
    non-model intermediary view objects (EMF.Edit),
        587-597
        drag-and-drop, 596
        object correction, 594-595
        Supplier class children, 587
        Supplier class create child property, dis-
            abling, 593-594
        Supplier class getChildren() method
            override, 588
        Supplier class non-modeled nodes, 588
        Supplier class OrdersItemProvider class, 589
        Supplier class SupplierItemProvider
            class, 590
        Supplier class TransientSupplierItemProvider
            class, 591-592
        SupplierItemProvider class dispose()
            method, 597
        SupplierItemProvider class getOrders()
            method, 593
addPreviousOrderPropertyDescriptor() method, 395
Address class, 275
alternative generated code patterns, 295
    performance optimization, 295-302
        Boolean flags, 295-298
        constant-time reflective methods, 301-302
        virtual feature delegation, 298-301
    suppressing EMFisms, 302-305
        EObject API, 302-303
        interface/implementation split, 305
        metadata, 304
        types, 303
annotated Java
    creating model files, 72-79
        Generator model location/name, 77
        model directory, creating, 74
        model importer, selecting, 78
        new wizard opening page, 76
        packages, selecting, 79
        PPOPackage interface, 76

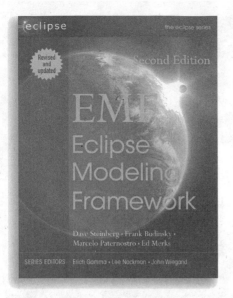

FREE Online Edition

Your purchase of **EMF: Eclipse Modeling Framework** includes access to a free online edition for 45 days through the Safari Books Online subscription service. Nearly every Addison Wesley book is available online through Safari Books Online, along with more than 5,000 other technical books and videos from publishers such as Cisco Press, Exam Cram, IBM Press, O'Reilly, Prentice Hall, Que, and Sams.

SAFARI BOOKS ONLINE allows you to search for a specific answer, cut and paste code, download chapters, and stay current with emerging technologies.

Activate your FREE Online Edition at www.informit.com/safarifree

> **STEP 1:** Enter the coupon code: JVIG-R4LG-LUJN-8JGV-Z853.

> **STEP 2:** New Safari users, complete the brief registration form.
> Safari subscribers, just log in.

If you have difficulty registering on Safari or accessing the online edition,
please e-mail customer-service@safaribooksonline.com